The Politics & Society Reader

edited by

Ira Katznelson
Gordon Adams
Philip Brenner
Alan Wolfe

with the assistance of Gerald Dorfman,
publishing director, POLITICS AND SOCIETY

David McKay Company, Inc. / New York

THE POLITICS AND SOCIETY READER

Copyright © 1970, 1971, 1972, 1973, and 1974 by Politics and Society, Inc.

ISBN: 0-679-30261-1   (paper)
     0-679-30260-3   (cloth)

LIBRARY OF CONGRESS CATALOG CARD NUMBER: 74-78400

MANUFACTURED IN THE UNITED STATES OF AMERICA

Acknowledgments

This book represents the first two years of *Politics and Society*. Since that time, we have been joined on the editorial board by Amy Bridges, David Gold, and Margaret Levi. All of us have benefited enormously from the sensibilities and qualities they have brought with them. We express our gratitude to them for their patience while we discussed a book which does not include their names on the list of editors.

To Gerald and Penny Dorfman we owe a special debt. Their collective labor, dedication, and incredible patience literally made *Politics and Society* possible. Roberta Mathews, our copyeditor, and Anne Russell and Kathy Armstrong, our administrative assistants, have made important contributions to the journal. Deborah Socolow Katznelson lovingly put up with periodic disturbances. Ed Artinian of David McKay encouraged us to bring out this book. J. David Greenstone, Lewis Lipsitz, and Kenneth Dolbeare gave useful editorial and organizational advice.

About the Editors

Ira Katznelson is associate professor of political science at The University of Chicago. He is the author of *Black Men, White Cities* and co-author of *Power and Choice in American Politics: A Critical Introduction* (forthcoming).

Gordon Adams is on the staff of the Social Science Research Council. He is completing a book on the role of the state in advanced capitalist countries.

Philip Brenner teaches political science at Trinity College, Washington, D.C. He was co-director of the Washington Mini-School, an experimental project in political education and is the co-editor of *Exploring Contradictions: Political Economy in the Corporate State.*

Alan Wolfe is associate professor of political science at Richmond College of the City University of New York. He is the author of *The Seamy Side of Democracy: Repression in America* and co-editor of *An End to Political Science.*

About the Contributors

Robert Alford is professor of sociology at the University of Wisconsin, Madison. He is presently extending the themes developed in his article to other sectors of the American political economy, and also studying pluralist, bureaucratic, and class paradigms of social structure and change.

P. Allum teaches in the department of politics at the University of Reading, England. His *Politics and Society in Postwar Naples* assesses the place of the Naples political machine in Italian national politics.

Isaac Balbus pursues an interest in critical theory and practice as associate professor of political science, City University of New York. He is the author of *The Dialectics of Legal Repression: Black Rebels Before the American Criminal Courts.*

Stephen Bronner is presently enrolled in the doctoral program in political science at the University of California, Berkeley, specializing in social theory.

William Connolly is professor of political science at the University of Massachusetts, Amherst. He is the author of *Political Science and Ideology,* and has edited *The Bias of Pluralism.*

Hans Peter Dreitzel teaches sociology at the Free University of Berlin. He edits the annual series *Recent Sociology.*

Susanne Jonas, a graduate student at the University of California, Berkeley, has been active in the North American Congress on Latin America.

David Kettler teaches political theory at Trent University, Canada. His work has revolved around the political vocation of intellectuals, including studies on Adam Ferguson and Karl Mannheim.

Kenneth Lutterman, formerly of the University of Wisconsin, is with the Behavioral Sciences Training Branch of the National Institute of Mental Health.

Judith May is assistant professor of political science at Rutgers University, Newark, and has been affiliated with the Oakland Project at the University of California, Berkeley. She has been concerned with the interrelationships between bureaucrats and clients under different structural conditions.

Bertell Ollman is associate professor of political science at New York University, and a member of the editorial board of *Kapitalistate*. He is the author of *Alienation: Marx's Conception of Man in Capitalist Society*.

Richard Pious is assistant professor of political science at Barnard College, Columbia University. His recent publications and research concern law and society, and executive politics.

Michael Paul Rogin is professor of political science at the University of California, Berkeley. He is the author of *The Intellectuals and McCarthy: The Radical Specter*.

James Russell teaches sociology at San Francisco State University, and is a doctoral candidate at the University of Wisconsin.

Maurice Zeitlin is professor of sociology at the University of Wisconsin, Madison, and the author of numerous articles of research and social commentary. He is the author of several books, including *Revolutionary Politics and the Cuban Working Class*.

Aristide Zolberg is professor of political science at the University of Chicago. His early research and publications were mostly concerned with tropical Africa. He is now studying aspects of the political development of Western Europe and the United States.

Contents

Introduction   1

Part One: Social Conflict in American Politics   5

1. MICHAEL PAUL ROGIN, Liberal Society and the Indian
   Question   9
2. MAURICE ZEITLIN, KENNETH LUTTERMAN, and JAMES RUSSELL,
   Death in Vietnam: Class, Poverty, and the Risks of
   War   53
3. JUDITH MAY, Two Model Cities: Negotiations in
   Oakland   69
4. RICHARD PIOUS, Policy and Public Administration: The Legal
   Services Program in the War on Poverty   101
5. ROBERT ALFORD, The Political Economy of Health Care:
   Dynamics Without Change   128

Part Two: Comparative Perspectives on Contemporary Politics   167

6. SUSANNE JONAS, Dependency and Imperialism: The Roots of
   Latin American Underdevelopment   171
7. P. ALLUM, The Neopolitan Politicians: A Collective
   Portrait   202
8. ARISTIDE ZOLBERG, Moments of Madness   232

Part Three: Political Interests and Class Consciousness   257

9. WILLIAM CONNOLLY, On "Interests" in Politics   259
10. ISAAC BALBUS, The Concept of Interest in Pluralist and
    Marxian Analysis   278
11. BERTELL OLLMAN, Toward Class Consciousness Next Time:
    Marx and the Working Class   305

Part Four: Radical Alternatives to Conventional Social Sciences   329

12. DAVID KETTLER, The Vocation of Radical
    Intellectuals   333

13. HANS PETER DREITZEL, Social Science and the Problem of
    Rationality   360
14. STEPHEN BRONNER, Art and Utopia: The Marcusean
    Perspective   378

Introduction

The articles in this reader represent the first two years of our attempt, as editors of *Politics and Society,* to encourage the growth of a critical tradition in the social sciences. *Politics and Society* came into being at a time when such a tradition was badly needed in America. The United States was involved in a genocidal war in Indochina; a prerevolutionary black revolt challenged the hegemony of white America in the streets; and students and community protests were growing in number and intensity. We, like so many social scientists, searched for ways to understand and act within the framework of these events.

American social science disappointed us. Much of its theory and analysis in the late 1960s was useless as an explanation of upheaval. Worse, the leaders of the disciplines were busy providing elaborate rationales for the Vietnam war and for policies of oppression at home. From their fertile minds, in collaboration with the military, sprung such policies as strategic hamlets and counterinsurgency in the ghetto. The enemy, we discovered, was within our own profession.

The problem we perceived in the social sciences was not restricted to repugnant individual acts. The very fabric of the approaches to social reality taught to undergraduate and graduate students claimed objectivity while it obscured real inequality, class dominance, and pervasive social control. As political scientists, we were aware that pluralist analyses of American politics were, in fact, celebrations of an unreal openness and responsiveness of American political processes. Increasingly, as we recognized racism, sexism, and class inequality in American society, we realized, with Schattschneider, that "the flaw in the pluralist heaven is that the heavenly chorus sings with a strong upper-class accent." The study of American foreign policy covered imperialism with benign intentions. Comparative political analysis, particularly of the developing countries, stressed social order and the desirability for developing countries to emulate the American way of capitalism. Political theory, as taught in the university, was either lost in the textual perusal of past theorists or busily developing new, supposedly value-free approaches, such as systems theory, which would threaten the real interests of nobody.

As social scientists, we were faced with a choice, not only about scholarly approaches, but also about our relationship with those in power. C. Wright Mills outlined the possibilities in *The Sociological Imagination:* the philosopher-king coveting political power (Henry Kissinger), the counsel who plays a subsidiary advisory role, or a third alternative—which we preferred. "It is to remain independent, to do one's own work, to select one's own problems, but to direct this work *at* kings as well as *to* publics." Our task was to hold those with power responsible for their decisions and to clarify for those without power the consequences of public decisions for their everyday lives.

Most of us had traveled this far intellectually when the Caucus for a New Political Science was founded in September 1967. At that time, the Caucus provided an organizational framework for students and professors who were dissatisfied with conventional political science. For those of us involved with *Politics and Society,* the Caucus became a home, a place to meet people with shared convictions, and a symbol that an alternative social science was possible.

By 1969, however, the limited, reformist politics of the Caucus dissatisfied some of us. Critiques of pluralism, assertions of scholarly independence, and the attempt to create a counterelite within a single social science discipline seemed insufficient as ways to understand and deal with social reality and the role of knowledge in society. Intellectually, other more critical modes of social analysis, such as phenomenology, structuralism, and Marxism, helped an increasing number of social scientists to transcend positivist frames of reference.

We saw the opportunity to create *Politics and Society* in 1969 as a way to provide an outlet, free of organizational connections, for this creative intellectual activity. An editorial board composed of Ira Katznelson (editor), Gordon Adams, Philip Brenner, Judith Coburn, Lewis Lipsitz, and Alan Wolfe began to function in the spring of 1970, assisted by an advisory board that included Peter Bachrach, Norman Birnbaum, Henry Kariel, David Kettler, Ralph Miliband, and Michael Parenti. We addressed our appeal initially to political scientists as a journal of real alternatives:

> The leading professional social science journals continue to be obsessed with technique at the expense of imagination, significance, and readability. Many of our colleagues have been uneasy about the absence of forums for the publication of well-written solid scholarship dealing with important political concerns. *Politics and Society* provides social scientists with an alternative forum. . . . We object to the depoliticization of the study of politics, to the paucity of critical analysis, to the unnecessary use of a parochial and often pseudo-scientific

> jargon. . . . We seek to promote a quest for the good community,
> polity, and society.

The volume of the response to this announcement exceeded our expectations, both in terms of subscribers and the submission of articles. A latent community of critical scholars was being activated, though its nature was somewhat ambiguous. Most of the manuscripts we received fell into two groups. Either they were critiques of the dominant pluralist approach, or they were devoted to the development of critical theory with little or no consideration of empirical reality. Although there were exceptions to this trend, several of which appear in this reader, we realized that we had to define our editorial intentions more clearly.

The themes and issues treated in the manuscripts we chose for publication in the first year suggested the directions we would take. Some articles strongly suggested that we, as critical social scientists, had to apply sustained reason and intelligence, as partisans in the movement struggles around us. This meant, in part, analyzing social issues such as imperialism and racism both empirically and theoretically. These issues had to be discussed with reference to more than American experience; we made a conscious effort to develop links with the scholarly and political Left both in the Third World and in Europe.

The journal's statement of intent for its second year made these implicit concerns self-confidently explicit:

> We have published and want to encourage work that confronts the
> realities of economic, political, and racial exploitation, imperialism,
> and dehumanization and environmental destruction in technologi-
> cally oriented societies. . . . *Politics and Society* is a radical journal
> of social science. The purpose of our inquiry emanates from our con-
> cern with the roots of society.

Increasingly, we have been able to match our performance to our intentions. Our progress has been facilitated by the gradual development of a community of radical scholars whose work transcends the narrow confines of a single discipline. As a group, for example, we no longer take our agenda of important political and scholarly issues from the discipline of political science. Although we began as critics of that discipline, four years of experience have helped us become intellectually independent.

As part of this process, we have made a conscious effort to break down the artificial barriers in the social sciences that separate the study of politics from the study of economics and society. Radical organizations were developing in all the disciplines in the late 1960s, including, most importantly, the Union for Radical Political Economics. We have developed close contacts with many of these groups.

This organizational development has an intellectual dimension, as the journal moves closer to the study of political economy, as opposed to the more narrow concept of political science. This clarification of our editorial self has led to an increase in the flow of radical scholarship to us. The critiques of pluralism have begun to disappear, and are being replaced by work with a truly critical theoretical and empirical perspective.

We are publishing this volume because of our belief that a serious intellectual and political task must now be undertaken. As the organizations of the New Left and the visible opposition ferment in American society wane, we feel that intellectual activity assumes a new importance. As in the period after the defeat of the 1848 revolutions and the workers' insurrection of 1850 in Paris when Marx turned to the British Museum, our hopes for rapid structural change have been disappointed. If a long-term revolutionary process is to be sustained, a high priority must be given to the development of alternative ways of understanding existing political reality.

This volume represents part of our contribution to this effort. It is structured in such a way—with sections on American Politics, Comparative Politics, Political Interests, and Political Theory—as to be accessible to students and researchers who work within the structures imposed by social science departments in the university. It is our hope that in this way the volume will provide a critical perspective on the issues being raised in such courses as Introductory American Politics, Introduction to Politics, Comparative Politics, and Political Sociology.

For us, the journal and this volume have been a labor of love and growth, personally and intellectually. We feel, however, that this work cannot be limited to relatively privileged intellectuals. Liberation involves all of us becoming social scientists, for the more we understand reality, the greater threat we pose to existing patterns of dominance.

Part One

Social Conflict in American Politics

The essays in this section illuminate the fundamental bases of inequality in the United States, and the ways these antagonisms of class and race are reproduced and managed by the state. Governmental institutions and everyday politics, in Gramsci's phrase, "are like the trench systems of modern warfare" which protect privilege and deflect discontent. From this perspective, American political history is not the benevolent unfolding of political liberty, but one of largely successful attempts by the privileged to exercise social control by securing the compliance of subordinates, thus forcing them to act against their interests.

The genocide practiced against the continent's indigenous Indian population has been the most chilling instance of the use of state power to reinforce and secure class and colonial privileges. Michael Rogin describes how state power was used to drive the Indians off their lands and to rationalize the process in terms of liberal ideology. The Indians were portrayed as infantile, in need of "parental" guidance. Indian removal was rationalized as an action intended for the Indians' own good, which they could not recognize. The suffering that followed only attested to their inability to adapt. Consequences were divorced from cause, since the intention of policy makers was said to be benevolent. Unfortunately, the Indians did not comprehend that, under capitalism, land is appropriated for private benefit. The government's extermination policy was thus rooted in the defense of private property.

If, in the case of the Indians, the state created the preconditions of private ownership, in the case of Vietnam it made America's working class and racially colonized pay the price of the country's imperial war in Asia. Maurice Zeitlin, Kenneth Lutterman, and James Russell document this reality by examining the draft in the state of Wisconsin during the height of the Vietnam war. They find that the poor and working class were overrepresented among America's battlefield casualties.

It might be said that Indian removal and Vietnam were exceptional cases, the product of crisis situations. Yet, as the other articles in the section indicate, the *routine* institutionalization and operation of American public policies deepens and widens the political trench that reinforces and protects privilege. Typically, state-established programs are run by apparently neutral technicians who claim to govern in the public interest. But as the black citizens of Oakland realized, according to Judith May, the imposition of "technical" decisions by "professional" administrators promoted their continued colonization. The conflict over the Model Cities program became a conflict over basic differences of interest. The technicians favored a policy of corporate economic growth on the grounds that the city's blacks would benefit in trickle-down fashion, while the black opposition sought a program of economic redistribution that challenged basic corporate interests.

Richard Pious describes a similar dialectic in the history of the Legal Services program of President Johnson's War on Poverty. At every turn, from legislation to implementation, there was a successful effort to keep control in the hands of lawyers who would not challenge the structural causes of poverty. As a result, the program, which might have allowed the underclass to challenge laws that place property above people, became no more than a new cumbersome way to give some poor people an opportunity to get legal services.

The Legal Service program thus came to reflect and reinforce the basic pattern of laws that protect the status quo. In a related analysis, Robert Alford shows how the key issue of health care is not a problem of citizen consumers; rather "the core problem of the structure of the *producing* institutions" must be studied. He discovers a relatively closed system of "dynamics without change" which prevents accessible quality health care and buttresses "the dominance of the private sector and the upper middle class." He examines various proposals for reform, and finds that they suffer from a common failing—they leave untouched the power of those who now control the fee-for-service health-care system.

These five articles on American politics are more than good case studies of the governmental process with regard to the basic elements of our society—health care, the legal system, local government, war, and racism. Taken together, they tell us a great deal about the complex web of political institutions and government actions that seek to strengthen existing patterns of dominance.

1. Liberal Society and the Indian Question*

MICHAEL PAUL ROGIN

Our conduct toward these people is deeply interesting to our national character.
Andrew Jackson, First Annual Message to Congress, 1829

I.

Underneath the "ambitious expansionism" of modern Western societies, writes Henri Baudet in *Paradise on Earth*, "with their economic savoir faire, their social ideology, and their organizational talents," lies "a psychological disposition out of all political reality. It exists independently of objective facts, which seem to have become irrelevant. It is a disposition that leads [its adherent] 'to die' rather than 'to do,' and forces him to repent of his wickedness, covetousness, pride, and complacency."[1] The worldly orientation, Baudet argues, points to history and practical consequences, the inner disposition to a primitiveness beyond history. The first is expansive, the second regressive. This regressive, inner disposition, Baudet believes, has fastened on images of the noble savage, the garden of Eden, and paradise on earth.

In America, however, "aggressive expansionism" encountered the "regressive impulse" as a "political reality." This, I will suggest, is the precise cultural meaning Americans gave to their destruction of the Indians. Their language teaches us some intolerable truths about regression, maturity, and death in liberal America.

At the outset the contrast between expansionist, liberal America's self-

*I am grateful to Paul Roazen for directing my early reading in psychoanalytic sources, to Leslie and Margaret Fiedler, and to the political theorists once together in Berkeley—Norman Jacobson, Hanna Pitkin, John H. Schaar, and Sheldon Wolin—for providing, with our students, the intellectual setting in which this essay was written. There have also been many helpful readings of the manuscript. These will be acknowledged, and more fully incorporated, in the larger study on which I am now engaged.

Portions of a draft of this paper were presented at the University of North Carolina Symposium, "Laws, Rights, and Authority," Chapel Hill, February 20-22, 1970; and at the Annual Meeting of the Western Political Science Association, Sacramento, April 3, 1970.

1. Henry Baudet, *Paradise on Earth* (New Haven, Conn.: Yale University Press, 1965), p. 8.

Herrenvolk democracy

conception and its image of the Indians seems clear enough. Liberalism insisted on the independence of men, each from the other, and from cultural, traditional, and communal attachments. Indians were perceived as connected to their past, their superstitions, and their land. Liberalism insisted upon work, instinctual repression, and acquisitive behavior; men had to conquer and separate themselves from nature. Indians were seen as playful, violent, improvident, wild, and in harmony with nature. Private property underlay liberal society; Indians held land in common. Liberal relations were based, contractually, on keeping promises and on personal responsibility. Indians, in the liberal view, were anarchic and irresponsible. Americans believed that peaceful competitiveness kept them in touch with one another and provided social cement. They thought that Indians, lacking social order, were devoted to war.

Disastrously for the liberal self-conception, however, its distance from primitive man was not secure. At the heart of ambitious expansionism lay the regressive impulse itself. Indians were in harmony with nature; lonely, independent, liberal men were separated from it, and their culture lacked the richness, diversity, and traditional attachments to sustain their independence.

hippies

The consequence was forbidden nostalgia, for the nurturing, blissful, and primitively violent connection to nature that white Americans had had to leave behind. At the core of liberalism lay the belief that such human connections to each other and to the land were dreams only, subjects of nostalgia or sentimentalization, but impossible in the existing adult world. Indian societies, suggesting otherwise, posed a severe threat to liberal identity. The only safe Indians were dead, sanitized, or totally dependent upon white benevolence. Liberalism enforced in action the world its theory said was the only one possible.

The intimate, historical encounter with the Indians still further undermined liberal identity. "In the beginning," John Locke had written, "all the world was America."[2] Then men relinquished the state of nature, freely contracted together, and entered civil society. But that was not the way it happened—in America. True, settlers had come to escape the corruption and traditional restraints of Europe, to begin again, to return to the state of nature and contract together. They aimed, as Hamilton put it in the *Federalist Papers,* to build a state based on "reflection and choice" rather than on "accident and force."[3] But while the origins of European countries were shrouded in the mists of obscure history, America had clearly begun not with

2. John Locke, *Of Civil Government* (London: Everyman's Library, 1924), *Second Treatise,* p. 140. For Hobbes and Rousseau, American Indian societies also demonstrated the historical existence of the state of nature. Cf. Hoxie N. Fairchild, *The Noble Savage* (New York: Russell & Russell, 1961), pp. 23-24.
3. *The Federalist Papers,* ed. Roy P. Fairfield (New York: Doubleday Anchor Books, 1961), no. 1, p. 33.

primal innocence and consent but with acts of force and fraud. Stripping away history did not permit beginning without sin; it simply exposed the sin at the beginning of it all.

In the popular culture of films, westerns, and children's games, seizing America from the Indians is our central, mythical, formative experience. Its dynamic figures prominently in the Vietnam War, providing symbols for soldiers, names for combat missions, and the framework for Pentagon strategic plans.[4] But historians have ignored the elimination of the Indians, and minimized its significance for American development. This was the one outcome American statesmen in the two centuries before the Civil War could not imagine. For the dispossession of the Indians did not simply happen once for all in the beginning. America was continually beginning again, and as it expanded across the continent, it killed, removed, and drove into extinction one tribe after another. I will focus here on the first half of the nineteenth century, and particularly on the "Indian removal" program of Jacksonian Democracy.[5]

Expansion across the continent was the central fact of American politics from Jefferson's presidency through the Mexican War. Indians inhabited almost all the territory west of the Appalachians in 1800; they had to be removed. The story is bloody and corrupt beyond imagining, and few American political figures escape from it without dishonor. From 1820 to 1844 one hundred thousand Indians were removed from their homes and transported west of the Mississippi. One-quarter to one-third of these died or were

4. Cf. Noam Chomsky, "After Pinkville," *New York Review of Books* 13 (1 January 1970): p. 10; Noam Chomsky, *American Power and the New Mandarins* (New York: Pantheon, 1969), pp. 279-280; Michael Rogin, "Truth is Stranger than Science Fiction," *The Listener* (7 July 1968), pp. 117-18; Richard Drinnon, "Violence in the American Experience: Winning the West," *The Radical Teacher* (Chicago), 30 December 1969, pp. 36, 45-46.

Hippie and New Left youth identify themselves, and are identified by their enemies, with Indian resistance to American culture. It is fitting that the leading academic defender of American traditions has written an intemperate attack on the "new barbarians" of the New Left. This "rebellion of small groups," is "rude, wild, and uncivilized," "wild and disorganized," demands "infant-instantism," is wholly un-American, and "cannot last, if the nation is to survive." See Daniel Boorstin, "The New Barbarians," *Esquire* 70 (October, 1968): 159-162, 260-262.

5. This essay interprets the prevailing cultural myth about Indians in antebellum America. It makes no effort to specify the social basis of that myth—class or mass, popular or elite, frontier or eastern, northern or southern, entrepreneurial or pastoral, speculator or backwoods. This forms part of the larger study on which I am working. The discussion here will indicate that our leading politicians shared the myth, and that it was particularly salient to those involved in Indian affairs. I believe that in some form the Indian myth reached deeply into all the social categories enumerated above. But it was sufficiently complex that different social types would stress different aspects. This sort of differentiation is not attempted here.

killed in the process.[6] Indian removal was Andrew Jackson's major concrete political aim in the years before he became president; Van Buren later listed it, along with the bank war, the internal improvements veto, and the nullification fight, as one of the four major achievements of Jackson's administration.[7] In the years from 1820 to 1852 six of the eleven major candidates for president had either won reputations as generals in Indian wars, or had served as secretaries of war, whose major responsibility in this period was relations with the Indians.[8]

How to reconcile the elimination of the Indians with the liberal self-image? This problem preoccupied the statesmen of the period. "The great moral debt we owe to this unhappy race is universally felt and acknowledged," Secretary of War Lewis Cass reported in 1831.[9] In our relations to the Indians, wrote Van Buren, "we are as a nation responsible *in foro conscientiae,* to the opinions of the great family of nations, as it involves the course we have pursued and shall pursue towards a people comparatively weak, upon whom we were perhaps in the beginning unjustifiable aggressors, but of whom, in the progress of time and events, we have become the guardians, and, as we hope, the benefactors."[10]

Van Buren and the others felt the eyes of the world upon America. They needed a policy and rhetoric permitting them to believe that our encounter with the Indians, "the most difficult of all our relations, foreign and domestic,

6. I am indebted to Mark Morris for this estimate. It is derived from Commissioner of Indian Affairs census records and other published sources. The figures in the text are conservative; removal during this period may have caused the deaths of forty thousand Indians.

7. Martin Van Buren, *Autobiography,* American Historical Association Annual Report, 1918, vol. 2 (Washington: American Historical Association, 1920): 275. Cf. Mary E. Young, *Redskins, Ruffleshirts, and Rednecks* (Norman, Okla.: University of Oklahoma Press, 1961), pp. 3-5, passim; Annie Heloise Abel, *The History of Events Resulting in Indian Consolidation West of the Mississippi,* American Historical Association Report of Proceedings, 1906. Indians are simply not mentioned at all in perhaps the two major contenders for synthetic interpretations of the Jacksonian period. Cf. Arthur Schlesinger, Jr., *The Age of Jackson* (Boston: Little, Brown, 1945); Marvin Meyers, *The Jacksonian Persuasion* (New York: Vintage Books, 1960). Thomas H. Benton's biographer largely ignores his important role in Indian affairs; Lewis Cass's biographer offers the most enormous, elementary, factual errors in his abbreviated account of the Secretary of War and Indian removal. Cf. William N. Chambers, *Old Bullion Benton* (Boston: Little, Brown, 1956); Frank B. Woodford, *Lewis Cass* (New Brunswick, N.J.: Rutgers University Press, 1950), pp. 180-183.

8. "Our Indian Affairs is ... the most important branch of the war department," Andrew Jackson wrote, offering the secretaryship to Hugh Lawson White. Cf. John Spencer Bassett, ed., *Correspondence of Andrew Jackson,* 6 vols. (Washington, D.C.: Carnegie Institution of Washington, 1926-1933), 4: 271. Hereafter cited as *JC.*

9. *American State Papers, Military Affairs,* 4: 714. Hereafter cited as *MA.*

10. Van Buren, op. cit., p. 295.

has at last been justified to the world in its near approach to a happy and certain consummation."[11] They needed to justify—the Puritan word means save for God—a society built upon Indian graves.

The theory and language American statesmen employed cemented the historical white-Indian tie with intimate symbolic meaning. America's expansion across the continent, everyone agreed, reproduced the historical evolution of mankind. "The first proprietors of this happy country"[12] were sometimes said to be the first people on earth. Early in time, they were also primitive in development. Human societies existed along a unilinear scale from savagery to civilization. The early, savage peoples could not coexist with advanced societies; civilization would inevitably displace savagery.[13]

So stated, the theory remained abstract; politicians and social commentators filled it with personal meaning. The evolution of societies was identical to the evolution of individual men. "Barbarism is to civilization what childhood is to maturity."[14] Indians were at the infant stage of social evolution. They were "part of the human family"[15] as children; their replacement by whites symbolized America's growing up from childhood to maturity. Winthrop Jordan writes, "The Indian became for Americans a symbol of their American experience; it was no mere luck of the toss that placed the profile of an American Indian rather than an American Negro on the famous old five-cent piece. Confronting the Indian in America was a testing experience, common to all the colonies. Conquering the Indian symbolized and personified the conquest of the American difficulties, the surmounting of the wilderness. To push back the Indian was to prove the worth of one's own mission, to make straight in the desert a highway for civilization."[16]

Not the Indians alive, then, but their destruction, symbolized the American experience. The conquest of the Indians made the country uniquely American. Yet Jordan is right; America identified at once with the conquered and the conquering. The Indians—that "much-injured race" who were

11. Martin Van Buren, "Second Annual Message," 3 December 1838, in James D. Richardson, *Messages and Papers of the Presidents,* (New York: Bureau of National Literature, 1917), 3: 500.

12. Secretary of War James C. Calhoun in *American State Papers, Indian Affairs,* 2: 190. Hereafter cited as *IA.*

13. Here and throughout I have relied heavily on Roy Harvey Pearce's seminal *The Savages of America* (Baltimore: Johns Hopkins Press, 1965). See also Winthrop D. Jordan, *White Over Black* (Baltimore: Penguin, 1969), pp. 89-91, 247-48, 477-81; George W. Stocking, Jr., *Race, Culture, and Evolution* (New York: Free Press, 1968), pp. 26-27, 75-100; Arthur A. Ekirch, *The Idea of Progress in America, 1815-1860* (New York: Columbia University Press, 1944), pp. 15-46.

14. Francis Parkman, *The Conspiracy of Pontiac,* 10th ed. (New York: Collier Books, 1962), pp. 182-83.

15. General Edmund P. Gaines in *MA,* 1: 684.

16. Jordan, op. cit., pp. 90-91.

once "the uncontrolled possessors of these vast regions"[17]—became a symbol of something lost, lost inevitably in the process of growing up.[18]

If the Indians were children, whites thought of themselves as parents. These parents did not simply replace Indians; they took upon themselves, to use Van Buren's words again, the obligations of "benefactors" and "guardians." What meaning can be given to a policy of death and dispossession, centrally important to the development of America, over which considerable guilt is felt, and which is justified by the paternal benevolence of a father for his children?

The myth of Indian disappearance, I will suggest, belongs to the pathology of family relations. The symbols of Indian policy expressed repressed anxiety at the premature separation from warm, maternal protection. Indians remain, in the white fantasy, in the oral stage, sustained by and unseparated from mother nature. They are at once symbols of a lost childhood bliss, and, as bad children, repositories of murderous negative projections. Adult independence wreaks vengeance upon its own nostalgia for infant dependence. The Indian's tie with nature must be broken, literally by uprooting him, figuratively by civilizing him, finally by killing him.

 Men in the new American world had left behind the authority provided by history, tradition, family connection, and the other ties of old European existence. Political authority, as Locke demonstrated against Filmer, must derive not from paternal relations but from interactions among free men. In a world where inherited and ascribed qualities were meant to count for so little, political and paternal authority would be fragile and insecure. But Indians were not liberal men. The paternal authority repressed out of liberal politics found its arena in paternalism toward Indians.

For whites to indulge their paternal wishes, Indians had to remain helpless children. Liberal paternal authority required its objects to have no

17. Andrew Jackson, "First Annual Message," 8 December 1829, in Richardson, op. cit., 2: 458. A few years later Jackson put on the headdress of the defeated Indian warrior Black Hawk shortly before receiving a delegation of petitioners for the United States Bank. "I don't think those fellows would like to meet me in this." Marquis James, *Andrew Jackson*, 2 vols. (Indianapolis: Bobbs-Merrill, 1933, 1937), 2: 366. Cf. *JC*, 3: 222.

18. Several interpretative works stress the American identification with nature and/or the Indians. Cf. Henry Nash Smith, *Virgin Land* (Cambridge, Mass.: Harvard University Press, 1950); Leo Marx, *The Machine in the Garden* (New York: Oxford, 1964); John William Ward, *Andrew Jackson, Symbol for an Age* (New York: Oxford, 1955), pp. 11-45. Perry Miller's breathtaking "Nature and the National Ego" demonstrates Jacksonian anxiety over the country's destruction of that nature which was the source of its identity; *Errand into the Wilderness* (New York: Harper-Row, 1964), pp. 204-16. Other discussions of nostalgia and regression in Jacksonian America include Meyers; Arthur K. Moore, *The Frontier Mind* (Lexington, Ky.: University of Kentucky, 1957); Charles G. Sellers, Jr., *James K. Polk Jacksonian, 1795-1843* (Princeton, N.J.: Princeton University Press, 1957), pp. 3, 92.

independence or life of their own; this was the only alternative to manly independence. As Andrew Jackson advised his nephew, "Independence of mind and action is the noblest attribute of man. He that possesses it, and practices upon it, may be said to possess the real image of his creator. Without it, man becomes the real tool in the hands of others, and is wielded, like a mere automaton, sometimes, without knowing it, to the worst of purposes."[19] In their paternalism toward the Indians, men like Jackson indulged their secret longing to wield total power. Explicitly the father was to break the child's tie to nature, so the child could grow up. The actual language and practice substituted for the tie to nature a total, infantilized dependence upon the white father, and the fragmented workings of a liberal marketplace and a liberal bureaucracy.

Liberalism broke the Indian's tie to nature in the name of independence; but the destruction of actual Indian autonomy suggested a dynamic to American expansion which contradicted professed liberal goals. The separation anxiety underlying liberal society expressed itself in a longing to regain lost attachment to the earth by expanding, swallowing, and incorporating its contents. Liberalism sought to regain the "dual-unity" of the primal infant-mother connection from a position of strength instead of infant helplessness, by devouring and incorporating identities culturally out of its control. In relation to Indians, whites regressed to the most primitive form of object relation, namely the annihilation of the object through oral introjection. America was pictured by defenders of Manifest Destiny as a "young and growing country," which expanded through "swallowing" territory, "just as an animal needs to eat to grow." Savagery would inevitably "be swallowed by" civilization. The "insatiable" "land hunger" of the whites struck alike critics of and apologists for Indian policy, and observers fell back upon oral metaphors to describe the traders and backwoodsmen "preying, like so many vultures, upon the vitals of those ill-fated tribes."[20] Indians were emancipated from the land only to be devoured by a white expansionism that could not tolerate their independent existence.

Child destruction was accomplished by a white father, whose maturity enabled him to accept Indian extinction with neither regret nor responsibility. Benevolence and greed, power and helplessness, were irrevocably split in this Jekyll-Hyde figure. The failure to achieve an integrated paternal

19. *JC,* 2: 441.
20. Sources for the quotations are: Albert K. Weinberg, *Manifest Destiny* (Chicago: Quadrangle Books, 1963), p. 195; T.H. Benton in *IA,* 2: 512; James W. Silver, *Edmund Pendleton Gaines: Frontier General* (Baton Rouge: Louisiana State University, 1949), p. 106. Grover Cleveland, signing a bill which opened the way for large-scale white appropriation of Indian land, remarked, "The hunger and thirst of the white man for the Indian's land is almost equal to his hunger and thirst after righteousness" (quoted in William T. Hagan, *American Indians,* University of Chicago History of American Civilization [Chicago: University of Chicago Press, 1961], p. 141).

figure who could accept responsibility for his actions recalls the failure to integrate childhood experience into the adult world. Just as these splits in the ego characterize schizoid personalities, so the inability to tolerate separation from the other, the longing to return to an egoless "dual-unity" stage, is a source of adult schizophrenia. But liberal society (and the men who carried out its Indian policy) neither disintegrated, nor underwent a genuine maturing; liberalism had the power to remove the Indian menace instead.[21]

At the outset this interpretation of Indian destruction must seem bizarre. The American myth about Indians was not the work of paranoids and social madmen, but a consensus of almost all our leading political and intellectual figures. The sources of white expansion onto Indian land, moreover, seem straightforward. Surely land hunger and the building of a national empire provided the thrust; at most the cultural myth sought to come to terms with the experience after the fact.

But the centrality of Indian dispossession in pre-Civil War America raises disturbing questions about the core of our politics that are hardly met by viewing Indian removal as pragmatic and inevitable. Precisely such basic encounters, inevitable as their outcome may be once they reach a certain point, form the history and the culture of a country. Hannah Arendt, for example, has suggested that the prolonged meeting of "advanced" and primitive peoples forms an important factor in the origins of totalitarianism.[22] Consider, as central to the American-Indian experience: the collapse of conceptions of human rights in the face of culturally distant peoples, with result-

John Locke cited cannibalism of fathers over children as the consequence of unrestrained paternal authority. See *Of Civil Government,* op. cit., *First Treatise,* p. 40.

21. The analysis summarized here seeks to join the psychoanalytic theories of Melanie Klein and Géza Róheim to a tradition of interpreting America as a liberal society. Cf. Géza Róheim, *The Origins and Functions of Culture* (New York: Nervous and Mental Disease Monographs, 1943), and *Magic and Schizophrenia* (New York: International Universities Press, 1955); Melanie Klein, *Contributions to Psychoanalysis* (London: Hogarth Press, 1948), and Melanie Klein et al., eds., *New Directions in Psychoanalysis* (London: Travistock, 1955). The treatment of America as a liberal society derives from Alexis de Tocqueville, *Democracy in America,* 2 vols. (New York: Vintage Books, 1959); and Louis Hartz, *The Liberal Tradition in America* (New York: Harcourt, Brace, 1955). Cf. M. Rogin, *The Intellectuals and McCarthy* (Cambridge, Mass.: M.I.T. Press, 1967), pp. 32-44, and Rogin, "Southern California: Right-Wing Behavior and Political Symbols," in Rogin and John L. Shover, *Political Change in California* (Westport, Conn.: Greenwood, 1970), pp. 178-201. Suggestive in bridging the gap between psychoanalytic theory and American society were Erik H. Erikson, *Childhood and Society,* 2nd. ed. (Middlesex, Eng.: Penguin Books, 1965); Kenneth Keniston, *The Uncommitted* (New York: Harcourt, Brace and World, 1965).

"Liberal" political movements, as Hartz makes clear, are not the sole repositories of the American liberal tradition. That tradition equally underlies American right-wing perspectives. The term "liberal" in this essay is not limited to a narrowly political referent.

22. Hannah Arendt, *The Origins of Totalitarianism,* 2nd ed. (New York: Meridian Books, 1958), pp. 192-97. See also her discussion of imperialism, pp. 124-147.

ing civilized atrocities defended as responses to savage atrocities; easy talk about, and occasional practice of, tribal extermination; the perceived impossibility of cultural coexistence, and a growing acceptance of "inevitable" Indian extinction; total war, with all-or-nothing conflicts over living space, and minimal combatant-noncombatant distinctions; and the inability of the savage people to retire behind a stable frontier, provoking whites' confidence in their ability to conquer, subdue, and advance over obstacles in their environment. Noam Chomsky asks, "Is it an exaggeration to suggest that our history of extermination and racism is reaching its climax in Vietnam today? It is not a question that Americans can easily put aside."[23]

Admit that white symbolization of Indians had to cover a proto-totalitarian situation; does that make the symbols themselves significant causes of Indian policy, rather than mere rationalizations for it? The issue of causality is complex, and I plan no extended defense of the importance of cultural myths to the ongoing cultural and political life of a nation. At the very least, attention to myth will tell us what whites made of their encounter with the Indians, what meaning it had for them. This meaning developed out of, and was enriched by, innumerable specific interactions and policy decisions before, during, and after the major events of Indian removal. It is a peculiarly split view of human existence in which symbolizations of meaning operate in a closed universe of their own, divorced from the "real" facts of historical causation. Men make history; they develop complex inner worlds because (from infant frustrations through their experience as historical actors) they do not make it in circumstances of their own choosing. These inner worlds, projected outside, become part of the continuing history men do make.

The search for historical causes, moreover, may well be misleading. In the present case historical explanation ought to aim at the fullest significant description of the matrix of white-Indian relations. Any description which, in the name of pragmatism, behaviorism, or vulgar materialism, omitted the symbolic meaning actors gave to their actions, would be radically incomplete.

Surely, however, if our concern is with actors' perceptions, Freudian categories and loose talk of madness are gratuitous intrusions upon the language actually employed. The problem is this: Americans uniformly employed familial language in speaking of the Indians; most historians and political scientists have been systematically deaf to it. Lacking a theory which sensitized them to such a vocabulary and helped them interpret it, perhaps they could not hear what was being said. Let us begin to take seriously the words of those who made our Indian policy.

23. Chomsky, "After Pinkville," op. cit., p. 10. Cf. Drinnon, op. cit., pp. 36-38, 44-46.

II.

The American family began, in the antebellum white imagination, with the mother and child. Indians were the "sons of the forest," "the children of nature."[24] Savages were children because of their unrestrained impulse life, and because they remained unseparated from nature. The metaphors resemble, to their details, psychoanalytic descriptions of fantasies of the oral stage of infant bliss.

T.H. McKenney, chief administrator of Indian affairs from 1816 to 1830, offered the typical picture of the aboriginal tribes in pre-Columbian times.

> Onward, and yet onward, moved the bands, clothed in winter in the skins of beasts, and in the summer free from all such encumbrances. The earth was their mother, and upon its lap they reposed. Rude wigwams sheltered them. Hunger and thirst satisfied, sleep followed—and within this circle was contained the happiness of the aboriginal man.[25]

Indians were perfectly at home in nature. They had a primitive, preconscious, precivilized innocence. They had not yet become separated from the earth, but enjoyed "almost without restriction or control the blessings which flowed spontaneously from the bounty of nature."[26] Savages lived in a world of plenty, protected and nurtured by mother nature. Their world was Eden, or paradise.[27]

24. These phrases enter almost every discussion of the Indian question. On the identification of savages with children, cf. Fairchild, op. cit., pp. 190, 230, 366-390.

25. Thomas L. McKenney, *Memoirs, Official and Personal,* 2 vols. (New York: Paine and Burgur, 1846), 2: 33. This sort of stock description of the noble savage endured in America after it died out in Europe, and was utilized precisely by the makers of Indian policy. Cf. Fairchild, op. cit., pp. 20, 79, 298-99, 363-64. For more of McKenney's comparisons of savages to children (for example, the infant King Alfred ruling his realm from a three-legged stool), see 1: 78, 82.

26. William Robertson, quoted in Bernard W. Sheehan, "Paradise and the Noble Savage in Jeffersonian Thought," *William and Mary Quarterly,* 3rd ser., 26 (July 1969): 337. Robertson was an eighteenth-century Scotch man of letters, whose writings on American Indians deeply influenced American perceptions. Lewis Cass, for example, cited Robertson as the foremost authority on the Indian, and incorporated Robertson's views wholesale in his own essays and reports. Cf. Drinnon, op. cit., p. 41.

27. In Sheehan's summary (op. cit., p. 328), "The noble savage was ... untouched by the hands of man. He was impulsive, unrestrained, unburdened by social conventions.... Rather than standing aside from his surroundings, as did the civilized man, altering them to his own specifications, the noble savage blended into the surface of paradise."

Indians themselves contributed to the dominant metaphor: "We love our land; it is our mother, and we do not think anyone would take it from us if we did not wish to part with it." "We have grown up as the herbs of the woods, and do not wish to be transplanted to another soil." Cf. *IA,* 2: 230; Silver, op. cit., p. 181n. Cf. also Angie Debo, *The Road to Disappearance,* Oklahoma University The Civilization of the American Indians Series (Norman, Okla.: University of Oklahoma Press, 1941), pp. 42-44.

Their connectedness to nature in no way restricted Indian freedom, in the white view. Aborigines were free to wander from place to place without losing the tie to nature. Manly and independent, they "never submitted themselves to any laws, any coercive power, any shadow of government."[28] Although Indians spoke often to whites of the land and the bones of their father, the savages' connection to nature and freedom from paternal, governmental authority semmed most to excite white imaginations.

Francis Parkman reduced the metaphor to its psychological essence:

> The Indian is hewn out of rock. You can rarely change the form without destruction of the substance. Races of inferior energy have possessed a power of expansion and assimilation to which he is a stranger; and it is this fixed and rigid quality which has proved his ruin. He will not learn the arts of civilization, and he and forest must perish together. The stern, unchanging features of his mind excite our admiration from their very immutability; and we look with deep interest on the fate of this irreclaimable son of the wilderness, the child who will not be weaned from the breast of his rugged mother.[29]

Why the sense of doom in Parkman's passage? Why cannot the bliss of the infant at the mother's breast be sustained? Why must the Indian relinquish Eden or die, and why can he not give it up? The whites gave two, related answers. First, the Indians would not work; they were improvident and lacked the "principles of restraint"[30] necessary to preserve themselves against adversity. Overlooking, for their own political and myth-making functions, extensive Indian agriculture (which had kept the first white settlers from starving), they perceived the Indians simply as wandering hunters.[31] They could not be made to turn to agriculture; they would not "subdue and replenish" the earth, as the incessantly quoted biblical injunction ordered. They would not forsake the primitive, oral, accepting relation with nature

28. The language is Jefferson's; cf. Thomas Jefferson, *Notes on Virginia* in Adrienne Koch and William Peden, eds., *The Life and Selected Writings of Thomas Jefferson* (New York: Modern Library, 1944), pp. 210-13, 221. Cf. also Pearce, op. cit., pp. 152-53; Sheehan, op. cit., pp. 352-55; Staughton Lynd, *Intellectual Origins of American Radicalism* (New York: Random House, 1969), p. 85.

29. Parkman, op. cit., p. 63. According to a 1794 school text, savage freedom kept the Indian "in a state of infancy, weakness, and the greatest imperfection." Quoted in Pearce, op. cit., p. 161.

30. Lewis Cass, "Annual Report of the Secretary of War for 1831," *MA*, 4: 714.

31. Pearce, op. cit., pp. 68-70; Debo, op. cit., pp. 19-21, 369; R.S. Cotterill, *The Southern Indians: The Story of the Civilized Tribes Before Removal*, Oklahoma University The Civilization of the American Indians Series (Norman, Okla,: University of Oklahoma Press, 1954), pp. 9-11; Wilcomb E. Washburn, "The Moral and Legal Justification for Dispossessing the Indians," in James Morton Smith, ed., *Seventeenth Century American Essays in Colonial History* (Chapel Hill, N.C.: University of North Carolina Press, 1959), pp. 19-23.

and try to control and subdue her. They would not accumulate property, build lasting edifices, make contracts, and organize their lives around rules and restraints. They would not, so to speak, move from the oral to the anal stage.

The typical description of this unwillingness revealed the writer's own sense of loss, his own envy of the presumed Indian condition. Lewis Cass, the politician with most dealings with northern Indians in the decades following the War of 1812, sympathized,

> It is easy, in contemplating the situation of such a people, to perceive the difficulties to be encountered in any effort to produce a radical change in their condition. The *fulcrum* is wanting, upon which the lever must be placed. They are contented as they are; not contented merely, but clinging with a death-grasp to their own institutions.... To roam the forests at will, to pursue their game, to attack their enemies, to spend the rest of their lives in listless indolence, to eat inordinately when they have food, to suffer patiently when they have none, and to be ready at all times to die ... how unwilling a savage would be to exchange such a life for the stationary and laborious duties of civilized societies.[32]

In McKenney's words,

> Who are they of all the race of Adam, that would surrender all the freedom, and the abundance, that were enjoyed by the North American Indian, when his country was first invaded by our race, and place himself, voluntarily, under the restraints which civilization imposes? It is not in the nature of man to do this. It requires, before he can bring himself to endure the labor and toil that attend upon the civilized state, the operation of that stern law—necessity.[33]

As long as the Indians held property in common, they could not break their tie to nature; they would not work and save. "Separate property in land is the basis of civilized society." "The absence of it is the cause of want and consequently of decrease in numbers." Without private property there was no individual incentive to appropriate the fruits of one's labor. Moreover, the stage before private property was, in the liberal view, the stage prior to the development of active, individuated egos. "The absence of the *meum* and *teum,* in the general community of possession ... is a perpetual operating cause of the *vis inertiae* of savage life... [Private property]

32. [Lewis Cass], "Removal of the Indians," *North American Review* 46 (January 1830): 75.

33. McKenney, op. cit., 1: 123-24. A Cherokee version of the familiar metaphor appears in a letter to Secretary of War Calhoun (*IA,* 2: 474): "The happiness which the Indians once enjoyed, by a quiet and undisturbed ease, in their primitive situation, before the face of the white man was seen on this continent, was now poisoned by the bad fruits of the civilized tree which was planted around them."

may not unjustly be considered the parent of all improvements." "At the foundation of the whole social system lies individuality of property. It is, perhaps, nine times out of ten, the stimulus that mankind first feels. With it come all the delights that the word home expresses."[34]

The oral stage, in Freudian theory, precedes development of a separate, individuated ego. White Americans implicitly applied the same personality theory to the Indians. Indians, in the white view, lived in an undifferentiated relation to nature. Nature appropriated to oneself through work underlay ownership and control of the self.[35] Lacking private property, Indians lacked a self they could call their own. Since they remained in oral dependence on nature, Indians could not take care of themselves.

But he who does not work cannot eat. The primitive bounty of nature, Americans insisted, was not inexhaustible. As the whites invaded Indian land, killed their game, and destroyed their crops, Indians began to starve in large numbers. This was taken as a sign of their improvidence; their alleged failure to use government rations frugally was further evidence.[36] Horace Greeley, crusading anti-slavery editor and future presidential candidate, explained after a trip through the West in 1859:

> The Indians are children. Their arts, wars, treaties, alliances, habitations, crafts, properties, commerce, comforts, all belong to the very lowest and rudest ages of human existence.... Any band of school-boys from ten to fifteen years of age, are quite as capable of ruling their appetites, devising and upholding a public policy, constituting and conducting a state or community as an average Indian tribe.... [The Indian is] a slave of appetite and sloth, never emancipated from the tyranny of one passion save by the ravenous demands of another.... As I passed over those magnificent bottoms of the Kansas ... constituting the very best corn land on earth, and saw their men sitting round the doors of their lodges in the height of the planting season,... I could not help saying, "These people must die out— there is no help for them. God has given the earth to those who will subdue and cultivate it, and it is vain to struggle against his righteous decree."[37]

34. U.S. Congress, *Register of Debates,* VI (1829-30): 1093. J.B. Kinney, *A Continent Lost—A Civilization Won* (Baltimore: Johns Hopkins Press, 1937), pp. 102, 109. Kinney is quoting from Reports of the Commissioners of Indian Affairs for 1832 (E.H. Herring) and 1838 (T.H. Crawford). This book is an invaluable (albeit unconscious) source book on white efforts to impose private property upon Indians.

35. Cf. C.B. McPherson, *The Political Theory of Possessive Individualism* (Oxford: Oxford University Press, 1964), pp. 53-70, 137-42, passim.

36. Among the many examples, cf. Captain Eugene F. Ware, "The Indian War of 1864," in Wilcomb E. Washburn, ed., *The Indian and the White Man* (New York: Doubleday, 1964), pp. 284-88.

37. Quoted in James Parton, *Life of Andrew Jackson,* 3 vols. (Boston: Mason &

The self-righteous sadism in this passage has several sources. Childish irresponsibility will bring deserved death upon the Indians; one need no longer pity them, or hesitate over expansion onto Indian lands. More deeply, even McKenney and Cass could not envy unambiguously the Indian world of childhood freedom and maternal protection. Such longing violated just the liberal independence and self-reliance which called it forth. Greeley's formulation directed rage at the need to forsake one's own private Eden against those who refused to forsake theirs. Having lost their own Eden, the whites could take Indian land as well.

The rage was not simply that of an anal society against its own fantasies of oral bliss. There was another argument, about another rage. The Indians, it was held, had given up their right to inhabit Eden by their own primitive violence.

In part those who emphasized Indian violence did not stress savage nobility. The mythology of violence turned Indians into "monsters in human shape." "Infuriated hell-hounds," they disturbed the "forest paradise" instead of inhabiting it.[38] The concept of the Indian was split into the noble savage and the "starved wolf", "the man who would scalp an infant in his cradle,"[39] was a literary cliché.

There was a deeper intimacy, however, between innocence and violence. Many writers, like Francis Parkman and Lewis Cass, stressed them both equally and found them inextricably related—as innocence and violent loss of self-control would be in children. Like children, Indians were not responsible for their violence; they lacked the intelligence and sense of responsibility of more advanced peoples.[40]

The common root of innocence and violence, in the liberal view of the Indian, once again recalls psychoanalytic descriptions of the oral stage. Melanie Klein has suggested that the infant at the breast has primitive rages as well as fantasies of bliss and plenty. He totally devours the breast, in these "body destruction fantasies," and enters the mother and devours her imagined bodily contents. In part these fantasies of the "manic feast" are innocent in

---

Hamlin, 1863), 1: 401n.

38. For some variations on the theme, see John K. Mahon, *History of the Second Seminole War 1835-1842* (Gainesville, Florida: University of Florida Press, 1967), pp. 265-70, 311; Malcolm J. Rohrbough, *The Land Office Business* (New York: Oxford University Press, 1968), p. 59; and Jackson in Parton, op. cit., 2: 451, and *MA,* 1: 705. Cotton Mather's "tawny serpents" is perhaps the most famous of these epithets. On Indians disturbing the forest paradise, see Parkman's "ungoverned children, fired with the instincts of devils." op. cit., p. 463, and pp. 323n, 436-37. Tennessee Governor Joseph McMinn, urging removal of the Indians from the old Southwest, explained that then "each southern and western inhabitant will cultivate his own garden of Eden" (*IA,* 1: 856).

39. McKenney, op. cit., 1: 112-13.

40. Cf. Fairchild, op. cit., pp. 90-91.

origin; in part they express the infant's primitive destructive impulses. Infant sadism is given added force from rage at the withdrawal of the breast. The infant wants to retaliate against the protective mother who has withdrawn her nurture. These vengeful fantasies are themselves intolerable, as the infant both creates from his projections a persecutory mother who must be destroyed, and blames himself and his devouring desires for the loss of the breast.

I am not sure what it means to speak of infant aggressive rages, or to allege that separation anxiety engenders in the baby elaborated fantasies of oral bliss and rage. Such language may well impose adult categories meaningless to infant experience. But the oral stage engenders both the energy for those fantasies and their content. Later childhood or adult longing to return to the imagined state of oral bliss is inseparable from vengeful rage against the mother, self-accusations, and persecutory fantasies.[41]

For our purposes two points must be stressed. First, oral bliss and primitive rage both aim to end the separation of the child from the mother; both involve "regression to the phase that precedes the evolution of the ego [and] ... the testing of reality."[42] In fantasy the mother and the separate ego are destroyed. Since oral rage aims at total unity and destruction, Mrs. Klein labels it "schizophrenic," or "insane."

Second, longing for union carries with it desire for vengeance. Those experiencing separation anxiety do not simply want union with the mother; they want to express primitive rage against her as well. But liberal men had no more right to primitive rage than primitive sustenance. Scapegoats, upon whom aggression was projected, would relieve the guilt engendered by these vengeful fantasies; they would embody violence, and could be punished for it.

Indians well served this function They were the bogeymen who frightened children at night in early America. Thomas McKenney makes the connection, in a passage perfectly introducing our discussion of Indian oral violence.

> Which of us has not listened with sensations of horror to nursery
> stories that are told of the Indian and his cruelties? In our infant
> mind he stood for the Moloch of our country. We have been made
> to hear his yell; and to our eyes have been presented his tall,

---

41. The psychoanalytic literature on the formation of a primitive, pre-oedipal superego is extensive and, in my view, convincing. See Melanie Klein, "The Early Development of Conscience in the Child," "A Contribution to the Psychogenesis of Manic-Depressive States," and "Mourning and its Relation to Manic-Depressive States," all in *Contributions of Psychoanalysis,* op. cit.; Sandor Rado, "The Problem of Melancholia," *International Journal of Psychoanalysis* 9 (October 1928): 420-38; George Gero, "The Construction of Depression," *International Journal of Psychoanalysis* 17 (October 1936): 423-61; Annie Reich, "Early Identifications as Archaic Elements in the Superego," *Journal of the American Psychoanalytic Association* 2 (March 1954): 218-38.

42. Róheim, *Magic and Schizophrenia,* op. cit., p. 224.

> gaunt form with the skins of beasts dangling around his limbs, and
> his eyes like fire, eager to find some new victim on which to fasten
> himself, and glut his appetite for blood.... We have been startled by
> the shriek of the dying mother; and hushed that we might hear the
> last sigh of the expiring infant....[43]

Melanie Klein comments about such childhood anxieties:

> We get to look upon the child's fear of being devoured, or cut up,
> or torn to pieces, or its terror of being surrounded and pursued by
> menacing figures, as a regular component of its mental life; and we
> know that the man-eating wolf, the fire spewing dragon, and all the
> evil monsters out of myth and fairy stories flourish and exert their
> unconscious influence in the phantasy of each individual child, and
> it feels itself persecuted and threatened by those evil shapes.[44]

White mythology pushed Indian violence back to the stage of the primitive, oral rage in several ways. First, Indian violence was exterminatory; it threatened ego boundaries and the self. Second, the quality of the violence itself, as McKenney's images suggest, was oral. Third, women and infants were its targets. Finally, the violence was perceived as presexual.

Indians were most commonly attacked in the name of self-defense. If we personify America, as was common in the nineteenth century, then this resistance to the Indians acquires the personal significance of defense of the self. Indians attacked America before the secure emergence of the country. They exemplified fears that the independent nation could not survive, fear that had led many Americans to intrigue at its dismemberment.[45] Indians were the first enemies the young country had to conquer. Expressing his gratitude for Jackson's invasion of Florida in pursuit of the Seminoles, Mississippi Senator Poindexter proclaimed, "You have protected us in the time of our infancy against the inexorable Red Sticks and their allies; you have compelled them to relinquish possession of our land, and ere long we shall strengthen into full manhood under the smiles of a beneficent Providence."[46]

43. McKenney, op. cit., 1: 230. Cf. Tennessee Senator Felix Grundy (quoted in Parton, op. cit., 1: 140): "If I am asked to trace my memory back, and name the first indelible impression it received, it would be the sight of my eldest brother bleeding and dying under the wounds inflicted by the tomahawk and scalping knife."

44. Klein, "Early Development of Conscience," op. cit., p. 268.

45. For example, during the War of 1812, Jackson feared America would be "apportioned amonghst the powers of Urope," and foresaw Russian intervention in the war (JC, 2: 32, 37). Before the adoption of the Constitution he had been sympathetic to a frontier intrigue to attach the Southwest to Spain, to insure navigation of the Mississippi and protection from the Indians. Cf. James, op. cit., 1: 58-61. He also could never convince himself that Aaron Burr in 1806 aimed at anything more than gaining new territory for the United States. Cf. James, op. cit., 1: 110, 126-38.

46. Quoted in Parton, op. cit., 2: 547.

Indians attacked the young nation at its boundaries, keeping them confused and insecure. Whites' images indicate that concern over the country's
boundaries aggravated, and was reinforced by, concern over the boundaries of
their own egos. A securely individuated ego requires a stable sense of boundaries between self and environment, and whites insisted America, too, needed
stable boundaries to mature. Mobility and expansion aborted stable environments in America, but these qualities were located on Indian culture, not
white. Indians, one nineteenth-century authority explained, were peculiarly
characterized by "the absence of private property," the "want of a home,"
the practice of "roaming from place to place," and "the habit of invading
without scruple the land of others." Only private property, whose significance for liberalism I have already noted, saved mobile, expansionist,
Jacksonian America from fitting this description.[47]

Indians not only embodied absence of boundaries; they also invaded white
boundaries. Peace talks with the Indians "infesting our frontier," wrote the
young Andrew Jackson in 1794, "are only opening an Easy door for the Indians to pass through to butcher our citizens."[48] As long as Indians remained
on Georgia land, complained Governor G.M. Troup, Georgia's "political organization is incompetent; her civil polity is deranged; her military force cannot
be reduced to systematic order and subordination; the extent of her actual
resources cannot be counted; and all because Georgia is not in the possession of
of her vacant territory."[49]

The vision of Indian violence threatening the selfhood of young America
reversed the actual situation. The expanding nation reiterated the claim of
self-defense as it obliterated one tribe after another. Self-defense against
the Indians excused expansion into Florida, Texas, and (less successfully)
Canada.[50] "An Indian will claim everything and anything," complained
Andrew Jackson, after including ten million acres of Cherokee land in a
treaty coerced from the Creeks.[51] Indians became the bad children, upon

47. James Hall, co-author with McKenney of the most important antebellum vol-
umes on the various tribes, quoted in Pearce, op. cit., p. 120. Compare Tocqueville's
description of America in "A Fortnight in the Wilds": "A nation of conquerors,... it is
a wandering people." Alexis de Tocqueville, *Journey to America,* ed., J.P. Mayer,
(London: Faber & Faber, 1959), p. 339. Southern author William Gilmore Simms,
criticizing the United States in 1843, wrote, "A wandering people is more or less a
barbarous one," in Ekirch, op. cit., p. 183.

48. *JC,* 1: 13.

49. *IA,* 2: 735.

50. Cf. George Dangerfield, *The Era of Good Feeling* (New York: Harcourt, Brace,
1952), p. 151; Abel, op. cit., pp. 327-29; Parton, op. cit., 2: 449-52, 498-99, 513-15;
Silver, op. cit., pp. 192-215; *JC,* 1: 331, 396-97; 2: 374-86, 395-98; 5: 423-24; 6: 278,
290; *MA,* 6: 1044-45; H.S. Halbert and T.H. Ball, *The Creek War of 1813 and 1814*
(Chicago: Donohue & Henneberry, 1895), pp. 270-72.

51. *JC,* 2: 271-72. Cf. p. 245 for an elaborate fantasy of Indian claims, which
simply reverses the specific progress of white expansionism. The Creek name for

whom was projected the whites' own aggressive expansionism.

Indians did threaten American identity, even if they could not destroy the country, since that identity required expanding over and obliterating savagery. In the name of attacking threats to the independent self, America could "swallow" one tribe after another.[52] Security was possible only once the Indian threat on the boundaries was finally stilled, and whites need not coexist with independent realities unconnected to them and out of their control. Indian threats to the self-defense of expanding white America suggest that early time when a secure self has not emerged, and is threatened with retaliatory extermination for its own aggressive rage.

White descriptions of Indian "atrocities" concretely expressed the terror of oral rage. Lewis Cass insisted that Indians were taught from infancy to take pleasure in war and in inflicting cruelty, that they loved scalping, and that a "man-eating Society" which devoured prisoners flourished among some tribes.[53] A nineteenth-century history of the eastern frontier was more graphic: "The Indian kills indiscriminately. His object is the total extermination of his enemies." "Those barbarous sons of the forest exercised ... the full indulgence of all their native thirst for human blood." Prisoners were saved "for the purpose of feasting the feelings of ferocious vengeance of himself and his comrades, by the torture of his captives."[54]

These passages and countless others like them pictured Indian violence as insane, exterminatory, and dismembering. Its method was oral; and it was protected by primitive magic. Melanie Klein and Géza Róheim describe the aggressive fantasies of adults experiencing separation anxiety in just these terms. The reality basis provided by methods of warfare among some tribes, isolated incidents, and acts by individual Indians or outlaw bands permitted these images to dominate the mythological Indian.[55]

---

settlers was "the-people-greedily-grasping-after-land." See Debo, op. cit., p. 54.

52. Thomas Hart Benton for the 1824 Senate Committee on Indian Affairs, *IA*, 2: 512.

53. [Lewis Cass], "Policy and Practice of the United States and Great Britain in Their Treatment of Indians." *North American Review* 55 (April 1827): 372-76.

54. Reverend Dr. Joseph Doddridge, "Notes on the Settlements and Indian Wars...," in Washburn, *The Indian and the White Man,* op. cit., pp. 271-73.

55. Erikson and Róheim suggest that child-rearing practices among some primitive peoples encourage oral aggression; this would clearly bear on white fears, but my anthropological literacy is far too inadequate for this line of speculation. Cf. Erikson on the Sioux, pp. 127-50; Géza Róheim, "The Evolution of Culture," in Bruce Mazlish, ed., *Psychoanalysis and History* (Englewood Cliffs, N.J.: Prentice-Hall, 1963), pp. 72-76.

Some tribes, although generally not those in the Southwest, did engage in torture. But incidents were exaggerated, universalized to all "bad" Indians, and in many cases tribes had only learned torture from Europeans who tortured them in the sixteenth and seventeenth centuries. See Nathaniel Knowles, "The Torture of Captives by the Indians of Eastern North America," *Proceedings of the American Philosophical Society* 82 (1940): 151-225. The fascination with Indian "atrocities" out of all proportion to their importance served political and, I will argue, psychological functions.

Indians on the warpath were always "maddened," and their aim was total extermination of the whites. Indians tortured and dismembered their enemies; scalping of corpses and other mutilations received prominent attention. Indian rage was oral; the aborigines were cannibalistic, and had a "thirst for blood." One Indian claimed, it was said at the beginning of the Creek War, that he "had got fat eating white people's flesh."[56]

Indians were protected by primitive magic. Prophets convinced them they were omnipotent, beyond harm from bullets. War cries and terrifying war paint indicated to the whites that Indians sought victory through terror and awe, rather than practical, adult methods of warfare. White generals and Indian agents, sometimes whistling in the dark, insisted that their soldiers were not children, and would not be frightened by Indian shrieks and costumes.[57]

Indians as monsters, then, carried out forbidden infantile violence. They at least partially embodied guilt felt over the child's own aggressive and destructive fantasies. Indian atrocities therefore not only justified wars against Indians; in response to Indian violence whites themselves engaged in fantasies and activities expressing primal rage. Punishing the criminal permitted them to participate in the forbidden criminal activity.[58]

Since Indian violence was exterminatory, whites could exterminate Indians. When a few Creek warriors killed some settlers at the outbreak of the 1812 War, the Tennessee legislature urged the governor to "carry a campaign into the heart of the Creek nation and exterminate them." The August *Niles Register,* commenting on the Second Seminole War, hoped that "the miserable creatures will be speedily swept from the face of the earth."[59] Andrew Jackson often called for extermination of his Indian enemies.[60] In 1816,

56. For examples, see Parton, op. cit., 2: 431; Washburn, *The Indian and the White Man,* op. cit., p. 444; ("The ferocious creature had tasted blood and could not restrain himself til he could be surfeited.") *IA,* 1: 843; and a host of letters reprinted in *IA* and *MA;* Congressional debates, etc.

57. *IA,* 1: 848; *JC,* 1: 337-38, 488; Parton, op. cit., 1: 524. The terror and flight of the Illinois militia during Black Hawk's War are described in William Hagan, *The Sac and Fox Indians,* Oklahoma University The Civilization of the American Indians Series (Norman, Okla.: University of Oklahoma Press, 1958), pp. 158-61.

58. The classic statement is Sigmund Freud, *Totem and Taboo* (London: Routledge & Paul, 1960), p. 72: "If one person succeeds in gratifying a repressed desire, the same desire is bound to be kindled in all the other members of the community. In order to keep the temptation down, the envied transgressor must be deprived of the fruit of his enterprise, and the punishment will not infrequently give those who carry it out an opportunity of committing the same outrage under cover of an act of expiation. This is indeed one of the foundations of the human penal system."

59. *JC,* 1: 416; Debo, op. cit., p. 78; Mahon, op. cit., p. 122.

60. During the Creek War, Jackson wrote, "I must destroy those deluded victims doomed to destruction by their own restless and savage conduct." He further insisted that all Creeks that did not fight with him against the hostiles should be treated as enemies. *JC,* 1: 422-23.

long after the end of the Creek War, he told a general serving under him to destroy every village refusing to turn over the alleged murderers of two whites. He had urged burning Creek villages well before the outbreak of that war, and continued burning them well after the last battle.[61]   A few years later he entered Florida, burned Seminole villages, and drove out the women and children on the grounds that "the protection of our citizens will require that the wolf be struck in his den."   In 1836 he urged that Seminole women and children be tracked down, and "captured or destroyed" to end the Second Seminole War. He continued to apply the metaphor of wolves and dens.[62] Violations of Indian truce flags, in that war and others, were common, on the grounds one need not observe civilized rules of war with savages.[63]

Indian wars also permitted verbal participation in savage violence. Jackson wrote to the governor of Pensacola in 1814 that, if the Spanish forts were not surrendered, "I will not hold myself responsible for the conduct of my enraged soldiers and Indian warriors." "An eye for an eye, tooth for tooth, scalp for scalp."[64]

Indians directed their primal rage, in the white view, against "aged matrons and helpless infants."   They "snatched the infant from the nipple of its mother, and bashed its brains out against a tree."   Men could presumably defend themselves; their killing had little symbolic significance. But "helpless women have been butchered, and the cradle stained with the blood of innocence."   "When we figure to ourselves our beloved wives and little, prattling infants, butchered, mangled, murdered, and torn to pieces by savage bloodhounds and wallowing in their gore, you can judge of our feelings." Jackson accused the Governor of Pensacola of receiving a "matricidal band" after "the butchery of our women and children," "as the Father his prodigal Son."[65]

Indians thus became the bad "children of nature," whose exterminatory aggression totally destroyed the mother and the "innocent babe." Purified

61. *JC*, 2: 238-39; *JC*, 1: 230, 500.

62. *IA*, 2: 162; *MA*, 1: 703; *JC*, 5: 468, 512.

63. Mahon, op. cit., pp. 198-300; Grant Foreman, *Indian Removal* (Norman, Okla.: University of Oklahoma Press, 1942), pp. 342-63. During Black Hawk's War a boat commander, whose crew had fired upon an Indian party, killing women and children, explained, "As we neared them they raised a white flag and endeavored to decoy us, but we were a little too old for them." Seymour Dunbar, *A History of Travel in America*, 3 vols. (Indianapolis, Bobbs-Merrill, 1915), 2: 464.

64. *JC*, 2: 42, 28-29, repeated 44.

65. The quotes in the text come, in order, from *JC*, 2: 386; U.S., Congress, *Register of Debates*, VIII (1831-32): 791; *MA*, 1: 720; *JC*, 1: 231; *JC*, 2: 28-29. The second is Congressman Buckner of Missouri; all the rest are Jackson. For still other Jackson variations, see *JC*, 1: 186, 225-26; *MA*, 1: 720; Parton, op. cit., 1: 213, 426. For other contributions, cf. Mahon, op. cit., pp. 247-48; Doddridge in Washburn, *The Indian and the White Man*, op. cit., p. 273; Parton, op. cit., 1: 546; *IA*, 1: 839, 843; Arthur W. Thompson, *Jacksonian Democracy on the Florida Frontier* (Gainesville, Fla.: University of Florida Press, 1961), p. 33.

by his elimination of these monsters, the good children could grow safely to manhood.[66]

Indians not only murdered white women; they also treated their own women badly. Savages gained innocent bliss at the expense of their women. The Indian reposed in nature on the lap of his mother, McKenney explained, but "his squaw" paid the price. "Alas! then, as now, her shoulders were made to bear the weight, and her hands to perform the drudgery of the domestic labor." Indians had to be civilized so they would learn to respect their women.[67]

McKenney shared the view of women prevalent in Jacksonian America. The pure, honored, and respected white female personified civilized virtues. At the same time expanding America attacked and subdued mother nature, and understood this victory in personal terms. Jacksonians' personifications of their enemies—whether effeminate aristocrats or the devouring, "monster hydra" bank—exhibited fear of domination by women.[68] The culture resolved its ambivalence over women by splitting femaleness into passionate and uncontrolled images, which had to be destroyed, and feminine enforcers of civilized values, who had to be protected. Because Indian men were not separated from savage, violent, rock-like nature, they brutalized Indian women. Once again Indians resolved white ambivalences in unacceptably self-indulgent ways, and had to be punished for it. Liberal self-indulgence came cnly in the punishment.

The Indian threat to women was not perceived as sexual, or oedipal. Indians did not kill men to possess women. Mothers, not fathers, were the targets of Indian violence. This violence, moreover, was not sexual. Sexual assaults played almost no role in stories of Indian atrocities, in striking contrast to the mythology of blacks. Winthrop Jordan writes,

> Negroes seemed more highly sexed to the colonists than did the American Indians.... Far from finding Indians lusty and lascivious, they discovered them to be notably deficient in ardor and virility.

66. Nathaniel Hawthorne's work, preoccupied with oedipal guilt and the "sins of the fathers," contains an example of Indians as surrogate father-killers. The hero of "Alice Doan's Confession" recalls a childhood scene, in which he stands over the body of his dead father and imagines he has killed him. In fact he is innocent; the killing was done by Indians. See Frederick C. Crews, *The Sins of the Fathers* (New York: Oxford University Press, 1966), pp. 44-45. On Indians and American women and children, see Leslie A. Fiedler, *The Return of the Vanishing American* (New York: Stern & Day, 1968), pp. 50-134.

67. McKenney, op. cit., 1: 33-34; cf. Parton, op. cit., 1: 401-402.

68. Cf. Fiedler, *Return of the Vanishing American;* and Fiedler, *Love and Death in the American Novel* (New York: Criterion, 1960). The bank "devoured the western cities in its jaws;" office-holders only wanted "a tit to suck the treasury pap;" etc. Cf. *JC,* 4: 14, '21; 5, 52; Bray Hammond, *Banks and Politics in America from the Revolution to the Civil War* (Princeton, N.J.: Princeton University Press, 1957), p. 259.

(Eventually and almost inevitably a European commentator announced that the Indian's penis was smaller than the European's.)
And the colonists developed no image of the Indian as a potential
rapist; their descriptions of Indian attacks did not include Indians
"reserving the young women for themselves." In fact, the entire
interracial complex did not pertain to the Indians.[69]

Jordan believes white mythology treated Indians more kindly than
Negroes. Blacks were sexual threats who had to be repressed; Indians were
the first Americans. Certainly there was greater sympathy and identification
with Indians. But this did not make the Indian danger any less threatening.
Blacks represented sexual threat and temptation; the relation had reached
the stage of forbidden love. The Indian was a fragment of the self, that
primitive, oral part which was dangerously pleasure-seeking and aggressive and,
therefore, in the name of self-defense, had to be destroyed. Indians represented the pre-ego state of undifferentiated bliss and rage. As Leslie Fiedler
puts it, if the blacks were about sex, the Indians were about madness.[70] The
blacks were a sexual, oedipal threat to white men; the Indians were a pre-
oedipal aggressive threat to the mother-child relationship.

The Indians lacked authority; fathers had not yet entered the picture. It
was the job of whites to introduce them. What kind of fathers would a culture which longed for the Indians' fatherless freedom offer them?

III.

American policy makers insisted upon their paternal obligations to the
Indian tribes; they sought to subject Indians to paternal, presidential authority. In legal relations, too, Indians were the "wards" of the state.[71] If one
takes seriously the evidence of speeches and documents, whites could not
imagine Indians outside the parent-child context.

"What then," asked Alabama Governor John Murphy, "is to be done for
this people, who had priority of us in the occupation of this favored land?...
The United States should assume a parental guardianship over them," and
extend the benefits of learning, religion, and the arts.[72] P.B. Porter, John
Quincy Adams' secretary of state, explained, "In their present destitute and
deplorable condition and which is constantly growing more helpless, it would
seem to be not only the right but the duty of the government to take them
under its paternal care, and to exercise over their persons and property the
salutory rights and duties of guardianship."[73]

69. Jordan, op. cit., pp. 162-63; cf. Mahon, op. cit., p. 125.
70. Fiedler, *Return of the Vanishing American*, pp. 178-79. Or, in the words of
a nineteenth-century American, the country's happiness was only threatened by "the
Negro in our bosom and the Indian on our borders."
71. See *Worcester v. Georgia,* VI Peters (1832): 512-559; Kinney, pp. 9-10, passim.
72. *IA,* 2: 246.
73. *MA,* 4: 4. It would be greatly in error to think that the language of fathers and

Such paternalism offered the Indians not simply help, but a redefinition of their identity. It defined them as children, which in fact they were not. The paternal metaphor forced the tribes into childish dependence upon white society. This was particularly devastating in a liberal culture which had eliminated legitimate, hierarchal authority and believed that "manly independence" offered the only proper basis for relations among men.[74] When such a society imported the family into politics, it was likely to impose an insecure and overbearing paternal domination. To insist that Indians be shown "their real state of dependence"[75] upon government was, I will argue, to infantilize them. Infantilization provides the major significance of the call for paternal authority.

The process of infantilization has been studied in many contexts: concentration camps; slave societies; total institutions such as insane asylums, old people's homes, and prisons; environments of isolation and sensory deprivation; schizophrenic families; housewives in suburban families; and efforts to manipulate mass publics for political purposes (such as to win support for the war in Vietnam). These environments, it is argued, break the social relations, cultural norms, and normal expectations of those subjected to them. "Ceremonies of degredation" destroy the victim's connection to his previously validated social self. Individuals lose social support for their own, personal experience of reality. The infantilization process, calling into question one's basic security in and trust of the environment, undermines the independent ego. Elimination of ties to objects in the environment produces an extreme sense of object loss, and consequent regression to infantile longings for protection, connection, and loss of self. Infantilization creates acute separation anxiety, and calls into question individuation beyond the oral stage.

The victim's blank and bare environment offers him only one remaining source of gratification, the authority who manipulates rewards and punishments. Thus the very oppressor becomes the source of values and sustenance. The infantilized victim, in the extreme case, identifies with his oppressor and seeks total dependence upon him.[76]

---

children was used only in communications to the Indians, not when whites addressed the problem among themselves. Indeed, Indians themselves often gave the rhetoric its peculiarly American significance. A Cherokee delegation, appealing to President Monroe, was "confident that his youngest children, as well as our elder brothers, will equally have a place in his mind, and that protection and measures for the amelioration of our condition will be pursued until we can rise from our present state of minority to a state of more perfect manhood, and become citizens" (*IA*, 2: 147).

74. On the weakness of paternal authority in the American family, see Tocqueville, *Democracy in America*, 2: 202-206.

75. *JC*, 2: 387n.

76. Among the studies of infantilization, cf. Bruno Bettelheim, "Individual and Mass Behavior in Extreme Situations," *Journal of Abnormal Psychiatry* 38 (October 1943); Bruno Bettelheim, *The Informed Heart* (Glencoe, Ill.: Free Press, 1960),

It could be argued that white rhetoric and policy did infantilize Indians, destroying tribal cultures and undermining, for large numbers, the simple will to live. The anhedonia which decimated thousands of Indians after a certain stage of white engulfment struck many observers. But infantilization has often been studied from the child's perspective. The infantilization imposed on victims may well serve needs for the self-appointed parent-figures. My concern is with infantilization from the parent's point of view.

Whites perceived Indians, I suggested, as children in a sustaining, oral relationship to nature. Since that relationship was a projection of forbidden white longings, it could not be permitted to remain a cultural alternative. But the forbidden oral longings would not disappear. With the parental metaphor whites substituted paternal domination over infantilized Indians for the dependence on nature. Now the white father and his instruments became the only source of gratification. As parents, while policy makers could participate in the dual-unity situation from the position of domination instead of dependence.

The model for the white father and his red children was not a family relation permitting growth, but a family with schizophrenogenic elements. Of the parents in such families Searles writes, "In essence, the parents need for security cannot allow him or her to feel the child as a separate identity, and the parent cannot give indication to the child that the child is capable of emotionally affecting the parent." The child must be "denied the experience of feeling himself to be an individual human entity, distinct from but capable of emotional contact with the parent."[77]

The theory of paternal assistance offered the Indians aid in growing up. But the very notion of growth was infantilizing. Indians were offered only the alternatives of civilization or death. The House Committee on Indian

pp. 107-263; Stanley Elkins, *Slavery* (Chicago: University of Chicago Press, 1959), pp. 81-139; Erving Goffman, *Asylums* (New York: Anchor Books, 1961); Harold F. Searles, *Collected Papers on Schizophrenia and Related Subjects* (New York: International Universities Press, 1965), pp. 254-283, 717-751; R.D. Laing, *The Divided Self* (Middlesex, Eng.: Penguin Books, 1965), pp. 172-205; R.D. Laing and A. Esterson, *Sanity, Madness and the Family* (Middlesex, Eng.: Penguin Books, 1970); Jules Henry, *Culture Against Man* (New York: Random House, 1963), pp. 322-474; Betty Friedan, *The Feminine Mystique* (New York: Norton, 1963), pp. 276-298; Walter O. Weyrauch, "Law in Isolation, The Penthouse of Astronaughts," *Trans-Action* (June 1968), pp. 139-46; Isidore Ziferstein, "Psychological Habituation to War: A Socio-psychological Case Study," *American Journal of OrthoPsychiatry* 38 (April 1967): 467-68. For a magnificent early formulation, see Victor Tausk, "On the Origins of the Influencing Machine in Schizophrenia," in Robert Fliess, ed., *The Psychoanalytic Reader* (New York: International Universities Press, 1948).

77. Searles, op. cit., pp. 40-42. Tocqueville's observations about the pioneer are to the point: "Even his feelings for his family have become merged in a vast egotism, and one cannot be sure whether he regards his wife and children as anything more than a detached part of himself." ("Fortnight in the Wilds," in ed., Mayer, op. cit., p. 339.

Affairs forecast in 1818, "In the present state of our country one of two things seem to be necessary, either that those sons of the forest should be moralized or exterminated."[78] Senator Thomas Hart Benton explained that the disappearance of the Indians should not be mourned. "Civilization or extinction has been the fate of all people who have found themselves in the track of advancing whites; civilization, always the preference of the advancing whites, has been pressed as an object, while extinction has followed as a consequence of its resistance."[79]

Such theories, as has often been noted, helped justify white occupation of Indian land.[80] Since the "hunting tribes" did not "subdue and replenish" the earth, more advanced agricultural societies could take their land. The decline of the barbarous people was necessary to the progress of civilization.[81] But I want to focus on a somewhat different significance of the choice between death and civilization.

In the white scheme, civilization meant, no less than death, the disappearance of the Indians.[82] They could not remain Indians and grow up; their

78. Quoted in Francis Paul Prucha, *American Indian Policy in the Formative Years* (Cambridge, Mass.: Harvard University Press, 1962), p. 220.

79. Thomas Hart Benton, "Speech on the Oregon Question," in C. Merton Babcock, ed., *The American Frontier* (New York: Holt, Rinehart and Winston, 1965), p. 223.

80. See the discussion in Part I, above, and the references cited in note 13. The bald argument that agricultural societies could take the land of hunters is stressed in the secondary literature somewhat out of proportion to its appearance in the sources; I may have, in retribution, slighted it here. A good, compact discussion is Mary E. Young, "Indian Removal and Land Allotment: The Civilized Tribes and Jacksonian Justice," *American Historical Review* 64 (October 1958):37-38.

81. E.g., Cass, "Removal of the Indians," op. cit., pp. 64, 77.

82. A southern Congressman tellingly exploited the logic of the sentimental friends of the Indians. Taking direct control of Indian land, Congressman Wilde began, "we should become their real benefactors; and we should perform the office of the great father...." He concluded,

> But the race of Indians will perish! Yes sir! The Indians of this continent, like all other men, savage or civilized, must perish.... What is history but the obituary of nations?... Whose fate do we lament? The present generation of Indians? They will perish like the present generation of white men....
>
> When gentlemen talk of preserving the Indians, what is it that they mean to preserve? Is it their mode of life? No. You intend to convert them from hunters to agriculturalists or herdsmen. Is it their barbarous laws and customs? No. You promise to furnish them with a code, and prevail upon them to adopt habits like your own. Their language? No. You intend to supersede their imperfect jargon by teaching them your own rich, copious, energetic tongue. Their religion? No. You intend to convert them from their miserable and horrible superstitions to the mild and cheering doctrines of Christianity.
>
> What is it, then, that constitutes Indian individuality—the identity of that race which gentlemen are so anxious to preserve? Is it the

only hope was to "become merged in the mass of our population."[83] "The ultimate point of rest and happiness for them is to let our settlements and theirs meet and blend together, to intermingle, and to become one people incorporating themselves with us as citizens of the United States."[84] Similar efforts to force indigenous peoples into a single "modernizing" pattern have continued to hypnotize our policy makers. "Merged" into liberal society, Indians would no longer offer subversive forms of experience, forcing whites to encounter identities not replicas of their own.

Requiring Indians to mature into whites or die irrevocably split childhood from adult experience. Savagery could maintain itself only by fleeing westward. Providence decreed that "the hunting tribes must retreat before the advance of civilization, or perish under the shade of the white man's settlements."[85] Alleged tribal willingness to leave their land for the West even indicated, in white projections, that childhood would not resist maturity.[86] Jackson and the other proponents of Indian removal promised the tribes that they could remain forever on their new land. But the spirit of the plan, and the actual outcome, was more accurately characterized by Cherokee agent R.J. Meigs. One educated Cherokee, he claimed, suggested that land given the Indians not be bounded on the west; the Indians could then continue to move west as the tide of civilization advanced from the east.[87]

But politicians who argued isolating the Indians would protect them also called for the march of civilization across the continent. The integrity of the

---

more copper color of the skin, which marks them—according to your prejudices at least—an inferior—a conquered and degraded race?

But alas! The Indians melt away before the white man, like snow before the sun! Well, sir! Would you keep the snow and lose the sun?

See *Register of Debates*, VI (1829-1830): 1088, 1103.

83. Andrew Jackson, "First Annual Message," in Richardson, op. cit., 2: 458.

84. Thomas Jefferson to Indian agent Benjamin Hawkins, quoted in Dangerfield, op. cit., p. 27. Jefferson advocated that Indians turn to agriculture, so they would need less land and could cede the excess to the advancing whites. In the sentence immediately preceding the one quoted in the text, he explained, "The wisdom of the animal which amputates and abandons to the hunter those parts for which he is pursued should be theirs, with this difference, that the former sacrifices what is useful, the latter what is not." "Castrated," to use Dangerfield's word, the Indians could safely merge with the whites.

85. From an 1834 pamphlet by Joel R. Poinsett, later Van Buren's secretary of war, quoted in Ekirch, op. cit., pp. 43-44.

86. It was said that Indians wanted to remain savage, and therefore desired to separate themselves from whites. Henry Wadsworth Longfellow explicitly presented Hiawatha as part of America's childhood; his willingness to go west showed Indians would not resist progress. Cf. Young, *Redskins*, op. cit., pp. 47-51; Pearce, op. cit., pp. 173-74.

87. *IA*, 2: 115.

savage experience could only ultimately maintain itself in death. Only dead or helpless Indians could safely be mourned. One historian, defending Jackson's Indian removal policy a generation later, explained that it permitted the inevitable Indian extinction to go on with less demoralization to the whites.[88]

Since civilization meant liberal uniformity, independent Indian growth could not safely be tolerated. Only embryonic liberals who had internalized adult values could be permitted freedom to grow. Indians were not liberal men; they required a greater exercise of paternal authority. The father's explicit task was first to break the Indian's tie to the land, and then to help him grow up. The process is better understood, however, according to the theory of infantilization. Breaking the Indian's tie to his customary environment, the white father sought to substitute paternal domination.

The Jacksonian policy of Indian removal transported Indians from their land, which whites coveted, to land west of the Mississippi. Large-scale transfer of native populations, in the name of security and modernization, has continued to appeal to our statesmen. Indian removal bears resemblance to "forced draft urbanization" in Vietnam, and urban renewal in our cities.[89] It sought to impose the American experience of uprooting and mobility upon the Indians. In Jackson's words,

> Doubtless it will be painful to leave the graves of their fathers, but what do they more than our ancestors did nor than our children are doing? To better their condition in an unknown land our forefathers left all that was dear in earthly objects. Our children by thousands yearly leave the land of their birth to seek new homes in distant regions. Does humanity weep at these painful separations from everything animate and inanimate, with which the young heart has become entwined? Far from it. It is rather a source of joy that our country affords scope where our young population may range unconstrained in body or mind, developing the power and faculties of man in their highest perfection. These removed hundreds and almost thousands of miles at their own expense, purchase the lands they occupy, and support themselves at their new homes from the moment of their arrival. Can it be cruel in the Government, when, by events which it cannot control, the Indian is made discontent in his ancient home to purchase his lands, to give him a new and extensive territory, to pay the expense of his removal, and support him a year on his new abode. How many thousands of our

88. Parton, op. cit., 3: 779.

89. Cf. Samuel Huntington, "The Bases of Accommodation," *Foreign Affairs* 46 (July 1968): 648-52; Chomsky, *American Power*, op. cit., pp. 11-13, 21, 53-56; Herbert Gans, *The Urban Villagers* (New York: Free Press, 1962), pp. 269-336; Marc Fried, "Grieving for a Lost Home: Psychological Costs of Relocation," in James Q. Wilson, ed., *Urban Renewal* (Cambridge, Mass.: M.I.T. Press, 1966), pp. 359-79.

own people would gladly embrace the opportunity of removing to
the West on such condition?[90]

How, then, come to terms with the resistance of the natives, their ties
to the land? Policy makers adopted strategies both of denial and rationalization. "Real Indians," the whites insisted, would offer no resistance to removal, since they led a wandering life anyway.[91] Denying Indian attachment to the land, whites called natural the wandering their policies imposed
upon the Indians. Whites turned Indians into wanderers by killing their
game; by destroying their crops and burning their villages; and by moving
a tribe from one location after another as whites wanted the land.[92] Jackson
innocently asked, "And is it to be supposed that the wandering savage has a
stronger attachment to his home than the settled, civilized Christian? Is it
more afflicting to him to leave the graves of his fathers than it is to our
brothers and children?"[93]

From another perspective, however, breaking tribal ties to the land was
urged and defended. As long as they were "clinging with a death-grasp"[94] to
their land, Indians could not be civilized. In 1826 the Chickasaws refused to
give up their land in Mississippi and move west, "fearing the consequence may
be similar to transplanting an old tree, which would wither and die away."
Commissioners Thomas Hinds and John Coffee replied,

> The trees of the forest, and particularly the most useless trees,
> are most difficult of transplanting; but fruit-trees, which are more
> particularly designated by the Great Spirit for the nourishment and
> comfort to man, require not only to be transplanted, but to be
> nourished, cultivated, and even pruned, in order to bring forth good
> fruit.[95]

Breaking the Indian relation to the land had concrete as well as symbolic
significance. To become civilized and grow up, Indians had to learn to work.
They would remain "idle," as the whites saw it, as long as they could live

90. "Second Annual Message to Congress," 6 December 1830, in Richardson, op.
cit., 2: 521. Cf. Lewis Cass's 1831 Report as secretary of war, *MA*, 4: 714. The comparison with white emigration was used, unsuccessfully, to convince several tribes to
move west. Cf. Jackson's 1830 talk to the Chickasaws in Dunbar, op. cit., 2: 575-76;
Jackson and General Thomas Hinds to the Choctaws, 1820, *IA*, 2: 235; Indian Commissioners to Cherokees, 1823, *IA*, 2: 430; Commissioners to Chickasaws, 1826, *IA*,
2: 720.

91. Abel, op. cit., p. 244.

92. This was common; some tribes were moved several times in a single generation.
Cf. Abel, op. cit., p. 267; Hagan, *American Indians*, op. cit., pp. 81-87.

93. "Second Annual Message to Congress, 6 December 1830 in Richardson, op. cit.,
2: 522. At other moments Jackson knew full well the problem lay in the peculiar
Indian attachment to his land. Cf. Parton, op. cit., 1: 433; and Florida Governor
DuVal, quoted in Mahon, op. cit., p. 53.

94. See p. 280, above.

95. *IA*, 2: 720.

purely by hunting and foraging. "The Indian must first find himself separated from his forests—and the game must be gone, or so difficult to find, as to expose him to want ... before he will [begin] ... earning his bread by the sweat of his brow."[96] "Necessity" was the "fulcrum" "upon which the lever must be placed" to civilize the Indians; they had to be situated so that they would starve if they did not work.[97]

The paternal interest of whites in Indian welfare thus required the government to take Indian land. Ohio politician and Cherokee agent R.J. Meigs explained,

> I would lead them into civilization without injuring an individual, until they gradually and almost imperceptibly became blended with ourselves. And to effect this, they must circumscribe their immense limits; for while they can roam through extensive forests, they will not make use of their physical or mental faculties to raise themselves up. Poor human nature, alone, revolts at the thought of the labor required and the sacrifices to be made to arrive at a state of civilization.[98]

Work, to antebellum Americans, meant agriculture. "A father ought to give good advice to his children," President Madison told the Cherokees, urging them to plant crops.[99] Work also required private property. In Secretary of War Crawford's words, "Distinct ideas of separate property ... must necessarily precede any considerable advance in the arts of civilization ... because no one will exert himself to procure the comforts of life unless his right to enjoy them is exclusive."[100]

For a century beginning in the Jacksonian period private property was the major weapon for teaching the Indians the value of civilization, and incidentally dispossessing them of their land. Requiring Indians to take individual plots of land released enormous amounts of leftover Indian land for white settlement. In addition Indians could further "sell," be defrauded of, or lose for "debts" or nonpayment of taxes their individual plots. Private property in fact was more important to the disappearance than the civilization of the Indians.[101] But this only illustrates the underlying identity we have seen between civilization and Indian death.

Liberating Indians from their land, whites offered them paternal assistance in growing up. But the paternal relationship was insisted upon most per-

96. McKenney, op. cit., 1: 124.

97. Cass, "Removal of the Indians," op. cit., p. 75.

98. *IA,* 2: 114. This argument was tried on the Indians, with little success. Tennessee Governor Joseph McMinn to the Cherokees, *IA,* 2: 487; Secretary of War John C. Calhoun to the Cherokees, *IA,* 2: 190.

99. Cass, "Policy and Practice...," op. cit., p. 382.

100. *IA,* 2: 26-27.

101. Cf. Hagan, *American Indians,* op. cit., pp. 130-150; Kinney, op. cit., pp. 81-311; Young, *Redskins,* op. cit., pp. 12-114.

sistently precisely at those moments when Indians by their behavior were denying its validity—expressing genuine independence, real power, or legitimate grievances. Indians were children; they could have no consciousness of grievances.102 They fought because "of the predisposition of the Indian to war,"103 not because whites were taking their land. Where wars, like the Second Creek War, were obviously the result of white aggression, it was best not even to mention this possibility. But where the tribes who fought were more distant from white settlements, as in the 1812 War, it seemed safe to insist they could not have fought to protect their land.

> It would disclose, not a mere trait of character, but a new feature
> of human nature, if these improvident beings with whom the past
> is forgotten and the future contemned, and whose whole existence
> is absorbed in the present, should encounter the United States in
> war, lest their country might be sold after the lapse of centuries.104

Lewis Cass wrote those words in 1827, long after whites had settled the land taken from hostile (and friendly) Creeks during the 1812 War, and during a period when he himself was arranging the transportation of formerly hostile northern tribes across the Mississippi.

Since the Indians were too immature to have grievances, any discontent must be the work of outside agitators, or half-breeds who took advantage of the fullbloods. In particular, "the real Indians—the natives of the forest"—wanted to emigrate, but were restrained by "designing half-breeds and renegade white men."105 In this metaphor white officials became the paternal protectors of the real Indians against the half-civilized or evil parents who exploited them. In fact, the aim was to make the Indians powerless and malleable. As Jackson wrote when his theft of Cherokee land met resistance, "If all influence but the native Indian was out of the way, we would have but little trouble."106

The most dangerous bad parents were the Spanish and British, who were to blame for every Indian war. Indians had to be "weaned" from the British and Spanish; "the savages must be made dependent on us."107 Where foreign intervention could not be discovered, the Indians must have been "excited

102. When the Creek chiefs refused to meet privately with Georgia's commissioners, during investigation of a fraudulent treaty, the commissioners insisted federal officials must be behind the Indian's refusal, since "no savage" could have thought it up on his own. *IA*, 2: 833.

103. Lewis Cass on the origins of the Second Creek War, in *MA*, 6: 623. He gives the same explanation for Black Hawk's War in the Northwest in his 1832 Report (*MA*, 5: 23-24).

104. Cass, "Policy and Practice...," op. cit., pp. 417-20.

105. *JC*, 2: 243-44, 300-304.

106. *JC*, 2: 269.

107. St. Louis Superintendent of Indian Affairs William Clark, quoted in Hagan, *Sac and Fox Indians,* op. cit., pp. 84-85; *JC, 1: 368.*

by some secrete [sic] influence."[108] Projecting evil designs onto bad parents justified America's aggressive expansionism. Men like Jackson directed paranoid rage against the foreign countries allegedly to blame for Indian wars; their influence was discovered everywhere. Illegally executing a Scottish trader and British adventurer captured on his 1818 Florida invasion, Jackson explained that he could not have punished "the poor, ignorant savages, and spared the white men who set them on."[109]

There was more rage against the British and Spanish than against the "deluded" savages.[110] But sympathy for the Indians simply infantilized them, and undercut their grievances. It did not, moreover, save them from destruction. Major Thomas Butler explained, speaking for Jackson, that the British "only use them so long as they might be serviceable, and ultimately abandon them to the mercy of the government which has had too much cause to punish with vigour the innocent savage who has been schooled to the murder of his friends and thus made the instrument of his own destruction."[111]

Jackson and Cass insisted on their parental responsibilities with most vehemence just when the southern Indians were, in white terms, growing up. Prior to 1820 it had been possible to gain Indian land through treaties, fraudulent or otherwise, and rely on the spontaneous workings of society— speculators, intruders, traders, whiskey, disease, and bribery—to make the Indians consent to leave. But in the first quarter of the nineteenth century the southern Indians took increasingly to agriculture, developed government institutions to protect themselves against whites, and refused to cede more land. In this context Jackson, the man responsible for obtaining the bulk of southern Indian land, developed the theory that treaties were not the proper way of doing business with Indians. Indians were subjects of the United States, not independent nations, and they had no right to refuse to cede their land. Congress, as "the proper Guardian," "should extend to the Indians its protection and fostering care." It should take Indian land as whites needed it, at the same time providing for Indian needs.[112] Jackson could not convince President Monroe to adopt this method, but he

108. *JC*, 1: 209. Cf. 1: 365-66.

109. Parton, op. cit., 2: 485. Jackson invaded Florida, on the pretext of an Indian war, to gain the territory for the United States. That story, and the "trial" of Ambrister and Arbuthnot, are reported in James, op. cit., 1: 300-30; Parton, op. cit., 2: 463-85, 513-515; *JC*, 2: 365; *MA*, 1: 700.

110. Jackson in *MA*, 1: 697. Preparing to seize a Spanish fort on his earlier Florida invasion, Jackson had written to the Pensacola governor, calling him "the Head which countenanced and exalted the barbarity. He is the responsible person, and not the poor savage whom he makes his instrument of execution." *JC*, 2: 28.

111. *JC*, 2: 154.

112. *JC*, 2: 278-80; also *JC*, 3: 31-32, 38; Prucha, op. cit., pp. 234-36; Abel, op. cit., pp. 276-85.

obtained considerable Indian land by telling tribes, untruthfully, that Congress planned to take their land if they did not cede it.[113]

As President, Jackson applied his interpretation to justify the extension
of state law over the Indians, in violation of treaty rights. Meanwhile, Cass,
soon to be Jackson's secretary of war, developed the paternal metaphor to
defend Jackson's approach. Cass argued that, instead of the system of treaties,
in which the whites left the Indians to look after themselves, the tribes would
have been better off if from the beginning the United States had adopted
the principle of "pupilage" in deciding which lands each party needed. The
Jackson administration, Cass believed, at last seemed to understand this.
"If a paternal authority is exercised over the aboriginal colonies ... we may
hope to see that improvement in their conditions for which we have so long
and vainly labored."[114]

Shortly thereafter Georgia Governor William Schley applied the Jackson-
Cass argument to the Alabama Creeks. The Creeks had been defrauded of
their land during Jackson's Indian removal, which Cass's paternalism had
sought to justify. Settlers and speculators had illegally occupied Creek land,
seizing Indian farms and other property. A few starving Creeks killed some
settlers, leading Jackson and Cass to end the fraud investigation and transport the entire tribe by force west of the Mississippi. Governor Schley had
urged this step: "These Indians must no longer be permitted to remain where
they now are, to murder our people and destroy their property *ad libitum.*
It is idle to talk of treaties and national faith with such savages. The proper
course to adopt with them is to treat them as wards or children, and make
them do that which is to their benefit and our safety."[115]

As helpless children, Indians had no independent identity. Bad Indians
became "monsters," lost their humanity, and could be exterminated. Helpless Indians became things and could be manipulated and rearranged at will.
Governor Wilson Lumkin of Georgia, urging the forcible removal of the
Cherokees without the formality of a treaty, wrote Jackson, "Have not these
Indians lost all claim to national character? Ought not these Indians to be
considered and treated as the helpless wards of the federal Government?"[116]

White greed for Indian land dominated Indian-white relations. It was
crucial, and disorienting, to insist on the purely benevolent concern of the
white father for his red children. The white father had no interests of his

113. "This plain language of truth," as he put it, "has brought them to their senses."
JC, 2: 387-88, on the Chickasaw treaty of 1818. Cf. the report of the 1820 Choctaw
treaty proceedings in *IA,* 2: 237-41.
114. Cass, "Removal of the Indians,"op. cit., pp. 80, 121. "We must frequently promote their interest against their inclination," Cass explained, "and no plan for the improvement of their condition will ever be practicable or efficacious, to the promotion
of which their consent must first be obtained." Quoted in Woodford, op. cit., p. 143.
115. *MA,* 6: 446.
116. *JC,* 2: 388; *JC,* 5: 351.

own, but only a concern for Indian welfare. In his 1830 Annual Message, Jackson explained, "Toward the aborigines of this country none can indulge a more friendly feeling than myself, or would go further in attempting to reclaim them from their wandering habits." He hoped that all true friends of the Indians would "unite in attempting to open the eyes of those children of the forest to their true condition," so they would remove west of the Mississippi.[117] As the House Committee on Indian Affairs asserted, "one common feeling, favorable and friendly towards the red children in question, pervades the bosom of every enlightened citizen in the Union."[118]

Such benevolence threatened to smother the Indians. It gave them no distance from the white father, and denied them the anger which would preserve their connection with reality, and their identity.[119] Nevertheless, it did not always work. Indians often responded with "ingratitude." Tribes were commonly accused of stubborness and recalcitrance, failing to appreciate how much the president had done for them.[120] Unlike the benevolent whites, the Indians were creatures of emotion; they had desires, particularly greed for their land and unwillingness to part with it.

True, some whites were also selfish and self-aggrandizing. But white predation was always split from, never contaminating, the Indian guardians. Indeed, the benevolent father would protect the Indians against the greed and violence of less-enlightened whites. James Gadsden explained to the Florida Indians, "Like a kind father, the President says to you, there are lands enough for both his white and his red children. His white are strong, and might exterminate his red, but he will not permit them. He will preserve his red children." He would, that is, if the Indians ceded the bulk of their Florida lands.[121] In this treaty, as in countless others, the split between benevolent and predatory whites permitted the former to use the latter to club the Indians, without taking responsibility for the contemplated violence and extermination.[122]

117. Richardson, op. cit., 2: 517-20, 523.
118. *IA*, 2: 408.
119. Cf. Goffman, op. cit., pp. 318-20.
120. E.g., Generals Thomas Hinds and John Coffee to the Chickasaws, 1826, in *IA*, 2: 723.
121. *IA*, 2: 436.
122. Jackson's early relations with the Cherokees are a good example. He had included ten million acres of Cherokee land in a treaty coerced from the Creeks in 1814. He had his friend John Coffee run the boundary line without authorization from Washington. Then he encouraged intruders to settle on the Cherokee land, while the secretary of war was ordering it returned to the tribe. Jackson resisted orders to remove the intruders, encouraged them to stay, and aimed, ultimately successfully, to use their presence to force the Cherokees to sell. But his posture was one of kindness to the Indians. They must be made to see, if they do not sell their land, "what is really to be feared, that is, their own destruction by an irritated people." Cf. *JC*, 2: 252-53; Abel, op. cit., pp. 278-81.

Benevolent whites could also expiate America's guilt over its treatment of Indian tribes. For some this altruism had a clearly personal meaning. Thomas McKenney saw himself as a messiah befriending "those desolate and destitute children of the forest" against the injustices they had suffered.[123] The Indian commissioner's charged language and obsessional parental imagery suggest he identified Indians with a lost childhood of his own. Defending Indians against predatory whites, he could help them grow up without his own sense of longing and loss.

McKenney, like many others concerned with Indian affairs, put this parental benevolence into personal practice. He adopted a Cherokee boy the same age as his son. According to the commissioner, race consciousness prevented the boy from duplicating the happiness of the McKenney household in the outside world. The Cherokee became a frontier lawyer, and killed himself when a white woman refused his offer of marriage. McKenney turned this story into a plea that Indians be permitted to become white.[124]

Andrew Jackson, fatherless at birth and orphaned at fourteen, adopted a Creek boy after his troops had killed the parents. "At the battle of Tohopeka," explained Jackson's close friend and future Secretary of War John Henry Eaton, "an infant was found, pressed to the bosom of its lifeless mother." Hearing that the Indian women planned to kill the baby, Jackson

> became himself the protector and guardian of the child. Bestowing
> on the infant the name of Lincoier, he adopted it into his family,
> and has ever since manifested the liveliest zeal towards it, prompted
> by benevolence, and because, perhaps, its fate bore a strong resem-
> blance to his own, who, in early life, and from the ravages of war,
> was left in the world, forlorn and wretched, without friends to
> assist, or near relations to direct him on his course.[125]

Lincoier lived for some years in the Jackson household, but died of tuberculosis before reaching manhood.

True benevolence required the white father to be strong as well as kind. The president, McKenney explained to the Committee on Indian Affairs, needed to employ military force to prevent Indian tribes from settling their disputes by war, and

123. McKenney, op. cit., 1: 78. The passage continues, "There were flowers and gems which needed only to be cultivated and polished, to ensure from the one, the emission of as sweet odors as ever regaled the circles of the civilized.... And yet they were, and are, neglected, trodden down, and treated as outcasts!

    At twelve o'clock on Monday, the signal gun for assembling of the council was fired—when were seen coming from all directions, the great multitude of the sons of the forest, to hear what their father had to say to them."

124. McKenney, op. cit., 2: 109-17.

125. John Henry Eaton, *The Life of Andrew Jackson* (Philadelphia: S.F. Bradford, 1824), pp. 436-37. Eaton himself subsequently adopted an Indian boy. Cf. Peggy Eaton, *Autobiography* (New York: Scribner, 1932), pp. 162-68.

> ... to enforce an observance of his fatherly councils. Our Indians
> stand pretty much in the relation to the Government as do our
> children to us. They are equally dependent, and need, not infre-
> quently, the exercise of parental authority to detach them from
> those ways which might involve both their peace and their lives.
> It would not be considered just for our children to be let alone to
> settle their quarrels in their own way.[126]

After calling the Indians our "fostered children," Secretary of War Eaton stressed the need for military posts in Indian territory because "moral influence can be productive of little benefit to minds not cultivated."[127] General Edmund Gaines agreed. "The poisonous cap of barbarism cannot be taken from the lips of the savage by the mild voice of reason alone; the strong mandate of justice must be resorted to and enforced."[128]

Force was necessary not only to civilize the Indians, but also to punish them for attacks on settlers. Here, too, the dominant metaphor was paternal. A strong father was necessary to "chastise" Indians when they went on the warpath. Occasionally, calls for extermination of the Indians were even brought within the family circle. Indian agent Joseph Street, seeking Sioux aid in Black Hawk's War, explained,

> Our Great Father has foreborne to use force, until the Sacs and
> Foxes have dared to kill some of his white children. He will for-
> bear no longer. He has tried to reclaim them, and they grow worse.
> He is resolved to sweep them from the face of the earth. They shall
> no longer trouble his children. If they cannot be made good they
> must be killed.... Your father has penned these Indians up, and he
> means to kill them all.[129]

For those who found the Indians essentially depraved, the need for strong, paternal discipline followed naturally. The only way to civilize the Indians, explained Georgia Congressman John Forsyth (later Jackson's secretary of state), was to destroy the tribes and make the Indians subject to state law. "You might as reasonably expect that wild animals, incapable of being tamed in a park, would be domesticated by turning them loose in the forest.... Wild

126. *IA,* 2: 264.
127. "Annual Report of the Secretary of War,"(30 November 1829), in *MA,* 4: 154-55.
128. *IA,* 2: 161. Jackson stressed the benefits to the Indians of the "exertion of our military power," as opposed to "feeding their avarice." *JC,* 5: 507.
129. Quoted in Dunbar, op. cit., 2: 461. Jackson and General Hinds, in their 1820 talk to the Choctaws (*IA,* 2: 237), warned that if the tribe refused to remove across the Mississippi, it would inevitably disintegrate. Some would join America's enemies. "We would be under the necessity of raising the hatchet against our own friends and children. Your father, the President of the United States, wishes to avoid this unnatural state of things."

nature was never yet tamed but by coercive discipline."[130]

But the parental ideal of the more hopeful and philanthropic school was only slightly less fierce. Thomas McKenney, during a trip among the southern tribes, illustrated the proper method of helping the Indians to civilization. A warrior had attempted to stab his mother-in-law, who had hidden his goods so he could not trade them for whiskey. McKenney asked Lewis Cass, then governor of Michigan Territory, what to do. The governor "answered promptly, 'Make a woman of him.' " McKenney placed the warrior in the center of a circle of a thousand Indians. He told him that henceforth he would be a woman, took his knife from his belt, thrust it into a flagstaff and broke it at the hilt. He then stripped the Indian of his mocassins, decorated leggings, blanket, silver earings, bracelets, and face-paint, describing the process later in loving, sadistic, detail. Dressing the brave in a petticoat, McKenney explained that women were to be protected and valued by men, not murdered. Good treatment of women differentiated savagery from civilization. According to McKenney, the Indian women approved of the punishment, while the braves would never again admit the warrior among them. The humiliated Indian exclaimed, "I'd rather be dead. I am no longer a brave; I'm a woman." "Now this form of punishment," McKenney concluded, "was intended to produce moral results, and to elevate the condition of women, among the Indians. It was mild in its physical effects, but more terrible than death in its action and consequences upon the offender.[131]

This "ceremony of degredation" epitomizes the psychic war against the Indians. McKenney's altruism required helpless and dependent children. The commissioner understood the connection between death and destroyed identity. Paternal benevolence permitted symbolic castration and infantilization; the Indian no longer confronted the white world with independent power and subversive cultural alternatives. McKenney participated in the crime as well as the retribution (except that his domination was not over women, but over a feminized man). The coldness, detachment, and tutelary quality of the punishment avoided intimacy and contamination. Relations with the Indians permitted that domination over men forbidden but longed for in liberal society. In a culture which undermined paternal authority, the father returned as a harsh and punishing figure in those areas where he was permitted to function at all.[132]

130. *Register of Debates,* VI (1829-30): 325.

131. McKenney, op. cit., 2: 121. For similar humiliations of Indian chiefs, see Cotterill, op. cit., p. 129, and the description of Black Hawk's tour of the cast in captivity, in Woodford, op. cit., p. 176. Cf. the fictional description of a child's punishment in an 1835 best seller analyzed in Bernard Wishy, *The Child and the Republic* (Philadelphia: University of Pennsylvania Press, 1968), pp. 44-49.

132. Only one political figure of the period, to my knowledge, rejected the parent-child metaphor. Missionary Jeremiah Evarts' "William Penn" letters sparked the opposition to the Indian removal bill. In this pamphlet Evarts accused the whites of imposing

IV.

Interaction among free, independent, and equal men had one crucial advantage over the theory of paternal authority. Liberal contractual relations diffused guilt; no one could be held responsible for the condition of anyone else. Since the Indians were offered only death or disappearance, it was particularly important to avoid the burden of guilt. The personal, paternal metaphor, therefore, was combined with another. The Indians were pictured as at once victims of mechanized and fragmented social processes for which no one was to blame, and at the same time free to choose their fate. This ultimate in the rhetoric of disorienting infantilization broke even the connection to a personified central authority, and left individual Indians to contend with an irresponsible social pluralism, allegedly driven by inevitable historical laws. Indians were infantilized and destroyed, but white leaders were not to blame.

For two centuries treaties—fraudulent, coerced, or otherwise—imposed liberal contractualism upon the tribes. But by the 1820's treaties were foundering on Indian intransigence. The parental president had to interfere, but in such a way that he could not be accused of coercing the tribes. At times the language maintained a personal connection between the father and his children. T.H. McKenney, for example, announced that he would not force Indians to leave their land.

> Seeing as I do the condition of these people, and that they are bordering on destruction, I would, were I empowered, take them *firmly* but *kindly* by the hand, and tell them they must go; and I would do this, on the same principle I would take my own children by the hand, firmly but kindly and lead them from a district of the country in which the plague was raging.[133]

This language implied coercion, however benevolent. More commonly, the only acknowledged coercion came from the tribal structure itself. Half-breed chiefs, it was alleged, prevented the fullbloods from emigrating. Indian commissioners commonly reported, after the failure of treaty negotiations, that a treaty would have been signed "had the authorities and the people

---

the language of great white fathers and little red children on the Indians to avoid dealing with the tribes as autonomous, independent societies. The pamphlet ends with an equally unique appeal to the law. Evarts personifies the law not as a strong, forbidding, and punitive father enforcing uniformity and obedience, but as a woman who can accept harmony and diversity in the world she rules. Cf. "William Penn," *Present Crisis in the Condition of the American Indians* (Boston: Perkins & Marvin, 1829), p. 101. A similar, religious-based metaphorical contrast appears in Tocqueville's *Democracy in America*, 2: 386-87.

133. Quoted in Francis Paul Prucha, "Thomas L. McKenney and the New York Indian Board," *Mississippi Valley Historical Review* 48 (March 1962): 653. The author cites this passage to prove McKenney opposed coercing Indians.

been left to the free and unrestrained exercise of their own inclinations and judgements."[134] "I believe every native of this nation left to themselves," said Jackson, "would freely make this election [to remove], but they appear to be overawed by the council of some white men and half breeds, who have been and are fattening of the annuities, the labours, and folly of the native Indians." Eliminate these "self-aggrandizing," "bawling politicians," and the freed Indians would emigrate.[135]

It was unwise to attack the tribal structure directly. Jackson rejected a Florida Indian agent's contention that he had to "rebuke the Indian chiefs as if they were wrong-headed schoolboys" for opposing removal, by stripping them of their titles.[136] The same purposes were better served through bribery, which was legitimate—given the good aims of the government and the selfish "avarice" of the chiefs,[137] and through signing treaties with un-representative groups of Indians sympathetic to white blandishments.

Break apart the tribal structure, and Indians would be free to choose their own best interests. Destruction of communal restrictions on individual free-dom by a strong central authority followed the tradition of early, European liberalism. If Jackson frowned upon direct dethronement of chiefs, he inter-vened in other ways to destroy tribal authority. He took from the Cherokee leaders the annual annuity that supported tribal government. It was divided into equal amounts of forty-two cents and given to each Cherokee, or at least to those who bothered to make the long journey to agent headquarters.[138] The Creek, Choctaw, and Chickasaw removal treaties gave individual plots of land to thousands of Indians. Each was then free to sell his plot and cross

134. Commissioner Duncan Campbell on the failure of a Creek treaty in 1824, *IA* 2: 574.

135. Jackson in *JC,* 2: 299, 300-304. This is Jackson's earliest use of the rhetoric of Jacksonian democracy, attacking leaders in the name of the people. Note the meta-phors of independence vs. oral dependence. Cf. also note 68, above.

136. Quoted in Edwin C. McReynolds, *The Seminoles* (Norman, Okla,: University of Oklahoma Press, 1957), p. 195.

137. John H. Eaton, Jackson's first secretary of war, told the commissioners sent to the Cherokees to keep their identities secret at first. "There is no doubt, however, but that the mass of people would be glad to emigrate; and there is no little doubt that they are kept from this exercise of their choice by their chiefs and other interested and influential men." It was necessary, Eaton continued, "to break the power that is warring with their best interests.... The best resort is believed to be that which is embraced in an appeal to the chiefs and influential men, not together, but apart, at their own houses, and by a proper exposition of their real condition, rouse them to think of that; whilst offers to them of extensive reservations in fee simple, and other rewards, would, it is hoped, result in obtaining their acquiescence." The plan failed here, and ultimately the Cherokees were removed by military force, many in chains. But similar efforts succeeded with other tribes. Eaton's letter is quoted by Senator Theodore Frelinghuysen in *Register of Debates,* VI (1829-30): 310.

138. Cf. Abel, op. cit., p. 387; Marion L. Starkey, *The Cherokee Nation* (New York: Knopf, 1946), p. 150.

the Mississippi, or remain under state law. Since the government had left each Indian free to make his own decision, it was not implicated in the extraordinary fraud, thievery, and violence which followed.[139]

The liberal principle behind such tactics was that only the central government was the source of coercion. If Indians were coerced by their situation to choose to sell their land, then they were not coerced at all. If each Indian could internalize his impossible situation, then he, not the president or the white society, would be responsible for the choices he made. Jefferson, for example, recommended establishing trading houses in Indian territory to increase Indian wants. Indians would then be forced into debt, and "we observe that when these debts get beyond what the individuals can pay, they become willing to lop them off by a cession of lands."[140] Jefferson's specific recommendations were followed in Chickasaw country, and tribal land there and elsewhere was later acquired through Indian indebtedness (often hugely inflated) to government and private traders. Here was an early example of what Margaret Mead would later call "democratic control," as opposed to totalitarian coercion and the Selective Service Board, "the American or indirect way of achieving what is done by direction in foreign countries where choice is not permitted." As a method of liberal planning it found its way into government social policies from agriculture to draft deferments.[141] The principle was to structure the environment so that the dice were loaded strongly in favor of a single alternative, and then give the target of social planning the onus of the choice.

Liberal planning demonstrated its advantages over federal coercion when Georgia, Alabama, and Mississippi extended their laws over the tribes residing within state bounds. The Supreme Court correctly held that this action violated Indian treaties and federal law.[142] But Jackson refused to enforce the decision, and acquiesced in the states' action. He and his friends favored the extension of state sovereignty, since it would eliminate Indians without attaching blame to the federal government.[143]

139. Cf. Cass, in *MA*, 6: 590; and, for the whole monstrous story, Young, *Redskins,* op. cit.; Foreman, op. cit., pp. 118-83; *MA*, 6: 575-780.

140. Quoted in Dangerfield, op. cit., p. 27; another Jefferson letter with the same message is in Samuel C. Williams, *Beginnings of West Tennessee in the Land of the Chickasaws* (Johnson City, Tenn.: The Watauga Press, 1930), p. 62. Cf. Cotterill, op. cit., pp. 139-49; Hagan, *Sac and Fox Indians,* op. cit., pp. 9-14; Dunbar, op. cit., 2: 419, 470-82.

141. Cf. Margaret Mead, *And Keep Your Powder Dry,* 2nd. ed. (London: Whiting & Wheaton, 1967), pp. 186-89; and the now-famous selective service pamphlet on "channeling," discussed in Richard Flacks, Florence Howe, and Paul Lauter, "On the Draft," *New York Review of Books* 8 (6 April 1967): 3-6.

142. *Worcester* v. *Georgia,* VI Peters: 512-559. Jackson wrote to his friend General John Coffee, "The decision of the Supreme Court has fell still born." Quoted in James, op. cit., 2: 304-305.

143. Cf. Coffee to Jackson, quoted in Young, "Indian Removal...," op. cit., p. 36.

State laws deprived the chiefs of their titles and power. Indians could not testify in state courts, and the state would not prosecute intrusions and depredations on Indian land. Georgia divided up Cherokee territory for auction in a state lottery.[144] Extension of state sovereignty, as everyone understood, meant death to the Indians who remained on their land. As the secretary of war put it, "by refusing" to remove, "they must, necessarily, entail destruction on their race."[145]

At the same time Indians were reputedly free to stay or go. Jackson explained, "This emigration should be voluntary, for it would be as cruel as unjust to compel the aborigines to abandon the graves of their fathers and seek a home in a distant land. But they shall be directly informed that if they remain within the limits of the states they must be subject to their laws."[146] "God forbid," said future President James Buchanan in support of the Indian removal bill,

> that I, or that any other gentlemen upon this floor, should enter-
> tain the purpose of using the power of this Government to drive
> that unfortunate race of men by violence across the Mississippi.
> Where they are let them remain, unless they should freely consent
> to depart. The State of Georgia, so far as we can judge from her
> public acts, entertains no other intention.[147]

What did this mean for the paternal metaphor? A Georgia senator explained that Jackson, "with a special regard for the welfare of the Indians," gave them a choice of land in the west or of remaining under Georgia law. "And this, sir, is [supposed to be] the language of a despot!... [It is only] a little friendly and parental advice from the President to the children of the forest."[148] The president was not a despotic father, but one who helped the Indians make their own decisions.[149]

If the Indians, failing to take the president's advice, remained and were destroyed, the president was not to blame. In Jackson's words, "I feel conscious of having done my duty to my red children and if any failure of my

144. Congressman Edward Everett complained that Georgia law, "by reducing them to a state of minority," "holds them to their infancy." See *Register of Debates,* VII (1830-1831): 696.

145. Eaton letter quoted by Senator Sprague in *Register of Debates,* VI (1829-30): 356. In Cass's words, "It is certainly better for them to meet the difficulties of removal, with the probability of an adequate and final reward, than, yielding to their constitutional apathy, to sit still and perish." "Annual Report of the Secretary of War," 21 November 1831, in *MA,* 4: 714.

146. "First Annual Message," in Richardson, op. cit., 2: 458.

147. *Register of Debates,* VI (1829-30): 594.

148. Ibid., 1034.

149. This meant, in practice, that Jackson coerced removal treaties from the Choctaws and Creeks by threatening otherwise to leave them to the mercy of the states. Cf. Young, *Redskins,* op. cit., pp. 30-39, and the next paragraph in the text.

good intention arises, it will be attributable to their want of duty to themselves, not to me." "I have exonerated the national character from all imputation, and now leave the poor deluded Creeks and Cherokees to their fate, and their annihilation, which their wicked advisers has [sic] induced."[150]

To free the government from responsibility for the Indian plight, however, was also to assert paternal helplessness. "Your great father has not the power to prevent" whites from moving onto Chickasaw land and Mississippi from extending its jurisdiction, Jackson told the tribe.[151] The workings of society were not the responsibility of the government, and it was powerless to control them. The government took no responsibility for traders, squatters, and speculators, who defrauded Indians and were major forces in the social pressure for removal. Contractors who won with the lowest bid the right to transport and provision Indians removing west, who fed them rancid meat, led them through diseased areas, clothed them inadequately for the freezing southwestern winters, and crowded them on dangerous flatboats were not, as independent businessmen, the responsibility of the government.[152] Paternal helplessness underlay the ideal of Indian freedom; the strong and benevolent father was not responsible for his acts.

The intractability of the Indian character also contributed, it was alleged, to paternal helplessness. Countless efforts to civilize the Indians, explained Cass, had foundered on Indian improvidence. With Indian removal the government was trying yet again, and any "failure must be attributed to the inveterate habits of this people and not to the policy of the government."[153] In spite of efforts to civilize the Creeks and Cherokees, "the great body of the people are in a state of helpless and hopeless poverty... The same improvidence and habitual indolence ... mark the northern tribes." A few years ago, Cass illustrated, Congress even had to appropriate money to feed the starving Florida Indians.[154]

Such arguments only revealed the function of the assertion of paternal helplessness. The Seminoles were starving, not because of the "inveterate

150. *JC*, 4: 169, 177. Commissioner of Indian Affairs Elbert Herring summarized Jackson's sentiments: "If it be consistent with their duty as chiefs to oppose removal, or to be passive on the subject, and to witness the consequent degredation and suffering of their people, they must take the responsibility and persist in their opposition" (*MA*, 6: 599-600). In the same fashion the American government blames Hanoi for the death it rains on the South Vietnamese countryside. If the Communists did not resist the government relocation program, villagers would not be killed. Cf. Chomsky, *American Power,* op. cit., pp. 131-32.

151. Quoted in Dunbar, op. cit., 2: 575-76.

152. Cf. Foreman, op. cit., pp. 56-69, 183-87, 258-63; McReynolds, op. cit., pp. 216-17, 238-42.

153. Lewis Cass, "Annual Report of the Secretary of War," 25 November 1832, *MA*, 5: 23.

154. Cass, "Annual Report of the Secretary of War," 1831, *MA*, 4: 714-15; Cass, "Removal," op. cit., p. 70.

habits" of the Indians, but because the government had moved them once to land upon which little could be grown, was now planning to move them to the west, and had burned their crops and destroyed their cattle in a government-provoked war.[155]   The demoralized Indians could hardly be expected to plant once again simply to leave crops behind or have them devastated. Assertions about the Indian character simply involved the refusal of the government to take responsibility for the consequences of its acts.

The worse the government policy toward Indians, the more insistent the attacks on Indian character. How else justify white crimes, particularly as the powerless Indians could not so easily be accused of provoking them. The remaining Indians were living reminders of white guilt; infantilization and dehumanization avoided the pain of experiencing their suffering. Cherokee leader John Ross wrote, "I knew that the perpetrator of a wrong never forgives his victims."[156]

Refusal to accept responsibility separated individuals from the consequences of their actions. This, as Tocqueville saw it, was the unique feature of America's conquest of the Indians. Americans' "cold and implacable egotism" toward the Indians narrowed drastically their own sense of responsibility. They could destroy nature and the Indians on an enormous scale, "setting coldly about deeds that can only be explained by the fire of passion." They did not intend that Indians starve, and therefore were not to blame if their actions caused famines.[157] Apologists for America's slaughter of Vietnamese peasants also explain that bombing the countryside is not meant to kill civilians. Of this claim Mary McCarthy writes, "Foreknowledge of the consequences of an act that is then performed generally argues the will to do it; if this occurs repeatedly, and the doer continues to protest that he did not will the consequences, this suggests an extreme and dangerous disassociation of the personality."[158]

America had begun with a radical assertion of the power of men to control their fate. But the country progressed through the destruction of another set of men, and responsibility for that destruction could not be faced. In Lewis Cass's words, white men were planted by providence on the "skirts of a boundless forest." Subduing it by industry, they advanced and multiplied

155. Abel, op. cit., pp. 327-31, 357-58; Mahon, op. cit., pp. 19-36; Foreman, op. cit., pp. 342, 363.

156. Quoted in Starkey, op. cit., p. 283. Cass put it a little differently. "It is due to the character of the government and the feelings of the country, not less than to the moral and physical imbecility of this unhappy race, that a spirit of kindness and forbearance should mark the whole course of our intercommunication with them." 1831 Report, *MA*, 4: 713.

157. Cf. Tocqueville, "Fortnight in the Wilds," in ed., Mayer, op. cit., pp. 331, 339; *Democracy in America*, I: 364-69.

158. Mary McCarthy, "Report from Vietnam III: Intellectuals," *New York Review of Books* 8 (18 May 1967): 13.

by providential decree. They had superiority in arts, arms, and intelligence. How, then, could whites be blamed for the Indian plight? "Their misfortunes have been the consequence of a state of things which could not be controlled by them or us." Cass drew practical lessons from this theory of history. If the Creeks who chose to stay in Alabama "finally melt away before our people and institutions, the results must be attributed to causes, which we can neither stay nor control."[159]

Cass still recognized that Indians might die in Alabama. In its most extreme form the process of denial reached reality itself. The worse the events, the less they could be admitted into consciousness. The roundup, detainment in stockades, and military removal of the Cherokees killed an estimated four thousand of the fifteen thousand members of the eastern branch of the tribe.[160] As the secretary of war described the process, "The generous and enlightened policy ... was ably and judiciously carried into effect by the General appointed.... Humanity no less than good policy dictated this course toward these children of the forest." The commissioner of Indian affairs amplified:

> A retrospect of the last eight months in reference to this numerous and more than enlightened tribe cannot fail to be refreshing to well-constituted minds.... A large mass of men have been conciliated; the hazard of an effusion of human blood has been put by; good feeling has been preserved, and we have quietly and gently transported eighteen thousand friends to the west bank of the Mississippi.[161]

Instead of facing actual deaths, Indian destruction became an abstracted and generalized process removed from human control and human reality. To face responsibility for specific killing might have led to efforts to stop it; avoiding individual deaths turned Indian removal into a theory of genocide. In Jackson's words,

> Humanity has often wept over the fate of the aborigines of this country, and Philanthropy has been busily engaged in devising means to avert it, but its progress has never for a moment been arrested, and one by one have many powerful tribes disappeared from the earth. To follow to the land the last of his race and to tread on the graves of extinct nations excites melancholy reflections. But true philanthropy reconciles the mind to these vicissitudes, as it does to the extinction of one generation to make room for another.[162]

159. Cass, "Removal," op. cit., pp. 107, 120-21.
160. Foreman, op. cit., p. 312n.
161. Quoted in Dunbar, op. cit., 2: 610.
162. "Second Annual Message," in Richardson, op. cit., 2: 520-21.

Weeping over Indian deaths was immature. History rescued a man from melancholy; he could tread on Indian graves in peace. "Independence of mind and action," to recall Jackson's advice to his nephew, could not be borne. Instead, a man like Jackson had to justify himself, in "the image of his creator," as a "real tool in the hands of" a devine Father, "wielded, like a mere automation, sometimes, without knowing it, to the worst of purposes."[163] To be a man meant to participate, separated from the actual experience, in a genocide.[164]

163. Compare pp. 274 and 275, above.
164. American servicemen defending the Song My massacre against public outcry write, "Grow up Americans." "Why must Americans be so childish," they ask, so "politically immature?" See San Francisco Chronicle, 31 December 1969, p. 26.

2. Death in Vietnam: Class, Poverty, and the Risks of War

MAURICE ZEITLIN, KENNETH LUTTERMAN
AND JAMES RUSSELL

Has every young American man had an equal chance of getting killed in the war in Vietnam, whatever his social origins? This is the central empirical question of this article. Socially relevant and politically significant, this question is also important from a sociological standpoint. There is ample evidence that the "life chances" of the poor and of workers in general suffer by comparison to those of more privileged strata in the United States. This is true not only of such diverse "opportunities" or "rewards" as formal education, access to health and medical care, decent housing and humane working conditions, but of mortality rates themselves. In a recent analysis of more than thirty studies—many of them in the United States—of "Social Class, Life Expectancy, and Overall Mortality," Aaron Antonovsky concluded that "despite the variegated populations surveyed, the inescapable conclusion is that class influences one's chances of staying alive. Almost without exception, the evidence shows that classes differ in mortality rates. . . . What seems to be beyond question is that, whatever the index used and whatever the number of classes considered, almost always a lowest class appears with substantially higher mortality rates. Moreover, the differential between it and other classes evidently has not diminished over recent decades."[1] Most relevant here is Antonovsky's conclusion that "when men are quite helpless before the threat of death, life chances will tend to be equitably distributed." The risks of death in war would seem to fit that category all too well, placing all fighting men on a par in their relative helplessness before the threat of death in combat.

Thus, our leading empirical question also has a special—and poignant—theoretical relevance: Does war equalize the threat of death? To what extent does the civilian class situation of the American fighting man determine his life chances in the armed forces, and the likelihood of his death on remote battlefields? Despite its importance, the question is apparently all but unresearched. A study by Mayer and Hoult of casualties in the Korean war, did find that, in Detroit, ". . . the lower the relative economic standing of a man's home area, or the greater the number of nonwhites in his area, the more likely it was that he would be a war casualty."[2] However, aside from

1. Antonovsky's article appeared in the Milbank Memorial Fund *Quarterly* 65 no. 2 (April 1967), and is reprinted in *Structured Social Inequality,* ed. Celia S. Heller (New York: Macmillian, 1969).

2. Albert J. Mayer and Thomas F. Hoult, "Social Stratification and Combat Survival," *Social Forces* 34 (December 1955): 155-59.

their important study, based on ecological analysis, we have found no others focusing on this question. So far as we know, moreover, ours is the only study to use income and occupational data on the individual servicemen themselves, and to differentiate them by their branch of service and rank.

Methods and Data

This study is based on data gathered systematically on every serviceman from the state of Wisconsin killed in the war in Vietnam through December 31, 1967. The names, rank, branch of service, date and cause of death, and nearest of kin of all but one of the 380 Vietnam dead from Wisconsin were obtained from the State of Wisconsin Department of Veterans Affairs. Data on the occupations and income of the parents of the servicemen were obtained through the cooperation of the Wisconsin Department of Taxation. We were not able to ascertain the parental income of seventy-one servicemen, or the father's occupation of seventy-eight servicemen, and they were excluded from the analysis, as is indicated in the specific tables in this article. We adjusted gross family income, with some slight modification, in accordance with the Office of Economic Opportunity's scale of poverty thresholds by size of family for 1959.[3] Thus, it should be clear that the "poor" in this study represent a minimum estimate, by official standards.

The occupational and income distributions of the casualties' parents were compared to the distributions of these attributes in a one-third random sample of the parents of male seniors in all of the public, private, and parochial schools in 1957 in Wisconsin. We believe that this matching cohort is much more adequate for the purposes of our analysis than any available from Census data. The 1957 sample provides a reasonably accurate estimate of the social characteristics of the parents of sons close to the age of draft liability, which the Census cannot provide. However, the high school cohort presents one important problem: Eleven percent of the school population has dropped out before reaching the senior year of high school. This cohort, therefore, probably understates the proportion of poor and manual workers among all age-peers of the 1957 seniors in the high school cohort. However, since school dropouts are quite likely to be very under-represented in the pool of inductees also, this may not be a major drawback for our purposes. Eighty percent of the "young men rejected for military service between 1958 and 1960 . . . because they could not pass the Army's examination in basic scholastic skills . . . were school dropouts."[4]

3. U.S. Office of Economic Opportunity, *Dimensions of Poverty,* Supplement I (Washington, D.C.: U.S. Government Printing Office, June 5, 1966).

4. Abraham J. Tannenbaum, *Dropout or Diploma* (New York: Teacher's College Press, Columbia University, 1966), p. 32. The 1957 cohort sample was gathered under

Findings

What, then, do we find concerning the relative representation of young men from different social origins among the servicemen who died in Vietnam? Our evidence clearly shows that the poor are highly *over*-represented: Whereas only 14.9 percent of the high school cohort came from poor families, nearly twice that proportion, or 27.2 percent, were poor. among the casualties of war.[5] The disproportion is especially striking among army privates, those most likely to have been draftees: There, 35.2 percent were from poor families. It should also be noted that, in contrast to the situation among privates and noncoms, the poor are *under*-represented among the officers killed in Vietnam (table 1).[6]

What about workers' sons? Have they, too, borne a disproportionate share of the casualties in Vietnam? We find that they have, although by no means as great as that borne by the undifferentiated poor: In the high school cohort, 51.9 percent are workers' sons compared to 60.3 percent of the war dead.

---

the supervision of K.G. Lutterman and William H. Sewell, for a study of the "effects of family background and ability on earnings"; we are grateful to them for making it available for this study. The parents of the high school cohort are likely to be slightly older on the average than the parents of those who died in Vietnam from 1962 through 1967. However, since the parents of both groups are in their prime from an earnings standpoint, we presume this difference to be irrelevant to our analysis. It should be noted also that because we required a precise cohort for comparison, it was preferable not to extend the study beyond the casualties through 1967.

5. This over-representation of the poor is not the result of any disproportionate numbers of black servicemen among the poor. We attempted to identify the "race" of servicemen from photos accompanying their obituaries. To the extent to which this provided us with reliable evidence, we found only nine blacks (2.4 percent) among the 380 dead servicemen. We have no information on the racial composition of the high school cohort. Using the less adequate Census figures, there were in Wisconsin in 1960, 1.8 percent blacks among males between the ages of five and nineteen. We obtained no information on the parental income or fathers' occupations of these black servicemen, so they are excluded in the tables in the text.

6. Given the structure of the conscription army until now, it seems plausible that sons from poor families would be less likely to acquire the education, skills, and motivations required to rise into the officers' ranks. What is known of the social composition of armed forces officers supports this supposition: Unskilled and service workers' sons were found, in the one study which has come to our attention, to constitute 5.3 percent of the officers in the army. Among Regular Army enlisted men, that is, excluding draftees, the proportion rises to 14.1 percent. From an unpublished study by Rufus Browning cited by Charles H. Coates and Roland J. Pellegrin, *Military Sociology* (University Park, Maryland: The Social Science Press, 1965), pp. 267-73.

That is, workers' sons are over-represented by roughly a sixth (1.162 times their proportionate share); and the over-representation is not particularly different for the sons of the skilled as contrasted to the semi-skilled and unskilled. The sons of fathers in no other occupational group are over-represented among the casualties as a whole. Once again, however, it is striking that whereas skilled workers' sons are more or less proportionately represented among dead officers, and the sons of the less skilled are *under*-represented among dead officers, the sons of professionals and technicians are highly *over*-represented among the officers, as are the sons of managers, officials and proprietors, although to a lesser extent (table 2).

Given that poverty cuts across the occupational strata, although greatest among semi- and unskilled workers and small farm proprietors in Wisconsin,[7] the question is how poverty affects the life chances of individuals *within* the different occupational groups; were the poor more likely to be killed in Vietnam, whatever their class? The answer is clear: The poor in every occupational group are over-represented among the war dead (table 3). Looking at the casualties in all ranks combined, we observe that the poor are over-represented by at least twice their share in all occupational groups, excepting the semi- and unskilled, perhaps because the latter form a more homogeneous stratum than the other occupational groups. The sons of poor farmers were particularly hard hit, constituting nearly two and one-half times their proportionate share of the casualties. It is also interesting to note that whereas the sons of poor semi- and unskilled workers, and of poor farmers, are most over-represented among privates, the sons of skilled workers and of the middle strata are most over-represented among noncoms—an unfortunate and unforseen consequence, perhaps, of their "social mobility" in the armed forces.

An equally important question concerning the relationship between class and poverty is whether the sons of workers, farmers, or middle strata families are proportionately represented among the casualties, *once we take poverty level into account*. For example, did even the sons of well-off (nonpoor) workers die disproportionately in the war compared to servicemen from other social origins, or does taking poverty level into account eliminate the class differences in casualty rates? The answer is that among the poor, the differences between the occupational groups diminish considerably. In fact, taken as a whole, the differences in casualty rates between the classes virtually disappear, among the poor. Their relative proportions in the cohort

7. The following is the distribution of poverty in the 1957 male cohort among the specific occupational groups constituting the "middle strata": 5.7 percent of the professionals and technicians; 11.7 percent of the managers, proprietors, and officials; and 11.1 percent of the clerical and sales group fell below the poverty line.

and among the casualties are roughly identical: Workers, for example, constitute 47.1 percent of the cohort poor and 48.8 percent of the servicemen who were from poor families. However, among those who were *not* poor, the sons of farm owners, and from middle strata families, are quite *under*-represented among the well-off servicemen killed in Vietnam, while even well-off workers' sons are *over*-represented. This is true of both skill-groups among the workers, as well as of the workers as a whole: 49.9 percent of the cohort nonpoor were from workers' families contrasted to 64.6 percent among the casualties who were not poor, or roughly one and one-third times their proportionate share (table 4). That even workers who were *not* poor constitute a disproportionate share of the casualties in Vietnam, underscores the pervasive and profound effect of the class structure on the individual's life chances; it is further evidence that the workers' location in the class structure of the United States, be their income sufficient to keep them above the poverty level or not, imposes disproportionate and cumulative disadvantages on them which severely restrict their life chances, indeed, their very survival, compared to individuals in other and more privileged classes.

Interpretation

The question is what processes lead to the disproportionate burden of the war's casualties being borne by the poor and by workers, even when they are not poor? The most plausible explanation is that they are over-represented among the dead because they are over-represented in the pool of draftees in the first place. That this country's system of military recruitment is, indeed, a "selective service" has been widely accepted; Senator Edward Kennedy, for example, has charged that the draft, because it virtually exempted college students, bore "down most heavily on the lower income brackets." Wisconsin's Republican Congressman Alvin O'Konski concluded, long before this study was completed in his state: "They say the poor are always with you. . . . If the draft goes on as it has, they may not be with us much longer."[8] Stewart Alsop, not usually given to radical pronouncements, has stated bluntly that the Selective Service System "is quite clearly based on class discrimination."[9] Others have argued, however, that because the mental,

8. Quoted in Jacquin Sanders, *The Draft and the Vietnam War* (New York: Walker and Co., 1966), p. 13, which was originally a *Newsweek* cover story on the draft; and in Bruce K. Chapman, *The Wrong Man in Uniform* (New York: Trident Press, 1967), p. 86.

9. "The American Class System," *Newsweek*, 29 June 1970, p. 88. Alsop reports also that "Yale, Harvard and Princeton, to cite three obvious examples, together have graduated precisely two—repeat, two—young men, in the whole course of the war, who were drafted and killed in action in Vietnam." He adds, however, that they had, respectively, thirty-four, thirteen, and thirteen young men who volunteered and were killed in Vietnam.

"moral," and physical disqualification rates tend to disproportionately exempt poor Americans from military service, they are probably *not* over-represented in the armed forces. In short, "the 'disadvantaged' do have an advantage in escaping the draft."[10]

A systematic ecological analysis of differential induction rates in Wisconsin, by Davis and Dolbeare, found that "the income related bias in present deferment policies is sufficiently great to overcome the countervailing effects of higher proportions of unfitness in the lower income areas and to establish an income-based pattern of military service. . . . The induction rate is higher in the low income areas and lower in the high income areas. This suggests," Davis and Dolbeare also point out, "that the higher service experience of registrants in low income areas is not due to enlistments, but quite the opposite, to inductions."[11] Thus, since the sons of the poor and of manual workers are generally far less likely to go to college, or to graduate, "college deferments" essentially defer the government from drafting those from the more privileged strata of American society.

In addition, more subtle processes may be involved than the mere enforcement of existing regulations. Draft board members are empowered to some extent to decide on deferments, to decide "who serves when not all serve." Most of them are from the middle strata (and white). Among local board members in the metropolitan areas of the United States, only 6.6 percent were from manual occupations during the period encompassed by this study; outside of metropolitan areas, the figure was 7.3 percent. In the state of Wisconsin, the figure was 8.3 percent.[12] We have little direct evidence regarding how the social composition of the draft boards affects the individual's chances of being drafted. One study of local boards in an urban area by a participant-observer, found that board members tended to rely on their evaluations of the registrant's personal appearance or even his choice of words in a letter when deciding on hardship or occupational deferments—the types of deferments most likely to be required, and the only available, for the sons of workers and the poor. Board members' judgments reportedly were based on such values as "thrift, education, morality, nativism, etc."[13]

In a very fundamental way, then, the operation of the Selective Service System, whatever its peculiarities, is exemplary of certain general processes

10. Chapman, *Wrong Man in Uniform,* pp. 81-86.

11. James W. Davis and Kenneth M. Dolbeare, *Little Groups of Neighbors: The Selective Service System* (Chicago: Markham Publishing Co., 1968), pp. 145-46.

12. National Advisory Commission on Selective Service, *In Pursuit of Equity: Who Serves When Not All Serve?* (Washington, D.C.: Government Printing Office, 1967), pp. 75 and 79.

13. A study for an unpublished dissertation by Gary Wamsley, cited in *Little Groups of Neighbors,* pp. 81-82.

involved in the relationship between the "state" and the class structure. The Selective Service System was established to operate in such a way, *whatever the conscious motivations involved*, as to protect the privileged strata from the ravages of wars fought in their interests. By giving legal and institutional support to the general social processes which redound to the cumulative disadvantage of the workers and poor in our political economy, the state (in this case the Selective Service System), as well as the personnel who compose its administrative apparatus, adversely affects the interests of the poor and of the workers while protecting and advancing the interests of the privileged and dominant classes.

The very same social processes may be recapitulated in the "universalistic" armed forces themselves. Even when they end up in uniform, those from professional, technical, or other middle strata homes may be less likely to see combat than workers' or poor families' sons. Subtly or explicitly, "well-qualified and intelligent young men" may be encouraged to take administrative or noncombat posts—which would not, in the first place, seem to require much encouragement. In general, the MOS or job assignment received by individual servicemen may be influenced by their social origins, and, perhaps, particularly by the formal education and skills brought with them (verbal and mechanical) from civilian life. Radar operatives or artillerymen, for instance, are probably less likely to have direct contact with the "enemy" or enemy action that subjects them to concentrated small arms fire, than riflemen or infantrymen. Similarly, men in supply service battalions or administrative MOS classifications are probably less subject to risk from enemy action.

To some extent, the nature of a war against a popularly based guerrilla movement, as in Vietnam, may diminish such differential risks. In wars with relatively clear rear and forward positions, where the front is identifiable, and where the terrain is relatively open, the distinction between "safe" and "hazardous" assignments is likely to be greater than in an expeditionary war against a national liberation movement. Here, the "enemy" is everywhere; fixed positions are few; women and children may be "enemy troops"; and "fighters by night and workers by day" and hidden snipers abound in the fight "against U.S. and allied forces in Vietnam."[14] When the NLF is capable of penetrating even the American Embassy in Saigon, a "safe" MOS will do little to protect its possessor.

14. Paraphrasis and quotes from Col. Robert B. Riggs, "Made in USA," *Army*, January 1968, pp. 24-31, reprinted in Maurice Zeitlin, ed., *American Society, Inc.* (Chicago: Markham Publishing Co., 1970).

The question, then, is whether or not, aside from the differential effects of the draft, there may be class-effects on the rates of death in combat. Once in the armed forces, do fighting men from certain classes still continue to have greater life chances than others? Or, here at last, do all men, whatever their social origins, find themselves more or less equally "helpless before the threat of death," thus evening out their relative life chances? The Defense Department distinguishes in its casualty lists between "deaths resulting from hostile action" and "deaths resulting from other causes," such as the same sort of accidents or diseases that might kill in civilian life. If one's social origins affect one's chances of death in combat, we should find noticeable differences between the proportions of poor and nonpoor, and of workers and non-workers, killed in "hostile action" in Vietnam. For this type of internal analysis, no external cohort is necessary or relevant.

What we find is that there is a very slight but noticeably systematic pattern of differences between the combat-death rates of the poor and the non-poor (table 5). In all ranks combined, in the army and other services, servicemen from poor families were somewhat more likely to be killed in hostile action than those who were not poor. This is true of privates *and* noncoms in the army, although this does not hold true of privates in the other services. The difference in combat death rates between the poor and the nonpoor is greatest among the noncoms in both the army and in the other services. Indeed, among the privates of all branches combined, the difference is negligible. We cannot test the following plausible explanation, but it is worth suggesting that this may result from the greater homogeneity of MOS assignments among privates than among noncoms, as well as the greater equality of the privates' helplessness before the threat of death.

When we look at the relationship between classes, poverty, and the rate of death in hostile action, one relatively clear pattern emerges (despite the paucity of cases in some categories): Among the sons of workers, farmers, and the middle strata, combining all ranks and branches of the armed forces, more sons of the poor died in hostile action than their more privileged fellow fighting men. The differences between the classes, on the same poverty level, are not systematic, although, again, one fact stands out: Of all groups, the highest proportion of combat deaths is among poor workers' sons (table 6).

We believe, therefore, that the cumulative evidence presented here clearly supports this conclusion: The sons of the poor and of the workers have borne by far the greatest burden of the war in Vietnam, in the measured but immeasurable precision of death.[15]

---

15. We should point out here that this distinction between deaths in hostile action and from other causes does not affect the findings presented in tables 1-4. When the same relationships are examined among only those who were killed in hostile action, the relationships do not differ in any essential way.

Table 1

Percent "Poor" Among the Parents of Wisconsin Servicemen Killed in Vietnam through December 31, 1967, Classified by Branch of Service and Rank, Compared to the Parents of Male Seniors in the Wisconsin High School Class of 1957[1]

| | High School Cohort | ARMY | | | |
		Privates	NCOs	Officers[2]	All Ranks
Poor	14.9%	35.2%	28.0%	9.5%	28.7%
Others	85.1	64.8	72.0	90.5	71.3
	100%	100%	100%	100%	100%
	(N=4080)	(N=71)	(N=82)	(N=21)	(N=174)

| | High School Cohort | MARINES, NAVY, AIR FORCE | | | | |
		Privates	NCOs	Officers	N.A.	All Ranks
Poor	14.9%	26.8%	26.6%	14.3%	-	25.2%
Others	85.1	73.2	73.4	85.7	(1)	74.8
	100%	100%	100%	100%		100%
	(N = 4080)	(N=41)	(N=79)	(N=14)	(N=1)	(N=135)

| | High School Cohort | ALL BRANCHES | | | | |
		Privates	NCOs	Officers	N.A.	All Ranks
Poor	14.9%	32.1%	27.3%	11.4%	-	27.2%
Others	85.1	67.9	72.7	88.6	(1)	72.8
	100%	100%	100%	100%		100%
	(N=4080)	(N=112)	(N=161)	(N=35)	(N=1)	(N=309)

1. Excluding those whose parental income was not ascertained.
2. This category includes two army warrant officers.

In his Master's thesis, James W. Russell also examined the rc onships of career-status—that is, whether servicemen were professional soldiers or draftees—with servicemen's deaths in Vietnam. This is clearly a distinction relevant to battle survival. He found the same essential relationships between class, poverty, and mortality rates among non-career and career men, although these relationships, as we might expect, were strongest among non-career men. Increased experience, training, and commitment would diminish the effects of one's civilian background on one's life's chances in combat ("Who Dies in Vietnam?" University of Wisconsin, 1968).

Table 2

Percentage Distribution of Occupations of Fathers of Wisconsin Servicemen Killed in Vietnam through December 31, 1967, Classified by Rank and Branch of Service, Compared to the Occupations of Fathers of Male Seniors in the Wisconsin High School Class of 1957[1]

Occupational Groups	High School Cohort[2]	ARMY			
		Privates	NCOs	Officers	All Ranks
Professional, Technical, and kindred	7.5%	1.4%	2.5%	23.8%	4.6%
Managers, Officials, and Proprietors (non-farm)	11.9	9.7	12.5	23.8	12.7
Clerical, Sales, and kindred	10.8	6.9	6.3	14.3	7.5
Skilled Workers	14.6	15.3	22.5	14.3	18.5
Semi-Skilled and Unskilled Workers	37.3	47.2	40.0	19.0	40.5
Farm Owners	17.8	19.4	16.3	4.8	16.2
	100% (N=4846)	100% (N=72)	100% (N=80)	100% (N=21)	100% (N=173)

Occupational Groups	High School Cohort[2]	MARINES, NAVY, AIR FORCE				
		Privates	NCOs	Officers	N.A.	All Ranks
Professional, Technical, and kindred	7.5%	10.0%	5.3%	23.1%		8.5%
Managers, Officials, and Proprietors (non-farm)	11.9	10.0	6.7	15.4	(1)	9.3
Clerical, Sales, and kindred	10.8	-	13.3	7.7		8.5
Skilled Workers	14.6	20.0	12.0	15.4		14.7
Semi-Skilled and Unskilled Workers	37.3	42.5	53.3	30.8		47.3
Farm Owners	17.8	17.5	9.3	7.7		11.6
	100% (N=4846)	100% (N=40)	100% (N=75)	100% (N=13)	- (N=1)	100% (N=129)

1. Excluding those whose father's occupation was not ascertained.
2. Technically, the distribution in the cohort is of the occupations of heads of households, though the overwhelming majority were fathers.

Table 2 (Continued)

Occupational Groups	High School Cohort	ALL BRANCHES				
		Privates	NCOs	Officers	N.A.	All Ranks
Professional, Technical, etc.	7.5%	4.5%	3.9%	23.5%		6.3%
Managers, Officials, and Proprietors (non-farm)	11.9	9.8	9.7	20.6	(1)	11.3
Clerical, Sales, etc.	10.8	4.5	9.7	11.8		7.9
Skilled Workers	14.6	17.0	17.4	14.7		16.9
Semi-Skilled and Unskilled Workers	37.3	45.5	46.5	23.5		43.4
Farm Owners	17.8	18.8	12.9	5.9		14.2
	100%	100%	100%	100%	-	100%
	(N=4846)	(N=112)	(N=155)	(N=34)	(N=1)	(N=302)

1. Excluding those whose father's occupation was not ascertained.

2. Technically, the distribution in the cohort is of the occupations of heads of households, though the overwhelming majority were fathers.

Table 3

Percent "Poor," by Father's Occupation, Among Wisconsin Servicemen Killed in Vietnam through December 31, 1967, Classified by Rank, Compared to the Male Seniors in the Wisconsin High School Class of 1957[1]

	High School Cohort (N)	Privates (N)	ALL BRANCHES NCOs (N)	Officers (N)	All Ranks (N)
Workers					
Skilled	7.6% (675)	11.1% (18)	22.2% (27)	0 (5)	16.0% (50)
Semi-Skilled and Unskilled	17.5 (1341)	29.4 (51)	21.4 (70)	12.5 (8)	24.0 (129)
(Workers combined)	14.2%	24.6%	21.6%	7.7%	21.8%
Farm Owners	23.6 (839)	65.0 (20)	50.0 (20)	(1/2)	57.1 (42)
Middle Strata[2]	10.1 (1225)	20.0 (20)	30.6 (36)	10.5 (19)	22.4 (76)[3]
Total:	14.9% (4080)	31.2% (109)	27.5% (153)	11.8% (34)	26.9% (297)

1. Excluding those whose parental income and father's occupation were not ascertained.
2. Professionals, technicians, etc.; managers, officials, proprietors; clerical, sales, etc. The number of poor in each of these occupational groups is too small to calculate percentages for meaningful comparisons.
3. One manager is included whose rank was not ascertained.

Table 4

Percentage Distribution of Occupations of Fathers of Wisconsin Servicemen Killed in Vietnam through December 31, 1967, All Branches, Compared to the Occupations of Fathers of Male Seniors in the Wisconsin High School Class of 1957, Classified by Poverty Level[1]

	High School Cohort		Servicemen	
	Poor	Others	Poor	Others
Professional, Technical, etc.	2.6%	7.6%	6.3%	6.5%
Managers, Officials, Proprietors (non-farm)	10.7	14.2	3.8	13.8
Clerical, Sales, etc.	7.1	9.9	11.3	6.9
(subtotal)	20.4%	31.7%	21.4%	27.2%
Skilled Workers	8.4	18.0	10.0	19.4
Semi-Skilled and Unskilled Workers	38.7	31.9	38.8	45.2
(subtotal)	47.1%	49.9%	48.8%	64.6%
Farm Owners	32.6	18.5	30.0	8.3
	100%	100%	100%	100%
	(N=608)	(N=3472)	(N=80)	(N=217)

1. Excluding those whose parental income and father's occupation were not ascertained.

Table 5

Percent Killed in "Hostile Action" Among "Poor" and Other Wisconsin Servicemen Killed in Vietnam Through December 31, 1967, Classified by Rank and Branch of Service.[1]

ARMY

	Privates (N)		N.C.O.s (N)		Officers (N)		All Ranks (N)	
Poor	92%	(25)	87%	(23)		(1/2)	88%	(50)
Others	89	(46)	78	(59)	74	(19)	81	(124)

MARINES, NAVY, AIR FORCE

	Privates		N.C.O.s		Officers		All Ranks	
Poor	75%	(11)	91%	(21)		(2/2)	86%	(34)
Others	80	(30)	79	(58)	75	(12)	78	(101)[2]

ALL BRANCHES

	Privates		N.C.O.s		Officers		All Ranks	
Poor	87%	(36)	89%	(44)		(3/4)	87%	(84)
Others	85	(76)	79	(117)	74	(31)	80	(225)[2]

[1] Excluding those whose parental income was not ascertained.

[2] Including one serviceman killed in hostile action, whose rank was not ascertained.

MAURICE ZEITLIN, KENNETH LUTTERMAN AND JAMES RUSSELL

Table 6

Percent Killed in "Hostile Action" Among Poor and Other Wisconsin Service-men Killed in Vietnam through December 31, 1967, Classified by Rank, and by Class.[1]

All Branches

	Privates	(N)	N.C.O.s	(N)	Officers	(N)	All Ranks	(N)
Workers[3]								
Poor	88%	(17)	95%	(21)	(1/1)		92%	(39)
Others	85	(52)	79	(76)	75	(12)	81	(140)
Farm Owners								
Poor	92	(13)	80	(10)	(0/1)		83	(24)
Others	(6/7)		70	(10)	(1/1)		78	(18)
Middle Strata								
Poor	(4/4)		82	(11)	(2/2)		88	(17)
Others	87	(16)	84	(25)	59	(17)	78	(59)[2]

[1] Excluding those whose parental income and father's occupation were not ascertained.

[2] One manager is included whose rank was not ascertained.

[3] We have sufficient numbers of sons of semi- and unskilled workers to view the relationship in this group alone:

	Privates	(N)	N.C.O.s	(N)	Officers	(N)	All Ranks	(N)
Poor Semi- and Un-skilled	93%	(15)	93%	(15)	(1/1)		93%	(31)
Other Semi- and Un-skilled	83	(36)	82	(55)	(5/7)		82	(98)

3. Two Model Cities: Negotiations in Oakland

JUDITH MAY

As colleague confronts colleague, so also do the constituent orders of the Roman Republic: the sovereignty (*imperium*) of the magistracy confronts the sovereignty (*majestas*) of the people not on a line of vertical subordination but horizontally coordinate. The Roman body politic is not one, but two. The two principles cannot operate except as they cooperate; so that, as Mommsen says, "law was not primarily, as we conceive it, a command addressed by the sovereign to the community as a whole, but primarily a contract concluded between the constitutive powers of the state by address and counter-address." The schism in the body politics known as the secession (not rebellion) of the plebs is only an aggravation of the inherent separation of the constituent orders. The extraordinary institution to which that secession gave rise, the tribunate of the people, with its veto over the acts of the magistracy, amounted to legalized, and institutionalized, civil war.

Norman O. Brown, *Love's Body*, p. 28

In Oakland, California, under the auspices of the Model Cities program, the federal government precipitated a conflict between the "sovereignty of

This paper is based upon three years of observation of the Oakland poverty and Model Cities meetings, interaction with the participants, and examination of available records, correspondence, and newspaper reports. This research was conducted under the auspices of the Oakland Project headed by Aaron Wildavsky and funded by the National Aeronautics and Space Administration and the Urban Institute. I am grateful to Professors Wildavsky and Matthew Stolz for unfailing support and stimulation, to Michael Lipsky, Paul Cobb, Percy Moore, Mel Mogulof, Ralph Williams, and John A. Martin for their valuable comments on an earlier draft, and to Carolina Helfer for editorial assistance.

This essay will soon appear in George Fredericksen, ed., *Politics, Public Administration and Neighborhood Control* (San Francisco: Chandler Publishing Co., forthcoming). It was presented at a conference on New Public Administration and Neighborhood Control held in Boulder, Colorado, May 1970, sponsored by the Center for Governmental Studies, Washington, D.C.

the magistracy" and the "sovereignty of the people," and the immediate consequence was the creation of a second government for the West Oakland community. West Oakland residents, in effect, declared their independence from the authority of the local government and established new institutions which they vested with legitimacy. Led by newly sanctioned leaders in their battle over Model Cities planning, they fought for the right to govern their own community in concert with city officials—to share authority on a large number of important matters. Their negotiated victory may prove short-lived; a small change in federal administrative or legislative policy could have an enormous effect on the viability of the West Oakland "government." Even should the Model Cities structure fail to survive, however, the contest will continue. At stake are alternative visions of the model city, one compatible with existing institutions and policies and the other premised upon major changes in them.

During the course of the negotiations, West Oakland leaders articulated with increasing clarity an alternative to the economic growth ideology held by city officials and embodied in the city's political institutions. In so doing they tackled some of the most politically repressive features of the institutional and intellectual changes which have occurred in this country since the advent of the welfare and warfare states: political legitimacy based upon conformance to procedures rather than performance; political authority delegated to experts; and governmental policy directed toward economic growth at the expense of economic redistribution—features which are found in many American governments, not only in the city of Oakland.[1] Social scientists are becoming increasingly sensitive to these developments and are beginning to see the inadequacies of the paradigms which have guided their research in recent decades. If, as I contend, we are witnessing the exhaustion of another generation of ideas, then perhaps at this point in time, when the search for a new paradigm is under way, social scientists should examine the reactions of those who are struggling with the overripe fruits of old ideas.

1. In arriving at these conclusions I found the following sources helpful:
James Weinstein, *The Corporate Ideal in the Liberal State, 1900-1918* (Boston: Beacon Press, 1968); Gabriel Kolko, *The Triumph of Conservatism: A Reinterpretation of American History, 1900-1916* (Chicago: Quadrangle Books, 1963, 1967); Barton J. Bernstein, "The New Deal: The Conservative Achievements of Liberal Reform," in *Towards a New Past: Dissenting Essays in American History*, ed. Barton J. Bernstein (New York: Random House, Vintage Books, 1967, 1969); Andrew Shonfield, *Modern Capitalism: The Changing Balance of Public and Private Power* (New York: Oxford University Press, 1965); John Kenneth Galbraith, *The New Industrial State* (New York: Signet Books, 1967, 1968); Herman P. Miller, *Rich Man, Poor Man* (New York: Signet Books, 1964); John C. Donovan, *The Politics of Poverty* (New York: Pegasus, 1967), pp. 93-110.

Economic Growth versus Economic Redistribution

City officials and West Oakland residents evaluated the possible benefits of the Model Cities program in terms of different conceptions of the proper relationship between government and economic life. In general, city officials and their supporters believe that Oakland's economic future depends upon the city's ability to attract and retain private capital investors. Economic growth will not only expand the city's tax base, creating resources which can be reinvested in the city's advancement, but will also create employment opportunities and result, thereby, in productive citizens rather than public liabilities. Recent changes in Oakland's population and economic base have increased the burdens upon the city. During World War II, its population increased rapidly as the demand rose for workers in the Oakland shipyards and war-related activities. A large minority population remained after the war and the white population began to move to the suburbs over newly completed freeways. Simultaneously, manufacturing decreased, while transportation, distribution, communications, and service industries expanded. Thus, while the skill level of the city's population decreased, the skill demands of its economic institutions increased. Nevertheless, Oakland's economic future is promising. Despite the many enterprises that have moved out, those that remain are attracted in large part by Oakland's location in a nexus of transportation facilities. These firms have a stake in Oakland and are potential supporters of long-range economic development strategies.

A relatively coherent strategy for achieving economic development has emerged. A private investor's willingness to invest in Oakland is affected by his confidence in Oakland's economic future. Public policy must be directed toward creating this confidence. Two means to this end have been identified: maintaining racial peace and programming public investment. In the short run, racial peace is achieved through a combination of coercion and co-optation, in the long run, through individual upward mobility.

Sources of public investment funds have changed in recent years. Bond elections have repeatedly failed and numerous structural innovations have been necessary to capture new sources of investment capital. As a result, government on the local level has become increasingly fragmented. Increasingly, capital resources within Oakland are provided by other governments which attach conditions to the use of these funds, conditions that dissipate the city's authority still further. A recent study, initiated by the mayor, found that the federal government spent a total of $487,356,372 in Oakland in 1968, $95,459,372 for non-defense purposes.[2] The Port of Oakland, whose commission members are appointed by the mayor with the

2. *Digest of Current Federal Programs in the City of Oakland* (October 1968), prepared for Mayor John H. Reading by Jeffrey L. Pressman with the assistance of the Redevelopment Agency of the City of Oakland.

concurrence of the city council, received $8,275,780. The relatively autonomous Oakland Redevelopment Agency and the Oakland Housing Authority received $8,158,110. The City of Oakland itself received $1,009,323. Under the circumstances, it is not surprising that city officials welcomed the Model Cities program and its promise that the city government would play a major role in coordinating federal programs within the city.

Despite its handicaps, the city government has used the capital investment resources it does control to increase the city's attractiveness to investors. Major bond issues have financed a museum, an airport, and a police and municipal court building. Several urban renewal projects are under way, and the present mayor, John Reading, hopes to revive the downtown area with a major hotel-and-convention center assisted with urban renewal funds. Despite these investments in Oakland's future productivity, the city has one of the highest unemployment rates among urban areas of its size in the nation.[3]

Recently, city leaders have begun to realize that there is no necessary correlation between economic growth and the alleviation of Oakland's social problems and have increased their support for programs which invest in human as well as in capital development projects. Mayor Reading, in particular, believes that reducing unemployment will solve all other social problems and that the key to increasing employment lies in raising the skill level of the population. Much of the money available for this purpose is administered by the OEDC, the community action agency in Oakland. Reading is convinced that the OEDC has spent its money unwisely and is unsuited (by virtue of its composition) to administer employment programs, and he has attempted to wrest control over the program from the agency's board. Embittered by the federal government's willingness to bypass the city government, he also tried to force the agency, then functioning somewhat autonomously though attached to the city government, to observe "normal administrative procedures," i.e., to funnel all communications through the city manager's office. These conflicts and their culmination in a break between the agency and the city overlapped the period of the preparation and revision of the Model Cities application.

When West Oakland residents viewed the results of the city's social and economic policies—as they experienced their effects on their daily lives—their general conclusion (though not expressed in this language) was that the objective of economic productivity was a long-run strategy which, in the short run, visited harsh consequences upon the low income and minority communities, and that city officials were more concerned with promoting

3. In 1966, 8.4 percent of Oakland's total civilian labor force was unemployed; in the West Oakland target area, the figure was 14.3 percent. Source: William L. Nicholls II, *Tables on Employment and Unemployment from the 701 Household Survey in Oakland* (Berkeley: University of California Survey Research Center, revised August 1, 1968), Table R-3, p. 19.

economic growth than with increasing political and economic equality. As a result of capital improvement projects—freeway and rapid transit constructions and urban renewal programs—West Oakland sustained a net loss of 5100 housing units between 1960 and 1966. A clearance project lay dormant for six years; when it was finally carried out, housing was constructed for moderate- rather than low-income tenants. A rehabilitation project in West Oakland advanced the interests of homeowners at the expense of renters; the coliseum and arena, museum, and police administration building were given priority, although many streets in West Oakland lack curbs and gutters. Nor did West Oakland residents benefit indirectly from public improvements: millions of local and federal dollars have been invested in the Port, but Port commissioners have resisted employment clauses which would increase job openings for ghetto residents. The city made little effort to enforce employment clauses, agreed to by industries moving into the Acorn clearance area, for fear the industries would move away. Employment training programs have become an acknowledged hustle, since few jobs are available at the end of the training period.

Furthermore, West Oakland residents had little hope of altering these policies through normal political processes. In Oakland, councilmen reside in districts but are elected at large in nonpartisan elections. They pride themselves on representing "the community as a whole" rather than special interests, and are notably conservative in ideology. Since 1937, when the council-manager form of government was installed, one-third of the council members achieved office through appointment to vacancies caused by death (eight) or resignation between election periods (eleven). Of the mayoral and councilmanic incumbents who ran for re-election between 1953 and 1969, eighty-five percent retained their seats. Two of the three minority representatives now on the council, one black and one Japanese, were originally appointed to office; the third, who is Chinese, defeated an eighty-year-old incumbent from West Oakland in his third campaign effort. The two Orientals share the conservative views of their colleagues; the black councilman was largely isolated from the rest of the black community until recently. Needless to say, the low-income and minority communities do not regard the city council as responsive to their interests. In Oakland, blacks compose approximately forty percent of the population and Mexican-Americans another ten percent; but lower registration and a high proportion of young people have so far reduced the electoral strength of the minority population.

Whereas city officials wanted to make everyone better off while retaining the existing relative shares, West Oakland residents wanted political and economic advantages distributed more evenly over all sections and classes in the city. Whereas city officials located the source of Oakland's problems in its change economy and the low skills of a large part of its population, West

Oakland residents pointed to the failure of the American government to assure political and economic equality to all of its citizens. Given these differences, it is not surprising that city officials and West Oakland residents also differed on the way in which decision making for the Model Cities program should be structured.

The Original Application: Advocacy Planning

Oakland has a weak-mayor, council-manager form of government. Members of the city council are accustomed to delegating responsibilities to the city manager and relying upon his advice. In October 1966, a month before the Demonstration Cities Act was passed, the city council directed its city manager, Jerome Keithley, to prepare an application. He assigned the task of preparing the application to Marshall Kaplan, a planning consultant, and assembled a task force of city and county agency heads to assist him. Since Kaplan had previously been hired by the Redevelopment Agency to appraise the existing urban renewal program within the city, he was able to draw heavily upon that report[4] and completed the application within a relatively short time. The city manager restricted participation in what he called "the pre-planning processes" to members of the task force on the ground of an imminent deadline (April 15, 1967) for submission of the application. When the application was nearly completed, two target area residents were added to the task force, and endorsements by various citizen boards, including the poverty board, were sought.[5]

The structure which Oakland officials projected for citizen participation in the Model Cities planning process relied upon the advocacy principle. In summary its premises were: (1) Although community residents in the past had been unable to "insert their views" into the policy-making process, they are able to do so if they are supervised by an established organization (the Oakland Economic Development Council, the community action agency) and

4. City of Oakland, Redevelopment Agency, *Oakland: A Demonstration City* (May 1966).

5. Kaplan opposed the addition of the two residents to the task force because it destroyed the pure advocacy model. This addition transformed the task force from an executive committee for the city into a policy-making body where city and community representatives would interact directly, and shifted attention from the quality of advocates possessed by each side to the parity of voting strength on the policy-making body. Kaplan feared that direct interaction would increase the severity of the conflict between public officials and West Oakland residents. For a defense of Kaplan's perspective and a detailed chronological account of the Model Cities negotiations, see his case study prepared for the Oakland Task Force of the San Francisco Federal Executive Board, *An Analysis of Federal Decision-Making and Impact: The Federal Government in Oakland*, vol. 2 (Washington, D.C.: Economic Development Administration, U. S. Department of Commerce, January 1969).

assisted by professional advocates; (2) Planning itself is a job for professionals who possess both technical skill and political sensitivity; plans for the Model Cities program are to be hammered out in negotiations between the city's planners and the community's advocates; (3) Responsibility for the plan's preparation is properly delegated to the city manager, who is the city's superintendent of administrative matters; (4) The Model Cities program concentrates resources within a particular area, but the interests of the whole community are to be given weight in the planning process; (5) Final policy determinations are properly made by the city council after all interested parties have had a chance to be heard.[6]

West Oakland Residents Propose Community Control

On November 16, 1967, federal officials announced that Oakland's application had been accepted conditionally. Among the five or six conditions attached to the contract was one that the city would have to clarify the role of community residents in the planning process before final approval would be granted. Federal officials held a meeting in Oakland on November 28 to explain their reservations. Immediately thereafter, the West Oakland Planning Committee[7] proposed a structure which eliminated all intermediaries between the spokesmen they selected and the political leaders of the city. In effect, they proposed the creation of a subgovernment for the West Oakland community which would author Model Cities plans subject only to the concurrence of the city council. In the city's original application, planners dominated the planning process; in West Oakland's proposal, community residents dominated. Oakland's experience suggests that both planners and community residents view the new federal interest in urban problems as an opportunity to reduce their past ineffectiveness in influencing urban policies; and each has invented an ideology which justifies this new route to communal upward mobility: "advocacy" in the case of planners, and "community control" in the case of community residents.

West Oakland residents wanted to control the Model Cities planning process because they thought city officials were neither willing nor able to plan and implement programs which met their needs as they defined them. As a result of their experience with the poverty program, they were strengthened in their conviction that only if they controlled the program would they obtain results that satisfied them. West Oakland leaders were among the indigenous target area representatives who fought for majority control over

6. City of Oakland, City Manager, *Application for Planning Grant, Model Cities Program*, City of Oakland (April 3, 1967).
7. Detailed discussion of this organization occurs in a later section.

the poverty board—the Oakland Economic Development Council.[8] Many of the attitudes and strategies which they brought to the Model Cities fight were formed in the evolving relationships between indigenous and at-large members of the Oakland Economic Development Council and between the Oakland Economic Development Council and the city. For that reason, the principal stages in the evolution of these relationships will be summarized here.

During the first stage, beginning in 1965, black professionals among the at-large members of the OEDC played a dominant role in defining the strategy followed by that body.[9] They assumed a tutelary role in relation to the poor and continued the strategy of "responsible opposition" to the city which they had developed as leaders of civil rights organizations. Through control over poverty funds, they hoped to enhance their effectiveness in negotiations with established agencies over the quality of services delivered to poor people. Their effectiveness depended upon their ability to maximize the amount of funds controlled by the OEDC (thereby increasing their bargaining leverage), to negotiate skillfully with federal and city officials, and to maintain an aura of "responsibility" about the poverty program, that is, to reduce visible conflicts both within the OEDC and between the OEDC and the city. Nevertheless, they acknowledged that the phrase "maximum feasible participation" legitimized direct participation by target area residents, and they sponsored the development of target area advisory committees and gradually added indigenous representatives to the council. However, they did not act swiftly enough in the view of some target area leaders who felt that maximum feasible participation required a larger role for the representatives of the poor.

The second stage begin when, at an OEDC program-review meeting on March 12, 1966, target area representatives walked out after demanding that the OEDC give them "fifty-one percent control" over the board and allocate more of its money to poor people than to agency administrators.[10] They

8. At the time of the Model Cities negotiations, the OEDC had thirty-nine members: four representatives from each of the five target area advisory committees, and nineteen "at-large" members representing public officials, business, labor, education, religious bodies, and civil rights organizations.

9. At this time, each of the four target area advisory committees was entitled to three representatives, and the fifth advisory committee for Spanish-speakers had not yet been created; thus, indigenous representatives constituted thirty-three percent of council membership.

10. With the advent of the poverty program in Oakland, in December 1964, the citizens' advisory committee of the Ford Foundation Grey Areas program (which had been operating in Oakland since early 1962) was transformed into the OEDC. The mayor appointed additional members creating a body broadly representative of the total community. At the first meeting the council approved fourteen programs for poverty-funding. The first direct representatives of the poor were added four months later.

argued that poor people could better define their own needs than these professionals. While at-large members continued to focus on changing the ways in which agency programs were run, the target area representatives wanted to run their own program. During this period, the at-large representatives retained effective control over the OEDC and their commitment to the negotiating strategy. However, since that strategy depended upon maintaining a low level of conflict within the OEDC, they acceded to some of the demands made by the indigenous representatives. A change in the guidelines permitted the OEDC to use Ford Foundation Grey Areas funds for financing indigenous projects, while continuing to use OEO funds to create negotiating leverage with established agencies. Thus, for a time, both the black professionals and the indigenous representatives were satisfied.

However, a number of changes occured which upset this equilibrium and initiated the third stage. A new city manager (Keithley) took office, a man who was less interested in social problems and less amenable to behind-the-scenes negotiations. At the same time, spurred by the indigenous representatives, the OEDC began demanding greater changes in city policy than city officials were willing to make (e.g., creation of a police review board). Through skillful negotiations by its at-large members, the OEDC gained control over a new federal employment program funded by the Labor Department; this thoroughly alienated the new mayor (Reading) who had vigorously opposed OEDC's expansion into this area. Each of these factors strained the relationship between the city and the poverty program and undermined the efficacy of the negotiating strategy. Early in 1967 the OEDC decided to sever its attachment to the city and become a nonprofit corporation. In June, the executive director of the OEDC—Dr. Norvel Smith, a staunch and skillful advocate of the negotiating policy—resigned. Reluctantly, in November, the city manager appointed the OEDC's choice for Dr. Smith's successor, Percy Moore; and, two months later, the OEDC began its independent existence as the OEDC, Inc. Moore's appointment marked the beginning of more open conflict between the OEDC and the city and within the OEDC itself.

Moore rejected the negotiating strategy. Using it, the OEDC could win no more than agencies were willing to concede. He urged the OEDC to use its funds to create an independent political base from which it could extract concessions that agencies were unwilling to make. Moore chafed at taking directions from those who had participated in the negotiating strategy, characterizing them as "brokers." Because he sometimes made aggressive public statements in the name of the OEDC without consulting them, he periodically alienated their support. He also antagonized some of the indigeonous representatives when, in an effort to strengthen the OEDC, he attempted to consolidate some activities which had been decentralized in the target areas. (And he angered the Mexican-Americans and some blacks by using the term "black," instead of "black and brown" or the less divisive term "poor.") Relations between the OEDC and the city were strained and conflicts within the OEDC were unresolved at the time West Oakland mobilized to revise the Model Cities application in negotiations with city officials.

The advocacy planning structure in Oakland's original Model Cities application was compatible with the negotiating strategy, since it preserved for black professionals a tutelary role in relation to West Oakland residents and a bargaining role in relation to the city. With the support of Percy Moore, West Oakland leaders rapidly demonstrated that they would not allow OEDC members to mediate between community residents and city officials. The OEDC's at-large members at first resisted West Oakland's declaration of independence from the OEDC on Model Cities matters because they feared that West Oakland leaders lacked sufficient skill and resources to carry on successful negotiations with the city. However, for a number of reasons, they soon acquiesced in the fait accompli and confined their activities to providing political support and advice upon request. For one, by then they were tired and angered by the arduous negotiations required to separate the OEDC from the city, and they wanted city officials to bear the costs in higher conflict for their failure to cooperate with the negotiating strategy. By then, too, target area advisory committees had won the right to authorize and oversee projects in their areas, and so West Oakland's demand for control over the Model Cities program in their area found support among other target area representatives. And, as West Oakland spokesmen pointed out, most of the at-large members of the OEDC lived in Oakland's affluent hills and not in West Oakland's flats "with the rats, roaches, and mosquitoes twenty-four hours a day." Overlapping membership between the WOPC Executive Committee and the OEDC lessened fears that an autonomous rival power center was being established. But perhaps the most important reason was that the OEDC could not control access to city and federal officials; and once the swiftly organized WOPC initiated its own contracts with these officials, its spokesmen could argue with great forcefulness that introducing intermediaries between them would be inefficient and would jeopardize the interests of West Oakland citizens.

For the first time, lower-class community residents and their chosen representatives carried on direct negotiations with city officials over the form and objectives of a social program. The strategy which they prepared for this confrontation reflected their response to the conflicts then occurring within the OEDC. They endorsed the strategy of negotiations, but insisted upon participating directly rather than through the mediators who had carried responsibility for past negotiations, and they elected to build an independent political base, but rejected the centralization of authority that Moore had urged. By their actions, West Oakland residents explicitly rejected definitions of themselves as deficient. Acting on their conviction that the City of Oakland was unresponsive to their "wants, wishes and desires," they created a parallel government for West Oakland. At first this "government" was largely symbolic. Ralph Williams (who had been chairman of a district council under the Grey Areas program and of a target area advisory committee under the poverty program) was referred to as the "mayor" of West Oakland, and West Oakland leaders cultivated other analogies with the city government. As a result of the Model Cities negotiations, however, West Oakland residents actually won the right to share authority with the city council on matters of importance to their community. The Model Cities structure itself was founded upon a contract concluded between "two sovereigns." Before negotiations began, each had prepared a Model Cities structure which reflected its political and economic objectives. Then by "address and counter-address" the constituted authorities and their sovereign constituents negotiated a contract whereby the Model Cities program would not operate except insofar as the two sovereigns could cooperate. Their experience may provide a model for legalizing and institutionalizing other urban civil wars. In the following sections I shall describe the evolution of those negotiations starting at the point when Wert Oakland prepared its response to the city's conditionally accepted original application.

The first task confronting West Oakland leaders was to create an organization which could legitimately claim recognition both from community residents and city officials as the spokesman for the West Oakland community. Given the divisions within that community, this task was not easy. Next, West Oakland leaders had to choose between controlling the administration of planning and governing a community. They chose to try to govern a community. Having made this choice, they first established their relation to experts within and outside the West Oakland community, and then they set out to determine the extent of their authority. They operated on the premise that control over Model Cities planning without control over the implementation of those plans would severely limit their ability to ameliorate or eliminate the coercive side effects of social change. They hoped that authority over the use of resources that others needed to accomplish their objectives would create opportunities to negotiate policies which were mutually beneficial. By means of this authority they hoped to bring about policies which were genuinely redistributive in their outcomes, rather than policies that sought to adjust West Oakland residents to the existing distribution of advantages and disadvantages.

RECLAMATION OF SOVEREIGNTY

In striving to build an organization and gain recognition as the legitimate spokesman of the West Oakland community, West Oakland leaders had (a) to create a structure which permitted the mobilization of a broad base of support while preventing old antagonisms from disrupting the new organization's unity, (b) to create trust among their constituents in their responsiveness and ability, (c) to gather political support in various forms from outside the organization, and (d) to establish their equality with city officials in negotiating a Model Cities "partnership." With support from a unified organization which had the confidence of the diverse factions and groups in the community, West Oakland's leaders could drive a hard bargain, capitalizing on the city's reluctance to lose promised federal funds.[11] Disunity would give city officials the opportunity to confer recognition on the most congenial faction, and thereby continue the practice of co-optation which they had used so effectively in the past.

Divisions Within the West Oakland Community

The pattern of conflicts within the West Oakland community threatened to prevent the mobilization of a broad base of support. Organizations ranging from fundamentalist churches to revolutionary parties operated in West Oakland, but three identifiable leadership factions, sustained by the citizen participation provisions of federal legislation and reflecting the class divisions within the community, have emerged in recent years. Each has experienced successes in its area of special competence.

The faction dominating the West Oakland Advisory Committee (WOAC)—who were to form the leadership core of the new Model Cities organization—had shared with other indigenous leaders the triumph of securing "fifty-one percent control" over the city-wide poverty board and of redirecting funds from established agencies to indigenous organizations. Most members of this faction had migrated to Oakland from the South during World War II. Many of them were veteran participants in community affairs (district councils, church and school groups, fraternal organizations). Upwardly mobile in spite of their low educational attainment and working-class occupations, a large number took advantage of the poverty program's "new careerists" employment opportunities.

The second faction had initially formed around the Peter Maurin Neighborhood House, a Catholic social service agency. They went on to form the Western-End Model Cities Organization (WEMCO) and were also active in various block clubs. Members of this faction live in the most dilapidated

11. How willingly "the City would surrender sovereignty to get Federal dollars" was not known to West Oakland leaders at the time they formulated their negotiating strategy, according to Percy Moore (memo to the author, October 31, 1969). During one particularly trying period, the city council threatened to move the Model Cities area from West Oakland to another section of the city where the leaders might be more grateful for the benefits of the program. However, West Oakland leaders refused to take this threat seriously, since they realized the city would be unable to complete rapidly the preliminary work for another Model Cities application.

section of West Oakland, separated from the rest of the community by a freeway, and are generally less mobile, less well-off, and less sophisticated politically than members of the other two factions. Nevertheless; with the assistance of Dorothy Kauffman, a white woman, and other volunteers from outside the community, they achieved a high degree of community organization, accomplishing such goals as the construction of a community nursery school which uses the Montessori teaching method, the conversion of several vacant lots into small recreation areas, and extensive painting and repair work. They are more concerned with improving local social services and living conditions than with local autonomy, and they antagonized the West Oakland Advisory Committee faction by using outside assistance as well as by having access to private resources. Moreover, their accomplishments undercut the WOAC's attempt to monopolize access to scarce resources[12] in their area. Bitter controversies frequently occurred between the two groups, which WEMCO appealed to the Oakland Economic Development Council.

The third faction, organized around the Oak Center Neighborhood Association, consisted primarily of middle-income homeowners, many of whom had lived in Oakland prior to World War II and who had long participated in community affairs (including social activities). The Oak Center Neighborhood Association, though preventing clearance of the Oak Center area and winning the right to be consulted by the Redevelopment Agency, has little concern with the problems of tenants within the rehabilitation area; it generally shares the Redevelopment Agency's goal for the area, namely, to re-create a middle-class integrated community in the central city. The poverty program has strengthened the ability of the upwardly mobile working class, represented by the West Oakland Advisory Committee, to challenge both the class-related views and the leadership dominance of this longer established, higher income group.

The Structure of the West Oakland Planning Committee

In a remarkably short time, a group of West Oakland leaders achieved their goal of creating a single organization, the West Oakland Planning Committee, which would bridge the divisions within the community and become the spokesman for the target area residents in negotiating with city officials a

12. The resources I have in mind are: membership on boards, money for indigenous programs, jobs in programs financed with poverty funds, enjoyment of social status or esteem, access to formal and informal information flows, opportunities for publicity and interaction with city officials and civic leaders. For illuminating discussions of political resources, see Warren Ilchman and Norman Uphoff, *The Political Economy of Change* (Berkeley: University of California Press, 1969); and Michael Lipsky, "Protest as a Political Resource," *American Political Science Review* 62 (December 1968), 1144-58.

revised application for Model Cities. The West Oakland Planning Committee was established as a delegate assembly. (The leadership could complete its work so quickly because they had previously experimented with this form.)[13] Any organization of at least ten members operating totally or partially within West Oakland could become a member by submitting the names of two representatives. Political, religious, social, economic, and professional organizations joined. At the organizational meeting (December 8, 1967), representatives from 65 organizations were present; by August 1968, 165 organizations belonged.

The West Oakland Planning Committee's structure, based upon group rather than individual membership, reduced the possibility that more than one organization would seek recognition as spokesman for the community. The fact that each member organization, regardless of its size, has two delegates, quieted fears that the planning committee could be dominated by a single faction or by large church congregations. The group membership policy of the planning committee encourages political entrepreneurship and rewards the politically active. Those who belong to more organizations have more opportunities to become delegates. An enterprising individual can create an organization to represent. Highly organized neighborhoods have a greater number of representatives than an electoral system provides, whether it bases representation on territory or population. Because membership on the WOPC is easily accessible to groups and leaders, any struggle over leadership is more likely to take place within the planning committee than between rival organizations. Because the selection and removal of delegates is left entirely to its member organizations, the WOPC is not subject to conflicts in filling vacancies. The policy of inviting all groups to join—bowling clubs as well as block clubs—eliminates contests over eligibility. This delegate-assembly structure enabled the West Oakland Planning Committee to organize quickly and with a minimum of conflicts.

The Leadership of the West Oakland Planning Committee

The West Oakland Planning Committee had not only to unite jealous factions, but also to create support for its executive committee, elected by the delegate assembly at the December 8 meeting. The executive committee

13. Another West Oakland Planning Committee forms the citizen participation organization for the Neighborhood Services Project, an OEO-funded project to establish a community-sponsored model multi-service center in West Oakland. This organization was established less than a month before the Model Cities organization, but West Oakland residents experienced its effectiveness as a planning body prior to the conclusion of the Model Cities negotiations.

consisted of nine regular and four alternate members.[14] At least one member was affiliated with each major division within the community, but nine of the thirteen were closely associated with a single faction, the West Oakland Advisory Committee. These leaders consequently had to overcome the distrust generated by their past political activities. In the West Oakland Advisory Committee, they had controlled the scarce resources (money, personnel, status, authority, and information) available through OEO legislation and had not wanted to share this control; therefore, they had used an assortment of techniques to control admission to membership. Now, as leaders of the West Oakland Planning Committee, they were seeking access to the much greater supply of resources made available under the Model Cities legislation, and to gain this access they needed a broad base of community support. For this reason, they fully endorsed the open membership policy of WOPC. In fact, they ritualized the inclusiveness of the organization with lengthy roll calls and elaborate solicitations of new memberships, called frequent mass meetings where the assembled delegates reviewed the actions of the executive committee and voted on subsequent steps, and stressed repeatedly that their power to act was limited to steps authorized by the delegate assembly.[15]

The ideology of community control united West Oakland leaders and their followers. A parenthetical explanation is necessary here. Although West Oakland is a predominantly black community, community control is not a specifically "black" response. Most West Oakland residents appear to be

14. Members of the executive committee chosen by the delegate assembly included: two clergymen, one Catholic and one Protestant; the chairman of the West Oakland Advisory Committee; the chairman of Western-End Model Cities Organization; two political entrepreneurs, the moderate chairman of BUMP (Blacks Unified to Motivate Progress) and the militant proprietor of the Western-End Help Center; the chairman of the McClymonds Youth Council; the chairman of the United Voters and Taxpayers Association, an organization formed to fight the first urban redevelopment project in Oakland (this man was also a member of the board of the NAACP); and the public relations director of the Concentrated Employment Program. Among the four alternates were the chairman of the Prescott Neighborhood Council; the chairman of an association of West Oakland small businessmen; a neighborhood organizer for the West Oakland Advisory Committee; and a member of the Oak Center Neighborhood Association. Four of those selected were currently serving on the Oakland Economic Development Council.

15. These actions to secure support actually increased the delegate assembly's control over their executive. The executive committee had called for several important votes during the negotiations, but once the negotiations were completed, the leaders attempted to revert to their West Oakland Advisory Committee practice of controlling access to scarce resources. At issue in the April 14, 1969, meeting of the West Oakland Planning Committee was the use that would be made of OEO Title 1-D Special Impact Funds. The delegate assembly asserted its authority by reversing an action taken by several members of the executive committee; the assembly's reasons for the reversal were partly substantive and partly procedural—the delegates had not been adequately consulted in advance.

motivated by righteous indignation, built up over long years of experience with an unresponsive government; only a few feel comfortable articulating this experience in the language of black ideology. The others do not lack racial pride; rather, they are rejecting an ideology that implies separation of West Oakland from the rest of the city. The apparent paradox dissolves on closer inspection: the goal West Oakland Planning Committee leaders call "community control" (and some observers term "black control of a black community") is premised upon a strong identification with the fate of the city as a whole. In the "model" city they hope to achieve, all races, all classes, and all communities share a common fate. To quote Ralph Williams, "The piano player has to play the black keys and the white keys together for the most harmonious, melody-ous music"—an observation he makes almost every time the issue of race arises. He and other leaders encourage pride in and a strong identification with West Oakland, but visualize its future as inseparable from the whole city's. As an ideology, community control was intended to unite the community across class lines and to reduce opportunities for established leaders to selectively co-opt individuals—a process that divides the community. Community control holds that the only lasting social mobility is communal and that communal mobility requires a political base from which redistributive policies can be either negotiated or coerced.

An organizational ideology, articulated by Paul Cobb (whose role is described in the next section), significantly increased the effectiveness of the planning committee leaders in negotiations with city officials. Called "functional unity," this ideology allowed the highly heterogeneous WOPC and its executive committee not only to survive despite its diversity, but to utilize that diversity to its own advantage. It was intended to reduce the envy and jealousy which flourish in all settings, but particularly where opportunities for power and status are relatively scarce. "Functional unity" acknowledges a division of labor and specialization within the political world, and promises support rather than negative sanctions to the exercise of political initiative. It encourages a permissive attitude toward conflict within the organization, but unity when confronting the opposition. However, it teaches that this unity is compatible with many different political styles. It calls, not for conformity to norms deemed appropriate by city officials—a complex of political virtues revolving about a rather sedate conception of "responsible" behavior—but for each member of the executive committee to participate in the negotiations in the manner best suited to his talents and skills. Any single meeting or negotiating session activated a wide range of political modes: invocation of religious norms, recitation of bombastic analogies, deferential behavior, ad hominem attacks, demagoguery, and pleas for unity, plus the standard political maneuvers. When city officials responded inflexibly, the West Oaklanders won a bargaining advantage.

Mobilizing Political Resources

The West Oakland Planning Committee's most powerful resource was its ability to speak for a wide range of groups in West Oakland, to communicate with these groups through their representatives, and to mobilize large numbers of community residents at crucial points in the negotiations. In addition, the WOPC needed to mobilize political resources outside their immediate organization in order to enhance its effectiveness in negotiations with city officials. West Oakland leaders systematically cultivated the support of city councilmen, newspaper reporters, a newly-formed coalition of white liberal and church organizations, and black public officials and political leaders.

The staff of the poverty board, the Oakland Economic Development Council, gave invaluable support. Percy Moore, the OEDCI executive director, outspokenly endorsed the goal of community control for West Oakland residents and the separation of the West Oakland Planning Committee from the OEDCI. Paul Cobb, planning director of the OEO-funded West Oakland Planning Center, headed a small staff based in West Oakland to assist residents with planning a model multi-service center, and he made his staff's services available to the West Oakland Planning Committee to prepare meeting notices, informational packets, organization charts, letters, and counterproposals. Cobb had been a member of the West Oakland Advisory Committee until appointed to the planning position, and he participated in every phase of negotiations as political advisor and staff man to the West Oakland Planning Committee. His willingness to work behind the scenes (rather than to insist on public recognition of his leadership role) won the confidence of indigenous leaders, although, in West Oakland's turbulent political environment, that confidence has to be continually rewon.

The administrative guidelines for the Model Cities program did not prescribe a citizen participation structure. The regional Model Cities administrators repeatedly reiterated that, within broad limits, they would accept whatever agreement was reached between Oakland public officials and West Oakland residents, but would not intervene to dictate a settlement in the event of a stalemate. However, they did play a facilitative role. For example, when city officials and West Oakland residents reached an impasse in their negotiations, they arranged a meeting on neutral territory in a federal post office building. They also rendered opinions on the acceptability to HUD of certain initiatives. By getting federal officials to legitimate their counterproposals, the executive committee used this noninterventionist posture to bolster their position.[16]

16. Informed observers consistently applaud Melvin B. Mogulof's refusal to step in and dictate the shape of the citizen participation structure in Oakland. (Mogulof was federal regional Model Cities administrator during the time of these negotiations.) In this

Winning Recognition from City Officials

West Oakland leaders insisted upon public acknowledgment of their peer status with city officials. To them, the rhetoric of "partnership" which surrounded the Model Cities program (marriage, divorce, and more ribald analogies abounded) meant that they were to be treated with dignity and respect and not as supplicants. They reasoned that they did not have to feel grateful for a program whose real objective was to buy racial peace, especially since the money came to Oakland because of deprivations they were suffering. They used visits of public officials to West Oakland as occasions for securing recognition of the various facets of their equality. They sought recognition of the legitimacy of their initial bargaining position, of their leaders, and, finally, of the West Oakland Planning Committee itself as the policy-making body for West Oakland.

The first such visit occurred on December 9, 1967, before the negotiations had actually begun. A tour group of federal officials and invited local guests crowded into the room where West Oakland leaders were conducting a large planning meeting. Business was interrupted briefly for an exchange of remarks between Walter Farr, federal Model Cities administrator, and Ralph Williams, planning committee chairman. Farr lent support to the planning committee's initial bargaining position by referring to Model Cities as a "partnership" between the city and the community to which both parties had to agree, and a friendly reporter from the *Oakland Tribune* recorded his remarks in a three-column banner and story.

A second visit took place the following month (January 4, 1968). This time the visitors were an assistant to the city manager and a city department head, and the planning committee meeting was held in a church basement in the heart of West Oakland. The WOPC officers purposely did not acknowledge the visitors' presence in the front row until the end of the meeting. In the interim the visitors sat through a long drawn-out roll call of member organizations, solicitation of new members, an emotion-charged review of the action of the executive committee in removing a member who could not reconcile himself to group rather than individual representation, and a detailed recounting of West Oakland planning committee history to date. What they witnessed supported West Oakland leaders' allegation that they were the duly selected spokesmen of a properly constituted and representative body to which they were accountable.

At the time of the third visit, the planning committee executives were insisting upon a "dual green light" approach to Model Cities planning under which both the West Oakland Planning Committee and the city council would

---

paper I focus upon observable events on the local level. Mogulof and John A. Williams, former OEO regional administrator, both have pointed out to me after reading an earlier draft of this paper that conflicts paralleling those described in this paper were simultaneously occurring among the federal administrators responsible for the program.

have to agree before a policy became binding. They wanted symbolic recognition that the entire planning committee—the delegate assembly as a whole—was West Oakland's policy-making body; thus, the executive committee had been calling for public negotiating sessions to be held in West Oakland in the presence of the delegate assembly. The city manager, speaking for the task force, refused an invitation to the February 7 meeting of the West Oakland Planning Committee on the ground that it had been issued on too short notice. The West Oakland residents who attended the meeting expected to see a public negotiating session, and instead heard supportive statements from miscellaneous public officials and black leaders there to help executive committee members save face with their followers. Near the end of the meeting, leaders of rival factions (the Western-End Model Cities Organization and the Oak Center Redevelopment Council) asked questions challenging the legitimacy of the executive committee and the delegate assembly. Their questions did little more than cause a stir in the audience, but their actions illustrated that the ability of the leadership to maintain its position depended on its effectiveness in dealing with the city.

By virtue of the fourth visit, on February 21, the executive committee won the recognition they sought from the city: the entire task force, including the city manager and the mayor, presented themselves for public negotiations before more than three hundred spectators at a meeting of the West Oakland Planning Committee in West Oakland. Executive committee members were jubilant. Their success in doing what had never been done before eliminated the possibility of serious challenge to their leadership from other factions within the community, at least for the period of the negotiations.

SUBORDINATION OF THE TECHNOCRATS

Examination of the issues raised during the actual negotiations can procede somewhat chronologically. In a letter to City Manager Keithley in December of 1967, Ralph Williams described the West Oakland Planning Committee's initial proposal for a Model Cities planning structure. He proposed that planning begin in open-ended study committees, receiving inputs from a miscellany of public officials and private citizens; that the WOPC Executive Committee (analogous to the city manager) supervise the staff, receive the products of the study committee, and prepare them for WOPC review; and that the West Oakland Planning Committee (analogous to a city council for the West Oakland community) be given the responsibility of approving the plans prior to direct submission to the city council for final approval. The city manager sent his formal response to the WOPC on January 15, 1968. He ignored the WOPC's effort to deal directly with the city council (an attempt to circumvent normal administrative procedure) and proposed instead a merger of his task force with the WOPC Executive Committee, to be designated the steering committee. He proposed (a) that the steering committee direct the Model Cities planning staff, receive proposals from the study committees, and prepare Model Cities plans for review first by the city manager and then by the city council; (b) that West Oakland residents be assured of majority control on the steering committee; (c) that the WOPC select West Oakland members on the steering and study committees. He further proposed that (d) the city manager select the project director from a list of three names submitted by a five-man screening committee acceptable to both sides; (e) that the project director act under his supervision; and (f) that the city council have final review authority, including the right to veto actions adopted by the steering committee.

Members of the executive committee were initially gratified by the concession of fifty-one percent control of the steering committee and pleased with the prominent role they would play. But further reflection led to divisions within the executive committee based on different aspirations for the future role of the West Oakland Planning Committee—whether it would be as the governor of an agency or the governor of a community, that is, whether the WOPC would confine its activities to selecting representatives to the steering and study committees in the manner outlined in the city manager's response or whether the WOPC as a body would retain ultimate authority for the West Oakland community over decisions in the Model Cities planning process, in the manner described in the West Oakland Planning Committee's original proposal.

Moore and Cobb[17] had been united in preparing the West Oakland Planning Committee's initial proposal; both had urged the WOPC to seek veto power over Model Cities planning, subject to the final authority of the city council. However, they now differed over the appropriate rebuttal to the city manager's response. Both sought community control, but they disagreed over timing and over locus of control. Surprised that city officials had conceded as much as they had, Moore was willing to settle for the city manager's response

17. After reading an earlier draft, Ralph Williams, chairman of the West Oakland Planning Committee, objected to the amount of space given to the statements of Moore and Cobb. Pointing out that Moore and Cobb, as employees of the Oakland Economic Development Council and the Neighborhood Services Project, respectively, were unable to take independent aciton, he recommended that, in every place where Cobb's name appears in this section, the words "executive committee" should be inserted and where Moore's name appears, the words "Oakland Economic Development Council." I have given his recommendation serious consideration and have decided that describing the positions articulated by Moore and Cobb in public meeting does not conflict with attributing responsibility to the West Oakland Planning Committee and its executive committee for making the ultimate determination on these important policy matters. I did not attend executive committee meetings and so cannot report the contribution of individual members to the final product. Thus, I can only treat Moore and Cobb as spokesmen for positions which divided the whole community.

with some modifications; Cobb disliked key features of that response and hoped that prolonging the negotiations might win larger concessions. In responding to the city manager's proposal, Moore's primary concern was *efficiency*, whereas Cobb's was *responsiveness*. Relying upon the administrative strategy of controlling the alternatives, Moore sought control over the Model Cities planning agency in order to control the actual *plans* submitted to the city council for final consideration. Favoring a more political approach, Cobb sought not only to control the alternatives, but also to create a political organization in West Oakland that would be strong enough to influence the *choices* the city council would make.

Ironically, this issue—the one which most severely divided the West Oakland Planning Committee—had little salience for the city's negotiators. Having made the decision to give community residents a veto at some stage in the planning process, they cared little whether that veto was exercised by WOPC's representatives on the steering committee or by the West Oakland Planning Committee as a whole, so long as the city council retained ultimate review authority. The conflict over the WOPC's future role occurred in the context of a struggle between the executive committee and the task force over how much authority the city manager would be able to exercise over Model Cities planning; however, West Oakland's negotiators could make little progress on that issue until the role of the West Oakland Planning Committee was decided.

Moore applauded the opportunity that the city manager's proposal gave WOPC Executive Committee members to interact as peers with agency administrators on the steering committee. He contended that, at the local level, administrators are more powerful than elected officials, and he regarded the steering committee as the proper focal point for West Oakland initiatives. He, too, believed that the planning committee as a whole should confine its activities to selecting leaders rather than to reviewing substantive policy; it should permit its leaders discretion in representing West Oakland's interests on the steering committee, subject to review in periodic elections. Since Moore opposed a more active role for the WOPC, he also opposed allocating funds to the organization for an independent staff. He felt that through majority control of the steering committee, West Oakland representatives would have adequate control over the Model Cities planning staff and that an independent staff for the WOPC would raise the possibility of a confrontation on every issue and gravely interfere with the efficiency of the planning process. In short, Moore assumed that the normal processes of local government were less in need of change than the decision makers, and with the assignment of a dominant role to West Oakland representatives, the planning process would be responsive to the needs of the West Oakland community.

Cobb felt that majority control of the steering committee was necessary but not sufficient in itself to increase the city's responsiveness to West Oakland's needs. He conceded that administrators might be more powerful than politicians in local government, but insisted that this need not be so. To him, a model partnership required recognition of the West Oakland Planning Committee as the peer of the city council, not merely recognition of the planning committee's representatives as peers of administrative officers. Parity between the city council and WOPC demanded that both groups review the work of the steering committee. Thus, he expanded the role of the West Oakland Planning Committee from that of an electorate to that of an active policy maker and required that the planning committee hold executive committee members accountable not only at election time for their overall performance but on a continuing basis for substantive issues. Cobb felt that administrative efficiency in planning was desirable, but that it was more important to alleviate residents' fears of the Model Cities program and spread support for change beyond a small circle of leaders and planners—goals which he hoped giving the WOPC an independent role would achieve. Cobb advocated a separate staff for the West Oakland Planning Committee. An independent staff would reduce the autonomy of the steering committee and the Model Cities planning staff; it would be an additional resource available to the executive committee, thus increasing their independence in interaction with other steering committee members and with the Model Cities staff and public officials. All West Oakland leaders have the ultimate objective of erasing inequality between the West Oakland community and other Oakland communities, and many of them share two interim goals: securing authority over federal funds in order to allocate resources in line with West Oakland priorities, and building a political base in order to gain access to larger amounts of resources. Moore advocated an administrative route to these ends, Cobb, a political route.[18] Cobb argued that the time was right not only to change decision makers, but also to alter the institutions which had consistently put West Oakland residents at a disadvantage.

Victory of the "Dual Green Light" Definition of the Model Cities "Partnership"

The relative merits of the positions defended by Percy Moore and Paul Cobb were not readily apparent to members of the executive committee and the WOPC, premised as they were on relatively subtle political and empirical

18. I do not mean to imply in making this distinction that administrators do not engage in politics. The distinction I draw is between setting priorities within an agency and setting priorities between agencies. I treat the first task as administrative, the second, political.

judgments. The conflict between these proposals took place in an atmosphere of great uncertainty over the prospects for mobilizing community support behind the WOPC leadership, the ability of indigenous working-class leaders to negotiate successfully with the city's spokesmen, and the options available under the provisions of the Model Cities legislation. Not surprisingly, during this period, the WOPC membership suffered bitter internal clashes and mounting anxiety. Disputes revolved, nevertheless, around the underlying problems of the proper relationship between professional and political decision makers and whether the WOPC would control an agency or govern a community.

With the assistance of Percy Moore, the WOPC Executive Committee prepared a counterproposal limiting the city manager's veto power and right to prevent the project director from carrying out steering committee instructions, but accepting the major part of the city manager's proposal. This counterproposal was passed out at the January 27 meeting of the West Oakland Planning Committee, but was never discussed. In subsequent actions, the WOPC progressively modified its counterproposal in the direction of incorporating additional features of its original proposal. Gradually the WOPC moved from virtual endorsement of Percy Moore's position to adoption of that championed by Paul Cobb. This movement occurred as the WOPC resolved particular aspects of the relationship between experts and community laymen.

As the conflict between Moore and Cobb emerged, so did a feeling of anxiety about the ability of executive committee members to hold their own in negotiations with professional administrators on the projected steering committee. In order to augment their bargaining skills, West Oakland leaders invited the Oakland Economic Development Council to participate as a "partner" of the West Oakland Planning Committee in negotiations with the city (January 24, 1968). When the OEDC accepted this invitation, they gained the assistance of more experienced negotiators and re-established ties between indigenous community leaders and black professionals. Subsequent revisions of the organizational chart for Model Cities planning included one representative from the OEDC on the steering committee. Significantly, WOPC leaders invited the OEDC representative to participate as their peer, not as an intermediary between them and city officials, the relationship which had precipitated the initial alienation of the WOPC from the OEDC.

However, addition of one OEDC representative to the negotiating team was not sufficient to quell mounting anxieties about the competence of WOPC representatives to negotiate with city officials. In the February 1, 1968, meeting of the WOPC, Donald McCullum, chairman of the Oakland Branch of the NAACP and vice-chairman of the OEDC, strongly urged that lay members of boards and commissions rather than professional

administrators represent agencies on the steering committee.[19] A vote in the
February 5 meeting endorsed this policy; another placed the WOPC on record
as supporting an independent staff to provide technical assistance to the
WOPC. It was but a short step from this proposal to that outlined by Paul
Cobb on February 7: that there be a "dual green light"—both must say "go."
By requiring that products of the steering committee be submitted to both
the West Oakland Planning Committee and the city council, the supremacy of
political decision makers over administrators would be maintained. This
arrangement relieved the fears of executive committee members that they
would be taken advantage of by the more knowledgeable agency heads on the
steering committee. Under Cobb's proposal, they would have a second chance
and their own technical assistance to correct any oversights in their effort to
protect and advance the interests of West Oakland.

In endorsing this structure, the West Oakland Planning Committee resolved
an important aspect of the debate over the relationship between experts and
citizen policy makers. Community residents trusted their own ability to
engage in politics, where conflicts are resolved through negotiated agreement,
more than their ability to compete with knowledgeable administrators on
technical matters. Resolution of the conflict within the West Oakland
community coincided with recognition of the West Oakland Planning
Committee as the legitimate spokesman for the West Oakland community by
city officials—at the fourth visit described earlier. In the public negotiating
session before the assembled West Oakland Planning Committee, the city
manager agreed with no demurrer that both the West Oakland Planning
Committee and the city council would have a veto over Model Cities plans.
Having resolved its internal split over role and won its point with the city, the
West Oakland Planning Committee was at last ready to negotiate its
differences about the city manager's authority.

The Role of the City Manager: Definition of Administration

A persistent theme in the negotiations between the WOPC and the city
concerned the role of the city manager. Recalling bitter experiences under the

19. This debate had another dimension. If professional representatives were seated,
Moore or his representative would become a member of the steering committee; if lay
representatives, McCullum would, or another of the OEDC members whom Moore
characterized as black brokers. Moore supported seating administrators because he feared
that "traditional 'brokers' would be designated and would gladly assume the role of
'leader' and generate internal conflicts within WOPC to maintain status and value to City
Hall." (Memo to the author, October 31, 1969.) Some West Oakland leaders may have
been influenced in deciding this issue by their resentment toward Moore who insisted
upon reserving a high degree of autonomy for himself as OEDC executive director. Even
if made on this basis, however, their decision turned, nevertheless, upon the issue of the
proper relationship between laymen and administrators.

poverty program when the city manager refused for months to attend an OEDC meeting in spite of repeated invitations from that body and failed to respond to community demands that they be involved in Model Cities planning "from the day one," West Oakland leaders were determined to reduce the city manager's role in Model Cities planning to the minimum necessary under the law. Three specific aspects of this issue caused Model Cities negotiators to miss two "deadlines" set by federal officials for submission of a revised application. The first concerned the manner in which the project director (an assistant city manager) would be selected; the second, the manner in which his work would be supervised; and the third, the right of the city manager to interpose himself as an independent review authority between the WOPC and the city council.

After several unsuccessful attempts to negotiate the three points of difference extending over two and one-half months, the city manager announced that he was unable to reach agreement with the WOPC and turned the matter over to the city council. The WOPC had requested meetings with the city council from the beginning and were pleased when they came to pass. In their first meeting on April 2, the two groups of political representatives rapidly disposed of *administrative* matters. The composition of the screening committee for selecting the project director, which up to that point had variously combined city and community representatives on a five-member committee, was set at three representatives from the city and three from the community, with one member of the city's three being determined in advance by the WOPC (John Williams, black executive director of the Redevelopment Agency); five votes were required for action, and final selection was to be made by the city manager from a list of three names submitted in order of preference. The project director was to be held responsible by the city manager for the day-to-day administration of planning and by the steering committee for "policy." Products of the steering committee were to be submitted to the WOPC for review and then to the city manager who was specifically enjoined from altering policy matters. Thus, the role of the city manager was limited, but not eliminated; however, the distrust expressed throughout the negotiations undoubtedly alerted city officials that community residents had a much narrower definition of "administration" than did the city manager, and that assumption of more than "technical" responsibilities would provoke outcries in the future.

The city council and the WOPC took longer to dispose of *political* matters, the subject of the next section.

THE STRUGGLE FOR AUTHORITY

The WOPC sought authority over the Model Cities program in order to be able to control the coercive side effects of "progressive" policies. Having won

the right to exercise authority in concert with the city council, the WOPC
turned to the next problem: authority over what?" Two subjects occupied
negotiators during the next four and one-half months: defining WOPC's veto
powers and drawing the boundaries of the Model Cities area. Little doubt
remained that, to the extent they were able, the WOPC leaders intended to
establish the WOPC as the governing body over a given territory rather than
merely to "insert the views" of the West Oakland community in the planning
process.

Broad Veto

Immediately after securing recognition for the WOPC as the legitimate
spokesman for the West Oakland community, WOPC leaders initiated the
next phase of the negotiations: clarifying the extent of their "veto." In a
press release issued February 29, WOPC leaders remarked: "They say that the
City Council and the West Oakland Committee shall have mutual veto power
but we do not know at what points this can be exercised if indeed it must." A
negotiating session with the city manager's task force on March 15 clarified
the matter somewhat; the WOPC was granted a veto over "block grant"
proposals initiated by the City. The WOPC also had the right to initiate
proposals for the use of these funds. Thus the WOPC secured access to
decision making on the expenditure of approximately five million dollars, the
amount it was estimated that Model Cities would bring to Oakland annually.
But the original intention of the Model Cities program was to "coordinate"
the use of federal funds within a particular area. In fact the size of the "block
grant" varied with the size of present federal commitments to projects in the
Model Cities area: the city would receive up to eighty percent of the local
contribution to these projects. Additional federal programs were anticipated
as a result of the effort to concentrate social and physical programming in a
specified area. Allocating this small amount of money was less important to
WOPC leaders than overseeing the expenditure of all federal funds within the
West Oakland community. They feared that local agencies, when thwarted by
Model Cities planning decisions, would use non-Model Cities funds to pursue
their objectives anyway. Having been recognized as the governing body for
West Oakland in respect to planning for the future of West Oakland, the
WOPC leaders sought authority to assure that those plans would be respected.

The WOPC followed two courses in seeking to broaden their veto powers:
(a) negotiations with federal officials to secure veto power directly and to win
recognition of the validity of an agreement between a local agency and the
WOPC granting such authority; and (b) negotiations with local agencies to
secure the right to review federally financed programs slated for the West
Oakland area. On March 27 Ralph Williams sent a letter to Mel Mogulof
regional Model Cities administrator, asking that a meeting of federal officials

be convened in West Oakland on April 10 to clarify the extent of West Oakland's veto. In the interim the WOPC Executive Committee met with the city council on April 2 and resolved the administrative matters which had divided the city and the community for so long. But the mayor and the city council reacted testily to West Oakland's desire for a "broad veto." The matter was postponed pending the outcome of the April 10 meeting.

At the April 10 meeting, federal officials representing the Departments of Health, Education, and Welfare, Labor, Housing and Urban Development, and the Community Relations Service, Economic Development Administration, and the Office of Economic Opportunity, were asked:

> Is your agency willing to grant a veto by the WOPC over all of its funding for West Oakland, whether or not it is part of the Model Cities program?; or,
>
> Is your agency willing to respect agreement between WOPC and your local counterpart agencies (such as the Public Housing Authority, the School District, etc.) granting veto authority to WOPC over the use of all federal funds for West Oakland through that agency?[20]

Significantly, the questions posed by WOPC leaders had not been dealt with in the federal guidelines. In their replies, federal officials indicated that they were more willing to respect local grants of authority than to grant such authority directly.[21] Although their replies were ambiguous, and relied in two instances on confusing the West Oakland Planning Committee and the West Oakland Advisory Committee, the poverty board in the West Oakland

20. Memorandum from Mike Kenney, Model Cities specialist, to Carl Shaw, CAP regional administrator, "Report of Meeting of 10 April with the West Oakland Planning Committee" (April 16, 1968).

21. Ibid. Of further interest in the same memorandum is the following:

"Examples of the kinds of issues WOPC raises concerning the use of Federal funds are:

a. Major public works projects such as the Bay Area Rapid Transit System station, the Oakland Stadium, highways, etc., which require demolition of residential sections and the destruction of the neighborhood and community.

b. According to the WOPC, EDA has put $23,000,000 into the Port of Oakland, and the Oakland Airport, yet this money has created no jobs for the people of West Oakland. Part of this development will mean a public recreation pier with concessions, restaurants, and small shops. WOPC points out that the EDA regulations requiring a substantial percent of local bank capital before EDA help is available to small businessmen assures that there will be no black owners of ventures in this complex since local banks will not lend to black people.

c. Difficulties of getting insurance and bank loans for homes and businesses in the ghetto.

d. Police brutality. WOPC wants to be able to stop Federal money from going to the Oakland Police Department because of a bitter and profound distrust of the Oakland Police Department for alleged police brutality."

community, the WOPC succeeded in having its questions taken seriously, and, consequently, established the legitimacy of future efforts to secure review authority over federal programs in the West Oakland area.

In a tumultuous meeting of the city council and the WOPC leaders on April 15, the deadline for concluding one phase of the negotiations, the issue of the "broad veto" was again discussed. The mayor and the city council maintained that they did not have the authority to grant West Oakland a veto over programs administered by other jurisdictions. WOPC leaders denied that they expected city officials to grant veto powers over nonmunicipal activities. In the end, they concluded their agreement with the city and announced their intention to negotiate with the other public agencies individually.

Boundaries

West Oakland is bounded on the south by the downtown business district and on the west by the Port of Oakland. City officials and their supporters assign important roles to both of these locations in formulating their strategies for the future economic development of Oakland. Both areas are projected to receive large amounts of federal funds. West Oakland leaders, working out their own strategy of economic development, perceived the value of reviewing how these funds would be spent. On April 23, the West Oakland Planning Committee received a copy of the city's proposed revisions of the Model Cities area and discovered that this draft, unlike previous ones, excluded both the site of a future downtown center redevelopment project and the Port. City officials had learned that inclusion of the downtown project in the Model Cities area would not increase the amount of federal funds for which the project would be eligible, and, thus, had no incentive to submit even employment plans (as West Oakland leaders subsequently requested) to WOPC review. The Port may previously have been included in the Model Cities area because West Oakland fronts on the Port and Model Cities boundaries had been drawn down to the water. However, these boundaries took on a new significance after the West Oakland Planning Committee won veto power.

With the issue still unresolved, events following the assassination of Dr. Martin Luther King had consequences for the Model Cities negotiations. As the militance of Oakland's black community increased in the aftermath of the assassination, so did the adamance of city officials against including the Port and the downtown project in the Model Cities area. On April 6, a shoot-out between some Black Panthers and the Oakland police took place, raising the salience of police brutality issues. In response to King's death, a group of black leaders, composed primarily of black professionals and civil rights activists, formed the Black Strike for Justice Committee and organized a boycott of a market serving the black community. They demanded that the

Downtown Retail Merchants Association petition the city council in support of their proposals to change the nature of police-community relations in Oakland.

Black strike activities angered the mayor (and the editor of the *Oakland Tribune*) and temporarily divided the West Oakland leaders who became less tenacious in pursuing their boundary demands in negotiations with the city. After May 1, the date when the boycott began, WOPC leaders were unable to change the city's position. In August, after fruitless negotiations held at irregular intervals, the WOPC withdrew its request to include the downtown project; and they declared that they would deal directly with the commission on matters concerning the Port. With these acts, the major differences between the city and the West Oakland Planning Committee were resolved.[22] However, the disposition of the final papers took several more months. (It was rumored that the city officials hoped that a Republican administration would take office and radically revise the Model Cities guidelines affecting citizen participation.)

CONCLUSION

Legitimacy Based Upon Procedures Rather Than Performance

West Oakland residents felt oppressed by the results of city policies, but were prevented by the existing structural arrangements from changing them through normal political processes. Oakland's political institutions do meet standard democratic criteria for determining who should rule: each elected official, in fact, represents a majority of the total Oakland electorate. Unfortunately, each city official represents the *same* majority. The classic problem in democratic theory, that of the relationship between a majority and an intense minority, has substantive content in Oakland. When West Oakland residents designed the structure of their subgovernment, they incorporated the lessons that experience with the existing institutions had taught them. The structure they created included representatives of all groups and opinions rather than just the majority group and its opinions. They accepted the inevitability of conflict and created a structure which encouraged the resolution of conflict within the community rather than with the intervention of outside assistance. Self-consciously, they created incentives for leaders to be responsive to the wishes of their constituents and to take responsibility for their continuing political education. These leaders were placed in the position of having to reconcile interests of the whole community with the particular desires of portions of the community; in order

22. According to Maurice Dawson, Oakland Model Cities administrator, the Model Cities contract was signed April 23, 1969. (Telephone interview, March 2, 1970.)

to do so, they were encouraged to create identification with the interests of the whole community while reducing disproportions in the costs of particular policies borne by segments of the community. Thus, West Oakland residents revealed their aspirations and their program for achieving government more responsive to their needs as they defined them. What are the lessons of their experience for social scientists?

In recent years students of American government have focused on the question of "who rules?" and have tended to ignore the related question of "who benefits?" Support for particular institutional arrangements depends upon the institution's ability to produce acceptable outcomes, not only upon its conformance with procedural norms; this fact suggests that institutional arrangements should be evaluated by performance as well as by process criteria. A political scientist must, of course, pay attention to behavior within political structure, that is, to process criteria—to who has a right to be heard in the political process, and to who the winners and losers are in particular contests. But, as the Oakland experience indicates, willingness to enter a contest and the content of the demands are influenced by assessments of the likelihood of winning. The more valid criteria for evaluating structures may well be some measure of their distribution of outcomes. Political behavior has certain universal characteristics; the relationship between characteristics of political structures and a desirable distribution of outcomes, however, vary with the situation. Investigation of the latter forces the political scientist to visualize and assess alternatives, to visualize a desirable series of outcomes in order to assess the appropriateness of particular structures, an activity distinguishable from but accessory to political decision making. When he engages in this activity, the political scientist is involved in work significant for public policy.

Political Authority Delegated to Experts

When West Oakland residents sought authority to make decisions affecting their lives, they found that they had to compete for this right with experts who wanted to "help" or "serve" them. In the course of their struggle to define the role of the West Oakland Planning Committee, whether as a decision maker for an agency or a community, they acknowledged that the city manager and his administrators exercise a preponderance of power under a weak-mayor, council-manager form of government, but they risked the loss of the Model Cities program in order to deal directly with the city council. They underscored repeatedly their insistence that the city manager confine his role to the technical tasks compatible with a strict interpretation of the politics-administration dichotomy. For themselves they reserved the role of citizens rather than subjects. Within their subgovernment, too, they subordinated technical assistance to political controls. Their preference for responsiveness over administrative efficiency had roots in their experience with previous social reform programs and professionalized public service.

Expertise is one kind of authority. Increasingly, it threatens to displace political authority. The determination of priorities and the allocation of scarce resources are *political decisions*. Experts speak of coordination, or advocacy, or planning, or use a host of other terms in such a way that the intrinsic political nature of priorities-and-allocations decisions are obscured. So long as these vital decisions are based on "technical" criteria to which only trained experts have access, there can be no parity between the city's professional representatives and the community's amateur representatives. The West Oakland leaders struggled to redefine "administration." The scope of technical questions was narrowed and allocative decisions were reclaimed for politics. As they explored the substantive possibilities of their newly won authority, the West Oakland leaders could now formulate their redistributive aims.

Economic Growth at the Expense of Redistribution

In Oakland, both the city government and West Oakland residents regard control over outside funds as vital to their economic development strategies. As a consequence of the Model Cities negotiations, they will share authority over some federal funds. The struggle between the "magistracy" and the "people" has brought into opposition differing conceptions of the solutions to the city's problems—one which places the primary emphasis upon economic expansion, and one which emphasizes economic redistribution; one which expects economic benefits to percolate down to West Oakland residents, and one which demands that governmental actively seek to change the economic status of West Oakland residents.

The Oakland case-study reveals that the interests of the contestants are not far apart on all issues. In some instances, West Oakland residents castigate the failure of officials and their supporters to carry out their stated objectives, not the objectives themselves. For example, they are not opposed to increasing employment opportunities for West Oakland residents by attracting private enterprises to Oakland; they are opposed to the abandonment of the goal of increasing employment opportunities when it increases the difficulty of attracting private capital. Some objectives, of course, genuinely conflict and are less susceptible to integrative solutions. West Oakland residents explicitly reject the condition that change is permissible only insofar as the result is compatible with the status quo. They insist upon owning some of the new enterprises as well as working in them. West Oakland's veto power over matters in which outsiders have vital concern (e.g., construction and labor contracts, the location and uses of public facilities) means that in each case, the various parties must create mutually agreeable solutions or suffer an impasse.

In Oakland the contention of the sovereignty of the magistracy and the sovereignty of the people during the negotiations over the Model Cities program resulted in the creation of a structure which acknowledged both the secessionist mood of West Oakland residents and the interests of the city as a whole in the future of the West Oakland community, and which provided the framework within which mutual interests might be negotiated. This structure may not survive for long or function as its authors hoped. However, in the absence of such a structure, the fundamental differences between the West Oakland community and the city will undoubtedly find other forms of expression. The value of an institutionalized political form seems evident. Political institutions are our principal mechanisms for reconciling the whole and the part. It is only political institutions that have the particular responsibility of integrating a community and advancing the interests of the whole. It is only political institutions that can pursue policies which assure acceptable processes *and* outcomes, which assure expertise *and* responsiveness, which assure productivity *and* equality.

4. Policy and Public Administration: The Legal Services Program in the War on Poverty

RICHARD PIOUS

The New Frontier and the Great Society used the intergovernmental grant and contract systems to deal with domestic social problems. By the end of the two Democratic administrations the number of such programs had multiplied from thirty to over four hundred, while expenditures had risen to more than twenty billion dollars annually. The intergovernmental programs were sponsored by a coalition of social scientists, bureaucratic professionals, political executives, and congressional committee leaders. The result was the development of "vertical function hierarchies" which reduced conflict between participants at each level of the intergovernmental program, but prevented the coordination of programs at the local or national levels across organizational lines.[1] For political scientists, the expansion of the intergovernmental system meant that students of both metropolitcan and national politics found their research interests converging on the relationship that existed between professional groups at the local and national levels and the new grant programs.[2] Policy making in the grant system, often delegated to the "professional guilds," became a subject of new importance.[3]

What follows is an account of policy making in one intergovernmental contract system, the Legal Services Program established within the Office of

1. Cooperative federalism is described in the following works: Morton Grodzins, *The American System* (Chicago: Rand McNally, 1966); W. Brooke Graves, *American Intergovernmental Relations* (New York: Scribner, 1964); and Daniel Elazer, *The American Partnership* (Chicago: University of Chicago Press, 1962). The development of the "vertical functional hierarchies" is discussed in Advisory Commission on Intergovernmental Relations, *Tenth Annual Report* (Washington, D.C.; 1969), p. 8.

2. Cf. Morely Segal and A. Lee Fritschler, "Policymaking in the Intergovernmental System" (Paper presented at the Sixty-Sixth Annual Meeting of the American Political Science Association, September 8-12, 1970); also "Symposium on Research in Intergovernmental Relations," *Public Administration Review,* May/June 1970.

3. This problem is dealt with by James L. Sundquist, *Making Federalism Work* (Washington, D.C.: Brookings Institution, 1969); also Harold Seidman, *Politics, Position, Power* (New York: Oxford University Press, 1970), p. 138, and Edward W. Weidner, "Decision-Making in a Federal System," in ed., Arthur W. MacMahon, *Federalism* (New York: Doubleday, 1955).

Economic Opportunity in 1965.[4] It shows how interest groups at the national and local levels can influence both the administrative structure of the grant system and its policy outputs. First is a description of the organization of the Legal Services Program (LSP) in the Office of Economic Opportunity in order to demonstrate how policy making in a grant program can be delegated to a coalition of program officials and interest group leaders; second is an analysis of the relationship between the administrative structure developed for the national grant program and the performance of the local legal service projects; and, finally, the third section discusses alternatives to the present system. I agree with Mr. Dooley's observation:

> Don't I think a poor man has a chanst in court? Iv course he has. He
> has the same chanst there he has outside. He has a splendid poor
> man's chanst.

I.

THE POLITICAL SETTING OF THE LEGAL SERVICES PROGRAM

Efforts to organize a program to provide civil legal services for indigents began in the Office of Economic Opportunity in 1965. A number of demonstration projects had been funded between 1963 and 1965 by the Ford Foundation and the President's Committee on Juvenile Delinquency and Youth Crime as part of community action prototype programs in New York City, New Haven, Washington, D.C., and Boston. For a number of reasons neither funding source was prepared to underwrite a massive program, and so the sponsors of local projects turned their attention to the newly formed War on Poverty.[5]

During the summer of 1964, Edgar Cahn, a special assistant to OEO Director Sargent Shriver, and his wife Jean Cahn, an attorney formerly in the New Haven demonstration project, organized an Ad Hoc Group to plan a legal services program in OEO. This group, consisting of friends of the Cahns, had very definite ideas about the purposes of such a program. It would not continue the traditional emphasis of the Legal Aid movement on individual case service, but instead would develop a *strategy* in providing legal services for the poor.

---

4. I wish to thank Clinton Bamberger, Jr., Earl Johnson, Jr., and Burt Griffin, former directors of the Legal Services Program, and Edgar and Jean Cahn, former consultants to the Office of Economic Opportunity, for discussing with me operations of the program. I also thank Burt Griffin for permission to use materials from program files. The Library Staff of the American Bar Center is thanked for permission to examine materials compiled by the Washington office of the American Bar Association. Opinions expressed in this paper are solely those of the author.
5. The demonstration programs are discussed in *Conference Proceedings: The Extension of Legal Services to the Poor* (Washington, D.C., 1964). The prototype community action agencies in which local programs were placed are discussed in Peter Marris and Martin Rein, *Dilemmas of Social Reform* (London: Routledge & Paul, 1967).

The Cahns and other members of the group were concerned with changing the decision-making process in the War on Poverty. In an article published in *The Yale Law Journal* in July 1964, they set out the goals of neighborhood legal projects.[6] They argued that the War on Poverty was organized as a military operation in which central staff planning and coordination was emphasized. Summarizing their own firsthand experiences in the New Haven prototype program in 1962-1963, they pointed out that:

> The most disturbing defect of CPI, viewed as a military service operation, lies in its record of enervating existing leadership, failing to develop potential leadership, undercutting incipient protest, manipulating local organizations so that they become mere instruments of the comprehensive strategy. [7]

A central planning model would not permit local residents to challenge the priorities of local programs. Professionals, interested in building up their reputations and in furthering their careers, would look upon local demands as obstacles to their operations rather than as useful information. The poor would become frustrated and alienated, while the program concentrated on problems easiest to solve and clientele amenable to manipulation, thus ignoring the most important problems.[8]

In order to offset the limitations of the comprehensive central planning model, the Cahns proposed to develop a "civilian perspective" in the War on Poverty:

> This means that the ultimate power to govern must not only reside with the governed, but that such power must be susceptible of continuous and effective, rather than nominal and sporadic, exercise. It must include both the power to give and to withhold assent. The ultimate test, then, of whether the war on poverty has incorporated the "civilian perspective" is whether or not the citizenry have been given the effective power to criticize, to dissent, and where need be, to compel responsiveness. [9]

In order to compel responsiveness on the part of the Community Action Program (CAP) in the War on Poverty, the Cahns proposed the funding of legal services projects in local communities which would impose the "civilian perspective" of the local poverty community onto the operations of agencies dealing with the poor. Each project would serve as the advocate for groups in the poverty community. Its priorities would be set by these groups. Projects would be affiliated with universities in order to draw on legal and social

6. Edgar S. Cahn and Jean C. Cahn, "The War on Poverty: A Civilian Perspective," 73 *The Yale Law Journal*, July 1964.
7. Ibid., p. 1330.
8. Ibid., pp. 1330-1336.
9. Ibid., p. 1336.

science research which would aid them in negotiating or litigating with community action agencies and other bureaucracies.[10]

In September 1964, the Advisory Panel on Legal Services (the formal name for the group organized by the Cahns) recommended that the OEO fund a program of legal services as a component of the Community Action Program.[11] On October 21 Shriver approved this recommendation and established a Task Force on Legal Services, which expanded the original promotional group.[12] Jean Cahn was appointed as an OEO consultant to plan for a White House Conference in April and to work with CAP officials in making grants for the program. In November and December CAP approved grants to begin programs in Oakland and Detroit, and to fund the existing demonstration programs in New York City and Washington, D.C.[13]

The Task Force decided that the program should be a component of the Community Action Program at the national level, and that each local project should be part of a local community action agency (CAA). There were three reasons why the legal service projects would be part of the structure they were created to litigate against. First, CAP already had statutory authority to develop a variety of programs in the CAA structure, so that a separate authorization (which might take a year) would not be needed to fund the program. Second, CAP had funds which could be used immediately. Third, the Cahns favored control by local governing boards rather than by national administrators. The Task Force believed that the decentralized grant program would fund local boards composed of activist attorneys, law school professors, and representatives of the poor. They hoped that programs would be sponsored by organizations in the poverty community, law schools, civil rights organizations, and militant CAAs.[14]

Until the end of December the planning for the program took place without the participation of either the American Bar Association (ABA) or the National Legal Aid and Defender Association (NLADA). These two organizations had for forty years developed and supervised the privately funded Legal Aid movement. The ABA, through its Standing Committee on Legal Aid and Indigent Defendants, encouraged local and state bar associations to sponsor Legal Aid Socieities and Lawyer Referral Services, and prompted the state bar associations to form committees to oversee the operations of such groups to ensure that professional standards were maintained and adequate funds supplied.[15] The NLADA, an affiliate of the

10. Interview with Edgar Cahn, 17 January 1968.
11. Memo from Jean Cahn to Sargent Shriver, 29 January 1965.
12. Ibid.
13. Ibid.
14. Interview with Edgar Cahn, 17 January 1968.
15. 42 *A.B.A. Reports* 437.   46 *A.B.A. Reports* 493, 48 *A.B.A. Reports* 374; also R.H. Smith, "Interest of the American Bar Association in Legal Aid Work," *The Annals* (Philadelphia, 1939).

ABA, provided technical assistance for local societies, published statistics of service provided, and conducted promotional campaigns to increase the number of societies. It also promoted improvements in the administration of justice, and conducted research on the shortcomings of the Legal Aid movement in order to improve operations of local societies.[16] Both groups insisted that the governing boards of the societies consist entirely or primarily of lawyers. Little civil rights or civil liberties litigation was encouraged, and the societies emphasized service in individual cases rather than test cases, appellate advocacy, or law reform.

Leaders of the ABA and NLADA watched the planning in OEO with concern. In November a Conference on the Extension of Legal Services to the Poor was held under the auspices of the Department of Health, Education, and Welfare, and both Attorney General Katzenbach and Commissioner of Welfare Ellen Winston agreed that a program of legal services to indigents should be organized by the OEO.[17] By December, when the OEO began making grants, bar leaders decided to intervene. On December 28, in response to a request from the Washington office of the ABA, the Cahns met with two ABA lobbyists, Don Channel and Lowell Beck, and with two members of the ABA Standing Committee on Legal Aid and Indigent Defendants, John Cummiskey and William McCalpin.[18] The bar leaders impressed a number of points upon the Cahns at that meeting. First, they told the Cahns that the HEW conference proceedings, which severely criticized the work of the societies, had antagonized NLADA and local bar leaders. The rhetoric of social change, confrontation politics, and community advocacy also worried bar leaders. They saw possible violations of the ABA *Canons of Ethics:* the use of community workers might mean practice of law by laymen; community representation might violate the ban against "stirring up litigation"; educational programs might violate the ban against advertising or soliciting.[19] They claimed that the proposed program would duplicate the efforts of the societies, and urged that the societies be given OEO funds to upgrade and expand their work. Then the bar leaders warned that, unless the ABA and NLADA were included in the planning for the program, the ABA House of Delegates would condemn it at the ABA Midwinter Meeting in New

16. Useful narratives of the history of the Legal Aid movement are, Reginald Heber Smith, *Justice and the Poor*, 3rd ed. (New York: Scribner, 1924) and Emery Brownell, *Legal Aid in the United States* (Rochester: Lawyers Co-Operative Publishing Co., 1951) and *Supplement* (Rochester: Lawyers Co-Operative Publishing Co., 1961). A summary of the research findings of bar groups is contained in Lee Silverstein, *Availability of Legal Services for the Poor* (Chicago: NLADA, 1968).

17. "Preface," *Conference on the Extension of Legal Services to the Poor* (Washington, D.C., 1964), pp. *vii-x.*

18. Memo from Jean Cahn to Sargent Shriver, 29 January 1965.

19. Ibid.

Orleans in February.[20]

The Cahns knew that the program could not be formed if the ABA and NLADA opposed it. Shriver was insistent that bar groups support it or remain neutral at the ver least. They had never intended to exclude the bar groups from the program, but had hoped to delay consultation with them until the spring so that their position could be strong. After the bar leaders' threat, however, the top priority for the Task Force was an accommodation with the bar groups.[21]

An agreement was reached between the OEO and bar leaders after the Cahns met with them on January 12 at the American Bar Center in Chicago. A joint OEO-ABA-NLADA Planning Committee for the proposed White House Conference was named, to be chaired jointly by Shriver and ABA President Lewis Powell. The bar leaders would also be named to an Advisory Committee to the program after the conference. In return, bar leaders agreed to support a resolution at the February meeting of the ABA House of Delegates which would support the program. They also agreed to reexamine the *Canons of Ethics* and to sponsor a session on "poverty law" at the summer meeting of the ABA. Finally, they agreed to help the OEO work with local bar groups and societies in the submission of grant applications.[22]

The agreement was soon implemented. On 8 February 1965, the ABA House of Delegates, after discreet prodding by bar leaders, duly passed the resolution supporting the program. One week later the Steering Committee (as the joint group was called) met for the first time to plan for the national conference. At that meeting full consultation with bar leaders was promised before any grants would be approved, and bar leaders were promised consultation in the preparation of policy guidelines for the program.[23] The spirit of the meeting is captured in the following exchange between Shriver and ABA leader Orison Marden:

> Orison Marden: I think we have in this country at this moment a very fine structure in some places, a very fine structure in many of our cities upon which we can build to put forward the program that you are heading up.
>
> Sargent Shriver: I think that our own experience, limited though it is, would substantiate what you are saying, namely that we do want to program existing institutions.[24]

The Task Force was not dissatisfied with the results of the first meeting. It appeared that the program would receive more than it would have to give

20. Ibid.

21. Ibid. Also interview with Jean Cahn, 18 January 1965.

22. Ibid.

23. *Proceedings, ABA-OEO Meeting: Legal Aid for the Poor* (Legal Services Program files), p. 105.

24. Ibid., p. 22.

away. The bar groups had endorsed it in exchange for access. They seemed cooperative: they did not ask for a local bar veto over grant applications, nor did they insist that only societies be given OEO funds. Task Force members felt that bar leaders were learning about the program and would soon come to support it. In this assumption they were quite mistaken.[25]

National bar leaders discussed the new program with Shriver and with CAP officials between January and March. The result of these discussions was a decision made by Richard Boone and Jack Conway of CAP in February to remove Jean Cahn as a consultant to the program and limit the influence of the Task Force in the program.[26] Jean Cahn was not informed of this decision until the middle of March, when Shriver refused to name her as director of the program.[27] At the end of March Bruce Terris of the OEO General Counsel's Office and Michael Rauh of the CAP program were placed in charge of the planning for the national conference and the preparation of the guidelines.[28]

Bar leaders and CAP officials had a number of reasons for joining together to remove the Task Force from control of the program. First, the Cahns did not favorably impress bar leaders with their talk of a "civilian perspective" and their ties to the academics who had downgraded the Legal Aid movement at the HEW Conference. Jean Cahn angered the NLADA leaders by refusing to approve a request they submitted for funds to engage in research on the legal needs of the poor. Bar leaders assumed that, if the Cahns directed the program, the societies would not receive fair treatment in the competition for funds. CAP officials and bar leaders agreed that, because the Cahns were an interracial couple (she was black, and he easily appeared to fit a stereotype of the "Jewish intellectual"), they could not effectively promote the new program at the local level, especially in the South.[29]

Terris and Rauh, the officials who replaced the Cahns, worked with bar leaders successfully to plan a national conference sponsored jointly by the OEO and the Department of Justice (after the White House declined to participate). But when they prepared a set of guidelines for the program, the bar leaders returned them with extensive recommendations for changes. Grants for local projects were held up pending a resolution of the controversy over the guidelines.[30]

25. Memo from Richard Boone to Jack Conway, "CAP and Law and Poverty," 25 January 1965.

26. Ibid.

27. Jean Cahn to Richard Boone, 15 February 1965; Richard Boone to Sargent Shriver, 15 February 1965; Stephen Pollak to Sargent Shriver, 15 March 1965; Michael Rauh to Sargent Shriver, 19 March 1965.

28. Stephen Pollak to Sargent Shriver, 15 March 1965; Michael Rauh to Sargent Shriver, 19 March 1965.

29. Richard Boone to Jack Conway, op. cit.

30. Bruce Terris, "Guidelines for Legal Services Proposals to the OEO" (LSP files,

The draft prepared by Rauh and Terris was unacceptable to the bar leaders because it envisioned that local projects would be component activities of the Community Action Agencies, directed by these agencies. Moreover, the applications for funds would be processed at the regional and national levels by CAP officials, who would propose modifications of the grant applications to add activities. Especially upsetting to bar leaders was the failure to restrict eligibility, and the provision for community participation in administering the projects. Bar leaders viewed this approach to local project organization just as unacceptable as the one proposed by the Cahns: if the "civilian perspective" and an activist governing board was unacceptable, so too was the imposition of the "lay" governing board of the local CAA over project professionals.

Bar leaders wanted to prevent CAP control of the program at the national level and CAA domination of projects at the local level. They were determined to gain two objectives: first, control of the administration of the national program to preserve its independence from CAP; and, second, a massive infusion of OEO funds channeled through the independent LSP to benefit the Legal Aid Societies and new projects sponsored by local and state bar associations free of the influence of CAAs.[31]

Shortly after the National Conference on Law and Poverty, held in June, bar leaders moved to eliminate CAP administration of the program. They held discussions with Shriver which resulted in his promise to ABA President Powell that:

> I am in full agreement that the Legal Services Program requires the leadership of a person who has the respect of the bar.[32]

He agreed that bar leaders could nominate a director for the program. CAP and the General Counsel's Office were not informed of this decision; just as they had teamed up with bar leaders to remove the Task Force, now they were being displaced from the program without warning.[33]

Bar leaders conducted the search for a program director during the summer of 1965. Professor Kenneth Pye of the Georgetown Law Center, a choice of some bar leaders, ruled himself out, but suggested Clinton Bamberger, Jr., an attorney in the Baltimore law firm of Piper and Marbury. Bamberger was active in a number of organized bar activities at the local and state level, and belonged to civic, cultural, and Catholic lay organizations. He was interviewed for the position by a number of bar leaders, and as Shriver stated later:

> He came to us with the *explicit* endorsement of the American Bar

13 April 1965); Bruce Terris to Lewis Powell, 8 April 1965; Lewis Powell to Bruce Terris, 16 April 1965; Junius Allison to Bruce Terris, 30 April, 1965; Theodore Voorhees to Bruce Terris, 14 June 1965; Bruce Terris to Theodore Voorhees, 18 June 1965.

31. Interview with Clinton Bamberger, Jr., 17 January 1968.
32. Sargent Shriver to Lewis Powell, 1 July 1965.
33. Bamberger interview, op. cit.

Association, and the National Legal Aid and Defender Association, and the personal recommendation of such distinguished figures as Lewis Powell, Theodore Voorhees, and Edward Kuhn. [34]

Once Bamberger had been nominated by bar leaders, he engaged in negotiations with Shriver in September before accepting the position. These negotiations were based on the goals of the bar leaders: removal of CAP influence from the program and assurance of funds for the Legal Aid Societies and bar-sponsored projects. Bamberger won independence from CAP: he was named a "program director" with his own budget and staff, and was to have direct access to Shriver. CAP would not make grants or supervise the grants made by the LSP staff. The LSP would develop its own guidelines in cooperation with the newly organized National Advisory Committee.[35] Although the local projects would be part of the CAAs, they would have separate governing boards which would determine program activities subject only to national guidelines. In short, Shriver agreed to professional control of the program by groups sponsored by the ABA and NLADA both at the local and national levels. He delegated the operation of the program to a "professional guild" which operated a "vertical functional hierarchy."[36] There would be no coordination at the national or local levels by the CAP program or the CAAs.

The *Guidelines* which were finally issued for the LSP after approval by bar leaders specifically endorsed law reform and appellate advocacy techniques, and community education programs. Dropped was any mention of representation of local groups, litigation against the local CAAs or other bureaucracies, or the "civilian perspective." Thus, the national bar leaders took a middle ground between the societies, which emphasized only individual service of clients, and the demonstration program concept which proposed major innovations.[37]

National bar leaders did not insist that the *Guidelines* provide automatic preference for applications submitted by societies or bar-sponsored groups. Since they had gained control of the program, there was no need for such explicit preference. The *Guidelines* also did not permit local or state bar associations to veto the formation of local projects. If such a veto had been instituted, the societies and bar-sponsored groups would have had no incentive to upgrade their services and include educational and law reform units in their operations. National bar leaders did want the larger projects to engage in these activities; if local groups were assured of funding or if they

34. Sargent Shriver to Hon. George Mahon, 22 October 1965.
35. Cf. "Basic Agreement: CAP-LSP" (LSP files), 5 November 1965.
36. Bamberger interview, op. cit., and interview with Earl Johnson, Jr., 14 December 1968, confirm this intrabureau delegation.
37. Ibid. The behavior of bar leaders in opposing restrictive congressional amendments confirms this point. See below.

could veto applications of competing groups, they would not make any changes in their applications. National bar leaders and LSP officials agreed that some measure of uncertainty about grant approval was necessary to gain the modifications in applications they felt would be necessary.

Once the bar leaders had gained a suitable administrative structure and grant-making process, their next step was to encourage Legal Aid Societies and local bar associations to submit applications for funds. A "sales campaign" was necessary due to the traditional reluctance of the societies to rely on public funding for their activities. Some of the bar groups suspected dark plots to promote confrontation or civil rights litigation in local communities, and opposed the projects on ideological grounds. Some bar groups feared that projects would take away business from the local practitioners.[38]

Bar leaders and LSP officials cooperated in the sales campaign. They appeared at the NLADA Convention in Scottsboro, Arizona, in November 1965 to put to rest fears about federal control and to encourage applications from the societies.[39] They sponsored regional meetings for representatives of state and local bar associations in the fall of 1965 and spring of 1966. They appeared at dinners and meetings of state and local bar groups.[40] The Young Lawyers Section of the ABA submitted reports to LSP officials which described areas of local opposition.[41] National bar leaders were instrumental in overcoming the resistance of local or state bar associations in Tennessee, North Carolina, Oregon, California, and New Mexico.[42] After eight months of effort, at the end of the 1966 Fiscal Year in June, the organized bar at the local level had sponsored seventy-four applications directly, participated in forty-two others, was not involved in fourteen, and opposed only six.[43] The

38. Example of local bar association opposition is found in 30 *Kentucky Bar Journal* 300, and 27 *Alabama Lawyer* 24.

39. Bamberger and Johnson interviews, op. cit.

40. Regional conferences were: Southwest Regional, Northwest Regional, and Pacific Southwest; meetings of state bar associations addressed by Bamberger included the following: Maryland, Pennsylvania, Virginia, South Carolina, California, Missouri, Massachusetts, Florida, and Montana. For an example of the rhetoric used to "sell" the program see Clinton Bamberger, Jr., "The Legal Services Program," in 51 *Massachusetts Law Quarterly*, 313-317.

41. Bert Early memo, 9 November 1965, "Possible Future Role of ABA in the OEO Program."

42. On Tennessee see Committee of the Tennessee Bar Association, *Report: Policy Concerning the Economic Opportunity Act of 1964* (2 April 1966), Voorhees to Bamberger, 14 June 1966, and Earl Johnson to Sargent Shriver, 19 August 1966 and 22 November 1966; on North Carolina see Johnson memo of 2 November 1966; on Oregon see R.W. Nahstoll to Lowell Beck, 5 October 1966; on New Mexico see Johnson to John Robb, 1 July 1966 and 19 September 1966; on California see Sue Fisher memo to Earl Johnson, "CRLA Relations with the State Bar," 17 March 1967 and "Agreement Between CRLA and the State Bar" 15 June 1967. (Materials found in LSP files.)

43. Earl Johnson to Theodore Berry, 14 October 1966.

pattern of bar participation continued in subsequent years without change.

The grant process created local projects which, for the most part, were dominated by local and state bar groups. The composition of most local governing boards was as follows:

1. A majority of board members were lawyers;
2. A delegation of state and local bar association members constituted either a majority or substantial minority of the board;
3. One-third of the members were representatives of the poor, but they did not have to be poor themselves;
4. Members of local and state judiciaries were placed on many boards to gain their support for project activities;
5. Civic leaders, who could be expected to follow policies set by professional bar groups, were chosen to complete the boards.[44]

There were exceptions in the grant-making process. In a very few programs governing boards were split between an activist faction and a bar faction, with a "swing group" of mutually acceptable members placed on the board to break deadlock. One demonstration program had a governing board which consisted solely of law school professors. A few boards were organized so that one-third of the members were professionals, one-third were representatives of the community, and one-third were from the poverty community. But such arrangements were the exception.

By the end of Fiscal Year 1967, lawyers consisted of fifty-five percent of the total membership of local governing boards, while representatives of the poor made up thirty-three percent.[45] Bar leaders had succeeded in placing most local projects under the control of "professionals" rather than lay groups. Both CAA officials and the lawyers who would apply the "civilian perspective" approach had been prevented from controlling the projects.

At the national level the support which organized bar groups gave to the program prevented congressional oversight of program administration. Bar leaders defended it in congressional committee hearings and lobbied with the Republicans to prevent the program from becoming a partisan issue.[46] In the first four years of the program there was only perfunctory interest shown in

44. Descriptions of negotiations are found in the following journals: 27 *Alabama Lawyer* 142; 35 *Detroit Lawyer* 47; 47 *Chicago Bar Record* 421; 3 *Georgia State Bar Journal* 211. These citations are illustrative; my conclusions are based on examination of fifteen state and fifteen local bar association journals, as well as OEO memos and directives.

45. Data on participation of the poor are found in Johnson memo to Shriver, 19 September 1966; on organized bar membership see Sue Fisher to Earl Johnson, 19 November 1966.

46. On lobbying efforts see Beck memo, 1 April 1966, 16 May 1966, Westwood to Beck, 23 May 1966, Johnson memo, 28 September 1966, Beck memo to project directors, 21 November 1966, and John Tracy memo to bar leaders, 5 October 1967.

its activities by the committees.[47]

Organized bar groups succeeded in gaining congressional ratification of the OEO delegation of operating authority to them through approval of a favorable statutory base. The language was drafted in 1966 by bar leaders and LSP officials, and was submitted to Senator Joseph Clark and Congressman Sam Gibbons for approval. It was adopted and placed in the 1966 Amendments by the two substantive committees.[48]

Bar groups protected the program when its operations became an issue on the floor of Congress. When amendments which would have modified the program were offered, bar leaders organized the opposition and provided the evidence and speeches used by its congressional allies. One amendment offered by Senator George Murphy in 1967 would have prohibited projects from engaging in lawsuits against any local, state, or federal government agency. It was defeated with the help of bar leaders on the Senate floor.[49] In 1969 when Senator Murphy introduced an amendment to permit a governor's veto over local project grants, bar leaders arranged for Senator Javits to sponsor a compromise which would permit the president to override the governor's veto. After the Senate passed this compromise, they worked to remove the amendment in conference.[50] With the exception of amendments that passed requiring consultation by LSP officials with state and local bar associations prior to final grant approvals, and that forbade projects from representing indigents in felony cases, the bar leaders were able to prevent amendments that would change the operations of the program.[51]

Support given by national bar leaders for test cases against government agencies, support of the neighborhood law firm concept, and opposition to the governor's veto all indicate that they were committed to innovative activities conducted by local projects, provided that the projects were controlled by governing boards dominated by professionals rather than laymen.

The national bar leaders could be counted on by LSP officials to support increased appropriations for the program. They organized local letter-writing campaigns to convince the Appropriations Committees to earmark funds within OEO for the program and to increase the funds requested for it by

47. The amount of oversight was negligible compared to almost every other OEO component program: see especially *Examination of the War on Poverty*, Vols. 1-15, *Hearings Before the Subcommittee on Employment, Manpower and Poverty*, 90th Cong., 1st sess.; also see *Consultants Reports, Examination of the War on Poverty*, Vols. 1-9, Committee on Labor and Public Welfare, 90th Cong., 1st sess.

48. *Economic Opportunity Amendments, 1966*, U.S., Congress, House, Rep. No. 2298, 89th Cong., 2d sess.

49. John Tracy to bar leaders, "OEO Legislation, 5 October 1967."

50. "OEO News Summary," 27 October 1969.

51. Earl Johnson to NAC, "Status Report on 1967 Legislation" 22 November 1967; also Bamberger and Johnson interviews, op. cit.

OEO officials. In these efforts they were unsuccessful. When they attempted to gain the support of the president they failed, and incurred the wrath of the White House staff and the Bureau of the Budget for attempting to use Ramsey Clark and Abe Fortas to lobby with the president on behalf of the program.[52] The result was that the CAP officials submitted low budget requests (in revenge for their failure to control the program), the Bureau of the Budget routinely approved these low requests, and the Appropriations Committees refused to change the figures or earmark money for the program. While the LSP never suffered a reduction of funds in any fiscal year, at one point it did have to cut back its operations by almost ten percent, and its rate of growth was minute in comparison to the initial expectations of bar leaders.[53]

Bar leaders helped the program in the bureaucratic infighting with CAP officials. When CAP sponsored a plan to reorganize the program in the regions so that the grant-making process would be placed in the hands of regional CAP officials and the LSP personnel would become simply technical advisers, the bar leaders threatened Shriver with a walkout from the program, the staff threatened mass resignation, and the plan was dropped.[54] Three years later, in the Nixon administration, bar leaders and their congressional allies were again successful in preventing a regionalization plan from being implemented, although in this fight the LSP director was fired.[55]

Finally, bar leaders prevented HEW from developing its own program in 1967. After consultations between HEW officials, bar leaders, and LSP officials, a plan was developed whereby HEW funds would be used in four programs to provide legal services for welfare recipients. Local LSP projects would be reimbursed for providing the services. Instead of a competitor, HEW became a future source of funds for local projects.[56]

The political setting of the Legal Services Program at the national level was characterized by a continuous series of transactions between LSP officials and

52. Howard Westwood to Justice Abe Fortas, 23 June 1966 and 22 August 1966; Howard Westwood to Lowell Beck, 9 November 1966.

53. In Fiscal Year 1967 the program requested $50 million, bar leaders asked for $90 million, and the program eventually received $28 million from the OEO; in Fiscal Year 1968 the program again requested $50 million, bar leaders called for $100 million, and the program received $38 million; in Fiscal Year 1969 the LSP requested $60 million, the bar asked for $100 million, and the program received $42 million from the OEO. The initial budget projections of LSP officials in fall 1965 assumed expenditures of $80 million by Fiscal Year 1969.

54. McKinsey and Company, Inc., "Developing Staffing Patterns for the CAP Regional Offices" (CAP files); also "Position Memorandum of the Legal Services Program on the McKinsey Report," 13 July 1967 (LSP files), and Charles Edson to Sargent Shriver, 10 August 1967, which refers to Shriver's decision not to implement the report.

55. *New York Times,* 21 September, 8 October, 12 November, 21 November, 15 December 1970.

56. Griffin memo to Bozman, 9 July 1968; 9 October 1968.

national bar leaders. The program was in reality administered by a coalition of bureaucrats and national bar leaders after an intrabureau delegation of authority from Shriver. This arrangement was ratified by congressional committees with jurisdiction over the program, and accepted by local and state bar associations which received the opportunity to participate in the program on favorable terms. In turn, the support of these bar groups prevented the grant system from becoming controversial with congressional delegations, thus maintaining the stability of the original intra-bureau delegation.

II.

NATIONAL POLICIES AND LOCAL PERFORMANCE

LSP officials were concerned in the first year with promoting the program and stimulating grant applications from reluctant Legal Aid Societies and bar associations. By June 1966 they had succeeded in developing almost 150 programs. Clinton Bamberger resigned in June to run for attorney general of Maryland, and Deputy Director Earl Johnson, a former attorney in the Department of Justice and with the demonstration program in Washington, D.C., became first the acting and then permanent director of the LSP with the approval of bar leaders.[57] Johnson in turn brought Gerald Caplan, a law school classmate, into the program as director of research in the fall of 1966. Together the two men developed a set of project goals, and a national strategy to encourage local projects to reach these goals.

Johnson and Caplan had three criteria for judging the performance of local projects: first, whether the project engaged in law reform and appellate advocacy; second, whether it engaged in community education; and third, whether it had representatives of the poor on its governing board.[58] Johnson emphasized law reform and appellate advocacy because he felt that it would enable projects to develop general principles which could aid large numbers of the poor. It would permit projects to cut down on their large caseloads by ending the abuses that led to the cases in the first place. In addition, such work would curb the abuses of bureaucrats and private individuals who preyed on the poor, and therefore would gain the support of bar groups and local community leaders. As Johnson stated:

> In the broadest sense, the program is neither liberal nor conserva-
> tive. It has elements of both, and should have an appeal which cuts
> across traditional lines of political philosophy and party politics....
> It utilizes existing institutions, existing law, professional personnel.
> It represents change within the system. [59]

57. Bar approval is discussed in Westwood to Voorhees, 15 August 1966, and Voorhees to Westwood, 20 September 1966.

58. Interview with Gerald Caplan, 14 December 1968.

59. Earl Johnson and Gerald Caplan, "The Neighborhood Lawyer Program: An

These goals were supported by national bar groups. The NLADA Convention in November 1965 revised its *Standards* for the societies to include law reform, appellate advocacy, and community education. In succeeding conventions panels were held on test cases and community education. At the 1967 convention resolutions were passed endorsing tenant rent withholding, reform of the welfare system through test litigation, and suits against federal, state, and local governmental agencies. The convention also voted to organize a number of committees to propose legislation in specific areas of poverty law.[60]

The NLADA Convention that passed these resolutions contained 240 programs funded by OEO, many of them new projects rather than older societies. The NLADA restructured its Board of Directors and committee system to include directors of projects and other attorneys involved in poverty law. By 1967 neither the NLADA nor the ABA were as traditional or insular as they once had been. They accepted reluctantly and then enthusiastically the law reform and appellate advocacy approaches of the projects. The change in attitude on the part of bar leaders was evolutionary and incremental rather than revolutionary and radical, but nevertheless it resulted in support for these goals in Congress when they were threatened by amendments.

The performance of local projects funded by the LSP did *not* match the policies enunciated at the national level by LSP officials or supported by bar leaders. The goals which were supported at the national level were often ignored by the local governing boards of projects and by the societies. The extent to which they adhered to the national goals can be measured by examining the annual evaluations of each project conducted by the LSP. These evaluations were prepared by teams consisting of national and regional program officials, law school professors, private attorneys, and national and local bar leaders. Although the reports were kept confidential by the program, letters summarizing the results were sent by the LSP director to the chairman of the governing board of each project. The letters understated the shortcomings of the project while encouraging it to improve its performance.

I prepared the table below after examining letters sent to projects in the Fiscal Years 1967 and 1968. Because the samples were furnished by program officials at random rather than through a systematic randomizing process, and because the number of letters in each sample is not large relative to the total universe of projects, the data presented in the table is suggestive rather than conclusive. The letters, moreover, did not always mention deficiencies. Therefore, the table *understates* the situation. Accounts published by former program officials, the comptroller general of the General Accounting Office,

Experiment in Social Change," 7 *University of Miami Law Review* 187.

60. *Proceedings of the National Legal Aid and Defender Association*, 45th Annual Convention, "Resolutions Enacted," 27 October 1967.

and interviews with former program officials confirm the results.[61]

The table below indicates the number and percentage of projects in the sample in each fiscal year which failed to perform the listed activities satisfactorily:

PROJECT DEFICIENCIES

Program Goal	FY 1967 (n=35)		FY 1968 (n=32)	
Law reform, appellate advocacy	20	(57%)	22	(69%)
Community education	20	(57%)	18	(56%)
Poor on governing board	7	(20%)	10	(31%)

(Source: LSP files)

The sample of evaluation letters indicates that a majority of projects did not adhere to national program goals. Moreover, the percentage of projects failing to comply with program goals increased in the second fiscal year when one hundred additional projects, many of them in small or rural communities, were funded. As for the representation of community groups envisioned by the original Task Force, it was not even mentioned in the evaluation letters since it was not a national goal or local activity.

To understand why program performance diverged so greatly from program rhetoric, it is necessary to examine the local political setting of the operating projects. This is best done through short cases which illustrate the ways in which local community leadership could control the activities of the projects and prevent adherence to national program goals.

III.
THE LOCAL POLITICAL SETTING OF PROJECTS

The most important single factor determining the performance of local projects was the composition of the governing boards. The boards chose the project director, who in turn hired attorneys subject to the approval of the board. The governing boards also determined the range of activities, subject to the "Work Conditions" and "Special Conditions" in their grants.

When staffing projects, many boards chose to hire "locals" rather than persons trained in techniques of poverty law. The local lawyers were susceptible to social and professional pressures exerted by local community leadership. Such attorneys were not inclined to take controversial cases which would isolate them socially or professionally. In the Pine Tree Legal Services program in Maine, for example, a local attorney in the project refused to

61. U.S., Comptroller General, *Review of Economic Opportunity Programs* (Washington, D.C., 1969), pp. 108-110; former program official "Clark Holmes" (a pseudonym) estimates that sixty projects engaged in law reform and appellate advocacy, *Washington Monthly,* June 1970, p. 21.

accept a case involving local cafeteria workers at a college who wished legal assistance in negotiating with the school administration for higher wages. Even though the incomes of the workers made some eligible for services, the attorney refused to represent them. Shortly thereafter he entered private practice in the community, which had been his ambition from the very beginning of his service in the program.[62]

Although projects were supposed to follow the conditions of their grants, some governing boards ignored this in setting down guidelines for the projects. The Houston Legal Foundation not only forced a project attorney to drop a school integration case, but it also established the policy, in violation of the terms of its grant, that it would not litigate in civil rights cases. After intervention by OEO officials the governing board promised to live up to the conditions of its grant, but it was clear that it would informally discourage such cases through its hiring practices.[63]

Only the few projects whose boards were not dominated by local and state bar delegations could be innovative. The Legal Services Unit of the Mobilization for Youth antipoverty agency was directed by a seven-man governing board consisting entirely of law school professors. The only dispute between the board and the project staff was over the amount of time to be devoted to pure research as opposed to test cases, community representation, and service functions. Eventually the board agreed to a policy of aggressive community and group representation and education.[64] Most governing boards did not offer the local projects such a choice.

Even if the governing boards had not been dominated by organized bar groups, it is doubtful that most projects could have long engaged in innovative activities involved in group representation and community advocacy. The state judiciaries would have exercised greater supervision of project activities. A nonprofit corporation may organize to provide legal services to indigents, but the courts generally must approve the application of the corporation so that attorneys hired by it may practice before the court. Approval is granted for a specific period of time and then must be renewed.[65] For the most part such approval was granted routinely since there

62. The author conducted a study of Pine Tree Legal Services, Inc. in Waterville, Maine, in the spring of 1968, and interviewed the project attorney.

63. Houston Legal Foundation, "Application to Legal Services Program" sec. II(B), "Services Offered," pp. 11-12, specifically stated that *all* types of cases could be litigated; also Earl Johnson to Sargent Shriver, 16 November 1966; Thomas M. Phillips to Shriver, 13 December 1966; Shriver to Phillips, 27 December 1966 (LSP files).

64. Charles Grosser, "The Need for a Neighborhood Legal Service and the New York Experience," in *Conference Proceedings: The Extension of Legal Services to the Poor* (Washington, D.C., 1964); the conflict between board and attorneys is found in "Memo, Advisory Committee to Edward Sparer" (MFY files, undated).

65. The leading case is Azzarello v. Legal Aid Society, 117 *Ohio App.* 471, 185 *N.E. 2nd* 566. Cf. "Note: Ethical Problems Raised by the Neighborhood Law Office,"

was no local controversy among professional groups about the organization of the project. Often members of the judiciary would be on the sponsoring board. Three leading opinions suggest the conditions under which such approval might be denied.

The first opinion denied the application of the New York Legal Assistance Corporation submitted to the Appellate Division of the New York State Supreme Court. The LAC was a holding company for ten smaller corporations which would actually provide services, and was in turn supervised by the New York City Council Against Poverty. The proposal included a complex set of governing boards, advisory committees, and fiscal agents at both the local and city-wide level. In rejecting the LAC application and that of two of the proposed corporations, Justice Charles Breitel, on 15 November 1966, laid down a number of guidelines for projects in New York State.

First, Breitel insisted that a single board make policy for the program. Second, he required that a majority of that board consist of attorneys who would be subject to the discipline of the courts. Next, he insisted that the range of proposed services be detailed in the proposal. The opinion then discussed the range of acceptable services:

> The proposed corporations are projected to allow them to represent groups as distinguished from individuals. Again, the lack of definition and standards for eligibility is woeful. It would be one thing to allow neighborhood law offices to handle poor man's credit unions. It would be quite another thing to have them handle, advise, and represent political factions or organizations of social and economic protest, however worthy. [66]

Later the opinion was even more explicit in rejecting both community advocacy and some law reform activities:

> Moreover the proposals are deficient, albeit in each case in varying degrees, in not prohibiting entirely and without evasive qualifications political, lobbying, and propagandistic activity.[67]

This restrictive decision should be compared with two opinions written by Raymond Pace Alexander, Judge of the Court of Common Pleas, Philadelphia County. On 29 June 1966, before the New York opinion came down, Judge Alexander approved the charter of the Community Legal Services Program in Philadelphia. This opinion took a broad position on the range of permissible activities. It specifically endorsed law reform, lobbying for legislation, and advocacy against schools, welfare agencies, and public housing authorities. Alexander also endorsed some group representation:

> A realistic view of any Community Legal Services Program must, of

41 *Notre Dame Lawyer* No. 6, Fall 1966.
   66. 274 *N.Y. 2nd* 789.
   67. Ibid., 790.

course, contemplate the possibility that lawyers in the program will
give lectures to indigenous groups on their legal rights and on the
availability of free services and may invite them to use their
facilities. [68]

The opinion also noted approvingly that "overall direction of the program
will be by the bar," and left open the inference that had the local bar
associations not approved the program, the judiciary would have rejected its
application.[69]

After the New York opinion came down, two Philadelphia lawyers (!)
filed appearances pro se for exceptions to the opinion and decree issued by
Judge Alexander. On 10 May 1967, addressing himself squarely to the issues
raised in New York, Judge Alexander handed down his second opinion. After
citing the restrictions placed on projects in New York, he asked:

> Are the poor to be denied a lawyer's advocacy and left without his
> peculiar assistance in forums beyond the judicial and in the cases
> whose ends encompass social and economic as well as legal justice?
> Surely this is a narrow view of the law.[70]

And he added:

> No acceptable jurisprudence can fail to recognize that "legal" rights
> have an intimate relation to social and economic justice, nor that
> these ends are legitimately sought in the judicial forum.[71]

These opinions reveal that state judiciaries could exercise supervision over
project activities. There was unanimity that overall direction of projects
should be by professionals, and that projects should cooperate with local bar
groups. Beyond that, opinions differed on the range of activities to be
permitted: even within the jurisdiction of the Appellate Division in New York
State the Legal Services Unit of Mobilization for Youth had its application
renewed when it was engaged in activities seemingly proscribed by the Breitel
opinion.[72]

Even if the judiciaries had permitted governing boards to develop
innovative activities, state and congressional leaders would have prevented
such activities in many areas. When the South Florida Migrant Legal Services
Program was being organized, for example, members of the Florida
congressional delegation, led by Sam Gibbons and Paul Rogers, intervened

68. "In re Community Legal Services, Inc.," C.P. March Term No. 4968, p. 23.
69. Ibid., p. 66.
70. "In re Community Legal Services, Inc.," C.P. March Term No. 4968, Number 4,
10 May 1967, p. 2.
71. Ibid., p. 3.
72. Supreme Court of the State of New York, Appellate Division, First Judicial
Department, "Application of MFY for Approval of Existence and Incorporation of
Legal Services Unit Pursuant to Section 280 of the Penal Law," and "Order, New York
State Appellate Division" (MFY files).

with OEO officials on behalf of the State Bar Association of Florida. The result was that the program was organized by a governing board whose members were subject to veto by congressmen, and the original coalition of migrant and civil rights groups was removed from the sponsorship of the program. Moreover, the state bar association received a special OEO grant to fund a corporation which would supervise all local projects in Florida.[73]

The governor's veto of local programs, which could be overridden by the OEO director, also affected the range of services offered in the more innovative programs. The application of California Rural Legal Assistance, Inc. (CRLA), often considered to be the most militant and innovative program funded by LSP, was changed before final approval in order to gain support of Governor Brown and the California congressional delegation.[74] When the grant came up for renewal the following year, restrictions were placed on representation of migrants and migrant organizations in order to satisfy the objections of the California State Bar Association, and the governing board was reorganized to give representation to state and local bar groups.[75] These modifications gained CRLA the support of the state bar association, which in turn convinced Shriver to make known that he would override a veto by Governor Reagan. This permitted the program to escape a veto by the governor.[76] The threat of a governor's veto in this case served to give the state bar association a crucial role in bargaining with CRLA for its needed support. The price of its support was the modification of its governing board and operations.

The conflicts which were resolved in Florida and California were exceptions to the general pattern of organization of projects rather than the rule. For the most part the judiciaries approved applications routinely,

73. Marshall Criser, "Law, Poverty, and the Florida Bar," 40 *Florida Bar Journal* 304-5; Johnson to Harding, 11 July, 14 July, 28 July, 18 September, 19 December 1966; and Johnson to Shriver, 18 May 1967.

74. Compare "Draft of Tentative Proposal for Legal Services for the Rural Poor," 8 December 1965, with the "Special Conditions to Amended CRLA Work Program" of May 2, 1966. The first condition prevented "legal representation to any labor union or political organization" and the second unit forbade aiding workers to join collective bargaining units. Another condition added state and local bar representation to the governing board, while another placed representatives of agricultural producers on the board.

75. The 1967 "Special Conditions" provided that the program could not represent a collective bargaining unit in litigation, or in negotiations with employers, or provide legal assistance to labor unions, or represent union officials in matters relating to union business. LSP officials admitted, "The rule will be more restrictive than OEO follows generally, but because of pressure on the program and its vulnerability in this area, whether or not a union is eligible, it cannot be provided with representation." Cf. "Fiscal Year 1967 CRLA Grant Application" (OEO files).

76. William Clark to William Horan, 10 January 1968; William Horan to Ronald Reagan, 13 January 1968; William Horan to William Clark, 13 January 1968 (CRLA files).

governors did not veto grants (except for isolated cases in California, New Hampshire, and South Dakota) and governing boards did not force projects to drop cases. These political controls on project behavior were not employed because they were not needed. Controversial activities were not ended, because they rarely were begun, given the nature of the grant-making process which gave control of most projects to the societies and bar-sponsored groups.

Had many more projects been organized free of local bar control, the local pressures on Congress to dismantle the program would have been successful. As it was, the members of the Kentucky and Missouri congressional delegations succeeded in placing requirements for state and local bar association consultation prior to final grant approval.[77] A member of the Florida delegation gained an amendment to the statute, which, in conference, eventually became a ban on all felony representation by projects because he was upset by a project representing alleged rioters.[78] The members of the California delegation almost succeeded in 1967 in placing a ban on all litigation by projects against local, state, or federal agencies, and in 1969 gained Senate approval for a governor's veto which could have been overridden only by the president.[79] Had any more controversy existed at the local level, it is likely that Congress would have accepted amendments to provide a local bar veto and prevent all community education and appellate bar advocacy. Or Congress might have scrapped the projects and established a "Judicare" program which would have reimbursed private practitioners for representation of indigents on a fixed fee schedule. As it was, only the lack of controversy and the strong intervention of national bar leaders prevented such amendments from passing.

National bar leaders and LSP officials could not force local projects to engage in innovative activities once they had funded them under the decentralized grant system. Instead, they relied on programs developed by Earl Johnson and Gerald Caplan to induce projects to engage voluntarily in law reform, appellate advocacy, and community education. They funded training programs, such as the National Training Institutes. A national fellowship program designed to recruit the best law school graduates and young practitioners into projects for a year to do law reform and test case litigation was funded. Another program provided pre-law education and law school scholarships to members of minority groups. Project attorneys were provided with a *Poverty Law Reporter* which enabled them to keep up to date with developments in poverty law, and relevant briefs and materials were

77. *Congressional Record,* 29 September 1966, pp. 23471-23486.

78. *Economic Opportunity Amendments of 1967, Report No. 1012,* 90th Cong., 1st sess., p. 30.

79. *Congressional Record,* 28 September 1967, p. S14162. Also "OEO News Summary," 22 October 1969.

made available to them by the National Clearinghouse. Grants were made to law schools to engage in legal research on problems involving education, medical care, housing, hunger, and the elderly.

These incentive programs were emphasized so long as Johnson and Caplan remained with the program. In June 1968 Johnson left to write a book about the program under a Russell Sage grant, and Caplan left shortly thereafter. The new director, Burt Griffin, a former director of the highly innovative Cleveland Legal Aid Society, downgraded law reform and appellate advocacy activities in favor of a strategy to improve the service functions of local projects while developing their ability to attract public and private investment into the poverty community. Griffin's idea is summarized in the following staff memo:

> There is beginning to emerge a pattern of using legal service lawyers
> to help groups of poor people structure, secure resources for, and
> operate neighborhood corporations which create economic enter-
> prises such as housing developments, retail stores, manufacturing
> concerns, and transportation services. By tradition and training
> lawyers are strongly oriented toward service in such projects.[80]

Griffin also wanted to widen representation on the National Advisory Committee to include groups such as the National Welfare Rights Organization, the NAACP and CORE, and Mexican-American and Indian groups.[81] Unfortunately, he resigned from the program because of a tragedy in his family after less than a year. The change in national program priorities which he introduced was temporary and had little effect on local program operations. Most projects did not adopt his strategy of grantsmanship, although upgrading service was accepted. After Griffin's departure the LSP emphasis once again returned to law reform and appellate advocacy at the national level. Projects continued to operate as they had before, and paid little attention to national programs designed to induce them to change their approach. Only a score of projects engaged in sustained law reform and appellate advocacy activities.

IV.

IMPROVING THE DELIVERY OF LEGAL SERVICES TO INDIGENTS

The preceding sections have demonstrated that the administrative structure of the national program was controlled by a professional group which made grants to its affiliated state and local groups. The results of this

80. Griffin memo, 16 July 1968. For a discussion of economic grantsmanship in this context, see Melvin N. Eichelbaum, "Economic Development in Poverty Areas," 75 *Case and Comment* 3. Griffin's skepticism about the efficacy of law reform efforts is found in *Proceedings of the Harvard Conference on Law and Poverty* (Cambridge, Mass.), pp. 27-28.

81. Griffin memo, 21 July 1968. Also interview with Burt Griffin, 16 August 1968.

intergovernmental grant-making process was to end the possibility of a "consumer perspective" model or a CAA-controlled model of project activities. Instead, law reform and appellate advocacy activities were promoted as national policies and ignored by most of the local projects dominated by the professional groups. In this section I will explore reasons a program with such a sorry performance is considered to be so innovative and worthy of support by liberals, and then discuss alternatives to the present program which offer the possibility of matching program rhetoric with reality.

LSP officials and national bar leaders understandably emphasized the program goals and the NLADA Resolutions rather than the actual performance of local projects. They aided the propagation of a Founders Myth, originally spread by the promoters of the demonstration programs, that the neighborhood offices differed radically from the Legal Aid movement.[82] Program officials argued that the neighborhood offices were more accessible to the poor, and that the extent of coverage had increased. They also argued that community education, law reform, and appellate advocacy activities were innovations of their program. The dichotomy between traditional Legal Aid work and the LSP projects is false; the societies were never as service-oriented, nor the projects as innovative, as is claimed.

Both the societies and the projects were deficient in the quantity of service offered. Both met only a fraction of the legal needs of the poor.[83] The Legal Aid movement and LSP sponsored research on the unmet needs of the poor in order to stimulate additional support. The LSP did gain additional funds and dramatic increase in services for the poor, but the problem was far from solved.

Both societies and projects restricted the cases they accepted. The former refused to accept divorce cases, motions for name changes, and most actions against bureaucracies. But the latter was forbidden by statute from accepting felony cases and usually did not engage in eligible civil rights litigation. It is difficult to sustain the proposition that the neighborhood offices differed much from societies in this regard.

Societies never restricted themselves to a service orientation based solely on the individual case approach. Especially in the early years of the movement (until the 1940s) service to individuals was only part of an overall strategy to improve the administration of justice through a restructuring of the judicial system. Societies helped create administrative forums and small

82. See, for example, the trenchant criticism of Legal Aid work written by Marvin Frankel, "Experiments in Serving the Indigent," in *Conference Proceedings: The National Conference on Law and Poverty* (Washington, D.C., 1965).

83. See, for example, the statement that the program was only a "drop in the bucket" made by Earl Johnson, *Economic Opportunity Act Amendments of 1967, Hearings before the Committee on Education and Labor,* 90th Cong., 1st sess., p. 912.

claims courts in which the poor would be able to represent themselves.[84] This approach was considered a novel way to help the poor at the time, although subsequently the emphasis has been on legal representation in administrative forums and in the specialized courts.

Legal Aid lawyers also engaged in law reform activities; only they called it "preventive law."[85] They lobbied for legislation involving landlord-tenant relations, installment contracts, pledge loans, garnishment and repossession, and personal bankruptcy. The successes of the Legal Aid movement in law reform and institutional reform match anything the projects have done in overhauling the practices of welfare bureaucracies or promotion of legislation.

Both the societies and projects dealt with the same issues: the unresponsiveness of particular public institutions to the needs of the poor; and unscrupulous private individuals such as merchants and landlords who preyed on the poor. Both relied on case litigation, negotiation, and legislation to curb abuses and restructure institutions. Both organizations could gain the support of local bar groups and community influentials sympathetic to the poor in cases of obvious abuse. By attacking the local villains (i.e., bureaucrats and the unscrupulous small businessmen) a coalition of do-gooders and professionals gained widespread community support for their activities. It is always easier for local leadership to regulate and castigate others than it is to examine its own relationship to the poor.

Neither the societies nor the projects moved beyond this limited approach to serving the poor. Neither movement used the grantsmanship approach suggested by former director Burt Griffin which would have attracted additional public and private investment into community corporations in order to increase the incomes of the poor. Neither movement emphasized changing local decision-making structures, or helped community-organizing or voter registration activities. In other words, the projects and societies never attempted to make a fundamental redistribution of economic resources or political power in the local communities.

LSP officials and national bar leaders do not wish to compare their program with the possibilities for redistributive activities suggested above. Instead, they prefer to compare the neighborhood offices and funded societies with the inaccurate picture of traditional Legal Aid work. In addition, they compare their program with the "Judicare" system of direct payments to private practitioners who litigate on behalf of the poor. Four small demonstration Judicare projects have been funded by OEO.[86]

84. R.H. Smith, *Justice and the Poor,* 3rd ed., op. cit., p. 39.

85. Cf. Otto G. Wismer, "Lobbyists for the Poor," 225 *The Annals* (Philadelphia, 1936), p. 172; also Robert D. Abrahams, "Legal Aid and Preventive Law," 16 *Legal Aid Briefcase* 68.

86. The largest program was funded in twenty-six rural Wisconsin counties. Cf. Joseph Preloznik, "Wisconsin Judicare," 25 *Briefcase* 91.

The bar leaders and LSP officials claim that the Judicare system would subsidize the least competent and least ethical members of the profession— the "ambulance chasers." Local practitioners would not engage in community education, law reform, or appellate advocacy, and would not know relevant developments in poverty law. Their offices would be less accessible than neighborhood offices, and their services would cost more than do the existing projects.[87] Bar leaders have a vested interest in attacking the Judicare system, since it threatens the geographic monopoly of the NLADA. LSP officials can raise the spectre of Judicare to argue that the neighborhood programs represent the best possibility for innovative activities on behalf of the poor.

In fact, the Judicare delivery system offers the possibility of major innovations in the provision of legal services to the poor. It is misleading to think that only the "ambulance chasers" and solo practitioners would practice law on behalf of the poor. Indigents could also be represented by civil liberties and civil rights lawyers, by associates in law firms interested in pro bono publico work, and by members of the "law communes."

It is not true that law reform and appellate advocacy would be eliminated under a Judicare system. In the first place, the research and demonstration programs affiliated with universities could be continued under an affiliation with a state-wide Judicare agency. Even if they were not, the additional funds which could be made available to the "private attorneys general" such as the American Civil Liberties Union and its state affiliates, the NAACP Legal Defense and Educational Fund, Inc., the Mexican-American Defense Fund, and the National Office for the Rights of Indigents under a Judicare system would permit them to expand their own appellate activity.[88] Finally, under a Judicare system there would be an incentive for each attorney to carry a case to the highest appellate level, since he would gain a local reputation which would aid him in attracting a clientele. If anything, a system would have to be devised to prevent frivolous appeals and a waste of available funds.

The range of activities could be increased under a Judicare system. Eligible students might ask for representation in litigation with the Selective Service System. Practitioners might be involved in union and management discrimination, sexism, the representation of students on campuses, external diseconomies and pollution abatement, and zoning practices. The projects have concentrated their energies on inconsequential reforms of a welfare bureaucracy soon to be abandoned. Judicare and private practitioners could hardly

87. Edward Kuhn, "Lawyers Must be Active in OEO if Profession is to be Preserved," 2 *Trial* February-March 1966, pp. 17-20; William McCalpin, "The Bar Faces Forward," 51 *ABA Journal,* June 1965, pp. 548-551; Orison Marden, "The Bar and OEO," 29 *Texas Bar Journal,* May 1966, p. 357.

88. On group litigation cf.: "Note: Private Attorneys General," 58 *The Yale Law Journal* 574; Clement Vose, "Litigation as a Form of Pressure Group Activity," 319 *The Annals* 20; Lucius Barker, "Third Parties in Litigation," 29 *Journal of Politics* 41.

compile a worse record, and might engage in litigation on the frontiers of American public law.

Judicare is a means of implementing the "civilian perspective." It offers the poor a choice, and permits them to set the priorities of the Legal Services Program through free market choice of counsel. It ends the geographic monopoly of the societies and projects and forces them to become responsive to the needs of the poor in order to retain their clientele.

Finally, it would probably result in increased services being made available to the poor. State and local bar associations would exert pressure in Congress to provide more funds: subsidies for the poor may not be popular, but subsidies to professional groups are in an old and more successful American political tradition.

The Nixon administration has been toying with the idea of expanding the Judicare concept by developing a number of state-wide corporations to administer the program. Unfortunately such a program may be accompanied by statutory restrictions which would limit its progressive features and emphasize subsidies to local practitioners for individual case service. The statute might provide for payment only to attorneys unaffiliated with litigating groups. Local and state bar groups may dominate the state corporations that distribute funds. They will probably be delegated the authority to draw up lists of eligible attorneys. Compensation will be restricted to members of the state bar, which will prevent outsiders from assisting in litigation or preparing briefs. Local committees may be delegated the authority to screen possible actions before approving them for referral. Only cases considered to be "reasonable actions" would be approved for compensation, which might be used to prevent some kinds of litigation. Finally, the statute might forbid litigation against government agencies.

Given the temper of the Nixon administration and the Congress, it is reasonable to assume that some of these restrictions might be placed on a Judicare system in its first or subsequent years of operation. But the number of restrictions might be minimized with some intelligent coalition building. The "private attorneys generals," the large law firms, and the societies and projects have a vested interest in seeing that organizations engaging in nonprofit representation of indigents be permitted to participate in the program. They might succeed in preventing the solo practitioners from gaining a monopoly in the program. National bar groups could be expected to support this approach.

Both the NLADA and ABA have endorsed appellate advocacy and law reform. They would probably support a continuation of these activities in a Judicare system. State and local bar associations might also do the same if the pot were sweetened for them by increasing the research grants to the American Bar Foundation, the NLADA, and the state bar associations. National bar groups can also be expected to support a continuation of research grants to law schools. The Judicare agencies at the state level may also operate research programs affiliated with the law schools or the bar associations.

Restrictions on the range of cases might also be opposed successfully. First, the *Canons of Ethics* oppose any restrictions on the representation of clients, and statutory restrictions may prove obnoxious to leaders of the legal profession. If local and state bar associations can be persuaded that such restrictions are a dangerous precedent, it may be possible to prevent their enactment. On the other hand, there is no guarantee that these associations will not support such restrictions.

Perhaps the best strategy in dealing with Judicare is to try an incremental approach. A gradual increase in the level of funding for Judicare agencies might not provoke congressional interest or the adoption of a restrictive statute. The present broad delegation of authority to the LSP officials and national bar leaders might be retained. Judicare would develop out of the present system, and the societies and projects could be gradually phased into the program while their grants were scaled down.

Given the performance of the present system, drastic modification is desirable, but the approach should be cautious and incremental lest the restrictions prevent innovation. An approach to the provision of legal services to the poor that taps the talents of the private sectors of the legal profession is long overdue. The Judicare approach offers one way to break the monopoly of societies and projects dominated by local bar associations. Whether or not Judicare is instituted in a form worthy of support, objective analysis of the actual performance of the *present* program suggests that its spirited defense by those interested in fundamental social change in America is somewhat out of place.

5. The Political Economy of Health Care: Dynamics Without Change*

ROBERT ALFORD

Introduction

Health care in the United States is allegedly in a state of crisis. High and rising costs, inadequate numbers of medical and paramedical personnel, a higher infant mortality rate in 1969 than thirteen other countries, a lower life expectancy in 1965 for males than seventeen other countries, and poor emergency room and ambulatory care are among the diverse facts or allegations which have justified a wide variety of proposed reforms. And yet the numbers of health personnel, the proportion of the gross national product spent on health care, and the sheer quantity of services rendered have grown considerably faster than the economy as a whole.[1]

If health care is in "crisis" now, then it was in crisis ten, twenty, and forty years ago as well. Several qualified observers have commented on the similarity between the 1932 analysis by the Committee on the Costs of Medical Care[2] and reports issued thirty-five or more years later. Dr. Sumner N. Rosen, an economist on the staff of the Institute of Public Administration in New York City, has said that the "catalogue of problems drawn up almost forty years ago strongly resembles the latest list—inadequate

*This paper was prepared under a grant to the Center for Policy Research, New York, from the National Center for Health Research and Development, National Institute of Mental Health. I am indebted to the Center for Policy Research for providing research facilities, and particularly for making it possible for Ann Wallace to serve as my research associate during 1970-71.

I wish to thank the National Conference of Social Welfare for permission to use part of an earlier version which appeared in *The Social Welfare Forum* (New York: Columbia University Press, 1971).

Too many friends and colleagues have commented on the paper by this time to allow their names to be mentioned here, but I hope they will recognize their impact on the final version and realize that their sometimes severe criticisms have been appreciated if not always heeded.

1. For a collation of a wide variety of health statistics, see the Committee on Ways and Means, U.S. House of Representatives, *Basic Facts on the Health Industry* (Washington, D.C.: U.S. Government Printing Office, June 28, 1971).

2. *Medical Care for the American People,* the final report of the Committee on the Costs of Medical Care, adopted October 31, 1932. (Reprinted, 1970, by the U.S. Department of Health, Education and Welfare.)

services, insufficient funds, understaffed hospitals. Virtually nothing has changed."[3] Economist Eli Ginzberg, summarizing the results of his study of New York City, concludes that "While changes have occurred in response to emergencies, opportunities, and alternatives in the market place, the outstanding finding is the inertia of the system as a whole."[4]

The overwhelming fact about the various reforms of the health system that have been implemented or proposed—more money, more subsidy of insurance, more manpower, more demonstration projects, more clinics—is that they are absorbed into a system which is enormously resistant to change. The reforms which are suggested are sponsored by different elements in the health system and advantage one or another element, but they do not seriously damage any interests. This pluralistic balancing of costs and benefits successfully shields the funding, powers, and resources of the producing institutions from any basic structural change.

This situation might well be described as one of "dynamics without change." This paper argues that both the expansion of the health care industry and the apparent absence of change are due to a struggle between different major interest groups operating within the context of a market society—professional monopolists controlling the major health resources, corporate rationalizers challenging their power, and the community population seeking better health care.

Although the paper generalizes from the scholarly literature as well as from documents and from interviews which took place in New York City, it should be regarded as a set of "outrageous hypotheses," in the spirit of Robert S. Lynd's classic *Knowledge for What?*,[5] rather than as a theory inferred from reliable empirical findings.

Market Versus Bureaucratic Reform

Pressures for change come largely from three types of reformers, of which the first two are most important. The first, whom I shall call the "market reformers," would expand the diversity of facilities available, the number of physicians, the competition between health facilities, and the quantity and quality of private insurance. Their assumptions are that the public sector should underwrite medical bills for the poor and that patients should be free to choose among various health care providers. The community population is

3. Sumner N. Rosen, "Change and Resistance to Change," *Social Policy* 1 (January/February 1971): 4.

4. Eli Ginzberg et al., *Urban Health Services* (New York: Columbia University Press, 1971), p. 224.

5. Robert S. Lynd, *Knowledge for What?* (Princeton: Princeton University Press, 1939).

regarded as consumers of health care like other commodities and is assumed to be able to evaluate the quality of service received. Market pressures will thus drive out the incompetent, excessively high priced or duplicated service, and the inaccessible physician, clinic, or hospital. The market reformers wish to preserve the control of the individual physician over his practice, over the hospital, and over his fees, and they simply wish to open up the medical schools to meet the demand for doctors, to give patients more choice among doctors, clinics, and hospitals, and to make that choice a real one by providing public subsidies for medical bills.

These assumptions are questioned by the "bureaucratic reformers." They stress the importance of the hospital as the key location and organizer of health services and wish to put individual doctors under the control of hospital medical boards and administrators. The bureaucratic reformers are principally concerned with coordinating fragmented services, instituting planning, and extending public funding. Their assumption is that the technology of modern health care requires a complex and coordinated division of labor between ambulatory and in-hospital care, primary practitioners and specialists, and personalized care and advanced chemical and electronic treatment. The community population is regarded as an external constituency of the health providers to be organized to represent its interests if necessary to maintain the equilibrium of the system.

These contrasting modes of reform are partly illustrated by recent articles by Harry Schwartz of the *New York Times* and Dr. Milton I. Roemer of UCLA, who represent the market and bureaucratic reform views, respectively.[6] Both recognize the rocketing costs, criticize duplicated facilities, and call for such reforms as health insurance. But they differ sharply both in their image of the health system and in their proposals for reform.

According to Schwartz, "these needed and useful improvements can be made within the context of a continued pluralistic system. Different people have different tastes and different needs. Those who want to use prepaid groups should be permitted to do so; those who want to go to a physician and pay him each time should be free to do so, too. The result may not seem to be as neat on an organization chart as a uniform national system, and it may have seeming inefficiencies and duplications. But the right of choice for

---

6. Harry Schwartz, "Health Care in America: A Heretical Diagnosis," *Saturday Review,* 14 August 1971, pp. 14-17, 55; and Milton I. Roemer, "Nationalized Medicine for America," *Trans-Action,* September 1971, pp. 31-36. These articles merely provide concrete illustrations of certain points, and it cannot be assumed that either man holds any views which I summarize under the general categories except those specifically quoted.

doctors and patients alike is worth such costs—at least in a really humane society."[7]

Schwartz argues that the pluralistic market society in the United States not only "provides choices for both physician and patients," but also "gives [the physician] an economic interest in satisfying the patient" and provides "reassurance and psychological support" to the patient because of the "intimate and humane" contact between physician and patient. He argues that a "nationalized and bureaucratic" system like that in Britain will reduce the amount of choice, reduce the incentives to please the patient, and thus depersonalize treatment.

This position is essentially a defense of the present system or an advocacy of further extension of the market principle. Critics of this position argue that the choices allegedly provided by the plurality of health care providers are not real for most people, that the economic incentives to physicians result in much over-doctoring, over-hospitalization, and over-operating, and that the alleged "intimate and humane" quality of most doctor-patient relationships is a myth.

Thus, Dr. Roemer, in sharp contrast to Schwartz, asserts that indeed "[o]ur spectrum of health services in America has conventionally been described as 'pluralistic.' More accurate would be to describe it as an irrational jungle in which countless vested interests compete for both the private and the public dollar, causing not only distorted allocations of health resources in relation to human needs but all sorts of waste and inefficiency along the way."[8]

The image of the ideal health system presented by Dr. Roemer is worth summarizing, because it appears in many reports and studies aimed at "coordinating" health facilities and services. Integrating the system is advocated simultaneously with differentiating its components into a rational division of labor. The ideal system provides "primary health centers" for every neighborhood, close to people's homes, staffed by general practitioners and "medical assistants," to provide basic diagnoses and preventive services. "Each person served by this health center would be attached to a particular doctor and his team of colleagues."[9] "For each four or five such health centers . . . there should be a district hospital" with 120 to 150 beds to handle relatively common conditions: maternity cases, trauma, less complex surgery. For the service areas of about 10 district hospitals, there would be a regional hospital with about 500 beds serving even "more complex medical or surgical problems" and engaged actively in medical research. "At the highest echelon, serving the population coming under three to five regional hospitals

7. Schwartz, op. cit., p. 55.
8. Roemer, op. cit., p. 36.
9. Ibid., p. 34.

(that is, from 1½ million to 2½ million people), should be a university medical center" providing basic medical training and treating all types of cases as part of their research and teaching objectives.

According to Dr. Roemer, "Ideally health care should be a public service like schools or roads, paid for from general tax revenues." All professional personnel would be salaried, with salaries varying "according to qualifications, skills and responsibilities." The quality of medical care would be assured by a "framework of authority and responsibility, backed up by continuous education. Surveillance and reasonable professional controls would also be provided, with rewards and penalties as necessary." In charge of the system would be a hierarchy of officials, beginning with the district hospital director who would serve as a "public health director" in the "broadest social sense," being responsible for seeing to it that "the whole health service operates effectively. . . . He would be responsible for coordination of the several parts of the system, through proper use of records, statistics and information exchange. . . . He would be responsible to a health official above him."[10]

Another plan for bureaucratic reform envisions automated multiphasic screening of patients upon first contact in order to use scarce medical manpower efficiently, and an integrated system of health maintenance organizations, clinics, and specialized hospitals. The greater supervision and checking of medical decisions in the hospital context is seen as far outweighing the possible loss of personal contact.[11]

Contrasting images both of present institutions and of the viability of reform are seen in Schwartz's and Roemer's analogy of health to education. Dr. Roemer cites the public school system as an "achievement" of the American political system which did not require a revolution, along with a sharply graduated income tax and an extensive social security program. These achievements constitute grounds for his optimism that a reorganized health system can be achieved without a fundamental modification of American political and economic institutions. Harry Schwartz, on the other hand, cites the public school system as a "debacle" and says that "[i]n every community, public school education is free to the recipients; yet, everywhere—or almost everywhere—there is bitter complaint of the failure of this system to teach effectively or to satisfy the psychological needs of our young people."[12]

These two contrasting diagnoses, images of the future, and proposals for

10. Ibid., p. 36.
11. See Sidney Garfield, "The Delivery of Medical Care," *Scientific American* 222 (April 1970): 15-23, for another model along these lines, which is criticized by Schwartz, op. cit.
12. Schwartz, op. cit., p. 55.

reform of health care are not opposing political ideologies which can be accepted or rejected only in terms of one's moral and political values. They are also analyses of the structure of health care resting upon different empirical assumptions about the nature of and power of the medical profession, the nature of medical technology, the role of the hospital, and the role of the patient (or the "community") as passively receiving or actively demanding a greater quality and quantity of health care.

Major Interest Groups

Strategies of reform based on either "bureaucratic" or "market" models are unlikely to work. Each type of reform stresses certain core functions in the health system and regards others as secondary. But both neglect the way in which the groups representing these functions come to develop vital interests which sustain the present system and vitiate attempts at reform.

For the market reformers, supplying trained physicians, innovating through biomedical and technological research, and maintaining competition between diverse health care producers are the main functions to be maintained. They view the hospitals, medical schools, and public health agencies as only the organizational framework which sustains the primary functions of professional health care and biomedical research. However, these types of work become buttressed through institutional mechanisms which guarantee professional control, and come to constitute powerful interest groups which I shall call the "professional monopolists." Because these interest groups are at present the dominant ones, with their powers and resources safely embedded in law, custom, professional legitimacy, and the practices of many public and private organizations, they do not need to be as visibly active nor as cohesively organized as those groups seeking change.

For the bureaucratic reformers, the hospitals, medical schools, and public health agencies at all governmental levels perform the core functions of organizing, financing, and distributing health care. Hospitals are seen ideally as the center of networks of associated clinics and neighborhood health centers, providing comprehensive care to an entire local population. The bureaucratic reformers view physicians and medical researchers as performing crucial work, but properly as subordinated and differentiated parts of a complex delivery system, coordinated by bureaucrats, notably hospital administrators. However, these large-scale organizations also become powerful interest groups, which I shall call the "corporate rationalizers." These interest groups are at present the major challengers of the power of the professional monopolists, and they constitute the bulk of the membership of the various commissions of investigation and inquiry into the health care "crisis."

A third type of reformer is relatively unimportant in the American context as yet: the "equal-health advocates," who seek free, accessible, high-quality health care which equalizes the treatment available to the well-to-do and to the poor. They stress the importance of community control over the supply and deployment of health facilities, because they base their strategies upon a third set of interest groups: the local population or community affected by the availability and character of health personnel and facilities. The community population is not as powerful or as organized as the other two sets of interest groups, but has equally as great a stake in the outcomes of the operations of health institutions.

Each of these three major interest groups is internally heterogeneous. The professional monopolists include biomedical researchers, physicians in private or group practice, salaried physicians, and other health occupations seeking professional privileges and status, who differ among themselves in their relationships to each other, as well as to hospitals, medical schools, insurance plans, and government agencies, and thus their interests are affected differently by various programs of reform. But they share an interest in maintaining professional autonomy and control over the conditions of their work, and thus will—when that autonomy is challenged—act together in defense of that interest.

The corporate rationalizers include medical school officials, public health officials, insurance companies, and hospital administrators, whose organizational interests often require that they compete with each other for powers and resources. Therefore, they differ in the priority they attach to various reform proposals. But they share an interest in maintaining and extending the control of their organizations over the conditions of work of the professionals (and other employees) whose activities are key to the achievement of organizational goals.

The community population constitutes a set of interest groups which are internally heterogeneous with respect to their health needs, ability to pay, and ability to organize their needs into effective demands, but they share an interest in maximizing the responsiveness of health professionals and organizations to their concerns for accessible, high-quality health care for which they have the ability to pay.

My assumption in making these key distinctions is that the similarities of structural location and interests vis-à-vis each other of each of these interest groups warrant an emphasis on the common interests within each group rather than on their differences. If my concern were to explain the actions of various individuals and groups with respect to a particular piece of legislation or administrative decision, lumping these diverse groups and individuals together into three such internally diverse groups would be entirely too crude. But for explaining the main contours of the present system and its resistance to change, finer distinctions would entail a short-term time perspective. Differences which are extremely important for tactics may be relatively unimportant in the long run.[13]

The danger of this mode of analysis, however, is that the internal contradictions within each interest group may be the source of potential strategic alliances which may have great long-term implications. For example, the vision of an ideal health system which erases the distinction between those who pay and those who don't is held up by the bureaucratic reformers as well as by the equal-health advocates. And, in the abstract, both the value of personalized care (defended by one group as viable only through fee-for-service medicine) and the value of coordinated, comprehensive care (defended by another group as possible only through hospital-organized health care) are hard to question.

But whether or not these values of personalized service and comprehensive care are sheer ideological rationalizations by one or another interest group of its power and privileges may be irrelevant if they can be used as a weapon for critical attack upon the inadequacies of health care. The corporate rationalizers properly accuse the professional monopolists of not providing the personalized care which justifies their claim to fee-for-service practice. The professional monopolists properly accuse the corporate rationalizers of not being concerned with personalized care in their drive for efficient, high-technology health care. The contradictions in both cases between rhetoric and performance provide an opportunity to the equal-health advocates to show the deficiencies in analysis and program of the dominant interest groups.

13. I assume also that there is a reasonably high correlation between ideologies and personal incentives of doctors, researchers, administrators, and the organizational interests of the medical profession, hospitals, or public health associations. That is, there is a high probability that elites will take a public position consistent with the interests of their organization. Career incentives probably require that collective myths be publicly sustained, even if there is considerable private cynicism or disbelief. More detailed analyses of particular events and conflicts would require taking into account contradictions and discrepancies between ideology, personal incentives, and organizational interests.

A further distinction can also be drawn between the objective interests of an individual or group (the consequences of certain policies) and its subjective interests (beliefs about those consequences). A group may be affected in important ways by the operations of an institution, but its members may not be conscious of those consequences and thus may not act either to defend themselves or to change the structure which produces the consequences. Or even if conscious of the consequences, the members may be unwilling or unable to act for a variety of reasons. See Isaac D. Balbus, "The Concept of Interest in Pluralist and Marxian Analysis," *Politics and Society* 1 (February 1971): 151-177, for a recent discussion of this point, and for an earlier but similar statement, Harry Eckstein, *Pressure Group Politics: The Case of the British Medical Association* (Stanford: Stanford University Press, 1960), pp. 9-12.

Differences between these interest groups should not be overemphasized, because both the professional monopolists and the corporate rationalizers are operating within the context of a market society. Both have a concern to avoid encroachments upon their respective positions of power and privilege, which depend upon the continuation of market institutions: the ownership and control of individual labor, facilities, and organizations (even "nonprofit" ones) by autonomous groups and individuals, with no meaningful mechanisms of public control. (The instruments of alleged political control available to the community population are discussed later.)

The corporate rationalizers may thus favor certain market reforms, if that will provide them with more doctors for their hospitals, more researchers for their medical schools, and more potential workers for medical corporations, and will subject these workers to market pressures which in turn will make them tractable employees. The professional monopolists may thus favor certain bureaucratic reforms, particularly those aspects of planning and coordination which safeguard their interests, or administrative rules in hospitals which guarantee their continued dominance of medical practice.

Nor should the seeming rationality implied by the term "interest group" be overemphasized, because one basic consequence of the plurality of interest groups is that health institutions in a real sense are out of control of *both* the professionals and the bureaucrats. A hospitalization that could be terminated in one week lasts two, because there is a week's waiting time for a barium enema. Or one-third of a high-cost ward may be occupied because convalescent or chronic care facilities are unavailable. These failures of "coordination" or "planning" are not due to a conspiracy, vested interests (except in a very narrow sense), or failures of information (the horror stories are endless).[14]

Investigations of the Health System

It is significant that most definitions and diagnoses of the "crisis" do not come from the health professionals. The AMA and other professional associations have largely reacted defensively, proposing alternatives and compromises only when other interest groups have raised challenges to existing practices. When institutions and laws continuously serve the interests of dominant interest groups, challenge must come from elsewhere.

From where has the challenge come? A clue lies in the composition of the numerous commissions of inquiry which have investigated the health delivery system in the last twenty years and made many recommendations for public

14. I am indepted to Dr. Joel Hoffman for some of these points.

policy. I can cite only a few examples here, but they are typical.[15] The thirty-six-member "Heyman Commission" which issued its report on New York City health services in 1960 included five city officials, twelve hospital administrators and executives of health associations or medical research institutes, fifteen corporate or bank executives or directors, one university president, one labor representative, and two persons representing private medical practice (both presidents of county medical societies). Of the corporate group, at least five were directors of voluntary hospitals or pre-paid health plans.[16]

Seven years later, the so-called "Piel Commission" reported its findings to Mayor Lindsay, and recommended the establishing of the Health Services Administration (1967) and the Health and Hospitals Corporation (1970). Its seven members included one publisher, one university professor, and five corporate and banking representatives, all of whom happened to hold directorships of voluntary hospitals or other health associations.[17] Of the fourteen M.D.'s comprising the "medical advisory committee" to the commission, four represented hospitals, six university medical centers, two the New York Academy of Medicine, one a health institute, and only one a county medical society.

At the federal level, such commissions are similar in composition. To take only one example, the Task Force on Medicare and Related Programs was composed of twenty-seven persons, five of whom held M.D.'s. Only one of these (according to the list of the affiliations in the report) was an unattached physician. Four others were associated with city or state health agencies or were directors of hospitals or medical schools. Of the remaining twenty-two members, seven were corporation executives (one a proprietary hospital chain), six were connected with universities (including medical schools), three with community or state health agencies, and three with hospitals.[18] The chairman of the task force was the president of Blue Cross, a private hospital insurance association.

15. For a content analysis and evaluation of seven of the some fifteen such reports dealing with health care in New York City between 1950 and 1971, see Robert R. Alford, *Interorganizational Outputs: Case Studies of Health Care in New York City* (New York: Center for Policy Research, 1972).

16. See the "Report of the Commission on Health Services of the City of New York," July 20, 1960.

17. See the report and staff studies of the Commission on the Delivery of Personal Health Services, *Community Health Services for New York City* (New York: Frederick A. Praeger, 1969). The report was officially released on December 19, 1967.

18. "Report of the Task Force on Medicaid and Related Programs," U.S. Department of Health, Education and Welfare (Washington, D.C.: U.S. Government Printing Office, June 29, 1970), cited henceforth as "Task Force."

While I may not have accurately classified the members' multiple affiliations, the relative absence of physicians, and especially physicians in private practice, is striking. Predominant in all of these commissions are hospital administrators, hospital insurance executives, corporate executives and bankers, medical school directors, and city and state public health administrators. These organizations represent a coalition of interest groups which I have called the "corporate rationalizers." They favor what the AMA attacked as the "corporate practice of medicine,"[19] favoring the coordination of health services by a combination of private and public health agencies, principally the hospital.

The analyses of the health "crisis" in these reports follow a number of common themes. A brief summary of one of them will illustrate both the character of the diagnosis of the crisis and the nature of the recommendations. The most recent example available from New York State is Governor Rockefeller's Steering Committee on Social Problems,[20] composed of seventeen members, only one of whom had an M.D. Of the sixteen men who took part in the study, fourteen were high executives of some of the country's largest corporations, banks, or brokerage firms, including U.S. Steel, Pan American World Airways, duPont, Equitable Life, AT&T, as well as Xerox and General Foods. The one M.D. was on the Yale medical school faculty; the other noncorporate executive was the president of the Committee for Economic Development.

Their report emphasizes that the health "crisis" is *not* a result of a shortage of anything, whether beds, physicians, dollars, or physician assistants (allied health manpower). Although the report does not generalize in this way, this overabundance might be termed an "anarchy of production," almost in the classic image of a capitalist economy.

With respect to manpower, "Boston, for example . . . has one of the nation's greatest complexes of medical institutions [but] a severe shortage of general care practitioners."[21] Two percent of medical school graduates in 1970 became general practitioners.[22] There are also "too many ancillary personnel—but . . . they are not adequately trained and not effectively deployed.". . .[23]

19. Quoted in Herman M. Somers and Anne R. Somers, *Medicare and the Hospitals: Issues and Prospects* (Washington, D.C.: The Brookings Institution, 1967), p. 136.
20. See the "Preliminary Report of the Governor's Steering Committee on Social Problems on Health and Hospital Services and Costs," April 15, 1971, henceforth referred to as "Preliminary Report."
21. Ibid., p. 12.
22. Ibid., p. 14.
23. Ibid., p. 22.

With respect to beds, "[w]e estimate that we need 450,000 short-term hospital beds—we now have 800,000 such beds."[24]

With respect to duplication of facilities, "[n]eedless competition [by hospitals for costly but under-used equipment] results in tremendous waste of scarce resources and funds."[25] And mortality rates were sharply higher in hospitals where surgeons performed few operations such as open-heart surgery.

With respect to funds, increasing costs and subsidies act as an incentive to expand facilities and add to inflation. Total expenditures on health rose from twenty-six billion dollars in 1960 to sixty-seven billion in 1970, from 5.3 percent of the gross national product to 7 percent. Two-thirds of the 1970 total was personal health expenditures, with half of this due to price increases, not more use of services or more advanced technology.

This "overproduction" of health manpower and facilities is distributed in such a way as to maintain a "two-class health system—one for the poor and a better one for those able to pay their own way. . . . The nation's poor people have been receiving inadequate and, at times, inexcusable care and treatment."[26]

Using the words of the 1967 National Advisory Commission on Health Manpower, the report summarizes the state of affairs: "Medical care in the United States is more a collection of bits and pieces (with overlapping, duplication, great gaps, high costs and wasted effort) than an integrated system in which needs and efforts are closely related." But, according to the Rockefeller committee, "The situation is more acute than four years ago, and deteriorating rapidly."[27]

This picture is restated in every diagnosis of the "crisis" of the health system. The figures portray dynamics without change: a rapid increase in almost every index of growth—dollars, manpower, programs—except those pertaining to quality, distribution, accessibility, and reasonable cost to the consumer.

It should be noted that the empirical criteria and basis for the judgments of quality and the adequacy of quantity and distribution are not given in this report, nor are the basic data available which would be necessary to evaluate either a specific health service or the character of coordination of diverse health institutions. The reasons for this absence of information will be discussed later in a more theoretical context, but the point is that the many critiques of the health "system" are not cumulative nor based on solid

24. Ibid., p. 21.
25. Ibid., p. 13.
26. Ibid., pp. 8, 15.
27. Ibid., p. 41.

research, and thus have an ideological character, rooted in images and theories about the proper way to reorganize and coordinate the "system."

The Rockefeller committee, without quite saying so, attributes many of the defects of health care to the interests of the physicians, the "dominant profession."[28] The physicians have defined "health and medical care in very restricted terms," leaving out preventive medicine.[29] "Most clinics serving poor people are structured for the convenience of the doctor, not the patient."[30] "Much care now given by a physician does not require a physician's level of training and education."[31] The physicians, and especially those allied occupations which have not yet achieved similar professional controls over their incomes and work, exhibit a "great deal of sensitivity about professionalism and status."[32] As a result, "[w]e are impressed with the number of meritorious proposals for change which have been ignored, and with the tendency of the health care establishment to resist such change."[33]

In a barely concealed attack on the interests of the professional monopolists in maintaining their power and privileges, the Rockefeller committee recommended coordinating all health services around hospitals, or "Health Center Complexes," employing "modern management approaches"[34], utilizing machinery for "internal planning and systems development," and, perhaps most important, establishing "utilization controls." The system recommended would, ideally, cover the entire population for seventy-five percent of their medical bills (one hundred percent for the poor).[35]

While not expressly advocating salaries for physicians, the utilization controls would exclude any public funds being used for health care services "found to be unnecessary in accordance with generally accepted practice"; nor would any charge be honored which "exceeds the prevailing level of charges in the community."[36]

It is quite clear that the committee accepts the hospital as the central health provider in our society. They see the hospital, with some qualifications, as the "core of a broader health care corporation responsible for assuring comprehensive health care to a defined service area."[37] It should

28. See Eliot Freidson, *Professional Dominance* (New York: Aldine, 1971), for a critique of the professional division of labor in health care.
29. "Preliminary Report," op. cit., pp. 18, 64.
30. Ibid., p. 38.
31. Ibid., p. 64.
32. Ibid., p. 65.
33. Ibid., p. 23.
34. Ibid., p. 57.
35. Ibid., p. 76.
36. Ibid., pp. 57-58.
37. Ibid., p. 52.

be franchised or licensed by a state and participate meaningfully in "area, state and regional health care planning and regulation."[38] The result will be a network of community preventive services, ambulatory and home care, integrated with in-hospital care, and linked to nursing homes and extended care facilities.

There is little to object to in this abstract image of an ideal health system, which is quite similar to Dr. Roemer's. The point here is not to criticize its assumptions, but to suggest that it is in fact a challenge by the corporate rationalizers of the professional monopolists. The proposals by the committee to end restrictive licensing of health professionals would challenge their attempts to control their markets and their own supply. The proposals to open up medical schools and reduce the length of time for training an M.D. also challenges professional control over their own supply.[39]

The proposals to establish physician assistants (or "surrogates"—a significant substitute term) would challenge the monopoly of M.D.'s over important areas of primary health care. As the report says, a Washington pilot program indicates that "such men can perform a series of jobs with even greater skill than most physicians."[40]

The proposals to expand prepaid group practice and review utilization and fees challenge the sole control by M.D.'s over their conditions of work and incomes, and thus directly undercut their professional monopoly.[41]

The proposal to allocate health professionals after their first training to areas short of health manpower, in return for waiving of loans, constitutes an invasion by government of the right of the new physician to choose his own area of practice.[42]

Thus, major proposals to reorganize and coordinate the health delivery system constitute several important challenges to the professional monopoly of the physicians.

What is the likely course of change? Given the central interests of each set of groups and the ease with which the equal-health advocates can be co-opted, change is extremely difficult. The interrelated activities of these groups account for the expansion of health care in providing units at the "bottom" of the system and the elaboration of bureaucratic machinery at the "top." Explanation of the "dynamics without change" of these processes are now my major concern, not the character of private medical practice.

38. Ibid., p. 54.
39. Ibid., p. 68.
40. Ibid., p. 70.
41. Ibid., p. 82.
42. Ibid., p. 72.

The Professional Monopolists

The professional monopolists are mainly physicians, specialists, and health research workers in medical schools and universities (but not hospital administrators, even if they have M.D.'s), who usually have an advanced degree and also a position—either an entrepreneurial one guaranteed by law and custom or an official one defined by the hierarchy of statuses within an organization—which entitles them to monopoly over certain kinds of work. Their incomes are derived from private practice or from foundations, governments, and universities, but they are able to exploit organizational resources for their personal and professional interests. They can be called "monopolistic" because they have nearly complete control over the conditions of their work, buttressed by the traditions of their professions and/or institutions, and because usually there is no other way to show effectiveness except through a demonstration grant, research project, or contract to them, or by contracting with them to perform their professional services. Frequently a clinic or health center will be set up which, although providing services, is established mainly for other purposes of the persons who hold power (not always or even usually the operating staff): research, training, professional aggrandizement, power within their home" institutions, the prestige of extending their professional empire, and so forth.

The major consequence of the activity of the professional monopolists is a continuous proliferation of programs and projects which are established in a wide variety of ways, under many auspices, and with many sources of funding, and which undoubtedly in most cases provide real services of some kind. The reason it is so difficult to describe or explain how these work is that the professional monopolists who set them up attempt to provide a symbolic screen of legitimacy while maintaining power in their own hand through various organizational devices. A continuous flow of symbols will reassure the funding or allegedly controlling publics or constituencies about the functions being performed, while the individuals or groups which have a special interest in the income, prestige, or power generated by the agency are benefiting from its allocations of resources.

Thus, the symbolic screen will put off attempts at control or supervision by making them difficult as well as less likely (because the nominally superior agency will be reassured). It is almost impossible to plan or coordinate or integrate the activities of the myriad projects and programs because important interests of the individuals and groups which establish and maintain them contradict the goals of those who wish to coordinate, plan, and integrate all of the functions implied or defined by the master symbols of the project: its title, the funding agency's contract with it, its annual report, and so on.

The professional monopolists, by and large, are satisfied with the status quo and do not form part of the "market reformers" who regard them as performing the core health functions. The physicians and biomedical researchers are not in the vanguard proposing reforms, except when their powers and prerogatives are threatened by others. That physicians are not heavily represented on the various reformist committees and that the AMA is losing membership and is continuously criticized for its political stance do not mean that physicians are losing power. The physicians in private practice and the voluntary hospitals still constitute the core of the health system. All of the federal, state, and local programs and projects which occupy so much time and energy of both types of reformers are still on the periphery of the health system. Almost none of the reports, commissions of investigation, presidential task forces, and so forth, which attempt to define the crisis and recommend solutions, ever mention invading the powers and territory of the private physicians and the voluntary hospitals.

The continuous control of the medical profession over the provision of medical services is a basic element of the American health system. As one author put it in 1932, "The legal ownership and ultimate control of the great bulk of capital invested in the practice of medicine in hospitals lies with the lay public, but the medical profession exercises a pervasive and in most instances a determining influence over the utilization of this capital and over the kinds of service which, through the use of this capital investment, are furnished to the community."[43] Twenty-three years later, the same author asserted that "the predominance of social capital has continued. Proprietary hospitals have diminished in absolute and relative importance. . . . More capital per physician is required than formerly."[44]

But in 1955 a third of American doctors worked entirely with organizations full time, and "a much larger number—about five-sixths, including the preceding group—work part time or full time with organizations—especially hospitals and clinics."[45] This trend has undoubtedly continued.

Thus, medicine seems to be a classic case of the socialization of production but the private appropriation of the "surplus" by a vested interest group—the doctors—who maintain control through their professional associations of the supply of physicians, the distribution of services, the cost of services, and the rules governing hospitals. The gradual decline of solo practice has created the social conditions for the challenge of this professional monopoly by the corporate rationalizers.

43. Michael M. Davis and C. Rufus Rorem, *Crisis in Hospital Finance* (Chicago: University of Chicago Press, 1932), p. 76.

44. Michael M. Davis, *Medical Care for Tomorrow* (New York: Harper and Brothers, 1955), p. 34.

45. Ibid., p. 35.

This generalization probably applies mainly to larger cities and perhaps most to New York City. In smaller cities the physicians still control the hospitals through the county medical societies. Administrators of the small-town hospitals are less professionalized than those in big-city hospitals and thus have a less independent view of the way their hospital should be run. A small town is also not likely to have a medical school, so that a potential coalition of corporate rationalizers from a medical school, hospital administrators, insurance companies, and public health agencies does not have the organizational or political base to challenge the control by the solo physicians of medical practice in the hospital.

Potential mavericks among the doctors are controlled by the power of the county medical board to refuse an appointment in the hospital. Small cities are less likely to have more than one hospital, so that a dissident physician has no place to go, except to change his place of practice.

Thus, small cities are less likely to exhibit open conflict over the organization, quantity, and quality of health care than large cities. (In the pluralist sense, no "power" is being exercised.) But there may actually be more unequal allocation of health care to various segments of the community and more chance that doctors and professional associations are unchallenged than in larger cities, where opposing interest groups have reached some threshold of effective organization.

The Corporate Rationalizers

The corporate rationalizers are typically persons in top positions in "health" organizations: hospital admininstrators, medical school directors, public health officials, directors of city health agencies, heads of quasi-public insurance (Blue Cross), state and federal health officials. Their ideology stresses a rational, efficient, cost-conscious, coordinated health care delivery system. They see the medical division of labor as arbitrary and anachronistic in view of modern hospital-based technology. The more successful they are in unifying functions, powers, and resources under a single glorifying symbol ("medical center," "comprehensive health planning"), the greater their incomes are likely to be and the higher their community and professional prestige. Thus, there are ample incentives for these individuals to attempt to expand the powers of their home institutions or organizations.

Sometimes the corporate rationalizers ally themselves with the professional monopolists within their own institutions as a way of gathering more financial resources and legitimacy, and also as a way of bringing more and more health care units into their domain, even if not under their control. But usually it is in the interests of the corporate rationalizers to attempt to control the conditions of work, the division of labor, and the salaries of their employees, in view of the exigencies of funding and the need to adopt technical and organizational innovations without the built-in resistances of professional (or union, for that matter) jurisdictions over tools and tasks. They, therefore, attempt to convert professionals, mainly physicians, into employees and in a variety of ways to circumscribe their power in the hospital.

Although great size and resources are equated with capability and performance in order to legitimate extending the domain of control of the corporate rationalizers, there is little evidence that even the internal structure of the giant hospital complexes is planned, integrated, and coordinated for the effective delivery of health services to a given target population, let alone the public as a whole.

"Outreach" neighborhood health centers established by a medical center may be advertised as a rational step toward coordination and integration, but instead are really needed as a source of patients and surgical material. Because of Medicare, physicians assume they will be reimbursed, and thus need not send poor patients with interesting diseases on to a university hospital. The goal in establishing a neighborhood health center is thus not coordination, but patients. Other cases of supposed coordinating mechanisms—ambulance services, referrals, communication of records and patient information—are notoriously poor in operation, and there is little evidence that the extension of control by one organization, whether via formal merger or not, results in more comprehensive care.

Even if the target of the corporate rationalizers' activity is to coordinate and integrate a number of organizations into a cohesive whole, the successful instituting of such bureaucratic controls means that democratic planning and coordination of the larger health system becomes *more* difficult. Generating enough power to integrate a portion of it successfully means, almost by definition, that this part is now insulated from outside influence and can successfully resist being integrated into a still larger system.

The rhetoric of the corporate rationalizers conceals this consequence by suggesting that social or political mechanisms can be created to unify and integrate the entire system. But such mechanisms do not exist—in government or anywhere else. The mere passage of legislation establishing "comprehensive health planning," for example, does not provide them with the necessary power and resources. If this is the case, then the act of creating another agency further complicates the system. As will be discussed later in more detail, historically legislators have responded to pressures for reform by establishing a series of agencies—none of which has sufficient power to do its job. Few of these are abolished, and subsequent legislation incorporates the previous agencies into the list of those to be "coordinated," thereby further complicating the system. The resources made available to these agencies, charged with planning and coordinating other agencies, frequently become part of the budgets controlled by the corporate rationalizers.

A major consequence of the activity of the corporate rationalizers is a constant expansion of the functions, powers, and resources of their organizations. One organizational device for doing that is the institution of a bureaucratic stratum designed to coordinate and integrate the component units. Unfortunately, this new stratum cannot carry out this function because it is a staff operation with little power and is usually the instrument of one particular leadership faction within the organization. Thus, their recommendations frequently fail to carry enough weight to be implemented. Also the planning or research staff tends to be drawn, because of lack of any other source of personnel, from the ranks of the professional monopolists, who have little stake in truly rationalizing the operation and see the planning or research functions partly as instruments for their own personal and professional ends. Where the goals of the professional monopolists within the organization and the sponsoring faction of the corporate rationalizers coincide, an effective staff function will be performed. In that case, the committed and motivated staff will usually come into conflict with a powerful element in the top officialdom of the organization—either another group of professional monopolists whose toes they are stepping on, or a faction among the corporate rationalizers.

Thus, the net effect of the activities of the corporate rationalizers is to complicate and elaborate the bureaucratic structure. The relationship between them and the professional monopolists is symbiotic in that the ever-increasing elaboration of the bureaucratic structure is justified by the need to coordinate the expansion of health care providing units at the bottom. No group involved has a stake in the coordination and integration of the entire system toward the major goal of easily accessible, inexpensive, and equal health care.

The Community Population

The third major set of interest groups comprises the community population affected by or needing health care. Their spokesmen are the "equal-health advocates," comprising various "community control" groups in both black and white communities, full- or part-time organizers, and some intellectuals. Because they are not part of the network of health institutions and agencies, they are free to demand more and better health services and also some voice in the decisions and policies which might affect health care. City bureaucracies, public health agencies, and the medical schools usually contain some supporters.

The efforts of these diverse individuals and groups, whether aimed at specific or general reforms, are likely to fail. If their demands are focused upon a particular program or need, the response is likely to be the establishment of a particular kind of program or clinic—drug, alcoholism, mental health. The professional monopolists will seize upon the demand as an opportunity to legitimate their efforts to establish another project or program. While some tangible services to some people may be the outcome, the overall result is the expansion and proliferation of still more highly specialized clinics, demonstration projects, or health centers which confuse people trying to find care and are highly expensive in both staff and administrative costs and, thus, lead to a further elaboration of the overriding bureaucratic structure.

If the demands of the equal-health advocates are directed toward reorganizing the health system, the activities of the corporate rationalizers are legitimated. New planning committees and new coordinating councils will be set up with representation from the community groups and with the avowed goal of rationalizing the system. But the community representatives do not have the information necessary to play an important political role; they do not know the levers of power, the interests at stake, and the actual nature of the operating institutions, and they do not have the political resources necessary to acquire that information since they are only minority members of advisory committees. The presence of equal-health advocates on one or another committee or council is a sign of legitimacy being claimed by either a set of professional monopolists or corporate rationalizers, or sometimes both, in their battle for resources and power.

Because the community is not self-conscious and knowledgeable about health facilities, and because the members of the community are likely to give food, jobs, housing, and schools priority over doctors and hospitals—since only a small proportion of the community needs health care at any given time—the equal-health advocates are likely to have a great deal of autonomy in representing community needs to official agencies. Advocates are not under much surveillance, there is little reaction to their decisions, and their victories have little collective impact. Thus, the isolation of equal-health advocates from the community increases the chances of their being co-opted into advisory boards, planning agencies, and other devices for advertising the representative character of "community participation" without much chance, let alone guarantee, that the community will be able to evaluate and control the actions of their advocates, let alone the health providers.

Thus, the major consequence of the activity of the equal-health advocates is to provide further legitimacy for both the expansion of specific research or service units controlled by professional monopolists and the expansion of the layers of bureaucratic staff under the control of the corporate rationalizers. Given the enormous discrepancy between the output of actual health services and their claims, there will be a continuous supply of persons from community groups ready to serve as equal-health advocates. However, persons who have played that role for some time are likely to become discouraged and leave, or will be co-opted into one of the established health organizations.

Other persons will arise from community organizations to replace them for a
wide variety of motives: prestige as a community representative, a chance to
mingle with high city and other officials and community leaders, and possibly
a chance for a better job or a political career. This chance for mobility may
be good for the individuals involved, but may be disastrous for the
accumulation of political and organizational experience by community
groups, if their leaders are constantly either being absorbed into the existing
health system or dropping out of activity.

Given the original diversity of health providers and the personal and
organizational stakes of the interdependent, although conflicting, network of
professional monopolists and corporate rationalizers, the demands of the
equal-health advocates are almost inevitably frustrated. In fact, the system as
a whole, as a result of their activities, moves in a direction exactly opposite to
that which they envision. Costs go up as a result of the establishment of new,
expensive programs. The accessibility of care goes down as a result of the
proliferation of specialized, high-technology, research- or teaching-oriented
health care units.

This description of a system in equilibrium is of course only partial. The
legitimacy gained for the dominant interest groups by the activity of the
equal-health advocates is precarious because it rests upon a continuous
contradiction between rhetoric and performance. Legitimacy is purchased at
the escalating cost of constantly expanding provider units which duplicate
each other and of continuously establishing new agencies which purport to
coordinate and integrate. To the extent to which equal-health advocates can
create consciousness among the community population of the causes of the
situation, the groundwork is laid for a more fundamental challenge to the
powers and privileges of the dominant interest groups.

The Consequences of a Community "Victory"

The preceding discussion of the activities of the equal-health advocates has
argued that their attempts to increase the quality and quantity of health
services available to them are likely to fail. Either they will become absorbed
with no real power in an "advisory committee" to existing agencies, or they
will play a minority role in planning committees for new health facilities
which take years to come to fruition. While some community participation
may lead to greater political consciousness, under present conditions
co-optation and stalemate are most likely.

Even if community groups become involved in planning committees for
new facilities, one highly likely consequence is that their activities by
themselves will block new programs and projects. Once community groups
are mobilized, they tend to conflict with each other and with the
professionals in health organizations over funding, priorities, timing, sites, and

control. Community participation is a classic instance of the "veto group" process leading to stalemate.

Such a typical pattern is no accident. The structure of participation maximizes the chances of stalemate by setting up the rules of decision making in such a way as to prevent any major interest group from being seriously damaged (the requirement of "consensus"), and by failing to allocate enough power to the decision-making bodies on which community groups are represented. Because these bodies are not given enough power, there is little incentive to set up procedures and create a composition which will lead to effective decision-making processes. Just the opposite incentives exist: to make them large and unwieldy—as "representative" as possible—so that all points of view will be heard but none implemented, save those interest groups who already hold power. The net result is many meetings, speeches, and reports. Committees are set up which plan, coordinate, and communicate—and ultimately evaporate when the planning grant runs out.

One consequence of this particular scenario is that even the professionals who started the project with a sincere desire to "get the community involved" will become cynical about the competence and skills of community groups and leaders. The next time around they will join the ranks of those who try to make the mechanisms of community representation as fictitious as possible in order to preserve at least some chance of getting a health facility organized, funded, and built.

But let us assume that, as a result of sustained community organization and pressure, a "neighborhood health center" is, at long last, established to provide accessible, inexpensive, and high-quality care. What are the consequences? Will it continue to do so? No, for several reasons: the consequences of excessive *demand*, its establishment as part of a two-*class* health system, and the likelihood of short-term *funding*. Each of these reasons why a community "victory" is likely to be short-lived is worth a brief discussion.

Neighborhood health centers are selected as the example of a community victory because of their recent emergence as the focus of demand in New York City and their actual funding under specific federal legislation; but there have been parallel programs in the past, and there will be others in the future under such names as comprehensive health center, district health center, health maintenance organization, neighborhood family care center, ambulatory care service, child health station, and mental health clinic. Such a "center" is likely to be set up only in an area where few M.D.'s are in private practice, where there are few hospitals, and where there is a heavy concentration of poor people. The market reformers can applaud such an innovation because it meets demand in a flexible way, establishes diversity in the system, and uses government resources where the private market has no incentive to compete. The bureaucratic reformers hail such a development because it usually will be established as an "outreach" clinic by an existing hospital, under public funding, and therefore add to the resources of a seeming movement toward integration and coordination.

Demand. Because of the inadequacy of other health facilities in poor areas, the very success of a neighborhood health center is likely to be its downfall. If it attempts to "deal comprehensively with patients' problems," the center becomes the "repository for all the unmet needs of our patients. . . ." The consequence of the "lack of adequate social services in our community will inevitably deaden staff's responsiveness to their problems."[46] Thus, even though the staff may have begun work there in the full flush of idealism, ready to serve the community's needs with great energy and devotion, their very commitment will cause patients to flood in demanding care. The resulting overload of work will reduce the quality of care, the enthusiasm of the staff, and the sense of gratitude of the patients.

Establishing a facility in a poor area which provides—at its beginning—easily accessible, inexpensive, and high-quality care will thus generate enormous demand, reflecting great unmet needs, which soon reduces both accessibility and quality. Thus, the activities of the equal-health advocates, if successfully focused upon the "realistic" end of getting an OEO grant for a neighborhood health center, let us say, are likely to be fruitless from the point of view of the system as a whole. If the total quantity of health services available to the population is increased, it can then be argued plausibly that the community is better off than it was before. But if the same characteristics—long waits, hurried physicians, and so forth—are reproduced after a while, the net effect may be cynicism on the part of the previously idealistic staff and a new sense of hopelessness in the population, which has been led to expect real improvement.

Where the poor community has become apathetic because of the successive failure of previous attempts to install new facilities, it may be difficult for the latest one, no matter how well-intentioned and well-staffed at the outset, to generate usage. If so, this becomes an obvious argument for dismantling the health center, particularly since it is likely to be set up as a demonstration project. *Lack* of demand thus will kill the facility.

Class. The same characteristics of the "old" system are reproduced not only by the demand on the facilities but also by the maintenance of a two-class system. In the case of the OEO neighborhood health centers, the requirement that service be only to the poor has meant "heavy-handed insistence"[47] by OEO on a means test, with all of the resulting downgrading

46. Martin Luther King Neighborhood Health Center, New York City, *Annual Report,* 31 December 1969, p. 15.
47. Ibid., p. 14.

of respect for the patients, lower status for the staff, and other characteristics of institutions designed for the poor.

Attempting to build health care institutions for *all,* providing free, accessible, and high-quality care, runs into an objection. Why serve the middle class? They can pay for it. Why not reserve these scarce resources for the poor who need it most? If you open up health care to all on the same basis, the argument runs, the middle class will monopolize services since they have the information and the resources to take advantage of the available facilities. This is a plausible argument, especially if one takes the position that political realism argues for a piecemeal approach to reform.

But, as already suggested, the consequences of a two-class institution are likely to be the extension of more of the same kind of services as before. To the extent that the sheer production of more health care facilities is better, such additions of facilities may be worthwhile, but they do not constitute reforms of the health system.

Funding. The argument that more is better assumes, for its plausibility, that these neighborhood health centers become part of the established array of health facilities available to the public, even on terms of existing costs, accessibility, and quality. This is not the case, however. The magic wand of financing moves from health area to health area and from crisis to crisis, causing one kind of facility to grow and flourish for a time, then another, leaving the first to dwindle or wither away. Community mental health centers, neighborhood health centers, and methadone clinics have each felt the impact of public concern.

Precisely because of community pressures, funding tends to flow to the kinds of facility which can be advertised as a legitimate response to community needs. When the "old" agency or facility fails to meet those needs, community pressure builds up again after a time, and a new agency surges forward, leaving the hollow shell of an under-financed, struggling agency in its wake. The old agencies are struggling partly because their failure to meet the needs has become obvious; they lose political clout, and their budgets are cut to make resources available to the new agencies, or at least they are not increased enough to enable them to do their jobs. Thus, they are further paralyzed.

The lack of permanent governmental commitment to such programs as the OEO neighborhood health centers—their definition as peripheral and supplemental programs to the main body of the private health sector—means that they are eternally precarious and starved for funds. The consequences for their internal operations are serious. They must seek the short-term payoff, the program which will bring in the maximum number of patient visits as tangible evidence that they are playing the political role which originally generated them: cooling out the community. If they seek maximum short-term "productivity" in terms of patient visits, they run the danger of overloading their facilities which were probably under-financed and under-staffed in the first place. Overloading, as we have seen, in turn reduces the impact on the community and the likelihood of community pressure demanding the project's continuation. In effect, the health center becomes after a few years just another component of the two-class health system, and its theoretical goal of providing comprehensive health care is contradicted by its practice.

Another consequence of dependence on short-term financing—itself also a result of the strategy of getting something rather than nothing for the poor—is that costs are likely to be high. In the first few years of any program, the setting-up costs—hiring, training, capital investment in buildings and facilities—are high. But in the context of "demonstration projects," where an evaluation of the costs will, at least seemingly, be one of the bases for judging whether or not the project will continue, these high initial costs become one of the negative features in the evaluation. A common point made about demonstration projects is that they are expensive and therefore cannot be continued.

Another reason that such projects are expensive is that the poor community has many sick, untreated people. If they ask for care once it is made available, the new, ambitious, and committed (let us assume) staff is put in a double bind. If they seek to meet all of these needs, they will quickly subject themselves to difficult work conditions, with all of the consequences listed above. If they attempt to insulate themselves against only the most pressing medical needs, and try to meet those needs in a humane, careful, and thoroughly professional manner, they inevitably set up barriers to treatment for the rest. Poor patients asking for help (and also testing the new facility for its humanity) will again be subjected to "official" treatment: the appointment hassle, the inquiries (Are you really sick?), and the not-so-subtle attitudes (What do you expect for nothing?). While the health care for those persons who ultimately reach a physician in the health center may be careful and competent, the cost of making it possible for their care to be of high quality may reduce the accessibility of care to many others. This consequence is a direct result of inadequate manpower and resources.

The auspices under which the neighborhood health center is organized might seem to make a difference. It is sometimes argued that linking such centers to medical schools will increase the chances of better care for the poor. This is not necessarily the case because of the exploitation of the poor for teaching purposes. The poor patients with rare diseases may, indeed, be selected for special and even superb treatment, but may be subjected to untested medicines or operations (for legitimate research and teaching purposes, of course) by inexperienced persons (medical students), who would never be allowed to practice their skills in that way on wealthy patients. The remainder of the patients, the poor with ordinary, uninteresting diseases which are useful for neither research nor training, are subjected to the normal indignities found in charity institutions of all types.

But the poor are no better off if the neighborhood health center is not connected to a medical school. In this case the medical staff, working in a lower-status facility precisely because it serves the poor and is not connected to a medical school, tends to be composed of foreign doctors, many of whom are not well-trained, below-average medical school graduates who cannot get better jobs or practices, young idealists who get discouraged after a few years and leave, or a few good physicians who have taken the job as part of their career but intend to move on as soon as possible. The staff tends to have a high turnover, and thus is relatively unable to build up continuous relationships with families in the area. [48]

To conclude, even if the equal-health advocates are victorious in their long struggle to get more health facilities in a poor area, the principles by which the rest of the health system already operates become reproduced in the new facility. The disillusionment which follows leads either to apathy or greater militance, depending on the concrete character of the experiences of the community population, the political skills of the equal-health advocates, and the broader social and political situation at the time.

The Role of the Political System

Up to this point we have dealt only with the interest groups active at the local level, and the resources for which they compete have been regarded as exogenous factors. The points might be made that all of the processes summarized above are due to vacillating financial support and that regular funding for health services would solve many problems, even if they were organized as at present. This may indeed be true, but then it is necessary to see if the sudden spurts of funds for new programs and then their drying up, and the continuous creation of new but under-funded and under-powered agencies, are characteristics of the political system which can be easily rectified.

Most new urban health programs depend on vacillating commitments under federal and state legislation. But most of the analyses of New York City's (or any other community's) programs regard these characteristics of the political system as exogenous factors to be taken account of, but almost like fate or the weather. The Ginzberg study, discussing ambulatory services and the city's plans for "neighborhood family care centers," says, "In the

---

48. The same problems plague the "free-clinic" movement as well. Sponsorship of a neighborhood health center in a poor area with few health facilities thus has little to do with the structural causes of its failure to become a long-range solution. See, for example, Health-PAC *Bulletin,* no. 34, October 1971.

presence of persisting financial strictures that are not likely to be loosened by the current federal administration . . . the city has nonetheless committed itself to a priority program. . . ." And the city's "ambitious program to establish neighborhood family care centers throughout the city was scarcely off the drawing board when it was undermined by Medicaid cutbacks at the state and federal levels as early as 1968."[49]

The federal government has been seen as a major force in reforming health care. Yet federal activity has intensified the problems. Government agencies are not independent forces for the public interest, regulating, coordinating, mediating, and planning. Instead, government agencies are likely to become instruments for one or another part of the private sector. The Small Business Administration, for example, has been used on a number of occasions by one group of hospital interests to finance expansion, even while the Hill-Burton Agency has been financing the expansion of another nearby hospital.[50]

And at the federal level, according to Dr. James A. Shannon, former director of the National Institutes of Health, health programs are a "broadly decentralized" and "highly fragmented" set of "patchwork" activities that make it "difficult to consider broad issues in a coherent manner." These activities touch on every problem of health care and delivery "without dealing decisively with any one," he said.

Federal programs have "come into being sequentially as unbearable defects are uncovered" in private health care systems, rather than as "elements in a complete and unified system." During the Johnson administration alone, the Congress enacted fifty-one pieces of health legislation that provided for some 400 "discrete" authorities. The establishment of Regional Medical Programs in 1965 and Comprehensive Health Planning Programs in 1966 are additional cases in point. According to Dr. Shannon, elements of these two programs are in "direct conflict" with each other.[51]

As the Task Force on Medicaid put it, "The existing programs that directly influence new development or change (Partnership for Health, Regional Medical Programs, National Center for Health Services Research and Development, Maternal and Child Health, Neighborhood Health Center, Community Mental Health Centers, and Hill-Burton) have each been established by specific legislation that limits and defines eligible populations, services and the roles that demonstration, experimentation, and research can

49. Charles M. Brecher and Miriam Ostow, "Ambulatory Services," in Ginzberg et al., op. cit., pp. 155-157.

50. *Federal Role in Health,* report of the Subcommittee on Executive Reorganization and Government Research, Committee on Government Operations, U.S. Senate, 91st Cong., 2d sess., Rept. 92-809 (Washington, D.C.: U.S. Government Printing Office, 1970), pp. 25-26.

51. Ibid., pp. 18-19.

play. Consequently, each program has its own grant policies, funding cycles, and requirements for review, reporting and accounting; and any group trying to develop comprehensive health care at the local level must thread its way through a maze of multiple grant applications, multiple sets of books, and inflated administrative cost—all too often to be rewarded with fragmented assistance."[52]

According to the Rockefeller committee, at the federal, state, and local levels, there are "68 different controlling agencies in the field. . . ."[53] The U.S. Department of Health, Education and Welfare is "replete with overlapping and duplicating funding programs which not infrequently work in contradiction to each other. . . . 25 major programs within HEW, funded at a current cost of $12.7-billion . . . bear upon various aspects of the health care problem and . . . operate largely independently of each other. More importantly, many of the programs have outlived their usefulness. . . ."[54]

Also, HEW has been "too politically defensive and not sufficiently assertive. Too frequently, it reacts to individual Congressional initiative, and, in the absence of an overall health strategy of its own, fails to provide . . . leadership. . . . Many of its programs address old issues, which have been inherited from earlier days and not been re-tooled to keep abreast of contemporary needs. Overlays are put on overlays, and instead of reform and new structures, old programs are continued in their old style while new ones are added as needed—and as legislative expediency permits."[55]

Congress cannot be looked to for help. "Congress . . . many years ago succumbed to categorical 'disease' programs and patterns [and] has, by its actions and control over appropriations through a variety of subcommittees, contributed to many of the problems of fragmentation which now plague the present system."[56]

The main consequences of Medicare and Medicaid have been the same. As a prominent medical sociologist says, "Whatever the merits of Medicare and Medicaid, they impressively illustrate that to increase substantially investments in health care without altering the framework in which services are delivered will only exacerbate the inefficiencies and absurdities of the current organization of medical care in America."[57]

Given the functions performed by the basic structure of the health care system for the dominant interest groups, legislation which allegedly

52. "Task Force," op. cit., p. 29.
53. "Preliminary Report," op. cit., p. 16.
54. Ibid., p. 17.
55. Ibid., p. 33.
56. Ibid., p. 17.
57. David Mechanic, review of Barbara Ehrenreich and John Ehrenreich, *The American Health Empire: Power, Profits, and Politics,* and Selig Greenberg, *The Quality of Mercy,* in *Science* 172 (14 May 1971): 701-703.

establishes new principles of operation and explicitly is designed to change
the "system" is almost inevitably distorted in ways which reinforce the
present system. For example, in commenting on the community mental
health centers established by federal legislation in 1963, Connery *et al.* say,
"Something appears to have been lost since the community centers program
was initiated. The 'bold new approach' of 1963 shows great promise of
becoming merely an expensive expansion of decentralized facilities closely
resembling the outpatient clinics predating its adoption."[58]

But the corporate rationalizers have faith in the power of the federal
government, despite their own account of its complex and fragmented
structure. I intentionally omitted some of the optimistic rhetoric surrounding
some of the above critique. The Rockefeller committee softens its criticism of
HEW above by asserting that HEW "fails to provide the leadership it can and
should be expected to give." Elsewhere it speaks of the "vital, major role" to
be played by HEW in "helping to shape and rationalize the health care
system."[59] And the Task Force on Medicaid asserts, "We must focus these
programs around a common Federal health-service policy, coordinate
financial and administrative requirements, integrate technical services and
spend what we save on new and improved services."[60] This brave rhetoric is
nearly meaningless. Why?

The answer is that politicians have to respond to crises. The "solution": a
continuing series of new programs which promise to respond to the crisis.
When one program fails, another will be offered, sometimes by the same
incumbent party and politician, sometimes by the next incumbent who may
have been propelled into office by his promises to provide leadership which
will solve the problems his predecessor promised to solve and didn't.

Thus, each impending election produces a spate of new programs which
show either or both how much the incumbent has achieved or how much his
challenger will achieve. Given the frequency of elections and the need to
provide patronage which will solidify the support of local constituencies, each
set of officials will attempt to institutionalize his programs in a new set of
agencies. The liberals go along, and even become the main proponents of
these "solutions" because of a politically realistic, pragmatic assessment of
the situation.

Thus, new programs are sold; they become political commodities on the
electoral market. But like other commodities their exchange value for
electoral support is more important than their use value—how much actual

58. Robert H. Connery et al., *The Politics of Mental Health: Organizing Community
Mental Health in Metropolitan Areas* (New York: Columbia University Press, 1968), p.
501.

59. "Preliminary Report," op. cit., p. 33.

60. "Task Force," op. cit., p. 29.

health care is provided. Once their price has been realized in the political market, new programs lose much of their value, except insofar as something tangible must be demonstrated at the time of the next election. But what is "tangible"? An agency, a building, a staff, a budget, funds being spent, but not, unfortunately, actual improvements in health services. In fact, attempts to demonstrate actual improvements are likely to show only the discrepancy between intentions (or claims) and performance and are, therefore, politically dysfunctional.

But this description seems to contradict the oft-made point that legislatures are losing control as more and more programs become firmly embedded in bureaucratic agencies. This is true, but does not contradict my thesis. Legislatures which fund new programs are, indeed, interested in maintaining their fiscal and statutory control over as much government activity as possible. This control is steadily weakening as more and more agencies become securely established and remove bigger and bigger chunks of the budget (whether city, state, or federal) from legislative power. What accounts for this contradiction?

The interest of the legislature as a whole in maintaining control over budgets and agencies is contradicted in specific cases by the interests of a given faction within it, which wishes to turn over programs to a permanent agency, stably representing in its policies and decisions the interest of a specific constituency. As a result of logrolling between various factions within the legislature, such bills are ultimately passed in many cases. Every faction, whether liberal or conservative, wants to institutionalize its own programs—embed them in permanently funded agencies beyond the reach of "political" decisions—and prevent other factions from doing the same for their interest groups. But the consequence of continuous expansion of such bureaucratic agencies—by definition, those which are renewed or refunded with little or no debate—is to reduce the power of the legislature as a whole.

The compromise which frequently resolves this contradiction, decision by decision, is to vote to establish a new program, thus responding to constituent demands, but on a "demonstration project" or year-by-year basis. This "solution" creates additional problems for legislative operations because it means that many programs must be brought up frequently for "review," cluttering up the legislative schedule. But at the cost of much seemingly ritualistic behavior (passing renewal legislation or another biennial budget by a unanimous vote), the legislature maintains control over as much of the budget and agencies as possible. If at any time a given program loses political support, becomes a liability, or becomes too "expensive" or "obsolete," it can be cut back or eliminated.

There is one sense in which it is in the interests of legislators to create public bureaucracies. Creation of an agency is a way of getting political pressure from interest groups off their backs. Depending on the cohesion, political resources, and consistency of the demands of the interest group with the dominant institutions of the society, the new agency will be a substantive rather than symbolic response to the demands.[61]

New agencies thus simultaneously reduce the power of the legislature vis-à-vis the proliferating array of public bureaucracies, but also are a sign of the power of those majority coalitions within the legislature which succeed in establishing the agency and in providing it with the power to respond substantively to outside constituencies. The point here is that the long-range effect of the actions of legislatures is to decentralize power into a wide variety of public bureaucracies. This is a necessary form of administrative fragmentation in a pluralist system, because it reduces "demand overload" on the legislature. The various recommendations to create instrumentalities to "coordinate" and "integrate" services ignore these political functions.

The consequence at the *operating* levels of health agencies of these processes at the *legislative* level is to create continuous uncertainty among the staff. Considerable time must be diverted from program into preparation of the annual budget report, grant application, or whatever other document must demonstrate the need for continuation of the project or program. To some extent, it might seem that this need continually to justify the program would maintain the priority of the original goals which established the program. This may in some cases be true. But also likely is a concern with tangible and manifest aspects of the program, those most easily measured in quantitative terms, such as adding new staff members, spending more money, adding divisions or departments which have new names, or building offices and new facilities. None of these has any necessary relationship to the presumed goals of the organization, but forms a visible part of the description of its recent achievements. Growth, expansion, and increased complexity can all be defined as progress toward the goals.

In addition to the pressure to develop these indicators of performance, there must be a continuing escalation of the rhetoric of claims of past performance and the promises for the next period of funding. In many situations, funds will be scarce, and different agencies will be competing against each other for them. Pressure is thereby created to exaggerate both reports and plans in order to create a favorable comparison. Because the granting agency does not want to lose its own control over decisions, it is not likely to release information about how generous the available funds are in any given year, and therefore how "honest" the applying agency need be in order to compete effectively with other applying agencies. In any case, the applying

---

61. See Murray Edelman, *The Symbolic Uses of Politics* (Urbana: University of Illinois Press, 1964), and by the same author, *Politics as Symbolic Action: Mass Arousal and Quiescence* (Chicago: Markham Publishing Co., 1971), for an elaboration of this point.

agency (whether for funds, legislation, a new program, or any other authority being requested) has nothing to gain from being honest, because it never knows at what moment a revelation of the shortcomings of a program—even if clearly provable to be out of control of the staff—will be used against it by one or another faction higher in the organization which holds a different conception of the relative importance of one or another component department or agency.

This pluralistic competition exists because there can be no central control mechanism for making national health policy which is in the general or "public" interest. While legislatures have that symbolic role, they are a congeries of representatives of specific interest groups. Sometimes bureaucratic agencies are regarded as "above politics," even if legislatures cannot be, and thus are potentially able to formulate general public policy. Many reforms aim at removing decisions from the legislature or the executive and placing them in a bureaucratic agency, for the reasons and with the consequences outlined above. These efforts assume that such agencies can become neutral instruments of general interests, but ignore the continuous distortion of their substantive decisions in directions which fit the pervasive presence of private economic and social power. In fact, the more apparently separate the agency is from legislative representative institutions, the more vulnerable it is to influence from private organizations and groups, such as the doctors and the voluntary hospitals, in the case of the health system.

Given this sketchy outline of the structure and the processes by which it changes, one might imagine that it would quickly become both bottom- and top-heavy and collapse. That is, the multiplicity of organizational units and the differentiation of existing ones in response to the pressures summarized above would cause such a high level of overlapping, costs, complexity, and inaccessibility that a fantastically expensive chaos of organizations failing to accomplish their stated goals would result. At what point such a system would become politically and socially unbearable is difficult to say. We may be close to that point.

But there is at least one political mechanism which militates against this process and serves to maintain some equilibrium. Although this is not their intention, one consequence of the legislatures' maintaining veto power over agencies by not making them permanent is to allow the dying off (or the killing off) of a certain proportion of agencies, programs, and projects.[62] Some agencies are eliminated, and some projects disappear, remarkable as it seems. There may be little or no correlation between the tangible services which an agency performs and the likelihood of its not being refunded. Certainly one should not assume from the cries of agony which are raised by the staff, its clientele, or its political sponsors when an agency is in imminent

62. I am indebted to Jonathan Cole for suggesting this possibility to me.

danger of being killed that, in fact, its continuation would be the best possible use of the human and material resources involved.

But from the point of view of the continuation of the existing system, the periodic elimination of some organizations may compensate for the continuous creation of new ones. Like political regimes, bureaucratic organizations may either accumulate so many liabilities that they lose political support, or they become so rigid—so "bureaucratic" in the pejorative sense—that they are no longer able to adjust to a situation to which their political sponsors want them to respond. In that case, even if the need which generated the organization remains unfulfilled, an existing organization may be allowed to die, and a new one may be created in its place. The new one may also be, as the old one may have been, merely a symbolic response to the need. But it is a response; the organization has a fresh new name and a fresh new staff—even though their jobs may be part of political patronage—and can thus be advertised as the actions of a responsible and innovative leadership.

The life history of any organization and the interests it serves thus cannot be seen in a vacuum. The organization, no matter how seemingly securely established by law, custom, or funding, will continue to exist only so long as the coalition of interest groups who benefit from its existence continue to support it. The more stable an organization seems, say one of the great voluntary hospitals in New York City, the more likely it is that its activities are continuously serving the interests of certain groups. Emerging conflict over the existence, purpose, funding, size, location, or any other characteristic indicates that the interests the organization has been serving are withdrawing their support, becoming weaker, or being challenged. Only when there is some chance of altering the balance of power and control over the organization are other groups likely to challenge its existence or character.[63]

Consequences for Health Research

The seemingly confident factual assertions above do not rest upon well-confirmed and repeated studies of health institutions, but are only hypotheses seeking to link scattered observations. In fact, little knowledge exists about how the present system works or what alternatives might be feasible. The 1967 "Report of the National Advisory Commission on Health Manpower" concluded that "there is a serious lack of the consistent and

63. See Richard D. Alba, "Who Governs—The Power Elite? It's All in How You Define It," in *The Human Factor* (Journal of the Graduate Sociology Student Union, Columbia University) 10 (Spring 1971): 27-39, for an elaboration of this point. Although it may be obvious, it should perhaps be made more explicit that my position here directly contradicts those who assert that power is seen or manifest only in instances of conflict, and that assessment of who wins in such conflicts is an adequate measure of power.

comprehensive statistical information that is required for rational analysis and planning, despite a surfeit of numbers about health."[64] The research director of the Kaiser Foundation Hospitals in Portland, Oregon, commenting like others on the lack of significant change between 1933 and 1967, added that, although many "conferences and papers" in thirty-five years have pointed out the "need for adequate medical care research," we still do not have "comprehensive, coordinated, and reliable research, systematically carried on to help solve the many complex problems in the organization of health care services."[65]

Although the community population has a real stake in accurate information on the quality and quantity of services and their costs, and also information on a structure of controls which would be responsive to community health needs, they have no resources with which to command that information. The main information which the system generates is internal management information for billing and tax purposes, individual patient data, and research data useful for certain professional and scientific problems, but not for assessment of outputs and the performance of the organization. But outside groups cannot easily obtain even these data to analyze for their own purposes, since the data might be used to show the ways in which the various parts of the organizations fail to achieve their ostensible goals, advertised far and wide in the efforts to achieve more funds. Even if available, information could not easily be aggregated with information from other sources to estimate the causal relationships between the inputs of money and manpower from one organization to another and the outputs of tangible health services. The professional monopolists, who tend to be strategically located in data-gathering and -processing positions, also have no incentive to release information to outside groups who might challenge their power to define their own work.

Because there is *no* "system" in the sense operations researchers define it, the oft-repeated solution of better information and better communication is no solution at all. Thus, while obeisance may be made to information gathering and data processing, these symbolic claims again serve to screen the absence of the basic data which could be used to measure the character of services and the performance of organizations. For the same reasons, the data do not exist which could allow the study of the health system as a whole. Almost no studies have been done which take as problematic the structure of health-care-providing institutions—their funding, control, relationships to each other, and impact on the quality and quantity of services. Most studies

64. "Report of the National Advisory Commission on Health Manpower," 2 vols. (Washington, D.C.: U.S. Government Printing Office, 1967), 1: 4.

65. Merwyn R. Greenlick, "Imperatives of Health Services Research," *Health Services Research,* 4 (Winter 1969): 259.

of the "delivery system" focus on the utilization of health services by different income, occupational, and ethnic groups, on the socialization of physicians and nurses, or on the impact of the internal organization of a hospital upon patient care. While all of these studies can be justified in their own terms, they do not touch the core problem of the structure of the *producing* institutions, but focus instead either upon the *consumers* of health care or upon a specific institutional, organizational, or professional context in which a particular kind of care is provided. Such a paucity of studies is no accident; such studies would challenge the primary interests of both the professional monopolists and the corporate rationalizers in maintaining the structure of health institutions as they now exist and in directing its "orderly" expansion.

Crisis and the Political Economy of Health

Periodic crises, notably those in the last ten years in New York City, have been precipitated by the corporate rationalizers in an attempt to arouse support for their goals, although media exposure which defines a crisis usually has nothing to do with any change in the basic performance of the health system. The series of investigations in New York City by private, city, and state agencies from 1950 to 1971 stress the fragmentation and lack of coordination of the system, a sure sign of the ideology of corporate rationalization—as are the various reorganizations of the hospitals carried out in the last decade. But none of the reforms has touched the basic power of the private sector and its institutions.

A few crises have been precipitated by equal-health advocates moving outside the established framework of representation and influence to take disruptive, militant action. These have produced specific responses, usually in the form of new programs or still more "representation," taking the forms already described.[66]

66. See Barbara Ehrenreich and John Ehrenreich, *The American Health Empire: Power, Profits and Politics* (New York: Vintage Books, 1971), a publication of the activist New York group Health-PAC, for a similar perspective, although the authors are more optimistic about the prospects for and consequences of militant community action isolated from broader movements than my argument would lead me to be. Michael Halberstam, "Liberal Thought, Radical Theory, and Medical Practice," *The New England Journal of Medicine* 284 (27 May 1971): 1180-1185, criticizes the "radical" position on health care for essentially accepting the position I have called "bureaucratic reform." Interestingly, this criticism would apply also to the proposals advanced by Robb Burlage, one of the founders of Health-PAC. (See his *New York City's Municipal Hospitals: A Policy Review* [Washington, D.C.: Institute for Policy Studies, 1967].) Halberstam, an M.D. himself, stresses the importance of reducing alienation and depersonalization and believes that only committed individual responsibility to a patient by a health professional can provide such personalized care. In this respect the "radical" position

Both market and bureaucratic reformers are likely to be upper middle class in their social origins, incomes, and occupational prestige, and thus they share an interest in moderating conflict and blunting "community" demands even if they are bitterly divided among themselves over the timing and scope of reforms. Noisy debate conceals an underlying unity of commitment to working through existing political channels, which may account for the unwillingness of the bureaucratic reformers—visibly more dissatisfied with the present organization of health care—to mobilize potential allies with the rhetoric and political tactics which could generate an effective movement for change. The ambiguous analyses of the various investigations recommending "coordination" and "planning"—and the fatal compromises which result (as in the case of the Health and Hospitals Corporation in New York City)—are the ideological corollary of a political commitment not to challenge the essential power of the professional monopolists.[67]

As Eli Ginzberg put it, "Each of the major parties insists that its essential power remain undiminished as a result of any contemplated large-scale change. . . . Inherent in pluralism is an overwhelming presumption in favor of incremental rather than large-scale reforms."[68]

An explanation of the deep-rooted character of the dynamics without change must thus ultimately go back to the dominance of the private sector and the upper middle class. As Ginzberg also says, "The industry remains dominated by the private sector—consumers, private practitioners, voluntary hospitals."[69] Thus, a major characteristic of the public sector is that it does not have the power to challenge the domination of the private sector. Given this domination, it seems a reasonable assumption that major characteristics of the health system are due to private control. Government policy is not fundamentally important, except insofar as the policy is *not* to interfere with the private sector, or only to come forth with financial subsidies for the private sector.

To say this does not mean that *any* program which increases the government's role will be an advance since any specific government policy

---

exhibits a curious schizophrenia between a faith in the potential rationality of large-scale organization and a faith in the redeeming power of community control. Perhaps the two can be reconciled, but there have been few serious efforts to think through the problem.

67. See Edmund O. Rothschild, "The Level of Health Care in Municipal Hospitals Is Shocking," *New York Times,* 27 November 1971, p. 131, for the most recent surfacing of the same old situation in the New York City hospitals, allegedly to be cured by the bureaucratic reforms recommended by the Piel Commission (op. cit.), including the Corporation. Rothschild was at the time he wrote the article an attending physician at Memorial Hospital for Cancer and a member of the board of directors of the Corporation.

68. Ginzberg et al., op. cit., p. 226.

69. Ibid.

may reaffirm the dominance of the private sector, provide additional subsidies for it, or further institutionalize the dichotomy between the public and private sectors. It would be possible, for example, to separate the public sphere of subsidies for the poor, or even government-owned clinics and hospitals, even further from the private sector; and this could be advertised as a step forward in public support for health services for the poor. But if the results were further to insulate the private sector from public mechanisms of funding and control, to set up new public institutions subject to the vacillating funding already discussed, and, further, to perpetuate a two-class system of care, these alleged reforms might be better regarded as a setback.

It is important to emphasize that Ginzberg in the quotation above includes the "consumers" as part of the private sector. If the upper middle-class consumers of the health care provided by fee-for-service practitioners and hospitals are, in fact, securing most of the medical services they need, then these particular consumers have no incentive to change the system, and, in fact, have compelling incentives to keep it the way it is. From their point of view, the only result of a merger of the private with the public sectors would be to *reduce* their capacity to buy care, because their access to the medical and hospital market would be restricted. And this would be most true for the richest consumers. If there were a move to open up the best hospitals and the best surgeons to the public on the basis of need rather than on the basis of the ability to purchase care, the only possible result would be to reduce their access to the market, unless the supply of manpower, beds, and machines were expanded to the point where all, regardless of income, had access to equivalent care. That, of course, would be enormously expensive.

For this reason, intrinsically related to the class structure of American society, the vision of merging the two systems—having only one set of offices, clinics, hospitals, beds, wards—is undoubtedly utopian. The symbiosis of upper middle-class consumers of health care, their private physicians, and their voluntary hospitals, constitutes a coalition of interest groups too strong to be defeated by hospital reorganization, comprehensive health planning legislation, or new neighborhood health centers—if the goal is equality of health care.

Given a system which cannot provide decent care for all because of the domination by the private sector, and thus a continuing "crisis," there is increasing pressure upon government to step in. But, again, because of the dominance of the private sector, government cannot act in a way which could change the system without altering the basic principle of private control over the major resources of the society. Thus, the health system exhibits a continuous contradiction between the expectations of the people for decent health care, the impossibility of the private sector to provide decent and *equal* health care for all, and the impossibility of the public sector to compensate for the inadequacies of the private sector.

Conclusions

To summarize and conclude the argument, the "crisis" of health care is *not* a result of the necessary competition of diverse interests, groups, and providers in a pluralistic and competitive health economy, nor a result of bureaucratic inefficiencies to be corrected by yet more layers of administration established by government policy. Rather, the conflicts between the professional monopolists—seeking to erect barriers to protect their control over research, teaching, and care—and the corporate rationalizers—seeking to extend their control over the organization of services—account for many of the aspects of health care summarized above.

These conflicts stem, in turn, from a fundamental contradiction in modern health care between the character of the technology of health care and the private appropriation of the power and resources involved. Health care, from the point of view of the most advanced technology, is a complex division of labor, requiring highly specialized knowledge at some points, routine screening at others, highly personalized individual care at still others. The integration of all aspects of the health care system—preventive care, outpatient checkups, routine treatment for specific minor illnesses, specialized treatment for rare diseases requiring expensive machines, long-term care for chronic conditions—would require the defeat or consolidation of the social power that has been appropriated by various discrete interest groups and that preserves existing allocations of social values and resources. Government is not an independent power standing above and beyond the competing interest groups.

An institutional and class structure creates and sustains the power of the professional monopolists and the corporate rationalizers. Dynamics are likely to continue in the direction proposed by the latter coalition. Change is not likely without the presence of a social and political movement which rejects the legitimacy of the economic and social base of pluralist politics.

Part Two

Comparative Perspectives on Contemporary Politics

A section on comparative politics in this reader makes sense only in the most superficial terms, i.e., that some of the articles published in *Politics and Society* deal with international affairs and with the domestic politics of societies other than the United States. Put another way, a section on comparative politics conforms to that rather uninsightful, historically rooted division of the American political science curriculum into "American" and "Comparative" politics. As if politics in other societies was carried on in some other way than it is in the United States, which allowed American social scientists, in their *hubris,* to lump the rest of the world together. Perhaps placing these three articles together will help erode that pernicious distinction, since each in its own way is critical of the failure of much of social science to interpret and understand political developments abroad.

Susanne Jonas focuses on the constraints the United States imposes on the development of Latin American countries. She points to their dependency on the United States as an explanation for the nature of their economic underdevelopment. The article is one of the first efforts in English that presents the ideas of a school of Latin American scholars who examine their continent as part of the nexus of advanced capitalist economies. She connects their work to an analysis of the process by which these ties are enforced through the cultivation of a local bourgeoisie dependent on the United States. In doing this she considers the larger question of how monopolistic enterprise in advanced capitalist countries operates to widen the gap between wealthy and poor nations.

Her analysis consequently transcends an approach that focuses on control as a fixed goal to be achieved in the face of diverse situations. The seemingly diverse situations are in fact systemically created by the structure of dependency in which Latin American countries locate themselves. Internal mechanisms of domination by the local bourgeoisie are not rooted in national sovereignty as traditional development theorists tell us, but in contradictions created by dependency relations which exploit the lower classes.

P. Allum's article is an effort to understand the dual way in which Neapolitan parliamentarians in postwar Italy operate. He finds that they acted in an arena characteristic of a *Gesellschaft,* of modern society (a modern parliament), while representing a *gemeinschaft* constituency, that is, traditional Naples. The theoretical perspective is both Weberian and Marxist. Allum finds that the politicians tended to come from the intelligentsia (law, teaching), and "not having anything else to do" (Salvemini), become parliamentarians. Once in parliament, they become bosses, preaching the general good to the Chamber and to their constituents, while thriving on the machine and the particularistic favor. Since they lack "roots in the real force of a social class" (Croce), they become agents of the ruling class in Italy, maintaining order in a time of transition from one form of society to another.

Allum thus explores the nature of control in a capitalist society with a partially unintegrated preindustrial subculture. The political institutions designed to service the needs of the advanced capitalist sector of the Italian economy compose the arena for men (few women) whose major task is to ensure that the preindustrial lower classes are kept in line. Hortatory orations are part of the myth-making process that seeks to link these masses' loyalty to the state. Private favors ensure this loyalty through direct purchase. Aristide Zolberg's apparently divergent article also touches on the theme of domination and social control. He focuses on moments when dominant classes had so routinized their politics and their mechanisms of control that new classes were able to make a perceptual break with the predominant ideology, because in his words, they were "bored." The moment of revolution, in this case France in 1848, is a moment of consciousness. People, workers, women, students— each became conscious of their oneness with their own kind and with other dominated groups. Although none of these moments sustained a level of consciousness, each left a contribution behind in terms of the evolution of society, or, perhaps, in terms of the ability of the new dominant class to control and to stave off the next revolutionary moment.

With a new dominant class, control takes on new forms. When

seen in this light, the loss of control by the former dominant class —that is, revolution—is not pathology but an integral part of the development of a country's political and social system. Beyond this, Zolberg also focuses our attention on the ties between art and political upheaval. Periods of upheaval seem to be related to times when creative or expressive elements of a society flourish.

Thus, on an underlying level, one theme reappears in all these articles: the maintenance and breakdown of mechanisms of social control in capitalist societies. Jonas deals most directly with the domestic (internal) mechanisms of domination and control (the compliant, national bourgeoisie) and the international mechanisms that are in charge. Control is constantly sought by rulers, devices to maintain it are constantly changed and developed, and new internal contradictions develop which risk upheaval (e.g., unemployed lower classes in Latin America).

Of course, this is also the general theme of the material discussed in section I on American politics. Hence, if this section demonstrates anything, it is that comparative politics and political science must be synonymous.

6. Dependency and Imperialism: The Roots of Latin American Underdevelopment

SUSANNE JONAS

> To overcome the injury done by [past United States] interventions [in Latin America], and to demonstrate that, while we strongly oppose communism, we nevertheless favor internal reforms essential to the rapid economic development of Latin America, the United States launched the much-publicized Alliance for Progress. The concept was novel, even noble. It was based on the belief that governments in Latin America, wherever necessary, would undertake fundamental land and tax reforms with a helping hand from the United States. Seven years later, the failure of that experiment must be acknowledged.... The faith we placed in the Alliance for Progress as an effective instrument for bringing about fundamental change must certainly represent the high-water mark of American innocence abroad.[1]
>
> — Senator Frank Church

> There is general frustration [in Latin America] over the failure to achieve a more rapid improvement in standards of living. The United States, because of its identification with the failure of the Alliance for Progress to live up to expectations, is blamed....[2]
>
> — Governor Nelson Rockefeller

Nine years ago any critic of the Alliance for Progress was dismissed as a cynic, a malicious troublemaker, or worse yet, a Communist. Today such criticism has become so respectable that these statements by Senator Church, the disillusioned liberal, and Nelson Rockefeller, the corporate hard-liner, came as no surprise to anyone, and caused hardly a ripple in Washington.

Quite aside from statements like these, there is far more eloquent testimony to the failure of the Alliance to promote development much less to achieve its stated objective of peaceful social and economic revolution in Latin America:

1. U.S. Sen. Frank Church, "U.S. and Latin America—Call for a New Policy," speech, 11 September 1969, reprinted in *Congressional Record,* 11 November 1969.
2. Nelson Rockefeller, "Letter to the President," in *The Rockefeller Report on the Americas* (Chicago: Quadrangle Books, 1969), p. 9.

1. Annual average growth rates during the 1960s were lower than those of the previous decade, and fell far short of the target (2.5 percent per capita) established in 1961;[3]

2. Social problems such as urban poverty, unemployment, and inequality of income distribution have been aggravated rather than resolved: e.g., while average per capita income is $410, the lower half of the population receives an average of $120, and the top 5 percent of the population receives $2600;[4] UN agencies estimate present equivalent unemployment to be about 25 percent of the labor force;[5]

3. The serious agrarian and tax reforms envisioned in 1961 have not been made: e.g., in no country other than Venezuela was more than 10 percent of the rural population resettled through agrarian reform;[6]

4. Given the declining value of Latin American exports, and the rising prices of goods imported by the region, Latin America faces an increasingly serious balance of payments crisis and a "virtual commercial deficit" in the coming decade.[7]

These examples indicate the magnitude of Latin America's underdevelopment problems (as characterized by declining growth rates, increasing poverty relative to the developed nations, worsening distribution of income and resources, and absolute impoverishment of certain sectors of the population, such as the Indian peasants in a number of countries),[8] and the failure of the Alliance to cope with these problems in terms of its own rhetoric and *stated* goals.

How can this failure be explained? American policy makers and social

3. U.N. Economic Commission for Latin America (CEPAL), *El Segundo Decenio de las Naciones Unidas para el Desarrollo: Aspectos Básicos de la Estrategia del Dessarrollo de America Latina* (Lima: CEPAL, 4-23 April 1969), pp. 7 ff.; and summary of report, *New York Times,* 20 April 1969; Keith Griffin, *Underdevelopment in Spanish America* (London: Allen & Unwin, 1969); pp. 54 ff.

4. CEPAL, *El Segundo Decenio,* op. cit., p. 12.

5. U.N. figures, cited by André Gunder Frank, "The Underdevelopment Policy of the United Nations in Latin America," *NACLA Newsletter,* December 1969, p. 7.

6. Simon Hanson, "The Alliance for Progress: The Sixth Year," *Inter-American Economic Affairs,* Winter 1968, p. 54 (taken from House Appropriations Subcommittee Hearings for 1969).

7. CEPAL, *Los Déficit Virtuales de Comercio y de Ahorro Interno y la Desocupación Estructural de América Latina* (Santiago: CEPAL), p. 45.

8. For the moment I shall adopt the commonly accepted notion of development as entailing overall economic growth and some measure of social welfare and restribution of income and resources to the benefit of the lower classes. I do so in order to establish some common ground for discussion with American policy makers and social scientists, and thereby to demonstrate the poverty of their analyses and strategies for resolving the problem as they define it. This in no way obviates the need to establish a new and more appropriate definition of development—as some have already done, (e.g., Paul Baran, *The Political Economy of Growth* [New York: Monthly Review, 1957], pp. 136, 164, 226 ff.)

scientists have devised endless ad hoc explanations. It has been said, for instance, that the United States did not send enough aid; the Latin governments failed to carry out their end of the bargain; inefficient use has been made of aid resources; extraneous factors (such as the fall in Latin export commodity prices) counteracted the benefits of the Alliance; and so on, ad infinitum. But in the first place, these "explanations" may be refuted partly on empirical grounds: e.g., the United States has authorized well over the one billion dollars per year pledged in 1961.[9] Second, to the extent that they have any factual basis, these "reasons" do not really *explain* anything. They shed little light, for example, on *why* the Latin governments have not carried out the necessary structural reforms. In the end, these sorts of explanations are unsatisfactory for one basic reason: they are based on the very same premises which gave rise to the Alliance in the first place. In short, the possibility is never considered that the basic assumptions and theories underlying the Alliance are themselves invalid—that in a very real sense, the failure of the Alliance to resolve the underdevelopment problems of Latin America reflects the bankruptcy of American theories for analyzing those problems.

Rather than listing and criticizing, point-by-point, the various theories devised by American social scientists to explain Latin underdevelopment (as I have done elsewhere),[10] I shall focus here upon the principal distortion underlying all of these theories: the failure—perhaps the refusal—to examine Latin America in terms of its relationship to the advanced industrial nations, particularly the United States. Most American social scientists have evaded this task either by (1) treating Latin countries as self-contained units, whose economic, social, or political systems can be analyzed in themselves;[11] or (2) arguing (or assuming) that the contact between Latin America and the advanced industrial nations has been such as to stimulate development in Latin America.[12] In both cases the fundamental problem of Latin underdevelopment is obscured. The first is a "closed-system" analysis, which ignores the basic condition of Latin society: its integration into an

9. Hanson, op. cit., p. 42.

10. Susanne Bodenheimer, "The Ideology of Developmentalism: American Political Science's Paradigm-Surrogate for Latin American Studies," *Berkeley Journal of Sociology,* 1970.

11. See, for example, the work of structural functionalists such as Gabriel Almond; see critique by Ralf Dahrendorf, "Out of Utopia," *American Journal of Sociology,* September 1958.

12. For the argument that foreign investment and aid stimulate development, see for example, W.W. Rostow, *The Stages of Economic Growth* (London: Cambridge University Press, 1962), pp. 142-43; Rostow and Max Millikan, *A Proposal* (New York: Harper, 1957), p. 56; Claude McMillan and Richard Gonzales, *International Enterprise in a Developing Economy* (Lansing, Mich.: Michigan State University Press, 1964); selections by Frederic Bonham and others in Gerald Meier, ed., *Leading Issues in Development Economics* (New York: Oxford University Press, 1964), pp. 131 ff.

international environment in which the developed nations prevail. The second, which maintains or assumes that there has been a net inflow of capital from the developed nations into Latin America (through foreign investment and aid) and that the region has benefited from that inflow, flies directly in the face of the facts.[13]

Recognition of this distortion in existing theories leads directly to the starting point for a critical analysis of Latin underdevelopment. *Latin America is today, and has been since the sixteenth century, part of an international system dominated by the now-developed nations, and Latin underdevelopment is the outcome of a particular series of relationships to that international system.* It is this thesis which will be developed in the dependency-imperialism model presented here.[14]

13. It has been shown in a number of studies that foreign investment by the U.S. and other industrial nations in underdeveloped areas has resulted in a net outflow of capital from the underdeveloped to the developed nations, a decapitalization of the former. In a number of Latin countries and for the region as a whole, the input from foreign private investment has been far exceeded by the outflow of profit remittances abroad. (According to U.S. Department of Commerce figures, the outflow from Latin America was $7.5 billion greater than inflow from 1950 to 1965.) This drain through foreign investment is aggravated by the clear deterioration of the terms of trade for the Latin nations and of their position in world trade. (Between 1950 and 1968 Latin America's share of world trade shrank from 11 percent to 5.1 percent) Foreign aid has become continually more "tied" to conditions imposed by creditor nations to meet their own balance of payments difficulties or to accomodate private business interests. Service (interest and amortization) payments on the foreign debt, as well as the flow of profits abroad, continue to mount in Latin nations, and consume an ever-increasing share of export earnings (now more than 35 percent for the region as a whole). By the mid-1960s the total paid by Latin countries in debt service payments exceeded the amount of new loans, and at the end of the decade the external debt had doubled since 1960. (These figures are taken from: Frank, "Sociology of Development and Underdevelopment of Sociology," *Catalyst,* Summer 1967, pp. 46-49; Frank, *Capitalism and Underdevelopment in Latin America* (New York: Monthly Review, 1967); Keith Griffin and Ricardo French-Davis, "El Capital Extranjero y el Desarrollo," *Revista Económica,* 1964, pp. 16-22; Luis Vitale, "Latin America: Feudal or Capitalist?," in James Petras and Maurice Zeitlin, eds., *Latin America: Reform or Revolution?* (Greenwich, Conn.: Fawcett, 1968); Maurice Halperin, "Growth and Crisis in the Latin American Economy," in Petras and Zeitlin, op. cit.; Griffin, op. cit., pp. 144-45; CEPAL, *Estudio Económico de América Latina* (annual) (Santiago: CEPAL); U.N. Dept. of Economic and Social Affairs, *Foreign Capital in Latin America* (New York: United Nations, 1955), p. 15; Harry Magdoff, "Economic Aspects of U.S. Imperialism," *Monthly Review,* November, 1966; U.S. Department of Commerce data (*Balance of Payments Statistical Supplements, Surveys of Current Business*); CEPAL, *El Segundo Decenio,* op. cit., p. 9; Miguel Wionczek, "El Endeudamiento Publico Externo y la Inversión Privada Extranjera en América Latina," mimeographed. Paper presented to Consejo Latinoamericano de Ciencias Sociales, Lima, October, 1968, p. 6.

14. It should be understood at the outset that this model is not a "finished" paradigm. My intention here is not to present conclusive proof for each proposition on which the model is based; to do so would require an entire book. Rather, the purpose of a model such as this is to suggest the importance of certain aspects of Latin under-

A. *The Dependency Model*

The basic premises of the dependency model, as first elaborated by a group of Latin American social scientists,[15] differ sharply from those of American social science development theories. "Dependency" is conceived as a "conditioning situation," i.e., one which "determines the limits and possibilities for human action and conduct"[16]—in this case, for development in Latin America. We shall accept the definition of dependency as

> a situation in which the economy of a certain group of countries is conditioned by the development and expansion of another economy, to which their own [economy] is subjected:... an historical condition which shapes a certain structure of the world economy such that it favors some countries to the detriment of others, and limits the development possibilities of the [subordinate] economies....[17]

What does this mean? That Latin America has fulfilled certain definite functions in the "world economy" or world market, and the domestic development of Latin America has been limited or conditioned by the needs of the dominant economies within that world market. To be sure, no nation has ever developed entirely outside the context of the world market nor does any nation operate without constraints upon policy choices. The distinguishing feature of dependent (as contrasted with interdependent) development is that growth in the dependent nations occurs as a reflex of the

---

development which have hitherto been ignored or distorted by American social scientists, and thus to reorient the specific questions asked and subjects investigated by Latin-Americanists. The ultimate validity of this model cannot be determined a priori, but will be judged rather on the basis of its utility for the analysis of concrete situations and problems in Latin America.

Although the two aspects of the model, dependency and imperialism, will be discussed separately, it should be understood that they are not basically separable from each other. They are two perspectives or emphases for understanding the same phenomenon: the international system. As presented here, the dependency model requires separate consideration insofar as it investigates the impact of imperialism upon the Latin American nations in more detail than most of the classical theories of imperialism have done (with some exceptions).

15. The specific impetus for the dependency theorists was their increasing dissatisfaction with an earlier Latin American model (that of the U.N. Economic Commission for Latin America, CEPAL), and particularly its failure to explain the economic stagnation and aggravation of social problems in Latin America during the 1960s. (See below, Section B.) Although my account of the dependency model is taken largely from the work of these Latin Americans, they should not be held responsible for those elements (e.g., the infrastructure of dependency) which I have added here.

16. Theotonio Dos Santos, "Crisis de la Teoría del Desarrollo y las Relaciones de Dependencia en América Latina," reprint from *Boletín del CESO,* October-November 1968, p. 28.

17. Ibid., pp. 26, 29.

expansion of the dominant nations,[18] and is geared toward the needs of the dominant economies—i.e., foreign rather than national needs. In the dependent countries, imported factors of production (e.g., capital and technology) have become the central determinants of economic development and sociopolitical life. And while the world market served as an instrument of expansion in European and American development, it restricts autonomous development in the dependent nations.[19] This historical dependency has been associated with underdevelopment in Latin America and can be shown in concrete cases to cause underdevelopment (i.e., insufficient growth, and unchanging or worsening income distribution).

Dependency means, then, that the development alternatives open to the dependent nation are defined and limited by its integration into and functions within the world market. This limitation of alternatives differs from limitations in the dominant nations insofar as the functioning of and basic decisions in the world market—to take only the most obvious example, with respect to commodity prices and terms of trade—are determined by the dominant nations. Thus the dependent nations must make choices in a situation in which they do not set the terms or parameters of choice.

Before proceeding any farther, we must clarify the concrete meaning of the "world market" and the "international system." By itself, the world market encompasses all flows of goods and services among nations outside the Communist trade bloc—all capital transfers (including foreign aid and overseas investment) and all commodity exchanges. But the world market is the core of a broader "international system": this international system includes not only a network of economic (market) relations, but also the entire complex of political, military, social, and cultural international relations organized by and around that market (e.g., the Monroe Doctrine, the Organization of American States, "Free World" defense treaties and organizations, and media and communications networks). The international system is the static expression and outcome of a dynamic historical process: the transnational or global expansion of capitalism.

By focusing on the international system, the dependency model takes as its point of departure a concrete datum which has conditioned Latin American history: that since the Spanish conquest—that is, since its existence as Latin American, as opposed to indigenous Indian, society—Latin America has played a certain role in the political economy of one or another dominant capitalist nation (Spain and Portugal in the colonial and early post-independence period, England during most of the nineteenth century, and the United States since the beginning of the twentieth century). Thus the Latin economies have always been shaped by the global expansion and

18. Ibid., p. 26.
19. Pablo González-Casanova, *Sociología de la Explotación* (Mexico: Siglo XXI, 1969, pp. 275-78.

consolidation of the capitalist system, and by their own incorporation into that system.[20] In this sense, Latin societies "brought into existence with their birth" their relation to the international system, and hence their relations of dependency.[21]

Although the particular function of Latin America in the international system has varied, the development of that region has been shaped since the Spanish conquest by a general structural characteristic of capitalist expansion—its unevenness.[22] "Unevenness" means that some nations or regions have developed more rapidly than, and often at the expense of, others. For Latin America this has entailed increasing relative poverty, as the gap in income and growth rates between the industrial nations and Latin America is constantly widening. (Since 1957, for example, the growth rate of per capita income in Latin America has been less than 1.5 percent a year, as contrasted with nearly 2.5 percent in the United States and 4 percent in Europe.)[23] Similar disparities have marked the uneven development of various regions within Latin America.

This unevenness has been manifested through an "international division of labor": while Western Europe and the United States industrialized, Latin America remained for centuries an exporter of primary raw materials and agricultural products. And even the faltering steps toward industrialization more recently have not altered the fundamentally complementary character of the Latin economies: the industrial sectors remain dependent on imports (of capital goods) and, as a result of the increasing foreign control over these sectors, growth is still governed largely by the needs of foreign economies. The international division of labor has persisted; only its form has changed.[24] Thus complementarity is not incidental but essential to the Latin economies. Moreover, the tendency in capitalist development is to attract the factors of

20. Thus underdevelopment in Latin America may be distinguished from the situation of "underdeveloped" societies, the latter referring to "the situation of those economies and peoples—ever more scarce—which have no market relations with the industrialized nations" (Fernando Cardoso and Enzo Faletto, *Dependencia y Desarrollo en América Latina* [Mexico: Siglo XXI, 1969]).

21. Aníbal Quijano, "Dependencia, Cambio Social y Urbanización en Latinoamérica" (Santiago: CEPAL, 1967), mimeographed, p. 5; see also Tomas Vasconi, "Cultura, Ideologia, Dependencia, y Alienación," in Jose Matos Mar, ed., *La Crisis del Desarrollismo y la Nueva Dependencia* (Lima: Moncloa, 1969), p. 145.

22. V.I. Lenin, *Imperialism, The Highest Stage of Capitalism* (Peking: Foreign Languages Press, 1965), pp. 72-73; David Horowitz, *Empire and Revolution* (New York: Random House, 1969), p. 42.

23. Griffin, op. cit., pp. 62, 265.

24. A recent call for a "more efficient" and "broadening" division of labor among the nations of the Western Hemisphere came in the Rockefeller Report [p. 102]—the argument being that "everyone"—both Latin America and the U.S.—"gains in the process." For Rockefeller, of course, Latin dependency and lack of autonomy (and consequent underdevelopment) is clearly an un-problem.

production (e.g., capital and skilled labor) away from the less developed areas, toward the more developed areas.[25] Thus, intensified contact with the more advanced capitalist nations produced underdevelopment in Latin America. And thus, as has been widely recognized, the periods of relative growth and development in Latin America (e.g., industrialization during the 1930s) have occurred during the phases of relative contraction in the world market (for example, during periods of international war or depression), when the region's ties to that market and to the dominant nations have been weakest.[26] Politically as well, Latin American development has been limited by the fact that policy decisions about resource allocation and all aspects of national development are conditioned, and options limited, by the interests of the developed societies.[27]

From the foregoing, it becomes clear that underdevelopment in Latin America is structurally linked to development in the dominant nations. European and American development and Latin underdevelopment are not two isolated phenomena, but rather two outcomes of the same historical process: the global expansion of capitalism.

Insofar as Latin American development has been limited since the sixteenth century by fulfilling one or another function in the international system, the *fact* of dependency has been a constant. But the *forms* of dependency in particular countries, at particular historical moments have varied, according to the specific characteristics of the international system at that time, and the specific functions of the Latin country within the system.

1. Characteristics of the international system, for example:

   a. The prevalent form of capitalism (mercantile or industrial, corporate or financial);

   b. The principal needs of the dominant nation(s) in the international system (agricultural commodities, minerals, cheap labor, commodity markets, capital markets, etc.);

   c. The degree of concentration of capital in the dominant nation(s) (competitive or monopolistic capitalism);

   d. The degree of concentration internationally (one hegemonic power or rival powers and, if one hegemonic power, which nation [Spain, England, or the United States]);

   e. Characteristics of world trade (mercantilism, "free trade," or protectionism).

25. Griffin, op. cit., p. 272.

26. Ibid., pp. 269-70; Albert Hirschman, "The Political Economy of Import-Substituting Industrialization in Latin America," *Quarterly Journal of Economics,* February 1968, p. 4; A. Kafka, "The Theoretical Interpretation of Latin American Economic Development," in H.S. Ellis, ed., *Economic Development for Latin America,* p. 8; Frank, *Capitalism and Underdevelopment,* op. cit., chap. 1 and passim.

27. Cardoso and Faletto, op. cit., Osvaldo Sunkel, "Política Nacional de Desarrollo y Dependencia Externa," *Estudios Internacionales,* April, 1967, p. 57.

2. Degree and nature of the Latin country's ties to and function within the international system, for example:

a. Its function primarily as a supplier of raw materials or agricultural products, as a market for manufactured goods, as a supplier of certain manufactured commodities, as an arena for direct foreign investment, or any combination of the preceding;

b. The degree of relative autonomy (periods of international war or depression vs. "normal" periods of capitalist expansion);

c. The degree of foreign control in the principal economic sectors;

d. The nature of political tie to the dominant power(s) (colonial or nominal independence).

The specific forms of dependency in Latin America in any given historical period are shaped by the characteristics of the international system and of Latin America's function within it. Latin America was first integrated into the international system in its mercantile phase, under Spanish dominance, and served primarily as a provider of raw materials and agricultural commodities. Thus dependency during the colonial period and during much of the nineteenth century was manifested primarily through the development of export-import "enclaves." The conditions which shape Latin dependency today are quite distinct. The international system today is characterized by advanced industrial capitalism (corporate integrated with financial capital); the dominant nations' need for raw materials and, more important, for commodity and capital markets; monopolistic concentration of capital; American hegemony (vis-à-vis Latin America); and increasing international integration of capital. Trade within the international system is increasingly protectionist (tariffs or quotas imposed by the dominant nations) and is increasingly incorporated within the structure of the multinational corporations. Latin America's function within the system is shifting from a supplier of raw materials and agricultural commodities to an arena where certain phases of industrial production are carried out—but still under the auspices of foreign corporations.[28] The degree of foreign control in the principal economic sectors is increasing; and more generally Latin America's integration into the orbit of the dominant capitalist nations is becoming more complete, despite nominal political independence.

These characteristics of the international system and of Latin America's function within it impose definite limitations on the possibilities for Latin development. Nevertheless, it would be an oversimplification to maintain that the international system causes underdevelopment directly; it does so indirectly, by generating and reinforcing within Latin America an *infrastructure of dependency*. What is the infrastructure (internal structures)

28. The proportion of U.S. private investment directed toward the industrial sector in Latin America has risen from 35 percent in 1951 to 60 percent in 1962. (CEPAL, *External Financing in Latin America* (New York: United Nations, 1965), p. 215).

of dependency? The international system affects development in Latin America by means of certain institutions, social classes, and processes (industrial structure, socioeconomic elites, urbanization, and so on). These aspects of Latin society become part of the infrastructure of dependency when they function or occur in a manner that responds to the interests or needs of the dominant powers in the international system, rather than to national interests or needs. It is through the infrastructure of dependency that the international system becomes operative within Latin America. And it is through the infrastructure of dependency that the legacy of Latin America's integration into the international system is transmitted and perpetuated within Latin America, thereby limiting the possibilities for development,[29] and thereby generating structural underdevelopment.

Let us take two examples of the infrastructure of dependency.[30]

1. Industrialization in the broadest sense implies far more than the construction of new factories and the production or processing of commodities. In many Latin nations the industrial sector has become central to the national economy; even in those nations which are still predominantly agricultural (as in Central America), industry is becoming an important factor in shaping decisions about the entire economy. In addition the quality of industrialization is integrally related to political decision making, social structure, urbanization, and so on. Industrialization is not by nature dependent; it becomes part of the infrastructure of dependency when the industrial structure is integrated into and complementary to the needs of foreign economies. Some specific characteristics of dependent industrialization are (1) increasing foreign control over the most dynamic and strategic industrial sectors (through direct ownership and control over production, control of marketing and distribution, or control of patents and licenses): in many sectors foreign corporations have been buying out formerly national industries;[31] (2) increasing competitive advantages for (often

29. Analytically it may be conceived in terms of successive limitations on the possibilities for development: while the international system establishes the general limits within which development is possible, the particular possibilities within these limits are redefined on the concrete level by the infrastructure of dependency. Schematically, the infrastructure becomes the intervening variable through which the international system affects development.

30. These examples—dependent industrialization and clientele classes—are two of the most salient, but by no means the only, examples of the infrastructure of dependency. Similar analyses have been made of dependent urbanization (see Quijano, op. cit.) and of the dependent or comprador state (see, for example, Marcos Kaplan, "Estado, Dependencia Externa, y Desarrollo en América Latina," in Matos Mar, op. cit.; Dos Santos, "Dependencia Económica y Alternativas de Cambio en America Latina," mimeographed.

31. CEPAL, *El Desarrollo Industrial de América Latina* (Santiago: CEPAL), p. 47; for a good case study of Brazil, see Dos Santos, "El Nuevo Caracter de la Dependencia" (Santiago: Centro de Estudios Socio-Economicos, CESO, 1968).

monopolistic) foreign enterprises over local firms, particularly in industries of scale;[32] (3) as a result of foreign ownership, outflow of capital (profits) abroad; (4) despite some production for the internal market, continued adaptation of the economic structure to the specialized needs of the buyers of Latin exports in the dominant nations; (5) introduction of advanced, capital-intensive foreign technology, without regard to size or composition of the local labor market, and consequent aggravation of unemployment[33] (which in turn results in restriction of the domestic market): in several countries (e.g., Chile, Colombia, Peru) employment in manufacturing industries actually declined as a percentage of total employment between 1925 and 1960);[34] (6) also as a result of foreign control over technology, its restriction to those sectors in which foreign capital has a direct interest; (7) lack of a domestic capital goods industry in most countries and, consequently, an increased rather than reduced dependence on imports, and rigidities in the composition of imports; (8) a high porportion of (generally foreign-owned) "industries" which really do no more than assemble or mix imported components, and in which, therefore, the local employment and other economic benefits generated are minimal. Thus, dependent industrialization has aggravated rather than resolved such basic problems as balance of payments deficits, unemployment, income disparities, and an insufficient domestic market.

2. Intersecting the process of dependent industrialization is another, equally fundamental, dimension of dependency; the creation and/or reinforcement of clientele social classes.[35] Clientele classes are those which have a vested interest in the existing international system. These classes carry out certain functions on behalf of foreign interests; in return they enjoy a privileged and increasingly dominant and hegemonic position within their own societies, based largely on economic, political, or military support from abroad. In this sense the clientele classes come to play in Latin America today the role historically performed by the comprador bourgeoisie (export-import mercantile elites, whose strength, interests, and very existence were derived from their function in the world market). Like their behavior, the ideologies of these classes reflect their dual position as junior partners of metropolitan

32. González-Casanova, op. cit., pp. 277 ff.

33. Quijano, op. cit ., p. 32; González-Casanova, op. cit., pp. 286-87; Griffin, op. cit., p. 57.

34. Cardoso and J.L. Royna, "Industrialización, Estructura Ocupacional y Estratificación Social en América Latina," mimeographed (Santiago: 1966), p. 13.

35. Without getting into an extensive discussion of what is meant by "social class," it should nevertheless be understood that the concept of "class" does not refer simply to one-dimensional income, occupational, "status" or "interest" groups. Membership in a particular class implies, in addition to a certain level of income, etc., a "mode of life" and a structural position in relation to other classes in the society, giving rise to a class consciousness, to class interests, and to sharp struggles with other classes.

interests, yet dominant elites within their own societies.[36] The clearest
example of clientele classes today are those elements of the Latin industrial
bourgeoisie which

> expand and thrive within the orbit of foreign capital ... [whether as]
> wholesalers ... or as suppliers of local materials to foreign enterprises
> or as caterers to various other needs of foreign firms and their
> staffs....[37]

The state bureaucracy and other sectors of the middle class—e.g., the
technical, managerial, professional, or intellectual elites—become clientele
when their interests, actions, and privileged positions are derived from their
ties to foreign interests. Particularly with the expanded role of the state in the
national economy, the state bureaucracy (including the military in many
countries) has been viewed by some as the key to national autonomy.
Nevertheless, when the primary function of the state is to stimulate private
enterprise, when the private sector is largely controlled by foreign interests,
and when the state bureaucracy itself relies on material and ideological
support from abroad (as in Brazil today), the "autonomy" of the state
bureaucracy must be illusory.

The alliances and conflicts of clientele classes with other domestic classes
are shaped to a considerable extent by their previous and present alliances
with foreign interests. Thus, for example, no less important than the alliances
or conflicts of a São Paulo industrialist with the Brazilian proletariat or
coffeegrowing interests are his economic and ideological alignments with Wall
Street bankers or foreign industrial interests; indeed the former are often
shaped by the latter. In the absence of these clientele classes within the
dependent nation, dependency could not be perpetuated. "The basic
correspondence between the dominant interests [of the dominant society and
those of the dependent society] is a *sine qua non* of dependency."[38]

From the preceding discussion, it may be seen that dependency does not
simply mean external domination, unilaterally superimposed from abroad
and unilaterally producing "internal consequences." The internal dynamics of
dependency are as much a function of *penetration* as of domination. It is in
this way that dependency in Latin America differs from that of a formal
colony: while the chains binding the latter to the mother country are overt
and direct (administrative control), those of the former are subtler and are

36. Vasconi, op. cit., p. 146.
37. Baran, op. cit., pp. 194-95.
38. Quijano, op. cit., p. 4; Dos Santos, "Crisis de la Teoría del Desarrollo," op. cit.,
p. 31. Thus dependency is not the confrontation of all interests in the dependent
society against those of the dominant society, nor does it imply the "alienation" of
Latin elites from their "real" interests. It represents, rather, a correspondence or convergence of interests which are materially based in the socioeconomic positions of the
dominant classes in the dependent society as well as of the dominant classes in the
dominant society. (Quijano, op. cit., p. 4; Vasconi, op. cit., pp. 142-46).

internal to the nation—and for that reason are much more difficult to break. In this sense, the infrastructure of dependency may be seen as the functional equivalent of a formal colonial apparatus—the principal difference being, perhaps, that since all classes and structures in Latin society have to a greater or lesser degree internalized and institutionalized the legacy of dependency, that legacy is much more difficult to overcome.

From this analysis follow certain political implications. On the one hand, if dependency is conceived as an internal structural condition, then the opposite of dependent development, autonomous development, in no way signifies the absence of *all* ties to other nations (even to more advanced nations). It does signify that the basis of these ties must be totally revised through a profound change within the now-dependent nations, so that those ties are no longer determinative of internal socioeconomic structures and no longer serve exclusively the interests of the dominant nations. Thus, for example, Cuba may trade with Western European nations and may even receive technical assistance without compromising its autonomy, because it has become clear that social structures and development within Cuba correspond to the needs of the great majority of the Cuban people.

On the other hand, for the rest of Latin America, even if the United States and every other dominant capitalist nation were to disappear suddenly, Latin American dependency would not be immediately ruptured. And thus, by implication Latin nations cannot break the chains of dependency merely by severing (or attempting to sever) their ties to the international system. A total rupturing of dependency as an internal structural condition of underdevelopment requires simultaneously—and indeed as a precondition for lasting autonomy or independence from the international system—a profound transformation, an anticapitalist, socialist transformation, of their own socioeconomic order.

Thus, as experience has demonstrated, the various efforts to build "bourgeois nationalist" or "national capitalist" or, more recently, "state capitalist" solutions must fail in the end because the social classes on whom such solutions are based (the bourgeoisie) are themselves limited by their role in the international system. They may advocate a foreign policy "independent" of the United States (as in Brazil during the early 1960s); or they may successfully expropriate foreign holdings in some sectors, as has been done in Peru and as may be increasingly the case in other countries. But so long as they follow the capitalist road of development, they will continue to depend upon foreign investment, and thus will eventually have to make their compromises with and cater to foreign interests. And regardless of their intentions to implement far-reaching domestic reforms, they will be limited in practice by the legacy of dependency as institutionalized within their own class interests and alliances, within the existing industrial base, and so on. To break out of dependency means, then, to break out of the capitalist order whose expression in Latin America is dependency.

B. *The Predecessors of the Dependency Model*

The dependency model was not the first attempt to relate Latin American underdevelopment to the region's function in the world market. Why, then, was this model in some sense "necessary"? In order to understand both the continuities and the differences of the dependency model with respect to its predecessors, it is necessary to examine briefly two previous "international system" analyses of Latin underdevelopment: the classical model of the U.N. Economic Commission for Latin America (CEPAL) and that of André Gunder Frank.

The starting-point of the CEPAL analysis is Latin America's "peripheral" status vis-à-vis the advanced industrial "centers," as manifested primarily in the region's historical evolution as an exporter of primary commodities. Until the 1930s, when some Latin nations began to industrialize, their economies (and the economy of the region as a whole) typified *desarollo hacia afuera* ("externally-oriented development"), geared to the needs of the then-industrializing nations which dominated the world market, rather than to the needs of their national markets. This historical condition finds its contemporary expression in the unfavorable position of the "peripheral" nations in world trade, stemming from the low income elasticity of demand for Latin American exports and the high income elasticity of demand for the industrial imports into these countries. As a means of overcoming Latin America's inherent disadvantage in the world market and excessive dependence upon one or a few primary exports, and as a means of stimulating internally- rather than externally-oriented development, the CEPAL solution has been import-substituting industrialization. Import-substitution was expected to lessen dependence on foreign trade, transfer the "centers of decision making" to Latin America, and expand production for the internal market. The rise of a national (industrial) bourgeoisie would weaken the traditional oligarchies (mainly landed and import-export interests). And, if coupled with an agrarian reform, import-substitution could lead to income redistribution and incorporation of the lower classes into the national economy. Since industrialization required far more capital than was currently available from domestic sources, foreign investment and foreign aid on terms favorable to Latin America were seen as necessary and desirable.[39]

Although the CEPAL thesis (which has been grossly oversimplified here) was fruitful when first put forth, in that it linked Latin American underdevelopment to the international economic system, it is limited in several respects. First, its explanation of why Latin America has been at such a disadvantage in the world market relies too heavily on the nature of

39. For a good example, see Raul Prebisch, *Toward a Dynamic Development Policy for Latin America* (New York: United Nations, 1963).

traditional Latin exports, and pays insufficient attention to the conscious policies and the specific needs of the developed nations. As has been seen above, it is no natural accident that the Latin countries have remained, until recently, exporters of primary products and importers of manufactured goods. Second, CEPAL's class analysis places the entire responsibility for retarded industrialization upon "traditional" or "feudal" oligarchies within Latin America. But the characterization of Latin society as having been "pre-capitalist" or "feudal" or dominated by feudal oligarchies is misleading, since Latin American society and modes of production since the sixteenth century have been mercantile, i.e., geared toward exporting to an international capitalist market.[40] In addition the CEPAL theorists assumed that an indigenous industrial bourgeoisie would be developmentalist, progressive, and nationalistic—a premise which clearly requires reexamination, in view of the actual behavior of that bourgeoisie.[41]

Third, and perhaps most important, the CEPAL analysis has been partially invalidated by facts: specifically, the increasing dependence upon the international system of those countries which have been import-substituting for more than thirty years (e.g., Argentina and Brazil), and the stagnation plaguing those nations in recent years, which is a symptom of the exhaustion of import-substitution possibilities. (To mention only three examples: since beginning to industrialize, Latin America has become more dependent than ever upon certain critical imports (heavy capital goods for industrial facilities); foreign ownership and control of industry have increased, thus contradicting the expectation that decision making would be transferred to Latin America; and growth rates for the entire region and for some of the most industrialized nations were lower during the 1960s than during the 1945-60 period.)[42] In short, the CEPAL diagnosis took insufficient account of the built-in limitations of the import-substitution solution, arising from Latin America's historical dependency.

Faced with the by now obvious bankruptcy of import-substitution during the 1960s, CEPAL has avoided a thorough reappraisal of its analysis by discovering yet another panacea: regional economic integration. But, in the absence of a transformation of the national economic structures, this panacea (supported by United States and international aid agencies as well as CEPAL) promises to be no more viable than import-substitution. This is true, first, because, unless accompanied by strict regulations on foreign investment,

40. See Frank, "Latin America: A Decrepit Capitalist Castle with a Feudal-Seeming Facade," *Monthly Review,* December 1963, and other works by Frank; Vitale, op. cit.; Sergio Bagú, "La Economía de la Sociedad Colonial," *Pensamiento Crítico,* April 1969.

41. See for example, Fernando Cardoso, "The Industrial Elite," in S.M. Lipset and Aldo Solari, eds., *Elites in Latin America* (New York: Oxford University Press, 1967); Dos Santos, "El Nuevo Carácter," op. cit.; Vitale, op. cit.

42. CEPAL, *El Segundo Decenio,* op. cit., p. 8.

economic integration will benefit foreign rather than local firms, the former having the capital and advanced technology to support regional enterprises which are beyond the capacity of local firms; second, because the increased scale and advanced technology of regional enterprises aggravate national development problems such as unemployment unless these negative effects are counteracted through deliberate policies; and, third, because regional integration of markets removes the pressure for drastic social reforms which would normally be created by industries of scale requiring large markets. Instead of enlarging the consumer base within each country by improving the economic status of the majority of the population, it is possible to combine middle- and upper-class consumer bases of several nations (as is currently happening in Central America). These factors do not imply the invalidity of the *idea* of integration, but rather the illusory nature of integration under present conditions as a substitute for basic structural changes.

On the grounds that capital shortage has been one of the main obstacles to industrialization, CEPAL recommends increased foreign investment and aid. But this recommendation flies in the face of considerable evidence that foreign investment and aid have served as channels for the outflow of capital from Latin America rather than the inflow.[43] Thus the CEPAL analysis calls for the intensification rather than the rupturing of ties to the dominant world powers—and (unintentionally) for the intensification of dependency.

In short, the CEPAL model provides at best a partial explanation of Latin underdevelopment; it confronts the symptoms rather than the basic causes. Perhaps this is more understandable in the light of its socioeconomic roots. The CEPAL strategy is the expression of a Latin bourgeoisie trying to be national, but confined by the contradictions of the national capitalist "solution" to dependency, and forced, in the end, to call for additional foreign capital as a requisite for development. The inadequacy of the CEPAL model represents the failure of a particular social class, with particular interests, to offer a long-range alternative to Latin America.[44]

The second "international system" analysis, which goes considerably beyond the classical CEPAL model, is André Gunder Frank's marxist model of relations between "metropolitan" and "satellite" nations. Frank traces the underdevelopment of Latin America and all the manifestations of that underdevelopment to the global expansion of capitalism and its penetration of the non-Western nations. "Underdevelopment [in Latin America] was and still is generated by the very same historical process which also generated economic development [in the U.S. and Europe]: the development of

43. See references in note 13 above.
44. The irony is that much of the empirical evidence which contradicts (and is used to refute) the classical CEPAL analysis and strategy comes from the very thorough annual and periodic studies made by CEPAL itself.

capitalism itself."[45] This process has resulted in a hierarchical chain of metropolis-satellite relations, in which each metropolis appropriates the economic surplus generated in its satellites, and "each of the satellites ... serves as an instrument to suck capital or economic surplus out of its own satellites, and to channel part of this surplus to the world metropolis of which all are satellites."[46] Within Latin America power has always rested with the subordinate metropolises, particularly the bourgeoisie, intimately tied to foreign interests, yet dominant at home.[47]

Frank addresses the major weaknesses of the CEPAL model. He provides a causal explanation for Latin America's unfavorable position in the world market, specifying clearly the role of the dominant classes in the developed societies as well as of the local metropolises (dominant classes and regions) in the Latin nations. He refutes the myth that Latin America is currently emerging from a feudal social order, which must be destroyed by the triumph of the national bourgeoisie over the feudal obligarchy.[48] He suggests why industrialization, import-substituting or otherwise, will not rupture the cycle of underdevelopment and dependency unless the existing structure of metropolis-satellite relations, both domestic and international, is overthrown. Thus he projects no hopes as to the "positive contribution" which might be made by foreign investment and aid; these are, in Frank's model, instruments for the extraction of capital from Latin America, rather than for its infusion into the region.

There remain, however, several problems in Frank's analysis. For the purposes of this article it is necessary to mention only the most relevant one. Just because his theory is so sweeping and "elegant" (in the sense of reducing complex phenomena to one basic set of principles and relationships), it tends to be one-dimensional. Although the extraction of economic surplus may be the basis for all metropolis-satellite relations, both international and internal, it is not the only important dimension of these relations or of Latin dependency.[49] The concept of dependency calls attention to many other aspects of Latin America's relation to the international system (e.g., ideological hegemony of the dominant nations and of local clientele elites) which cannot be reduced to the extraction of economic surplus. It is for this reason (among others)[50] that the dependency theorists did not simply adopt

45. Frank, "The Development of Underdevelopment," *Monthly Review,* September 1966, p. 23.

46. Ibid., p. 20.

47. Frank, *Capitalism and Underdevelopment,* op. cit., p. 116.

48. E.g., Frank, "Capitalism and the Myth of Feudalism in Brazilian Agriculture," ibid.

49. José Luis Reyna, "Subdesarrollo y Dependencia: el Caso de América Latina," *Revista Mexicana de Sociología,* October-December 1967, p. 661.

50. See critique by Dos Santos, "Crisis de la Teoría del Desarrollo," op. cit., pp. 24-26.

Frank's model as it stood, but developed a somewhat different version of the same basic thesis: that Latin underdevelopment and dependency are an expression and a consequence of the global expansion of capitalism. Thus the dependency model has incorporated the important theoretical contributions of its predecessors, while attempting to avoid their problems and limitations.

C. *The Limits of the Dependency Model and its Integration with a Theory of Imperialism*

Insofar as the international system lies at the heart of dependency, that system must be understood in its entirety—not only at its point of impact on Latin America, but also at its origins in the dominant nations. It is at this point that we reach the limits of the dependency model. While providing the basis for an analysis of the impact of capitalist expansion and the functioning of the international system in Latin America, by itself it is not very explicit about the reasons for the expansion of capitalism or the roots of the international system in the dominant nations (for our purposes, the United States). Furthermore (although a certain conception is implicit within the writings of a number of the dependency theorists), the relation between the state and private capital in the American political economy is not made explicit. Private capital remains the driving force in the international system; nevertheless, the state or public sector of the dominant nations plays an important role in relations with Latin America and even in the operations of private capital. It is in terms of the relation between the state and private capital in the dominant nations that we may understand why the international system perpetuates underdevelopment in Latin America—and ultimately why policies such as the Alliance for Progress cannot resolve the underdevelopment problem.

In attempting to fill the "gap" left by the dependency model, we may choose from among several alternative theories which presume to explain American relations with Latin America. For this analysis these theories may be classified in three groups: international relations theories, non-Marxist theories of imperialism, and Marxist theories of imperialism. After suggesting the insufficiencies of the first two bodies of theory for the specific problem at hand, I shall indicate why the third provides an appropriate complement to the dependency model.

In most conventional international relations theories the international context is depicted as an arena in which independent (though not necessarily equal) players bargain about competing or conflicting national interests, and in which war occasionally erupts when the bargaining process breaks down. In the case of United States relations with Latin America this model is inappropriate. It assumes that Latin American nations are bounded units, led by autonomous decision makers. It implicitly or explicitly postulates a clear dichotomy between internal and international structures, thus precluding at the outset the notion of Latin American dependency (as defined above).[51] In addition, international relations theories tend to deal with "policy choices," the implication being that Latin governments, acting autonomously, could make alternative decisions. In fact, so long as they remain within the international capitalist system, the range of alternatives open to these governments is limited to changing certain minor aspects of their relation to the dominant nations (e.g., gaining trade concessions, more economic or military aid). This restricted range of options is, in fact, a principal feature of Latin American dependency.[52] Moreover, as the dependency model makes clear, the autonomy of Latin American decision makers is not to be taken for granted: while they may go through the motions of deciding policy, the substance of their decisions often reflects foreign interests more nearly than national interests.

From the stand-point of the United States as well, international relations theories tend to obscure the essentials of United States-Latin American relations. They generally treat these relations in terms of policies and policy-choices, which presumably could have been or could be changed by more "enlightened" policy makers. (Thus, for example, the Alliance for Progress and, thirty years earlier, the Good Neighbor Policy[53] were seen as real "departures" from previous United States policies.) To be sure, American strategies and policies toward Latin America *do* change; but those changes represent variations of a less flexible underlying relationship between the United States and Latin America, rather than alterations in the basic relationship. The exclusive focus on United States policy also precludes attention to the institutions and social groups in the American socioeconomic system which shape these policies. Given the dichotomy between domestic politics and "relations that take place across national boundaries,"[54] the only "domestic factors" which receive any consideration are rather obvious ones, such as congressional pressures.[55] As part of the state (public) apparatus, foreign policy is assumed to reflect the public interest, and thus is seldom examined in terms of dominant private interests within the United States. By obscuring the essential relationship between public policy and private interests, international relations theories must devise ad hoc explanations—or excuses—for the failure of policies such as the Alliance for Progress; their own

51. This distinction may be found (implicitly, at least) in several selections in Stanley Hoffmann, ed., *Contemporary Theory in International Relations* (Englewood Cliffs, N.J.: Prentice-Hall, 1960), e.g., Frederick Dunn, "The Scope of International Relations," p. 13.

52. Sunkel, op. cit., p. 57.

53. E.g., Bryce Wood, *The Making of the Good Neighbor Policy* (New York: Norton, 1967); Samuel Bemis, *The Latin American Policy of the United States* (New York: Norton, 1967).

54. Dunn, op. cit., p. 13.

55. John D. Montgomery, *The Politics of Foreign Aid* (New York: Praeger, 1962).

assumptions preclude a real understanding of its roots, and thus of its consequences.

The basic assumption of most international relations theories, that there exists at least a minimal autonomy and freedom of action for all nations as actors in the international arena, is challenged by all theories of imperialism. The notion of an imperialistic relation between two or more nations implies (regardless of the particular theory of imperialism) a decisive inequality between those nations, an exploitative relationship (i.e., one which serves the interests of the dominant nation at the expense of the subordinate nation), and the crippling of the latter's autonomy. The subordinate nation becomes, to one degree or another, the object of the needs and interests of certain groups in the dominant nation. Beyond the very general notion of imperialism as exploitative, however, Marxist theories differ sharply from most non-Marxist theories in analyzing the nature and causes of imperialism.

Given the great diversity of non-Marxist theories of imperialism, these remarks must be limited to those tendencies which have direct bearing on Latin American dependency.[56] First, there is a tendency to associate imperialism with expansionism (territorial expansion or protracted political domination) and/or the military aggression and intervention generally accompanying such expansion.[57] By associating imperialism with a phenomenon that has characterized international political relations since the beginning of time, this conception is so broad as to deprive the term "imperialism" of any specific meaning. Nor does it contribute toward an explanation of dependency in Latin America: for dependency is not created by occasional military interventions or even gunboat diplomacy (which historically involved prolonged occupation and/or overt political control by the United States or other hegemonic powers). Rather, dependency has been a chronic condition of Latin development, maintained by the day-to-day and, for the most part, peaceful relations between Latin America and the dominant nations. The very identification of imperialism with physical or direct coercion projects an oversimplified image of overt domination, and almost automatically excludes from examination the subtler mechanisms through which dependency has been internalized and perpetuated in Latin America.

Second, non-Marxist theories tend to dissociate imperialism from the

56. A notable non-Marxist exception to the following discussion is Hobson, *Imperialism* (Ann Arbor: University of Michigan Press, 1965). Some theorists included here as non-Marxist theorists of imperialism do not acutally use the term "imperialism" to describe their concern (e.g., Juan Bosch, *Pentagonism: A Substitute for Imperialism* (New York: Grove, 1968), preserving the term "imperialism" in its Marxist meaning. I include them, nevertheless, because they do deal with exploitative relations among nations.

57. E.g., Joseph Schumpeter, "Imperialism," in *Imperialism: Social Classes* (New York: Meridian, 1955), pp. 4-5; John Strachey, *The End of Empire* (New York: Praeger, 1964), pp. 7-8, 319; Richard Barnet, *Intervention and Revolution* (New York: World Publishing, 1968).

economic system (for our purposes, capitalism) in the dominant country. Thus they may resort to ideological-political-military explanations (such as: the obsessive anti-Communism of American leaders, the doctrine of the "American responsibility" held by the "national security bureaucracy," independent of economic interests,[58] the needs of the defense establishment,[59] and so on). Or they may argue that imperialism is "unprofitable"[60] or "irrational" in a capitalist society, basically a "vestige" or "atavism" surviving from a pre-capitalist era.[61] By conceptualizing imperialism too narrowly in terms of the actions of the state, or implicitly distinguishing a priori the interests of the state ("national security") from those of the dominant socioeconomic classes, these theories do not consider that imperialism may be systemically related to capitalism. But if imperialism is dissociated from capitalism, then it must be regarded as little more than a policy; in this respect the logical conclusions of many non-Marxist theories of imperialism almost converge with those of international relations theory. And if imperialism is dissociated from the global expansion of capitalism on the international level, the concept loses its potential as an explanation of dependency in Latin America.

In contrast to the above, a Marxist theory of imperialism[62] addresses itself directly to the economic basis (as well as the political-military aspects) of American policies and to the causes of dependency and underdevelopment in Latin America. For our purposes the adoption of a Marxist framework implies an integral relation between the actions of the United States government abroad and the structure of the American socioeconomic system; it analyzes Unites States relations with Latin America as one aspect of American capitalism. In this sense American imperialism is not "irrational" or "accidental," but, rather, is a necessary extension of capitalism. It is not a fleeting policy, but *a stage in the development of capitalism as a world*

---

58. Barnet, op. cit., p. 17.
59. Bosch, op. cit.
60. Strachey, op. cit., p. 340.
61. Schumpeter, op. cit., pp. 7, 64-65.
62. It is a Marxist theory in the sense of remaining within the Marxist tradition—even though Marx himself left little in the way of an explicit *theory* of imperialism. This does not necessarily imply blanket acceptance of the writings of Lenin, Rosa Luxemburg, or any other individual Marxist. Even among Marxists there is considerable controversy as to the specific nature of modern imperialism. Moreover, many of the classical Marxist writings on imperialism are specific to a particular historical era (e.g., the late nineteenth and early twentieth centuries.) For varying interpretations of the nature and driving force of imperialism, see Hobson, op. cit.; Rosa Luxemburg, *The Accumulation of Capital* (New York: Monthly Review); Victor Porlo, *The Empire of High Finance* (New York: International Publishers, 1956); Lenin, op. cit.; Heather Dean, "Scarce Resources" (Ann Arbor: Radical Education Project); Michael Barrat-Brown, *After Imperialism* (London: Heinemann, 1963), among others.

system.[63] Moreover, while recognizing the importance, necessity, and inevitability of military or coercive actions abroad, a Marxist analysis understands these not as the essence of imperialism, but rather as the ultimate recourse, when the subtler mechanisms of imperialism are insufficient to contain a threat to the existing international system. This analysis is appropriate to a specific feature of contemporary United States relations with Latin America: namely, the attempt to avoid, and to obviate the need for, overt military intervention or direct political control wherever possible.[64] It should be stressed that to accept a theory of economic imperialism as a general hypothesis does not imply the reduction of every *specific* political or military action by the state to pure economic motives; political factors are always important, and there are occasions (such as the Cuban missile crisis) when "security" considerations become determinative. This theory insists, however, that isolated military or political actions be understood in their overall context, which is the preservation of capitalism as an economic order.

To introduce the model of contemporary imperialism, we begin with a skeletal description of the main units of contemporary capitalism and imperialism. This sketch is based on a particular Marxist model which takes *monopoly capital* as the defining feature of the American political economy today:[65]

> Today the typical unit in the capitalist world is not the small firm
> producing a negligible fraction of a homogeneous output for an
> anonymous market, but a large-scale enterprise producing a signifi-
> cant share of the output of an industry or even several industries,
> and able to control its prices, the volume of its production, and the
> type and amounts of its investments. The typical economic unit, in
> other words, has the attributes which were once thought to be
> possessed only by monopolies.[66]

These economic units have four outstanding features, which can be stated briefly. (1) The first is increasing concentration of capital and resources under

63. This Marxist critique of non-Marxist theories of imperialism (which see imperialism as a policy, which divorce the politics of imperialism from the economics, etc.) goes back to Lenin's critique of Kautsky, in Lenin, op. cit., pp. 107-12, 142 ff.

64. James O'Connor, "The Meaning of Economic Imperialism" (Ann Arbor: Radical Education Project), p. 18.

65. The emphasis given here to the monopolistic corporations is not meant to detract from the importance of the institutions of financial capital (particularly banks) nor to underestimate the extent to which corporate and financial capital have been integrated. In a sense the entire dispute about financial *vs.* corporate capital is distorted: Lenin himself defined "financial capital" as "the concentration of production; the monopolies arising therefrom; *the merging or coalescence of the banks with industry*" (Lenin, op. cit., p. 52, emphasis mine).

66. Paul Baran and Paul Sweezy, *Monopoly Capital* (New York: Monthly Review, 1966), p. 6.

the control of fewer units, through the traditional forms: horizontal integration (increasing concentration of control over the production of a commodity or class of commodities) and vertical integration (increasing concentration of control over all phases of the production process, from the supply of raw materials to the marketing and distribution of the commodity to consumers). (2) Another is a growing tendency toward conglomeration or diversification: that is, the control by a smaller number of corporations over production in various different and often unrelated sectors, thus augmenting the corporation's strength, and simultaneously minimizing the risks of production or marketing, in any one sector.[67] (3) A further characteristic is increasing "internationalization" or "multinationalization" of the operation (*not* the ownership or control)[68] of capital. Multinational corporations are

> plants that purchase inputs from one branch of a corporation
> located in the same or a different country and sell outputs to
> another branch of the same corporation located elsewhere....
> [They] are able to mobilize, transform, and dispose of capital on a
> regional or even world-wide scale—in effect constituting themselves
> as extra-territorial bodies.[69]

In short, the (non-Communist) world has replaced the nation as the arena for their operations in both production and marketing. (4) A final feature is the progressive shift from rivalry among the capitalist powers (such as prevailed, for example, during the heyday of colonialism, from 1870 to 1914) toward closer integration of the capitalist world, and inability of the secondary capitalist powers thus far to offer a serious challenge to American hegemony.[70] (This is especially the case vis-à-vis Latin America.)

These characteristics of contemporary capitalism give rise to certain generally shared interests of the multinational corporations with respect to their overseas operations.[71] First, there arises a need to control all aspects of

67. "Notes on the Multinational Corporation," *Monthly Review*, October 1969, pp. 12-13; Celso Furtado, "La Concentración del Poder Económico en los Estados Unidos y sus Proyecciones en América Latina," *Pensamiento Crítico* 20, 1968.

68. "Notes on the Multinational Corporation," op. cit., pp. 3 ff. Even where, as in Latin America, "local capital is the most important source of financing for wholly owned subsidiaries of U.S. corporations" (O'Connor, op. cit., p. 14); see also J. Behrman, "Foreign Associates and their Financing," in Raymond Mikesell, ed., *U.S. Government and Private Investment Abroad* (Eugene, Ore.: University of Oregon Press, 1962), p. 103), control over the disposition of that captial remains in the hands of the U.S.-based parent corporation.

69. O'Connor, "The International Corporations and Economic Underdevelopment," manuscript, pp. 5-6.

70. Magdoff, "The Age of Imperialism," *Monthly Review*, June 1968, p. 24; Horowitz, op. cit., pp. 239-41.

71. The following account of generally shared interests of the multinational corporations should not be taken to imply the absence of conflicting interests between individual corporations (or even within one conglomerate); indeed such conflicts exist

the production process, including the sources of supply and processing of raw materials, as well as the markets or outlets for commodities.[72] Second, as the scale, monopolistic concentration, conglomeration, and internationalization of private capital increase, the dependence upon immediate profit returns from overseas investments is reduced. The emphasis shifts toward long-range planning, maximum security and avoidance of risk,[73] and preservation of a favorable climate (ideological, political, and social, as well as economic) for the *perpetuation* of corporate operations and for long-range profits.[74] To insure against sudden changes in the "rules of the game," controls over the political situation in Latin America—generally informal and indirect—must be tightened. And in the international environment there is need of an apparatus to guarantee not only "the rationalization of international capital flows and monetary transactions,"[75] but also maximum political stability. "Hemispheric security" comes to mean protection not against interference by non-hemispheric powers or even "international Communism," but rather against the threat of truly independent regimes of any type in Latin America.

Third, corporate capitalists acquire an interest in a limited measure of "development" in Latin America. A moderate redistribution of income in Latin America provides a larger market for American exports, as well as a safeguard against potential political instability. A relatively healthy Latin economy improves the climate for investment and trade. In this sense modern imperialism has an element of "welfare imperialism."[76] Under these conditions, however, Latin development responds primarily to the needs of the foreign corporations, rather than national needs; it is, in short, fragmented, dependent, and ultimately illusory development. Fourth (and partly as a response to the failure to achieve real income redistribution or

---

and remain important. But given the essentially monopolistic (rather than competitive) nature of contemporary capitalism, particular interests are often superceded by the overriding common interests of corporate capital.

72. Magdoff, "The Age of Imperialism," p. 23; Horowitz, op. cit., p. 236.

73. Magdoff, "Economic Aspects of U.S. Imperialism," op. cit., pp. 18-19; Baran, op. cit., p. 197.

74. This concern, often expressed by American business, is illustrated in a recent article in *Fortune* on the investment climate in Latin America:

> [U.S. investors in Latin America] find the rules that govern foreign investment constantly changing, almost always in what, from the American investor's point of view, is an undesirable direction. Day-to-day operations are becoming more and more difficult, and planning for the future uncertain and sometimes futile....

(Juan Cameron, "Threatening Weather in South America," *Fortune*, October 1969, p. 99; see also speech by Sal Marzullo of the Council for Latin America, "The Role of the Private Sector in Latin American Development," January 1970, p. 10.)

75. Johnson, op. cit., p. 26.

76. O'Connor, "Public Loans and Investments and Latin American Underdevelopment," (manuscript).

expansion of the domestic market in Latin countries), there is an interest in regional integration of markets. As *Fortune* points out the advantages of integration, it not only eliminates tariff barriers, but also provides "the chance to move to the broader, more competitive, and potentially more profitable task of supplying a market big enough to be economic on its own terms...."[77]

Finally, the nature of private corporate operations overseas is such that they require protection by the (imperialist) state. Thus the multinational corporation has an increasing stake in consolidating its influence over "public" or (United States) government decisions, i.e., over the apparatus of the state.[78] This implies not only a strong influence over government foreign policies, but also "the active participation of the state in international economic relationships" which serve their interests.[79] As the interests of the state come to overlap with those of the multinational corporations, "the state enlists more and more private capital in its crusade to maintain world capitalism intact," and there arises a "partnership" between public and private capital.[80] The full import of this partnership between the state and private capital goes far beyond the scope of this discussion. For our purposes its significance is that the state performs certain services which are essential to the overseas operations of the multinational corporations.

Rather than attempt to present an exhaustive catalogue of the services performed by all agencies of the United States government, I shall take as an example the functions of one branch of the state: the United States economic aid agencies—both national (AID) and United States-dominated international (e.g., World Bank, International Monetary Fund, Inter-American Development Bank). Foreign aid is a useful example because it involves far more than the transfer of capital: loan funds are generally designated for specific uses (e.g., education, labor unions, transport and communications facilities), and are accompanied by sizable teams of American "experts." Thus, aside from their economic effects (foreign debt, balance of payments, etc.) aid programs affect political decisions about development, the socialization and training of certain sectors of the population, and so on. Insofar as contemporary imperialism is characterized by the attempt to avoid direct military intervention or political control, American interests muat be preserved through the reinforcement of the infrastructure of dependency—*Latin American* institutions and social classes which are oriented toward foreign interests. It is largely through aid agencies that this has been done—that

77. "A Latin American Common Market Makes Common Sense For U.S. Businessmen Too, " *Fortune,* June 1967.

78. Furtado, op. cit., p. 174; O'Connor, "The Meaning of Economic Imperialism," op. cit.

79. O'Connor, "The Meaning of Economic Imperialism," p. 9.

80. Ibid., p. 20; Mikesell, op. cit., p. 7; O'Connor, "Public Loans," op. cit., p. 6.

public education, urbanization, the training of certain elites, fiscal and industrial policy, and other aspects of development policy have been shaped in accordance with United States corporate interests.

· The services or functions of foreign aid are essentially of four types: aid provides "points of entry" for private investors in Latin America; aid socializes the indirect operating costs of the multinational corporations (transferring those costs from the corporations to the public sector, i.e., American or Latin American taxpayers); aid creates advantages for American firms over actual or potential local competitors; and aid facilitates long-range planning and minimizes the risks of foreign investments for the corporations.[81]

Foreign aid agencies provide an "opening wedge" or "point of entry" for private capital (especially in the modern industrial sectors of Latin economies) by: (1) making loans directly to the corporations, both for feasibility studies and for actual operations; (2) making these feasibility studies for the corporations; (3) sponsoring aid programs such as Food for Peace (under which the United States government makes loans to American corporations in local currencies (acquired from the sale of surplus agricultural commodities), in order to finance the local costs of investment.[82] Foreign aid functions to socialize the indirect costs of private investors[83] by: (1) setting up programs, in Latin or United States universities, technical institutes, "productivity centers," etc., to train managerial personnel and skilled labor for local branch plants of the multinational corporations—and government bureaucrats who

81. Sources for this list range very widely, from books and articles on aid (e.g., Montgomery, op. cit.; various works by Mikesell; Hamza Alavi, "Imperialism, Old and New," *Socialist Register*, 1964; William Caspary, "American Economic Imperialism" [Ann Arbor: Radical Education Project] ; and others) to AID and other agency documents and interviews.

Economic aid programs here include technical assistance and other non-military grants, as well as loans. The importance of the "services rendered," as enumerated below, has been repeatedly confirmed by U.S. corporate and aid agency officials. To take one example, former World Bank President Eugene Black asserts that "our foreign aid progarms constitute a distinct benefit to American business," and then lists the specific ways in which business is benefited. Black, "The Domestic Dividends of Foreign Aid," *Columbia Journal of World Business*, Fall 1965, p. 23.

82. Mikesell, *Public International Lending for Development* (New York: Random House, 1966), p. 92.

83. The overall importance of state capital in financing capitalism overseas is dramatically illustrated by the fact that nearly 75 percent of all loans and investments to the underdeveloped countries now originate in the public sector. While state capital outflows have increased, private outflows have greatly declined (since overseas operations are financed primarily by locally raised capital). It should be noted, however, that since most non-military aid programs are loans rather than grants, the indirect operating costs of the multinational corporations overseas are ultimately borne by the Latin American rather than the American taxpayers (O'Connor, "The Meaning of Economic Imperialism," op. cit., pp. 17-18).

work in cooperation with foreign private corporations; (2) subsidizing unviersity research projects, both in Latin America and the United States directed chiefly toward the technological and scientific problems of the corporations; (3) promoting (granting loans for) infrastructure projects (roads, communications facilities, etc.) which are of more benefit to the foreign corporations than to the indigenous population.

Foreign aid creates advantages for American firms over local competitors by: (1) refusing loans to local firms which might compete with American companies; (2) providing United States corporations with vital information which is not available to local firms; (3) "lobbying" (sometimes pressuring) the host government to adopt policies favorable to United States private interests; (4) specifying that loan contracts for construction, supervision, accounting, etc. (especially for large infrastructure projects) must be given to either an American firm or a local firm, but adding further stipulations (e.g., that the entire project must be completed by one firm or that a high bid bond must be paid) which in effect eliminate smaller local firms from the competition; (5) promoting regional economic integration, which requires industries of scale and advanced technology, far beyond the capacities of local enterprises.

Finally, and perhaps most important, foreign aid facilitates long-range corporate planning and minimizes the risks to the corporations of longe-range overseas investment by (1) establishing investment guarantee programs, which insure United States firms against losses from expropriation, incontrovertibility, war, revolution, and insurrection, thus providing a hedge against risks in unstable areas, and transferring to the United States state an increasing responsibility for what were originally disputes between American corporations and Latin American governments; (2) further stabilizing the local investment climate through such measures as: training (in conjunction with big United States labor and international labor confederations) of tame, "responsible," fiercely anti-communist union leaders, "open-minded" enough to see both sides in labor disputes; penetration of indigenous popular organizations (e.g., labor unions, peasant, and community organizations) or establishment of parallel institutions to compete with indigenous organizations, in order to channel potentially revolutionary demands into manageable social institutions; use of the mass media and educational institutions at all levels to promote the ideology of free enterprise; structural and curriculum reforms in the Latin American universities designed to "depoliticize" them (or change prevailing political orientations); (3) sending into the country "expert" personnel to supervise, advise, and in some cases directly administer aid programs from within the Latin American government ministries; through those experts, foreign interests acquire increasing control over policy formation and development strategies;[84] (4) persuading (or pressuring) local

84. Alavi, op. cit., p. 19.

government planners to tailor their development policies to the long-range needs of American corporations; (5) centralizing and rationalizing the world capital market through international agencies such as the World Bank and IMF (which also insure monetary stability in the Latin nations by making all international loans contingent upon rigorous fiscal stabilization policies).

In addition to these specific functions performed by aid agencies for the multinational corporations in their overseas investments, foreign aid continues to fulfill its more general functions for the preservation of American capitalism as a whole (beyond the interests of specific firms investing in Latin America), such as: gaining Latin government cooperation with foreign business interests by offering loans or grants as rewards, or alternatively threatening to withhold aid; providing large budget loans or grants to pro-American governments which are in trouble (e.g., Balaguer regime after the 1965 Dominican Republic revolt); and providing markets and stimulating new markets for United States goods and services (through such mechanisms as "tied aid," and the Export-Import Bank, which subsidize American exports—secure a market for them, often at artificially high prices).[85]

In addition to the foregoing, other state agencies also perform important services to United States corporate interests. For example, the CIA, the State Department and the Pentagon provide training for local military "civic action" and counterinsurgency programs, military assistance, and ultimate direct protection of United States investors—and in extreme cases of noncooperation by Latin governments, they have played decisive roles in overthrowing those governments; the in-country embassies provide crucial information to the corporations, represent their interests to the local governments, and influence local government policies; and the United States Treasury Department exerts pressures for tariffs and quotas on imports from Latin America which are competitive with United States goods, etc. These and other services are no less important than those of the economic aid agencies. In fact, given the current cutback in aid appropriations, it may well be that the importance of the aid mechanism was fairly specific to the era of the Alliance for Progress, the era of "welfare imperialism." If this is the case, the particular role of the state vis-à-vis the multinational corporations will be somewhat modified (as was proposed in the Rockefeller and subsequent

85. The importance of aid as a means of stimulating American exports was well summarized in a House of Representatives report on the Alliance, enumerating the ways in which, "While helping our neighbors, we have helped ourselves"—through EXIM-Bank and AID loans "tied" to U.S. purchases; through P.L.-480 programs ("our farm sector has not been neglected in the Alliance for Progress"); through stipulations that no less than 50 percent of all goods purchased with American loans be shipped in American-flagged ships: and so on. ("New Directions for the 1970's: Toward a Strategy of Inter-American Development," report by the Subcommittee on Inter-American Affairs of the Committee on Foreign Affairs of the U.S. House of Representatives [Washington: Government Printing Office, 1969], pp. 6-7).

reports to the President).[86] Whatever new agencies may be created to super-
cede the present aid apparatus, the state will continue to play an important
role in assisting overseas investors.

This analysis is not to imply that the state *never* acts independently of, or
even in direct opposition to, private corporate interests in particular
situations; indeed there have been notable instances of such actions.
Moreover, the state is sometimes faced with conflicting interests among
the multinational corporations.[87] In short, the state (and even the
corporations themselves) are sometimes forced to sacrifice specific interests in
order to serve the "higher interests"—the preservation of the capitalist system
as a whole. In this sense the overriding task of the modern capitalist state is
the stabilization and rationalization of world capitalism and imperialism as a
socioeconomic order.

We may now draw together the two parts of the analysis. By itself the
dependency model provides a view "from below." It traces Latin American
underdevelopment to that region's function in the world market and
international system, which is governed by the interests of the dominant
nations. The theory of imperialism provides a view "from above"—an
explanation of the specific nature of the international system and its roots in
the dominant nations. Through it the principal force which has conditioned
Latin development—the global expansion of capitalism, which is the engine of
the international system—is personified. For the theory of imperialism
specifies *whose* particular needs or interests in the dominant nations—i.e.,
those of the corporate and financial capitalists—are served by the international system. And on the basis of the ties between the state and private
interests in the dominant nations, the theory offers an account of American
relations with Latin America, thus converging with the dependency model.
Dependency and imperialism are, thus, two names for one and the same
system.

D. *Instabilities and Contradictions in the System*

On the basis of this analysis of dependency and imperialism in Latin
America, let us return briefly to the starting-point: the failure of the Alliance
for Progress. The Alliance was billed as a massive infusion of capital to
promote a peaceful social and economic revolution in Latin America. From
the perspective of the dependency-imperialism model, it becomes evident that
the Alliance *could not have* succeeded: first, because, contrary to the

86. *Rockefeller Report*, op. cit., pp. 46-48.
87. Such a case occurred, for example, when the Peruvian government expropriated
the holdings of the Standard Oil subsidiary, the IPC, in 1968, and there were pressures to
cut off the Peruvian sugar quota. These pressures were eventually resisted by the Nixon
administration—not least, perhaps, because the W.R. Grace Co. was the second largest
producer of sugar in Peru.

assumption that foreign aid and investment make a positive capital contribution to Latin development, the thrust of the empirical evidence (see note 13 above) is that these have served as mechanisms for the *extraction* of capital; and, second, because the cumulative effect of Latin America's contact with the dominant capitalist nations has been and remains the generation of dependency as an internal condition. Thus the Alliance was merely one more means of integrating Latin America into the international system which creates dependency and hinders development in that region.

From this perspective we must also reconsider the original objectives of the Alliance. The stated goal was to promote development through reform. This may have been a partial motivation for the Alliance. Far more important, however, was the *unstated* objective: to stabilize Latin America, and to make the region perpetually safe for private American investment. Some reform would be desirable—but only insofar as it was perceived as a necessary precondition for stability in Latin America and for preservation of the international capitalist system in the Western Hemisphere. (In case there is any doubt about this hidden agenda of the Alliance, let us recall that it was initiated simultaneously—and by no coincidence—with the Bay of Pigs invasion and with the establishment of counterinsurgency campaigns wherever a threat to stability existed in Latin America).

But this stability is precisely what was not, and could never have been, achieved by strengthening Latin America's ties to the international system and thereby intensifying Latin dependency. For the international system and Latin American dependency are fraught with serious contradictions, of which only a few can be mentioned here. First, because it is dependent—because it is controlled by monopolistic foreign corporations and adapted to imported capital-intensive technology—industrialization has generated not employment but unemployment. Those very social classes which were to have been incorporated within the national economy have been progressively marginalized. Not only does this create the usual threat from an increasing reserve army of the unemployed. In addition, it limits the expansion of the domestic market, which is a necessary condition for the expansion of foreign investment in Latin America (as well as for Latin development). Thus the multinational corporations are creating the conditions which will ultimately limit their own expansion in Latin America.

Second, because it is a dependent bourgeoisie—one which is closely allied, yet a junior partner in that alliance, with foreign capital—the once-national industrial bourgeoisie loses whatever potential it had for mobilizing a nationalist united front within Latin Ameria; with its internationalization, the Latin industrial bourgeoisie loses its ideological hegemony and control over other popular nationalist forces. Thus the international system is reinforcing a bourgeoisie which will in the long run be incapable of maintaining Latin America within the orbit of the international capitalist system. Third, as underdevelopment is intensified and new sectors of the population are radicalized, dependent or comprador governments, subservient to foreign interests, are forced to employ overt repression, not only against revolutionary movements but also against popular movements (e.g., peasant land invasions, as in Chile; resurgent labor movements, as in Argentina; and students). When these movements spread and, in response, the measures of repression are generalized to the entire nation, opposition to the government increases (even, as in Brazil, among sectors of the middle class which initially brought it to power), and the repression-resistance cycle becomes chronic. Or, as in the case of the Dominican Republic, the imperialist power is finally forced to intervene directly, thereby transforming a reformist movement into a potentially revolutionary force.

The real and ultimate failure of the Alliance for Progress, then—and of any other policy designed to intensify Latin America's integration into the international system—was the failure to stabilize Latin America. It had to fail, because dependency is not a stable or stabilizing condition for Latin American development. As one Latin American put it,

> The process of internationalization has two faces: one dependent
> face (the present) and one liberating face (that of the future). The
> dependent face and the liberating face present themselves in one and
> the same process.... 88

88. Dos Santos, "El Nuevo Carácter de la Dependencia," revised and reprinted in Matos Mar, ed., op. cit., p. 24.

7. The Neapolitan Politicians: A Collective Portrait

P. ALLUM

Naples is full of royal palaces which remind one of its glorious past as the capital of an independent kingdom. It has no town hall, much less a parliament building. The city council meets in the old Sala dei baroni in Castel Nuovo. These architectural traits are a vivid reminder that, if the parliamentary system of government evolved in Western Europe in the course of the change from feudalism to capitalism, the old Kingdom of the Two Sicilies made little contribution to that process. The problems which parliamentary government endeavored to resolve—the new relations between state and society, rulers and ruled—were little felt in Naples before 1860. Like all new political arrangements, the parliamentary system was a curious mixture of invention and imitation. Invention was in the van in the field of political ideas, what Gaetano Mosca baptized the "political formula," and imitation in the field of political institutions, in what he called the "political mechanism" of government.[1]

The "political formula" which sanctioned the triumph of the European capitalist bourgeoisie over the landed aristocracy, Parliament over the Absolute Monarchy, was the immortal expression of the principles of 1789, "Liberty, Equality and Fraternity." The authority of the state, these principles proclaimed, was no longer derived from above, but from below. Political sovereignty was henceforth to be vested in the people and the representatives of the people were to be endowed with political authority, not the representative of God. The model for the "political mechanism" was the old unreformed English constitution, suitably interpreted and transformed by the French revolutionary leaders. The people were to express their collective opinions through their representatives in parliament elected by universal suffrage. This paper is a study of Neapolitan parliamentary representatives who mediate the relations between Neapolitan society and the Italian state.

Italian journalists and Neapolitan historians have been at one in abusing the incompetence and corruption of Neapolitan politicians. Treatises have

---

1. G. Mosca, *Teorica dei governi e governo parlamentare* (Milano: Giuffrè, 1968), pp. 27-30, 127 ff.

been written about the deleterious effects of *clientelismo* and its cousin *trasformismo*,[2] but nobody has studied the Neapolitan politician as a social type with the detachment necessary for finding out what sort of man he is. To discover the man behind the colorful images of journalists and historians requires the gathering of a representative sample of parliamentarians and parliamentary candidates. We collected this information on the candidates and deputies for the seven major Italian national parties for the five general elections held between 1946 and 1963. However, to understand not only the sort of man the Neapolitan politician is, but also the way he behaves requires a frame of reference that places his activity in a larger context. Thus, this paper outlines a simple theoretical model to explain the nature of Neapolitan politics; then examines the social background and careers of Neapolitan deputies and parliamentary candidates; and finally considers the role of members of Parliament in the larger world of Italian parliamentary politics.

The Framework of Analysis

For the purposes of analysis we decided to adopt a scheme of "social polarity";[3] that is, we decided to postulate a pair of contrasting models of political activity. The reason was quite simply that Naples has been defined[4] as a city of transition between the European type—where industrialization has begun to create the problems associated with the "affluent society," and the old Mediterranean type—where the problems of modern industrial society have yet to be resolved. These conceptual devices, which merely point to the more important features, of reality, are themselves to be found nowhere in their pure form.

The models used are derived from Tönnies' *Gemeinschaft und Gesellschaft*[5] with appropriate modifications to suit the task at hand. *Gemeinschaft* is a social formation based on feeling, in which every individual considers each other individual as an end in himself, knows him personally and shares a great deal in his private life. The individuals who compose it intrinsically value their mutual relationship and the fact that they are a vital part of such a social entity. In contrast stands *Gesellschaft,* a social formation

2. See, for example, the ample literature on the Southern Question, and particularly, P. Turriello, *Governo e governati in Italia* (Bologna, 1889), 2 vols.; for details, M. L. Salvadori, *Il mito del buongoverno, la questione meridionale da Cavour a Gramsci* (Turin: Einaudi, 1960).

3. For the concept of "social polarity," see S. Giner, *The Theory of Mass Society,* (Ph.D. diss., University of Chicago, 1969), pp. 218-52, 431-39.

4. By Francesco Compagna. See his "La *Casbah* a Napoli," in *Atti dell'Accademia Pontaniana,* NS, X, 1960-1, pp. 297-305.

5. F. Tönnies, *Community and Society* (New York: Harper Torchbook, 1963).

founded on interest, in which the individual considers the others as the means, knows them impersonally, and shares his external life only with them.

Unlike Tönnies, Marx and Weber focused on social relations rather than on social formations. "It is quite obvious from the start," Marx wrote in *The German Ideology*, "that there exists a materialistic connection of men with one another, which is determined by their needs and the mode of production, and which is as old as men themselves."[6] While insisting on the differences between types of society as denoting particular stages of development in the history of mankind, Marx recognized that the one between the various types of precapitalist agrarian society and industrial capitalist society was fundamental in the modern world. Tribal, ancient, and feudal societies were all "based on a community" (*Gemeinschaft*), whereas "the basis of the *modern* State is civil society (*bürgerliche Gesellschaft*) and the *individual* of civil society, that is, the independent individual, whose only link with other individuals is private interest and *unconscious*, natural necessity, the *slave* of wage labour, of the *selfish* needs of himself and others."[7]

Marx gave little attention to the actual mechanics of political organization. It is here that Weber is useful. Although he followed Marx in centering his analysis on social relations and not social formations he accepted Tönnies' formulation of *Gemeinschaft* and *Gesellschaft* as polar social formations. He based them on two different types of social relations, *Vergemeinschaftung* (communal social relations) and *Vergesellschaftung* (associational social relations).[8] Weber rejected what he conceived as the Marxian notion that politics is directly based on economic interest. He accepted the concept of class, but surrounded it with the additional concepts of "status" in the social sphere and party in the political sphere, giving an independent dimension to institutional arrangements, their organization and control.

If *Gemeinschaft* and *Gesellschaft*, personal and organizational domination, are taken as representing the outer limits of a series of parallel, but nonlinear, continua, we can envisage a number of transitional situations. In the first place, there is the breakup of one social formation and the nonemergence of the other, i.e., the breakup of *Gemeinschaft* and the nonemergence of *Gesellschaft* so that, although both are present, neither is predominant.[9] In the second place, one type of social formation may be predominant, but the norms and forms of the other might be imposed from outside as with the

---

6. K. Marx and F. Engels, *The German Ideology* (London: Lawrence & Wishart, 1965), p. 41.

7. Ibid., p. 49.

8. See R. Bendix, *Max Weber, An Intellectual Portrait* (London: Methuen, 1966), p. 288.

9. See S. Hoffmann, "The Paradoxes of the French Political Community," in *In Search of France* (New York: Harper Torchbook, 1965), pp. 1-118.

imposition of parliamentary regimes in the colonies of the European imperial powers. From this discussion we derive the following typology of parliamentary political organizations:

TYPES OF DOMINATION	SOCIAL FORMATION		
	Gemeinschaft	Transitional	*Gesellschaft*
Personal Domination	Aristocrat/ Notable	Boss	
Organizational Domination		Political Machine	Interest Group/ Mass Party

Translating this discussion into terms relevant to our study of parliamentary politics in Naples, we start with two sociological models: a simple, precapitalist agrarian society and an advanced, capitalist industrial one. The significant areas of contrast for our purpose are the division of labor, types of role, social relations and values predominant (because never exclusive) in both types of society. Simpler societies are *Gemeinschaft* because they have little division of labor and little role specialization, while more complex societies, which are *Gesellschaft,* have developed an extensive division of labor and so role specialization. Social relations in *Gemeinschaft,* are ascriptive, and are founded on primary groups (family, godparenthood. neighborhood, and friendship) which embrace most aspects of the individual's life. In consequence, the social hierarchy is founded on status, deference and tradition; it is a static society. In contrast, social relations in *Gesellschaft* are achieved; and are fashioned by secondary groups or associations (parties, unions, industrial companies, professional groups and cultural associations). As a result, the social hierarchy is functional in relation to the means of production. Finally, we must stress the contrast in the political ties provoked by these type of social relations. In *Gemeinschaft,* political ties are vertical and are determined by traditional patterns of deference to established authority; in *Gesellschaft* they are horizontal and are formed by the functional relations of class and occupational groupings.

From Weber's analysis we derived two forms of political domination, personal and organizational, which gave rise to two forms of political organization, patriarchy and bureaucracy. The first type of political organization is what we may call the aristocrat or parliamentary notable. The classic example was the Andalusian *cacique;*[10] he was a landowner with more land than he could exploit economically, the child of the *latifundia.* He cultivated a small part only of his estate and rented the rest to tenants on

10. See, for example, G. Brennan, *The Spanish Labyrinth, An Account of the Social and Political Background of the Spanish Civil War* (Cambridge, England: Cambridge University Press, 1962), pp. 7 ff.

very short leases and in very small plots. The peasantry settled on a latifundium, lived in less than subsistence conditions and were, therefore, totally dependent on the landlord. In consequence, he (or his bailiff) was its born parliamentary representative: to demonstrate their fidelity to his person by voting for him (or his candidate) was the first duty of a rural population dependent on a landlord. The landlord was generally not interested in economic gain but in preserving his social position; power over his dependents through vertical political ties of subordination was an admirable weapon for this purpose in parliamentary politics. It made him the incontestable master of the politics of his locality and gave him a position from which to defend his interests in the national political arena. With the rise of the bourgeoisie, the gentry (families who acquired land through urban wealth or professional services) infiltrated or replaced the aristocracy, and the parliamentary notable took the place of the aristocrat, although their political activity remained unchanged. In fact, the parliamentary politics of an agrarian society is no more than the factional struggles of the leading families.

In contrast to aristocrat and parliamentary notable, the mass party and the interest group aspire to be the organized expression of social classes and occupational groupings. Their basis is a society organized along broadly functional lines in which a considerable degree of class consciousness has developed along with the division of labor. In the *Communist Manifesto,* Marx has outlined the key factors in the development of this type of society as market expansion and its concomitant, political centralization: "independent, or but loosely connected provinces, with separate interests, laws, governments, and systems of taxation, became lumped together into one nation, with one government, one code of laws, one national class-interest, one frontier and one customs-tariff."[11] Members of a class or occupational group form coherent organizations to pursue and defend their group interests. In general, these organizations, parties, unions, and interest groups of various kinds, are highly structured, nationally based and locally articulated. They have a permanent structure which is organized to pursue class or group interests on the basis of principled political views and not those of single individuals. Moreover, they undertake the political education and formation of members in addition to formulating collective demands. Their leaders and officials are elected and appointed through formal procedures and speak for the class or group they organize. They are the servants of the organization and are accountable for their activity in the fulfillment of their mandates. This principle remains true despite abuse of trust and manipulation by party leaders and domination of officialdom. The parliamentary politics of organized mass parties and interest groups is, therefore, the cut and thrust of program and principle.

11. Now in K. Marx and F. Engels, *Selected Works,* 1:38.

The model of political organization in transitional or intermediate social situations is the political boss and/or political machine. The political boss is a political entrepreneur who provides votes on his own account and at his own risk. He is usually a lesser professional man who organizes a *clientela*.[12] He thrives in a nonindustrial urban society which is formed of a mass of marginal elements who do not yet form a class-conscious proletariat. It is among the big city poor of *casbah* and *bidonville* (two notorious Mediterranean urban locations), among the irregularly and semi-employed, the depressed artisans and shopkeepers, that the city boss finds supporters in need of a protector. Since they are a mass of individuals who are incapable of organizing themselves, the boss organizes them into a political machine. Moreover, since he cannot count on traditional political ties to ensure loyalty, he must be in a position to obtain favors and advantages for them. In such societies, dominated by the lack of economic resources, the chief source of wealth is the state treasury; hence the boss must have access to it. He is a middleman or broker—which explains the advantages of being a lawyer—and his power derives from this position which limits his freedom of maneuver compared with the aristocrat and the old notable. Nonetheless, with a modicum of ability and entrepreneurial capacity, the judicious use of street gangs when necessary, he can employ the electoral support which he controls with relative freedom or, at least, more than the mass party leader, because, in the final analysis, he is master of the decision of what is in the interest of his troops. Finally, a political machine exists when the organization of the boss is capable of reliable and repetitive control of the electorate in its constituency; it can be defined as an organization interested in securing and holding office for its leaders solely for the patronage and booty that it can lay its hands on and distribute. As Weber noted, machines "seek profits solely through political control, especially municipal government, which is the most important object of booty."[13] The parliamentary politics of a nation of bosses and political machines is unbroken maneuvers, and payoffs between cliques and *camarillas.*

These models of political organization should enable us to identify the predominant pattern and its implications in a concrete social and political situation. Moreover, we can take the process one stage further and elaborate the various components of these models. From this it will be seen that the aristocrat has a quasi-absolute power over his dependent peasantry in direct

---

12. The classic study of a *clientela* still remains W. F. Whyte, *Street Corner Society: The Social Structure of an Italian Slum* (Chicago: University of Chicago Press, 1955).

13. In H. H. Gerth and C. Wright Mills, eds., *From Max Weber* (London: Routledge & Kegan Paul, 1948), p. 110. An exemplary, if old-fashioned study of a political machine is H. F. Gosnell, *Machine Politics, Chicago Model* (Chicago: Phoenix Books, 1968).

TABLE 1 – TYPOLOGY OF SOCIAL FORMATIONS, CLASS RELATIONS,
SOCIAL GROUPS, POLITICAL DOMINATION, POLITICAL ORGANIZATION,
IDEOLOGICAL APPEAL, POLITICAL TIES, METHODS OF POLITICAL
CONTROL, AND RELATIONS WITH STATE APPARATUS IN A
PARLIAMENTARY SYSTEM.

Predominant Traits	Types of Society		
	Simple agrarian	Transitional	Complex industrial
Social formation	Gemeinschaft		Gesellschaft
Class relations	Estates	Fragmented	Classes
Social groups	Primary		Secondary
Types of domination	Personal		Organizational
Forms of political organization	Aristocrat/ Notable	Boss/ Political Machine	Mass Party/ Interest group
Territorial organization	Local	Local/ National	National/ Supranational
Ideological appeal	Religious (Divine right)	Populist	Materialist (Class struggle/ Technocracy)
Nature of political ties	Vertical	Narrow Vertical	Horizontal
Methods of political control	Consent/ Coercion	Manipulation/ Coercion	Consent/ Manipulation
Relations with state apparatus	Certain autonomy	Total dependence	Certain autonomy

proportion to the isolation of his estate, i.e., the greater the isolation, the
greater his power, and vice versa. This explains his relations with the state
apparatus; his only interest is in the nonintervention of the state power in his
locality. In fact, in default of an adequate state power, the aristocrat or
notable often organized his own system of order maintenance, as, for
example, the *mafia*.[14] The position of the political boss is different, he needs
to add individual favors and material rewards to the lack of moral pressure he
can exert on his clients. Thus, he needs direct access to the state treasury for
patronage and the state apparatus for protection. In consequence, he is
totally dependent on the state for the satisfaction of his clients and the
maintenance of his position. He will support the government clique that will
satisfy his patronage requirements and which leaves him free to enjoy local
political supremacy. In a party regime, he will build his political machine
within the governing party.

Mass parties attempt to organize classes and occupational groups on the
basis of an ideology appealing to their collective interests. Although oriented

14. See Pantaleone, *Mafia e politica* (Turin: Einaudi, 1962). (Eng. trans., *The Mafia
and Politics* (London: Chatto & Windus, 1964).

towards the conquest of state power for the implementation of their programs, they are semi-independent of the state machinery in their daily activity. Indeed, the measure of their autonomy is their ability to survive long periods of parliamentary opposition when they have no immediate prospects of office. In this connection, it is worth making a distinction between working class and bourgeois mass parties.[15] The latter are concerned to maximalize electoral support; hence their ideological appeal is less precise and more pragmatic. The bourgeois mass party seeks to establish "consensus" and avoid party realignment by limiting the political participation of members and reducing party activity to fighting elections. It is generally assisted in this by the information manipulation of the mass media. Moreover, since it is electorally oriented, it is much more dependent on the state power for its survival than working-class parties. Loss of the prospect of power is often sufficient to sound the doom of bourgeois mass parties.

Recruitment: A Sociological Analysis

Having outlined the theoretical premises of our analysis, we are now in a position to examine the empirical data on Neapolitan parliamentarians. In so doing we must continually keep our theoretical framework in mind since it is the element which informs the detailed observations we shall make, and which links them to the wider context of political analysis.

A preliminary observation concerns candidatures: the number in the Naples-Caserta parliamentary constituency declined between 1946 and 1963 from 408 in twenty-three lists to 361 in eleven lists. This contrasts with the number of seats which increased from thirty to thirty-eight in keeping with the growth of the electorate from 1.4 to 1.8 million. The large number of lists and candidatures in the early postwar years was a result of the confusion and uncertainty in the political situation following twenty years of dictatorship. In 1946 and 1948 many lists and candidates tried their luck for the most part with little or no success. The *Uomo Qualunque* Movement which did very well in 1946, electing four deputies, disappeared in 1947, almost as suddenly as it had appeared two years earlier. By 1953, the situation had more or less stabilized itself: the number of candidatures dropped from 452 in twenty-four lists to 366 in fourteen lists in 1953. Recent events since the "hot autumn" of 1969 have increased political uncertainty once again, and this has been reflected in the rise in both the number of candidatures and lists contesting the general elections of May 1972.

15. Kirchheimer's "catch-all" party is the obvious example of the bourgeois mass party. See O. Kirchheimer, "The Transformation of Western European Party Systems," in J. LaPalombara and M. Weiner, *Political Parties and Political Development* (Princeton: Princeton University Press, 1966), pp. 177-200.

The social and demographic characteristics of candidates and deputies of the principal political groupings shows remarkable homogeneity (see Table 2.) In the main, candidates are mature, middle-class men, born in urban communes, professional men and clerks by occupation, with little experience of manual labour. Deputies (successful candidates) are generally older than candidates, in late middle age, and of solid upper- or middle-class status and income. Almost without exception, they have had no experience of wage or lower salaried employment. They are, in short, in and of the new and old upper classes of Neapolitan society.

TABLE 2 – CHARACTERISTICS OF CANDIDATES AND DEPUTIES
OF PRINCIPAL POLITICAL GROUPINGS, 1946 to 1963[16]

	PCI		Soc		DC		Right		Total	
	c.	d.	c.	d.	c.	d.	c.	d.	c.	d.
1. Place of birth										
Within constituency	72%	75%	82%	75%	71%	75%	75%	70%	76%	71%
Outside constituency	28%	25%	18%	25%	29%	25%	25%	30%	24%	29%
Urban communes	83%	95%	66%	70%	62%	70%	79%	75%	74%	77%
Rural communes	17%	5%	34%	30%	38%	30%	21%	25%	26%	23%
N.	(150)	(37)	(270)	(19)	(178)	(77)	(506)	(60)	(1104)	(192)
2. Sex										
Men	92%	90%	98%	100%	95%	94%	95%	100%	95%	95%
Women	8%	10%	2%		5%	6%	5%		5%	5%
N.	(150)	(37)	(270)	(19)	(178)	(77)	(506)	(60)	(1104)	(192)
3. Age*										
Under 30 years	4%	0%	8%	0%	1%	0%	3%	0%	5%	0%
31-50 years	85%	80%	75%	40%	54%	45%	45%	40%	60%	50%
51-65 years	8%	20%	15%	60%	42%	50%	35%	47%	25%	47%
Over 65 years	3%	0%	2%	0%	3%	5%	17%	13%	10%	3%
N.	(72)	(16)	(144)	(10)	(72)	(28)	(216)	(15)	(504)	(69)
4. Social Class										
Upper and Middle	45%	85%	35%	90%	70%	97%	75%	100%	62%	95%
Lower Middle	25%	5%	55%	10%	30%	3%	25%		31%	3%
Working	30%	10%	10%	0%	+	0%	+		7%	2%
N.	(150)	(37)	(270)	(19)	(178)	(77)	(506)	(60)	(1104)	(192)

* = Data for only two elections, 1958 and 1963.
+ = Figures of less than 1%.
(Sources: Material supplied by parties, supplemented by press accounts.)

16. We have followed the procedure of André Siegfried, "préoccupé surtout de la réalité je me suis donc moins attaché aux partis–classifications superficielles–qu'aux tendences de fond," in *Tableau politique de la France de l'Ouest* (Paris: Colin, 1913), p. xxiv. The four main political groupings have been defined as follows: Communism = PCI in all elections; Socialism = PSIUP in 1946, PSI and PSDI thereafter; Catholicism = DC in all elections; Right = UQ, BNL and UDN in 1946, MSI, BN and Monarchists in 1948, and MSI, PLI and Monarchists thereafter. The PRI and local lists were left out of our analysis because they did not elect a deputy between 1946 and 1963.

The high proportion of local candidates and deputies, and particularly of Neapolitans (over 40 percent of candidates were born in the City of Naples) is in keeping with the city's intense local patriotism, an appeal which has been used constantly to woo the support of the Neapolitan city poor. The predominance of urban-born candidates over rural-born ones would appear to reflect the economic transition of the constituency from agriculture to industry and services, but this hypothesis may be incorrect. It is probable that, if we had comparable evidence for the origins of pre-fascist deputies, we would have found that the same situation existed then. Most landed proprietors were absentee landlords and from families that had lived in the city for at least a century. Moreover, the lack of educational facilities in rural areas has always acted as a spur to the families of richer peasants and small bourgeois to move into towns. Nonetheless, the percentage of candidates and deputies born in rural communes is not drastically smaller than the proportion of the population living in rural communes. The only partisan differences we need note are the contrast between the PCI and right-wing candidates and deputies, on the one hand, and the Socialist and DC ones, on the other, which is in keeping with the characterization of their electoral support, particularly that between PCI (urban and industrial) and the DC (rural and agricultural). This suggests, a priori, some relationship between candidates' origin, party electoral support, and preference voting.

The lack of women candidates reflects the politicians' traditional view of politics: that it is a man's occupation. Indeed, only three women, Vittoria Titomanlio (DC), Luciana Viviani, and Maria-Antonietta Macciocchi (PCI) have been elected to the Chamber in the constituency. Experience of more industrialized societies does not lead one to believe that the development of industry will increase rapidly the number of women in politics.[17]

The age distribution of candidates and politicians illustrates a number of interesting points. First, the average candidate is younger than the average deputy: success at one's first election is rarer than re-election; this is above all the case with Socialist deputies, as we shall see below. Second, left-wing candidates are younger than right-wing ones. Third, the PCI differs from all other formations in that the majority of its deputies are under fifty years of age. This is due to two factors: (1) its existence as a mass party dates only from 1945 and (2) the party has actively pursued a policy of switching candidates (over fifty percent changed at each election) to give as many local leaders as possible the experience of an electoral campaign and to emphasize that a parliamentary seat is in no way superior to party office. The greater age of the right-wing deputies illustrates that these parties provided a refuge for politicians active under earlier regimes. The age of DC deputies was kept

17. See M. Duverger, *The Political Role of Women* (Paris: UNESCO, 1956).

down by two factors: (1) the pressure of new generations of leaders to enter the Chamber; and (2) the transfer of "notables" to the Senate. The "notables" preferred to sit in the Senate because the constituencies were smaller and easier to control. Indeed, many were what one might call "safe DC seats." Thus, the average age of Senators is consistently higher than that of deputies.

One area where there are significant differences between political groupings is that of social class. Upper- and middle-class candidates compose a minority of PCI and Socialist candidates but a large majority of DC and right-wing candidates. Moreover, nearly a third of the PCI's candidates are of working-class origin. This is what we should expect since both the PCI and PSI define themselves as working-class parties. However, this observation is of limited political relevance since it is not reflected in similar differences between PCI and Socialist deputies, on the one hand, and DC and right-wing deputies, on the other. In fact, if successful candidates only are considered, the homogeneity of politicians' backgrounds reappears. It is true that the only working-class deputies have been elected in the PCI list, but their number, ten percent, was small. This suggests that their inclusion in the list was dictated more from a desire to identify the party's list in the minds of the electorate than to elect working-class representatives. However, the proportion of PCI working-class candidates also reveals that the party has a strong working-class, middle-level leadership.

The class characteristics of Neapolitan deputies are of considerable interest because, according to Sartori's study of the Italian Parliament,[18] the Campanian representatives in the Chamber are the most upper-class in Italy. In fact, one-quarter of the Italian upper-class deputies and one-eighth of the upper-middle-class deputies are elected in Campania. This consideration is supported by his figures of their class origins: only 5 out of 127 had fathers who were skilled workers or peasants, while the fathers of 40 were from the small bourgeoisie, 58 from the middle class and 9 were the sons of the nobility. The relevance of these figures is this: if, as Sartori has argued on the basis of his study, the Italian parliament has been characterized in the postwar period by a high degree of social mobility among its members and more open access [19] (higher than that of all other power centers except the ecclesiastical hierarchy), then it has occurred in the region of Campania, and in Naples in particular, less than any other region of Italy. Thus, not only are Neapolitan politicians in no way a representative cross-section of the Neapolitan people, but they have come to political success from reasonably

18. See G. Sartori et al., *Il parlamento italiano, 1946-1963* (Naples: ESI, 1963), p. 61.
19. Ibid., p. 346.

prosperous family circumstances. They were children whose fathers were unusually economically well-off and socially well-placed. Insofar as the chances of a successful political career rests upon family background, they have had the chances denied to the majority of Neapolitans: their families could give them the advantages in education and position requisite for the pursuit of political careers.

However, the specific character of the Neapolitan politician lies elsewhere. It can best be discerned in the socio-professional distribution of candidates and deputies (see Table 3). To stress its significance, we have subdivided occupations in the table into five sectors of activity: agriculture, industry and business, the professions, domestic life, and professional politics. This classification points to two privileged sectors: one so far as candidatures and

TABLE 3 – SOCIO-PROFESSIONAL OCCUPATION OF
CANDIDATES AND DEPUTIES, 1946 - 1963.

Occupation	PCI		Soc		DC		Right		Total		Sectors of activity
	c	d	c	d	c	d	c	d	c	d	
Landowner			3	3	4	2	9	3	16	8	*Agriculture*
Small holder	1		2		1				4		cand.: 24 3%
Agric. Labr.	2						2		4		dep. : 8 3%
Businessman			2		5		41	15	48	15	*Industry/Business*
Employee	6		19		12		20		47		cand.: 151 16%
Shopkeeper	1		8		1		10		20		dep. : 15 8%
Artisan							1		1		
Worker	26		15		1		1		43		
Lawyer	16	4	60	8	42	25	124	15	242	52	*Professions*
Doctor	6	1	18	1	18	10	31	7	73	19	cand.: 638 64%
Engineer	3		2		5	3	38		48	3	dep. : 123 60%
Journalist	3	1	4		9		24	6	40	7	
Magistrate			1		1		1	1	3	1	
Civil servant	3		18		11	4	16		48	4	
Teacher	11	1	24		20	12	23		79	13	
Univ. lecturer	5		9	3	13	6	27	5	54	14	
Army officer			1		6	3	25	7	32	10	
Housewife	2		6		3		17		29		*Domestic*
											cand.: 29 3%
											dep. : 0
Party official	40	23	10	4	7	4	1	1	59	32	*Prof. politicians*
T. Union											cand.: 143 15%
official	25	7	31		13	8	7		76	15	dep. : 47 25%
Not known			37		6		88		131		
Total	150	37	270	19	178	77	506	60	1104	193	

(Sources: Material supplied by parties, supplemented by press accounts.)

deputies go, the professions; the other for electoral success, professional politics. In Naples, the overwhelming majority of professional politicians are recruited from the same social area as are the professional men, the intelligentsia. Thus, the key social character of the Neapolitan politician is that he is usually a member of the intelligentsia.

Before considering the implications of this predominance of the intelligentsia, we should note three other points: (1) the systematic underrepresentation of the productive sector of society: agriculture, industry, and business account for less than twenty percent of candidatures and ten percent of deputies. This means that very few leaders of Neapolitan economic life are politicians. Achille Lauro, the big shipowner and Monarchist leader, and his clan of speculative businessmen are the exceptions which prove the rule: that there is generally a distinction between economic and political leaders. Most of the leaders of Neapolitan industry live in Rome and the North, since Neapolitan industry comprises in the main the subsidiaries of foreign and Northern private companies and state-holding companies, and Northern managers have preferred to refrain from participating in Neapolitan politics. Hence, the distinction is not so clear as it would appear, nor are its implications those which first come to mind. (2) No working-class candidate has been elected simply as a manual worker. Those few who have been elected were trade union officials. It can be argued that their real occupation was more intellectual than manual—which underscores the fact that it is virtually impossible for an active manual worker or peasant as such to be elected to parliament. Thus the peasants' and manual workers' refrain: "I have no time and work is my first worry.... Politics is for those who have the spare time...." remains substantially true. The number of worker candidates has remained stationary over the six postwar elections.

(3) There are privileged individual professions within the privileged area of the professions as a whole: law is the most obvious, but others are medicine and teaching. There has been a national tendency for the number of lawyers and university teachers in the Chamber to decline, for doctors to hold their own, and for schoolteachers to increase their proportions quite considerably. These trends can be observed in Naples, but with much less clarity than elsewhere. Thus lawyers are still predominant and schoolteachers have come to the fore much less. Finally, in 1968, the number of civil servants successful in the DC and Socialist lists doubled. Much has been written about the privileged position of lawyers in the world's legislative assemblies: that their verbal skills are similar to those demanded of politicians; that their involvement in bargaining and negotiation is a useful training ground for parliamentary politics; that politics is a useful and easy adjunct to professional legal activities since it publicizes the practice, etc. To this we need add only that Naples has a great legal tradition—its bar is the most famous in the peninsula—and many "idols of the Neapolitan Courts"

have been elected to the Chamber: Giovanni Bovio, Arnaldo Lucci, Enrico De Nicola, Giovanni Porzio. In fact, Porzio won the highest preference vote in Naples in 1946, and Giovanni Leone, the leading Catholic deputy, has continued the tradition of De Nicola by becoming president of the Chamber and president of the republic.

However, what we should like to stress is the strategic position of the lawyer in Neapolitan society: he understands the law (*Gesellschaft* rules) in a prevalently *Gemeinschaft* condition. Moreover, his clientele, like that of a doctor, provides an admirable base for Neapolitan-style parliamentary politics. The strength of this strategic position was made explicit, albeit unwittingly, by Pasquale Schiano, former Socialist deputy, in his evidence at the *De Lorenzo-Espresso* trial.[20] General De Lorenzo, the former chief of the general staff, alleged that Schiano had "organized a kind of private information service among the officers of the *Carabinieri* in the regions of the South." Schiano denied this insinuation, but admitted that he gained his knowledge of the preparations of the so-called coup of 14 July 1964, "in the course of (his) activity as a lawyer." The lawyer is, therefore, at the nodal point of two strategic areas: personal relations, like the doctor, and information, like the civil servant (and teacher). As information becomes public, i.e., as mass communication replaces face-to-face contact, so the new-style professions take the place of the old, as elsewhere in Italy. The strength and importance of old-style politicians in Naples is a valuable index to the dominant style of politics.

Neapolitan politicians are, indeed, the professional men, the educated and better class of people whom their constituents identify them as being. To be more precise, we have seen that they are recruited, by and large, from the intelligentsia. We have no exact figures of their educational attainment, but a rough surmise on the basis of our evidence indicates that, at least, ninety percent of deputies have a university degree. As regards unsuccessful candidates, the figure must be lower because of the proportion of lower-class PCI and Socialist candidates, but it must be in the region of sixty percent. This is natural, since the majority of politicians come from well-to-do families. In fact, most candidates give so many qualifications in their propaganda—Macciocchi has said that candidates seem to view an election as a *concorso per titoli!*[21]—that one has the utmost difficulty, in some cases, in determining the candidate's true occupation. Most of them claimed to be *dottore, Ingegnere, Avvocato* (even if they never practiced), *docente*

20. In R. Martinelli, *SIFAR—Gli atti del processo De Lorenzo-L'Espresso* (Milan: Musia, 1968), pp. 82, 145.

21. See M.–A. Macciocchhi, *Lettere dall'interno del PCI a Lousi Althusser* (Milan: Feltrinelli, 1969), p. 237.

universitario (even if they never taught) etc., and probably many were civil servants.

What the recruitment of politicians from the intelligentsia means for the politics of a disintegrated society such as that of Naples was made clear by Gaetano Salvemini in a celebrated article of 1911.[22] It is worth recalling the key passage, if only because Salvemini declared in 1955 that he found the activity of the Southern intelligentsia in the postwar period similar to what he had described four decades earlier. It was the stratum "which supplies the personnel for the government administration, the local administration and the parties, all the parties." "Not having anything else to do, they can devote all their time to public life, winning the top posts in the parties, becoming men of confidence, the holders of secrets, the guardians of the most delicate and strategic positions." In short, he suggests that they are middlemen and fixers in a society of scarce resources.

A Set of Middlemen I: Analysis of Parliamentary Activity.

Salvemini's suggestion is particularly useful because it furnishes the elements of our basic hypothesis which can be formulated thus: Neapolitan parliamentarians play the role of middlemen between the Italian state machinery and Neapolitan society; and this role determines their activity both in parliament and outside in their contact with local civil society. If this hypothesis is correct, given the contradiction between the rules of the national system which reflects the institutional arrangements of *Gesellschaft* and activity in a region where local values are still formed in largely *Gemeinschaft* conditions, we should expect: (a) that particularistic or *Gemeinschaft* orientations prevail over general or *Gesellschaft* orientations in the Neapolitan politicians' parliamentary activity; and (b) that the Neapolitan politicians' political activity will be characterized by a marked dualism between public and private conduct.

In order to appreciate the parliamentary activity of Neapolitan deputies, it is necessary to outline the main pecularities of Italian legislative practice and procedure. First, as a result of the universality of parliament's competence, and historical precedent (no defined area of administrative regulation; fascist use of decree-laws with force of legislation), everything is now considered to be within the domain of legislation.[23] This means that legislative production is very great—2317 laws were passed in the First Parliament (1948-53) and

22. "La piccola borghesia intelletuale del mezzogiorno d'Italia," in *Scritti sulla Questione meridionale, 1896-1955* (Milan: Einaudi, 1955), pp. 412 ff.

23. The figures quoted here come from M. C. Sforza, *L'Uomo Politico* (Florence: Vallecchi, 1963), pp. 233-34; and A. Predieri, "La produzione legislative," in G. Sartori et al., op. cit., pp. 205-76.

1767 in the Fourth Parliament (1963-68)—and that it is often confused, fragmentary and conflicting. Concomitantly, it means that the legislative pressure is immense. This can be seen in: (1) the number and constant increase in bills laid before parliament, which rose from 3,662 in the First Parliament to over 5,000 in the Fourth; and (2) the increase in Private Members' Bills over Government Bills from thirty-eight percent (forty-seven percent in the Chamber) in the First Parliament to seventy percent (eighty percent in Chamber) in the Fourth. Second, the Italian Parliament can, and does, legislate by committee: this unique device alone makes it possible to pass the bulk of legislation. The greater part of the time in full sessions is dedicated to formal ideological discussion of motions, interpellations, budgets, etc. On the other hand, legislation by committee is legislation behind closed doors by a small number of parliamentarians. Since it needs only the request of a fifth of committee members to get the matter discussed on the floor of the house, and since seventy-five percent of all legislation is passed in committee, and ninety percent of this is approved unanimously, it is clear that the area of agreement between all parliamentarians (including the PCI)[24] is very great, however violent the ideological clash on the floor of the houses in open sessions. Hence, non-public legislation by small groups with all the undemocratic behavior that it permits is characteristic of the Italian parliament.

One result of this situation has been a rise in the proportion of Private Members' Bills approved during the life of a parliament from twelve percent in the first to twenty-five percent in the third. In fact, the system clearly encourages the presentation of Private Members' Bills in favor of either restricted numbers of individuals, or occupational categories or pressure groups. In addition, in some cases Private Members' Bills are inspired and drafted by sectional interests in the administration. According to Professor Predieri's analysis,[25] twenty-eight out of the twenty-nine Private Members' Bills approved in the first semester of 1960 were bills for sectional interests (*leggine*). Lastly, because individual committees are often composed of parliamentarians with special interests in the committee's field (lawyers in the Justice Committee, teachers in the Educational Committee, former civil servants in the Public Works Committee, etc.), the committee often promotes and facilitates legislation favoring sectional interests. Indeed, rare, and getting rarer, are the Private Members' Bills discussed outside committee (less than

24. For a study of the PCI's legislative activity in the Third Parliament (1958-63), see P. Ferrari, in P. Ferrari and H. Meisl, *Les groupes communistes aux assemblées parlementaires italiennes (1958-63) et francaises (1962-67)* (Paris: PUF, 1969), pp. 28-101.

25. Predieri, op. cit., pp. 266-67.

twenty percent in the First Parliament and less than five percent in the Fourth).

The two areas where we have investigated the parliamentary activity of Neapolitan deputies are those of Private Members' Bills and Private Members' Questions for written answer. In the period, 30 April to 10 August 1969, four hundred bills were laid before the Chamber of Deputies;[26] forty-eight of these were associated with the names of Neapolitan deputies, in groups for the most part. While we were not able to gauge accurately the contribution of other constituencies, this number appeared higher than for most constituencies, particularly Northern constituencies. Seventy-five percent of the bills concerned occupational categories; eight percent Parliamentary Enquiries; two percent local matters; and the remainder (thirteen percent) were matters of general national interest. Typical of the former type were:

> Di Nardo (PSI), n. 1421 of 9 May 1969, "Extension of social security institutions to pensioners"; Napolitano F (DC), n. 1799 of 10 August 1969, "Amendment of the regulations of the Guardia di Finanza" (provision of rank of General); Lobianco and others, n. 1404 of 5 May 1969, "Entry of directive personnel in the ranks of State Professional Institutions"; Di Stasio (DC), n. 1597 of 18 June 1969, "Transfer by request to the category *'a disposizione'* of Lieut. Colonel pilots on regular commissions in the Air Force, who have been judged suitable for promotion at least three times but have not been placed on the promotion list"; Lobianco, Mancini V (DC), n. 1477 of 22 May 1969, "Confirmation of Chemist shop licenses to those managed on a provisional license for at least three years."[27]

Those of a general interest included:

> De Lorenzo (PLI), n. 1407 of 7 May 1969, "Road traffic"; Barbi, Bosco, Allocca Lobianco (DC), n. 1400 of 30 April 1969, "Direct Popular Election of Mayor"; Riccio, Napolitano F, Lobianco, Scotti, D'Antonio, n. 1565 of 10 June 1969, "Rules regulating the opening and operation of Gaming Houses."[28]

In the last year of the Fourth Parliament (March 1967 to February 1968), the Neapolitan deputies asked 345 questions out of a total of 3,394 asked in that period. This represents a percentage of 10.5% which is approximately double that of their numerical strength in the Chamber (6.2%). The content of these questions was as follows: *local* constituency problems, fifty-four percent; *other* (i.e., non-Neapolitan) constituency questions, five percent;

---

26. *Atti parlamentari*, Camera dei Deputati, Va. legislatura.
27. Ibid.
28. Ibid.

occupational group problems, thirty-five percent; general national problems, six percent. Typical examples of the first group of questions were:

> Jacazzi (PCI), "Telephone dialing in the zone of Aversa"; Abruzzese (PCI), "Aid for craftsman, Gaetano di Benedetto of Capri"; Romano (PSU), "Playing fields for Secondigliano"; Barba (DC), Public works in the Neapolitan area"; Riccio (DC), "Provisions for the economic and social development of the zone of Gragnano"; Riccio (DC), "Telephone kiosk in Massalubrense"; Carioti-Ferrara (DC), "Help for the Orfei circus of Castellammare."[29]

Typical examples of the third category included:

> Abernante (PCI), "Employment of war widows and orphans"; Caprara (PCI), "Promotion of NCO's in the *carabinieri*"; Bronzuto (PCI), "Promotion and appointment of *carabinieri*".[30]

A typical example of a general national question asked by a Neapolitan deputy was:

> D'Antonio (DC), "The suicide of singer Luigi Tenco".[31]

We can conclude, therefore, that Private Members' Bills and Questions concerned patronage and welfare for sectional (category) interests and narrow local constituency problems.

There seems to be a different tactical use of these procedures (see Table 4.) according to whether the deputy was associated with the government or in opposition. The observer would expect the opposition parties to present more Private Members' Bills (because in Italian terminology these include all non-governmental bills) than the government parties. But the PCI bills are either presented corporately by the parliamentary group in opposition to government bills or in motions. Thus there would seem to be a division of labor: the government leaving it to its back-benchers to introduce all sectional measures; and the PCI coordinating prospective opposition legislation through the party group and leaving less initiative to its ordinary members of

TABLE 4 – USE OF PRIVATE MEMBERS' BILLS AND QUESTIONS BY POLITICAL FORMATION

	PCI	Soc.	DC	Right	Total	N.
Private Members' Bills presented	8%	20%	52%	20%	100	(400)
Private Members' Questions	49%	16%	11%	24%	100	(3394)

(Sources: Analysis of Atti parlamentari)

29. *Atti parlamentari,* Camera dei Deputati, IVa. legislatura.
30. Ibid.
31. Ibid.

parliament. It is clear, moreover, that the PCI prefers to concentrate its influence in committee while conducting its political campaigns in plenary sessions.[32] Last, the government does not use the liberty of action that this division would appear to give it to prepare and push through general legislation because it is just such legislation that the postwar governments have singularly failed to pass. As regards Private Members' Questions, it is the opposition, and the PCI, as we should expect, which monopolizes this procedure to sap the government's prestige and standing.

Giorgio Galli[33] has indicated that Italian parliamentarians spend most of their parliamentary time in vague and imprecise politico-ideological speech-making. In fact, six out of seven arguments of speeches analyzed by the Cattaneo Institute[34] were found to relate to reciprocal contests between members of different parties to appropriate for themselves the epithets "honest" and "democratic." In addition, five percent only of PCI members' arguments referred to Marxism and ten percent only mentioned capitalism, i.e., had some specific theoretical content. The rest were indeterminate as were the arguments of members of other parties. Despite this, the difference in tactical approach between government and opposition is reflected in the style of Neapolitan deputies. The important thing for all, including ministers, is to remind constituents that they are continually doing things for them. The *Atti parlamentari* (the official record) can be dispatched to the constituents concerned. Hence, a DC member like D'Antonio, can introduce a bill to include primary school teachers in the lists for the special recruitment examination with the following protestation, knowing full well that the beneficiaries will learn of his efforts. This explains why his appeal is addressed more to his electors than to his colleagues:

> The present bill brings here the echo of much pain and suffering. It represents the thread of hope of a thousand or so generous and abandoned teachers who have now got white hair and a family to support and who face the specter of hunger after having devoted decades of worthy service to education, as is testified by their qualifications . . . . My real intention is to call on the legislature to make an act of reparation . . . .In this respect the South, as always, has been worst hit . . . . Our bill is not therefore the usual end of legislature Private Members' Bill to nourish hope and snatch a few votes from the poor occupational category concerned. As an old parliamentarian, this is not our habit. It is a case of people in need,

32. Ferrari, op. cit., pp. 87-90.

33. Galli, in *Il bipartismo imperfetto, comunisti e democristiani in Italia* (Bologna: Il Mulino, 1966), pp. 299 ff.

34. Results reported in ibid., pp. 300-302.

who ask that the legislature's intentions be respected: the settlement
of a category by examination. This appeal can be accepted without
calling on public funds. It means increasing the number of posts and
adding this worthy category to those destined for the teachers'
special examination . . . . We are sure that our request will find a
favorable response in the hearts of all colleagues . . . [35]

The individual PCI member prefers to use his initiative to attack the
government for what it has not done. This kills, electorally speaking, two
birds with one stone: it proves (1) his interest in those concerned; and (2) the
government's disinterest. Thus Abernante asked the Minister of Labor:

what measures he proposed to take against the ex-Biglia Company
of Sant'Antimo which had been sold to FAX, after having obtained
public financial assistance, and which had extorted letters of
resignation from the dependent workers by threat of dismissal . . . and who were now deprived of compensation for loss of
employment . . . . [36]

A question can also be used to suggest improper behavior and discredit an
opponent, as when Abernante (PCI) asked the minister of health about the
conduct of the veterinary surgeon of Sant'Antonio Abate; and the local
prefecture's inaction:

Finally, the questioner wants to know if the Prefecture's conduct
was linked to the fact that the above-mentioned dott. Cafiero is a
crony and *"grande elettore"* of Senator Gava, and brother-in-law of
Avv. Roberto Gava, the Senator's son.[37]

The government has, of course, much more powerful means for keeping in
touch with the electorate during the legislature. It not only controls much of
the mass media, particularly television, but many of its acts affect the
ordinary citizen directly in his everyday life. Moreover, as Alfredo Reichlin,
the PCI deputy, declared in the Chamber during the debate on the economic
measures for the South in spring 1969, a minister does not lose an
opportunity of informing his constituents of his activity on their behalf:

And I think On. di Vagno, of all those years spent in Bari when not
a day passed, it can truthfully be said, without one reading on the
first page of the *Gazzetta del Mezzogiorno,* a telegram from On.
Moro (Prime Minister) announcing a new provision (*provvidenza*), so
you say, it appears to me, in your charitable language, and when I
add all these telegrams to those of the various DC, and even alas, the
Socialist notables which appear in *Il Mattino, Giornale della Sicilia,*

35. *Atti parlamentari*, CD, seduta del 25 genn. 1968, p. 42744.
36. *Atti parlamentari*, CD, seduta del 19 guigno 1967, p. 9873.
37. Ibid., p. 9980.

> *Unione Sarda,* you will allow me ... to ask if you intend to
> continue along this road.[38]

A few days after the debate had finished in the Chamber, the following news item appeared in the columns of the Casertan edition of *Il Roma*:

> One can read in a telegram sent by Minister Bosco to Prof. Bruno
> Visentini, chairman of Olivetti: "Further to my telephone call I
> wish to let you and members of Olivetti Board know my deep
> appreciation for sensibility which Directors showed decision enlarge
> factory Pozzuoli and set up new factory Marcianise as contribution
> to economic development of South etc." . . . Once again our fellow
> townsman and minister has been very active in a question vital for
> the industrial development of Terra di Lavoro. He will continue to
> be active—we can be sure—given the strong local spirit which
> animates him. . . .[39]

The final way in which the parliamentarian can keep contact with his electorate is to be active in, or nurse, his constituency. We have noted elsewhere that most deputies retain local office—provincial or municipal councillorships—after their election to the Chamber. Local contact is the main reason for this. Frequent visits to the constituency, local party activity in the area, etc., are all parts of this endeavor. One method of combining one's parliamentary role with direct association with one's constituents is leading delegations of protest. These are frequent and depend on the gravity of the local problem: either the all-party delegation of solemn protest to the head of government or that of a specific social category to the minister concerned. Thus, on the one hand, we read in the local press that "Mayor Moscati, accompanied by all the Neapolitan deputies, took advantage of the new name for the old poverty of Naples to call on the head of government to explain to him the real evils which afflict the Neapolitan social body,"[40] while, on the other, "400 employees of the Prince of Naples Hospital are going to Rome today to request the approval of measures that will increase the contribution to the institution from 70 to 500 billion lire a year. The delegation will be led by a DC Parliamentary group who presented the bill, among whom will be On. Davide Barba; they will request the reorganization of the institution's financial situation, which is in grave deficit; it is unable to pay the employees' wages."[41]

From this brief survey of their parliamentary activity, we can conclude that the Neapolitan deputies tend to play a middleman's role. Certainly, particularistic orientations prevail over general ones. Indeed, deputies are

38. *Atti parlamentari,* CD, seduta del 17 aprile 1969, p. 6803.
39. Issue of 4 May 1969.
40. *Il Risorgimento,* 3 December 1948.
41. *Il Mattino* of 8 March 1968.

continually concerned to use their national position to reinforce their local political position and remind their electors of their national activity in the local interest. In many ways, this situation is inherent in representative politics. All politicians face, in fact, a conflict between normative rules and practical conduct. Giorgio Galli has argued that it is singularly acute in the Italian parliament where he contrasts "the ideological diatribes on the floor of the house with the costly compromises in committee."[42] Is it more acute for the Neapolitan deputies? We believe that it is because the parliamentary system which they work is liberal/democratic (i.e., *Gesellschaft*) in inspiration whereas the political methods they employ are more suitable to an oligarchic regime with strong *Gemeinschaft* overtones. This impedes them from making a normative justification of their activity in its own terms and forces them to adopt a Jekyll and Hyde attitude to it. On the one hand, they will exalt their activity as dedicated to the common good: Giovanni Leone, for instance, has written of "a ruling class that . . . has demonstrated a strong capacity for action and achievements, the close relationship between the people's aspirations and the active conscience of the many men called to be responsible for the destiny of the nation."[43] And, on the other, they will vociferously deny responsibility for any of the deleterious aspects of the system. Silvio Gava, as an example, claimed that "we don't pretend that the clientelistic phenomenon has completely disappeared; on the contrary we note with apprehension and sorrow certain localized reappearances which don't come from our side."[44]

A Set of Middlemen II: Analysis of Political Dualism.

The second set of sub-hypotheses generated by the role of middlemen exercised by Neapolitan Parliamentarians concerns the permanent dualism in their political conduct. Neapolitan electoral activity is founded essentially on personal relations, on what we have characterized as vertical ties of political loyalty. It permeates all levels of Neapolitan political activity from the most modest to the most exalted. We have noted elsewhere the importance of the training of the "secretaries of the secretariat" and recruitment by co-option by important political leaders in parliamentary careers. The necessary corollary of such a situation is that an individual politician's position is measured in terms not only of the votes he can mobilize but the number of political messengers and "go-betweens" he can command. Neapolitan politics in point of fact revolve round the diplomacy of the personal emissaries of the

42. Galli, op. cit., p. 318.
43. G. Leone, *Testimonianze* (Milano: Mondadori, 1963), p. 9.
44. S. Gava, *La parte di Marta, Testimonianze di vita politica* (Naples, ESI 1968), p. 484.

various political leaders, with all the weapons, reciprocal favors and veiled threats, which such activity implies. For example, the correspondence between Giovanni Leone and Angelo Corsi, chairman of the National Institute of Social Security (INPS), published by *L'Espresso* in 1966, contains the following exchange describing their communications when Leone was Prime Minister in 1963. Corsi wrote inter alia on 13 December 1965:

> [T] he second fact, clearer and more significant that you cannot forget is that . . . you charged On. Renato Morelli, who visited me at my home and asked me strangely if I had nothing against a meeting with the Prime Minister and whether I would be favorable to Morelli's presence at the meeting. I expressed considerable surprise at such a procedure because a simple telephone call would have been enough for me to accept the Head of Government's request; in any event I accepted the double request. The meeting took place in your private office in Palazzo Chigi and you asked me to reintegrate Prof. Di Maria, now lecturer at the University of Catania, in the service, which I believed was contrary to the regulations in force.
>
> But before telling me of that, you spoke to me at length complaining about my refusal to suspend the transfer of Prof. Babolini in September, 1963, and you told me candidly that, if it had taken place, "all Naples would have attributed it to Giovanni Leone," because, you added, "I opposed the candidature of Babolini in the last parliamentary elections" (and so made clear the ethnic and linguistic reasons that led you to want only Neapolitan-speaking candidates). Finally, you added that you lost over 50,000 votes in the last elections.[45]

Leono's reply of 16 December contained the following passages:

> At this point I am obliged to open a parenthesis: Prof. Di Maria, of whom I will speak below, has been for many years your intermediary with me for soliciting my intervention in your favor when it was a question of having you confirmed as chairman of the Institute (it is worthwhile recalling that the last confirmation was much disputed and was made on the undertaking that you gave to President Gronchi of retiring after two years). The same Di Maria was mobilized by you to intervene with me to induce me to delay the legislative procedure of approval of the above-mentioned bill [reorganizing the INPS]. It is true that I did not accept such a suggestion because of my duty of impartiality . . . .
>
> The opinion that your act was an act of reprisal connected with this

45. Documento n. 10, in *Il libro rosso dell'INPS,* supplemento all'*Espresso* of 13 March 1966.

parliamentary affair known to me, the belief that it was an illegitimate procedure and a sense of chivalry towards Babolini induced me to intervene. Here it is necessary to refer to my position with regard to Babolini. As I told you in the meeting at Palazzo Chigi . . . I, in spite of my esteem and appreciation of Babolini, professionally and morally, opposed his candidature for Parliament in the Naples constituency, on the grounds that he was not a Neapolitan but only living "temporarily" in my city. This convinced Babolini that his political aspirations had been sacrificed; but accustomed as I am, not to reprisals but to generosity–I thought I could do something for him. And I did so with great tact, not taking advantage of my power as Prime Minister but using the services of an intermediary and friend, whose assistance you had asked for several times when you found it useful, i.e., Prof. Di Maria. I knew that he had been your doctor for many years and so closely associated with you that he had always given you, *free of charge,* a long, successful and devoted professional attention. You are well aware that the Prime Minister could, at least on personal grounds, invite you into his office, but I did not wish, not even formally, to draw attention to my position. I preferred not to interrupt your holidays at Salsomaggiore and accepted the courtesy of Di Maria in informing you of the position I have outlined above . . . And we come to the meeting at Palazzo Chigi in the presence of our common friend Morelli. That meeting was determined by the spontaneous and generous initiative of Renato Morelli, to whom I had mentioned, by chance, your pitiless reprisal against Prof. Di Maria as a result of the attempt at mediation which you so decisively refused; and Morelli asked me if I had any difficulty in meeting you (Morelli, in fact, remembered that you had on occasion appealed to me, through Di Maria, for confirmation as chairman of INPS, because your confirmation was linked to his) . . . . [46]

These letters and other documents are full of all the world of personal diplomacy: Leone's protestation of acting personally and not as prime minister runs, moreover, like a *leitmotif* through his letter. It is interesting to compare his language in this letter with that of his speeches; the former is self-righteous and the latter upright and moralizing. The first masks an iron fist in a silk glove and the second reveals the soul on the tip of the tongue:

It is certain, declared leone in his peroration celebrating the twentieth anniversary of the DC in Naples, that Providence ought to be our guide and inspiration; but ours is the task of preparing the

46. Ibid., documento n. 12.

minds and consciences so that the elections of 1963 renew the pact
of love between the DC and Italy and mark for us a new and more
intensive phase of work for the good of the country, for an
ever-growing and stable well-being for our people and those classes
on whose behalf the work of justice and progress was begun and still
needs to be completed .... In the light of our outstanding
traditions, in the name of our dead leaders who live in our reverent
memories, in memory of so many battles fought in the name of the
purist ideals and won with generous popular support, let us prepare
minds and souls for the next, but not least hard-fought battle. Raise
your hearts, O Christian Democrats of Naples and Province, in the
service of the fatherland, so that the progress of our country may
continue in order, in liberty, and with justice .... [47]

or again in the 1963 election campaign:

[T]he last centers of paternalism, exloitation and cries of popular
suffering must be destroyed to make a platform for the deeds of the
last Masaniello! Naples has waited over a century for its own social
resurrection.... [48]

The problem which Leone, like all Neapolitan politicians of whatever
political persuasion, face is that their electoral and personal politico-diplomat-
ic activities cannot be justified in straight *Gesellschaft* normative language.
Gesellschaft norms imply a rational basis, those of *Gemeinschaft* the goodwill
of established authority. In short, the one appeals to the principles of a
political argument and the other to the quality of the person making it; or,
again, the one talks in terms of Rights and Duties and the other in terms of
Vices and Virtues. In consequence, the Neapolitan politicians clothe their
activity in the full-scale normative respectability of principles which
ill-disguise their *Gemeinschaft* inspiration. The result of this confusion is the
sentimental rhetoric which we have just observed in Leone's speeches.
Moreover, it leads them into considerable misunderstanding or misrepresentation of events. A classic example was the claim made by Leone in an
interview he gave on giving up the presidency of the Chamber to become
prime minister in 1963:

Quite frankly, I was very sorry indeed, he said, to give up the
Presidency. You will understand that I was Vice-President for five
years and President for eight .... But as a Neapolitan I have the
sense of state (*lo senso dello stato*) and I accepted this new
responsibility in a difficult situation for the country ....
Neapolitans in all social classes have the sense of state to the point

47. G. Leone, op. cit., pp. 414-5.
48. Quoted in *Il Tempo* of 17 April 1963.

> of exasperation .... I will never forget seeing this monarchical city literally delirious in its enthusiasm for the President of the Republic, when I accompanied Einaudi from Naples to Campobasso as Vice President of the Chamber ....[49]

This claim that the Neapolitans have a "sense of the state" indicates either misunderstanding or misrepresentation because of the widespread estrangement of large sections of the population from the state and its institutions. However, that Leone's claim springs from misrepresentation rather than misunderstanding seems clear from the example which he provides to support his assertion: the belief that the acclamation of the president of the republic had any overt political significance outside the traditional flattery of established authority in the hope of *largesse*.

It is only fair to add that Leone's language was in no way unique: his eloquence may have been more rhetorical as befits a celebrated lawyer. Achille Lauro and Giorgio Amendola, to take two leaders from opposite poles of the political spectrum, employed similar techniques; they appealed to established, but strictly nonaccountable authorities, like the king or Antonio Gramsci, as symbols or *suppositiones*. There were, moreover, some politicians who dispensed with the *Gesellschaft* clothing to their political appeals altogether. Senator Buglione, one of the Monarchist leaders, was wont to open his speeches in pure *Gemeinschaft* language: "Neapolitans, last month I was with our beloved King and he said to me, dear Buglione, go out among the Neapolitans and kiss them for me, one by one"[50]

A paternalistic conception of politics "as doing good," *fare del bene* (virtue) is a basic element of the southern Catholic tradition of the Neapolitan upper classes. The politician was traditionally conceived as a sort of worldly pastor, looking after the material interests of his constituents, as the shepherd does his flock; the government was seen as a good family father, *"buon padre di famiglia."*[51] It underlay the DC Southern policy of 1947 in the celebrated slogan, "The South, the commitment of honor of the DC."[52]

This political attitude, which we can define as typical of *Gemeinschaft*, has three implications that have informed the whole of the DC's conduct in the South in the postwar period. First, the inferiority of the South was the condition of its need of help. Second, it needed interceders with the government to get that help. Third, help is a good in itself; hence criticism of

49. Reported by C. Cederna, in "C'e un Moro ai piedi di Leone," *L'Espresso* of 20 October 1963, p. 14.

50. Quoted in *Il Piccolo* of 17 April 1963.

51. See Gava's speech of resignation as minister of the treasury (January 1956) in Gava, op. cit., pp. 200-201.

52. Ibid., pp. 501-2.

the costs or methods of getting that help are not only irrelevant but
ungrateful. The inferiority of the South in the postwar period has formed a
part of the general patrimony of all politicians. On the other hand, typical of
the exaltation of intercession and its achievement as a positive value (which is
also a normative justification of the whole procedure) is this passage from
Senator Gava's eve of poll speech:

> [W]e send instead our message of gratitude, not only to Minister
> Pastore, but also to Prime Minister Moro—Prime Minister today, and
> we hope tomorrow—who the day the work on Alfa-Sud was
> initiated promised me, who had asked him in the name of all the DC
> deputies of Naples, his immediate interest which has revealed itself
> today to be so prompt, efficient and decisive for the approval of the
> plan . . . .[53]

Lastly, charity (*caritas*) is the traditional Catholic concept which makes help
or any governmental measure providential and justifies it as a good in itself.

A second area where the dualism of the politicians' conduct can be found
is the differences in their local and national political positions, i.e., between
those assumed in Naples and in Rome. Before fascism, local power was
dependent on access to state patronage and to secure it the local deputies
were prepared to change allegiance to support the government. The
mechanism still works but has changed considerably in form with the
development of organized political parties. Today it must be sought in the
government parties in the subtle play of factions. The most notorious
examples concern the DC, because it is the major government party. In 1954,
for example, Senator Gava, although a minister in the ruling "Centrist
coalition of DC, PLI, PSDI and PRI," launched his "Holy Alliance" in
Castellammare with Achille Lauro and the Neofascists to win control of the
commune from the Left, and succeeded by a few hundred votes. Again, in
1961, although nationally a supporter of the "opening to the left" (alliance
with the PSI), Gava did not hesitate to sponsor the "Magnificent Seven"
operation and the formation of a city administration in Naples with the
support of the Monarchists. On both occasions he denied that there was any
incompatibility or incoherence in his action of promoting local alliances with
reactionary opposition parties.[54]

Similarly, Senator Bosco (DC Minister and boss of Caserta) has aptly been
described as a past master of this kind of political maneuver in his federation.
A respondent commented on Bosco's career: "He has controlled the Casertan
federation since 1954. He is a *fanfaniano* but above all his is a power faction.

---

53. Ibid., p. 503.
54. For details of both, see P. A. Allum, *Politics and Society in PostWar Naples,*
(Cambridge, England: Cambridge University Press, 1972), chap. 9.

He is a centrist . . . and opposed the "center-left," but he accepted it in order to remain in power."[55] This dualism arises from the fact that the deputy plays the role of link-man between the state machinery and Neapolitan society. In consequence, local and national power in the DC are mutually interdependent: national power in the party is based on local power and vice versa. The politician has to control both at the same time and the loss of one could cause the loss of the other. The local DC parliamentarians were forced to qualify their positions ideologically in the national arena because *Gesellschaft* was dominant there. The local dominance of *Gemeinschaft* made this superfluous in Naples. An ideologically active young DC leader analyzed this phenomenon at the time of the "Opening to the Left" in these terms:

> A second aspect of the problem of political method inside the DC concerns the ambiguous conduct of many Neapolitan political leaders . . . . They are politicians who lead a double life: they pose as supporters of popular action and progressive policies in Rome, while in Naples one finds them supporting positions which are barely democratic. In Rome, recently paladins of the center-left, in Naples defenders of the *status quo,* of the *clientele* system and their own power positions. . . . The rhetoric and demagogy of their speeches and writings serve both in Rome and Naples as a mask for deception.
>
> It is yet another example of the old technique of only formal differences in the worn-out mold of traditional southern *trasformismo;* but even today, the deception works and only a few have realized what is happening (this is why the center-left, with so many defenders, failed in Naples; only a few of the many who talked about it, really wanted it).[56]

It should be said that the same kind of factionalism can be found in other parties; relations with Saragat were the key to power positions in the PSDI for many years;[57] relations with the central ruling group—the apparatus—appears to be the key in the new situation that has arisen in the PCI.[58]

Conclusion

The case we have been arguing cannot be proven in all particulars. It has to stand or fall on the balance of probabilities. Its key proposition is that

55. Allum Interview n. 23, p. 9.

56. "Un problema di metodo all'interno della DC napoletana," in *Hermes,* 15 November 1962, p. 4.

57. PSDI, *La federazione di Napoli dalla gestione commissariale al XIV congresso provinciale* (Naples: Cortese, 1964).

58. See M.–A. Macciocchi, op. cit., pp. 325 ff.

Neapolitan politics is carried within the framework of the boss system rather than exercised in terms of ideological commitment towards mass society. In support of this proposition a fundamental place devolves on the nature of the political ties between the deputy and his constituent. The evidence of personal influence and so of narrow vertical political ties, is impressive, if not overwhelming. Thus, although no more can be said of our other propositions than that they are interrelated and interdependent, this does mean that the whole is greater than the sum of the parts.

The Neapolitan politician, as we saw, is a member of the intelligentsia who aspires to upper-class income and status which entry into the Italian parliament secures. He will have made a career through party responsibilities, usually at the provincial level, and in local public office; family and political connections will have opened doors; and in the course of his political career, particularly if he started on the Right, he may well have changed party. Lastly, if he is a member of the government party, or rallied to one of them, he can expect a public appointment on defeat or retirement from the Chamber; if he is a member of the PCI he can expect the party to give him a new assignment.

The political dualism of the Neapolitan politicians, analyzed in this article, both in their role as middlemen in the distribution of patronage and in their political activity, is a symptom, not a cause of their situation. It points up a clear prognosis: the intelligentsia is a parasitic stratum and, as Croce noted of nineteenth century liberals, it lacks "roots in the real force of a social class."[59] Its lack of an autonomous economic base means that it must be on the side of the classes which control the state. In Italy since unification these have invariably been the dominant classes of the North. This has not prevented certain members of the intelligentsia from becoming leaders of the class parties opposed to the dominant national class, nor does the action of individuals change the overall activity of the mass of the intelligentsia. As a result, while individual politicians may act from altruistic motives, the mass of successful parliamentary politicians are forced by their class position in Naples to act as middlemen. Croce observed that the nineteenth century liberals remained "superior, abstractly superior to the country, outside and ignorant of it"[60] and the only sorts of contacts which the majority of Neapolitan parliamentarians have with their constituents are clientelistic ones. Hence, it is not to be wondered at that they were, for the most part, representatives of conventionality, empty rhetoric, weakness and opportunism, whose role has been, in Marx's words "to misrepresent the people in Parliament."[61] In so acting, of course, they were doing no more than playing

59. B. Croce, *Una famiglia di patrioti* (Bari: Laterza, 1918), p. 30.
60. Ibid., p. 40.
61. Marx and Engels, *Selected Works*, 1:521.

a well-rehearsed historical part: that of " 'agents' of the ruling class for the subordinate functions of social hegemony and political government"[62] in a political situation marked by a substantial lack of social consensus.

62. A. Gramsci, *Gli intellectuali e l'organizzazione della cultura* (Turin, Einaudi, 1949), p. 9.

8. Moments of Madness*

ARISTIDE ZOLBERG

I.

If politics is "the art of the possible," what are we to make of moments when human beings living in modern societies believe that "all is possible"? We know with assurance that such moments occur, if only because those who experience them are acutely conscious of their unusual state. Speaking with tongues, they urgently record their most intimate feelings. Furthermore, they are often aware of affinities across time and space with others in similar circumstances. Are they moments when politics bursts its bounds to invade all of life, or on the contrary, are they moments when political animals somehow transcend their fate? So much in the conventional paraphernalia of political science is founded on axiomatic instrumentalism that we do not know what to make of events in which the wall between the instrumental and the expressive collapses. Is this politics or prophecy? Is this politics or poetry?

We might more comfortably cast these pentecosts beyond the pale of our scholarly concerns were it not for their ineluctable reality and historical significance. Since we cannot ignore them, we tend to segregate them from our main concern, the universe of "normal" political events. As occasional pathologists, we make room in our discipline for the study of revolutions, and sometimes even include near- or quasi revolutions; more recently, taking our cue from sociology, we have also begun to study "collective behavior" more generally. It is possible, however, that this prejudgment as to what is normal and what is not hampers our understanding of politics, and that the meaning of moments when "all is possible" can be better apprehended if we seek instead to share the experience of participants in order to understand the place of these moments in the political life of a modern society.

*In addition to the sources cited below, I would like to acknowledge my debt to Vera Zolberg, Annie Kriegel, Nathan Leites, Clifford Geertz, Cherry Turkle, and the students in my seminar on "Politics and the Contemporary Arts" at the University of Chicago for their stimulating responses to the ideas contained in this paper. I have also benefited from the unpublished paper by Victor Turner, "Passages, Margins and Poverty: Religious Symbols of Communitas," and generally from the works of Harold Rosenberg. An earlier version of the essay was presented at the September 1971, meetings of the American Political Science Association in Chicago. I am grateful to Carey McWilliams, panel chairman, for his encouragement. The subsequent comments of Lloyd Fallers, Roger Masters, Mark Kesselman, and Sidney Verba prompted several revisions.

For this purpose, the most interesting case is France. In the Paris of May 1968, innumerable commentators, writing to celebrate or to deplore proffered a vast range of mutually exclusive explanations and predictions. But for all of them, the sensibility of May triggered off a remembrance of things past. By way of Raymond Aron, himself in touch with Tocqueville, readers of *Le Figaro* remembered February 1848; by way of Henri Lefèbvre, French students remembered the Proclamation of the Commune in March 1871, as did those who read Edgar Morin in *Le Monde;* French workers listened to elder militants who spoke of the occupation of factories in June 1936; and most adults, whether or not they had been in the Resistance, relived August 1944, the liberation of Paris.

These connections across one hundred and twenty years establish a tangible set available for analysis. Although other modern societies have experienced moments of political enthusiasm when "all is possible," in France alone have these moments been so recurrently visible at the very center of society, and hence become so embedded in the political consciousness transmitted by the national culture. That is indeed what makes the French case such an inviting starting-point. Paradoxically, the considerations that lead to the selection of France may reflect such a unique constellation of factors as to make France no "case" at all. Unique or not, the French experience provides an opportunity to penetrate somewhat more easily the inherent strangeness of a political phenomenon shared to a greater or lesser extent by all modern societies.

II.

Edgar Morin and Raymond Aron, among the first to record and to analyze May 68, remain the most valuable commentators because they emerge brilliantly at opposite ends of the range of interpretations. Morin hailed the student uprising as the dawn of an age; Aron shivered in the dusk of civilization. That they were both immensely wrong matters little for our present purpose. What is more remarkable is that, when one reads between negatively and positively loaded lines, their perceptive observations of the spirit of May are strikingly similar. Although Aron wrote *La Révolution Introuvable* against Morin's *La Brèche,* Morin had already stated that it was a "quasi or peri-revolution."[1] Where Morin was carried away by "the great festival of youthful solidarity," the "permanent game" which was also a

---

1. Raymond Aron, *La Révolution Introuvable. Réflexions sur la Révolution de Mai* (Paris: Fayard, 1968), especially pp. 14, 31, 145; Edgar Morin, Claude Lefort, and Jean-Marc Coudray, *Mai 1968: la Breche. Premières réflexions sur les évènements* (Paris: Fayard, 1968), especially pp. 20-33. Throughout this paper, all translations from the original French are my own.

serious strategy, in which revolutionary incantations achieved a "genuine socialization," Aron, mixing compassion with contempt, perceived "youthful brotherhood in a semi-delinquent community," a moment in which "feelings were more important than words," a "psychodrama" which might have become "drama," a "tragi-comedy" which might have become "tragedy." Aron's forthright statement of his intention to "demystify" and "desacralize" perhaps constitutes the best confirmation of Morin's identification of the moment as strange and extraordinary. Both captured the exaltation; but the "ecstasy" of the one was "delirium" for the other.

"All is Possible!"—expressed in pamphlets, speeches, posters, or be-ins: ecstasy or delirium? Rather than arbitrate let us merely note that in this as in other moments, both words—or others like them—are used for the same phenomenon and that it is usually a matter of which side the observer is on. And rather than dwell on May 68, let us rapidly explore the earlier moments which it evoked. The nearest one, for Frenchmen, was the liberation of Paris. In that case, for understandable reasons, the record is one-sided. When Leclerc's men march through the streets after several days of uprising, Adrien Dansette records a moment of "communion."[2] Liberated Parisians and victorious warriors "live a dream more beautiful than dreams, a dream which they have not imagined." He cites the words of a diarist: "An eruption of volcanic happiness," of "absolute magic." To demonstrate that "the rhythms, habits, modes of thought and of feeling of daily life are engulfed in the intoxication of the present moment," Dansette cites an anecdote which demonstrates that "amidst the general exaltation, money is no longer a thing of value." De Gaulle expressed the same sentiments in his first radio address: "And why should we hide our emotion? And why should we hide what grips us? . . . Each of the moments we are living transcends our own lives, our poor lives."[3]

The atmosphere of the streets was congruent with the sensibility of Parisian intellectuals and of the *Résistance* generation more generally. According to Simone de Beauvoir, fear returned on the morrow of the liberation as German missiles fell on Paris and as the war continued,

> But it was rapidly swept away by joy. Day and night with our friends, talking, drinking, strolling, laughing, we celebrated our liberation. And all those who celebrated it as we did, nearby or far away, became our friends. What an orgy of brotherhood! The darkness which had imprisoned France was bursting.[4]
>
> . . . .
>
> This victory erased our old defeats, it was our own and the future it

2. Adrien Dansette, *Histoire de la Libération de Paris* (Paris: Fayard, 1946), p. 365.
3. Quoted in Dansette, ibid., p. 403.
4. Simone de Beauvoir, *La Force des Choses* (Paris: Gallimard, 1963), p. 13.

> opened belonged to us. Those in power, they were members of the
> Resistance, men whom, more or less directly, we knew. Among
> those in charge of the press and of the radio, we counted numerous
> friends. Politics had become a family affair, and we intended to
> make it our business. "Politics is no longer dissociated from
> individuals," Camus wrote in *Combat* at the beginning of
> September. "It is a direct speech by man to other men." To speak
> to men, that was our role, for us writers.[5]

The moment of immense joy, when daily cares are transcended, when
emotions are freely expressed, when the spirit moves men to talk and to
write, when the carefully erected walls which compartmentalize society
collapse, is also a moment of political harmony. As Simone de Beauvoir
records it:

> In this climate, all oppositions became shadowy. That Camus was
> hostile to the Communists, that was a subjective trait of little
> importance since, struggling to bring about the implementation of
> the C.N.R. [National Council of the Resistance] charter, his
> newspaper defended the same positions as they did. Sartre, albeit
> sympathizing with the Communist party, nevertheless approved
> *Combat's* position, so much so that he even once wrote its editorial.
> Gaullists, Communists, Catholics, Marxists, fraternized. A common
> thought was expressed in all the papers. Sartre granted an interview
> to *Carrefour*. Mauriac was writing in *Les Lettres Françaises*. We all
> intoned in chorus the song celebrating tomorrows.[6]

That the moment was fugitive—her next paragraph begins, "Soon, *Les
Lettres Françaises* fell in to sectarianism . . . "—should not blind us to its
radiance. Indeed, we must rid ourselves temporarily of our compulsive
concerns with causes and consequences to empathize properly with the
phenomenon under consideration which is itself characterized by a
suspension of these concerns. We must do so in approaching the Popular
Front, eight years before the liberation of Paris, without denying that France
was profoundly divided at the time, that the Popular Front may have been a
Comintern trap, and that even sympathetic historians have since pointed to
grave mistakes in the Blum government's social and economic policies.
Nevertheless, concluding their balanced appraisal of its achievements, L.
Bodin and J. Touchard can state with assurance that

> The balance sheet of the Popular Front cannot be based only on the
> number of laws voted or of decrees signed; the essential thing
> appears to be of another order. As there was a spirit of 1848, so

5. Ibid., p. 14.
6. Ibid., p. 18.

> there was a spirit of 1936, which infused life into a whole ritual of
> rallies and parades, of slogans and songs, of gestures and flags.[7]

And they end the book with:

> The Popular Front was something other than a mere electoral
> coalition, and it is undoubtedly difficult to bring it back to life, in
> our own day, otherwise than in a picture book.[8]

The keynote of the Popular Front was a sentiment of liberation: political, economic, and social—of minds and bodies. This was especially visible among the workers who, even as Léon Blum formed his government, launched an immense wave of sit-in strikes: "A few million workers were affected by the most spectacular movement in French social history,"[9] replicated after the publication of Bodin and Touchard's book in 1968. Although much was written at the time on the causes of this movement (A Trotskyite plot? A Stalinist stab-in-the-back? Bourgeois provocation?), observers from different sides agree on its spirit. Simone Weil, the mystical martyr of French labor, found "joy" in the factories where she herself had worked a few months earlier. She noted that the workers were not merely concerned with grievances:

> After having always bowed, suffered everything, taken it all in
> silence for months and years, it is a matter of finally having the guts
> to stand up. To stand upright. To take one's turn to speak. To feel
> like men, for a few days.[10]

The good-hearted happiness in the factories is confirmed by Bertrand de Jouvenel:

> The beginnings of all revolutions demonstrate that Jean-Jacques
> Rousseau was right. Nothing puts man in a better mood than to
> escape the boredom of his routine and the laziness of his
> obligations. He laughs, he walks around, and you think that he is
> naturally good.
>
> For three days I went from factory to factory. . . . I didn't see a
> single case of brutality . . . of damage to a single machine. The
> "sit-down strike" is a protracted picnic.
>
> An effort must be made to remember that we are witnessing a
> battle. Who is the enemy? Where is the enemy?
>
> . . . Amidst this camp life, a sort of warmth arises, a human
> contact which is never useless between the one who commands and

7. L. Bodin and J. Touchard, *Front Populaire. 1936* (Paris: Armand Colin, 1961; "Kiosque"), p. 164.

8. Ibid., p. 232.

9. Ibid., p. 107.

10. Quoted in Bodin and Touchard, ibid., p. 112.

those who carry out his orders. But the boss in most cases stayed home.[11]

Reviewing the evidence, Bodin and Touchard stress that the spirit of 1936 was not limited to the workers:

> Brotherhood, solidarity, hope, the great illusion of happiness and of peace: all these feelings experienced with confused intensity by the hundreds of thousands men and women who brought to power the Popular Front are to be found in the literature—and also in the films—of 1936.[12]

Bodin and Touchard connected 1936 with 1848. But the Commune, whose memory was celebrated in the first great manifestation of the Popular Front on May 24, 1936, and whose hundredth anniversary was not celebrated in the appropriate spirit in 1971 perhaps because that had already been done three years earlier, stands between those two dates. To what extent did Henri Lefèbvre transform the Paris of 1871 into a cause of the Paris of May '68? A parenthetical question, of some interest here because Lefèbvre's critique of daily life in advanced industrial societies and his advocacy of the "festival" as an appropriate revolutionary remedy were much better known in France than the writings of Marcuse.[13] He undoubtedly influenced the "situationists" (the nearest French thing to Yippies or to Kabouters) when he taught at Strasbourg, and Cohn-Bendit in Nanterre, providing a logic for the activities of cultural revolutionaries' manipulating the prank as a terrorist weapon. In any case, *La Proclamation de la Commune,* presented as a "completion of Marx," is a critical book for our purpose.[14]

Without mincing words, Lefèbvre states that "the question of style dominates all others" in the historiography of the event and asserts that "the style particular to the Commune was that of the Festival." He writes,

> The Paris Commune? It was first of all an immense, a grandiose festival, a festival which the people of Paris offered to themselves and offered to the world. Festival of spring in the City, festival of the disinherited and of the proletarians, revolutionary festival and festival of the Revolution, total festival, the greatest of modern times, it unfolds first in magnificence and joy.[15]

The "style" is confirmed by Jacques Rougerie, a much less ideologically committed historian, who gives us, among other eyewitnesses to the

11. Ibid., p. 114.
12. Ibid., pp. 167-68.
13. See especially *La vie quotidienne dans le monde moderne* (Paris: Gallimard, 1968, "Idées").
14. Henri Lefèbvre, *La Proclamation de la Commune. 26 mars 1871* (Paris: Gallimard, 1965), p. 11.
15. Ibid., pp. 20-21.

exaltation of Paris in the days after the municipal election of March 26, Jules Vallès:

> What a day! The warm and clear sun which gilds the maws of cannons, the scent of flowers, the flutter of flags, the murmur of this revolution which flows by, tranquil and beautiful as a blue river, the light tremors, the lights, the brass bands, the bronze glimmers, the explosions of hope, the perfume of honor, there is enough to intoxicate with pride and joy the victorious army of republicans. . . . Embrace me, comrade, who shares my grey hair! And you, little one, playing marbles behind the barricade, come to me as well! March 18 saved you, urchin! You might have grown up like us, in the fog, trampled in mud, rolled in blood, died of shame, suffered the unmentionable pain of those without honor! It's over! . . . Child of the desperate, you shall be a free man! I have my money's worth of happiness. . . . It seems to be no longer mine, this heart torn by so many ugly wounds, and it seems that the very soul of the crowd now fills and expands my chest. Oh! If only death could get me, if only a bullet could kill me in this radiance of resurrection.[16]

Reviewing the overall evidence concerning the character of the Commune, Rougerie acknowledges that participants honored violence against enemies as a fundamental virtue but adds, "I must immediately counterpose—was it a virtue?—*good nature.*" He points out that these insurgents "who spoke such a violently terrorist language were the least terrifying men in the world, and this undoubtedly cost the Commune a great deal. Very few went from their frightening words to acts (except in the exceptional circumstances of the Bloody Week). The guillotine was burned; and all together fewer than one hundred hostages were massacred. He concludes, "The Commune, it was first of all the festival, not the barbaric and criminal orgy so comfortably described by the 'witnesses' on the Versailles side."[17]

Although he criticizes Lefèbvre for the use to which he put his findings, Rougerie credits him for "restituting to the men of '71 this genuine an-archizing virtue which was theirs, which was until now poorly perceived (or else knowingly hidden), as was the case yesterday for the *sans-culottes.*"[18] His own analysis of original data and documents demonstrates that, before its degeneration into sectarian quarrels, the Commune was genuinely united on a "Declaration to the French People" (April 19) and that this constituted "a *program,* reasonably constructed and ultimately coherent even if it does not resolve all questions after so many

16. Quoted from *Le Cri du Peuple,* March 29, 1871, in Jacques Rougerie, *Paris Libre 1871* (Paris: Editions du Seuil, 1971, "Politique,") pp. 146-47.
17. Ibid., p. 233.
18. Ibid., p. 235.

ambiguities and contradictions, in which one has a premonition that the genuine revolution will be 'the antithesis of the State.' " Even Marx, he points out, agreed.[19] Furthermore, analyzing the Commune's policies, Rougerie concludes that its ideology was an original one, not to be seen through the eyes of sectarians who later fought for possession of the Internationale. The Commune was Socialist, of a Socialism "which still resembles in many traits the experience attempted in 1848. It was not merely a matter of giving work to those who were unemployed, even if that was an urgent task. Everything rests on the cooperative and free association of workers." These were not the "degraded and petty businessmen's cooperatives" of the Second Empire, but growing cooperatives which would irresistibly, they thought, take over the administration of things. That socialism was to be accomplished *"Thanks to the Commune,"* which was not a weak non-state, but "the absolute right for the communal group to create its political organ as a means to bring about the liberation of labor."[20]

In the light of independent confirmation by Rougerie of the overall character of the Commune, some of Lefèbvre's conclusions are not so farfetched. He writes, among other things:

> 1. The insurrection of March 18 and the great days of the Commune that followed constituted an unlimited opening toward the future and the possible, without care for the obstacles and the impossibilities which barred the way. A fundamental spontaneity . . . sets aside secular layers of sediment: the State, bureaucracy, institutions, dead culture. . . . In this movement prompted by the negative, and therefore creative, elements of existing society—the proletariat—, social action wills itself and makes itself free, disengaged of constraints. It transforms itself in one leap into a community, a communion in whose midst work, joy, pleasure, the achievement of needs—and first of all social needs and the need for sociability—will never be separated. In the wake of economic 'progress,' man will free himself of economics. Politics and political society will disappear by merging into civil society. The political function, as a specialized function, will no longer exist. Daily life will be transformed into a perpetual festival. The daily struggle for bread and work will no longer make sense.[21]

Therefore, Lefèbvre concludes, the Marxist thesis of the end of human prehistory was no mere utopia. "For a few days, this utopia, this so-called myth, was actualized and entered into life."[22]

19. Ibid., p. 157.
20. Ibid., pp. 186-87.
21. Lefèbvre, *La Proclamation*, op. cit., p. 389.
22. Ibid., p. 390.

III.

If, as Lefèbvre insists repeatedly, the Commune was the greatest festival "of the century and of modern times," what are we to make of the February Revolution of 1848? The ambiguity of the moment is captured in all the writings surrounding that event. It is not merely that men wrote for or against, as with all other revolutions, but rather that the most brilliant contemporary analysts were both for and against. This fundamental ambivalence has persisted down to the present as in the work of the late Georges Duveau who writes within a few pages of "the lyrical illusion" and of "the miracle of 48."[23] Duveau, like all others, is a prisoner of history and experiences the greatest difficulty in perceiving February 1848 without being overwhelmed by its sequels; nevertheless, he does conclude that although there was some initial violence, "in spite of all frictions, one experiences on the morrow of the proclamation of the republic, an extraordinary impression of freedom, of happiness, of fulfillment."[24]

Among the many talented writers who personally lived the Paris of February, Flaubert and Tocqueville are unsurpassed witnesses because, both having reached a negative evaluation of what was a central event in their lives, they struggled relentlessly to record its truth. Although the statesman was as antiromantic as the novelist, and although each wielded irony and sarcasm as the weapons of reason, each provides us with a glimpse of the irresistible exaltation of the moment.

Flaubert traveled to Paris in order to participate in the demonstrations announced by the opposition newspapers and was eventually drafted into the Second Republic's National Guard. In L'Education Sentimentale (published in 1869) the revolution erupts as Frédéric Moreau, the provincial bourgeois youth "subject to all weaknesses,"[25] "in order to better violate in his soul Mme Arnoux," his elusive romantic love, brings a fancy prostitute "to lodgings prepared for the other."[26] The revolution begins as he possesses her. Then, suddenly awakened by the sound of shots, Frédéric wanders through a long chapter in which his personal life and history mingle. When are we seeing through Frédéric's naive eyes, when through the bitter wisdom of the novelist? No matter, for the time being.

Paris is a torrent of words: "Men possessed by a frenzied eloquence harangued the crowd on street corners."[27] Flaubert repeats this observation

23. Georges Duveau, 1848 (Paris: Gallimard, 1965; "Idées"), p. 61 and p. 69.
24. Ibid., p. 71.
25. Gustave Flaubert, L' Education Sentimentale (Paris: Editions Garnier Freres, 1964), p. 300.
26. Ibid., p. 285.
27. Ibid., p. 287.

throughout, often giving us glimpses of what the torrent contains. It is a sometimes incoherent amalgam of possible and impossible aspirations to change the world. Quite independently of Marx and, as we shall see, of Tocqueville, Flaubert points to the theatrical quality of it all:

> Frédéric, caught between two deep masses, did not move, indeed fascinated and having a marvelous time. The falling wounded, the stretched out dead, did not look like real wounded, like real dead. He felt as if he were watching a spectacle.[28]

What an exalting spectacle it is! Showing his awareness of how close it comes to horror by interspersing his narrative with pejorative words and images, Flaubert nevertheless records the joy, the playfulness, and the harmony of the crowd. In the palace, after the crowd throws the throne out the window, "a frenzied joy burst out, as if, instead of the throne, a future and unlimited happiness had appeared. . . ."[29] It is a time for games: "Since they were victorious, shouldn't they have a good time?"[30] The contents of the palace become toys. Improvising like children, rather than following a script like actors, the people play "dress up" in a way that verges on obscenity. Outside, Frédéric (who is taken in by the spirit of the crowd) and Hussonet (who is not) meet Dussardier, a genuine revolutionary. "Ah! What happiness, my poor old buddies!" The People is triumphant! Workers and bourgeois are embracing! Ah! If you knew what I've seen! What wonderful people! How beautiful!"[31]

Dussardier will be wounded while repressing the popular insurrection of June; while recovering, he is tortured by the idea that he fought against justice; and he will be killed resisting the coup d'état. By then, Frédéric, absorbed in his sentimental pursuits, will have become indifferent to politics. But in February, Frédéric was caught up in "the magnetism of the enthusiastic crowd. He inhaled voluptuously the thundery air, full of the scent of powder; and yet he shivered in an exhalation of immense love, of supreme and universal tenderness, as if the heart of all of mankind beat in his chest."[32] Has Flaubert suspended ironic disbelief? Perhaps, as when he describes the festive atmosphere of the city. Everyone is in the streets. Like Saul Bellow observing turned-on New York through Mr. Sammler's one good eye, Flaubert takes change in dress as an indication of departure from ordinary times. In the Paris of 1848, "negligence of dress attenuated differences of social ranks." And he goes on: "Hatreds were hidden, hopes were displayed, the crowd was full of softness. The pride of a conquered right

28. Ibid., p. 288.
29. Ibid., p. 290.
30. Ibid.
31. Ibid., pp. 292-93.
32. Ibid., p. 294.

burst out on faces. There was gaiety as in a carnival; it looked like a bivouac. Nothing was as much fun as the way Paris looked in the first days."[33]

If Flaubert ever departs from irony, it is not for long. Joy fostered political unity. It is not only Frédéric, caught up by the moment of "universal madness,"[34] who joins the Republic, but everyone else as well. First of all, Frédéric's mistress, the prostitute. But Flaubert immediately adds that she was merely doing "as Monsignor the Archbishop had already done, and as were to do with marvelously hurried zeal the Magistracy, the Council of State, the Institute, the Marshals of France, Changarnier, M. de Falloux, all the Bonapartists, all the legitimists, and a considerable number of Orleanists."[35] Among them was Alexis de Tocqueville.

As a member of the constitutional opposition under the July Monarchy, Tocqueville had warned his friends against actions that might lead to a revolution they might not be able to control. Was the revolution which did occur a mere parody, as for Marx? Tocqueville, in his *Souvenirs,* is much less one-sided: "Our French, especially in Paris, easily mix memories of literature and of theater into their most serious demonstrations."[36] Thus, the *spectacle* aspect is not fortuitous; it is not merely a phenomenon in the eye of the beholder, it is an aspect of action; art becomes a determinant of political life. This process, Tocqueville continues, "often lends support to the belief that the sentiments they are displaying are false, while they are in reality merely awkwardly adorned." In 1848, "the imitation was so visible that the terrifying originality of the events was hidden by it."[37]

Tocqueville wanders through Paris the day after Flaubert's Frédéric. The monarchy has fallen. The city is peaceful as if "on a Sunday morning."[38] He meets some soldiers strolling about without arms. Writing from hindsight in the winter of 1850-51, he observes: "The defeat which these men had just experienced had left in their soul a very vivid and very lasting impression of shame and of anger; we've seen that since. But nothing of it showed at the time; among these youths all other feelings seemed to be absorbed by the pleasure of finding themselves free. They walked without care, stepping lightly."[39] The soldiers were going home. But the streets must not have remained empty all day because, continuing his walk throughout the afternoon, Tocqueville says he must record two dominant impressions: First, "the uniquely and exclusively popular character of the revolution which had

33. Ibid., p. 295.
34. Ibid., p. 300.
35. Ibid., p. 294.
36. Alexis de Tocqueville, *Souvenirs d'Alexis de Tocqueville* (Paris: Gallimard, 1942; "Mémoires du Passé pour servir au temps présent"), p. 63.
37. Ibid.
38. Ibid., p. 78.
39. Ibid.

just occurred," and specifies that he means that the revolution "gave overwhelming power to the people properly speaking, that is to say, to the classes that work with their hands, over all others."[40] We get a sense of the *visibility* of their presence in Paris for the first time. This gives a concrete specificity to Tocqueville's second impression which is "the paucity of passionate hatred, and even, to tell the truth, of vivid passions of any sort displayed in this first moment by the lower people who had suddenly become the masters of Paris."[41] Peace and harmony were very prevalent; Tocqueville notes the absence of disorder in spite of (or because of?) the invisibility of the police. And he records an impression of unity:

> It was for the first time in sixty years that priests, the old aristocracy, and the people were meeting in a common sentiment, a sentiment of grievance, in truth, and not of affection; but that is already a great deal where common hatreds almost always provide the foundation of friendships. The genuine and only losers of the day were the bourgeois, but even those had little to fear.[42]

Remember Rougerie's contrast between the violent language of the *Communeux* and their good-natured behavior? Tocqueville notes that the languor of the people was in contrast

> to the bombastic energy of the language and the terrifying memories which the language brought to life. The truth is that never had a greater change in the government, much more, in the condition of a nation, been the work of citizens possessed of so little emotion.[43]

Historical works and especially plays had made the Terror fashionable; "the names and examples of illustrious wicked men were cited all the time, but nobody had the energy nor even the sincere desire to imitate them."[44]

Early in his account, Tocqueville hints at the "terrifying originality" underlying the spectacle. What was new was that

> This time, it was not merely a matter of insuring the triumph of a party; there was an aspiration to found a social science, a philosophy, I could almost say a religion suitable to be learned and followed by all men. There was the really new part of the old scene.[45]

That newness is to be discovered in the torrent of words. There was little disorderly conduct, but

> an extraordinary agitation and unheard of disorder in the ideas of the people. As early as February 25, a thousand strange systems

40. Ibid., p. 79.
41. Ibid.
42. Ibid., pp. 81-82.
43. Ibid., p. 82.
44. Ibid., p. 82.
45. Ibid., p. 80.

> issued impetuously from the minds of innovators and spread
> through the troubled mind of the crowd. Everything was still
> standing except the monarchy and parliament, and yet it appeared
> as if society itself had crumbled into dust under the shock of
> revolution, and as if a contest had been launched for the design of
> the edifice to be erected in its place. Every man submitted his plan;
> this one put it in the newspapers; that one on the posters which
> soon covered the walls; and this other cast it to the winds in
> speech. . . .[46]

Uniting the "thousand strange systems" was one word: "socialism."

Tocqueville was no Frédéric Moreau. But from the depth of his winter of discontent in Sorrento, consigning his most intimate thoughts to the privacy of his memoirs, he must explain, at least to himself, how even he joined the Revolution, submitting himself to the demotic arbitration of universal suffrage. It pains him to do so, he tells us, because even if one wishes to be sincere, "one is too close to oneself to see clearly. . . . The innumerable tiny paths known poorly even to those who walk on them prevent them from discerning the highways followed by the will to reach the most important conclusions."[47] Nevertheless, relentlessly treading the paths leading away from the conscious self, he reaches the truth. And so the confession begins:

> I will therefore say that, when I came to peer attentively into the
> deepest reaches of my own heart, I discovered there, with some
> surprise, and a certain relief, a sort of joy mixed with all the sadness
> and all the fears which the revolution was bringing to life. This
> terrifying event made me suffer on behalf of my country, but it was
> clear that I did not suffer on my own behalf; it seemed to me, on
> the contrary, that I was breathing more freely than before the
> catastrophe.[48]

Even for Tocqueville, the moment was irresistibly liberating. Out of the destruction of the old political world,

> There issued indeed, it is true, a disordered and confused society,
> but one in which cleverness became less necessary and less prized
> than disinterestedness and courage; in which character was more
> important than the ability to speak well or to manipulate men, but
> especially in which there was no longer any room for intellectual
> uncertainty: here lies the country's salvation, there its downfall. No
> more mistakes to be made about the road to follow; we would walk
> on it in broad daylight, sustained and encouraged by the crowd.[49]

46. Ibid., pp. 82-83.
47. Ibid., p. 88.
48. Ibid., pp. 88-89.
49. Ibid., p. 92.

And therefore Tocqueville went to Normandy, seeking a mandate from the people.

IV.

Ecstasy or delirium, the thing happened and it was unmistakably political. The recurrence of these moments over one hundred and twenty years, recognizably the same in spite of variations, gives the phenomenon a persuasive concreteness each event may not possess individually. The evidence contained in the purposely heterogeneous testimony gathered in this essay is remarkably consistent. Whatever the attitudes of the writers at the time of writing, whatever role they played in the events, whatever their mode of writing, they record intense moments of festive joy, when an immense outpouring of speech, sometimes verging on violence, coexists with an extraordinarily peaceful disposition. Minds and bodies are liberated; human beings feel that they are in direct touch with one another as well as with their inner selves. The streets of the city, its objects, and even the weather take on harmonious qualities. Falsehood, ugliness, and evil give way to beauty, goodness, and truth. Factions and parties appear unreal while personal networks appear strong as steel. The private merges into the public; government becomes a family matter, a familial affair. Simultaneously, there is a disposition to encounter the *déjà vu;* through the medium of collective memories recorded in sophisticated or demotic culture, in historical works or in folklore, human beings connect the moment with others. Liberated from the constraints of time, place, and circumstance, from history, men choose their parts from the available repertory or forge new ones in an act of creation. Dreams become possibilities.

The connections among the elements that contribute to the fugitive apparition of this exalted sensibility become somewhat more apparent when we examine the circumstances in which the Parisian moments occurred. Two of them, 1871 and 1944, came after periods of severe physical and mental deprivation. The liberation of Paris after four years of Nazi occupation marked not only the end of an absence of political freedom, but also, as Simone de Beauvoir points out, the end of humiliation. That it did not mean the immediate end of scarcity of food, clothing, and shelter was not known at the time; in fact, in the joy of liberation, these things were unimportant. Mind prevailed over matter and scarcity was abolished by a change of values through an act of the human will. That is the process which links 1944 with 1871. Paris rejoiced in the proclamation of the republic on September 4, 1870; but afterwards, the city experienced an unusually harsh winter compounded by the Prussian siege and during which relations between Paris and the national government steadily deteriorated. The Parisians felt abandoned, humiliated, and betrayed; they were being punished for their history. After several abortive attempts, the democratic and socialist victory in the municipal elections of March triggered an explosive springtime of freedom in which scarcity was again transcended into abundance. These elements were also present in 1848, which came not only after several years of increasingly arbitrary and rigid rule, but also after a famine and a cholera epidemic. Although the Popular Front followed the Great Depression and arose in the face of an impending Fascist threat, the specific combination of material and political deprivation was not clearly present; it was of course even less to be found in 1968. The occasional absence of the combination altogether as well as the fact that "moments" do not always occur when it is clearly present suggests that we should seek other commonalities. Some of them become visible only *after* the fact.

On the very first day of the revolution of 1848, a week before the provisional government unanimously decreed universal suffrage, the people was born to political life. Indeed, the speed with which the decision concerning universal suffrage was taken, at a time when popular participation belonged to the realm of utopia, and realized—very imperfectly—only in the nowhere that was America, confirms the sudden visibility of hitherto invisible men recorded by Tocqueville. Visibility, birth, entrance of human beings hitherto excluded from society: a cataclysmic phenomenon repeated in each of the moments considered.[50] In 1848, it was the people as a whole; but it was also specific categories of people. In spite of Tocqueville's initial belief, "those who work with their hands" did not become all-powerful in 1848. They irrupted into society again in 1871, reasserting their rights as political citizens, but remained deprived of the economic benefits of that membership, even after they forced the door again in 1936, exalted once more by the amazing spectacle of their strength. What they failed to achieve in 1936 was at the center of their aspirations thirty-two years later when the factories were again turned into joyous bivouacs in the name of participation.

Barely noted by historians is the fact that those who entered society in 1848 also included women. Anticipating some of our own contemporary stereotypes, Flaubert gives us Mademoiselle Vatnaz, *La Vatnaz,* "one of these unmarried women of Paris ... who dream ... of everything they lack. Therefore, like many others, she hailed in the Revolution the coming of revenge;—and she carried on frantic socialist propaganda."[51] This woman, who believes the Fourierist gospel that "the liberation of proletarians will be possible only by means of the liberation of women" is no mere caricature; her presence in *L'Education Sentimentale* is historically correct. Flaubert's sarcasm notwithstanding, he was probably in touch with that aspect of the

50. I am indebted to the Turner paper cited supra for the focus on "entrance" of the "marginals" and the relation of this process to *Communitas.*
51. Flaubert, *L'Education Sentimentale,* op. cit., p. 299.

Revolution through his friend George Sand. "The illustrious Madame Sand" herself appears in Tocqueville's *Souvenirs*, seated next to him at dinner. "I was gravely prejudiced against her," he confesses, "because I hate women who write, expecially those who disguise the weaknesses, of their sex by erecting them into a system . . .; but in spite of that, I liked her."[52] Surprised to find in her "something of the natural manner of great minds," he remembers speaking with her "for a whole hour of public affairs," adding, as if to explain this unlikely statement, "Besides, she was at that time a sort of politician." Although they did not talk about women—he only tells us how well informed she was about workers—her very presence contributes to the present point. Just as workers entered more than once, so did women: recent historiography has set the record straight about the *pétroleuses* of the Commune; the Popular Front government was the first one to include women; the liberation gave women voting rights and, even more significantly, saw a since unequaled number of women elected to public office at the municipal level.

The prominence of students in May 1968 requires little elaboration. Edgar Morin hinted at the very process under discussion when he stated that "the great festival of youthful solidarity, the great syncretic game of revolution were, at the same time, on an individual plane, an entrance examination into society (which, at the moment and for most people, seemed preferable and much superior to school examinations), and, on a collective plane, the will to assert themselves in and against society."[53] But can we view students as an excluded group in the same sense as the people, the workers, the women? Their situation in society evokes privilege rather than deprivation, especially in France. It may be that the particular student aspect masks a more general aspect which connects 1968 with the other moments in the series. In each of them, observers noted the prominence of youth. It is only in our own time that many of them are students; but even in 1968, young workers were especially visible among those who occupied factories.

An emphasis on biological age may itself hide more than it reveals. Most likely, the phenomenon under consideration involves the sudden entrance of a *generation* into public life. The rhythm of such events is irregular because the formation of generations is the result of a combination of demographic and political factors. In particular, it may involve the shared experiences of growing up in times when political life is suspended, as was the case between 1940 and 1944, or between 1851 and 1870. In those cases, there is a connection between the formation of a generation, exclusion, and deprivation. But a generation can also share the experience of growing up in a particular ideological camp at a time when the camp does not have access to

52. Tocqueville, *Souvenirs*, op. cit., pp. 134-35.
53. Morin et al., *La Brèche*, op. cit., p. 21.

power, as with the French Left in the decades preceding 1936 or 1968. Or, more problematically, it may involve coming of age during a period when the game of politics is unusually routinized and boring.

Boredom is perhaps the best thread to guide us through the labyrinth. Youth is unusually sensitive to its prevalence in a particular age; they share this flair with others who are especially attuned to sensibility, chroniclers and artists. Together they constitute the intolerant vanguard which may trigger off the mechanisms that transform the world into an attractive place. Shortly before May 1968, Pierre Viansson-Ponté repeated on the front page of *Le Monde* the grievance Lamartine had hurled at the July Monarchy: *La France s'ennuie!* Jean-Luc Godard had already expressed the same message surrealistically in *Week End,* released in late 1967. After the fact, Raymond Aron agreed that the dullness of routinized Gaullism was among the causes of May. A generation earlier, for the vast majority of West Europeans, the consequence of the wartime deprivations and humiliations noted earlier was boredom rather than tragedy. Through the works of Sartre and Camus, this concrete experience was amplified into an interpretation of the human condition. Engagement through participation in the Resistance was one way *out* of boredom and *into* a better life, and it was the spirit of those who refused to be bored which transformed Paris in August 1944, as it had brought joy into the factories in 1936. Lefèbvre's work on the Commune further contributes to our perception of the connections between physical deprivation, exclusion, the absence of freedom, and the rebellion against dullness which ensued. But whether or not we accept Lefèbvre's view that the boredom of daily life is the form which alienation takes in contemporary societies, we should not stop with 1871 because it was 1848 which was the first revolution against boredom.

Of that there is hardly any doubt. Tocqueville makes the point twice, in very different ways. First, at the very beginning of his *Souvenirs,* he writes concerning the July Monarchy:

> In this political world . . . what was most missing, especially toward the end, was political life itself. It could hardly come to life or be sustained within the legal sphere delineated by the Constitution; the old aristocracy had been defeated, the people excluded. Since all affairs were treated among the members of a single class, in its interest, in its spirit, it was impossible to find a battlefield where great parties could wage war. This singular homogeneity of position, of interest, and consequently of the views that prevailed in what M. Guizot called the legal country, removed from parliamentary debates all originality, all reality, hence all genuine passion. I spent ten years of my life in the company of very great minds, which constantly busied themselves without being able to warm up and

who used all their perspicacity to discover subjects on which there
could be deep disagreement, without being able to find any.[54]

And in case the message is not clear, he writes in the next paragraphs that at the level of the political class, "there reigned nothing but languor, impotence, immobility, boredom" and that "the nation was bored listening to them."

Almost unwittingly, Tocqueville provides us with a second assertion concerning the importance of boredom. Crediting Lamartine, the poet who became a member of the Provisional Government and who yearned to be the George Washington of France, with "having contributed more than anyone to the success of the February revolution," Tocqueville charges that the poet was unwilling later to sacrifice himself to save the country. Stressing his lack of character, he writes:

> I don't know whether I ever encountered, in this world of selfish
> ambitions, in the midst of which I have lived, a mind more empty of
> the thought of the public good than his. I have seen in that world
> many men make trouble in the country in order to make themselves
> great; that is the run-of-the-mill perversity; but he is the only man, I
> believe, who always seemed to me ready to turn the world upside
> down to divert himself.[55]

Unlike Lamartine, Tocqueville was unwilling to launch a revolution against the boredom he too found unbearable. Once others had done so, however, did not Tocqueville also feel an irresistible elation? "I discovered . . . with some surprise . . . a sort of joy. . . . I was breathing more freely than before the catastrophe."

V.

If 1848 was, at least in part, a revolution against boredom, then we might ask why Lefèbvre chose instead the Commune as his subject. He says, remember, that the spirit of the Commune demonstrates that the Marxist thesis of the end of human prehistory was no mere utopia because "for a few days, this utopia, this so-called myth, was actualized and entered into life." *Marx's Utopia?* The utopia that was fugitively actualized in 1871 and in each subsequent moment of joy was the utopia of 1848. It was not Marx's, but that of the socialists upon whom he heaped his scorn. The thread we have followed leads us to the most underrated prophet of modern times and through him to an understanding of some important connections between politics and art in the past century.

It required intellectual courage for the late Georges Duveau to argue, in the France of 1954, that Marx's thunderings against the utopian socialists

54. Tocqueville, *Souvenirs,* op. cit., pp. 29-30.
55. Ibid., p. 112.

"are not always justified, because it is possible to fail in the face of immediate events while being right in the long run. The utopists of '48 were not mistaken about the direction of history, but about its speed. More presbyopics than dreamers."[56] Fourier, in particular, "anticipated Freud; his vision of human nature is richer, more modern than that of the well-thinking men of his time."[57] And long before they became once more respectable, Duveau predicted the ultimate triumph of the utopian socialists over Proudhon and Marx because "urban man runs the risk of wilting and must renew himself in contact with nature." More recently, Frank Manuel summarized Fourier's teachings as follows:

> Fourier's "passionate series" centered around psychological differences. The bringing together of eight-hundred-odd recognizable psychological types under one roof was a precondition for happiness in a phalanstery; otherwise the variety of relationships necessary for total self-fulfillment in the State of Harmony would be lacking. Since work without love was a psychological burden, a pain to be eradicated from utopia, Fourier developed the mechanism for making labor "attractive," a free expression of the whole self, never divorced from erotic inclinations.[58]

Having earlier pointed to the *boredom* inevitably engendered by the unchanging state of previous utopias, Manuel concludes: "Fourier widened the dimensions of utopia beyond anything that had been dreamed of before, and in retrospect he emerges as the greatest utopian after More."[59]

Fourier died eleven years before 1848, but his genius was widely recognized for decades afterwards. Here is a tribute first published in 1880:

> [W]e find in Fourier a criticism of the existing conditions of society, genuinely French and witty, but not upon that account any the less thorough. . . . Fourier is not only a critic; his imperturbably serene nature makes him a satirist, and assuredly one of the greatest satirists of all time. . . . Still more masterly in his criticism of the bourgeois form of the relations between the sexes. . . . But Fourier is at his greatest in his conception of the history of society.[60]

The voice is that of Engels, praising Fourier only better to damn him: "To

---

56. Georges Duveau, *Sociologie de l'Utopie et autres "Essais"* (Paris: Presses Universitaires de France, 1961), p. 31. The work, published posthumously, is a collection of essays published separately in the early 1950s.

57. Ibid., p. 124.

58. Frank Manuel, "Toward a Psychological History of Utopias," *Daedalus* 94, no. 2 (Spring 1965): 307.

59. Ibid., 308.

60. Friedrich Engels, *Socialism: Utopian and Scientific,* in Lewis S. Feuer, ed. *Marx and Engels: Basic Writings on Politics and Philosophy* (Garden City: Doubleday Anchor Book, 1959), pp. 76-77.

make a science of socialism it had first to be placed upon a real basis."[61] Although this is not the place to undertake an analysis of the views expressed by Marx and Engels throughout their writings concerning the utopians, the quotation is sufficient to reveal the *ambivalence* that we should find. This is not surprising since, in spite of his condemnation of the utopian-inspired movements which competed with the ones he supported, Marx partly shared the sensibility of his enemies. If Fourier sought a way to end boredom, Marx's genius, as Duveau put, "was to have understood that democracy gave life a whimpering, fastidious, schoolroom tone: history is drama."[62]

But the condemnation of the utopians contained in the *Communist Manifesto,* written at the height of their influence and published amidst signs of the impending doom of the revolution their spirit inspired, is most severe. The *Manifesto* charges that "historical action is to yield to their personal inventive action, historically created conditions of emancipation to fantastic ones. . . ."[63] It speaks further of "such fantastic pictures of future society, painted at a time when the proletariat is still in a very undeveloped state," of "this fantastic standing apart from the contest," of "their fanatical and superstitious belief in the miraculous effects of their social science."[64] What were Marx and Engels getting at? Perhaps that Fourier and the others were poets and painters, seeking to promote salvation by altering the *vision* human beings had of society. And this condemnation of "revolution as art" evokes Flaubert's parallel scorn for the opposite phenomenon. In the crucial chapter discussed earlier, Pellerin has contributed to the revolution by means of a painting: "It represented the Republic, or Progress, or Civilization, in the shape of Jesus Christ driving a locomotive, which traveled through a virgin forest." In case we don't get it right away, Flaubert speaks through Frédéric, who exclaims: "What garbage!"[65]

Conclusion

In the course of seeking to achieve some understanding of a disturbing feature of the political life of modern societies, we have come to focus on France around 1848, when some political thinkers and many acute participant observers perceived a tension between the growth of instrumentalism as a dominant aspect of institutionalized political processes and the persistent yearning of an expanding citizenry for a more dramatic political process in which fulfillment could be achieved through the act of

61. Ibid., p. 82.
62. Duveau, *Sociologie de l'Utopie,* op. cit., p. 33.
63. Feuer, *Marx and Engels,* op. cit., p. 37.
64. Ibid., pp. 38-39.
65. Flaubert, *L'Education Sentimentale,* op. cit., p. 300.

participation itself. We have also recorded, albeit sketchily, some evidence which indicates that the yearning is by no means utopian, in the sense of a longing for the imaginary or the impossible, but rather genuinely Utopian, in the sense of an actualization of the project modern Utopians had conceived. In short, that project, repeatedly achieved at least in part, consists in the immediate transformation of society through a drastic change of the conceptions human beings have of that society and of themselves. It is the politics of poets and prophets rather than of princes and priests.

As a first step, the present essay raises more questions than it answers. Some are perhaps not answerable at all; nevertheless, they suggest directions for further exploration.

1. Are the moments of madness recorded here merely another French disease? At one level, their occurrence can be viewed as a variant of Crozier's analysis of the crisis as the main adaptive mechanism of French bureaucratic culture.[66] From the point of view of the study of French politics, the present essay suggests the possibility of analyzing the historical origins of one pattern of French political culture. It may be that, rather than history being a projection of the psychological stresses of individuals, historical events become encoded into culture as patterns of socialization.

Were it to be demonstrated, by way of comparative analysis, that the phenomenon under consideration was peculiarly French, it would become necessary to account for this peculiar feature of French political development. One possibility is that, although France is often regarded by social scientists as "backward" from the point of view of modernization generally or as having experienced a premature broadening of participation in relation to institutionalization, France was in fact precocious in at least one respect. There, more than anywhere else, political authority was rationalized very early in the form of a centralized bureaucratic state. Moments of enthusiasm, during which authority can be made to disappear and the community rules itself—in a genuine state of an-archy—are the congruent, but obverse, process. But that possibility leads to a further thought: Could the French experience not be anticipatory? As other societies, in which the growth of political rationality has been mitigated or inhibited by other factors, become more modern in this particular respect, they may be in the process of becoming more French in their responses as well. In that sense, an analysis of France may enlighten others about themselves.

2. The tension between the two kinds of political processes noted above evokes and is part of the more general tension between instrumental and expressive aspects of life in contemporary societies. It is once again in France during the middle third of the nineteenth century that one aspect of this

---

66. Michel Crozier, *Le phénomene bureaucratique* (Paris: Editions du Seuil, 1963), particularly pp. 359-61.

tension, the relationship between politics and art, first became manifest. Although little has been said here of artists, even a cursory glance at literature and the plastic arts suggests that Paris was at that time a once-only place where political and artistic radicals not only shared many elements of a common Utopian sensibility, but also acted together. For many of them, politics and art were not merely complementary pursuits; they were different versions of the same attempt to transform the world. How come Paris? To what extent the roots lay in Rousseau, and to what extent Rousseau himself amplified a cultural trend related to the early bureaucratization of both political and religious authority in France, would itself warrant investigation. In any case, because Paris was one of the political centers of the West, and without a doubt the artistic center, the coming together of the two vanguards there was an historical event of vital importance in the relationships between political and artistic pursuits in the West as a whole for the next century. That politics and art were soon torn asunder is of equal significance.

Egbert's monumental survey notwithstanding, a thoroughly satisfactory analysis of these relationships does not exist.[67] However, some guidance is available. Duveau believed that the emergence of the doctrine of "art for art's sake" was closely related to the failure of 1848, just as that failure also provided the foundations for scientific socialism.[68] Indeed, for a long time afterwards, Socialists became ever more concerned with organization until, in the Bolshevik version, it became an end in itself. On the artistic side, Flaubert ends *L'Education Sentimentale* with a conversation between Frédéric and Deslauriers: "And they summarized their life. They blew it both, the one who had dreamed of love, the one who had dreamed of power."[69] The only thing left, then, is the writer and his novel. Although Poggioli dates the separation from the Commune rather than from 1848, his central proposition is also that afterwards, political radicals and the artistic avant-garde became engaged in mutually exclusive projects.[70] The artists achieved utopia in their bohemia rather than on the barricades. The immense liberation of human expression accomplished through the birth of the modern truly destroyed the old world

67. Donald Drew Egbert, *Social Radicalism and the Arts: Western Europe* (New York: Knopf, 1970).

68. Duveau, *1848,* op. cit., p. 221. He attributes the idea about art to Jean Cassou, whose work I have not studied at this time. "Art for art's sake" originated before 1848; it might be more accurate to say that 1848 contributed to the founding of what Harold Rosenberg has called "the tradition of the new" (see note 71, below).

69. Flaubert, *L'Education Sentimentale,* op. cit., p. 426. Jean-Paul Sartre's new work on Flaubert undoubtedly deals with the present subject but I have not yet been able to study it.

70. Renato Poggioli, *The Theory of the Avant-Garde* (New York: Harper and Row, 1971), pp. 94ff.

or, rather, in the words of Harold Rosenberg, revealed "what is already destroyed. Art kills only the dead."[71]

Except fleetingly, what was torn asunder has never been reunited. Although artists have continued to associate themselves with a variety of revolutionary movements, they do not survive success. At their worst, the rulers of contemporary societies kill art by imposing upon artists their own instrumental ways: Art must serve *their* revolution. The artistic avant-garde, Poggioli argued, can survive only in liberal societies; but the artists are necessarily alienated from the very societies which make their survival possible. Writing in the post-World War II world, he believed that through this process, the avant-garde contributed to those societies a unique form of cultural experimentation.

Has this, too, become a thing of the past? Egbert firmly believes so, and entitles the last section of his book, "The End of Traditional Social Alienation in the Arts and of the Traditional Conception of the Avant-Garde."[72] That there is a malaise, stemming from the incorporation of many products of avant-garde art into the liberal societies of the West as entertainment, is obvious. But Egbert's elegy is perhaps premature. In the last half-century, beginning with Dada, Western artists themselves have rebelled against the paradoxical boredom of the avant-garde. Some reached the dead end of solipsism; others sought to discover yet a new world. So, lifting the proscenium arch or freeing themselves of the constraints of plastic media, they sometimes escape from the now-luxurious bohemian ghetto into the political world, where they embrace, in a great moment of enthusiasm, the expectant rebels against boredom. Ecstasy or delirium? Together, as children engaged in a magnificent prank, they momentarily restore magic to the world.

3. What are the consequences of political action based on the belief that "all is possible"? Moments of madness have had a very bad press in the social sciences. What followed the Parisian experiences of 1848 and of 1871 probably contributed significantly to the diffidence of contemporary social theory, which was then in the process of being born, toward participation of the sort discussed in this essay. That this Parisian spirit was reborn in Berlin immediately after World War I, when once again there was a fleeting conjunction of political radicalism and artistic innovation, contributed to the further transformation of diffidence into pessimism. What we remember most is that moments of political enthusiasm are followed by bourgeois repression or by charismatic authoritarianism, sometimes by horror but always by the restoration of boredom. Even those who record the joy of living in a good place at a good time almost always take it back. It is as if the old adage, *Post*

71. Harold Rosenberg, *The Tradition of the New* (New York: McGraw-Hill, 1965), p. 76; see also the surrounding discussion of "Revolution and the Concept of Beauty."
72. Egbert, op. cit., pp. 741-45.

coitum omnia animal triste, had been made into a rule of historiography. It has by now become something of a self-fulfilling prophecy: Backlash of some sort is expected, and perhaps the guilty disposition of those who let themselves go helps bring it about.

Although the present essay has not dealt systematically with this question, it has suggested that the prevailing negative view, which focuses on obstacles and reactions, distorts the truth. It neglects the lasting political accomplishments that are perhaps made possible only by the suspension of disbelief in the impossible which is characteristic of moments of madness. As a general proposition, it can be asserted that the Utopian project is a feasible strategy of social and political change, and perhaps even a necessary one. It brings about significant transformations in three distinct ways. First of all, the "torrent of words" involves a sort of intensive learning experience whereby new ideas, formulated initially in coteries, sects, etc., emerge as widely shared beliefs among much larger publics. This may be the manner in which certain forms of cultural change that are relevant to politics occur in the highly institutionalized cultures of modern, literate, societies. Secondly, these new beliefs expressed in new language are anchored in new networks of relationships which are rapidly constituted during such periods of intense activity. From the social structural point of view, stepped-up participation is like a flood tide which loosens up much of the soil but leaves alluvial deposits in its wake. Thirdly, from the point of view of policy, including the creation of new political institutions and the launching of new programs, although the dreams transformed into realities seldom evolve unilinearly afterwards, the instant formulations become irreversible goals which are often institutionalized in the not-very-distant future. The moments do not collapse the distance between the present and the future, as those who experience them yearn to do. In that sense, moments of Parisian madness and others like them are always failures. But they drastically shorten the distance, and in that sense they are successful miracles. Perhaps they are necessary for the political transformation of societies, especially after the foundations of modernity have been established.

Presentation of appropriate evidence must await a longer work. But since the third point, in particular, is likely to arouse much skepticism among political scientists, some illustration is appropriate. In 1848, for example, universal male suffrage *was* established in France within a few days, and much more thoroughly than in Europe's Utopia, the United States of America. Although much of the literature emphasizes reversals and setbacks, within France, and the advantages of gradualism elsewhere, what has been insufficiently stressed in studies of the political development of Western Europe is that France's accomplishment set an irreversible standard of political democracy for the rest of the world and that, for all its gaps and imbalances, as a result of that irreversible fact of political life, France alone among Latin countries in Europe became a leading liberal democracy in the nineteenth century. The ideal of a universal right to secular education left behind by the Commune was realized in less than a quarter of a century. Whatever else the Popular Front accomplished, it firmly established the right of the working class to leisure. As for the "all is possible" of 1944, one historian's assessment is that afterwards, "in the space of two years, a series of decisions are taken which constitute the most impressive whole ever realized in France since the Revolution. . . ."[73]

4. Because the emphasis here has been on macro-analysis, the phenomenon under consideration has not been viewed from the point of view of the aggregate experiences of individuals. Yet, it is through drastic changes in the experiences of individuals, already socialized into the existing society, that the transformational processes noted above occur. How does this happen? Beneath the macro-events lies a multitude of micro-events experienced by the participants, whether actually or vicariously. At any one time, only a minority of unusual persons are capable of resolving through their own devices the dialectic tension between the self and the world through which human beings manage to exercise some control over their fate. In societies where the *rite de passage* has never been fully institutionalized, or where it has become routinized and boring, is it farfetched to believe that those imbued with extraordinary sensibility provoke moments of exaltation, when the meek can more easily enter the kingdom?

73. Jacques Julliard, *La IV_e République* (Paris: Calmann-Levy, 1971; "Naissance et mort"), p. 32. He goes on to give details.

Part Three

Political Interests and Class Consciousness

Suppose someone told you it was in your interest to support a revolutionary movement in the United States, and someone else claimed that it was in your interest to pursue a corporate career that would make it possible for you to earn a good deal of money. How would you know who was right? What criteria could you use to find it out?

Conventional treatments of politics would find it hard to deal with these questions, since they take off from a purely *subjective* definition of interest: people's interests are no more and no less than what they think they are at any given moment. But often people do not know for sure what their interests are, or even how to go about reckoning their interests in the face of conflicting claims.

In its own way, each of the articles in this section argues that the conventional, subjective approach to the concept of interest is thus too narrow; adherence to it makes it impossible to develop critical perspectives that transcend the status quo. William Connolly notes that the "interests one accepts will determine what sorts of conflict become prime candidates for moral arbitration." A subjective approach to interest based on people's perceived policy preferences, he argues, is the most narrow of possibilities, since it removes moral judgement from the arena of politics. Connolly also critiques two other bases of approaching the question of interest: an approach based on utilitarian criteria, and one based on theories of basic human needs that equates needs and interests.

Instead, he proposes an approach rooted in people's *real* interests: "Policy X is more in A's interest than policy Y if A, were he to experience the *results* of both X and Y, would choose X as the result he would rather have for himself."

Isaac Balbus, too, is profoundly critical of the dominant approach to the concept of interest. He insists on a rigid distinction between subjective and objective concepts of interest. "Our ordinary language," he writes, "recognizes an objective meaning entailed by the concept 'interest,' so that when we say an individual has an 'interest in' something we mean that he has a stake in it or is 'affected by' it." In this sense, the existence of an objective interest does not depend on the individual's awareness he has such an interest. Pluralist conceptions, which deal only with subjective or perceived interests, necessarily ignore "the prior and decisive problem of the 'conversion' of objective interests to subjective interests, i.e., the development of consciousness, a phenomenon which any adequate political theory cannot ignore."

Balbus attempts to demonstrate that Marxist theory provides the most coherent alternative since "it recognizes both types of interest and is, above all, concerned with their interrelationship." Bertell Ollman directly deals with this interrelationship by questioning Marx's expectations that workers who constitute a class *in* itself sharing objective interests would become a class *for* itself sharing subjective interests. He details the sequential steps necessary for class consciousness to emerge, and locates a key source of difficulty in the early childhood experiences of workers.

Thus, while these essays do not provide answers to the question, What is your interest?, taken together they give us guideposts to the formulation of answers that have individual and collective meaning. The more we can conceptualize for ourselves where our interests lie, the greater the possibility for their realization.

9. On 'Interests' in Politics[1]

WILLIAM CONNOLLY

The Import of Disputes About Interests

An explanatory theory of politics generates a set of normative considerations for the assessment of political institutions and public policies. And the conceptual system within which a given explanatory theory is framed delineates a range of evidence liable to conversion into reasons for or against particular moral claims.[2] If the above two statements are true, and I will presuppose rather than argue in detail for them here, then it is surely true that the concept and interpretation of *interests* in politics provides a central medium for that conversion process.

Statements such as "*A* wants *x*," "*A* prefers *x* to *y*," and "*x* enhances the contentment of *A*" are licenses for making prima facie judgments that *x* is good or desirable. While "good" is not equivalent to any set of descriptive statements, statements which refer to the wants, purposes, and preferences of persons are conceptually linked to ascriptions of good. And talk about interests carries into political discourse that conceptual connection between description and normative appraisal. For although various notions of *interests* have been employed in political literature, each of those seriously advanced includes somewhere in its definition a significant reference to the wants, preferences, and purposes of persons implicated in political life.

Once the normative *function* of talk about interests is understood, the import of disagreements over the descriptive conditions or *criteria* of the concept's application also becomes more clear.[3] For one set of criteria will draw our attention to particular wants and preferences formed under specified conditions and deflect attention from other possible wants, etc., formed in different circumstances. The effect is to privilege certain actual or

1. My thanks to Glen Gordon, George Kateb, David Kettler, and Felix Oppenheim for their insightful criticisms of an earlier draft of this essay.
2. For a strong argument in support of this thesis see Charles Taylor, "Neutrality in Political Science," in Peter Laslett and W. G. Runciman, eds., *Philosophy, Politics and Society,* 3d ser. (New York: Barnes and Noble, 1967), pp. 25-57. See also: Kurt Baier, *The Moral Point of View* (New York: Random House, 1965).
3. See the distinction between the "material" and "formal" elements of a concept drawn by Julius Kovesi in *Moral Notions* (London: Routledge and Kegan Paul, 1967). Kovesi's approach to conceptual analysis suggests a profound critique of the approach conventionally adopted by political scientists.

potential conative states for purposes of normative appraisal and, often, to blind us to possible considerations operating outside those boundaries.

If the very notion of interests one adopts exerts an influence on the "materials" from which normative appraisals are forged, an explanatory theory employing that notion will generate more sharply defined normative implications. Such a theory purports to tell us what interests citizens in various settings have; how the political system nourishes and protects some interests while dampening others; whether those dampened interests could be advanced by, say, a more vigorous application of pressure; why and how particular segments of society fail to recognize some of their interests; to what extent pressures exerted on government reflect not interests but those unattainable fantasies and wishes citizens sometimes project onto politics. The explanatory theory, in short, "sets the crucial dimensions through which the phenomena can vary"; and, through its assessment of the possibilities, costs, and risks of satisfying those wants and needs identified as interests, it informs us "how we are to judge of good and bad."[4]

In the light of these remarks, it is surely not surprising that sharp disagreements have persisted among political analysts concerning the proper notion and theory of interests. While most of the participants in these debates have tried to limit themselves to lines of argument permitted by a positivist disjuncture between explanatory inquiry and moral commitment—thereby debating which notion of interest is more "operational" or, vaguely, of greater "theoretical importance," lurking in the background has been the tacit understanding that talk about interests carries normative implications in political discourse.

Our reflections will provide more illumination, then, if we bring this tacit understanding to the conscious level. For when we grasp that "by the 'moral point of view' we *mean* a point of view which furnishes a court of arbitration for conflicts of interest,"[5] we must also acknowledge that the *notion* of interests one accepts will determine what sorts of conflict become prime candidates for moral arbitration, while the *theory* of interests advanced will demarcate a range of claims to be assessed from the moral point of view. I would not myself argue (as the quote from Baier might suggest) that "interests" is the only concept in politics which serves as a bridge between explanatory and normative judgment, but it *is* one of the central concepts performing this crucial function.

---

4. Taylor, op. cit., pp. 30 and 40.

5. Baier, op. cit., p. 96. For examples of other essays which explicitly place "interests" in the center of moral discourse see Stanley Benn, "Egalitarianism and the Equal Consideration of Interests," in Hugo A. Bedau, ed., *Justice and Equality* (Englewood Cliffs, N.J.: Prentice-Hall, 1971), pp. 152-167; and John Rawls, "Justice as Fairness," *Philosophical Review* (1958), pp. 164-94.

Interests as Policy Preference

I will consider four alternative efforts to elucidate the descriptive criteria of "interests," arguing that the notions improve successively as we move from the first to the last.[6]

Most American political scientists, working largely within the confines of a pluralist theory of politics, have not explicitly defined "interests," but have tended to equate the concept in practice with the political pressure an agent (individual or group) brings to bear on government, perhaps merely as his policy preference.[7] Since the criticisms advanced here apply to either of these formulations we will treat them as interchangeable.

Typically, too, this conceptual focus is sharpened when the scholar is presenting a methodological critique of explanatory theories which purport to find "false consciousness" among some segments of society. Thus Nelson Polsby rejects on methodological gounds C. Wright Mills's assertion that "false consciousness" is "the lack of awareness of and identification with one's objective interests." Polsby's alternative view holds,

> at least presumptively, that decisions affect people's interests differentially, and that people participate in those areas *they care about the most.* Their values, eloquently expressed by their participation, cannot, it seems to me, be more effectively "objectified" [emphasis mine].[8]

6. I omit reference here to "explications" of the following sort which seek to bypass the issues involved: "Well, what is an *interest* then? . . . But for our purposes in this volume at least that is exactly the kind of question we have tried to avoid. The *scientific procedure* is to observe and isolate certain acts (or behaviors) and actions, and connect these into 'bundles' whose interconnections may prove fruitful. 'Interest group' being just a convenient label for one such 'bundle,' it need have no connection at all with the meaning of its two constituent terms." (!) Graham Wootton, *Interest Groups: Foundations of Modern Political Science Series* (Englewood Cliffs, N.J.: Prentice-Hall, 1970), p. 18.

7. Probably because the concept has received increased attention lately in philosophical literature, few political scientists today argue as confidently for interest as policy preference. But the concept is still commonly *employed* that way, largely on the grounds to be considered shortly, of operational rigor. For earlier statements, see David Truman, *The Governmental Process* (New York: Alfred A. Knopf, 1951), pp. 50-51; Glendon Schubert, *The Public Interest* (New York: The Free Press, 1960).

8. Both quotations are from Nelson Polsby, "The Sociology of Community Power," *Social Forces* (1959), p. 235. I should note that in private correspondence Polsby has denied that he defines interest as policy preference and has suggested that "interest" is not a central category in his work on community power. While it is not central to my argument whether he does or does not employ the term that way and while he has not given an explicit definition of the term in the works considered here, the following two points are relevant: (1) "interests" must be a central category for Polsby, for

The notion of interest as policy preference is open to several telling criticisms.[9] (1) The debate between pluralist theorists and their critics hinges in strong measure on the extent to which specific groups in the society fail to identify and press policy proposals which could substantially improve their well-being. But, by defining interests merely as policy preference, pluralists help to push the issue dividing them and their critics outside the reach of empirical inquiry. For, given that definition of interest, there simply cannot be "unarticulated interests"; those without particular policy preferences in certain areas must be viewed as not having an interest in a given policy result. If it is possible to formulate a concept of interest, meeting reasonable methodological standards, which does enable us to ask questions such as "Does group Q have unarticulated interest Y?" that explication will be preferable on the ground that it avoids settling by definitional fiat an important question that might be studied empirically.

(2) Equating "interest" with policy preference collapses an important distinction sanctioned in ordinary discourse between one's support for a policy because of a perceived moral obligation and his support for it solely on the grounds of self-interest. Failure to sustain this distinction clearly in political inquiry lends illicit (because unargued) support to the view that political man must act only, or at least primarily, in his self-interest. The pernicious effects of such an unexamined assumption, both for political inquiry and for the considerations governing the political commitments of citizens, can hardly be overstated.[10]

"proposition 4" of the "stratification theory" that he is out to refute holds that the "the upper class power elite rules in its own interests." (*Community Power and Political Theory* [New Haven: Yale University Press, 1963], p. 11) (2) Statements such as the following are found at several junctures in his book when he is criticizing "stratification theorists" for imputing interests to groups which the groups themselves don't acknowledge: "However, 'real' conflicts apparently can take place in the view of stratification analysis without overt disagreements . . . . For the moment, rejecting this presumption of 'objectivity of interests,' we may view instances of intra-class disagreement *as* intra-class conflicts of interest and interclass agreement *as* interclass harmony of interest. To maintain the opposite seems perverse [emphasis mine]." (Ibid., p. 22.)

9. I deal with the criticisms briefly here in order to get to more intriguing notions. For other criticisms with which I largely agree, see Isaac Balbus, "The Concept of Interest in Pluralist and Marxian Analysis," *Politics and Society* 1:2 (1971): 151-78; Brian Barry, *Political Argument* (New York: The Humanities Press, 1965), chap 10; Richard Flathman, *The Public Interest* (New York: John Wiley, 1966).

10. Pernicious for inquiry because, accepting that assumption, students of political "socialization," for example, forget to explore the central question perplexing Rousseau: Under what conditions of social life and education do citizens develop the capacity to support justice and the public interest even when that support requires a sacrifice of private advantage? Pernicious for political conduct because the assumption that political

(3) If, as suggested above, to say "policy x is in A's interest" is to provide a prima facie justification for that policy, defining interests in terms of policy preferences, and then viewing actual political participation as the best indicator of policy preference, combine to sanction perverse normative judgments. Since a high level of participation is correlated with high socioeconomic status, this view of interests supports the claims of the various segments of society in inverse proportion to their need. By thus restricting the application of the concept while tacitly retaining its conventional function in normative assessment, a significant bias is insinuated into materials from which normative conclusions are forged.[11]

Yet such criticisms, impeccable as they may be, fail to speak to the central counterargument wheeled out by those adopting this notion of interests. The argument, suggested by Polsby's statement quoted above, is that alternative notions of interest generally advanced incorporate the possibility of attributing false consciousness to citizens, thereby encouraging researchers to impute interests arbitrarily to groups which the groups themselves do not acknowledge. The more modest notion of interest as policy preference forces the investigator to confront the hard facts about the preferences and behavior of people in political life. It is a more operational definition.

It is not my intention here to argue generally against the myth of operationalism which has unjustifiably confined the scope of contemporary political inquiry.[12] Two points, though, are particularly pertinent to the question at hand. (1) Even if the notion of interest as policy preference is more operational than alternative explications to be considered, this advantage

---

acts (almost always) will be self-interested helps to justify particular acts of *selfishness* as part of the human condition. For an intriguing effort to raise the Rousseauian question see Lawrence Kohlberg, "Moral Development," *International Encyclopedia of the Social Sciences* (1968), 10: 483-94.

11. There are many arguments for the presumption to remain close to ordinary discourse in explicating conceptions such as "power," "interest," and "politics." One argument stands out sharply here: Concepts, as vehicles for thought and action, have complex rules governing their use which are never fully stated. Since a particular concept receives its full meaning only in relation to the entire conceptual system in which it is embedded, a change in one of its dimensions is likely to produce unnoted implications for its ability to perform its several conventional functions. Such a consideration does not militate against conceptual revision, but against such revision lightly undertaken. Concept revision is more analogous to a heart transplant than to a watch repair.

12. See William Alson, *Philosophy of Language* (Englewood Cliffs, N.J.: Prentice-Hall, 1964), last chap.; Max Black, "Reasoning with Loose Concepts," in his *The Margins of Precision* (Ithaca: Cornell University Press, 1970), pp. 1-13; George Schlesinger, "Operationalism," *Encyclopedia of Philosophy* 5 (1967): 543-47; and especially Friedrich Waismann, "Verifiability," in Anthony Flew, ed., *Logic and Language*, 1st ser. (Oxford: Basil Blackwell, 1951) pp. 115-45.

might well be outweighed by its other manifest deficiencies. (2) That notion of interest, when elaborated more fully, is not as neatly operational as its proponents suggest. Since a reasonable assessment of the first claim must await arguments yet to come, I will limit my attention here to the second.

There is, initially, the obvious problem of discovering the policy preferences people actually have. The preferences people express do not always converge with their unexpressed and latent preferences. A survey of blacks just prior to the Detroit riots surely would not have detected "preferences" clearly discernible during the riot and in studies shortly thereafter. Also, policy preferences expressed to middle-class researchers bearing on legalization of dope, protection of homosexuality, legalized prostitution, etc., may well distort the actual orientations of maverick groups in the society. Distortions of these types are likely to lend the investigator to overplay the extent and depth of consensus in contemporary politics.

More importantly, the term "preference," in this usage, ranges over choices of at least two kinds, and these differences must be unsorted in any appraisal of interests. We have noted the distinction between supporting a policy because I prefer it for itself and, alternately, because it seems morally appropriate to do so even though I would choose otherwise if moral considerations did not intervene. Hence, a farmer might prefer to continue using DDT on his crops when considering only his own benefit, but decide, on balance, to vote in favor of making its use illegal. Surely an advocate of interest as policy preference will accept this distinction once drawn, for otherwise he would allow an important question deserving empirical study (i.e., when people's policy preferences are self- or other-regarding) to be obscured by conceptual sloppiness or, more likely, settled by definitional fiat. But then he is forced to distinguish between "self-regarding" and "other-regarding" preferences, and the problem of applying that distinction in research practice will be severe indeed. It will force the dissolution of those crude indicators of interest commonly employed, such as collecting statements from interviewees about their policy preferences and observing the participation of group leaders in support of particular policies. To apply this distinction in research practice will require the subtle assessment of multiple cues in concrete settings.

Finally, since one always *prefers* something to other specified alternatives, the range of alternatives taken into account is crucial to the preference adopted. I might prefer democracy to communism, communism to death, and death to prolonged torture by the secret agents of a democratic society. But attention to this conceptual point complicates the effort to "operationalize" policy preference as interest. Is the range of alternative preferences considered to be limited to those which reach governmental arenas for serious attention? If so, the preferences scales uncovered will be biased in favor of whatever groups benefit the most from existing processes of issue formation. If the range of preferences considered is broadened beyond these limits, the question of how far must be faced. For surely a policy preference must be distinguished from a mere wish. If a trade union leader lobbied in favor of a policy which would ensure the immortality of blue collar workers, Professor Polsby, for example, would surely concur in labeling that a "pipe dream" rather than an interest of the workers. Such distinctions must be made, but no set of *operations* has been specified that enable investigators to determine even roughly the point in contemporary politics where policy preference shades off into political fantasy.

In practice these multiple discriminations are presupposed by research assumptions rather than tested by impersonal operations. Such presuppositions generally go unnoted when shared by a community of scholars. But when the theory of pluralism within which this notion of interests is embedded is challenged, when the props are exposed, the impressionistic status of the discriminations themselves becomes apparent. Among the central disagreements between, say, a C. Wright Mills and a Nelson Polsby are diverging interpretations of the unexpressed and latent preferences of the underclass in American society, of the occasions when political actors are guided by moral imperatives rather than self-interest in their political conduct, and, especially, of those aspirations within contemporary society which can properly be construed as political preferences rather than mere wishes or pipe dreams.[13] The notion of interest as policy preference does appear moderately operational when appraisals of interest are made within the framework of the theory in which this concept functions. When that context itself is in dispute, the tenuous connection between the concept and any particular set of operations becomes apparent.

Utilitarian Interests

Utilitarianism, narrowly defined, takes the wants, desires and inclinations of persons as given and asks how to maximize their attainment. In this sense, Brian Barry can be said to advance a utilitarian notion of interests. He considers a

> policy, law or institution [to be] in someone's interest if it increases
> his opportunities to get what he wants . . . whatever that may be.[14]

13. Thus, even the equation of interests and policy preference makes "false consciousness" of a sort possible. Polsby, op. cit.; Mills, *The Power Elite* (New York: Oxford University Press, 1959). Such comparisons are developed in W. E. Connolly, *Political Science and Ideology* (New York: Atherton Press, 1967), chap. 2.

14. Quoted from "The Public Interest," in Connolly, ed., *The Bias of Pluralism* (New York: Atherton Press, 1969), p. 163. Barry is not, of course, strictly a utilitarian. For he considers ideals which are not "want regarding" relevant to the appraisal of public policy. He is utilitarian only in the sense that he makes interest a want-regarding concept. See *Political Argument*, op. cit., chap. 3.

Now this definition, once the term "want" is appropriately clarified, constitutes a clear improvement over the first notion of interest considered. First, in line with usage in ordinary discourse, this definition makes it possible for an agent to be mistaken about his interests. For misinformation, poor calculation, or failure to consider feasible but unarticulated policy alternatives might lead one to prefer a policy which does not, on a comparative basis, maximize his "opportunities to get what he wants." A low-income citizen, for example, might want to maximize his disposable income but then favor a state sales tax over an income tax because of a mistaken view about the relative effects of each type on the amount of his disposable income. His policy preference, in this instance, would be at odds with his interest.

The definition, as clarified by Barry, also sustains the distinction between supporting a policy because it is in my interest and because of moral reasons. And since one's interest in a policy with this view has no conceptual linkage to participation in the political process, the illicit normative bias built into the first definition is avoided.

The limitations of this notion, though, become more apparent when we probe the phrase "opportunities to get what he *wants*." With one qualification, Barry takes the prevailing wants of persons as given for purposes of appraising their interests.[15] But the wants we have, as Barry knows, are shaped to a large degree by the society in which we mature. Without regard now to questions of truth or falsity, there is surely a *prima facie meaningfulness* to the claim that a perfectly adjusted slave or a well-socialized consumer has wants at odds with his real interests. Social theorists as diverse as Karl Marx and Emile Durkheim, as Ortega y Gasset and John Kenneth Galbraith have advanced interpretations which rest upon just such claimed distortions in processes of interest articulation. We should not accept a notion of interest which excludes such statements unless serious efforts to explicate the concept in ways that accommodate them are shown to be vitally flawed.

Barry's use of "want" limits "interest" in another questionable respect. For the kind of wants Barry considers relevant to ascriptions of interest seem

---

15. The qualification is this: It might be in one's interest to sacrifice the satisfaction of a current want if its attainment will impede his ability to satisfy future wants he might have. (Ibid., p. 184). Thus legalization of heroin might help me to get what I now want but limit my ability to attain future wants (and even affect my future wants themselves?). But a qualification posed along a *purely* temporal dimension is necessary but insufficient to handle conventional uses of interest. We need to specify in addition, conditions which enable us to ask, and bring evidence to bear on, whether it is in the slave's interest to escape slavery even if he now prefers that state to all known alternatives and *always will as long as he remains a slave*. A purely temporal qualification will not handle this paradigm case or the numerous other situations which more or less approximate it.

to be egoistic wants. Put more clearly, although Barry emphasizes that persons can consciously choose to act against their interests, the paradigm case of "doing what I want," is that of securing objects and advantages for my *private enjoyment.* When I act as a want-regarding creature, other persons are viewed merely as means or obstacles to my attainment of "life, liberty, health and indolency of body, and the possession of outward things such as money, houses, furniture and the like."[16] As Barry states the point elsewhere while distinguishing an interest from an ideal, "results concerning people other than *A* are not directly relevant" in the ascriptions of an interest to *A*.[17] This restriction, I shall argue, is too confining.

To be clear about interests we must specify the kinds of persons we are talking about and what aspects of their activity we have in mind. Some definitional statements draw our attention to the "interests" one has when one acts egoistically, but it seems to me that we can also speak sensibly about the interests a person has as a social being. When I act egoistically I seek such things as food and leisure for myself; the satisfactions (or dissatisfactions) I attain do not themselves involve a reference to other people. They are private gratifications not in the sense that I am the one who experiences them (for that is true of all *my* states) but in that other people are seen only as *means* or *obstacles* to my states and not as themselves implicated with me in *relationships* which are mutually gratifying.

When my interests as a social being are at stake, more than private wants are involved. Certain kinds of relationship with others are fostered—relationships which involve trust, friendship, shared conventions, and the like. One who cherishes the social dimension of life may often be willing to sacrifice purely private satisfaction for the mutual benefits of social life. For instance, a person might decide to forgo attaining certain material benefits in the interests of maintaining a relationship of trust with another. He might simply cherish for itself the kind of life implied by sustaining such relationships more than he prizes the sacrificed material benefits. He is surely acting in his interest in this case. There is a sacrifice here, of course, but not in the sense that an act of altruism is the sacrifice of one's interest. The person is simply sacrificing a lower-order interest for the higher-order interest he has as a social being.

Interests I have as a social being are those which make "essential reference to reciprocal states of awareness among two or more persons."[18] Thus

16. Barry's quotation from John Locke to illustrate the "kinds of ways in which a policy, law, or institution must impinge on someone before it can be said to be 'in his interest.' " *The Bias of Pluralism,* op. cit., p. 163.

17. *Political Argument,* op. cit., p. 182.

18. Robert Paul Wolff, *The Poverty of Liberalism* (Boston: Beacon Press, 1968), p. 181. See also Isaac Balbus, "The Concept of Interest in Pluralist and Marxian Analysis," op. cit.

workers might, as Marx contends, have an interest in policies supporting a
work life in which they interact creatively in the productive process. Citizens
might, as Herbert Morris believes, have an interest in a system of punishment
which treats one, when accused of a crime, as an agent capable of acting
responsibly in one's relations with others.[19] Human beings in general might,
as Durkheim believes, have an interest in policies enabling each to share with
others a set of social norms which give regularity, purpose, and direction to
their interaction. It isn't that Marx, Morris, and Durkheim are necessarily
correct in their assessments of the interests we have as social beings or in the
extent to which those interests override purely egoistic interest, for these
three theorists disagree among themselves and one or all of them might
indeed be seriously mistaken in his assessment of interests. But if a reasonable
notion of interest can be advanced which enables us to cope with conflicts
between egoistic and social interests, on the same plane, so to speak, we will
be able to sharpen and clarify those fundamental issues lying beneath the
surface of contemporary debates about political life.[20] We will be able to
make sense of the kind of claim advanced when someone says: "John favors
that policy because he wants to increase his income but his real interest
would be promoted further if the social conditions of this work life were
reformed."

Interests as Need-Fulfillment

We can speak rather easily of the interests one has relative to an accepted
standard of social life. Thus, given the principle of respect for persons, it is in
the interests of the slave to be freed even if he has been conditioned to accept
slavery. But is it in the slave's real interest to be treated with such respect?
How could we warrant or undermine such a claim when advanced by another
for the slave?

American social scientists who have approached this problem have most
often posited a set of universal human "needs" which are thought to stand
above and beyond variations in social structure and patterns of socialization
and to provide a standard of achievement against which particular social
arrangements can be assessed.[21] The term *need* is not always defined

19. Herbert Morris, "Persons and Punishment," *The Monist* (1968), pp. 471-501.

20. Those issues are tapped effectively in Fred Dallmayr, "Empirical Political Theory
and Images of Man," *Polity* (1970), pp. 443-78.

21. Thus Amitai Etzioni, in his defense of a theory of basic human needs, describes
the function of such a theory: "Theories which assume autonomous human needs
provide an independent basis with which to compare societies to each other, as more or
less consonant with basic human needs." See "Basic Human Needs, Alienation and

carefully in this literature, but Christian Bay's definition typifies a wider usage: A need is "any *behavior tendency* whose continual denial or frustration leads to pathological responses."[22] Needs are not reducible to wants here, for wants are specifically oriented to particular goals while an unmet need *may* find expression as malaise, vague anxiety, or unfocused tension. Bay, for example, takes suicide, alcoholism, psychosis, delinquency, and drug addiction to be among the symptoms of need-frustration. And he holds that these pathologies sometimes develop when "higher-level" human needs are frustrated—such as those to develop cognitive capacities, to act as responsible agents, and to enter into intimate relationships with others.

Even if this notion of needs were fully serviceable, "need" and "interest" would not be synonymous. For innumerable personalized and localized cases of need-frustration might remain beyond the reach of effective public policy. But, with this view, a *policy* would be in someone's interest to the extent that it, by comparison with other alternatives, promoted need-fulfillment or increased opportunities to promote need-fulfillment.

Such a definition does underline deficiencies in the first two formulations considered. For there are situations where people have, as C. Wright Mills would say, "troubles" not yet translated into firm wants, let alone into a set of political claims which could speak to them. "Instead of troubles defined in terms of values and threats—there is often the misery of vague uneasiness, instead of explicit issues there is often merely the beat feeling that all is somehow not right [sic]."[23] To the extent that the first two concepts of interest slide over situations such as this, they divert conceptual attention from possible tensions simmering just below the surface of pluralist politics. Conceptual blinders of this sort help to explain the failure of liberal social scientists of the last generation to anticipate the political crises of the sixties and seventies (Mills, of course, is the exception), to detect those troubles shuffled out of pluralist politics, and to formulate the political issues implied by their presence.

And yet this definition, too, has serious deficiencies. For a simple test will show, I think, that the suggested conceptual connection between needs and interests may well impose severe limits on the theory of interests which

---

Inauthenticity," *American Sociological Review* (1968), p. 878. See also, Christian Bay, "Politics and Pseudo-politics: A Critical Evaluation of some Behavioral Literature," *American Political Science Review* (1968), pp. 870-84, and James C. Davies, *Human Nature in Politics* (New York: John Wiley, 1963).

22. Bay, "Needs, Wants, and Political Legitimacy," *Canadian Journal of Political Science* (1968), p. 242.

23. Mills, *The Sociological Imagination* (New York: Oxford University Press, 1959), p. 11.

results. These limits are both contrary to the intentions of those who advance
the notion of human needs and, I shall argue later, unwarranted.[24]

Consider a hypothetical situation in which we (as investigators) have full
and direct knowledge of the tensions and behavioral inclinations of a
subservient population. We find the population to have all its needs met
(defined as behavioral tendencies); there are no "pathological" responses, no
blockage of felt inclinations and no vaguely felt tensions. The creatures we
are to visualize are well-fed and clothed; they exhibit a strong sense of
security; they even express a doglike warmth in their personal relationships.
What they lack, though, is the ability to choose reflectively among alternative
courses of conduct, to act responsibly, to express the complex reactive
attitudes of love, resentment, grief, guilt, remorse, and outrage which we
associate with the social life of human beings.

I do not wish to argue that the condition described is likely to occur
anywhere. But, if it were to occur, we would surely be tempted to say that
the people's lack of felt inclinations to develop, say, their deliberative
capacities to a high pitch was not conclusive proof that it would not be in
their interests to do so. This is not only because they might find such skills
necessary to the fulfillment of other vaguely felt inclinations—a consideration
need theories could easily accommodate. But human beings might, in some
settings, lack inclinations or urgings of any sort to achieve states they would
prize for themselves once attained; they might possess strong dispositions to
resist the attainment of those very modes of life they would find the most
gratifying once having experienced them; and they might even find that
certain arrangements prized for themselves necessarily include tensions and
anxieties as part of the prized condition.

Need theories typically start with a plausible statement of primary needs
tied to observable behavioral tendencies and inclinations. But as one advances
up the hierarchy of postulated needs a subtle conceptual shift emerges. From
"needs" as a noun defined in terms of inclinations we shift increasingly
toward "needs" as a verb construed as those conditions instrumental to the
attainment of one's full development as a person. And at the upper end of the
hierarchy, the connection between what one needs to become a person and
any set of behavioral inclinations becomes increasingly tenuous. Indeed, need
theorists display a tendency to tolerate those tensions and anxieties which
might accompany attainment of the highest postulated states.

To avoid this tendency toward equivocation—a tendency supported by
ordinary usage—it is advisable to treat "need" as a verb in our theoretical

24. The next two paragraphs are a somewhat revised version of my critique of a
paper given by Christian Bay at the *Ripon Conference on Rights and Political Action*,
Ripon College, October 8-10, 1970. The "Critique," along with other conference
proceedings, is published in *Inquiry* (1971), pp. 237-43.

work. This form calls attention to the fact that need statements are always triadic: "Person *A* needs *x in order to* (do, be, or become) *y*." And *y* in this triad is always the crucial variable. One might need something in order to survive, to survive comfortably, to develop the capacity to act responsibly, to polish his shoes, or to eliminate all sexual urges. Thus, when we translate need statements into this form, we can see that to say "*A* needs *x*" is not necessarily to say either that *A* is inclined towards *x* or that it is a worthy object for him to pursue. Such judgments must await consideration of what *x* is needed for.

My charge, then, is this: The conceptual connection between needs and interests seems plausible only when the equivocal use of "need" in need theories goes unnoted. But when need is defined consistently in terms of behavioral inclinations we can both imagine inclinations which it might not be in our interests to promote and identify possible interests not manifested by our most inchoate behavioral tendencies. Any view which anchors interest exclusively in felt behavioral tendencies runs the risk of celebrating uncritically those inclinations cultivated by dominant socialization processes while deflecting conceptual attention from possible gratifying modes of existence bypassed by those same processes. If the intellectual enterprise aims to recover worthy aspirations that have been lost, to render intelligible modes of life that are now only dimly glimpsed, then a definition of interest *restricted* to felt behavioral tendencies can hardly suffice.

Real Interests

Need theories are informed by the right questions; it is only the answer given which is inadequate. Can we, though, articulate a notion of interests which will speak more effectively to these issues? I think we can. But first I must mention a feature of definitions of this sort too often ignored by analysts of political concepts. As Friedrich Waismann has shown, no concept is ever completely defined; every concept is incorrigibly "open textured." In our definitional statements we limit a concept in particular directions, but there are "always other directions in which a concept has not been defined."[25] The definitional statement I will make, then, is only a first approximation. The accompanying text will help to make the import of the initial definitional gloss clear, but will not "limit the concept" in all important directions. That gloss will be useful if it provides a basis from which further clarifications and adjustments can be made when new circumstances are confronted. To say that is not to preface my definitional effort with an apology but merely to point to a little noted dimension of all such efforts. As a first approximation, then, consider the following:

25. Waismann, "Verifiability," op. cit., p. 126.

> Policy *x* is more in *A*'s interest than policy *y* if *A*, were he to
> experience the *results* of both *x* and *y*, would *choose x* as the result
> he would rather have for himself.

Several clarifying comments are in order.[26]

(1) The definition focuses on the results of policy rather than on attitudes toward the policy itself, bypassing problems posed in the first definition considered. Furthermore, following Barry's lead here, too, it treats interest as a comparative concept because for "any given proposal there is nearly always one that compared to it is in someone's interest and at least one that compared to it is contrary to someone's interest."[27] Defining the concept in this way encourages people to state explicitly the terms of comparison implicitly adopted when they tell us something is or is not in our interests.

(2) The key criterion is the choice of the agent involved, but the privileged choice is one made after the fact, so to speak, rather than before it. This does require investigators to make different judgments, in many situations, about the choices a person would make if he had had the relevant experiences, but such a reference to counterfactual conditions is required by most concepts employed in contemporary political inquiry (e.g., power). And the definition does enable us, I think, to *say* all of the things about interests we find people in ordinary discourse saying, thereby retaining for political inquiry not only the function that interests plays in normative discourse but the full range of activities it covers in performing that function.[28] It allows one to say that something *might* be in another's interests even though the other does not now

26. Since I am especially indebted to S. I. Benn's views about how one should construe interests in political inquiry ("Interests in Politics," *Proceedings of Aristotelian Society* (1960), 123-40), I should specify the point at which I disagree. I agree that "to say something is in a man's interest is not to say that he will be glad of it immediately; but it does seem to imply that one would expect him to be glad of it at some time" (p. 130). But, Benn then suggests, there "may be a sense" in which something is in a person's interest even if he doesn't want it, would not want it if he rightly understood the position, or even that, want it or not, he would be pleased if he got it" (ibid.). It would be in his interests, Benn thinks, *relative to a valid norm of conduct,* even if that norm is one the agent could never prize for itself. But if he himself did not, once he understood and "lived up to" the norm, come to be pleased with it for itself, then I don't see how we can appropriately say that policies which help him to see and achieve it are in his interests—even though it might be *right* for him to support such policies.

27. Barry, "The Use and Abuse of the Public Interest," in Carl Friedrich, ed., *The Public Interest* (New York: Atherton Press, 1966), p. 198.

28. I do not accept ordinary language as the final court of appeal here, especially since an atomistic view of human nature continues to infect talk about interests. But I do think any definition should at least cover the paradigm cases of "interest" sanctioned by ordinary discourse (remembering that "ordinary discourse" means not the definitions people give but the rules they actually follow), and then give reasons for any proposed extensions or modifications. To the extent I modify usage, my reason is simply that the

(or might never if prevailing social conditions persist) want it. It allows, further, for the possibility of having an interest in some result which I presently have strong inclinations against. And, as I shall argue next, it allows persons to have interests as social beings as well as in those results whose enjoyment does not essentially involve reciprocal states of awareness.

(3) Clarification of the phrase "the result he would rather have" is required to understand what *kind* of choices made after the fact are relevant to ascriptions of interest. If the phrase is interpreted too loosely, we risk merging "interest-regarding" choices with those which reflect a sense of obligation, selfless benevolence, and, perhaps, fear of reprisal. Interpreted too narrowly, it would rule out the kinds of considerations people tacitly have in mind when they counsel us about our "real interests" or our "best interests" as social beings. Thus Erik Erikson thinks that social arrangements and policies which help to nourish relationships of "mutuality," (that is, the sort of relationship which "strengthens the doer as it strengthens the other") are clearly in the real interests of the parties involved even if neither party fully recognizes that fact. For, in a relationship of mutuality between parent and child,

> a parent dealing with a child will be strengthened in *his* vitality, in
> *his* sense of indentity, and in *his* readiness for ethical action by the
> very ministrations by means of which he secures to the child
> vitality, future identity, and eventual readiness for ethical action.[29]

As I see it, then, the distinction between interest-regarding choices and other kinds of choices social beings might make can be formulated, roughly, along the following lines: An agent's choice is interest-regarding when or to the extent that (for many choices will reflect several kinds of considerations) it takes into account the quality of the result for the agent himself and includes a reference to others insofar as his relationships to them are of the sort he would choose as gratifying and fulfilling in themselves. Much more could probably be said about the demarcation line I seek to sustain here. For example, I would hope to argue that it is in my interests to develop the capacity to act as a morally responsible agent even though the very perfection of that capacity could, on particular occasions, enjoin me to act against my

---

atomistic conception of human nature (partially) reflected in contemporary usage is faulty; when those faults are recognized we can also see that relationships we prize as social beings have much in common with other conditions and objectives we cover with the language of interests. My general approach here reflects, I hope, the spirit of John Austin: "Certainly, then, ordinary language is not the last word: in principle it can everywhere be supplemented and improved upon the superseded. Only remember, it *is* the first word." "A Plea for Excuses," In V. C. Chappel, ed., *Ordinary Language* (Englewood Cliffs, N.J.: Prentice-Hall, 1964), p. 49.

29. Erikson, *Insight and Responsibility* (New York: W. W. Norton, 1964), p. 233.

interests. Even with further clarification, though, boundary problems will persist between those actions which are in my interests in one capacity or another and those which are indifferent or contrary to it. This, however, is not a problem peculiar to the definition I propose; those definitions couched in terms of preferences and private wants face, at different junctures, their own boundary problems, as in sorting among "privately oriented," "publically oriented," and "ideal-regarding" wants.[30]

(4) What if a person, after experiencing the results of a policy which legalizes heroin, chooses that as the result he would rather have? Does this apparent counterexample, and others like it, undermine the proposed definition? I think not. It impels us, rather, to clarify further the meaning of "choice." For if the person regrets those previous actions which now make him an addict, if he wishes he could choose to give up the habit but knows he cannot, or even if we are convinced he would now choose otherwise were he fully capable of choosing freely, then we can properly say that his present capacity to choose freely has been impaired. The appropriate question in this context is not "What does he now want?" but "What would he choose if, knowing what he now knows, he could freely make that choice again?"[31] Situations like this raise difficult questions of judgment which we must approach with some humility, but it is also certain that occasions do arise when we cannot avoid making judgments of this sort, occasions when the question becomes not if, but how and on what grounds. We are focusing here on the grounds.

Indeed, I am inclined to urge here that any current choice the implications of which deeply impairs one's capacity to make future choices—such as the

30. See Barry, *Political Argument,* op. cit., pp. 35-41 and 295-99. For formulations which move in the direction I seek to sustain see William Alston, "Pleasure," *Encyclopedia of Philosophy* 6 (1967), 341-47, and Alasdair MacIntyre, "Egoism and Altruism," *Encyclopedia of Philosophy,* 1, op. cit., 462-66.

31. I realize, of course, that the charge of "elitism" will be hurled here. But the charge moves too far too fast. First, all of the definitions adopted finally end up, as I have noted, acknowledging that people might be mistaken about their interests on occasion. And on most usages most people would agree that certain actions which go against the inclinations of individuals are nevertheless in their interests—as in the cases of some policies toward children and idiots. One needs only one example to raise the question I pose here *of the grounds for making such judgments.* Second, for me to say that you are mistaken about your interests is not necessarily to imply that I will jam my view down your throat. Only authoritarian types leap to that implication. I might simply try to persuade you or to bribe you. Indeed, persuasion is usually the most justifiable approach to take for one who celebrates cultivating the capacity for choice. Third, there are some occasions in politics when we simply cannot avoid taking positions on issues which affect the interests of others. Here we must simply exercise our best judgment, remembering human fallibility and privileging to some extent the views of those affected by that judgment.

agreement to accept enslavement—always weighs heavily against one's interests. For one of the things we include as part of being a person is the capacity to make choices based upon reasoned deliberation *and* to reconsider those deliberations and those choices on future occasions. We are speaking here, after all, of the interests persons have; and reflection about interest-regarding choices is part of the process of deliberation into what it means to be a person. To illuminate one of these areas is to shed some light on the other.

Appraisals of Real Interests

Finally, we must confront, if briefly, the question of testability. There are some easy cases where the choice criterion can be applied in ways which would settle the issue for most investigators. Thus the worker who changes his preference scale as between more income and a more creative work life after having experienced benefits produced by the latter can be said to provide solid evidence in support of the view that the policies promoting a more creative work life were more fully in his interest after all. But often, and surely with regard to the broadest and most fundamental questions about interests, the conclusions we reach will rest on an assessment of indirect evidence and will have a more or less precarious status.

The kinds of indirect evidence we can draw upon are varied. Consider, for example, the claim that it is in our interests as citizens to have a legal system which provides punishment for crimes committed by responsible agents, against our interests to treat every criminal as a victim of circumstances who needs therapy. Assume also that the therapy and punishment models of punishment are equally effective as deterrents, so the issue will have to be settled on other grounds. A line of inquiry pursued by J. D. Mabbot, P. F. Strawson, and Herbert Morris into the tacit commitments built into our use of such terms as responsibility, guilt, love, and resentment suggests that the application of these concepts to people treats them, under appropriate conditions, as persons having a capacity to form intentions, deliberate, enter into relations of trust, and so on.[32] If we were to expunge these concepts from our language (provided that were possible) we would indeed strip ourselves of the ability to view each other as members of a moral community; we would impoverish our lives by restricting the variety of shared experiences within our reach. Since the "preparedness to acquiesce in that infliction of

32. Mabbot, "Punishment," in F. A. Olafson, ed., *Justice and Social Policy* (New York: Prentice-Hall, 1961), pp. 39-54; Morris, "Persons and Punishment," op. cit.; and Strawson, "Freedom and Resentment," in Strawson, ed., *Studies in the Philosophy of Thought and Action* (New York: Oxford University Press, 1968), pp. 71-96.

suffering on the offender which is an essential part of punishment is all of a piece with this whole range of attitudes," our operating commitment to treat each other as persons tends to support the institution of punishment.[33] And once we peer into these conceptual connections carefully we are both more likely to choose a *system* (not necessarily individual acts) of punishment as in our interests as social beings and likely to choose "respect for persons" as a standard relevant to appraisals of interest. I am not trying to argue for this particular conclusion here, though I find arguments in support of it persuasive. The point is that conceptual clarification can inform the choices we make about interests by helping us to see more profoundly what turns on each alternative.[34]

A second line of inquiry involves one's vicarious and actual immersion in alternative modes of social life, in variable "life-styles." A participant study of kibbutzim, various tribal forms, feudal communities, and alternative styles in industrial society provides the materials from which comparative judgments can be made about possible interests not actively sustained by prevailing social arrangements.

These lines of inquiry surely help to bring suppressed presuppositions to the point of more conscious deliberation and choice, but what is the evidential status for the ascription of interests of such choices once made? The problem is not only that investigators must ask what the result would be if a particular practice or institution were introduced into an alien setting; nor is it merely that the persons who undertake these lines of inquiry are likely to have a deep investment in protecting a certain interpretation.

The paradox is this: The very process of preparing oneself to make the most reflective choice about one's interests affects the evidential status of the choice one makes. Consider the judgment of the girl radicalized by her experiences in the antiwar movement of the middle sixties. It was not only her obligation to join the movement, she now believes, but her involvement generated results which were, in a profound sense, in her own interests.

> Now that I look back on that job, if I had known what I was accepting, I probably would not have done it, because of the insecurities and what seemed so many threatening things . . . . (Kenneth Keniston: Was it a rough time then?) No, it was great. I was totally absorbed in the work. (K.K.: You mean that now you would do it again, but at the time, if you had known, you wouldn't have

---

33. Strawson, op. cit., p. 93.
34. The ways in which conceptual clarification can inform choices of the sort discussed here are explored with some care by Richard Flathman, "From Therapy to Theorizing: Conceptual Analysis and Political Philosophy" (Paper delivered at Annual Meeting of the American Political Science Association, Los Angeles, California, September 8-12, 1970).

done it?) Yes, that is what I am saying. I think that one of the
valuable things was that I was open. I was looking . . . .[35]

In one sense this judgment, made *after* having experienced two styles of
life, is impressive evidence in favor of the latter alternative. But, in another, a
different person is making the choice and that affects its status as evidence.
For her recent experience is mediated through new orientations,
expectations, and investments which themselves are supposed to be part of
the conditions to be appraised. Even under ideal conditions of choice, then,
elements of conjecture and speculation will enter into our assessment of the
extent to which alternative modes of social life are more or less in our
interests.[36] This incorrigible feature of efforts to appraise "higher-level"
interests should be reflected in the way we hold and defend views about these
matters and in the kind of action we are willing to sanction in support of
those who understand their own interests differently from the way we do.

Conclusion

Clarity about what "interest" means does not ensure that disputes about
what is in our interests can be neatly resolved. But it does help to sharpen the
issues implicated in these disputes and to point towards kinds of evidence
most fruitfully pertinent to the core issues. That is the best, I think, we can
expect. To promise more, to offer to "translate" these issues into a series of
neat hypotheses amenable to precise and impersonal test, is inevitably to
corrupt the enterprise undertaken. The outcome, as suggested by past
performance, would join surface precision to profound obscurity.

35. Quoted by Kenneth Keniston, *Young Radicals: Notes on Committed Youth*
(New York: Harcourt, Brace and World, 1968), p. 121.

36. To focus the problem more sharply, consider the case of a rather contented
person who is convicted of a crime, and, several years later, comes to prefer the security
and routine of prison life to freedom in the larger society. Many of us would want to ask
if that choice could be explained away as the result of the prison's constricting influence
on the convict's perception and understanding. Stephen Lukes explores problems
inherent in making such judgments in the context of deciding between a Marxist and
Durkheimian view of human development. "Alienation and Anomie," in Laslett and
Runciman, op. cit., pp. 134-56. The comparison is particularly pertinent since I suspect
that Marx and Durkheim tacitly share the *notion* of interest I have elucidated, but
diverge significantly as to what is most in our interests as social beings.

10. The Concept of Interest in Pluralist and Marxian Analysis

ISAAC BALBUS

Introduction

The purpose of this paper is to delineate and explore fundamental differences between Pluralist and Marxian political analysis by focusing on the way in which each "school" treats the concept of "interest." My argument will be, in brief, that the Marxian treatment of the concept "interest" is far more consistent with the variety of meanings that our ordinary language acknowledges are entailed by the concept, and that, as a consequence, Marxian analysis has both explanatory and normative advantages over Pluralist analysis. More specifically, I will argue that the Marxian recognition of the objective as well as subjective status of interests provides the basis for (a) the explanation of the development of consciousness and (b) trans-subjective criteria for judging the worth of a given policy or polity which Pluralist analysis cannot provide by virtue of its persistent refusal to recognize any interests but the subjective variety.

I. General Considerations on the Concept "Interest"

The concept "interest" has long been at the heart of both normative political discourse and explanatory political analysis. At least since the seventeenth century, political theorists have agreed on the one hand that the satisfaction of individual interests is a primary political goal, and on the other that an understanding of an individual's interests is essential for an explanation of the way in which he behaves.[1] As marked as this consensus as to the centrality of the concept for both normative and explanatory purposes has been, however, there has been an equally marked dispute over the proper meaning of the concept. Indeed, one could with justification assert that some of the central disputes within political theory since the seventeenth century have centered precisely over the question of the logical status of "interest," and "today there are few terms in political discourse used in a more diverse and shifting manner."[2]

Recently, however, ordinary language analysis has managed to bring some conceptual clarity to bear on the "diverse" and "shifting" uses of the concept

---

1. Richard Flathman, *The Public Interest* (New York: John Wiley and Sons, 1966), chap. 2.
2. Ibid., p. 15.

which will aid our comparison of its use in Pluralist and Marxian analysis.[3] In particular, two very different yet equally important meanings have been delineated—one which we will call the subjective and the other the objective definition of "interest." On the subjective meaning of the term, "interest" is equivalent to "interesting"; if a person is said to have an interest in something, it is because he finds it interesting or likes it. "Interest" in this sense is purely subjective because it refers to a psychological state in the mind of the person who is said to have the interest. If a person says he has an interest in music, meaning that he finds music interesting or that he likes it, it is impossible to bring any evidence to bear which will demonstrate that he is "wrong." This, then, is one typical way in which the concept "interest" figures in ordinary discourse.

On the other hand, our ordinary language recognizes an objective meaning entailed by the concept "interest," so that when we say an individual has an "interest in" something we mean that he has a stake in it or is "affected by" it. In this objective sense of the term the existence of the interest is not contingent upon the individual's awareness that he has the interest, i.e., upon any psychological state in the mind of the individual. A person may be affected by something whether or not he realizes it; hence evidence can be marshalled to demonstrate that an individual has an interest even if he is not aware of it or even that what an individual thinks is in his interest is in fact not in his interest. Thus, we say for example that "a child has an interest in a diet which provides a certain quantity of protein,"[4] "a consumer has an interest in the state of the market economy," or "an individual has an interest in the quality of the air he breathes" because all these things—the diet, the economy, and the air—affect the individual's life-chances whether or not he is aware of the effect. "Interest" in this sense, then, is objective because it refers to an effect by something on the individual which can be observed and measured by standards external to the individual's consciousness. In assigning this objective status to the concept "interest," our ordinary language, in effect, recognizes the complex interdependencies within our society which bind men together and shape their destinies.

Both senses of the term, then, express important realities, and both are important for normative and behavioral political analysis. Everyone agrees, for example, that an individual's subjective interests—what he likes, finds pleasurable, etc.—ought to be consulted in the determination of public policy, but to suggest that subjective interest alone is a sufficient political criterion

3. See, for example, Flathman, *The Public Interest;* Hannah Pitkin, *The Concept of Representation* (Berkeley: University of California Press, 1967), pp. 156-162; Brian Barry, *Political Argument* (New York: Humanities Press, 1965), chap. 10, and Barry, "The Public Interest" in *The Bias of Pluralism,* ed. William E. Connolly (New York: Atherton Press, 1969), pp. 159-177.

4. Flathman, op. cit., p. 17.

is to deny the reality of objective interests and the possibility that an individual may be unaware of, or mistaken about, his interests, i.e., that he may be unaware of, or may misjudge the effect that something has on him. In other words, our confidence in the Liberal dictum that "everyone knows his own best interest" is either likely to derive from a purely subjective use of the term (the equation of the desired with the desirable), in which case the statement becomes trivial or tautological, or else is likely to be ill-founded and disproved.[5] Similarly, the use of subjective interests as the sole criteria for evaluation leads one to the perverse conclusion that there is no normative problem of political representation with respect to individuals whose life-chances are seriously affected by a given policy but who do not perceive any effect. Reliance on subjective interest alone as a standard of political evaluation, in short, leads to conclusions that most of us would not want to accept. If it is individual interests which a polity is supposed to represent, then these must include those interests of the objective variety which ordinary language recognizes that our society in fact generates.

Similarly, although everyone agrees that subjective interests will in part determine a man's behavior, and that a focus on subjective interests is therefore essential for behavioral political theory, a sole focus on subjective interests ignores the social fact which our ordinary language recognizes that "it is precisely the presence of 'objective interests' which prompts the emergence of subjective awareness";[6] i.e., that an individual's subjective interests are not merely *given,* or *randomly* generated, but rather are systematically determined by the way in which his life-chances are objectively affected by objective conditions. To rely solely on subjective interest is to ignore the prior and decisive problem of the "conversion" of objective interests to subjective interests, i.e., the development of consciousness, a phenomenon which any adequate political theory cannot ignore.

Any adequate normative or empirical political theory, then, must recognize the existence of both types of interest which are recognized by our ordinary language, since together they raise important normative and behavioral questions which neither one alone can raise. Combining the two dimensions of interest—the objective and the subjective—and dichotomizing them yields a logically exhaustive and mutually exclusive classification of the possible relationships between objective and subjective interest:

5. Robert Paul Wolff, *The Poverty of Liberalism* (Boston: Beacon Press, 1968), pp. 27-28.

6. Flathman, op. cit., p. 19.

	Subjective Interests	
Objective Interests	Aware	Unaware
affected by	consciousness	lack of consciousness
unaffected by	false consciousness	x

This operation reveals three empirically interesting possibilities, none of which is revealed by sole reliance on either objective or subjective interests, and two of which are not revealed by an unwarranted equation of objective and subjective interests. The equation of the two reduces a complex reality to the single possibility represented in the top left-hand cell, where an individual who is affected by something is aware of the effect, i.e., has consciousness. The table, also reveals two other possibilities, however, which, I would contend, are empirically probable and hence normatively and behaviorally interesting. The first, *lack of consciousness* (top right-hand cell), occurs when an individual whose life-chances are materially affected by something is unaware of the effect; the second, *false consciousness* (bottom left-hand cell) occurs when an individual who is aware that his life-chances are being affected misperceives or misjudges the cause of this effect. Both of these possibilities—which, to repeat, are not logical possibilities if one recognizes only subjective interests or only objective interests, or equates the one with the other—represent empirical probabilities for which any adequate normative and explanatory political theory must be able to account. In the following pages I will attempt to demonstrate that Marxian theory, *because it recognizes both types of interest and is, above all, concerned with their interrelationship* is both behaviorally and normatively superior to Pluralist analysis, which consistently refuses to recognize any but subjective interests.

II. *Pluralist Analysis*

A. The Roots of Pluralism

Pluralism both as normative doctrine and as behavioral analysis has often been correctly diagnosed as a modern version of Classical Liberalism which substitutes the group of contemporary industrial orders for the atomized individual of early Capitalism as its basic unit of social interaction yet otherwise conforms in fundamental respects to the Liberal model of political behavior.[7] Nowhere is the parallel between Classical Liberal political theory

7. See, for example, Robert Paul Wolff, op. cit., chap. 4; Theodore Lowi, *The End of Liberalism* (New York: Norton, 1969), chap. 2; T.B. Bottomore, *Elites and Society* (London: C.A. Watts & Co. Ltd., 1964), chap. 6; and Hannah Pitkin, op. cit., p. 159.

and Pluralist theory more apparent than in their common treatment of the concept "interest." In fact, the roots of contemporary Pluralist theory are directly traceable to the way in which "interest" is conceived by Classical Liberalism and to the inadequate epistemology of Classical Liberalism which underlies this conception.

Underlying Classical Liberalism's confidence that the worth of a given polity is a function of the extent to which it leaves the individual free to pursue his own interests is a tendency to define "interest" in purely subjective terms. As Robert Paul Wolff notes, the logical persuasiveness of Mill's defense in *On Liberty* of governmental noninterference in what he called the "Private Sphere" rests entirely on the unexamined premise that every individual is the best judge of his own interest, a premise which as we have seen is either true by definition (if by "interest" we mean "subjective interest") or, probably, false (if by "interest" we mean "objective interest"). Consequently the plausibility of Mill's argument for maximum "individuality" derives from our tendency to interpret "interest" in the subjective sense and thus to interpret Mill's dictum that every individual is the best judge of his own interest as tautological:

> Mill's claim that each man is the best judge of his own interest become[s] the claim that each man is the only judge of his own interests. Since interest is defined in terms of choice, this is equivalent to the tautology that each man makes his own choice. A good deal of the plausibility of Mill's argument derives from our tendency to interpret it in this tautological way.[8]

In short, if "the test of what is desirable is whether in fact men do desire it,"[9] i.e., if a person's subjective perceptions are definitive of his interests, as both Bentham and Mill agreed, then no amount of governmental intervention in the "Private Sphere" can possibly serve the interests of the individual as well as the individual himself can serve them. Having denied the objective status of "interests," and hence providing no logical space for the problem of lack of consciousness or false consciousness, Classical Liberalism necessarily upholds as the best polity one which allows maximum freedom for individuals to pursue their own desires.

If Classical Liberalism's purely subjective definition of interest leads to serious normative problems, the fact that subjective interests necessarily form the starting point of Classical Liberal behavioral or explanatory theories leads to serious explanatory inadequacies as well. Since subjective interests are taken as a *given*, they are necessarily treated as random, i.e., as unstructured by the form of social organization as a whole.[10] The economic model

8. Wolff, op. cit., p. 28.
9. S.S. Wolin, *Politics and Vision* (Boston: Little, Brown and Company, 1960), p. 339, quoted in Flathman, op. cit., p. 34.
10. Talcott Parsons, "Social Classes and Class Conflict In The Light of Recent

which derives from Classical Liberalism, for example, takes individual utility functions as a given and enables one to predict how individuals with constant utility functions and a given order of preferences within the utility function will decide; what it does not do and can not do is explain the origins of, and changes over time in, utility functions. In order to do this, one would have to assume for heuristic purposes that the structure of social organization as a whole determines utility functions, i.e., what people want, and begin to theorize about the relationship between forms of social organization and the content and structure of utility functions. In other words the theoretical problem is to understand the relationship between the way in which individuals interact to objectively affect each other's life-chances and the way in which they perceive these interactions, i.e., to understand the origins of consciousness. In order to do this, however, one would have to abandon the epistemological individualism of Classical Liberalism—the notion of a society composed of self-contained, "independent centers of consciousness"[11]—along with the purely subjective definition of interest which is a reflection of this epistemology.

The refusal of Classical Liberalism to assign an objective meaning to the concept "interest," in short, is a product of a blindness to the complex social interdependencies which determine individual behavior and which our ordinary language recognizes by acknowledging that men have interests which are collectively shaped even if they are unaware of them. In the sections which follow, it should become clear that contemporary Pluralist analysis is characterized by the same refusal and is guilty of the same blindness, with the result that Pluralism suffers from virtually the identical normative and explanatory problems which plague Classical Liberalism.

B. The Group Theorists

Although the concept "interest" is equally central to both the work of Arthur Bentley, the so-called "father" of the modern interest group approach, and the work of subsequent Pluralists, Bentley's sensitivity to the complexities of the concept was never duplicated by either his Pluralist epigones or his Pluralist critics. More specifically, Bentely's writing in the *Process of Government* reflects, like no other Pluralist to follow him, a constant (if completely unsatisfactorily resolved) tension between the objective and subjective definitions of interest.

It is well known that Bentley stated boldly that "when the groups are adequately stated everything is stated. When I say everything, I mean everything."[12] He also stated that

---

Sociological Theory," in *Essays in Sociological Theory* (New York: Free Press, 1954).

11. Wolff, op. cit., p. 142.

12. Arthur Bentley, *The Process of Government* (Chicago: University of Chicago Press, 1908), pp. 208-209.

> There is no group without its interest. An interest...is the equivalent
> of a group...the group and the interest are not separate....If we try
> to take the group without the interest, we have nothing at all.[13]

Bentley thus equated "group" with "interest"; that is, his groups were defined by the common interests of the individuals who comprised them. As to the definition of interest, Bentley warned of "two serious dangers."[14] The first was the danger of "taking the interest as its own verbal expression of itself; the danger of estimating it as it is estimated by the differentiated activity of speech and written language which reflects it."[15] Here, then, Bentley appears to reject the purely subjective definition of interest of Classical Liberalism. At the same time, he warned of what he felt was the opposite extreme, i.e., the danger that we "disregard the group's expressed valuation of itself, and that we assign to it a meaning or value which is objective."[16] He thus also rejected a purely objective definition of interest. Bentley, it is clear, was trying to find a middle ground between sole reliance on a subjective definition of interest—in which the perceptions and evaluations of the individual are definitive of his interests—and sole reliance on an objective definition of interest—in which factors purely external to the individual consciousness are definitive of his interests.

Bentley's solution to this dilemma—of how to avoid the "spooks" of subjectivity on the one hand and a purely mechanical determinism on the other—was ultimately unsatisfactory, and even succeeded in completely robbing the concept "interest" of any normative or explanatory power.[17]

13. Ibid., pp. 211, 213.
14. Ibid., p. 213.
15. Ibid.
16. Ibid.
17. One "middle ground" which he might profitably have taken, but did not, is implied by the following passage in *The Process of Government*:

> It is common for cities to prescribe the width of average wheel tires in proportion to the load carried so as to save the pavements from the injury caused by narrow tires and heavy loads. In a city in which such a regulation does not exist, but where conditions make it important, a movement for it is begun. Some of the taxpayers will organize, they will lead the others. These others, however, although actually suffering in equal degree, will be indifferent, and often really ignorant of the fact that any such movement is under way. *Common speech will say they do not know their own interests.* Success will not be easy to achieve; nevertheless, the movement or some substitute for it...is bound to win...because the organization that leads it *genuinely represents* the mass of indifferent taxpayers. It will win because it will be clear that these indifferent taxpayers are potentially comprised in the group activity...If sufficiently goaded *they will certainly come to know their own interest*. (Emphasis added.) Bentley, *The Process of Government*, op. cit., 226-227.

The middle ground he arrived at was the equation of *interest* with *activity*. He argues that

> The interest I put forward is a specific group interest in some definite course of conduct or activity....Group and Group activity are equivalent terms....The interest is just this valuation...of the activity not as distinct from itself but as valued activity itself. It is first last and all the time strictly empirical. There is no way to find it except by observation.[18]

Behaviorally, it should be clear that the equation of "interest" with "activity" robs the concept of any independent explanatory or predictive power. If the interest of a group is simply its course of behavior, then "interest" becomes merely a redundant descriptive category rather than a means of linking up the problem of group formation with "objective" factors in the social structure. If, in short, the interest *is* the activity, then the interest can not possibly help explain the activity. If "groups are everything" that the political scientist need study, and groups are defined as activity, then all the political scientist need do—indeed all he can do—is *observe* the process of group activity. Thus the entire question of the conditions of group formation in the first place, of which one would be the development of consciousness, is banned radically from the scope of the enterprise. Acting groups are taken as the starting point of analysis, as a given, and there thus can be no effort to relate the formation of these groups to underlying economic and social interdependencies. Here Bentley's analytic problem closely parallels that of [Classical Liberalism: although there is a shift in the definition of "interest" from perception and evaluation to mere behavior, and although the "interests" are now attached to groups rather than individuals, in either case "interests" are treated randomly, as unstructured by the form of social organization as a whole.

Bentley's definition of "interest" in terms of "activity" also serves to deprive the concept of any normative value whatsoever. If groups are everything, i.e., if the political process is nothing but overt group activity, and if interests are manifested solely through overt group activity, then it is logically impossible to say that certain interests are being ignored, distorted, or discriminated against in the policy-making process.[19] By equating "interest" with behavior, in short, "interest" no longer becomes a normative standard by which to evaluate behavior.

In this remarkable passage Bentley demonstrates a sensitivity to both the objective and subjective meanings of "interest" and to their interrelationships. Unfortunately, the passage is almost an aside and its logic is contradictory to the main thrust of Bentley's argument, and (as we shall see) has never been reflected in the work of later Pluralists who claim a debt to Bentley.

18. Ibid., p. 214.
19. See Myron Q. Hale, "The Cosmology of Arthur F. Bentley," in Connolly, op. cit., pp. 35-50.

Bentley's treatment of "interest" thus leaves us no better off—and perhaps worse off[20]—than that of Classical Liberalism. Nevertheless, his work demonstrates both an awareness of the subtleties of the concept and an awareness of the inadequacies of Classical Liberalism's purely subjective definition. David Truman, however, to whom we principally owe the "rediscovery" of Bentley, demonstrates in *The Governmental Process* no such awareness. In fact, although *The Governmental Process* is allegedly an "elaboration" and "extension" of Bentley's work,[21] Truman chooses to ignore entirely Bentley's warning concerning the purely subjective definition of "interest" and defines "interest" solely in terms of *shared attitudes*. Thus he explains that "as used here 'interest group' refers to any group that, on the bases of one or more *shared attitudes*, makes certain claims upon other groups of the society for the establishment, maintenance or enhancement of forms of behavior that are implied by the shared attitudes," and goes on to assert that "the shared attitudes, moreover, constitute the interest."[22]

Truman's "raw materials" for political analysis, his starting point, are thus groups defined in terms of the shared attitudes of their members. This definition allows Truman to distinguish between what he calls *potential groups*, i.e., interests or shared attitudes which at a given time are not the basis for an *organized* group, and *interest groups*, which are identifiable organized groups, organized around certain shared attitudes. One advantage of this definition, then, is that it permits one to theorize about the conditions under which shared attitudes crystallize into organized groups, i.e., to theorize about the organization of subjective interests. Given this theoretical opportunity, one would presume that potential groups would be the starting point of Truman's analysis. It quickly becomes clear, however, that Truman's *actual* starting point is in fact organized groups and that potential groups are relegated to the status of a residual category which is invoked for the purpose of bolstering up his explanation when it becomes clear that political behavior cannot be explained fully in terms of the interactions of organized groups.[23] Thus Truman devotes nearly five hundred pages to organized groups—to their internal cohesion and above all to the conditions which determine their degree of access to the institutions of government.[24] In other words, although Truman's definition of "interest" allows one to treat the problem of the conversion of potential groups to interest groups as problematical, the overwhelm-

20. At least the Classical Liberal definition of "interest" in terms of preferences distinguishes, where Bentley's does not, between "interest" and behavior, and thereby provides some standard, if inadequate, by which to judge and explain behavior.

21. David Truman, *The Governmental Process* (New York: Alfred A. Knopf, 1951), p. *ix*.

22. Ibid., pp. 33-34.

23. See, for example, ibid., chap. 16.

24. Ibid., chaps. 6-15.

ing bulk of his own work ignores the distinction between the two types of groups and leads one to presume that the conversion of potential groups to interest groups is in fact non-problematical, i.e., not worthy of study. Truman thus excludes from the scope of his inquiry an entire set of questions relating to the differential formation of organized groups, e.g., which shared attitudes are more likely to become organized than others, that any adequate theory of political behavior must include. As we shall see, most Pluralists to follow Truman are guilty of this same omission, i.e., of the failure to examine a problem which even the Pluralist, purely subjective definition of "interest" admits is a crucial problem, and the arguments of critics of the Pluralists such as Bachrach and Baratz can be profitably understood as an objection to precisely this omission (rather than to the purely subjective definition of "interest" itself).

But the more serious problem with Truman's treatment of the concept "interest," however, relates to the fact that it is purely subjective. As we have seen with Classical Liberalism, taking attitudes as the starting point of analysis precludes any systematic specification of the *determinants* of attitudes, any specification of the linkages between the objective social and economic factors which affect the life-chances of individuals and the development of attitudes, ideology, or consciousness. In other words, Truman's interest groups, be they potential or organized, are treated as random and free-floating, as unstructured by the form of social organization as a whole. We are back to the Classical Liberalism of John Stuart Mill, for whom individual preferences were taken as a given, as an independent variable rather than as a variable radically determined by social organization itself. In both cases, for both Classical Liberalism and contemporary group theory, society continues to be viewed as a collection of "independent centers of consciousness" rather than the interdependent set of interactions which our ordinary language recognizes it to be.

Normatively, the definition of "interest" in terms of shared attitudes leads one to the conclusion that people do not have interests unless they are aware of them and that, therefore, the only legitimate criterion for evaluating governmental performance is whether policy making adequately reflects the inter-play of conscious preferences. In other words, the entire question of political representation can only be framed in terms of the responsiveness of political institutions to the *felt* needs of individuals; on this conception of "interest" one could not claim that a given number of individuals whose life-chances were similarly affected by similar objective conditions but who did not perceive their common interest were going unrepresented in the political process: if they do not perceive the interest, they simply do not have it. It is probably true that a good deal of the contemporary Pluralist confidence in the representative, responsive, and Democratic character of the American system rests precisely on this tendency to define "interest" in purely subjective terms. If, on the other hand, we were to define "interest" in such a way as to admit of the possibility that individuals may not perceive or may be mistaken about their interests, our confidence in the representative quality of the American system is bound to decline. Similarly, the confidence of Pluralists like Truman that the concept "Public Interest" has no legitimate cognitive status is likewise clearly connected to their purely subjective definition of "interest," for, if "interest" is defined objectively, then conflicts of political preferences and conflicts in political behavior can in no sense be taken as evidence for the proposition that no public interest exists.[25]

C. Pluralist Theories of Community Power

Nowhere is the parallel between the Pluralist school of "Community Power" and the earlier group theorists more clear than in their common treatment of the concept "interest." Like the group theorists such as Truman, Pluralist students of "community power" such as Dahl, Polsby, and Banfield have consistently defined "interest" in purely subjective terms and denied the objective status which ordinary language assigns to the concept. In fact, the explanatory and normative inadequacies of the Pluralist concept of "power" are in large part a direct function of the inadequate treatment of "interest" which underlies it.

The basic premise common to Pluralist analyses of community power is that political power manifests itself most clearly, most unambiguously, in the disposition of political issues. Thus Banfield says, for example, that "a political situation may often be viewed as one in which a proposal is to be adopted or not adopted."[26] Political power or influence, then, is manifested in the struggle over the question whether a given proposal should or should not be adopted—i.e., in the competition among preferences. For all practical purposes the Pluralist reduction of the question "Who Rules?" to the question of the nature of political decision making or issue disposition is further reduced to the question of the characteristics of the participants in the decision-making and the question of the degree of "success" of the participants in the decision-making.[27] To observe who it is that participates in "key political issues" and who prevails in them is to determine who in the com-

25. Barry, "The Public Interest," in Connolly, op. cit., pp. 159-177 and see Truman, op. cit., p. 51.

26. Edward C. Banfield, *Political Influence* (New York: Free Press, 1961), p. 6.

27. Polsby initially includes a third question, namely "Who gains and who loses from alternative possible outcomes?" but rejects it as unanswerable from the point of view of a decision-making methodology. The logical step would be to expand or transcend the Pluralist decision-making methodology, but this is not the step that Polsby takes. Rather, he rejects the importance of the third question for a power analysis on the grounds that "Value distributions occur without explicit decisions taking place, hence may tell us nothing about decision-making." [!] Nelson Polsby, *Community Power and Political Theory* (New Haven: Yale University Press, 1963), p. 132.

munity holds political power.28

Now, as Bachrach and Baratz have amply demonstrated, this focus on overt issues as the focal point for a power determination is plausible or defensible only if one assumes a non-problematical conversion of individual preferences or *wants* into political issues;29 otherwise one would have to include in one's power calculus those efforts undertaken to prevent *wants* from becoming *demands* ("those wants that the members of the system would wish to see implemented through political outputs") and demands from becoming *issues* (those demands "which are *seriously entertained* by the members of the system as possible binding decisions").30 Much of the force of Bachrach and Baratz's powerful critique of the Pluralists revolves around their denial of the plausibility of the assumption of a non-problematical or one-to-one conversion of wants into demands and demands into issues, and their concept of "non-decision making" is thus intended to expand the scope of the "power arena" to include the process by which wants are converted into demands and demands into issues.31

For our present purposes, it is important to note that Dahl, Polsby and Banfield's treatment (or, rather, lack of treatment) of the conversion of preferences to issues is almost perfectly analagous to Truman's treatment of the relationship between potential groups and interest groups. Just as Truman's theoretical starting point was shared attitudes, which in principle enabled him to examine systematically the conditions under which shared attitudes become the basis for political organization, so their theoretical starting point is individual preferences, which enables them in principle to examine systematically the process by which preferences are converted into issues as the initial focus of their power methodology. It is clear, however, that just as for Truman organized groups are the real starting point, for Dahl and the later Pluralists issues become the actual starting point, the *given* of their analyses.32 Common to all Pluralist analysis—to both the early group theor-

28. As Bachrach and Baratz note, Pluralists typically fail to provide an independent definition of "key political issues." See Peter Bachrach and Morton S. Baratz, "Two Faces of Power," *American Political Science Review* 56 (December 1962): 947-952.

29. Dahl, for example, justifies the focus on issue disposition on the grounds that in a Pluralistic, competitive democracy, all "significant" preferences will become political issues. But he has already said that the issue-disposition or decision-making methodology is the only means to determine whether a system is Pluralistic in the first place. His defense of his methodology thus rests on a hopeless circularity. See Robert A. Dahl, *Who Governs?* (New Haven: Yale University Press, 1961), chap. 8.

30. David Easton, *A Systems Analyses of Political Life* (New York: John Wiley and Sons, 1965), pp. 71, 143.

31. Peter Bachrach and Morton S. Baratz, *Power and Poverty* (New York: Oxford University Press, 1970), chap. 3.

32. Banfield, for example, says that

[Where there are no issues] the influence relationship, having been established some time ago and not having been called into question,

ists and the students of community power—is this unwarranted and indefensible tendency to ignore for all practical purposes the theoretical distinction (which they acknowledge) between individual preferences or subjective interests on the one hand and the mobilization or organization of subjective interests on the other.

But just as we have seen that Truman's major inadequacy was not his failure to follow up on his own theoretical distinction between potential groups and interest groups but, rather, was his theoretical formulation of potential groups in terms of purely subjective interests in the first place, so the later Pluralists' fundamental weakness lies not with their failure to investigate the empirical relationship between (their analytically distinguished) preferences and issues, but rather with the fact that they accept preferences or subjective interests as the theoretical starting point of their analyses. (This point must be made very clear, for if the major problem with the Pluralist approach to community power were not a theoretical one but rather simply the failure of Pluralists to follow up empirically on their own theoretical distinction, then one could take Merelman's argument that Pluralist assumptions and methodology are perfectly suited to investigate the process by which wants are converted into demands and demands into issues as a complete vindication of Pluralist theory.[33] The critique of the Pluralists must therefore be expanded beyond Bachrach and Baratz's criticisms if one is to demonstrate the *theoretical* and not simply the empirical inadequacies of the Pluralist approach to community power.) Even if the acceptance of wants or preferences—i.e., subjective interests—as the starting point does not logically prevent one from raising a number of important questions about power which Pluralists typically ignore, it *does* prevent one, it will be argued here, from raising behavioral and normative questions fundamental to an adequate analysis of politics which can only be raised if the objective status of the concept of interest is recognized.

Consider for a moment Polsby's treatment of "interest" in *Community Power and Political Theory*. In the midst of a critique of the assumption of elite theorists such as Hunter and Mills that some group necessarily dominates every community, Polsby says that "Pluralists refuse to regard particular groups as necessarily implicated in decisions when the groups themselves reject such involvement."[34] In other words, when individuals do not participate in political issues or decisions—or, to push things back a step or two,

---

lies outside the ken of the researcher who associates influence with controversy. In such "steady state" situation nothing "happens" and therefore case studies cannot be written.
    Banfield, *Political Influence,* op. cit., p. 10.

33. Richard M. Merelman, "On the Neo-Elitist Critique of Community Power," *American Political Science Review* 62 (1968): 451-460.

34. Polsby, op. cit., p. 116.

when they do not have any preferences with respect to them—they do not have any *interest* in them. Now, as we have seen, if by "interest" we mean subjective interest, this last statement is true by definition. Thus, it seems plausible when Polsby states categorically in a footnote that "of course, most political issues are entirely uninteresting to most people."[35] If however by "interest in" we mean "affected by," then it scarcely follows that individuals who do not participate in or express preferences with respect to a decision are not implicated (interested) in the decision; nor is it likely that "most political issues are entirely uninteresting to most people." As we have suggested, it is certainly possible, indeed likely, that political issues or decisions implicate individuals, in the sense of altering dramatically their life-chances, even if they express or hold no preferences with respect to them. We would certainly want to say, for example, that individuals who did not have any preferences with respect to governmental fiscal or monetary policies were interested in—i.e., affected by—changes in these policies which might drastically affect their chances for employment.

If we grant that this is so, that individuals' life-chances are objectively affected irrespective of their awareness of the effect and/or the cause, then Polsby's casual, sanguine remark that "most political issues are entirely [subjectively] uninteresting to most people" becomes a normative problem of the highest order. In fact, if true it would constitute a severe indictment of the American political system. Is there not something fundamentally wrong, we might ask, with a political system in which the majority of people whose life-chances are affected by political issues and decisions do not take a conscious, subjective interest in these issues and decisions? By defining interest in purely subjective terms, Pluralist analyses such as Polsby's are thereby able to define away a central normative problem and a major potential objection to the American political system. Indeed, instead of treating the datum that most Americans do not express interest in most political issues as a normative problem or defect, Pluralists have typically attempted to transform this defect into either a "natural law" of politics or else a political virtue![36] Non-participation—i.e., the failure of citizens to express preferences with respect to those things which affect their life-chances—doesn't mean there is anything wrong with the political system; it simply means, according to the Pluralist line of reasoning, that there has been something wrong with those theories of democracy which have emphasized the critical importance of citizen participation. For the Pluralists, what the datum of non-participation suggests is not that the system is not democratic, but rather that previous definitions of Democracy have been insufficiently realistic. Thus do the Pluralists, with the aid of the purely subjective concept of "inter-

35. Ibid., p. 128.
36. Ibid., p. 117; and see Dahl, op. cit., chap. 27 for the concept of "slack in the system."

est," transform the "Is" into the "Ought"; thus do social scientists become the apologists for the established political order.

If the purely subjective definition of "interest" on the part of the Pluralist theorists of community power leads inevitably to decidedly conservative normative biases, it also entails explanatory inadequacies which parallel those of the early group theorists. If preferences or wants are taken as the starting point of theoretical analysis, then the *origin* of preferences or wants is not amenable to empirical investigation. As in the case of Truman's interest group, on Pluralist assumptions of subjective interest, preferences or wants necessarily become random or free-floating; i.e., consciousness is given no structural basis and is therefore not subject to systematic analysis. Consequently it becomes impossible to account for differential rates of want formation; if for example lack of political (subjective) interest is considered "natural," how are we to explain changes in the extent and scope of political awareness? In order to explain changes in want formation, in short, it would be necessary to assume that wants or preferences are socially and politically determined, in which case it no longer becomes justified to take wants or preferences as the starting point of political analyses in general and the study of political power in particular.

There seem to be two choices, each of which has the same practical consequence. Either we restrict our definition of "power" to the process by which wants or preferences are converted into decisions, and call the determination of wants something other than "power," or we should include the determination of wants in our definition of "power." In either case we have greatly expanded our notion of what is politically important over the Pluralist approach which takes wants or preferences as a given. By the same token, either Bachrach and Baratz's concept of non-decision making must be expanded to include the processes by which wants are structurally determined, or else Bachrach and Baratz have taken us no further theoretically than the Pluralists.

It is precisely at this point, however, that Bachrach and Baratz in their latest work shrink before the task required of them. In the course of a general defense of the concept of "non-decision making" against Merelman's attack that it is non-empirical and hence non-falsifiable, Bachrach and Baratz concede, as Merelman had argued, that it is not possible to draw any inferences about the exercise of power from mere consensus or the absence of overt conflict within political systems.[37] Thus they assert that

> A non-decision can be identified only within the context of a power
> struggle that is known by the investigator....it is only identifiable
> within the context of a power relationship, or, to be more precise,
> a power struggle. For in the absence of a power struggle, there is no

37. Bachrach and Baratz, *Power and Poverty,* op. cit., chap. 3.

way to judge whether the major thrust of a decision will frustrate a potentially threatening demand from being raised against the decision maker. *If the demand does not exist then neither does the non-decision.* For purposes of a power analysis, a power struggle exists when either both contestants are aware of its existence, or only the less powerful party is aware of it....The most difficult case arises when the status quo is universally subscribed to by non-elites and elites alike. Here, admittedly, there is no way to determine empirically whether community adherence to a belief is the product of elite manipulation...or a genuine consensus. An analysis of this problem is beyond the reach of a power oriented approach and perhaps can only be fruitfully analysed philosophically. (Emphasis added.)[38]

In short, Bachrach and Baratz themselves appear to confine their political analysis to the conversion of wants, taken as a given, into demands, issues, and decisions and thereby exclude the problem of the generation of wants in the first place.

Bachrach and Baratz argue that this is only a minor concession, since in most polities there will always be overt, observable conflicts which are amenable to their non-decision-making methodology.[39] But if we remember that taking as one's starting point overt conflicts (of wants or demands) necessarily prevents one from theorizing about the structural origins of conflicts in the first place, from linking up the development of consciousness with changes in the socio-economic structure, then it becomes clear that their "concession" to Merelman is a far more serious one than they appear to appreciate. By refusing at this point to acknowledge the utility of an objective definition of "interest" Bachrach and Baratz necessarily encounter the same normative and empirical problems which have plagued the Pluralists and the Classical Liberals before them. As we shall see in the next section, however (and as Bachrach and Baratz themselves seem to understand in the chapter of their latest work which follows the one in which their "concession" to Merelman appears), their "concession" was totally unnecessary and unwarranted if one accepts the theoretical logic of a class analysis based on the heuristic assumption of contradictory objective interests as the starting point of political analysis.

III. *Marxian Class Analysis*

It is perhaps not surprising that our examination of the behavioral and normative inadequacies of Pluralism has led us to Marx, for a principal animus

---

38. Peter Bachrach, "Non-Decision Making and the Urban Racial Crisis" (Paper prepared for delivery at the Annual Convention of the American Political Science Association, New York, September 1969), p. 3.

39. Ibid., p. 4.

of Marx's work was precisely the effort to transcend the epistemological and
theoretical framework of Classical Liberalism, which, as we have seen, is at
the root of contemporary Pluralism. In the course of a critique of the Liberal
Political Economy of his day, Marx warned that

> It is above all necessary to avoid postulating "society" once more
> as an abstraction confronting the individual. The individual *is* the
> *social being*. The manifestation of his life—even when it does not
> appear directly in the form of a social manifestation, accomplished
> in association with other men—is therefore a manifestation of *social
> life*.   Individual human life and species-life are not different
> things.[40]

In this remarkable passage, Marx directly attacks the atomistic, Classical Liberal view of the relationship of the individual to society which pictures society
as a collection of "independent centers of consciousness" or "isolated
monads" who confront "society" only as an abstraction, an alien power
which limits the pursuit of their self-interest.[41] Marx's radical opposition
to this Classical Liberal dualism between the individual and society and his
assertion that all "individual" activity is both socially determined and has
social consequences led him inexorably to the view that the nature of social
organization determines the life-chances of the individual *whether he is aware
of this social determination or not*. Thus he wrote, "As in private life we
distinguish between what a man thinks of himself and what he really is or
does, so in historical struggles we must distinguish even more carefully the
catchwords and fantasies of parties from their real interests, their conception from their reality,"[42] and "In the social production which men carry
on they enter into definite relations that are indispensible and *independent
of their will*."[43] Consequently, individuals whose life-chances are similarly
affected by similar objective social conditions are said to have a *common
interest* whether they perceive any such interest or not.[44] Marx thus demonstrates that he fully understands the logic of the objective concept of "interest" wherein "interest in" is equivalent to "affected by."

This objective meaning of "interest" is the theoretical starting point—but
only the starting point—of all Marxian class analysis. Classes are in the first

---

40. Karl Marx, *Economic and Philosophic Manuscripts* in *Karl Marx: Early Writings*
(New York: McGraw-Hill, 1963), ed. T.B. Bottomore, p. 158.

41. The phrase "isolated monads" is Marx's in *On The Jewish Question*, in Bottomore, op. cit.

42. Marx, *The 18th Brumaire of Louis Bonaparte*, quoted in Ralf Dahrendorf, *Class
and Class Conflict in Industrial Society* (Stanford: Stanford University Press, 1959),
p. 15.

43. Marx, *A Contribution to the Critique of Political Economy*, in *Marx and Engels:
Basic Writings on Politics and Philosophy* (New York: Anchor Books, 1959), ed. Lewis
S. Feuer.

44. Dahrendorf, op. cit., p. 174.

instance—but only in the first instance—aggregates of individuals in what Marx called a "common situation,"[45] i.e., individuals whose life-chances are similarly affected by similar objective conditions. Thus he asserts that "the shared interest of a class exists not only in the imagination, as a generality, but above all in the mutual interdependence of the individuals among whom labor is divided,"[46] and that "insofar as millions of families live under economic conditions which separate their way of life, their interests and their education from those of other classes of people and oppose them to these, they constitute a class."[47] Classes in the first instance are thus objective in that their reality is external to the consciousness of the individuals who compose them; they are, to repeat, aggregates of individuals whose life-chances are similarly affected by their common position in the division of labor.

Nothing more can profitably be said about the Marxian concept of "class" without first recalling the overriding goal of Marx's sociology. As Dahrendorf rightly emphasizes, the fundamental problem with which Marx's sociology was concerned was the explanation of large-scale, structural changes in society, a problem to which he brought to bear the assumption that "social structures are not only subject to change, but create permanently and systematically some of the determinant forces of their change within themselves";[48] i.e., social structure is defined in terms of a domination-subjection relationship which produces a conflict of interest which acts as the motor of social change. It is of fundamental importance to realize that Marx's concept of "class" can only be understood insofar as it is understood as inseparably linked to this dialectical model of society, i.e., as an integral part of Marx's theory of conflict and change. "Class" for Marx, then, is above all a "tool for the explanation of changes in...society."[49]

Because Marx's concept of "class" is inseparably linked to a theory of conflict and change, the class society is normally defined by Marx in dichotomous terms; that is, his model is a two-class model. Since conflict always entails a two-sided relationship, involving two parties with incompatible objectives, any concept of "class" which seeks to illuminate and explain the structural basis of conflict must proceed from the heuristic assumption that the structure of any given society or association generates two contradictory, mutually incompatible sets of interests. In this sense, "class" for Marx is an analytic or heuristic concept, not a descriptive category; it is designed to facilitate the development of empirically verifiable hypotheses, rather than

45. Ibid.
46. Karl Marx and Friedrich Engels, *The German Ideology,* quoted in Dahrendorf, op. cit., p. 14.
47. Marx, *The 18th Brumaire of Louis Bonaparte,* quoted in Dahrendorf, op. cit., p. 13.
48. Dahrendorf, op. cit., p. *viii.*
49. Ibid., p. 19.

itself being empirically verifiable. Thus those who would object to the two-class model by arguing that in the "real world" there are a multitude of classes—a middle class, a lower-middle class, an upper-middle class, etc.—make the error of treating the concept of class as if it were a descriptive category rather than an analytic construct designed to illuminate the structural basis of conflict and change in society. Since the theory of class

> has its place within a wider context of the analysis of structural
> changes caused by social conflicts...it is evident that, however one
> may choose to define classes, they must always be regarded as
> groupings related to each other in such a way that their interplay
> is determined by a structurally conditioned conflict of interests.
> In this sense, one class alone is a contradiction in terms; there must
> always be two classes.[50]

The question is not whether two or more than two classes "exist," but rather whether the assumption that social structures generate in and of themselves incompatible sets of interests helps us to explore systematically the origins of conflict and change in society.

Marx's theory of class, then, is, to begin with, founded on an objective definition of "interest" which is wedded to an heuristic assumption that every society or association necessarily generates two such interests which are contradictory in substance and direction. However, while "class" in the sense of an objectively defined common social situation is thus in Marx's scheme the *necessary* condition for the emergence of conflicts important enough to produce major social changes, Marx knew full well that it was not the *sufficient* condition. That is, for conflict among the two classes to emerge, individuals must become *conscious* of their class interest, i.e., the development of class conflict requires the emergence of class consciousness. In other words, what Marx called a class "an sich"—a class in itself, or a class in the sense of an aggregate of individuals similarly situated in the division of labor and whose life-chances are thus similarly affected by similar objective conditions—must be transformed into a class "für sich"—a class for itself, or a community of individuals who are aware of their common interest in opposition to another such class. Classes in the full sense, then, are manifestly political entities: "Individuals form a class [in the full sense] only insofar as they are engaged in a common struggle with another class."[51] "Thus the Proletariat stands in opposition to the Bourgeoisie even before it has organized itself as a class in the political sphere" but "this mass is [only] a class in opposition to capital, but not yet a class for itself."[52] The transformation of objective interests to subjective interests, so to speak, is thus the necessary *and* sufficient condition for the emergence of class conflict; Marx's distinc-

50. Ibid., p. 134.
51. Marx and Engels, *The German Ideology,* quoted in ibid., p. 14.
52. Karl Marx, *The Poverty of Philosophy,* quoted in ibid., p. 14.

tion between a class *an sich* and a class *für sich* perfectly parallels the distinction between the objective and subjective definitions of "interest" and demonstrates that he was—unlike the Classical Liberals and the Pluralists to follow them—sensitive to the two-fold meaning of "interest" which our ordinary language recognizes.

Marx also realized that the relationship between the two types of "interest" and classes is a problematical one. Thus in his celebrated analysis in *The 18th Brumaire* of the limited revolutionary potential of the French peasantry, Marx noted

> The small independent peasants constitute an enormous mass, the members of which live in the same situation but do not enter into manifold relations with one another. Their mode of production isolates them from each other instead of bringing them into mutual intercourse. This isolation is strengthened by the bad state of French means of communication...every single peasant is almost self-sufficient and thus gains its material of life more in exchange with nature than in intercourse with society. [Insofar as] the identity of their interests does not produce a community, national association and political organization they do not constitute a class [in the full sense].[53]

This passage reveals that Marx's analysis of class and class conflict was not predicated on a strict mechanistic determinism; it reveals, rather, that he viewed the transformation of "objective" class interests to overt class consciousness and action as empirically contingent, i.e., as a function of the existence of a number of specifiable empirical conditions. Although in the above passage he alludes to some of these conditions—which we might call "conversion variables"—he never systematically specified the logically exhaustive list of such conditions which would be essential to a fully developed theory of class and class conflict.

This specification is beyond the scope of this paper, whose present purpose is simply to delineate the logic of class analysis and to differentiate it clearly from that of Pluralist analysis. This can be done with the aid of the convenient terminology of Ralf Dahrendorf, who has recently formalized Marx's rather obscure distinction between a class an sich and a class für sich by distinguishing between *latent* and *manifest* interests and between *quasi-groups* and *interest groups*. Latent interests, corresponding to a class an sich and thus to "interest" defined objectively, are structurally defined role orientations—either in the maintenance or modification of the class structure—which the analyst imputes to incumbents of superordinate and subordinate positions within associations. Within every association, two such contradictory inter-

53. Marx, *The 18th Century Brumaire of Louis Bonaparte,* quoted in ibid., p. 183.

ests are said to exist. A collectivity of individuals with a common latent interest is referred to as a quasi-group; for purposes of class analysis, then, in any association there are two and only two such groups. Manifest interests, on the other hand, correspond to a class für sich and thus to "interest" defined subjectively, in that they are "psychological realities," conscious goals relating to either the maintenance or modification of the asymetrical class relationship. Individuals united by and organized around common manifest interests are said to be members of an interest group. The fundamental problem in the theory of class conflict formation, then, is the systematic specification of variables which determine the conversion of latent interests to manifest interests and quasi-groups to interest groups, i.e., variables which determine the conditions under which individuals whose life-chances are similarly affected by similar objective conditions will become aware of their common interest and unite to defend it.[54] In other words, the central problems of Marxian class analysis concern the development and the organization of *consciousness.*

Thus for Marxian analysis, in contrast to Pluralist analysis, the question of the *formation* of interest groups becomes a theoretical problem of the highest order. In the first place, we have seen that Pluralists like Truman and Dahl do make a theoretical distinction between "potential groups"— i.e., manifest interests—and interest groups, but that they typically fail to investigate empirically the link between manifest interests and their organization and that their actual starting point is organized groups. More importantly, given their purely subjective definition of "interest" in the first place, Pluralists *necessarily* treat what Marx called a class für sich or what Dahrendorf calls manifest interests as a given, as the starting point of analysis. In other words, *the* crucial question for class conflict analysis—the question of the determinants of consciousness and the role of consciousness in the development of conflict and change, or of the conversion of "interests" defined objectively (latent interests) to "interests" perceived subjectively (manifest interests)—is entirely beyond the scope of Pluralist analysis. Marxian class analysis thus introduces a set of questions which Pluralism by its very defining assumptions does not and can not raise—a set of questions which must be raised and addressed by an adequate political theory.

A fully developed theory of the origins of interest groups and interest conflicts—in short, a fully developed theory of political change—can only be

54. Dahrendorf tends to equate the transformation of latent to manifest interest and the transformation of quasi-groups to interest groups, and his "conversion variables" thus apply to both conversion processes. Strictly speaking, however, the two conversion processes are analytically distinct. It is perfectly feasible, for example, to have manifest interests (or consciousness), which have not yet become mobilized into interest groups (the organization of consciousness), so that each conversion process is more usefully viewed as a function of *separate* "conversion variables."

developed within the framework of a theoretical analysis which acknowledges the objective status of the concept "interest." If the only type of "interest" that one recognizes is subjective interest, then it becomes impossible to specify the differential potential for interest group formation, since this potential is related to the structural generation of objective interests, i.e., to the "definite relations" which men enter into which are "independent of their will" and which are "indispensable" in that they affect dramatically their life-chances. The failure to distinguish between objective and subjective interests and to theorize about their interrelationship necessarily leads to a static political analysis of which Pluralism is an outstanding example.

Another point of central importance for an appreciation of the logic of class analysis is that within its framework "power" is treated as an analytic or heuristic concept rather than as a descriptive category. The Marxian approach to "power" necessarily follows from its concern with the systematic explanation of conflict and change. Since, as we have seen, the systematic explanation of conflict requires a two-class model, and since the two classes are defined in terms of an asymmetrical relationship of dependence, of superordination and subordination, "power" is necessarily defined as a zero-sum concept. That is, class theory assumes that in any "imperatively coordinated association, there are two groups or aggregates of persons, of which one possesses authority [power] to the extent to which the other is deprived of it."[55] The utility of this formulation, of course, depends entirely on the extent to which it allows for the development of empirically verifiable hypotheses concerning the emergence of conflict and change.

This point—the heuristic or analytic nature of the Marxian concept of "power"—must be underscored since Pluralists typically treat "power" as a descriptive rather than an analytic concept. Pluralists thus ask "who governs?"—i.e., who actually *has* power—rather than *define* power in a certain way for the purposes of the explanation of conflict and change. Whereas class analysis defines power for heuristic purposes in dichotomous, i.e., zero-sum, terms, Pluralists attempt to determine empirically the *distribution* of power within political systems. The Pluralist analysis of power, in short, is fundamentally *static,* whereas Marxian class analysis is above all concerned with the *dynamics* of political change.[56]

This distinction helps clarify the status of Bachrach and Baratz's "concession" to Merelman, which is discussed in the last section. Bachrach and Baratz, it will be remembered, apparently conceded to Merelman that for the purposes of a power analysis no inferences can be drawn from the absence of overt disagreements, i.e., the presence of an apparent consensus, and that

55. Dahrendorf, ibid., p. 170.
56. This distinction also differentiates class analysis from elite theory, which is also fundamentally static. See Dahrendorf, ibid., pp. 198-200; and Bottomore, *Elites and Society,* op. cit., passim.

the concept of non-decision making must therefore be restricted to the analysis of the process by which wants (subjective interests) are converted into demands and issues. In so doing, as was observed earlier, they, too, are forced to treat the origins of wants in the first place as a given, and thus fall victim to the same explanatory inadequacies as the Pluralists. Their "concession," however, is properly understood as unnecessary as soon as it is seen to be based on a failure which they share with Merelman to appreciate the distinction clarified here between the descriptive and heuristic uses of the concept of "power."

If one's goal is to *empirically measure* power, then it is of course true that one cannot empirically establish the distribution of power from the mere existence of apparent consensus or absence of overt conflict, "since there is no way to determine empirically whether community adherence to a belief is the product of elite manipulation...or genuine consensus."[57] If however the goal is not the empirical measurement of power but rather the explanation of *changes* in the allocation of values in society, then it is useful to establish *by definition* the existence of contradictory latent or objective interests and thus latent conflicts as characteristic of the political system. Such an assumption does not require empirical proof that the absence of overt conflict is a product of elite manipulation, since it is not an empirical proposition at all, but rather an assumption whose utility can only be measured in terms of the degree to which it enables one to explain or predict political change.

At times Bachrach and Baratz appear to be aware of this fundamental shift in focus, as when they indicate that

> Rather than asking "who Rules?" [our approach] asks which persons in the community are especially disfavored under the existing distribution of benefits and privileges? [and] to what extent does the utilization of power...shape and maintain a political system that tends to perpetuate "unfair shares" in the allocation of values; and how, if at all, are new sources of power brought to bear in an effort to alter the political process and in turn lessen inequality in the value allocation.[58]

Their concession to Merelman, however, seems to have been made in the belief that they, too, were still principally concerned with the problem of measuring power, for, if they had fully understood that their goal was the explanation of political change, they would have not felt obliged to concede Merelman's point. Once the focus on political change becomes explicit, then the force of Merelman's objection that the notion of "false consensus" is not empirically verifiable evaporates, since within the confines of class analysis the question is not whether it is empirically correct to characterize a political

57. See footnote 38.
58. Bachrach and Baratz, *Power and Poverty,* op. cit., p. 50.

system as a system of contradictory interests in the maintenance or modification of the political status quo, but rather whether this formulation, this assumption, allows one to generate powerful predictive or explanatory hypotheses concerning political change.

An awareness of the static bias entailed in the Pluralist effort to measure power thus leads to an appreciation of the possibilities of a Marxian class analysis based on the assumption of contradictory objective interests. Although, as we have suggested, Bachrach and Baratz apparently have not fully understood the fundamental differences between the two types of enterprises, their latest perspective on the political system nonetheless moves in the direction of Marxian class analysis. Thus in chapter 4 of *Power and Poverty*—immediately following the chapter in which their "concession" to Merelman appears—they develop a model of the political system whose defining characteristic is a struggle or conflict between persons or groups "committed to existing values" and those persons or groups who "seek reallocation of values."[59] That is, their very definition of the political system entails the assumption of contradictory interests and the expectation of dichotomous conflict over these contradictory interests. Their analysis is thus within the classical Marxian framework which assumes for heuristic purposes that society may be defined in terms of a domination-subjection relationship and that this domination-subjection relationship is the motor of social change.

Their specification of the membership of each of their two "classes" is also consistent with Marxian assumptions. Thus they note that persons and groups seeking reallocation of values include "latent and potential groups who are currently uninterested [subjectively] in the policy making process... but who are likely in the future to become active and capable of exercising power...within the political system" and that persons and groups committed to existing values include both active *and* potential supporters of ongoing programs.[60] Here it is clear that the defining criterion for class membership is common objective interests, of individuals being in what Marx called a "common situation." Clearly there would be no grounds for including within the two classes groups and persons who are currently "uninterested" unless one assumed that those currently "uninterested" in the subjective sense nevertheless share certain objective interests with the active participants. Consequently it is clear that in their latest model of the political system Bachrach and Baratz do not take wants or subjective interests as a given, as a starting point, but rather open the theoretical door for the study of the determination of want formation or the conversion of objective to subjective interests. Indeed, they suggest briefly that wants are determined at least in part by the feedback from political outputs or policies, i.e., that the formation of

59. Ibid., pp. 53, 56.
60. Ibid.

wants is not random but is rather determined by structural properties of the polity itself.[61] Perhaps without fully realizing it, they thus pave the way for a class analysis of American politics in general and local politics in particular.[62]

Let me close this exposition of Marxian analysis by briefly discussing its normative advantages over Pluralist analysis. As we have seen, the Pluralist, purely subjective definition of "interest" robs the concept of any value as a trans-subjective evaluative criterion. Pluralism thus translates the Democratic formula that a polity must be responsible to the interests of its members into the formula that a polity must simply be responsible to conscious individual preferences, while refusing to acknowledge that there is any normative problem of political representation with respect to individuals—regardless of their life-conditions—who do not express such preferences. At the same time, Pluralism reduces the Democratic goal of participation to the notion that a polity is healthy to the extent that those who are most interested in a subjective sense participate in political affairs, necessarily overlooking the problem that the life-chances of *all* citizens are affected by political affairs whether they participate or not and even whether they acknowledge the effect or not.

Marxian analysis, in contrast, recognizes that all individuals are objectively interested in, i.e., affected by, social and political decisions, and that the Democratic formula therefore requires that *all* citizens participate in their determination. One trans-subjective evaluative criterion which Marxian analysis provides, in other words, is precisely the degree to which individuals in a polity become subjectively interested in those things in which they are objectively interested, i.e., the degree to which they become aware of, concerned about, and participants in decisions which affect their life-chances. This means that to the Marxist there is, ipso facto, something fundamentally wrong with a polity in which only a minority participates in political affairs.

This also means, moreover, that to a Marxist there is something fundamentally wrong with a polity in which events of major social importance, i.e., events which dramatically affect the life-chances of millions of individuals —such as the workings of the economy—do not even become "political affairs" and hence the object for collective decision making,[63] since under

61. Ibid., p. 63.
62. Their criterion for class membership, i.e., those seeking "reallocation of values" and those "committed to existing values" is far too vague to provide the basis for a satisfactory class analysis, since on this formulation there could be as many different class alignments as there are different values in the society. What is necessary is a specification of a structural conflict of interest which would remain constant from issue to issue. See David J. Greenstone, *Labor in American Politics* (New York: Knopf, 1969), p. 380.
63. Robert Paul Wolff, op. cit., chap. 3.

these conditions individuals are literally prevented from expressing subjective preferences concerning those things in which they are objectively interested. The Marxist refuses to accept that

> Democratic government, which requires of the individual independent judgment and active participation in deciding important social issues, will flourish when in one of the most important spheres of life—that of work and economic production—the great majority of individuals are denied the opportunity to take an effective part in reaching the decisions which vitally affect their lives.[64]

In short, the logic of the Democratic formula, coupled with the logic of the objective concept of "interest"—both of which underlie Marxism—is the logic of *social democracy.* The Marxist recognizes that "it [is] a profound error to separate man as a citizen (i.e. as an individual with political rights) completely from man as a member of civil society (i.e. as an individual engaged in family life and in economic production)."[65] As Marx himself put it,

> Human emancipation will only be complete when the real individual man has absorbed into himself the abstract citizen; when as individual man, in his everyday life, in his work and in his relationships, he has become a *species-being*; and when he has recognized and organized his own powers as *social* powers so that he no longer separates this social power from himself as political power.[66]

Conclusion

The preceding discussion should in no way convey the impression that the *application* of class analysis to a particular society is an easy matter, or that Marx's specification of the criterion of class membership in terms of private ownership of the means of production is not open to serious objections. Rather, the purpose of the preceding section has been to delineate the logic of class analysis in order to demonstrate that it is able to raise important political questions of both a behavioral and a normative nature that Pluralist analysis by virtue of its logic is unable to raise. This advantage, we have tried to show, is in large part a function of the fact that Marxian analysis, in contrast to Pluralist analysis and to Classical Liberalism in which Pluralism has its roots, is faithful to the logic of the concept "interest" as it is used in our ordinary language. By violating the logic of the concept and recognizing only subjective interests, Pluralism denies the reality of social interdependence which the objective meaning of "interest" acknowledges. The behavioral and normative superiority of Marxian class analysis rests on its capacity to recog-

64. Bottomore, *Elites and Society*, op. cit., p. 115.
65. Ibid.
66. Marx, *On The Jewish Question* in Bottomore, ed., *Karl Marx: Early Writings*, op. cit., p. 31.

nize both objective and subjective interests and its awareness that the explanation and evaluation of human behavior requires a systematic examination of their interrelationship.

11. Toward Class Consciousness Next Time: Marx and the Working Class

BERTELL OLLMAN

I.

Why haven't the workers in the advanced capitalist countries become class-conscious? Marx was wont to blame leadership, short memories, temporary bursts of prosperity, and, in the case of the English and German workers, national characteristics.[1] In the last fifteen years of his life he often singled out the enmity between English and Irish workers as the chief hindrance to a revolutionary class consciousness developing in the country that was most ripe for it.[2] The success of this explanation can be judged from the fact that it was never given the same prominence by any of Marx's followers. Engels, too, remained unsatisfied. After Marx's death, he generally accounted for the disappointing performance of the working class, particularly in England, by claiming that they had been bought off with a share of their country's colonial spoils.[3] The same reasoning is found in Lenin's theory of imperialism, and in this form it still aids countless Marxists in understanding why the revolution Marx predicted never came to pass in the advanced capitalist countries.

Despite these varied explanations (or, perhaps, because of them), most socialists from Marx onward have approached each crisis in capitalism with the certainty that this time the proletariat will become class-conscious. A half-dozen major crises have come and gone, and the proletariat at least in the United States, England, and Germany are as far away from such a consciousness as ever. What has gone "wrong"? Until socialists begin to

---

1. Instances of such explanations can be found in Karl Marx, *Letters to Dr. Kugelmann* (London, 1941), pp. 107, 135; Marx and Friedrich Engels, *Selected Correspondence,* ed. and trans. Dona Torr (London, 1941), pp. 249, 256-57, 350, 502; Marx and Engels, *Selected Writings* I (Moscow, 1951), p. 249; A. Lozovsky, *Marx and the Trade Unions* (New York, 1935), pp. 38, 58-59.

2. Marx, *On Colonialism* (Moscow, n.d.), p. 201. See, too, *Selected Correspondence,* pp. 280-81.

3. Engels, *Briefe an Bebel* (Berlin, 1958), pp. 82-83. See, too, Lozovsky, *Marx and the Trade Unions,* p. 61.

examine the failure of the proletariat to perform its historically appointed task in light of their own excessive optimism, there is little reason to believe that on this matter at least the future will cease to resemble the past. It is the purpose of this essay to effect such an examination.

II.

"Men make their own history," Marx said, "but they do not make it just as they please; they do not make it under circumstances chosen by themselves, but under circumstances directly encountered, given and transmitted from the past."[4] In his writings, Marx was primarily concerned with the circumstances of social and economic life under capitalism, with how they developed and are developing. His followers have likewise stressed social and economic processes. As is apparent from the above quotation, however, the necessary conditions for a proletarian revolution were never mistaken for sufficient conditions: real, living human beings had to react to their oppressive circumstances in ways that would bring needed change. The theoretical link in Marxism between determining conditions and determined response is the class consciousness of the actors.

The mediating role of consciousness is sometimes hidden behind such statements as: "The question is not what this or that proletarian, or even the whole of the proletariat at the moment considers its aim. The question is what the proletariat is, and what, consequent on that being, it will be compelled to do."[5] But compelled by what? Marx responds by "what the proletariat is." However, what the proletariat is is a class of people whose conditions of life, whose experiences at work and elsewhere, whose common struggles and discussions will sooner or later bring them to a consciousness of their state and of what must be done to transform it.[6] Though industrial wage earners are in the forefront of Marx's mind when he speaks of proletariat, most of what he says holds for all wage earners, and he generally intends the designations "proletariat" and "working class" to apply to them as well.

Class consciousness is essentially the interests of a class becoming its recognized goals. These interests, for those who accept Marx's analysis, are objective; they accrue to a class because of its real situation and can be found there by all who seriously look. Rather than indicating simply what people

    4. Marx, "Eighteenth of Brumaire," *Selected Writings* I, p. 225.
    5. Marx and Engels, *The Holy Family,* trans. R. Dixon (Moscow, 1956), p. 53.
    6. Marx speaks of the proletariat on one occasion as "that misery conscious of its spiritual and physical misery, that dehumanization conscious of its dehumanization and therefore self-abolishing." Ibid., p. 52.

want, "interest" refers to those generalized means which increase their ability to get what they want, and includes such things as money, power, ease, and structural reform or its absence. Whether they know it or not, the higher wages, improved working conditions, job security, inexpensive consumer goods, etc., that most workers say they want are only to be had through such mediation. Moreover, the reference is not only to the present, but to what people will come to want under other and better conditions. Hence, the aptness of C. Wright Mill's description of Marxian interests as "long run, general, and rational interests."[7] The most long-run, general, and rational interest of the working class lies in overturning the exploitative relations which keep them, individually and collectively, from getting what they want.

Becoming class-conscious in this sense is obviously based on the recognition of belonging to a group which has similar grievances and aspirations, and a correct appreciation of the group's relevant life conditions. For workers this involves divesting themselves of many current delusions—the list is as long as the program of the Democratic party—and acquiring a class analysis of capitalism akin to Marx's own. Such class consciousness also includes an *esprit de corps* that binds members of the class together in opposition to the common enemy.

As a social relation, class consciousness can also be seen to include the social and economic conditions in which recognition of class interests occurs (or can occur). Consequently, any large-scale exposition of this theory would have to involve an analysis of the major developments in capitalism—ranging from the factory floor to the world market—from Marx's time to our own. In providing the beginnings of such an analysis, Marxist writers have tended to underplay the psychological dimensions of the problem. Rather than denying their important contribution, my own focus on the individual worker is best seen as an attempt to redress the imbalance.

Finally, the step from being class-conscious to engaging in action aimed at attaining class interests is an automatic one; the latter is already contained in the former as its practical side. It makes no sense in Marx's schema to speak of a class-conscious proletariat which is not engaged in the activity of overturning capitalism. Workers bursting with revolt stage revolts, or at least prepare for them by participating in the work of a revolutionary party or movement. The revolution takes place when "enough" workers have become class-conscious, and, given the place and number of the proletariat in modern society, its success is assured. The essential step, therefore, is the first one. If class consciousness is to play the role Marx gave it of mediating between determining conditions and determined response it must be taken in a broad enough sense to include this action component.

7. C. Wright Mills, *The Marxists* (New York, 1962), p. 115.

Another approach to class consciousness is offered by Lukács who defines it as "the sense become conscious of the historical situation of the class."[8] By conceptualizing consciousness as a part of a class's objective conditions and interests, Lukács can treat theoretically what is only possible as if it were actual. However, if workers always possess class consciousness because they are members of a class to which such consciousness attaches, then we are not talking about real workers or, alternatively, "consciousness" applies to something other than that of which real workers are conscious. In any case, if all workers are class-conscious, in any sense of this term, we can no longer distinguish between those who are and those who are not, so that nothing concrete in the way of revolutionary activity follows from being class-conscious. Lukács only succeeds in avoiding our problem by begging the question.

A similar misconception, and one widespread in Marxist circles, has "class consciousness" referring to the workers' general resentment and feeling of being systematically cheated by the boss, where any aggressive action from complaining to industrial sabotage is viewed as evidence. Here, too, all workers are seen to be more or less class-conscious, and, as with Lukács, such consciousness leads nowhere in particular. Though obviously components of class consciousness, resenting the boss and the insight that he is taking unfair advantage are not by themselves sufficiently important to justify the use of this concept.

Nor is "class consciousness" a synonym for "trade union consciousness" as Lenin seems to suggest in *What Is To Be Done,* where he ties together the "awakening of class consciousness" and the "beginning of trade union struggle."[9] Despite this suggestion, an important distinction is made in this work between "trade union consciousness," or recognition of the need for unions and for struggle over union demands, and "socialist (or Social Democratic) consciousness," which is an awareness on the part of workers of the "irreconcilable antagonism of their interests to the whole of the modern political and social system."[10] Class consciousness, as I have explained it, has more in common with Lenin's notion of socialist consciousness, and Lenin, on one occasion, even speaks of "genuine class consciousness" with this advanced state of understanding in mind.[11]

8. George Lukacs, *History and Class Consciousness,* trans. Rodney Livingstone (Cambridge, Mass., 1971), p. 73.

9. V. I. Lenin, "What is To Be Done?" *Selected Works,* 12 vols. (Moscow, n. d.), II:77.

10. Ibid., p. 53.

11. Ibid., 88-89. For a useful survey of other interpretations of class consciousness see H. Wolpe's "Some Problems Concerning Revolutionary Consciousness," *The Socialist Register 1970,* ed. Ralph Miliband and John Saville (London, 1970), pp. 251-80.

III.

For Marx, life itself is the hard school in which the workers learn to be class-conscious, and he clearly believes they possess the qualities requisite to learning this lesson.[12] In so far as people share the same circumstances, work in identical factories, live in similar neighborhoods, etc., they are inclined to see things—the most important ones at least—in the same way. They cannot know more than what their life presents them with nor differently from what their life permits. However, the less obvious aspects of their situation, such as their own objective interests, often take some time before they are grasped. What insures eventual success is the ability Marx attributes to people to figure out, in the long run, what is good for them, given their particular circumstances. For Marx, no matter how dehumanizing his conditions, an individual is capable of seeing where his fundamental interests lie, of comprehending and agreeing to arguments which purport to defend these interests, and of coming to the conclusions dictated by them. It is such an ability that Thorstein Veblen labels the "calculus of advantage."[13]

Rather than the proletariat's conditions serving as a barrier to such rational thinking, Marx believes the reverse is the case. The very extremity of their situation, the very extent of their suffering and deprivation, makes the task of calculating advantages relatively an easy one. As part of this, the one-sided struggle of the working class—according to Engels, "the defeats even more than the victories"—further exposes the true nature of the system.[14] The reality to be understood stands out in harsh relief, rendering errors of judgment increasingly difficult to make.

The workers' much discussed alienation simply does not extend to their ability to calculate advantages, or, when it does—as in the matter of reification—it is regarded as a passing and essentially superficial phenomenon. Marx maintained that "the abstraction of all humanity, even the semblance of humanity" is *practically* complete in the full blown proletariat."[15] A loophole is reserved for purposive activity, which is the individual's ability to

12. According to Marx, "The contradiction between the individuality of each separate proletarian and labor, the conditions of life forced upon him, become evident to him himself, for he is sacrificed from youth upwards and, within his own class, has no chance for arriving at the conditions which would place him in the other class." Marx and Engels, *The German Ideology,* translated by R. Pascal (London, 1942), p. 78.

13. Thorstein Veblen, "The Economics of Karl Marx: II," *The Place of Science in Modern Civilization and Other Essays* (New York, 1961), p. 441.

14. Engels, "Preface," Marx and Engels, *The Communist Manifesto,* trans. Samuel Moore (Chicago, 1945), p. 5.

15. *Holy Family,* op. cit., p. 52 (my emphasis). For a discussion of the workers' alienation, see B. Ollman, *Alienation: Marx's Conception of Man in Capitalist Society* (Cambridge University Press, 1971).

grasp the nature of what he wants to transform and to direct his energies accordingly. Marx held that productive activity is always purposive, and that this is one of the main features which distinguishes human beings from animals.[16] Class consciousness is the result of such purposive activity with the self as object, of workers using their reasoning powers on themselves and their life conditions. It follows necessarily from what they are, both as calculating human beings and as workers caught up in an inhuman situation.

The workers are also prompted in their search for socialist meaning by their needs as individuals. For Marx, society produces people who have needs for whatever, broadly speaking, fulfills their powers in the state in which these latter have been fashioned by society. These needs are invariably felt as wants, and since that which fulfills an individual's powers includes by extension the conditions for such fulfillment, he soon comes to want the means of his own transformation; for capitalist conditions alone cannot secure for workers, even extremely alienated workers, what they want. Job security, social equality, and uninterrupted improvement in living conditions, for example, are simply impossibilities within the capitalist framework. Hence, even before they recognize their class interests, workers are driven by their needs in ways which serve to satisfy these interests. And, as planned action—based on a full appreciation of what these interests are—is the most effective means of proceeding, needs provide what is possibly the greatest boost to becoming class-conscious.

Though rooted in people's everyday lives, class consciousness is never taken wholly for granted. The main effort of socialists from Marx to our own time has been directed toward helping workers draw socialist lessons from their conditions. Marx's activity as both a scholar and as a man of action had this objective. Viewed in this light, too, the debate initiated by Lenin regarding the character of a socialist party has not been over *what* to do, but rather over *how* to do it. Essential, here, is that among socialists the conviction has always existed that sooner or later, in one crisis or another (with the help of this form of organization or that), the proletariat would finally become class-conscious.

Both critics and defenders of Marx alike have sought to explain the failure of the working class to assume its historic role by tampering with his account of capitalist conditions. Thus, his critics assert that the lot of the workers has improved, that the middle class has not disappeared, etc., and, at the extreme, that these conditions were never really as bad as Marx claimed. His defenders

16. Though encased in another set of concepts, this is one of the main conclusions to emerge from Marx's discussion of natural and species powers in the *Economic and Philosophic Manuscripts of 1844* (henceforth referred to as *1844 Manuscripts*), trans. Martin Milligan (Moscow, 1959), esp. pp. 74-76, 156-58.

have tried to show that it was relative pauperization he predicted, that big businesses are getting larger, etc., and, after Lenin, that imperialist expansion permitted capitalists to buy off their workers. Such rejoinders, however, whether in criticism or defense, miss the essential point that for the whole of Marx's lifetime the situation in the capitalist world was adequate, by his own standards, for the revolution he expected to take place.

Martin Nicholaus, in his widely read article, "The Unknown Marx," has argued that the mature Marx (Marx of the *Grundrisse,* 1858) put the socialist revolution far into the future, in effect after capitalism was thoroughly beset by problems of automation.[17] Though Marx does speak of such a possibility, this is not his first projection. Marx was dealing after all with trends in the capitalist economy, and particularly, though not exclusively, with their *probable* outcome. On the basis of his research, he not only hoped for but expected revolutions on each downturn of the economic cycle. In 1858, the year of the *Grundrisse,* he wrote to Engels, "On the continent the revolution is immanent."[18] And twelve years later he declared: "The English have all the material requisites necessary for a social revolution. What they lack is the spirit of generalization and revolutionary ardor."[19] Does this sound like a man who thought capitalist conditions were not sufficiently ripe for the workers to make a revolution? Though it is true that Marx became progressively less optimistic (and always took account of other possibilities) he never really believed he was writing for a century other than his own.

If it was not conditions which failed Marx, it could only have been the workers. More precisely, the great majority of workers were not able to attain class consciousness in conditions that were more or less ideal for them to do so. Marx's error, an error which has had a far-ranging effect on the history of socialist thought and practice, is that he advances from the workers' conditions of life to class consciousness in a single bound; the various psychological mediations united in class consciousness are treated as one. The severity of these conditions, the pressures he saw coming from material needs, and his belief that workers never lose their ability to calculate advantages made the eventual result certain and a detailed analysis of the steps involved unnecessary.

IV.

Class consciousness is a more complex phenomenon—and, hence, more fraught with possibilities for failure—than Marx and most other socialists have

---

17. Martin Nicholaus, "The Unknown Marx," *The New Left Reader,* ed. Carl Oglesby (New York, 1969), pp. 105-6.
18. *Letters to Dr. Kugelmann,* op. cit., p. 107.
19. *Selected Correspondence,* op. cit., p. 118.

believed. With the extra hundred years of hindsight, one can see that what Marx treated as a relatively direct, if not easy, transition is neither. Progress from the workers' conditions to class consciousness involves not one but many steps, each of which constitutes a real problem of achievement for some section of the working class.

First, workers must recognize that they have interests. Second, they must be able to see their interests as individuals in their interests as members of a class. Third, they must be able to distinguish what Marx considers their main interests as workers from other less important economic interests. Fourth, they must believe that their class interests come prior to their interests as members of a particular nation, religion, race, etc. Fifth, they must truly hate their capitalist exploiters. Sixth, they must have an idea, however vague, that their situation could be qualitatively improved. Seventh, they must believe that they themselves, through some means or other, can help bring about this improvement. Eighth, they must believe that Marx's strategy, or that advocated by Marxist leaders, offers the best means for achieving their aims. And, ninth, having arrived at all the foregoing, they must not be afraid to act when the time comes.

These steps are not only conceptually distinct, but they constitute the real difficulties which have kept the mass of the proletariat in all capitalist countries and in all periods from becoming class-conscious. Though these difficulties can and do appear in other combinations, I believe the order in which they are given here corresponds to the inherent logic of the situation and correctly describes the trajectory most often followed. What we find then is that most workers have climbed a few of these steps (enough to complain), that some have scaled most of them (enough to vote for working-class candidates), but that relatively few have managed to ascend to the top.

To begin with, if we accept Marx's portrayal of the proletariat's dehumanization as more or less accurate, it is clear that there are workers who simply cannot recognize that they have interests of any sort. They have been rendered into unthinking brutes ("idiocy" and "cretinism" are Marx's terms), whose attention does not extend beyond their immediate task.[20] Given the conditions which prevailed in Marx's time, many workers must have suffered from this extreme degradation. And, when treated like animals, they reacted like animals, tame ones. Marx, himself, offers evidence for such a conclusion in telling of occasions when the workers' already impossible lot worsened without raising any protest from them.

In 1862, during a depression in the English cotton trade, a factory inspector is quoted as saying, "The sufferings of the operatives since the date of my last report have greatly increased; but at no period in the history of

---

20. *1844 Manuscripts*, op. cit., p. 71.

manufacturers, have sufferings so sudden and so severe been borne with so much silent resignation and so much patient self-respect."[21] Even a member of Parliament from one of the worst affected areas cannot refrain from commenting, nor Marx from quoting, that in this crisis, "the laborers of Lancashire have behaved like the ancient philosophers (Stoics)." Marx adds, "Not like sheep?"[22]

What conclusion did Marx draw from these events, events which were by no means that unusual? None at all. Despite his angry retort, his purpose in relating this incident was to show the conditions in which the workers were forced to live and work, and not how uncomplainingly they had submitted to these conditions. So bludgeoned by life that they cannot conceive they have any interests, many workers are condemned to submit to their earthy travail with as much thought as an ox before the plow. Admittedly, this malaise was more prevalent when the working day averaged fourteen hours than now when eight hours is the rule, but I am not convinced that it has completely disappeared.

For workers who recognize that they are human beings with interests, the next step in becoming class-conscious is to see their interests as individuals in their interests as members of the working class. It is not immediately apparent that the best way to obtain a good job, more pay, better conditions, etc. is to promote the interests of one's class. On the contrary, the practical isolation that capitalism forces on all its inhabitants makes the very notion of shared interests difficult to conceive. It was Marx, himself, who noted that the individual in capitalist society is "withdrawn into himself, wholly preoccupied with his private interest and acting in accordance with his private caprice."[23] The character of the ensuing struggle is well brought out in Marx's definition of "competition," its all purpose label, as "avarice and war among the avaricious."[24] Throughout society, calculator meets calculator in the never ending battle of who can get the most out of whom. "Mutual exploitation" is the rule.[25]

With so much indifference and hostility ingrained in the way of life and outlook of everyone, it is not surprising that the competition between workers for a greater portion of the meager fare which goes to them as a class is no less intense. Marx is eminently aware that, "Competition makes individuals, not only the bourgeoisie, but still more the workers, mutually hostile, in spite of the fact that it brings them together."[26] This competition

21. Marx, *Capital* III (Moscow, 1959), p. 128.
22. Ibid., p. 135.
23. Marx, "Zur Judenfrage," Marx and Engels, *Werke* I (Berlin, 1959), p. 366.
24. *1844 Manuscripts,* op. cit., p. 68.
25. Marx and Engels, *Deutsche Ideologie* in *Werke* III (Berlin, 1960), p. 395.
26. *German Ideology,* op. cit., p. 58.

first rears its head at the factory gate where some are allowed in and others are not. Inside the factory, workers continue to compete with each other for such favors as their employer has it in him to bestow, especially for the easier and better paying jobs. After work, with too little money to spend, workers are again at each other's throats for the inadequate food, clothing, and shelter available to them.

The cooperation that characterizes industrial labor hardly offsets the atomizing affect of so much inner-class competition. The scales are even more unbalanced than this suggests, since the individual worker, without a conception of his identity in the group, is incapable of appreciating the essential links between his own labor and that of his co-workers. Cooperation is something of which he is only dimly aware. So it is that both his social activity and product are viewed as alien powers. To be able to see one's interests as an individual in one's interests as a member of the working class under these conditions is no little achievement.

After workers realize they have interests, and class interests at that, it is essential next that they adopt Marx's view of what these latter are. I accept that there are objective interests which accrue to a class in virtue of its social-economic position, and, also, Marx's understanding of what these are for the workers, including their overriding interest in transforming the system. However, his belief that most workers will sooner or later come to agree with us has received little support from history. Without a doubt, this is the step at which the greater part of the proletariat has faltered.

When Samuel Gompers, the early leader of the AFL, was asked what the workers want, he answered, "More." And, as much as I would like to dispute it, this strikes me as an accurate description of how most workers have conceived their interests then and now. Most workers who have grasped that they have interests as workers have seen them in terms of getting a little more of what they already have, making their conditions a little better than what they are, working a little bit less than they do. As limited, cautious men, the workers have little, cautious designs. Their horizons have been clipped off at the roots. As with most of their other personal shortcomings, this is a result of the alienation Marx so eloquently describes. It is simply that their conditions have so limited their conceptions, that these conceptions offer them little opportunity to break out of their conditions.

While Marx was aware that most workers did not share his view of their interests, he refused to acknowledge the real gap which separates the two positions, or to devote serious study to its causes and likely consequences. Thus, when Jules Guesde came to London to seek Marx's advice about an election program, Marx could write, "With the exception of some trivialities which Guesde found necessary to throw to the French workers despite my protest, such as fixing the minimum wage by law and the like (I told him: 'If the French proletariat is still so childish to require such bait, it is not worth while drawing up any program whatever') . . . ."[27] But the proletariat, not only in France but throughout the capitalist world, were so "childish," and they remain so.

Marx's inability to grasp the staying power of the workers' trade union designs is due, in part, to his belief that the capitalists would not and could not accede to most of these demands; having got nowhere for so long, the workers would not fail to see that their real interests lay elsewhere. In part, he believed that whatever minor benefits whey managed to force upon the capitalists could only be temporary, acquired in booms, in periods of rapidly expanding capital, and lost again in depressions. And, in part, he thought that whatever improvements withstood the test of time were so clearly insignificant that this fact would not be lost upon the workers themselves. These were the "crumbs" which, he said, do nothing to bridge the "social gulf" between the classes.[28] In capitalism, even when the workers get higher pay, this is "nothing but better payment for the slave"; it does not "conquer either for the worker or for work their human status and dignity."[29] The successes of the English Factory Acts in ridding capitalism of its worst abuses are treated in the same light.[30]

However, it is one thing for us to agree with Marx's characterization of such improvements as "crumbs" which do not win for the workers their "human status and dignity," and quite another to believe that most workers agree as well, or that they ever have, or that they ever will. On the contrary, the same conditions which so limit their horizons that a higher wage is considered the acme of their interests make it likely that a few dollars added to their pay packet will be regarded as a major success. In keeping with this Lilliputian perspective, rather than being disappointed with "crumbs," they will use their collective bargaining power to obtain more. Organized into unions, they have managed to retain many of the gains made in prosperous times through the reoccurring crises, and, with the steady growth of society's absolute product, they have succeeded in acquiring a higher standard of living than Marx thought possible. Given the time and the patience, even pyramids can be built of crumbs. But most workers have never wanted anything else, nor have they ever conceived of their interests in other terms.

Once workers accept that they have class interests and that Marx is right about what these are, the step they must take is to consider these interests more important than ties of nation, religion, race, etc. In the

27. Marx, *Letters to Americans,* trans. Leonard E. Mins (New York, 1953), p. 124.
28. Marx, "Wage Labor and Capital," *Selected Writings* I, p. 91.
29. *1844 Manuscripts,* op. cit., p. 81.
30. Marx, *Capital* I, trans. Samuel Moore and Edward Aveling (Moscow, 1958), pp. 279 ff.

Communist Manifesto (1848) Marx declared that the proletariat had already lost both religious and nationalist attachments.[31] This is one conclusion he was later forced to qualify, as least as regards English and Irish workers. The hopes for a growing proletarian brotherhood received an almost fatal setback by the chauvinistic behavior of the European working class during World War I. With such divisions firmly entrenched in the psychology of most workers, an all too frequent reaction in time of economic hardship has been to seek for scapegoats among their class. It is against those who compete with them for scarce jobs, against fellow workers who can be easily distinguished because of their nationality, religion, or race that much of their pent up ire is directed.

One does not have to offer a theory of where these prejudices come from and how they operate to hold that the weight Marx attached to them is seriously inadequate. Oddly enough, Marx provides the framework for such a theory in his account of alienation and the mystification which accompanies it, where we also learn that the tenacity of these prejudices is a function of the degree of distortion present. How could such deprived people be expected to operate with abilities they have lost? How could workers, who are manipulated more than any other group, overturn the results of this manipulation in their own personalities?

Besides causing conflicts among workers, the excessive attachment to nation, religion, and race is also responsible for a lot of inter-class cooperation, workers and capitalists of the same nation, etc., joining together to combat their alien counterparts.[32] In these circumstances, the hatred workers should feel for their exploiters, which is another requirement for class consciousness, is all but dissipated. The whole education, culture, and communication apparatus of bourgeois society, by clouding the workers' minds with noncontroversial orthodoxies, has succeeded admirably in establishing numerous links between the classes on trivial matters. Aren't we all fans of the Green Bay Packers?

The workers, with relatively few exceptions—depending on the country and the period—don't really and deeply hate capitalists, because they cannot distinguish them sharply enough from themselves, because they have never been able to set off a sufficiently unencumbered target to hate. Whatever class mobility exists—this is a more significant factor in America than elsewhere—merely serves to compound the problem. And if some workers are aided in making this distinction by having a capitalist with a long nose or different colored skin, they are more likely to become incensed against his religion or race than against his class.

31. *Communist Manifesto,* op. cit., p. 28.
32. *On Colonialism,* op. cit., p. 301. In "Civil War in France" (1871), however, Marx still treats the German and French proletariat as if they were devoid of strong nationalist sentiment.

One excruciating result of such bourgeois successes is that workers, including socialist workers, often admire capitalists more than they hate them. Workers who live vicariously through their employer are not limited to those with a stunted conception of their interests. And their envy is not of a man who has more, but who is in some sense better. Such an admission is already contained in the widespread drive for respectability and prestige, for "status." Actions acquire status according to a particular social code, which is set and promulgated in every society by the ruling social and economic class. To be interested in acquiring status is to submit to the social code that determines it. It is to accept the legitimacy of existing society, and to admit, however feebly, that one's interests as a citizen are somehow superior to one's interests as a worker.

Marx and Engels were often made aware of this failing, which affected many of their own stalwarts, particularly in England. If Tom Mann, one of the truly outstanding leaders of the English working class, was—as Engels relates—"fond of mentioning that he will be lunching with the Lord Mayor," what could one expect of the others?[33] Yet, Marx and Engels always treated this "bourgeois infection" (Marx's term) as something skin deep and of passing importance.[34] My own conclusion from such evidence, which has not diminished with the years, is that the vast majority of workers, including some devotees of Marxist parties, have never really and decisively rejected the society which has despoiled them, but have always been more concerned to be accepted by it than to change it.

The next step up the ladder to class consciousness is that workers must have an inkling, however vague, that their situation can be qualitatively improved. It does no good to know what they need and to have the proper likes and dislikes if they believe that nothing can be done about it. For, in this situation, lotteries and football pools remain the only escape from the lot that has befallen them. We have all heard such rejoinders as "The world will never change" and "Rich and poor will always be with us." What it is important to realize is that it is not only workers whose horizons stop at "more" who are afflicted with this pessimism, but also many who share Marx's conception of their interests. Clearly, the relevant question is how could people who are so battered by their reality believe otherwise? A vision requires hope, and hope requires a crack in the ceiling, such as few good landlords in any society permit.

33. *Selected Correspondence,* op. cit., p. 461.
34. Ibid., p. 147. In 1863, Marx wrote to Engels, "How soon the English workers will free themselves from their apparent bourgeois infection one must wait and see." Engels had just written him, "All the revolutionary energy has faded practically entirely away from the English proletariat and the English proletariat is declaring his complete agreement with the rule of the bourgeoisie." Ibid.

Frederick Lessner, a working-class acquaintance of Marx, says of his introduction to Weitling's book, *Guarantees of Harmony and Freedom:* "I read it once, twice, three times. It was then it first occurred to me that the world could be different from what it was."[35] But how many workers would read this kind of book work even once? Yet, it was only through such sustained mental effort that a man who became a model for his class could obtain a major prerequisite for engaging in socialist activity, the idea that a more just society can be constructed. More recently, disappointment with the Soviet experiment has served as another kind of block to the workers' imagination.

Once workers who have accompanied us so far accept that change for the better is possible, the next hurdle is becoming convinced that they have something positive to contribute to this effort. A widespread phenomenon in our time, which we can only assume was also present in Marx's day, is the feeling of powerlessness, the self-reproach that there is nothing one can do which matters. Most people simply feel themselves too small and the establishment which requires overturning too large and imposing to see any link between individual action and social change.

Each person must make his own decision whether to join others for political action, and must justify to himself and, perhaps, to his family the time and energy this new commitment will take. In this situation, even people with strong socialist views are prone to say, "One more, one less—it won't make any difference." Everything from going to vote to manning the barricades is affected by this doubt. Socialist views come coupled with the duty to act upon them only where the individual is convinced that somehow or other, sooner or later, his participation will count. In Marx's day, many of the most restless spirits among the European proletariat immigrated to the New World simply because they did not believe there was anything they personally could do to improve the old one.

Assuming we cross this hurdle, we are now confronted with workers who have grasped what Marx takes to be their interests, who possess the proper attitudes toward co-workers and capitalists, who believe it possible to create a better world, and who think that they can help effect this change—it is essential, next, that they consider the strategy advocated by Marx or their Marxist leaders to be the right one. Marx was thoroughly pragmatic when it came to the means for achieving social change, favoring the ballot where it

35. Frederick Lessner, "Before 1848 and After," *Reminiscences of Marx and Engels,* no editor, (Moscow, n. d.), p. 150.

36. Engels tells us that Marx thought the transition to socialism in England, for example, might be peaceful and legal. Engels, "Preface to English Edition," *Capital* I, op. cit., p. 6.

could work and revolution where it could not.[36] Because national circumstances and traditions vary so greatly and because of the many peculiar "accidents" that cannot be systematized, Marx felt he was in no position to offer detailed advice; and, despite the reams written on Marx's theory of revolution, there is none. Most of his comments on this subject are very general, as when he says, the "social disintegration" will be "more brutal or more human, according to the degree of development of the working class itself."[37]

Nor did Marx ever speculate on what is the proper kind of political party or movement to make the revolution. The First International was a loose coagulation of working-class unions, educational associations, and parties whose first aim was to promote class consciousness. This, as we will recall, is also how Marx saw his task. When enough workers became class-conscious, they would know what to do and how to do it.

If Marx had no theory of revolution, he equally had no theory of democracy, and certainly felt no commitment to use "democratic" and "constitutional" methods. With his mixture of contempt and distrust for bourgeois democracy, his bias on the side of revolutions is a clear one. Once his followers were permitted to operate inside the constitution, however, many of them ceased thinking of their goals as outside it. For better or worse, they were determined to believe that it was possible to obtain what they wanted by obeying the rules (and even the customs) of the political game. What began as a tactical means became an end, displacing in the process their former end. Yesterday it was the Social Democrats and there are indications that the same metamorphosis is occurring in many Communist parties today.

Marx's correspondence is full of complaints against working-class leaders, many of them close students of Marxism, for their tactical bungling, usually for engaging in compromising actions with the bourgeoisie. He most often attributes their mistakes to personal faults, and, in this way, manages to exonerate their following. Ernest Jones, the Chartist leader, is described as the general of an army who "crosses over to the camp of the enemy on the eve of battle."[38] The army, apparently, was ready to fight. Again, my conclusion is more severe, for the evidence has been compounded many times over since Marx's day. The rules and practice of the capitalist political game, with its perpetual promise of the half-loaf, poisons the socialist rank and file as well as their leaders. For the workers to take up revolutionary tactics, it is essential that they be completely disillusioned with all reformist leaders and methods. But, in democracies, such leaders and methods are generally able to secure a small part of what they promise. The result is that the workers are

37. Ibid., p. 9.
38. *Letters to Americans,* op. cit., p. 61.

kept dangling, wed to solutions which cannot solve; yet, temptation, and with it hope, never ceases.

One final step remains. Once workers grasp what they need as workers, who their friends and enemies are, that a better world can be created, what must be done to create it possess the confidence that they have something to contribute and that by avoiding the trap of reformism they can succeed, what is still required is that they have the ability when the time comes to act. An imprisoned class consciousness that cannot be translated into revolutionary action is no class consciousness at all. Waiting for the German proletariat to provide a revolutionary initiative which never came, Rosa Luxemburg—whose politics ran a close parallel to Marx's own—paid for the delay with her life. Yet, in the aftermath of World War I, Germany probably had more workers who had climbed all previous steps than any capitalist country either before or since. But when the opportune moment for action arrived, most of them held back. This does not excuse the betrayal of the German Social Democrats who argued against rebellion and helped put down the outbreaks that occurred; it only helps explain, at least in part, their unfortunate success. Luxemburg's fate may very well have been Marx's had he lived in a more troubled land at a more troubled time. Or, would he have read the handwriting which had been on the wall since 1848 or thereabouts and become—a "Leninist"?

Marx's mistake was to believe that understanding things correctly, in a way that calls for a particular action, necessarily leads to people taking this action. First of all, in the case before us, there is the very real fear of being hurt. Very few workers have the courage which comes with having nothing to lose, simply because they always have something to lose, their lives if nothing else. In recent years, of course, they have much more to lose, the growing number of objects which they have purchased. Because they have relatively few possessions, and ones they have worked very hard to obtain, the proletariat have become as petty as the petty bourgeoisie have always been about their goods. In this situation, the tendency is to look not at what one has to gain, but at what one has to lose in any radical change. This is the same affliction that the peasants have always suffered from.

But such last minute restraint can also be attributed to two related psychological mechanisms about which Marx knew very little. It has often been remarked how people in authority browbeat others to act against their recognized interests, how awe, respect, and habit combine to overturn the most rational conclusions. This falling into line under any circumstances if part of a syndrome which T. W. Adorno and others have popularized as the "authoritarian personality."[39] Rooted in the habit of taking orders, a habit

39. T. W. Adorno, *The Authoritarian Personality* (New York, 1950). Marx had some conception of this failing as it applied to German workers. Of them, he says, "Here

which extends back to the earliest years of education and family training, it eventually succeeds in being felt as a duty. So great is the emotional compulsion to obey that the adult, who has been conditioned in this way, may actually feel physical pain when he disobeys.

How exactly this effect is created or the precise mechanism through which it operates cannot be gone into at this time. For my purposes, it is enough to state that it exists, and that the conditions in which most workers are raised—admittedly, more so in some cultures than in others—are only too well suited to producing authoritarian personalities. Thus in moments of crisis, many workers find themselves emotionally incapable of departing from long established patterns of subservience, no matter how much they rationally desire to do so.

The second psychological malfunction working to disrupt Marx's expectations is the security mindedness of the proletariat, what Erich Fromm has called their "fear of freedom."[40] People not only refuse emancipation because choosing against habitual patterns is painful, but because they irrationally fear what is to be chosen. What is new and unknown is more terrifying to many than the terror which is known. They think at least they have been able to live through the troubles they have had. How do they know they will be able to deal as well with the new troubles which await them?

People lack confidence in the future, essentially, becuase they lack confidence in themselves; but nothing in the lives of workers has enabled them to acquire such confidence. Again, those who are most in need of freedom are the very ones whose wretched, ego destroying existence has acted to make them afraid of freedom. In such straits, there will always be workers who desire to see the future conform to the past except at the limits of despair. This failing, admittedly, like the irrational need to obey, is more likely to afflict those who are not poised to act against the system. However, diseases—and what I have been describing are emotional diseases—generally have little respect for the political sophistication of their victims.

After removing workers for this, that, and the other shortcoming, and many for a combination of them (the actual combinations as I have indicated may vary), what is left? How many workers were class-conscious in Marx's time or are now? How many could have become class-conscious then or could

---

where the workers are under the thumb of bureaucracy from childhood on and believe in authority, in the constituted authorities, it is a foremost task to teach them to walk by themselves." Lozovsky, *Marx and the Trade Unions,* op. cit., p. 42. In the same year, 1868, he writes to Engels, "For the German working class the most necessary thing of all is that it should cease conducting its agitation by kind permission of the higher authorities. A race so schooled in bureaucracy must go through a complete course of self-help." *Selected Correspondence,* op. cit., p. 249.

40. Erich Fromm, *Fear of Freedom* (London, 1942), esp. pp. 1-19.

become so now? How many workers who became class-conscious were able to
remain so (for if character alters, it alters in both directions)?

V.

From the foregoing account, it appears that class consciousness is an
extraordinary achievement of which very few workers at any time have
shown themselves capable, and that there is little reason to believe this will
change. Indeed, with greater inter-class mobility, increasing stratification
within the working class, and the absolute (not relative) improvement in the
workers' material conditions in our century, some of the factors which have
helped bring about class consciousness where it did exist have lost much of
their influence. The pessimistic import of such truths has led to the demise of
more than one socialist and is at least partly responsible for the slight
attention paid to problems of class consciousness by socialist writers.

Yet in trying to account for the past failures of the working class, my
intention has not been to predict the future but to affect it. This is only
possible, however, after frankly and fully admitting the real psychological as
well as social barriers that exist to proletarian class consciousness. On the
basis of the foregoing analysis, the problem with which socialists are
confronted may be stated as follows: in order to have a revolution, there will
not only have to be other severe crises in the capitalist system (these will
occur), but a large segment of the working class will have to develop
characteristics that will enable them to respond to one or another of these
crises by becoming class-conscious.

This manner of posing the problem is not affected by differences of
opinion regarding how quickly class consciousness can arise. The French
events of May 1968 found workers climbing many of the steps to class
consciousness in short order (just as the aftermath found many of them as
quickly descending). Particularly impressive was the way workers initially
rejected the gigantic wage increases won by their trade union leaders. Clearly,
at this stage, a large number of workers wanted fundamental social change,
though most were still uncertain as to what exactly that was or how to get it.
The events of May were not only a result of preceding conditions and events,
social, economic, and political, but as well of the ability of the most radical
working class in any advanced capitalist country, with the possible exception
of Italy, to respond as they did. And this response, when and to the limited
degree that it occurred (whatever the guilt of the French Communist party),
is evidence of the speed at which under certain pressures the barriers to class
consciousness can be overcome. We have not been dealing, however, with how
fast workers can become class-conscious, but with all such consciousness
contains. While the complexity of this condition suggests slow or staggered
development, it is clear that particular events can greatly speed the process.

It is time now to examine more closely the causes for Marx's own excessive optimism. Marx was forever expecting the proletariat to become class-conscious, essentially, because in his scheme for understanding man and society there is no niche put aside for their continued refusal to do so. We have already seen how the needs people have are conceptualized as one with the wants they feel for whatever it is that will satisfy these needs. Marx is aided (and, perhaps, even encouraged) in constructing this knot by the German language where *Bedingungen* means both "need" and "want." As a result, Marx is inclined to believe that people want or will soon come to want that for which they have needs, or, by extension, which serves as the means to acquire what they need. Yet, people may have needs for which they never consciously want relief, and others—as Freud has shown—of which they never become aware, and still others the means to the satisfaction of which they never directly want.

Marx's position that life-activity is purposive brings him to a similar conclusion whenever the self is treated as the object. But, again, the necessity Marx finds is one he himself introduces into his concepts. In fact, people may act without purpose, without consciously seeking any particular development or goals. It was such faulty conceptualization which led Marx to treat consciousness, despite qualifications to the contrary, as the mental reflection of surroundings and kept him from correctly estimating the real gap between objective and subjective interests.

In this manner, the link between conditions and character—for all the space it gets in Marx's writings—remains undeveloped. The problem of the receptivity of character to new influences, its malleability, particularly relative to age, is nowhere discussed. Marx is obviously correct in holding that the individual is to a remarkably high degree the product of his society, and that by changing his living conditions we change him, but there are at least two questions that still have to be answered: are the changes which occur in character always rational, i.e., in keeping with the new interests that are created? How long does it take for new conditions to produce new people?

Marx believed that the effect of conditions on character was rational and relatively quick acting. The evidence examined in this paper argues against such beliefs. Before attempting to modify Marx's conceptual framework, however, we must first realize that very little that passes for irrationality here is sheer madness. For the most part, it is a matter of too little attention paid to some factors and too much to others, or of the right amount of attention paid too late. Given where his calculations should take him and when, the individual's response to his environment is distorted; he has become fanatical in his devotion to some needs and a cold suitor to others.

One factor, in particular, which has received less than its due in Marx's writings is the sexual drive. Young people are more interested in sex, devote more time to thinking about and trying to satisfy this drive, and are immensely more effected by it (by not having sex even more than by having it) than most adults, even after Freud, would care to admit. If one doesn't eat, one starves to death. But what happens if one doesn't satisfy the sexual drive, or does so only rarely, hurriedly, and with a lot of guilt? One doesn't die, but how does such abstinence effect the personality? Which qualities does it reinforce and which does it weaken? There are no conclusive answers, but it is my impression that sexual repression among the workers, as among other classes, has contributed significantly to their irrationality.[41]

By the right amount of attention paid too late, I have in mind the time lag which exists between the appearance of new conditions and resulting changes in character. Though Marx accepted the necessity of some such lag, he did not make it long enough; nor did he properly estimate the potential for mischief which this delay carried with it. People acquire most of their personal and class characteristics in childhood. It is the condition operating then, transmitted primarily by the family, which makes them what they are, at least as regards basic responses; and, in most cases, what they are will vary very little over their lives. Thus, even where the conditions people have been brought up in change by the time they reach maturity, their characters will reflect the situation which has passed on. If Marx had studied the family more closely, he surely would have noticed that as a factory for producing character it is invariably a generation or more behind the times, producing people today who, tomorrow, will be able to deal with yesterday's problems.

Even children, whose characters are more affected by existing conditions, don't become all these conditions call for, since the family, which is the chief mechanism through which society bears upon them, is staffed by adults whose outlook reflects the previous state of affairs. If, for adults, existing conditions come too late, for the young, who can do little about them in any case, they are reflected through a prism that both modifies and distorts the influence they would otherwise have. As a result, only in extreme cases do new conditions make people behave as they do (and these are generally young people); more often, old conditions determine their actions, and then, for the reasons given, this takes place in an irregular and distorted manner. In a society, such as capitalism, which is changing (albeit, in its superficial aspects) very rapidly, this means that the character of most people never catches up with their lives. They seem destined to be misfits, whose responses are forever out of date.

In order to allow for the irrationality which comes from this time lag, I would introduce into Marx's conceptual framework the idea of character structure, understood as the internalization of early behavior patterns, as

41. For an illuminating discussion of the role of sexual repression in helping to produce such irrationality, see Wilhelm Reich, *Mass Psychology of Fascism,* trans. Theodor P. Wolfe (New York, 1946), esp. pp. 19-28, 122-43.

organized habit. Such characterological hardening of the arteries derives whence character derives, but is a product apart, exercizing a relatively independent influence on how one will respond to future events and conditions.

The idea of character structure does little violence to Marx's basic framework; the interactions he describes go on as before, except that something now mediates between conditions and response, between needs and wants, between objective and subjective interests, between activity and consciousness, something into and through which the one must be translated to become the other. As such, character structure is both a product of alienation and, with the real conditions of life, a contributing cause of alienated activity. With the introduction of this new factor we can better explain why workers so often find their inclinations in conflict with the demands of the current situation, why they consistently misunderstand and are incapable of responding to it in ways that would promote their interests. We can better explain, too, why people today are driven to act in ways that might have been rational a generation ago, in a war, a depression, or a boom which existed then but no longer does. The concept of character structure also helps account for the proletariat's "fear of freedom" and their submissiveness before authority, which are, after all, simply attempts to repeat in the future what has been done in the past. Finally, character structure helps to explain the distorting sentiments of nation, race, and religion, as well as the worker's pessimism regarding a better form of society and his own role in helping to bring it about by treating them as expressions of early behavior patterns that, internalized within the individual, have acquired a dynamic and power of their own.

Thus, whenever the system has been in crisis, when it was in the workers' interests to construct new solutions, their character structure has disposed them to go on seeking old nostrums, where they can continue to act as they have been and know how to. To be sure, new social and economic conditions did develop with the growth of imperialism, workers' movements were often cursed with poor leadership at critical moments of their history, and capitalists have sought to exacerbate national and racial antagonisms—all this, as Marxists rightly maintain, has served to inhibit the development of proletarian class consciousness. What those who accept Marx's analysis have seldom admitted is that the character structure of most workers has also been at fault. With the introduction of this concept into Marx's framework, workers must be viewed not only as prisoners of their conditions, but of themselves, of their own character structures which are the product of previous conditions.[42]

42. Useful discussion of the concept of character structure can be found in Reich's *Character Analysis,* trans. T. P. Wolfe (New York, 1961), esp. 22 ff; and in Hans Gerth

VI.

The introduction of the concept of character structure into Marx's scheme, substituting a sense of retarded rationality for the sense of irrationality toward which so much of this study seemed to point, has great significance for a socialist strategy. If, as part of their alienation, workers cannot react to their conditions, no matter how bad they get, in a rational manner, then all efforts to attain widespread class consciousness are doomed to failure. They are, that is, unless some manner can be found to affect their character structure during its formative years, to make sure that the behavior patterns internalized there never develop or, more to the point, never acquire the degree of durability they now have. Looked at in this way, the focal point of a socialist strategy must be those conditions which most affect the young. For it is possible to alter the character structure of workers by fighting against its construction, by counteracting the disorienting influence of family, school, and church, whatever in fact makes it difficult for the individual once he becomes an adult to make an objective assessment of his oppression and to act against it.

The concrete aims of radical activity, on the basis of this analysis, are to get teen-age and even younger members of the working class to question the existing order along with all its symbols and leaders, to loosen generalized habits of respect and obedience, to oppose whatever doesn't make sense in terms of their needs as individuals and as members of a group, to conceive of the enemy as the capitalist system and the small group of men who control it, to articulate their hopes for a better life, to participate in successful protest actions no matter how small the immediate objective, and to create a sense of community and brotherhood of all those in revolt. The purpose is to overturn (or, more accurately, to undermine) the specific barriers that have kept past generations of workers from becoming class-conscious. Full class consciousness can only occur later on the basis of adult experiences, particularly in the mode of production. Making allowances for exceptions on both ends of the scale, what can be achieved now is essentially a predisposition to respond to the conditions of life in a rational manner, what might be called a state of

---

and C. Wright Mills, *Character and Social Structure* (London, 1961), pt. 2. Another attempt to revise Marx's conceptual scheme is found in Marcuse's distinction (though barely suggested in Marx's writings) between "true" and "false" needs. *One-Dimensional Man* (Boston, 1964), p. 6. Rather than having to overcome or undermine barriers rooted in character structure, Marcuse states the problem in terms of a struggle between two kinds of needs. In focusing on this broad distinction, however, the change-producing levers in human personality are disassembled. The same reconstruction leads Marcuse to overemphasize those elements in the population (particularly students) in whom liberating needs are dominant as agents of revolutionary change.

preconsciousness. Capitalism willing, and capitalism is periodically willing, revolutionary effects will follow.

To insist on the necessity of altering character structure is not to argue that only new men can create a new society, but to reaffirm that changes in both people and conditions are needed for a socialist revolution to occur. The opposition between idealism (where men are held responsible for transforming society) and vulgar materialism (where material conditions are) is, in any case, a false one. There is a constant, many-sided interaction going on, and the problem has always been how to capture (and conceptualize) the dynamics of this process so as to participate in it more effectively.

The conditions that now exist in the United States (more so than in other capitalist countries) are exceptionally well suited to the strategy I have been urging. In stressing the importance of social conditions in determining what people are and how they act, Marxists have not given sufficient attention to the fact that some conditions have a greater effect on what people are and others on how they act. This is chiefly because the people referred to in the two instances are not the same. Since we acquire the greater part of our character when young, it is conditions which most affect the young that most affect what people are (or what they are a generation later when the once young have become adults); whereas adults are the subject of conditions, generally more extreme, which are said to affect how people act.

Recent events have thrown up a number of important new conditions which exercise their predominant effect on what people are. Among these are the Vietnam War in which the young are expected to fight as well as to believe, a pause in the cold war and with it in anticommunist ideology, an increasingly evident racism that goes counter to taught ideals, the hunger and suffering seen daily on television, frequent disruption of community services and schools, growing unemployment among the newly trained and among incoming skilled workers of all sorts, the pill and drugs, and the new obscurantist puritanism that has arisen to combat both. In each case, a pattern of behavior in which the older generation grew up and which, through its transformation into character structure, contributed significantly to a passive acceptance of their lot is changing into behavior that in one or more respects opposes adolescents to the existing social and political system. It remains for socialists, especially young socialists, to make the most of these conditions, not to instigate a youth revolt (whatever that is) or to create an auxiliary of the working class, but to alter the character structure of the next generation of workers.

It is not possible for a paper that argues for a particular strategy to canvass all possible tactics that can be used to advance it. The choice of tactics requires detailed study of the time, place, and parties involved. Still, the strategy advocated here does suggest that the effort some radical groups are putting into high school "organizing" and publishing high school papers should be greatly expanded, especially in working-class districts, even at the expense of other activities in poor communities and among adult workers. Also, insofar as the aim is understood in the negative sense of breaking up existing behavior patterns, the hippies and Yippies—by holding up establishment ways and virtues to contempt and ridicule—may have as much to contribute as the more orthodox forms of protest. The means of keeping young people open to a rational calculus of advantages later in life may be quite different from those required to help them make the calculus itself. What exactly these means are needs further investigation, but for the moment I would not rule out any form of protest that increases or clarifies young people's discontent and their opposition to established authority.[43]

If the "revolution" is, as most socialists will admit, at a minimum decades away, then it is proper—given the conservative function of character structure and its greater malleability early in life—that we begin preparing for it among workers who will be around and relevant at the time. Samuel Gompers and his successors in the AFL-CIO sacrificed the revolutionary potential of the working class to the immediate needs of real workers; today, paradoxically, socialists with their limited means must pay less attention to real workers, certainly to workers over thirty (thirty-five?), so that they can help to develop a revolutionary working class.

43. For further discussion of some of the tactics advocated in this paper, see Reich's "What is Class Consciousness?", trans. Anna Bostock, *Liberation,* vol. 16, no. 5 (October, 1971), pp. 15-49. Though Reich devotes more attention to the problem of promoting class consciousness in adults than I feel is justified by his analysis of character structure, his stress on youth is unique in the serious literature on this subject. Reich's important contribution to Marxism in this area is summarized in B. Ollman, "The Marxism of Wilhelm Reich; or the Social Function of Sexual Repression," in *The Unknown Dimension: European Marxism Since Lenin,* ed. Karl Klare and Dick Howard (Basic Books, 1972).

Part Four

Radical Alternatives to Conventional Social Sciences

The most commonly repeated indictment of contemporary political science by its impatient practitioners was its complacency, its inclination to accept whatever existed as close to ideal. The obvious solution was to substitute a critical political science for an apologetic one. But what is a critical science of politics? This section is an effort to approach that question.

There is a recognized tradition in Europe called critical theory, centered in the Institute of Social Research in Frankfurt. Critical theory begins with a hostility to apologetics for any existing political system, whatever its proclaimed intentions. From that, it searches for a methodology in which assumptions must be approached with an open mind. Those Western liberals who began their work with the notion that liberalism had solved all the world's problems were condemned equally with Sovet ideologues who saw in Comrade Stalin the personification of human goodness. A basic article of faith for critical theory is that very few things are known for certain, and in the face of that, it is best to approach all philosophical questions anew.

Since politics is at the root of critical theory, it is imperative that the study of politics learn from it. Happily the real world of politics intruded on the closed cottage of conventional political science, and as a result, some form of critical political science has begun to emerge in the United States in the past ten years. While no coherent statement of principles has yet been issued, it can be suggested that the task of a critical political science is, first, to explode the assumptions of a discipline which is only ideology; and, second, to contribute political knowledge to the process of human liberation, by using ideas to expand people's ability to control their own lives, rather than to restrict it. The first task is deceptively easy, the second fiendishly difficult; but if it is not done, the movement toward a critical political science will eventually fail. This section represents some first attempts to build alternatives, radical and critical alternatives, to mainstream political science, all with the goal of aiding human liberation.

One essay, that by David Kettler, is a plea for the application of reason and intelligence on the part of leftist and critical scholars, who must adopt the role of "counselors" to political movements. In its emphasis on integrity, Kettler's article is very much part of the tradition of critical theory. Hans Peter Dreitzel examines the role of social science in an era dominated by rationality and technocratic decision making by focusing on the technocratic ideology itself. By example, this is an indication of one of the tasks of a critical social science. Herbert Marcuse is one of the most famous exponents of critical theory, and in the final article of this section, his ideas on aesthetics are critically examined by Stephen Eric Bronner, who finds Marcuse's notions strangely apolitical. The import of this article is that a critical theory criticizes itself as well as the much easier targets of the conventional wisdom.

Besides their critical nature, a common thread to these essays is their insistence on clarity of thought and their celebration of reason. In other words, standards upheld as ideals by conventional political science, but never reached, are themselves appropriated by the critics. Instead of offering new goals, they lay claim to be better able to reach the old ones. From this common point each essay goes on to explore its own unique problem, be it that of commitment, rationality, or aesthetics. Here, as well, the inspirations are not new culture heros but instead nineteenth-century writers Marx, Weber, Kierkegaard. The paradox is striking but nonetheless realistic, that the building of new alternatives must explore their links with the past, that a critical political science must not be alienated from but connect with a social theory that has shaped the modern world. The three essays in this section do not by themselves create a radical alternative to existing social science (that will be the work of a generation, or even two generations), but they posit what some of the tasks may be and they take the first steps along the road to fulfilling those tasks.

12. The Vocation of Radical Intellectuals

DAVID KETTLER *

I.

In transmitting his detailed commentary on the Gotha Program, Marx made it clear that he considered it his duty to criticize erroneous statements and concepts, even at the risk of offending political allies and personal friends, because the pervasiveness of theoretical confusion tends to "demoralize the party." It is indeed true that "every step of real movement is more important than a dozen programmes," he continued, but such political progress is "bought at too high a price" if it involves regression in theoretical understanding.[1] Alliances for political action must be entered without sacrificing the rigor of one's own thought. These injunctions are worth recalling at this time because there is demoralization and confusion among many of us, for whom Marx serves as model in the striving to integrate the struggles for knowledge and for human liberation. Radical scholars and intellectuals have been excited by the resurgence of radical aspirations and militant actions against prevailing authorities and orders in the United States, France, the Federal Republic of Germany, Czechoslovakia, and elsewhere in the developed nations and by the bitterly courageous revolutionary movements and groupings in many poor lands. But they have frequently not known how to think about these developments and about their own relationships to them without doing considerable violence to the sorts of canons of theoretical integrity which Marx applied to the Gotha Program and which must now be honored, if the demoralization is to be countered and the political movement itself is to be kept from a dead end in rhetorical posturing.

Three preliminary illustrations, deliberately drawn from the work of men I respect, will serve as symptoms of the demoralization. First, the following passages appear in a paper prepared for *Les Temps Modernes* by Georges Rozos as a characteristic and important part of an essay purporting to explicate the thought of Régis Debray:

> In my estimation, this line of anti-bourgeois thought and action
> which culminated in Nazi metapolitics holds the key to certain
> forms of struggle that might again become prominent in the near

* Peter Larmour helped bring this paper about. If he had not felt compelled to leave the Ohio State University in protest against a political firing, this would have been a joint paper and would have been tougher and better.

The essay will appear in an anthology to be published this fall in Dutch and Swedish and then, presumably, in other major languages. Godfried van Benthem van Den Bergh and David Kettler, eds., *Truth Against Power: Intellectuals in the Modern World* (Amsterdam: van Gennep, 1970).

1. Karl Marx to Wilhelm Bracke, May 5, 1875, in Karl Marx, *Critique of the Gotha Programme* (New York: International Publishers, 1938), pp. 34-35.

future....It should not be forgotten that a 'madman' called Hitler
mobilized and commanded hitherto untapped forces of tremendous
magnitude through what appeared to his opponents as irrational
methods....In a country or region that is culturally dominated by
bourgeois elements, a radical movement has to turn against culture,
and in the process reach a meta-political, or even nihilistic state,
before it can start to think in terms of social and economic reforms.[2]

The confusion between humanist radicalism and fascism must be ascribed
to Rozos and not to the author or movement he exploits; but the possibility
for such occurrences is given by our situation. The second example is far
less extreme, and typifies a widespread determination to give theoretical
expression to the political and personal admiration for the courage of those
who put themselves on the line. An able young political scientist, Marvin
Surkin, reports on his discovery of "the modes of thought originating in the
existentialism of Kierkegaard and the phenomenological philosophy of Hus-
serl, which have been synthesized by such writers as Sartre and Merleau-Ponty
in France, Heidegger in Germany, and John Wild and Alfred Schutz in this
country":

This approach transcends the world of objective reality and subjective reality by returning to preconceptual knowledge and mean-
ing-construction...As a methodology of the social sciences, phenomenology links thought and action; it rejects the arbitrary sanctity of intellectual thought over existential experience and the human and social knowledge of the mundane world, and instead attempts to revitalize what William James called "the world of the
street." The world is what "I live through" not what "I think," and

2. Georges Rozos, "Régis Debray et la Radicalisation de la Révolution," *Les Temps
Modernes* 24(August-September 1968) no. 266-67, pp. 443-479. The passages quoted
do not appear in the French edition. I have taken them from the English manuscript cir-
culated by the author. That the author's ideas are given circulation in a prominent journal without this revealing application of his basic thesis offers depressing commentary
on the intellectual situation.

Compare with this the following diagnosis, written by the Russian philosopher Mikhail Lifshitz in 1934, characterizing the elements dominant in the "bourgeois ideology"
of the time:

...conversion of the crisis of the old social structure into an eternal
cosmic problem of harmony and chaos, ultra-radical criticism of
liberal bourgeois traditions; transitions from the ideals of the 'free'
and the 'normal,' the 'harmonious' and the 'beautiful' to the ideals
of violence, harshness, and power at any cost; apology for barbaric
heroism, for infractions of moral and aesthetic norms, for ugliness
on principle; and finally interpretation of this reactionary extrem-
ism, this revolt of bourgeois violence against bourgeois civilization
as a revolutionary manifestation of the greatest significance.

(Mikhail Lifshitz, "Johann Joachim Winckelmann and the Three Epochs of the Bourgeois Weltanschauung," trans. in *Philosophy and Phenomenological Research* 7[1946]
no. 1, p. 80).

> the meaning of life is manifest in human experience as it is consti-
> tuted by the intentional structure of consciousness. In a very real
> way, Julius Lester, Stokely Carmichael and Eldridge Cleaver are the
> social scientists of the Black Ghetto rather than Daniel P. Moyni-
> han.[3]

The obvious danger in such an approach is that the effective rhetoric
obscures the rational consequences: Would it not follow equally well from
the general methodology that the most racist cop is as much a "social scientist" as Cleaver and the rest or that Weitling and Eric Hoffer are the "social
scientists" of the working class and not Marx or Mandel?

What makes the third illustration the most disturbing of all is the insight
it offers into the theoretical disorientation prevailing among writers who have
contributed as much as anyone to the resurgence of radical scholarship in the
United States. A serious discussion between Eugene Genovese and Staughton
Lynd about ways of formulating a radical analysis eventuates in the following:

> Lynd's other question—"Does he favor shooting conscientous objec-
> tors in socialist countries?"—is contemptible....This whole section of
> Lynd's letter is a thinly veiled effort to make it appear that I have
> criticized his work from a Stalinist perspective. His course compels
> me to say plainly what I have been willing to leave implicit in my
> review: I have a deep abhorrence for what Lynd stands for because
> his doctrine of absolute morality and absolute political truth had
> proved the ideological foundation for every form of totalitarianism
> that we have faced and are now facing; and notwithstanding his
> pious speeches on non-violence, his philosophy is an incitement to
> totalitarian violence.[4]

Since Genovese is correct in his characterization of Lynd's attack on him,
we are faced with the spectacle of rational discourse degenerating into ex-
changed accusations of "totalitarianism."

All three instances originate in the United States. They may reflect the
intellectual underdevelopment of the American Left. However, they are not
taken from the countless easy cases which could be culled from the so-called
theoretical literature which neatly equates American students with Marx's
revolutionary proletariat or "niggers." This thinking measures the revolutionary significance of political developments by the degree to which slogans and
ventures anathematize the existing order—however insignificant the participation in the events or their time and place. The contentions advanced by
Althusser and others in France, by Habermas and his associates in Germany,
by Sedgwick in England, moreover, indicate that the problem is by no means

3. Marvin Surkin, "Sense and Nonsense in Politics" (paper prepared for the meeting
of the Caucus for a New Political Science at the Center for the Study of Democratic
Institutions, May 1, 1969), mimeographed, pp. 23-24.

4. Eugene Genovese, "Letter to the Editor," *New York Review of Books* 11
(19 December 1968) no. 11, p. 36.

limited to the United States. The weakness of contemporary radical theorizing has in fact become a cliché, and no useful purpose would be served by another hand-wringing exercise. The need is to specify the weaknesses, to identify the key confusions which generate the demoralization, and to find strategies for moving out of the impasse. It is not the purpose of this paper to question or defend radicalism as. a general orientation to social and political life. I share the basic radical experience of the world as a place where men are made to suffer more than they must and where they become less than they could, through the workings of deeply rooted but changeable complexes of human arrangements. Radical movements have been concerned to identify and to transform such complexes. We are concerned with the relationship between theoretical work and such efforts.

In sum, the continuing excitement among radicals, countered in the political world by an increasingly determined and effective repression and countered in the theoretical sphere by an increasingly complex and sophisticated scientific apparatus hostile to radical visions, creates an urgent need to rehabilitate the theoretical enterprise among radicals, to reinstate distinctions between slogans for mobilization and analyses for orientation, between polemical annihilation and mutual criticism, between ideas as political instruments alone and theory. The absence of adequate strategic perspectives able to account for setbacks and incoherences as well as for openings and new directions leads to escalation of violence, to search for the "betrayer" within, to comfort in slogans and formulas, and/or to total disillusionment and passivity. As noted, many writers on the Left have become aware of the need, and substantial efforts to meet it are under way. But the central issues have not been faced honestly and modestly enough, and in any case it is not enough to have individual writers affirm the integrity of theory. One vital constituent of integrity for the kind of theory I am talking about is the existence of a critical but receptive public, able and willing to weigh contrasting claims of theorists and to generate explicable standards and criteria which will distinguish the more adequate formulations from the less; and this is not identical with another constituent of the radical theoretical enterprise, to be discussed later, a continuing interaction with the political work itself. The question is not simply about the place of theory and reason in the doctrine and utterances of the radical movement, in other words; it is also about the place of intellectuals and their institutions within the structure of whatever political movements unfold and in their visions of the future.

It is doubtless convenient to bypass such problems by a seemingly radical and even "Marxist" manipulation of terms like "ideology," "consciousness," and "practice." Then all uncomfortable objections can be written off as the "ideology" of some regressive class; one's own views can be rendered immune from legitimate criticism and the need for rational argument obviated by a proclaimed identification with the "consciousness" of the progressive class; and all incoherences can be sanctified by a general condemnation of mere theory and theoreticians in the name of "practice." Marx, of course, proceeds quite differently. In the *Critique of the Gotha Programme*, for example, he applies three important theoretical criteria. First, he demands accuracy in theoretical formulations. In objecting to the opening statement of the proposed program, "Labor is the source of all wealth and all culture," Marx points out that labor is only one of several natural forces which combine to create useful objects. Only then does he extend his commentary to inquire into the interested motives or other social functions subserved by the criticized formulation. He contends that it is a "bourgeois phrase" because it distracts attention from the private appropriation of the other natural productive factors and thus obscures the circumstance that, as Marx puts it, "it follows precisely from the fact that labor depends on nature, that the man who possesses no other property than his labor power must, in all conditions of society and culture, be the slave of other men who have made themselves the owners of the material conditions of labor."[5] An imprecise, rhetorical statement with a revolutionary ring is thus shown to draw attention from circumstances actually central to the domination being attacked. This kind of criticism runs through Marx's commentary, as well as his other writings. Marx's painstaking encounter with all the major political economists would make no sense at all if they could be all simply lumped together as bourgeois ideologists and thereby deposited on some historical rubbish-heap. There *are* statements which Marx treats as having no interest or meaning other than their social function of making sense of a certain destructive and exploitative way of being in the world, as mere ideology in other words, but such treatment presupposes a sweepingly negative theoretical judgment. I have drawn this distinction between theoretical assessment and ideological interpretation in Marx from his actual conduct of theoretical work and not from the same few suggestive but cryptic passages which have been pored over so much in efforts to explicate his views on these questions.[6] This follows logically from the nature of our indebtedness to Marx. His work is paradigmatic in its range of questions, its strategy of inquiry, and the general tendency of its product; but it is not an authority which supercedes the criteria which the paradigm itself generates. The distinction between operating principles and formal explication of those principles must be maintained not only in a consideration of Marx but also, as will be discussed below, in the evaluation of contemporary work in social science and social theory. For Marx, explicating the ideological bearing of a doctrine or statement plays an important part in an encounter with influential material which can be shown to have serious theoretical flaws, but the explication presupposes that the degree of adequacy can be shown. Marx's early formulations form part of an attempt to account for the possibility of truth being known and to account for the prevalence of error, especially in social theory; they cannot take the place of standards of truthfulness and they are not used in this way in Marx's major theoretical

5. Marx, op. cit., p. 3.
6. *Communist Manifesto, German Ideology, Preface to the Contribution to the Critique of Political Economy*. This conclusion agrees with the judgment of Althusser (Lire le Capital I, pp. 35-36), although we are not now prepared to commit ourselves to his demanding analysis as a whole.

works.

In addition to the application of criteria distinct from an assessment of ideological role, Marx's attack on the Gotha Program exemplifies two other principles too often neglected in contemporary evasions of the theoretical enterprise. He insists on the distinction between beliefs, however salutary from a political point of view or gratifying to the believer, and knowledge, and he sharply criticizes the retention of slogans like "iron law of wages" and "people's state" even though they have political appeal.[7] Finally Marx broadens his stand against converting one's own theoretical utterances into mere political instruments when he rejects a passage sweeping all social elements other than the proletariat into "one reactionary mass." He asks whether this was the line taken at the last election, in appealing to artisans, peasants, and others, and clearly implies that the adoption of merely tactical slogans (either as electoral tactic or as inner organizational tactic) is a disservice to the theoretical effort and to the political one as well, since anything which makes participants in the political movement stupid serves to demoralize that movement. It is not always necessary to say everything; but it is fundamentally wrong to inculcate confusing and disorienting notions. Marx, in short, leaves no doubt about the validity and integrity of the theoretical enterprise in his work, or about its relevance to the broader political movement.

We have suggested that contemporary radical thought displays disturbing signs of disorientation and demoralization, that a central source for this disturbance is confusion about the nature of theory and the place of the theorist, and that—contrary to the claims of many who consider themselves followers of Marx—Marx does not give license to such confusion or offer any comfortable way of bypassing the detailed and demanding work of theoretical criticism and construction. But present difficulties cannot be understood as products of wanton foolishness among contemporary thinkers; nor can they be countered by some earnest cry of "Back to Marx!" The Marxian approximation of what is involved in adequate interpretative theory drew on two major resources which are not readily available to serious theorists today. First, it operated within an intellectual setting where there was no serious challenge to the contention that the accurate and complete comprehension of the social universe constitutes knowledge in the fullest sense of the term and contains answers to the questions which constitute the search for practical orientation by a judging and acting man: to know what the world is like, in other words, tells you what it "makes sense" to do and to wish. The writers he criticizes were "liberals" or "conservatives" and they proceed in materialist or theological ways, but they are involved in search of

7. In his attack on the term "free state," Marx says: "The question then arises: what transformation will the state undergo in Communist society? In other words, what social functions will remain in existence there that are analogous to the present function of the state? This question can only be answered scientifically and one does not get a flea-hop nearer to the problem by a thousand-fold combination of the word people with the word state." (op. cit., p. 18).

a rational vision.[8] Marx seeks to make the activity more "scientific" than he found it, to introduce certain kinds of intellectual controls which the idealist writers of his acquaintance tend to disregard; he builds on and expands the intellectual strategy which identifies the historical process as the locus of meaning, in place of reliance on some natural forces. But he is not called upon to state and defend the whole range of contentions upon which a theoretical enterprise of such dimensions rests. When Marx attacks "philosophy" or criticizes "political economy," he is not thinking of an academic specialization; he sees each of these at their best as a complex and distinct phase within one and the same rational enterprise: Hegel and Feuerbach culminate the philosophic phase, Ricardo, the phase of political economy. Conceptions of theoretical work prevalent today, however, require us to support any such modes of conceiving the scope and capacities of theory in ways which Marx did not need and require us to refine and to make explicit detailed standards of theoretical adequacy which Marx could invoke by allusion, counting on a consensus among those who approach serious theoretical work.

During the three or four generations since Marx worked, philosophers of science have steadily narrowed the range of questions to which scientific inquiry could claim to provide accurate answers, and this has had particularly striking effects in sociology, economics, and political science—disciplines which derive from the old moral philosophy and whose subject matter constitutes the stuff of any political or social doctrine. That science itself says nothing about "morals" in the strict sense was a matter of indifference or enthusiastic approval to Marx, but that it cannot itself legitimately create a "consciousness" which includes awareness of one's own mission as well as a comprehensive view of "reality" (including understanding of historical stages, causes, and the rest) did not become the most influential scientific judgment until after Marx's work was done.[9] Marx could simply align himself with the most advanced, hard-headed intellectual currents of his time in all the disciplines, but especially in the physical sciences, against theologians and speculators and literary men of good will. Today that does not seem to be possible. The choice is widely considered to be one between, on the one hand, submission to scientific disciplines which ascetically deny themselves any ac-

8. This is the quality which C. Wright Mills sought to evoke in his plea for "sociological imagination." "Vision" is here used in the sense developed by Sheldon Wolin, *Politics and Vision* (Boston and Toronto: Little, Brown, 1960). Wolin's work in general influences the present argument. See, most recently, "Paradigms and Political Theories" in Preston King and B.C. Parekh, eds., *Politics and Experience* (London: Cambridge University Press, 1968). The many striking parallels to the work of Jürgen Habermas became clear only after completion of the ms.

9. It may be worth exploring whether Engels' apparent departures from Marx's position in the direction of greater "scientism" or "positivism" in fact derive from his being called on to deal with questions about the relationship between Marxism and science which Marx himself was free to ignore. So, for example, he undertook to specify what might be meant by a dialectical scientific law in the *Anti-Dühring,* following the principles governing scientific laws which had become widely accepted by the time that work was written.

complishment except the steady improvement of predictive theoretical models through empirical testing, or, on the other hand, celebration of some route to knowledge wholly different from and superior to scientific inquiry.[10]

Whether the issue is *properly* put in this way will be further discussed; we intend at this moment simply to report on a circumstance in our present intellectual setting which differs markedly from Marx's own case. Well into the twenties and thirties, writers who professed themselves as Marxists or other sorts of radical theorists could easily move in the company of all those who had no theological or moralistic scruples against telling the truth about power and myth in society. As often as not, the issues they faced were cast into some easily managed form, like questioning whether "spiritual values" were sufficiently respected by a "scientific" view. Since the Second World War, however, except in occasional academic pockets in England, questions have become a lot harder and this coalition of "anti-idealist" has everywhere burst apart, bringing radical theorists into all sorts of curious alliances with Romantics, phenomologists, spiritualists, and mystics. Marx, in short, could confidently see his own work as a particularly thorough application to social reality of modes of inquiry generally recognized as scientific; this easy orientation to the scientific community is not available today.

A similar change has attacked the second point of reference by which Marx took his bearings, the revolutionary movement of the working class. This is not the place to enter into details concerning his relationship to actual political movements. There is no doubt that he sought to shape and to direct these movements, as anti-Marxist writers stress;[11] but there is equally little doubt that he learned from the movement or that his identification with that movement came to control his conception of relevance. The relationship to the working class, moreover, provided his answers to the crucial "epistemological" questions which had in some way or other to be met by every serious writer after Hume: How is it possible that man can have knowledge relevant to action and how is it possible that such knowledge, even if attained, can be efficacious, can have practical effect? Most of the writers considered "scientific" in his generation managed these questions through

10. Karl Popper, as has been noted, is the philosopher for this view most influential among social scientists at this time. For a clear and authoritative recent statement, which makes clear the contrasts between the kinds of knowledge supported by this conception of science and the kinds of knowledge claimed by Marx and perhaps required for a rationally adequate interpretation able to guide political orientation and practice, see Robert Dubin, *Theory Building* (New York: The Free Press, 1969), especially the discussions of "summative units," pp. 63-76 and 196f. and distinctions between "belief systems" and scientific theory, pp. 227ff. Recent reports of work in Eastern European countries indicate that such a conception of science has also come to dominate most serious discussions of social science there too, except for ritual occasions when fairly standardized Marxist texts are invoked. See the forthcoming study by Peter Ludz.

11. Not only from the bourgeois side: the picture of Marx the authoritarian, who sought to dominate the working class in the interest of his own power-seeking, stems above all from anarchists. See James Joll, *The Anarchists* (Boston: Little, Brown, 1964), chap. 4.

various plays on the word "nature," as in "vulgar materialism." The contentions presented as scientific knowledge, in this view, were bound to have
actual effect on the shape of things since they were in accord with the
"nature" of man and of things. The non-scientific writers, whether called
"idealists" or not, variously invoked spiritual forces presumably decisive in
human affairs and subject to mobilization by the supposed truths of their
claims. Marx, in contrast, came to conceive of knowledge as the *consciousness* of that class in society which is destined by its factual situation to create
reality, as the clarifying vision perceived by an effective actor, revealing what
he is about. It is worth stressing again, that this conception served Marx as an
account of how it could be that there is potent knowledge; it did not serve as
a standard of knowledge in his actual theoretical work.[12] Such a conception
of the place of the working class survived disappointments and missed opportunities, but it is hard to see how it can operate at all when there is grave
suspicion that this class has cast its lot with the repressive order sustained by
illusion and served by untruth, or how this intellectual strategy can be revived
when there is no confidence that other actors can play the role assigned by
Marx to the proletariat. The relationship of theory to action, like the relationship of comprehensive and interpretive theory to science, appears far
more problematical at this time than it appeared to Marx (or even to Lenin).
Important weaknesses in contemporary radical theoretical efforts must be
understood in terms of these new difficulties, and the work of overcoming
these weaknesses must be organized on the basis of such understanding.

II.

Especially instructive with regard to all these issues is the case of Herbert
Marcuse and his Marxist critics. Any critical treatment of Marcuse's work,
however, must begin by acknowledging the debt owed to him by many of us
who have been concerned during these past ten or twenty years to express in
our theoretical work our revulsion against the human suffering produced by
a society whose spokesmen denied the very possibility of such suffering (so
that the victims were derided for calling out in pain). The author first encountered Marcuse in 1951. Marcuse had come to Columbia as a special
lecturer on Marxism, under the sponsorship of the State Department, and
those few of us who were caught by the Marxist vision but could see no
serious way of relating it to our time and place went to hear him with vast
scepticism. But he, like his friend Franz Neumann, showed us that the radical tradition of interpretation and commentary retained great power and that
it could organize the materials of the social sciences in ways which focused
attention on impediments to human freedom and happiness. Marcuse and

---

12. The distinction between theory of knowledge and standards of knowledge is
commonplace in philosophical discussions drawing on Kant's clarification of the issues,
but is not included among the vague ideas which make up the beliefs concerning epistemology among most social scientists and intellectuals. For a somewhat labored but
helpful analysis, see Karl Mannheim, "Die Strukturanalyse der Erkenntnistheorie"
(in Kurt H. Wolff, ed., *Wissenssoziologie* (Neuwied: Luchterhand, 1964).

Neumann taught by example; they embodied a humanistic and critical conception of the intellectual vocation and gave us inspiration; they legitimized our general sense that Marx and Engels were indeed "after something" that we were right to pursue; they were symbols of an opposition to Merton and Lazarsfeld and their Bureau of Applied Social Research. The very fact that Marcuse was housed at the Russian Institute along with the émigrés and crusaders during his first years at Columbia was a source of reassurance and hope: here is someone at the heart of information about the terror and the slave camps, some of us thought, but he does not call for the war of annihilation and he does not abandon the tradition so cruelly compromised by the facts we knew but resisted. Bernard Stern, Robert Lynd, and C. Wright Mills were at Columbia, too, of course, and for some students they were more important. But they suffered from being under the academic power of the victors within the sociology department; they had the stigma of being losers and the material disadvantage of being relegated to odd corners of the curriculum. Above all, Marcuse and Neumann had the magisterial quality of being in command, of ordering their materials to something that seemed to be a distinctive and comprehensive general theory and approach. We delighted in the fact that Kingsley Davis taught a sociology course entitled "Theories of Social Change" while Marcuse named his course starkly "*The* Theory of Social Change," and we rejoiced in the sweeping judgments of Neumann: "That's not true," "That's too rationalistic," and in his rejoinder to the student who questioned whether his conclusions did not rest simply on his own private value judgment—that he would not enter into discussion with anyone who did not begin with the commitment to human freedom. Marcuse was asked to comment on theories of history which contend that history repeats itself; he leaned across the lectern, then asked in definitive astonishment, "Do you really think it does?" and proceeded with his lecture. Those who imagine that all this describes the weakness of youth looking for dogmas and authorities do not understand the situation. They were our liberators: they freed us for a quest, but they gave us examples and dark and brilliant sayings rather than fixed doctrines. When Marx was nineteen, he composed several revealing epigrams on Hegel, one of which captures part of our own experiences:

> I teach sayings, compounded in a machinery of devilish complexity/
> Then let everyone think what it pleases him to think/ At least he is
> never hemmed in by constricting limitations/ For just as the poet
> conjures up for himself words and thoughts of the beloved out of
> the foaming stream plunging from the soaring cliff/ And recognizes
> his musings as knowledge and builds his musings on his feelings/
> Just so everyone can extract for himself the nectar which revives
> wisdom/ I tell you everything because I have told you a nothing[13]

13. Karl Marx, "Hegel Epigramme" in Karl Marx, Friedrich Engels, *Werke*, Erganzungsband, Schriften bis 1844, Erster Teil (Berlin: Dietz, 1968) pp. 607-608. The German text is: "Worte lehr' ich, gemischt in damonisch verwirrtem Getriebe,

Capped by this epigram, this account appears paradoxical if not contradictory. On the one hand, it is said that Marcuse conveyed the power of "critical theory," on the other, that he told us "a nothing." The paradox can be resolved by saying that Marcuse said magisterially suggestive and apt things about situations which mattered, but that he could not convey to us a technique for saying and, most importantly, for supporting such sayings. We could appreciate what he was doing, but we couldn't learn from him how to do it—except in the indirect way of making our own the complex intellectual tradition whose accumulated capital he simply took for granted. It was to be taken as a matter of course that the way to discuss the present condition of industrial societies, for example, was to relate it to the historical patterns displayed by the development of Greek and Roman societies, and that the way to discuss that was to "compare" the "theories" of Alfons Dopsch, Voltaire, Gibbon, Rostovzeff, Toynbee, Max Weber, Gustave Glotz, and so on. Out of such comparison, based on a standard no more expressly specific than requiring that the theory be based on "a viewpoint of totality" and an "ability to distinguish foundational dimensions from other dimensions," somehow emerged the adequate view, *the* theory of social change.[14] The actual support for such theory came, above all, from the circumstance that one could now take active part in the discussion among the various exponents of the great tradition in social theory; one knew what "the issues" were and could assimilate some historical and empirical studies to a general frame of reference. Historical and empirical studies which did not directly elucidate the issues could then be put aside as irrelevant. This sounds like a viciously uncritical scheme, basically hostile to science and destined to reinforce the prejudices of teacher, students, or both. In fact, it was a lot better than that. The critical standards actually applied were often much more demanding than is suggested by the way they have been described, and the injunction to take seriously the great classical works opened the way to self-clarification and self-education for the students. In no case, however, were we allowed to for-

---

Jeder denke sich dann, was ihm zu denken beliebt./ Wenigstens ist er nimmer geengt durch fesselnde Schranken,/ Denn wie aus brausender Flut sturtzend vom ragenden Fels, / Sich der Dichter ersinnt der Geliebten Wort and Gedanken,/ Und was er sinnet, erkennt, und was er fühlet, ersinnt,/ , Kann ein jeder sich saugen der Weisheit labenden Nektar./ Alles sag ich euch ja, weil ich ein Nichts euch gesagt!"

14. This draws on detailed lecture notes from a 1952-53 course. In these notes, by the way, one encounters somewhat disturbing indications that the diagnosis of a peculiarly post-industrial society as such, and that the complex argument in the later works about the special manipulative control prevalent in the "one-dimensional society" reinstate earlier contentions resting on Max Weber's and Werner Sombart's psychological theories of capitalism, that industrial and capitalist society rests on the internalization of certain norms and on the consequent adjustment of the psychic economy. For an account of parallels between Marcuse's conception of modern society and the views of German "conservative" sociologists, especially Hans Freyer, see Claus Offe, "Technik und Eindimensionalitat. Eine Version der Technokratiethese?" in Jürgen Habermas, ed., *Antworten auf Herbert Marcuse* (Frankfurt: Suhrkamp, 1968), pp. 73-88. What is disturbing about this is that it adds weight to the doubt that Marcuse's recent conclusions rest in any important way on the arguments which surround them.

get or confuse the distinction between theory and ideology or to abandon the search for a true, critical, theoretical way of encountering social reality as men destined to be free. What took place was solemn initiation into the discipline of interpretive social and political theorizing. With this, we were, however, left heir to all the inner conflicts and uncertainties within this tradition as well as to its outer conflicts with those older foes who attacked its disrespect for mysteries and with the newer foes who attacked it for mystifications.[15]

There are two justifications for this lengthy autobiographical excursus. First, the story may alert us to values and appeals in Marcuse's works which help to explain his contemporary influence. And, second, the story throws into sharp relief the curious (but far from unprecedented) twist in his teachings which appears to bring them into conflict with that very commitment to theory and to the major tradition in social theorizing which has been their basic spirit and prime strength. A *paideia* founded on Marcuse's most recently stated principles would make it impossible to understand those principles, not to speak of the arguments which support them.

In the course of those lectures at Columbia, Marcuse discussed the collapse of "critical rationalism" at the end of the Roman era. He noted that the primary philosophical tradition is transmuted into ideology in one of three ways: (1) ideas are given a locus in some transcendent sphere irrelevant to concrete conditions of man; (2) ideas are internalized, so that fulfillment becomes a matter of inner reordering; (3) the vision contained in ideas is reserved to an elite. Alternately, he pointed out that social protest against the repressive conditions expressed itself in three tragic and powerless variations of Utopia: (1) the dissemination of Utopian novels and visionary tales; (2) a fantastic conception of revolution from above; and (3) the pathetic and disastrous eruption of slave revolts. The extraordinary thing is how many of these elements, from the typology of ideology as from the typology of Utopia, are brewed together in Marcuse's writings of the past ten years. If Marcuse is pursuing an intellectual strategy founded upon a conviction that the possibility for "critical rationalism" is really not given by the present situation, then we are compelled to treat his work as symptom and not as diagnosis. Marcuse's work shows how much more pressing and bewildering the questions of how theory is possible, how it can be done, how it shall relate to political work have become in recent years. What had been a suggestive area of ambiguity, effort, and allusive insight in his earlier work now becomes a center of confusing paradox and a source of irrationality.

15. In *The Spirit of Russia,* Masaryk exemplifies a beautiful trust in this tradition. He writes, "The philosopher of history, the man who has read and understood Kant's *Critique* and Goethe's *Faust* will know how to discriminate between a needless popular rising and an indispensable revolution" (II, p. 538). In the same work, Masaryk also identified the elements combined against the tradition: "In 1850...(to prevent the spread of radical ideas in Russia) philosophy was reduced to courses upon logic and psychology which had in future to be delivered by theologians" (I, 112). Thomas Garrigue Masaryk, *The Spirit of Russia* (London and New York: Macmillan, 1919, 1955).

One passage in *One-Dimensional Man* most starkly dramatizes the difficulty:

> Philosophy approaches this goal (of becoming therapeutic) to the degree to which it frees thought from its enslavement by the established universe of discourse and behavior, elucidates the negativity of the Establishment (its positive aspects are abundantly publicized anyway) and projects its alternatives. To be sure, philosophy contradicts and projects in thought only. It is ideology and this ideological character is the very fate of philosophy which no scientism and positivism can overcome. Still, its ideological effort may be truly therapeutic—to show reality as that which it really is, and to show that which this reality prevents from being.[16]

As has been remarked by several critics, most valuably by Wolfgang Fritz Haug and Peter Sedgwick, this conception of philosophy as therapeutic ideology makes it all but impossible to understand how Marcuse's own work can make rational claims for itself. The terms of opprobrium are so sweeping—"enslavement by the established universe of discourse"—that no room is left for a communicable theoretical defense and critique of his argument. How would one proceed to question the innumerable contentions in Marcuse's work about the structure and dynamics of the human mind, about the totally integrating impact of industrial work, about the full effectiveness of contemporary public economic policy, and so on, without bringing in details from mere reality and without invoking concepts and procedures from the universe of discourse which presumably enslaves all of us, except...? It is embarrassing to be stuck with such inadequate journalistic concepts as "the establishment" on pain of revealing our slavishness, and it is crippling to shape our interpretation of emerging reality by consideration of what has and has not been "abundantly publicized." Most shocking is the perhaps ingenuous avowal that all this is "ideology," combined with the claim "to show reality."[17]

Although this is not the place for a detailed review of the problems, it is important to pin down this misleading use of the term "ideology." As normally employed by Marx, the term refers to two distinct but for him related aspects of an activity, usually of an intellectual sort. First, the activity falsifies reality: it designates as important things which are not important; it considers as fixed and "natural" things which are changing and which are products of changeable power constellations; it directs energy into concerns and efforts which are contrary to those called for by a true conception of what

16. Herbert Marcuse, *One-Dimensional Man* (Boston: Beacon Press, 1964), p. 199.
17. Wolfgang Fritz Haug, "Das Ganze und das ganz Andere. Zur Kritik der reinen revolutionaren Transzendenz." This is the most comprehensive and telling essay in the generally useful collection edited by Jürgen Habermas, op. cit. Peter Sedgwick, "Natural Science and Human Theory: A Critique of Herbert Marcuse," in Ralph Miliband and John Saville, eds., *The Socialist Register* (New York: Monthly Review Press, 1966).

man is about. When "ideology" presents itself as "theory," then, it is untrue; in its other guises, it might best be considered as hostile to truth. The second approach to ideology, in this usage, takes the activities characterized as ideological and subjects them to such explanation as social theory provides for any social activity: it discusses how such activities come about and what are the consequences of their occurrence. Most characteristically, of course, Marx found that ideology is produced by or under the auspices of the ruling class which benefits from the form of exploitation prevalent at a given time and that the effect of ideological activity is to preserve and promote that domination, or that ideology derives from the longing of other unhistorical classes to give themselves some account of and consolation for their bewildering fate.

The characteristic strategy of the ideologist, moreover, is to subsume events and relationships under categories loftily removed from the concrete empirical qualities of things and interlinked by connections as far removed as possible from the causal linkages which Marx discerns in the real world (spiritual affinities above all). A given utterance or discourse may partake of theory and ideology both, as we address ourselves to it at a given time, coming closer to the truth about things than other ideologies, and this ambivalent status is then explained by Marx by reference to the social theory of the knowability of social truth. Truth comes into the world as the consciousness of what they are about possessed by those who are doing what must be done, given the logos immanent in the historical process, and capable of doing it by virtue of their situation within that process. The political economists admired and criticized by Marx write to make sense of the world as it is encountered by the bourgeoisie during its period of creativity and progress; this helps to account for the fact that their work contains important elements of truth. In another respect, this is also true of Hegel. But at a time when new possibilities and a new class challenge that domination, giving notice that the creative period has ended, the doctrines are used to justify the existing order. They can function as ideology in this sense because they are partial truths only—and therefore false from the standpoint of the new possibility they could not anticipate. Interpreting the doctrines as ideology—that is, explicating their social character—has two justifications in serious critical assessment and theoretical work (apart from its contribution to the theory of ideological activity as such):

> (1) It directly refutes the contentions about the sources
> and consequences of theoretical activity which expressly
> underlie the doctrines being criticized, thus undertaking
> to remove the prop placed by the "ideologists" under their
> conception of how theoretical work ought to be done and
> how it may be judged.[18]

18. It may be recalled that the term "ideology" was coined by French thinkers following the tradition of Locke, Hume, and Condillac, who, beginning with the standard empiricist contention that ideas derive from experience, concluded that the prime critical task of philosophy is to subject concepts to an analysis which will strip from them the excrescences generated by social and cultural artificialities, bring them to the

(2) The theory of ideology comes to identify certain typical distortions of reality, and an interpretation stressing the ideological aspect of a doctrine may focus attention on these characteristic distortions more economically than a detailed assessment of the doctrine; but the truth of the theory and the judgment of distortion must ultimately rest on criteria developed elsewhere.

Marx's use of the term depends entirely on the possibility of distinguishing false consciousness from true, and thus on the distinction between an *ideology* which falsifies a reality destructive of human possibilities by treating it as if it were rational and a *social theory* which makes sense of the struggle for human liberation as it really happens and as it defines the world. This is also how Marcuse understood social theory in *Reason and Revolution*, although he did not there expressly address himself to the problem of ideology.[19] Not only the possibility of true consciousness and theory is presupposed by the Marxist use, but also the possibility of practical efficacy for such true theory. There is, in other words, nothing about social theory which removes it from the concrete needs of acting men, and it is not true that ideology possesses some special distinction by virtue of the fact that its being

---

pristine form where they correspond exactly to the natural and universal experience, and thereby reveal the elements of a true universal theory. Napoleon and others converted the term into a word of scorn for airy philosophical speculation not least because the ideologues came to attach wildly exaggerated importance to their pedagogical schemes for purging the language and education of misleading conceptions accumulated through history. What may well have attracted Marx to the term in *The German Ideology* was a conception of the ideologues as a paradigm for the way in which intellectuals misperceive and exaggerate the importance of intellectual work (taking the place of theology in large measure). "Empirical" and "idealist" conceptions converge according to Marx, in other words, because both abstract from the concrete accumulation of knowledge connected with the experience of successive collective historical actors. This is a plea for a historical empiricism in place of a psychological universalizing one. Marx uses the term in *The Holy Family* only once, and then the reference is clearly to the "Ideologues," as is clearer from the German text than from the English. Cf. Karl Marx, *Fruhe Schriften I* (Stuttgart: Cotta-Verlag, 1962), p. 818, with the 1956 Moscow edition, p. 166. Marx's vituperations against Destutt Tracy, leading ideologue, helps to support this speculation, as well as to underline the distinction between Marx's response to such writers as this, whose work comes to notice only in its quality as ideology, and his treatment of classical economists. At *Capital* I, p. 80n, Marx draws the distinction between classical and vulgar economics, and then at *Capital* II, p. 488, he caps an assult on Destutt with "Voilà le crétinisme bourgeois dans toute sa béatitude" (Moscow, 1954, 1961).

19. Herbert Marcuse, *Reason and Revolution*, 2nd. ed. (Boston: Humanities Press, 1954), p. 257 and pp. 258-262. In *One-Dimensional Man* itself, pp. 141f., Marcuse restates the Marxian conception in general terms. The difficulty arises when he comes to apply the detailed criteria of "social theory" as developed by Marx to his own work and finds that he cannot claim for it the decisive quality of "making sense" of the real transforming effort by a class whose time has come. George Lichtheim, *The Concept of Ideology* (New York: Random House, 1967), is generally right on this point, although hard to credit when he ascribes to Marx a vision of a time when consciousness will determine being.

believed makes a social or political difference. Despite some special overtones, the classical statement of this position, true to Marx and influential
on Marcuse's programmatic formulations (as distinct from the self-charac-
terization of his work as ideology) remains the old passage by Lukács:

> Only when becoming conscious signifies the decisive step which the
> historical process must take towards its goal—the goal constituted
> by human volitions but not dependent on human arbitrariness, not
> contrived by some "spirit of man"—, when the historical function
> of theory consists of making this step practically possible, when a
> historical situation exists in which the correct comprehension of
> society becomes for a class the immediate condition for its self-
> assertion in struggle, when for this class its self-comprehension
> signifies at the same time an accurate comprehension of society
> as a whole, when consequently for such comprehension this class
> serves at once as subject and object of comprehension and in this
> way the theory intervenes directly and adequately in the transfor-
> mation process of society: only then does the unity of theory and
> practice become possible, the precondition for the revolutionary
> function of theory.[20]

   Marcuse's language in the passage cited earlier moves him toward a dangerous contemporary confusion. Both of the challenges to the Marxist conception of theoretical work cited above, the changing implications of doing
science and the changing character of radical political prospects, manifest
themselves in revised uses of "ideology". It comes to be used as a term for
all doctrines which offer ostensibly linked statements purporting to interpret
the meaning of the social and political world, including in their statements
the claim to identify "the sense" or "the point" of what men are to do.
Within its purview, then, come most of the doctrines which had been presented as social or political "theory" through the nineteenth century—the
works of Marx as well as of those he criticized, of course. Since theory, in
its correct sense, is thought to be unable to answer such a range of questions,
the special term calling attention to the social or personal uses of such
pseudo-theory is applied. Some writers retain the critical edge of the term in
this new usage, and look forward to a time when theory and practice both
can be freed from ideological distortion. For these writers, the critique of
ideology, so understood, helps develop rigorous theory, and the destruction
of scientific claims on behalf of ideology helps foster realistic practice concerned to meet immediate and concrete needs. Other writers consider ideology in this sense as desirable or inevitable, and look for ways of judging competing ideologies, given the impossibility of applying criteria of truth to them.

   20. Georg Lukács, *Geschichte und Klassenbewusstein* (Berlin: Der Malik-Verlag,
1923), pp. 14-15.

We are not now concerned with differing theories of how it is that ideologies arise and have effect; the point is that in all this literature the claims of such doctrines cannot be taken on their own terms and that this stems not from the special content of this or that "ideology" but rather from the scope of the claims themselves.[21]

In speaking of philosophy as therapeutic "ideology," Marcuse gives up the fight for the distinction between theory and ideology and opens the way to those who defend contentions about the way the world is and what it means on the grounds that such contentions make them feel good or make the bastards feel bad. He fought that fight for a long time and does not now abandon the distinction easily or lightly. Throughout *One-Dimensional Man* and the works written since there are the echoes of alternate formulations— the preference for science against obscurantism, the classical and idealist conception of the mission of philosophy and of its discipline, and, indeed, some elegant reformulations of the Lukács-Marxist conception of theory.[22] But Marcuse despairs about two central things: the consequences of applying the critical techniques associated with science to social theory in the Marxist sense, and the availability of a social locus of criticism and radical transformation which can be shown to be an inherent part of social "reality" and a force for social revolution. The former of these despairs manifests itself in the attempt to show that science and philosophy oriented to science inherently turn on principles of domination and enslavement; the latter, in the contentions about the wholly integrative character of the existing social-political system.

Critics of his work have been able to show that his reasonings on both of these points are deficient; his picture of philosophy of science is misleading and is especially weak in comprehending what physical and even social scientists actually do, as distinct from what they say they do; the psychology and sociology of total integration rests on self-contradictory and inaccurate conceptions of the interaction between men and circumstances.[23] Moreover, they have called attention to Marcuse's own reliance on metaphor and anal-

21. Best known among recent American works developing such an argument is Daniel Bell, *The End of Ideology* (Glencoe, Illinois: Free Press, 1961). A useful compilation of characteristic pieces is Edgar Litt, ed., *The Political Imagination* (Glenview, Illinois: Scott, Foresman, 1966). Very influential in Germany has been Theodor Geiger, *Ideologie und Wissershaft* (Stuttgart: Humboldt-Verlag, 1953). In general, this shift in the concept was prepared by Karl Mannheim, who did not intend this outcome. The kinds of questions which sociologists and social psychologists generally explore in connection with this concept are conveniently surveyed in Giovanni Sartori, "Politics, Ideology, and Belief Systems," *American Political Science Review* 63(June 1969), pp. 398-411. Another paper would be needed to warn in detail against two errors: (1) a "defense of ideology" which accepts the leveling of rational differences among interpretive doctrines; and (2) ignoring all the findings of these social scientists on the grounds that their inquiries derive from a conception of ideology which is itself ideological in the Marxist sense.

22. Marcuse, *One-Dimensional Man*, pp. 186-67; 127f; 141-42.

23. There is much sharp, persuasive comment on both of these points in Sedgwick,

ogy instead of analysis. "The pure negativity of the 'great refusal,' " Haug
writes, "has undeniable advantages over Marxism: it is easily transmitted,
portable, not easily gotten a hold of, yet easily grasped."[24] With all the
critical power and specificity of these commentaries they still arouse at the
end a sense of nostalgia, because they haven't faced the issues. Marxism
isn't a scientific theory in the way that scientific theory is now commonly
understood, because it claims to answer questions which most writers on
social science relegate to the sphere of "ideology" or "value judgment." It
may well be, as Sedgwick contends, that contemporary findings in information theory and elsewhere support a model of the social process a good
deal less incompatible with that envisioned by Marx and Engels than someone like Marcuse imagines science to produce; but that theory does not itself
provide the focus on slavery and liberation which Marx supposed to be inherent in the rigorous theoretical enterprise as such.[25] And Marxism does
not identify the locus of rationality in contemporary society (even assuming
that one can make the search for "locus of rationality" a disciplined investigation), because the revolutionary movement of the class-conscious proletariat simply does not exist or give any signs of emerging.[26] The challenge
is to find sustainable and productive ways of managing and moving towards
overcoming the issues to which Marcuse responds with moving and heroic but
also confusing and infuriating prophecy.

op. cit., as well as in the essays in the Habermas volume. The points emphasized include
a challenge to Marcuse's presentation of operationalism and of its influence, his ambivalence about technology, his acceptance of a fixed-energy quantum in psychology.
Sedgwick effectively states a common theme: Marcuse ascribes to himself and to his
readers, he notes, "information-handling models of perception and action" instead of
the blind and conditioned responses to libidinal drives presumed to be repressively
dominating everyone else; "The stimulus-response paradigms," he says, "...hold good,
as in the writings of most cultural sociologists of this kind, only for a different sort of
people, i.e., for other people" (Sedgwick, p. 182).

24. Haug, op. cit., p. 57. The German reads "nicht fassbar and doch leicht fasslich."

25. Cf. the citation from Critique of the Gotha Programme, p. 3, discussed above.

26. It may be argued that this judgment is far too sweeping, either because it disregards some supposed objective character of the proletariat as revolutionary force,
regardless of appearances, or because it disregards the revolutionary movement of the
Third World. The former objection can be easily dismissed. Any direct but serious
reading of Marx—say, of The Holy Family—reveals that Marx was struck by and built
upon ordinary and visible signs of socialist agitation and movement among French and
English workers and not upon some abstract logical category. Surplus value may be an
analytical concept; but the revolutionary proletariat cannot be. The second objection
is more difficult. Nevertheless, the following comments by a writer who contends that
a revolutionary proletariat in the simple Marxist sense is indispensable are very telling:

The old ideological practice of the Revisionists and radicals of the
Right, locating the class-enemy preferably on the other side of the
national boundary, reappears in a new guise. Transformed so that
now the revolution too should preferably take place outside the
country. The contemptible notion that the revolution can be delegated like a political mandate presupposes that the world revolution
will be fought out in the sphere of consumption. The "Lumpen-
proletariat" of the Third World can hardly enter into a revolu-

III.

I persist in the search for a social and political theory with the scope of inquiry exemplified by the work of Marx, because I am persuaded that the alternative to interpretations subjected to as much rational control as possible is utter dependence on more or less explicit ideologies. In the absence of ready-made specific and rigorous rules according to which such theory can be constructed and judged, we find ourselves directed to an enterprise, an ongoing complex dialogue over time constituting a tradition of social and political theory. Within the framework of that enterprise, there have been major achievements upon which we can build—the development of interpretive categories like revolution, resistance, terror, alienation, democracy—and certain disciplining procedures (or a range of such procedures) govern the discussion.

But a return to that company strikes many of us as a disappointing, if not dangerous, course. The elements of such a response deserve separate consideration. First, there is the recognition that precisely this enterprise also generates ideology in its many forms and that most participants in such exchanges will work out of an ideological frame of reference and in its behalf. Secondly, there is the fear that accepting such a theoretical vocation means that theory is once again radically removed from the realm of practice, that the theorists become irrelevant to the concrete struggles for human liberation (even assuming that they do not enlist as ideologists on the side of repression). Before treating some of the issues raised by these serious and well-founded objections, let us be clear as possible as to how we got to this point: we have concluded that classical Marxist formulations of how theoretical work is possible and how it must proceed no longer suffice to comprehend and to deal with the specific problems which we encounter today in the effort to construct political and social theory. They do not enable us to integrate the work of science in the way that we find we must do, and they rest upon assumptions about social reality which we do not find borne out by events. Marx's work remains the most interesting and useful effort to reconstruct the theoretical enterprise after the ancient philosophic formulation had been fundamentally challenged by Hobbes, Hume, and the rest. Furthermore, the content of his theory provides a number of especially fruitful questions for inquiry. This is not an idiosyncratic conclusion, even among those who present themselves and are widely accepted as radical theorists: such a conclusion is the energizing principle of work by Marcuse and C. Wright Mills and all the yearners after phenomenological shortcuts and invokers of the cult of immediacy. There are "orthodox" Marxists who are not dogmatists or hacks; but they fall essentially into two categories. There are those who devote themselves to a relatively narrow range of problems,

tionary class struggle over the control of the means of production, because monopoly capital and means of production are not located in the Third World but in Europe and North America (Hans G. Helms, "Fetisch Revolution," in *Ad Lectores 8* [Neuwied: Luchterhand, 1969], p. 134).

which they then explore with the help of concepts and hypotheses derived from Marx—say, certain problems of economic analysis or historical investigation. Such a selection of problems makes it possible to avoid close scrutiny of those aspects of Marxist thought which are most problematical and unclear. Characteristically, such writers then presume that the habitability of the rooms they occupy testifies to the soundness of the edifice as a whole. The second sort of authentic "orthodox" Marxist proves on closer inspection not to be a theorist at all. He uses Marxist terms as starting points and metaphors in the course of explaining himself during political action. But such use stands in ambiguous relationship to the theoretical enterprise. On the one hand, it can often provide new insight or raise new questions; on the other, it often subordinates the language to the political requirements of inspiration, conciliation, obfuscation (as happened in the Gotha Program). Once the importance and special character of political leadership is recognized, it is both possible and essential to stand in an appropriately dual and discriminating relationship to the utterances of such political leaders without necessarily declaring political war on them. There is no inherent contradiction between participation in political movements which express themselves in the language of Marxism and a sober recognition of the serious inadequacies of contemporary Marxist thought and of the hard work which radical thinkers must do. The questions is whether such work can indeed be done and fostered by entering into intimate relationship with the historical and contemporary theoretical universe (which means, in sociological terms, association with academic disciplines, universities, and similar institutions) despite the fact that much of it is not animated by radical concerns and is in fact hostile to them.[27]

From time to time writers like Karl Mannheim have appeared who have offered some general solution to the problem created by the fact that the arena within which it is proposed to carry on the pursuit of theory is also the spawning ground of ideology. But there is no general solution. The struggle against ideological influences and the recovery from ideological misadventures cannot be anything other than a continuing confrontation with details and concrete instances. Historians and social scientists cannot disregard the evidence, for example, which links revolutionary doctrine and practice with the

27. This discussion concentrates on academic disciplines and universities as the sociological loci for disciplined inquiry. Such an emphasis may unduly slight the possibilities of several alternate forums which have been elsewhere discussed, including periodicals, discussion gruops, various party-educational agencies, teach-ins, and the like. It seems clear that these all serve either as auxiliaries to the basic university centers, and they may be extremely important as such, or partake of the confusion characteristic of the radical sects. Recent developments in Germany raise the question whether publishing houses and cooperatives may not come to serve as counter-universities. See *Ad Lectores 8*, published by the sociological readers of Luchterhand Verlag, especially Frank Benseler, "über literarische Produktionsverhaltnisse." But the very fact that these provocative discussions appear in what is little more than a beautifully done advertising brochure for a commercial publishing house altogether dependent upon what happens in German universities for its writers and readers again justifics our present emphasis.

social and psychological type of "the saints" even though such evidence is commonly presented in the context of genteel disdain for radical social change or of venomous defense against critical challenge to prevailing privileges.[28] Radical critics who take refuge in identifying "the functions" ostensibly performed by such studies within "the system" as substitute for such concrete confrontations contribute to our disorientation—especially since concepts like "function" and "system" are themselves among the more dubious products of social-science theorizing pervaded with ideological motifs. The important struggle against ideological distortions produced by contemporary American political scientists, to take another instance familiar to us, is being waged more by writers who identify and explode pluralist illusions (or impostures) in political science literature, those who show in detail how certain results are built into certain questions and how evidence is misinterpreted, rather than by those who undertake to show that, given the nature of the society as a whole or given the epistemological errors presumably inherent in certain modes of inquiry, the science produced must be wrong by logical necessity.[29] Most seriously, the confused relationship to empirical social science leads radical students and intellectuals in general to fall back on pseudo-radical rationalizations for failures to cope with the technical demands of contemporary literature, which involve familiarity with statistical and other mathematical material. There is something grotesque about a radical intelligentsia which builds its social vision on the possibilities created by modern technology but which can see no way, as is common among Americans at least, of relating its own efforts to the mathematical disciplines upon which these possibilities rest.[30]

28. See Michael Walzer, *The Revolution of the Saints: A Study on the Origins of Radical Politics* (Cambridge, Mass.: Harvard University Press, 1965). While this excellent work is part of an overall effort to develop a viable radical posture, it builds on and contributes to a body of literature which expressly supports defensive ideology. See Norman Cohn, *The Pursuit of the Millenium* (Fairlawn, N.J.: Essential Books, 1957, 1961), J.L. Talmon, *The Origins of Totalitarian Democracy* (London: Secker & Warburg, 1952), and the work of Popper, Von Hayek, and Michael Oakeshott. A conception of radicalism which cannot come to grips with the materials in such studies simply blinds itself to realities.

29. See, for example, the essays collected in William Connolly, ed., *The Bias of Pluralism* (New York: Atherton Press, 1969) and the works in the bibliography. Or see the work of Noam Chomsky, often cited in this volume. Very important, despite serious difficulties, is Theodore J. Lowi, *The End of Liberalism* (New York: Norton, 1969). See also Robert Paul Wolff, *The Poverty of Liberalism* (Boston: Beacon Press, 1968) and Henry Kariel, *The Decline of American Pluralism* (Stanford: Stanford University Press, 1961).

30. Among American radical writers, John McDermott is one of the few who makes a continuous effort to know enough about the details of technology to be able to address himself critically to relations between technological development and social theory. He is also an important opponent of the view that radical intellectuals ought to abandon the universities. A recent valuable illustration of the former undertaking is John McDermott, "Intellectuals and Technology" *New York Review of Books* 13 (31 July 1969), pp. 25-35.

Radicals work within existing disciplines because those disciplines are valuable to the theoretical search. The work will almost always have a critical direction, especially at the points where scientific work fits itself into the broader, usually ideological framework of meaning, but it will make use of disciplinary norms and findings as prime resources for its own development. Adequate radical theory if far from being the same thing as social and political action which implements a radical vision, and the prime objective of struggle within disciplines and within the professions which give the disciplines organizational form is the advancement of theory. The first obligation to a radical movement owed by radical intellectuals is criticism and counsel founded on adequate theory—not the slaying of hydra-headed ideologists. A healthy and valuable development in the United States has been the formation of such groups as the Caucus for a New Political Science and similar entities among economists, sociologists, psychologists, and students of literature; but these groups will dissipate their energies and get caught in the senseless escalation of expectations to the point of cynical passivity if they do not recognize that their political activities within these associations and professions must first and foremost serve the theoretical goal of making the disciplines places where we can do our work, including of course work between teachers and students. It is bravado and imposture to speak of "taking over" the disciplines, first, because radicals are now so far from having a monopoly on doing theoretically important work that they do damned little of it and are often dependent on commercial exploiters of sociological clichés for their information about society or cling with little examination to such journalistic categories as "the power structure," "the establishment," "the military-industrial complex," "hippies," and the rest. Second, it is bravado because it disregards one of the things we do have reason to know about the sociology of intellectual work, which is that in any settled system of domination the chore of battling ideologies is endless and largely useless. Contrary to the view which Marx considered typical for ideologists (but which enjoys a curious vogue among those who profess to follow him), it is not ideologists who constitute a given order, and therefore demolition of their product at any moment will not in itself decisively affect that order. We are in the disciplines and in the professions because we need them in our search for such truth as we can find, and we struggle against ideological domination over these spheres of activity primarily by working within them, helping and criticizing each other in the course of this sustained encounter.

But, it may be objected, all this is still abstract and does not identify the prime social circumstance of this kind of intellectual life which disqualifies it from contributing to radical theory. To speak of work within the disciplines and professions means, above all, work as professors and students in the universities, and the university is structurally geared to the performance of a number of vital tasks within American society, all of them fundamentally antithetical to the kinds of expectations here raised. The university is not only the chief repository of knowledge and culture in America, it is also the source and prime disseminator of the American ideology and, in the pure sciences and technical disciplines, a prime resource of American power. The university is a service center for corporate interests and for commerce and industry in general; it screens and recruits and develops trained manpower for the corporate economy; it is a key element in the class structure of modern America, granting respectability with the degree earned largely through spiritual docility; it is the primary pathway for social ascent from the lower classes and the institution for the recruitment of competence for the upper classes. The announced and ceremonial objectives of the university, disinterested pursuit of knowledge and education of the young, sustain the morale of those who carry on these tasks and provide a quasi-objective cover for the process of social selection; but the supposition that these objectives actually dominate, or, say the critics, could be made to dominate is a matter of delusion or deception. Those who deny that radical intellectuals can function within the universities call attention to the power of the basic imperatives within the institutions: professors may indeed teach Marx or whatever they like—one more noise within the cacophony makes no important difference—but they may not and will not give *A's* to all the students in the freshman survey course which screens aspirants to social elevation; students and teachers will collaborate in the so-called "free universities" parallel to the real ones, but the teachers will depart when it becomes necessary for them to prepare the publications needed for tenure or promotion, and the students will stop coming to classes when their "real" examinations loom. Employment in the universities, it is said, is collaboration in one of the most repressive institutions in the society.

This analysis does not support the moralizing absolutistic conclusion attached to it. What is shows is that work in the universities has immediate political as well as theoretical bearing, precisely because the universities are important economic and social institutions. In the university context, even trade union work among professors may have considerable significance if it helps to break down the status mechanisms which control conduct and make for a cooptive political culture. Movements of anti-war students and black students present the kind of immediate challenge and illumination which it is the task of radical theory to mediate, and they offer opportunities for political action within the concrete sphere of life where radical intellectuals are at home and at work. Problems of education, grading, university organization, channeling of university resources, impact on local communities— all provide significant focal points for commitment and self-definition. All this does not mean that work in the universities is superior to all political work elsewhere or even that the good reasons for working for social change at this part of the overall social structure always outweigh reasons which may arise for shifting energies elsewhere. It does mean that the case for and against participation in universities must be developed in strategic and specific terms and cannot be deduced from universal generalizations about the presumed imperatives of ideological institutions.[31]

31. Contrasts between two American groupings of university intellectuals show the

As this discussion illustrates, adequate radical theory must be able to comprehend complexities, ambiguities, a multi-layered reality. The contrary view derives from a failure to distinguish between the categorical judgments embodied in action, and the critical assessment which reviews, interprets, and evaluates such judgments on the basis of as adequate a theory as may be available at any time. Writing in 1962 about Stalin, Georg Lukács developed a set of pertinent considerations. He notes, first, "It is the Stalinist tendency to exclude everywhere so far as possible any sort of mediating concepts and to bring into direct connection the crudest matters of fact with the most abstract theoretical positions."[32] This means that Stalinism does not allow for tactical or strategic thinking, as he contends Leninism does: every action or deed is justified as an immediately necessary consequence of Marxism-Leninism (and not as a tactical or strategic response to certain concrete circumstances). He cites the terrible impact upon the international Communist movement of the Stalin-Hitler Pact and claims that this event would not have been so disorienting and disruptive if it had not been presented as a necessary response to the struggle between imperialist factions undifferentiated by any principled difference, etc. Lukács comments that such utterances were nothing more than pseudo-theoretical justifications for the actions of the day and consequently played directly into the hands of the anti-Marxist commentators who characterize Marxism as a political "ideology" no different from all the rest. Practice under such circumstances is no longer a concretization and testing of theory; instead, theoretical formulations are subjected to ruthless vulgarization in order to fit them to the supposed practical needs of the moment. Lukács cited in this connection Stalin's supposed discovery that every economic system has an underlying principle which can be summed up in a single sentence. "Stalin's 'basic laws' express trivialities, explain nothing at all, but fill certain circles with the illusion of knowing everything better than anyone else."[33]

All this, according to Lukács, points to the underlying subjectivism of such an approach, and this expresses itself most clearly in the Stalinist notion of partisanship. Lenin had developed a conception of partisanship with two elements, subjective and objective. The former constitutes a clear commit-

difficulties of these questions. The New University Conference has gravitated increasingly towards the view that universities are to be treated only as hostile social institutions, a conception which disregards the extent to which its membership depends on these institutions, intellectually as well as economically (and it is an anomaly of latter-day radicalism that the realities of livelihood are equated with materialist corruption). Leading members of the Socialist Scholars Conference, in contrast, emphasize the intellectual mission of the universities to such an extent that they tend to ignore the tensions between higher objectives and lower realities, and, in consequence, they often oppose changes and programs (like the lowering of certain kinds of academic standards for the benefit or sake of social equalization) which may have intrinsic or instrumental value within a more comprehensive strategy of social change.

32. Georg Lukács, "Brief an Alberto Carocci," in Georg Lukács, *Schriften zur Ideologie und Politik,* Peter Ludz, ed. (Neuwied: Luchterhand, 1967), p. 664.

33. Ibid., p. 668.

ment to the class struggle; the latter, an objectivity more thoroughgoing than that professed by pseudo-objective bourgeois scholars whose determinism proves to be a defense of the facts as established by a given order of domination. Stalin cast aside all pursuit of objectivity as "objectivism." The methodological thrust of all this is towards a reversal of the "classics of Marxism," Lukács says, where "it was self-evident that science produces the materials and points of view on the basis of which political judgments are made. Propaganda and agitation receive their material from a practice comprehended scientifically. Stalin reversed this relationship. For him...agitation was the prime thing. Its needs determine what science is to say and how it is to be said."[34] This methodological pattern links up with the well-known total mobilization of Stalinism: "The elimination of mediations itself contains the tendency to treat all phenomena of life as altogether monolithic. By means of making permanent the acute revolutionary situation, this tendency is considerably strengthened. Every person is wholly subsumed—in the totality of his existence, in all details of his personality and of his life's work—under that role which he plays (in fact or allegation) at the moment within a situation so conceived."[35] Thus the victims of the purge trials were sweepingly condemned as lifelong foes of socialism on the basis of quite specific political positions which might, Lukács remarks, have been antithetical to socialist development at the moment (or may, of course, simply have run athwart Stalin's designs). That the patterns identified by Lukács are not unique to Stalinism will be clear to anyone who follows political and "theoretical" discussions on the contemporary Left, and the confusion about the place of intellectuals and of their institutions has been heightened by this fundamental misconception of theory itself.

In the last analysis, however, the decisive question turns on the relationship between theoretical work and practical political activity. As I have presented the argument, it appears that the energies of those who will carry on theoretical work are wholly absorbed in that work itself and in the political tasks which must be fulfilled in order to make that work possible (i.e., activity within the professions which structure disciplines and within universities). The objection to such a conception on grounds of practical "relevance" may be raised from two sides. Radical intellectuals may argue that such a vocation denies to intellectuals their proper leading role in the major political actions of "the movement" or of "the revolution"; it represents a "cop-out" or retreat to an ivory tower. Political leaders may see the situation quite differently, as perpetuation of a special elite role for intellectuals, implying a claim for leadership and direction without the dirty hands of actual political struggle. Such objections, like many others discussed in this article, identify real problems, temptations, and tendencies; but they do not suffice to overcome the basic argument. What is required in radical theory and prac-

---

34. Ibid., p. 671.
35. Ibid., p. 673.

tice is an adequate conception of the politics of counsel.[36]

The conception of a counselor is by no means identical with that of the "expert," who presumably makes available instrumental knowledge which can effectively implement any value specified by his principal. But neither is it (or need it be) a dishonest way of presenting the Mandarin or the Platonic philosopher-king. Closely related to the role of teacher, the role of counselor is one which we encounter in our practice but whose explication has been relegated to literature, largely because it presupposes the possibility of "wisdom" (in the sense of possessing the kind of comprehensive theory discussed above), and because such a possibility is excluded from most of our more rigorous discourse. Together with the rehabilitation of the theoretical enterprise, however, comes a reinstatement of this concept as something other than a cant-word to cover the Bernard Baruchs. The norms defining counselors to the radical democratic movement cannot be simply churned out and proclaimed; they require careful development. But several elements of a code of etiquette can be simply stated:

1. The theorist gives advice, not commands.
2. The content of his advice will likely be an assessment of what has been done, an interpretive statement of where things stand, and then some projection of what is to be done.
3. The form of his advice will be reasoned argument and explication.
4. The occasion and forum of his advice will be appropriate to his relationship to the political movement: it is not proper to say all things in all places and at all times.

These are homely little truths, awkward to write down, but they bring us back to some balanced perspective on radical politics. Not all intellectuals will be prepared to submit themselves to the multifold discipline involved in counselorship. Those who will not should make other sorts of contributions, perhaps the far greater one of sharing political leadership in a democratic movement. Political leadership will always distrust demanding counselors and prefer the more convenient ones. There is no theoretical hocus-pocus which can overcome this circumstance, and the tension can be valuable in itself. Given the temptations of Platonism, political leadership should be suspicious; given the temptations of excessive accommodation to power (even "our own"), intellectuals ought not be too cozy. These general observations gain in force when they are applied to our present circumstances

36. The political theorists who cut through the medieval ideology, according to which all political rule is a function of a wisdom composed of harmony with natural laws, stressed the distinction between command and counsel. That they did this in order to attack competitors to political authorities does not vitiate the theoretical worth of the distinction or preclude our building on their work. Thomas Hobbes repeatedly returns to the issue of counsel in *Leviathan*, and makes a useful distinction between counsel and exhortation. See especially chapter 25 of the second part.

in the United States today. Like Marcuse and others, we see radical energies and aspirations embodied today above all in black strivings for "liberation," the struggle against an imperialist foreign policy, and in resistance among the youth to various aspects of dominant culture and society. Some sort of total fusion between the pursuit of adequate theory and this discordant and often incoherent "movement" quite literally makes no sense: to speak of it is simply to attach a misleading metaphorical label to some altogether different sort of relationship. The student movement, for example, has a turnover in members and leaders every two years or so, and every one of these butterfly generations quite properly seeks to redefine the activity in its own way. That radical professors should submit themselves to these changing conditions and styles is simply ludicrous. They must respond to them, try to comprehend them, offer counsel where this is appropriate (by the time-and-place rule of etiquette), accept challenges, ally with them on common political tasks. But the vocation of the radical academic intellectual has its distinct character and tasks. To deny these for the sake of some presumed political effect is a self-dramatizing indulgence which helps to confuse us in our real work.

13. Social Science and the Problem of Rationality *

HANS PETER DREITZEL

I.

As both member and observer of the community of social scientists, I have noticed recently in Europe as well as in America, in the East as well as in the West, a growing uneasiness about the meaning of our enterprise as social scientists—an experience which has drawn me to reconsider the rationale of our doings. Indicatively enough, Alvin Gouldner has recently published a voluminous statement on *The Coming Crisis of Western Sociology*.[1] But this crisis is neither a coming one nor a specifically Western problem. It gradually becomes clear that Eastern European sociologists are now joining the majority of their colleagues here in seeking to develop the behavioral sciences in such a way as to gain a better understanding of people's problems in order to better control their seemingly irrational behavior. Furthermore, more and more sociologists, particularly the younger ones, are developing an uncomfortable feeling about their own profession. During the fifties, the social sciences were a rapidly expanding field behind a whole generation of sociologists who had functionalism written on their banner. Those were the years of the cold war, when America was still so smugly confident in having basically solved her major problems. To be sure, some still remained to be solved, but that was considered no more than a question of time and better application of expertise. Today, the scene has radically changed: during the sixties cracks developed in the American creed, and by now disillusionment on the one hand, and a new radicalism on the other, have become a mark of all industrialized societies. The social sciences, originally developed in the

---

*This essay is the revised version of a lecture given at York University, Toronto, in March 1971 at the invitation of the Division of Social Science, and repeated at the New School for Social Research, New York, in April 1971.

1. Alvin Gouldner, *The Coming Crisis of Western Sociology* (London, 1971).

name of progress and predictability, could not be left unaffected by this crisis.

One knows, of course, that the question "Knowledge for What?" is not a new one in our field.[2] Sociology, like other social sciences, is an offspring of philosophy in the age of enlightenment. Emancipation from a self-perpetuated state of immaturity, to paraphrase Kant, was the declared goal of social science from Condorcet to Saint-Simon, from Lorenz von Stein to Karl Marx. Still, the tools on which this hope was based were the newly developed technology and, early enough, techniques of social control. It was in these same tools, in reaction to the French Revolution, that such early law-and-order prophets as de Bonald and, later, Comte, placed their hopes. More important than such conservative reactions, however, was the early development of a technocratic ideology—an enthusiastic overestimation of the liberating potential of rational means and tools, as displayed by some of the forerunners of modern sociology—most notably the Saint-Simonian school.[3]

This basic ambiguity of the new rationality is characteristic of the origins and all later history of sociology. The roots of this rationality can be found in a peculiar shift that took place in the philosophical mind during the seventeenth century. In the decades between Galileo, Descartes, and Newton something happened—a new concept of reason was developed, and applicability and observability gradually became the prevailing standard. With modern science, technological rationality emerged. What actually happened and why it did remains a matter of debate. But, however we describe it, it deeply changed our whole world view to the point where history is no longer comprehended as a matter of human fate, but as a human project—and society no longer as a sacred organism but rather as a secular organization.

My following remarks are but a few comments on the more recent phases of an old development: the increasing rationality of behavior and its relation to social science. Today, the question is how *reasonable* our rationality still is—in science as well as in life in general. There is surely no final answer to this altogether intriguing question. But it can be approached and reflected upon, provided the question of how our knowledge is applied is considered together with our modes of abstraction, which, again, are rooted in our forms of perception. I should therefore like to develop my argument on three different, though related, levels. First, I shall make some comments on the methodological rationality of the social sciences. Second, I shall be concerned with analyzing briefly the application and applicability of social scientific knowledge and will try to make a characterization of the experts involved in such application. Third, I would like to add some general sociological

2. See Robert Lynd, *Knowledge for What?* (New York, 1938).
3. See George G. Iggers, *The Cult of Authority; The Political Philosophy of the Saint-Simonians* (The Hague, 1958).

considerations regarding the relationship of social class and rational behavior. The focus, however, will be on the relationship between the production of social scientific knowledge and its utilization, my hypothesis being that the link is to be found in the kind of rationality used. After having presented some admittedly loose arguments for this case, I shall finally try to offer some suggestions toward a solution of the present crisis in social science.

II.

Today the production and distribution of scientific and scholarly knowledge are institutionalized according to the functional imperatives of industrialized social systems. The process of research can no longer be separated from the utilization of the products of research. However, the natural and social sciences differ in this respect: the products of scientific work are in principle value-free in the sense that they can be made to serve quite different social and political purposes. It lies in their nature that they are neutral toward any kind of utilization, be it "constructive" or "destructive." Hence the fundamental ambivalence of technological progress. For scientific products are subject to the utilization interests of private or state capital and cannot be immunized from such interests. Scientists cannot prevent a utilization of their work for purposes adverse to their own social and political inclinations; in certain clear cases they may refuse to participate in a research project, but, generally, they cannot reach a point beyond the state of moral uneasiness which the Oppenheimer case revealed.

In contrast, the products of social science are neither value-free nor neutral in regard to their utilization. The social function of social science research is determined not only by the choice of the problem area under study but even more so by the methodological approach used. For, in social science, the methodology is always an integral element of what we call sociological knowledge. Hence methodological controversies have been part of the history of social science until this day.

It has been argued that the quest for social scientific knowledge stems basically from an emancipatory drive inherent in the human condition as such, or in other words, from an interest in mastering the natural and social forces which govern our lives.[4] However, if we take a look at the methodological viewpoints presently represented in the social sciences, such interest in emancipation is hardly prevalent. Today only a minority of scholars defend social science as a hermeneutical enterprise in interpretation. Instead, the majority is dedicated to the positivistic program of a unified behavioral science, a program which, in its more refined versions of

4. Jürgen Habermas, "Knowledge and Interest," in *Toward a Rational Society* (New York, 1971).

behaviorism, is methodologically oriented toward the sciences, and, especially in the general theory of action, conceptually oriented toward a bureaucratized society's understanding of rationality. It was, of course, Max Weber who first developed this concept of rationality which is, in fact, both a description and an apologia for those strategies of action determined and enforced by the capitalist process of exchange.

Four methodological positions can presently be distinguished in sociology.[5] First, the positivistic view which wants to distinguish between two different sociologies: one dedicated to the nomological program of behavioral science and which raises sole claim to being a social *science,* and another which is disqualified as "mere" writing of history in a sociological perspective. A second view, presently shared by the majority of sociologists, holds that the aim of sociology is the construction of general theories of action, be they grand theory or middle-range theory, in which historical processes are integrated in the social system as "dynamic elements." This position rejects the positivistic view which holds that theoretical knowledge can only be attained by reconstructing interaction systems in terms of variables of observable behavior, that is, by a reduction of sociology to behavioristic social psychology. Its starting point is a theory of rational behavior extended to the level of motivation and its tool the model of a "homo sociologicus." A third view still maintains ties to the older evolutionary tradition of developmental theories in sociology; like positivism, this approach remains skeptical about the logical possibility of nomological historical theories. Yet it considers the historical development of societies as the real object of sociology. This position of a historical sociology is held by scholars in the neo-Marxist tradition. In a fourth category, finally, we would find a variety of approaches derived from phenomenology and symbolic interactionism. This position disregards history, but this time in favor of the construction of an anthropological theory of intersubjectivity based on concepts of the intentionality of action, symbolic communication, and ego-identity formation. The present debate in France on Marxism and Structuralism is but one expression of the difficulty in bridging the hiatus between the anthropological and the historistic claims to a humanistic sociology.

In the social sciences different methodological positions produce different kinds of knowledge. If we disregard the fact that empirical positivistic research tends mainly to produce trivia, it can be said that its chief yield is the production of social techniques. Today we have learned that such knowledge is as neutral in terms of its utilization by vested interests in the intensified exploitation of the labor force and in the maintenance of mass

5. See in a similar view, Jürgen Habermas, *Logik der Sozialwissenschaften* (Frankfurt, 1971).

loyalty[6] as are the products of science toward utilization by interests in profit and warfare. Knowledge produced by the theories of action, on the other hand, has a tendency to obscure relations of production and their historical context. Understood this way, it functions as an ideology which today contributes to establishing and maintaining the technocratic consciousness of the educated middle classes.

It seems to me that only a combination of the third and the fourth positions presents a possibility for creating a social science which would produce neither techniques of social control nor ideologies, but which would provide a contribution to a critical understanding of the historical situation, its typical forms of repression, and its potential for liberation. This, for Marx as well as Weber, was the guiding interest in their scientific work. Still, one detects a hidden positivism in the economic determinism of the later Marx which lent itself to a reified interpretation of history in dogmatic terms.[7] And for Max Weber the emphasis on the subjectively intended meaning of social action and the hermeneutic elements of his methodology did not prevent him from claiming that social science sets out to provide "knowledge about the techniques of controlling life—external things as well as the actions of people—by calculation."[8]

For both Marx and Weber, this ambivalence is a result of their view that the ongoing rationalization of our social relations is an inescapable product of the development of capitalism. Both, in their analysis of capitalism, reject the use of isolated psychological categories such as the acquisitive drive or the profit motive. Instead, under a capitalist economy, individual behavior must be oriented toward the *principle* of profitability, toward market chances and the calculation of capital accumulation and investment. Here, the separation of workshop from household, the existence of free labor, and a rational judicial system have proved to be necessary preconditions for the development of the capitalist mode of production. The common denominator in these elements is a general tendency to apply the principle of formal rationality to all spheres of social life, the principle being the calculation of choices between alternative means for given ends, namely, the growth of productivity and profit. Since Weber defined expedient rationality as the optimization of means and ends, we have experienced the development of what Habermas has termed "sub-systems of instrumentalist behavior"[9] in

6. One of the first to acknowledge this fact was Loren Baritz in his study on the uses of industrial sociology, *The Servants of Power* (Middletown, Conn., 1960).

7. See Albrecht Wellmer, *Kritische Gesellschaftstheorie und Positivismus* (Frankfurt, 1969).

8. Max Weber, *Aufsätze zur Wissenschaftslehre* (Tübingen, 1922), S.591 (my translation).

9. Habermas, *Toward a Rational Society,* op. cit.

which such calculated rationality has reached various levels of refinement, so that (a) even in the more private spheres it has by now become a common characteristic of social behavior to make use of technologically devised tools and strategies to attain given ends. (b) System analysis and game theory are attempts to rationalize the *choice* between alternative strategies, attempts which leave no room for values and needs except as irrational elements. (c) The final stage, however, is only reached when the choice of strategies begins to dominate any thoughtful consideration of goals involved. Technological society suffers from a tendency to utilize economically or politically whatever tools and strategies have been developed, regardless of what effect their utilization may have on social value systems—with the result of a growing overkill potential in ever more social areas.

The prevailing positivistic fashion in social science research has contributed much to this development of a computational concept of rationality; hence it is not surprising that social scientists should have played an active role in the development and application of social techniques for dubious purposes. The involvement of social scientists in counterinsurgency research in Indochina and the notorious project Camelot are, of course, prime examples.[10] The fact that a number of social scientists have become public figures by virtue of their direct or indirect service to the corporate system is not only indicative of the growing importance of so-called expert knowledge in public affairs but also of its ideological function. It seems that a closer examination of the social role of technocratic knowledge is needed.

III.

Technological as well as social scientific knowledge can only be used if mediated and transformed by a group of experts who understand this kind of knowledge and can adjust it to the strategic needs of those using it: the state and the corporations. These experts who work as science administrators, planners, coordinators and advisers I shall call technocrats. As the entrepreneur and customer of most expert knowledge, the state is not simply an independent political agency but has become a supercorporation of its own which in many ways acts in collusion with other corporations.

10. According to *Der Spiegel* 25, no. 47: 158, the Pentagon has by now spent nearly seven hundred million dollars on research on the strategy of the Viet Cong, which is yet only a fraction of the Pentagon's yearly research expenditures of about seven billion dollars. These figures demonstrate dramatically the extent to which scientific knowledge is bought by the state. The article quoted points out, however, that the bulk of the research results on the strategy of the Viet Cong have been completely ignored by the political decision makers and, if contradictory to the opinions of the military establishment, have often enough been officially suppressed. This already indicates the ambiguous position in which technocrats are placed in the power structure.

Therefore, technocrats, in serving the state, are serving not the interests of a diffuse "public" but, rather, the interests of the corporate system. It should be mentioned here that the relationship that ensues determines the class position of the technocrats—a point I shall return to.

Let us first consider the uses of expertise in and by the corporate system. In regard to power relations such knowledge has, generally considered, two functions:

1. to balance conflicts between divergent interests within the corporate structure—in other words, the function of coordination;
2. to balance conflicts between the ruling elites and the working classes—in other words, the function of social and welfare planning.

In a more specific sense, the expertise provided by technocrats is a specific type of know-how, namely, how to transform technological and social scientific knowledge into politically useful material and instrumental strategies. This transformation has four functions:

1. The development of strategies for the attainment of set goals which as such remain unquestioned. The planning of counterinsurgency strategies for the Vietnam War is an example.
2. The development of strategies which are goals in themselves, in other words, the realization of what is profitable regardless of what the outcome may be. Examples of this can perhaps be found in the SST and in educational programing.
3. The production of alibis for public and private policies which are subject to public criticism. Regardless of what their motivation and self-image may be, there are social scientists who occupy themselves with the production of ideologies and the creation of pseudoscientific smoke screens. Daniel Bell's proclamation of the end of ideology or Walt Rostow's theory of developmental stages may serve as examples. More obvious, however, is the neutralizing function of presidential committees or similar commissions, which, in effect, use scientific or judicial inquiry to put urgent, politically loaded issues on ice, while history goes on: the "Kerner Report" or the federal report on the Kent State killings are good examples here.
4. A fourth function lies in enlightening the public as well as in advising the state and the corporations as to where in nonstrategic areas they could give in to public pressure. The Wolfenden Report in England, for instance, has served this purpose, while in America the debates on health and welfare programs fall under this heading.

Of course, there is a considerable discrepancy between the image technocrats have of themselves and the objective functions they serve. It is, however, important to know how they define their own roles because under some circumstances such interpretations can have a modifying effect on the conditions under which they operate. The famous statement by W. I. Thomas that "if men define a situation as real it is real in its consequences" has a certain truth even where power relations are involved.

Technocrats differ in how they interpret their individual roles depending on their methodological standpoint and their experience with public or corporate agencies. We can observe four such ways in which social scientists define their role in working to transform scientific knowledge into strategies for use on the public:

1. *The expert on application.*

He sees society as lagging behind the development of science and technology: the knowledge is available; it only needs to be applied. He feels that, if politicians were not so involved with values and vested interests, social progress would result automatically from scientific progress. Everything depends on the application of established rules and devices. This is the most primitive role definition, current among military psychiatrists[11] and behaviorists in general.[12]

2. *The expert on expediency.*

In this role, the scientist sees himself as an expert for if/then relations, analyzing the compatibility of different means with given goals which as such are not questioned. The scientist simply sells his knowledge to those who define the goals and can afford to buy his knowledge. However, in contrast to the first type he is not satisfied with what is already known: while he sees himself as an expert for the transformation of existing knowledge, he also tries to initiate new research to discover knowledge applicable to yet unsolved strategic problems. This type is found quite frequently, usually working with the university or at various think tanks, but he also turns up on boards which distribute research money. Some scientists of this type even form their own corporations to sell their particular kind of goods.[13]

3. *The expert on strategies.*

In this role the expert is not only concerned with means and ends but also with organizational procedures, political forces, and strategies of persuasion. He usually does not sell his own products but tries to implement the knowledge of others through various political channels, pressure groups, and connections. This type is most often found among those science managers and advisers who are no longer involved in research but act either as government or corporation employees or as independent dealers in scientific and technological knowledge. They often count among the more progressive forces within the public agencies.

11. See, for instance, Arlene K. Daniels, "The Social Construction of Military Psychiatric Diagnoses," in H. P. Dreitzel, *Recent Sociology,* no. 2; *Patterns of Communicative Behavior* (New York, 1970) p. 182-205.

12. A good example of this attitude is the new book by B. F. Skinner, *Beyond Freedom and Dignity* (New York, 1971).

13. See James Ridgeway, *The Closed Corporation; American Universities in Crisis* (New York, 1968).

4. The expert on the definition of needs.

In this role the scientist is concerned not only with the means available or to be developed or with devising strategies by which to implement them, but also with the rationality of the goals themselves. He sees his task in formulating alternative policies and his role as essentially that of the "rational critic." In defining his role this way, the social scientist makes it almost impossible to work within the corporate framework because it is this very framework which prevents the redefinition of public needs he feels called upon to provide. Most often this type is to be found among those scientists who use their professional prestige to stir up public debate on alternatives on the political scene.[14] Only under two conditions can this role definition be brought into line with professional praxis: (1) if social science is redefined as a critical enterprise, and (2) provided that social scientists must find or create an organizational basis from which they can set out to implement this type of expertise. These conditions are seldom given. The story of the attempts to reorganize professional associations as a radical platform speaks for itself.

These four role definitions have to be understood as *ideal* types; in reality one would find various mixtures of the four. As categories, they have been developed from the findings of an unpublished study on scientific advisory committees to the West German government.[15] I assume that these categories can be applied on this continent as well, since science and technology have a universal quality and produce similar attitudes in all who are working to transform scientific knowledge into workable strategies.

The role definitions of technocrats are not necessarily identical with their actual behavior, much less with their objective functions. They can, however, *influence* these functions in relation to *the level of rationality inherent in a role definition and to the degree to which role performance is brought into accordance with the definition.* For the above-mentioned role definitions reflect different levels of rationality. The technological rationality of types (1) and (2) gives way to the political rationality of types (3) and (4), where instrumental techniques are combined with communicative patterns. In another dimension, types (1) and (3) can be termed functional rationality, because they are concerned with the *process* of action, while types (2) and (4) are concerned with the results and *effects* of action and can be termed substantial rationality.[16] Thus, four different levels of rationality can be

14. Paul Goodman's speeches and writings may serve as a good example. See, for instance, his address to the National Security Industrial Association, reprinted in *New York Review of Books,* 23 November 1967.

15. A sample of 150 scientific members of advisory boards to the West German government was intensively studied by Doris Dreitzel in 1966/67.

16. The distinction between functional and substantial rationality is made by Paul Diesing, *Reason and Society* (Urbana, Ill., 1962).

distinguished, loosely corresponding to the role definitions technocrats empirically assume, and to the objective functions they perform. On each level we would find different degrees of sophistication; yet the intentionality of behavior clearly distinguishes the levels from each other. On the first level we can speak of a *rationality of application.* Max Weber has demonstrated that this type of rationality is characteristic for the kind of bureaucratic organization that is based on the standardization of applicable rules and must be understood as one of the historical preconditions for the development of the corporate system. The second type can be called *expedient rationality;* it is concerned with the optimization of ends-means relations and is characteristically found in modern economies. The third type focuses on the *rationality of the decision-making process;* the communicative structure of organizations can be more or less rational depending on how many people can be involved at what time in a decision process. The fourth type then would be the *rationality of problem solving;* its characteristic fields are science and politics.

Types of Rationality

	Formal	Material
	Technical Rationality	Political Rationality
functional	I. Rationality of application	III. Rationality of the decision-making process
(focus on the *process* of action)	(*a*) bureaucracy (*b*) application of rules (*c*) knowledge of the rules	(*a*) organization (*b*) bargaining (*c*) influence
substantial	II. Expedient Rationality	IV. Rationality of problem-solving
(focus on the *result* of action)	(*a*) economy (*b*) calculation (*c*) "expert knowledge"	(*a*) politics (*b*) realization of goals (*c*) creativity

(*a*) = typical sphere of relevance
(*b*) = type of rational behavior
(*c*) = necessary role attributes of the actor

The essence of all four types of rationality is an optimization process—the optimization of applications, of means-ends relations, of decision-making and problem-solving processes. However—and this would be my case against the presently fashionable antitechnological radicalism—it is important to understand that these types of rationality are as *types* rooted in one another and cannot be isolated: *the display of rational behavior on each level presupposes that such behavior is also based on the lower levels of rationality*—provided our present level of technology and organization is to be preserved. There is no political rationality which does not encompass the level of technological rationality a society has historically reached. "Back to nature" cannot be the formula for the solution of our problems, even if, in view of the ecological catastrophe, our Western attitude towards nature needs to be revised.

On the other hand, the development of technological rationality can itself become irrational when the political and moral dimensions lag behind. Indeed, our present problem seems to be that the rationality of our political organizations does not meet the standard of our technological rationality. The calculation of procedures and strategies is not followed, much less preceded, by a thoughtful consideration of the rationality of goals and values. Instead, instrumental strategies often become goals in themselves. As Habermas has remarked, science and technology have become an ideology. Considering the evidence of the Pentagon Papers, Hannah Arendt has observed that "the problem-solvers did not *judge,* they calculated; their self-confidence did not even need self-deception to be sustained in the midst of so many misjudgements, for it relied on the evidence of mathematical, purely rational truth. Except, of course, that this 'truth' was entirely irrelevant for the 'problem' at hand."[17] The irrelevancy of most instrumental knowledge is a result of the incapability of our political system to reflect rationally upon goals and values.[18] This is not to assume that goals and values can be *made* rational (as some system theorists seem to think), but is to say that values can be weighed against each other and the available instruments for their realization in a public discussion which would give every citizen a chance to participate and express his own needs and attitudes. This would exclude a superficial redefinition of value-based goals as a cosmetic job that

17. Hannah Arendt, "Lying in Politics; Reflections on the Pentagon Papers," in *New York Review of Books,* 18 November 1971, p. 37 (italics in text).

18. This is true not only in regard to our own values and goals but also distorts our image of others. "It seems that no ivory tower of the scholars has ever better prepared the mind for wholly ignoring the facts of life than the various think tanks did for the problem-solvers and the reputation of the White House for the President's advisers," quoted from Hannah Arendt in the article cited above, p. 37. The numerous errors in making a sound judgment of the attitude and strength of the Viet Cong are a result of the subtraction of values from the "facts of life."

cannot resolve the inherent tension produced by the superimposition of instrumental rationality. A redefinition of our standards of rationality is a political task which involves a change of the power structure including the service function of technocrats. In fact, the supposition of values through strategies, of ends through means, is the very essence of the technocratic mind. In order to explain this phenomenon I should like now to make some brief remarks about the relationship of social class and rational behavior.

IV.

Rational action in everyday life as well as in any subsystem of instrumental behavior presupposes affective control. As Norbert Elias in his great study on the process of civilization has demonstrated, the development of an "apparatus of self-constraint" is historically a result of the monopolization of violence and the growing chains of economic interdependencies and of action and reaction.[19] This process has run parallel to the development of capitalism, which in turn is connected with the history of a growing internationalization of external constraints, or—to put it simply—self-control. The important fact, however, is that, as Elias has pointed out, the rationalization of behavior, the separation of the individual from his social roles, and increasing affective control are processes which were developed, initially, in the economically *dominating* classes. Only gradually, by thrusts and starts, did similar patterns of restrained behavior come to prevail in the middle and lower classes. At each moment in history we can see simultaneously coexisting behavioral patterns which actually relate to different historical stages: the lower classes lag behind in their consciousness, and display historically older modes of behavior. We can see this today: the relative incapability of working and underclass families to develop modes of socialization which would guarantee individual success in a middle-class world is—among other reasons—an indication of an anachronistic consciousness, which, however, serves as a social defense mechanism against their relative deprivation in this world and is insofar as necessary an expression of their objectively ambivalent situation. As research on the situation of the working class shows, the much discussed embourgeoisement of some parts of the working class destroys the defense mechanisms that had developed out of a historically older type of communal solidarity, a loss which, so it seems, can only be compensated at present by better opportunities for consumption. On the other hand, this tendency in the working class to develop what Lockwood has called "privatized" behavior[20] shows that, in accordance with the

19. Norbert Elias, *Über den Prozess der Zivilisation; Wandlungen des Verhaltens in den weltlichen Oberschichten des Abendlandes,* 2 (Bern and Munich, 1969).

20. See David Lockwood and John H. Goldthorpe, *The Affluent Worker* (Cambridge, 1968).

changes going on in the sphere of production, behavioral changes in this class take the same direction as such changes did in the middle classes in an earlier period.

If the present situation of the working class is thus an ambivalent one, the middle classes are in no better situation: socialization toward a strong ego-identity and an internalized, self-controlled rationality no longer has the function it did in the earlier stages of competitive capitalism. With the growing functionalization and industrialization of the work situation at the white-collar and even professional levels, the work roles the middle classes assume tend to become as repressive as those of the working class. With more and more external controls, the necessary ego-involvement in role performance is suppressed to such an extent that the individual no longer sees rational action as a result of his *own* personal effort but as enforced by the system. This situation indicates a new level of alienation.

An essential feature of this alienation is the repression of the emotional dimension in role play, a repression which tends to spread from work roles to other types of roles. Originally it was a matter of affective control; today it becomes affective repression. The growing rationalization and functional entanglement of all spheres of life demand affective neutrality, and call for a calculable role performance bereft of all emotional involvement. Under such circumstances the *autonomous* personality, as may be characterized by a deferred gratification pattern, a restrained self-representation in role play and a flexible superego,[21] becomes more and more a "bourgeois"—or in terms of the relations of production—an anachronistic ideal of socialization even for the middle classes.

Having made these observations, we may come to a better understanding of the class consciousness of technocrats. Being a privileged and relatively independent upper middle-class group, technocrats (with the exception of type 4) do not as yet experience in themselves the very alienation which is, among other factors, a result of their function. The scientistic attitude revealed in the role definition the majority give themselves is a comfortable stance as long as *they* are the planners and not the planned for. Although, of course, for technocratic positions the corporations tend to favor those social scientists who are best socialized and adjusted to the norms of the corporate system, technocrats usually ideologize their work as being independent and rational: a neutral power, committed only to social progress. At the same time they tend to see the state as an agency independent of corporate power which mediates the divergent interests of a pluralist society. Of course, this attitude not only reflects their upward mobility—and they do enjoy upper-class privileges to some degree—but also is a function of their

21. Jürgen Habermas, *Thesen zur Theorie der Sozialisation,* Vorlesungsskript, 1968, p. 8-15, Raubdruck.

ambiguous class position. They can be understood as a caste working within the framework of the corporate structure. Their socioeconomic interests favor those who can make use of their specific talents and who can buy their kind of knowledge. In a corporate society, then, the technocrat always works within the profit structure, just as he is the product of that structure.

Yet these technocrats can also objectively *function* as a relatively independent group within the system, provided—as André Gorz has noted—that three preconditions are met:[22]

1) There should be no plausible alternative to the prevailing technological rationality of the system nor may alternatives be seriously discussed, thereby demasking the system as one bent on predetermining the people's needs and means of need fulfillment.

2) It must be generally accepted that anticorporate forces are incompetent to manage state and economy. An explicit and successful anticorporate alternative would threaten the technocrats' prevailing ideology that they *have* to serve the corporate system because they alone will be able to solve its contraditions.

3) Yet the working class and possibly certain grass-roots movements have to be strong enough to countervail partially the pressure exerted by finance and industry on the state and, therefore, on the technocratic caste itself. This could possibly insure that the technocrats do not become *mere* handmaidens of established power.

The linkup between social class and rational behavior goes back to the fact that what Weber calls the rationalization process was originally a product of the economically ruling classes and the intelligentsia that served them. What Karl Marx said in regard to ideas is generally true for behavioral attitudes as well: the ideas of the rulers are the ruling ideas. The technocratic ideology cannot be separated from our capitalist system; the one-dimensional emphasis on technological rationality is a function of the prevailing relations of production.

It should not, however, be overlooked that capitalism as classically defined and developed in our Western societies, has no monopoly on technological rationality. The highly bureaucratized socialist systems of the East do not display any more political rationality than Western societies do. The stress under which the ego-identity is placed by the extension of the individual role budget, by repressive norms of affective neutrality in organizational roles and by the separation of behavioral spheres is much less resisted in present-day socialist countries than it is by the New Left and some related groups. Basically, it is the antiauthoritarian refusal to develop and display a socially functional, i.e., function-oriented, ego-identity at all which marks a new resistance against the rationalization of behavior. We do not

22. See André Gorz, *A Strategy for Labor* (New York, 1968).

know as yet whether this movement signals the beginning of the end of a long history of a particular kind of individual identity formation and affective control or whether the system will be able to integrate the free-floating affectivity. It seems that in any case—next to the ongoing competition struggles that lead to larger and larger monopolistic, functional units—it is this conflict which will largely determine the future of our industrialized societies. To quote Norbert Elias: "The complementary concepts of 'rationality' and 'irrationality' are defined by the relative proportion between shortlived emotions and longterm thought models of observable reality as expressed in the individual conduct of behavior. The more weight the latter . . . have, the more *'rational'* is the behavior—provided the control of affective impulses does not become too tight; for *their* pressure and satisfaction are in themselves an inherent element of human reality."[23]

It seems characteristic for the present domination of technological rationality that the emotional and sensual spheres themselves are labeled irrational and as such are almost despised. The rebellion of the counterculture against the prevailing computational rationality cannot help but be doomed to failure, however, if it continues to reject a political rationality rooted in and encompassing the developed levels of technological rationality in favor of various modes of body politics and politics of ecstasy. In this case, the forecast would not only be what the Bergers in a recent article called "the blueing of America,"[24] namely, a mere circulation of the technocratic elites in favor of working-class mobility; indeed, the system will easily be able to maintain mass loyalty on the basis of the privatized character of the presently emerging new mood of religiosity.

V.

In the light of these observations let me add a few final remarks on the present crisis of social science. There are circumstances when rational arguments lose their forward-looking aspect and become a hindrance to progress. The rejection of the prevalent mode of rationality by the new radicals may be inspired by a *different standard* of reason. After all, computational rationality has done nothing to prevent the present disastrous state of world affairs. University social scientists and administration technocrats have been proved wrong in their predictions that what is called "post-industrial" society would produce a greater degree of *political* rationality or reason—a failure in judgment that is in sharp contrast to their self-advertised strategical cleverness.

23. Elias, *Die höfische Gesellschaft* (Neuwied, 1970). (Italics in text; my translation)
24. Brigitte Berger and Peter L. Berger, "The Blueing of America," in *New Republic,* 3 April 1971.

I sympathize, admittedly, with the radicals' distrust in the present state of the social sciences, which have failed to bring forth any convincing general theory to explain the present deadlock between the alienated but silent majorities and the privileged yet radicalized intelligentsia. Nor has social science demonstrated much predictive power in regard to the effects computational rationality, applied to production and destruction, are and will be having.

What can be done? In regard to the social sciences I should like to suggest three complementary directions for research:

1. It would seem desirable to have much more research on the *social history* of societies. By this I mean an attempt to uncover the economic conditions and circumstances involved in the history of oppression, focusing at the same time on the development of corresponding psychic structures. Although much progress has been made over the past decade in certain areas of social history,[25] contact between sociologists and historians—if it occurs at all—is still generally limited to declarations of good will. Even worse is the situation in regard to psychological history. While some attempts have been made to subject historical figures to retrospective psychoanalysis, the main problem—to explain the history of the changing "social character" of particular groups and classes—has not even been recognized by most historians. Yet without such an approach it would be quite impossible to explain adequately the shifts and stages of socialization patterns and their effect on the—up to now—growing internalization of external constraints. The history of family life and the respective socialization patterns in Europe and America has yet to be written.

2. In *social theory* I would suggest a methodology which is critical in the sense of historical theory and hermeneutic in the sense of a science of interpretation. As I see it, what is needed to begin with is a critical revision of the notions of "rationality" and "irrationality," without immediately shying away from the use of other than formal logical categories—namely, the aesthetic dimension of what Weber has called the "element of composition" in the construction of theories. It would be a pity to forget that one of the best traditions in our field is the sociological essay. To be sure, social science remains a rational enterprise. As Alfred Schütz in his essay on "The Problem of Rationality in the Social World" has put it: "The postulate of rationality implies . . . that all other behavior has to be interpreted as derivative from the basic scheme of rational action. . . . Science does not have at its disposal other methods than rational ones and

25. An excellent report on the present situation of social history is provided by E. J. Hobsbawn, "From Social History to the History of Society," in *Daedalus* 100 (1971), no. 1: 20-45.

it cannot, therefore, verify or falsify purely occasional propositions."[26] It remains, however, an open question what exactly the principle of rationality in methodology means. Schütz has, on the other hand, emphasized the postulate of adequacy which "requires that the *typical* construction be compatible with the totality of *both* our daily life and our scientific experience.[27] For the construction of theories, this means that sociological imagination is as important as the logic of a system. It seems to me that such approaches as Adorno's aesthetical sociology, Habermas' critical sociology, Lefèbvre's Marxist sociology, Goodman's utopian sociology, Cicourel's cognitive sociology and even Gouldner's postulated reflexive sociology are more promising as programs than any further refinement in the general theory of action in the functionalist framework would be.

3. In *empirical sociological research* the only chance I can see to escape the mechanisms of utilization of knowledge by corporate interests on the capitalist marketplace and to develop a truly emancipatory social science is to bring about a methodological integration of theory and praxis, or, to be more precise, an integration of the empirical research process with practical political involvement. Such research would be guided less by what is simply representative and quantifiable than by concern with direct sensual perception. We must find ways to express and interpret sensual communicative experiences in a methodologically controlled manner. Methods of participatory observation should be refined and allowed to play a much more important role, since they demand direct contact with the phenomena under study. The most important methodological rule, however, is to control our processes of abstraction during the research process. As far as I can see, ethnomethodology at present represents the most promising methodological attempt at such an integration.[28] The formation of hypotheses, the codification of data and the interpretational rules should become an object of empirical research in their own right—not separated as a special discipline as, for instance, an empirical sociology of science, but rather as an integral part of any field work. Only in this way can it be scientifically demonstrated that social research is not a methodologically directed focalization by the subject on a given object,

26. Alfred Schütz, "The Problem of Rationality in the Social World," in D. Emmet and A. Macintyre, eds., *Sociological Theory and Philosophical Analysis* (New York, 1970), p. 112.

27. Ibid., p. 113 (my emphasis).

28. For a critique of traditional research techniques, see Aaron V. Cicourel, *Method and Measurement in Sociology* (Chicago, 1964). For his ethnomethodological approach, see *The Social Distribution of Juvenile Justice* (New York, 1967), especially the first chapter and the conclusion, which are a much clearer statement of this technique than H. Garfinkel's writings.

but rather a symbolically mediated understanding—a methodologically directed *communication* between subjects, the goal of which is to bring about emancipatory change in *all* participants. This means, however, that empirical research becomes political praxis. I have no illusions about the consequences of so radical a proposal: the price would be a sharp reduction in empirical research, something I think, however, we can accept as long as we have so few empirical studies which give us more insight than any good novel does.[29] It must be admitted, however, that the epistemological rather than the political consequences of the unity of theory and praxis in empirical research have to be most seriously considered: our methodological standards of verification and falsification would have to be modified so that they are applicable to the control of the communication process in question rather than to the mere control of the cognitive process of the observer.

The implementation of such standards would create a social science which is perhaps less *rational* in terms of the prevailing technological norms, but which would certainly be more *reasonable* in respect to the alienation that prevails.

29. This is true even for journalists; see, for instance, the excellent observations on the status games of the middle class by Tom Wolfe, *The Pump House Gang* (New York, 1968).

14. Art and Utopia: The Marcusean Perspective

STEPHEN BRONNER

At times, in the following pages, the criticism which will be directed at Professor Marcuse will be very sharp. Consequently, there are a few remarks which need to be made at the outset. To begin with, Marcuse's work is grossly underestimated by many academicians who seem unable to comprehend that his extraordinary influence upon students and intellectuals (ranging from Jürgen Habermas to Norman O. Brown) stems, in large part, from the alternative which he offers to the emptiness and sterility of contemporary philosophy and political science. In opposition to an often absurd, mundane, and "neutral" operationalist mentality, Marcuse has asserted the power of the critical intellect and the dialectical method. Indeed, in the present context, he attempts to prevent art from falling into a societal quietude reminiscent of classicism and/or the pedanticism of "art for art's sake," through his concern with the force of the imagination. But, perhaps, what is most important is that he has brought words like beauty, softness, and sensuality back to the political vocabulary. In contrast to those who fawn over the status quo, Marcuse has a vision of, and makes manifest the desire of many for, a *qualitatively* different mode of life. It is this critical capacity to question the deepest premises upon which our lives are founded, as well as the breadth of the alternatives that he offers, which assures his importance as a thinker.

Now, in the final analysis, there are only three ways to critique a philosophical conception. The first lies in attacking the central thesis from without, through rejecting an (and/or positing a different) *a priori* assumption. Secondly, one can show that the argument runs counter to empirical reality. The first involves a simple dismissal of the entire line of reasoning, while the second necessarily anchors its criticism from within the status quo. There is a third type, however, and this may be termed "immanent" criticism. This form is by its very nature dialectical, in that it enters the process of the argument and calls the internal reasoning into account. Therefore, while retaining the structure of the initial argument and the process of the reasoning, immanent criticism is not limited by being tied to the status quo. Moreover, since the influences of the German idealists, Marx, and Freud are so pronounced, and since Marcuse's own conception is dialectical, it is this type of critique which his thought requires.

In order to furnish such a critique, it is first of all necessary to explicate Marcuse's ideas on art and his utopian conception. Consequently, the first section of this paper will attempt an exegesis of Marcuse's thought, which, while drawing on other examples and different writers, will still seek to remain faithful to Marcuse's argument. Then, in the second section, the analysis will be explored and the criticism developed. This introduction may avoid any unnecessary confusion and, hence, possibly increase the clarity of both Marcuse's position and my own.

*   *   *   *

In a dialectical manner, Marcuse clearly attempts to understand society by comprehending it as a totality. Therefore, it is virtually impossible to consider Marcuse's ideas on art and utopia without briefly sketching his general view of present-day society.

For Marcuse, the traditional dialectical contradictions within society have "flattened out." Although class contradictions within society still exist "objectively", the "subjective" necessity for radical change has been rendered ineffective by the affluence and technological progress of advanced industrial society.[1] This, in turn, is seen as restricting the possibility of utilizing the potential, which exists, for a change to a society with a qualitatively different mode of life. Consequently, in this situation, the traditional types and effects of art must change also.

Civilization, for Marcuse, is "first of all progress in work for the procurement and augmentation of life."[2] However, this involves a denial of "Eros," the life instinct, with its desires for immediate gratification. This denial of Eros and "containment of the pleasure principle" occurs when man first confronts the "reality principle," which is fundamentally based on economic scarcity. Under capitalist society, in fact in its very creation, the reality principle assumes specificity as the "performance principle" and "under its rule society is stratified according to the competitive economic performance of its members."[3] What occurs under these circumstances (and especially as society becomes more affluent and efficient) is that, above and beyond that level of repression which is indispensable for human interaction, additional controls are put into effect. This is so that the progress of the society may be channeled in terms of an expansion of the status quo. Institutionalized, these controls (i.e., the perpetuation of the monogamic-patriarchal family, the continuation of the hierarchical division of labor, mass

---

1. Herbert Marcuse, *An Essay on Liberation* (Boston: Beacon Press, 1969), p. 54.
2. Marcuse, *Eros and Civilization* (New York: Vintage Books, 1962), p. 74.
3. Ibid., p. 40.

media intrusion into the private sphere, etc.) become instruments for what Marcuse calls "surplus repression."[4]

As with Marx's surplus value, surplus repression is quantitative in character. Although he considers a certain minimal amount of repression as necessary to preserve civilization, Marcuse sees the present level of surplus repression as being unnecessary, and therefore, in Hegelian terms, irrational.[5] Moreover, since "reason presupposes freedom, [which is] the power to act in accordance with knowledge of the truth, the power to shape reality in line with its potentialities,"[6] to the degree to which this level of surplus repression hinders the actualization of the potential freedom, to that degree do the individuals live in a state of un-reason and un-freedom. To that degree also is the present system stagnant and repressive. Further, this surplus repression appears in the very productivity of advanced industrial society, by the creation of "false needs," which are then satisfied as new ones are produced.[7] This, in effect, "reproduces" the repressive hopes and desires of the society within the individuals themselves. Consequently, though surplus repression is, in itself, quantitative in character, the effects it produces in the "infrastructure" of the individual members of the society, are qualitative. It is this, then, which makes necessary a qualitative break from the "vicious cycle of progress," and it is here that the basis for Marcuse's utopian conception emerges. If Marxism and the dialectical method are to remain valid, they "must risk defining freedom in such a way that people become conscious of and recognize it as something that is nowhere already in existence."[8] The potential for the utopian condition lies within the present society, and the potential utopia becomes "the determinate socio-historical negation of what exists."[9]

From here, too, does the revolutionary importance of art in present-day society arise. For Marcuse, it is Eros which first builds culture through its sublimation into art. It is in art, which retains the life instincts and their

4. Ibid., p. 34.

5. For a clear explication of the implications of the dialectical relationship between rationality and necessity, see Frederick Engels, *Ludwig Feuerbach and the End of Classical German Philosophy,* in Karl Marx and Frederick Engels, *Selected Works,* 3 vols. (Moscow: Progress Publishers, 1969) 3.

6. Marcuse, *Reason and Revolution: Hegel and the Rise of Social Theory* (Boston: Beacon Press, 1969), p. 9.

7. It should be noted that the "total organization of society under monopoly capital and the growing wealth created by this organization can neither undo nor arrest the dynamic of its growth: capitalism cannot satisfy the needs which it creates." From Marcuse, *Counter-revolution and Revolt* (Boston: Beacon Press, 1972), p. 16.

8. Marcuse, "The End of Utopia," in *Five Lectures,* trans. Jeremy J. Shapiro and Shierry M. Weber (Boston: Beacon Press, 1969), pp. 68-69.

9. Ibid.

validity within itself, that "the truth of the human condition [which] is hidden, repressed—not by a conspiracy of some sort, but by the actual course of history"[10] may be perceived. In the face of a repressive society, art holds out to humanity *"la promesse de bonheur"* (Stendhal). It is in this manner that art acts, at one and the same time, as the hope and "inner truth" of civilization—as the "second history" of man.

Then, in Marcuse's view, if the principle on which civilization is built is repression of Eros and the denial of its freedom, the truth of art lies "in the negation of the principle that governs this civilization . . . [art] is attained and sustained fulfillment, the transparent unity of subject and object, of the universal and the individual."[11]

Therefore, the spheres of societal and artistic reality are simultaneously antagonistic and complementary. Art, as the "inner truth" which contradicts the existing society, retains the freedom of shaping reality with regard to its potentialities, through the imagination. Art, then, must embody a certain transcendence, a "rational transgression [which becomes] an essential quality of even the most affirmative art."[12] Consequently, art contains its own dynamic, which is inherent and which, in a sense, connects "affirmative" and "negative" art.

In Marcuse's thought, the distinction is important. Affirmative culture, which especially marked the early phase of bourgeois development, was based on the belief of an inner sanctity and freedom, set apart from that external world with its misery, ugliness, and want.[13] The idea becomes clearer by considering a stanza from Keats's "Ode to a Nightingale."

> Away! away! for I will fly to thee,
> Not charioted by Bacchus and his pards,
> But on the viewless wings of Poesy,
> Though the dull brain perplexes and retards:
> Already with thee! tender is the night,
> And haply the Queen-Moon is on her throne,
> Cluster'd around by all her starry Fays;
> But here there is no light,
> Save what from heaven is with the breezes blown
> Through verdurous glooms and winding mossy ways.[14]

In this case, the flight is the flight of the heart and the freedom which is felt is internal. Even though Keats, like most of the romantics, looked back to

---

10. Marcuse, "The Affirmative Character of Culture," in *Negations,* trans. Jeremy J. Shapiro (Boston: Beacon Press, 1969), p. 230.

11. Marcuse, *Eros and Civilization,* p. 105.

12. Marcuse, *One-Dimensional Man (Boston: Beacon Press, 1964), p. 63.*

13. Marcuse, *Counterrevolution and Revolt,* pp. 92-93.

14. Richard Wilbur, ed., *Keats* (New York: Dell, 1959), pp. 96-97.

an idealized Gemeinschaft community in response to the misery of the industrial revolution, the flight of the heart is possible for everyone, since it depends on a spiritual communion with nature and is totally dissociated from the conditions of the society at large. By the same token, this concept would also apply to a classicism, which, rather than creating new forms of freedom and expression, recreates old forms in ministering to the existing order.[15]

In the existence of this dichotomy between the internal and the external, a "resolution can only be illusory. And the possibility of a solution rests precisely on the character of artistic beauty as illusion (*Schein*)."[16] Believing that happiness can exist internally, independent of the actual external living conditions, this type of art abrogates its socially critical function, and serves to perpetuate the given state of affairs. Indeed, it is this illusion which, in fact, "renders incorrect even one's own assertion that one is happy."[17]

Just because this conception considers the inner realm sacrosanct, it blinds itself to the possibility of the external realm subverting this inner sanctum. Marcuse sees this as happening in advanced industrial society, through the introjection into the individuals of the "happy consciousness." With this complacent consciousness, the individuals lose the desire for change and come to terms with the society and its evils. So, for example, the individual is thrown "back upon himself, learn[ing] to bear, and in a certain sense, to love his isolation."[18]

This decisive division within affirmative art would parallel the *bourgeois/citoyen* split which marks bourgeois democracy. In affirmative culture, freedom is purely privatistic and divorced from social institutions and concrete social activity; it forms no bond between man and his neighbor, and removes itself from the interaction between the individual and his community. In like manner, the bourgeois privatistically pursues his interests (in "freedom"?) but is only able to assert his "universality" as a citizen once every four years when he votes, thereby denying the possibility of fulfilling his potential as a "species being," (Marx) or as a "whole" man.

With the advent of the twentieth century, an art of all-encompassing protest sharpens the critical faculty and reasserts the utopian dream and its possibilities. The "Great Refusal" becomes the negation of what is, and this is accomplished by increasing the distance between the societal and artistic

---

15. It must be emphasized, however, that in this poem in particular, as well as in the aesthetic form of affirmative culture as such, indeed in all art, "there is the expression against plastic deeroticization. Beauty stands as the 'negation of the commodity world and of the performances, attitudes, looks, gestures, required by it.' See Marcuse, *Counterrevolution and Revolt*, p. 182.

16. Marcuse, *Negations*, p. 118.

17. Ibid., p. 122.

18. Ibid.

spheres, through the effect of estrangement (*Verfremdungseffekt*). It is important to note, that this technique of estrangement, which is now consciously used and often misused by many modern German playwrights, was originally introduced by Brecht. In contrast to the manner in which it is used now, Brecht neither wished to remove the work, as a totality, from the audience, nor to empty art of feeling as such, nor did he wish the audience to forget that they were in a theater. Even in an early work, such as *In the Jungle of the Cities,* the author immediately establishes a rapport between the audience and the work through the didactic prologue. By retaining form, and the communicative quality of form, he allows the audience to recognize intellectually the plight of the masses in the cities. Indeed, by making them aware of their own condition under capitalism, the work becomes a virtual call to arms.

In using this "Verfremdungseffekt," Brecht forces the audience to realize their own estrangement by the effect of the play. In eliminating *elements* of feeling—mawkishness, sentimentality, empathy (*Rührung*)—he endeavors to achieve a certain result: the audience's recognition of their condition, and how this condition affects them as individuals. Perhaps it is best expressed by what Brecht said in 1920:

> I can compete with the ultra-modernists in hunting for new forms,
> and experimenting with my feelings. But I keep realizing that the
> essence of art is simplicity, grandeur and sensitivity, and that the
> essence of its form is coolness.[19]

However, within the Great Refusal, what occurred was that through their integration into a new aesthetic form, "words, sounds, shapes and colors were insulated against their familiar ordinary use and function: thus they were freed for a new dimension of existence."[20] Although the Great Refusal actually came into prominence only in the first three decades of the twentieth century, culminating in German expressionism and surrealism, Lautréamont may be viewed as one of its founding fathers. In *Les Chants de Maldoror,* there is already the search for a new mode of expression and feeling, as in the marvelous description of Maldoror's copulation with a shark. Still later, Rimbaud in his poetry attempts to transform the whole totality of language and experience, as he travels the whole range of emotions in *Le Bateau Ivre* and *Une Saison en Enfer.*

It is Marcuse's contention that this distance is now being narrowed in contemporary society, that the transcendent quality of art is being impaired.

19. Bertolt Brecht, *Collected Plays* 1, ed. Ralph Mannheim and John Willett (New York: Vintage Books, 1971): xvii.

20. Marcuse, *Counterrevolution and Revolt,* p. 98.

The power of the second dimension of civilization is seen as being encompassed by the first. Indeed, Marcuse believes that through the mass diffusion of art, the individual works become

> part of the technical equipment of the daily household and of the daily work world. In this process, they undergo a decisive transformation; they are losing the qualitative difference, namely the essential dissociation from the established reality principle which was the ground of their liberating function. Now, the images and ideas, by virtue of which art, literature, and philosophy once indicted and transcended the given reality are integrated into the society, and the power of the reality principle is greatly extended.[21]

Earlier in the century, the Bauhaus movement attempted to wed art to industry and technology (as in the work of Gropius, Moholy-Nagy, etc.). Then, socialist realism made art the handmaiden of a political policy. However, today we can go to a concert and hear music performed and created by an electronic instrument which sits alone on the stage. Or, we can simply watch television, and by listening to the commercials hear excerpts from Beethoven to Stravinsky in the background, as the announcer tries to sell us a product. A Campbell's soup can becomes an ornament, while prints decorate our homes. The result is the transformation and integration of fine art.[22]

The difference in the manner of integration between the aforementioned movements and society, and the absorption of the liberating potential of art by advanced industrial society is qualitative and threefold. First, in the latter case, integration is not the desired aim of the work itself, and consequently the conscious intent of the work loses its importance. Second, as advanced industrial society is able to use the work as a commercial product, the content of the work when performed as an *oeuvre* is also affected. Finally, as part of a movement with an artistic intent, the work retained its identity as a work of art, as a singularly human product. Under present circumstances, technology and the given society become an intrinsic part of the work, perhaps even subsuming within it that which makes the work a human product.

This becomes more apparent when it is seen that through the increasing specialization of the division of labor and the unprecedented technological

21. Marcuse, "The Obsolescence of the Freudian Concept of Man," in *Five Lectures*, p. 58.

22. It is interesting that this transformation of fine art was already perceived by Hegel, in that it had even then "become more or less obligatory for a cultivated man to possess some acquaintance with art, and the pretention to display oneself as a dilettante and connoisseur [was] pretty universal. From "Vorlesung über die Aesthetik," in Georg W.F. Hegel, *On Art, Religion, Philosophy*, ed. J. Glenn Gray (New York: Harper Torchbooks, 1970), p. 38.

advances which require this specialization, a situation has come about in which "mechanization has penetrated into the subconscious of the artist,"[23] a situation in which there is a complete subordination of art to technique. Also, the amount of capital outlay necessary for television, movies and radio is such that "artistic expression is subordinated to a censorship of money or the state."[24]

Under these circumstances, one can see that the grandeur of the work can easily be affected. This effect assumes specificity in the function and effects of the hero(ine). Traditionally, the hero was the man or woman who either transcended reality through his concrete or spiritual feats and/or by the sensitivity or strength of emotional makeup. As with Oedipus or Odysseus, the traditional hero negated and transcended the hypocrisy and pettiness of the society, its misery and stagnation, by the enormity of his sacrifices, strengths, or quests. The potential hope, and the pathos, of humanity is there incarnate.

In the literature of the refusal, this is no longer the case. The hero is transformed into the antihero—Gide's immoralist Michel, or Kafka's Joseph K. These antiheroes are either on the outside of society, or are ordinary men who find it difficult, or impossible, to cope with their condition. Indeed, the antihero need not even act, as in the case of Goncharov's *Oblomov*. Oblomov is a lazy procrastinator, who is simply acted upon by the society. In each case, however, be it through recognition, empathy, or disgust, the reader is forced to come to grips with his condition. The antihero leads the reader to consider what could be, by showing that which is not.

However, for Marcuse, in advanced industrial society, neither the hero nor the antihero is any longer functional. The technological achievements of society itself have surpassed the quests of the traditional hero. It was the United States that landed a man on the moon: a collective effort of the government, the Pentagon and the scientific estate; it was not the feat of a "hero." On the other hand, the antiheroes "are no longer images of another way of life but rather freaks or types of the same life, serving as an affirmation rather than negation of the established order."[25] Poverty and misery are no longer visible in daily life, as they once were, for the majority of the population. Through the creation, satisfaction and re-creation of false needs, the individuals who are acted upon learn only to enjoy and value life in accordance with the set of values propagated by the status quo. They are satisfied, complacent, introjected with the "happy consciousness." The

23. Jacques Ellul, *The Technological Society*, trans. John Wilkinson (New York: Vintage Books, 1964), p. 129.

24. Ibid., p. 128.

25. Marcuse, *One-Dimensional Man*, p. 59.

potential incarnated within the hero, and the critical negation manifested by the antihero are both vitiated through the inability to value even the possibility of a different enjoyment, a real peace, and a more embracing gratification. The conception of a life which is not subordinated to productivity is denied.

As contradiction is more easily assimilated, the possibility for "negative thinking," which, for Marcuse, is the only source of art, is necessarily diminished. The negation inherent in the *oeuvre* is itself negated by the industrial society. The works, therefore,

> suffer the fate of being absorbed by what they refute. As modern classics, the avant-garde and the beatniks share the function of entertaining without endangering the conscience of the men of good will. This absorption is justified by technical progress; the refusal is refuted by the alleviation of misery in the advanced industrial society. The liquidation of high culture is a by-product of the conquest of scarcity.[26]

With this assimilation of contradictions, the societal heroes, themselves, act as repressive instruments.

> The stars, the consorts of royalty, the kings and champion sportsmen, have the function which demigods had in mythology; they are human to a superlative degree and therefore to be imitated; their behavior has a normative character. But as they are not of this world one can only imitate them in a small way, on one's own level, and not to presume to match oneself with them in reality.[27]

Once again, an illusion is held out before the members of the society: the illusion that "happiness" lies with them, the demigods. Supplanting the traditional hero with the potential and transcendence which he embodied, through the exposure which he receives, the demigod is also able to overpower the critical negation of the antihero. Handsome, rich, and smiling, he relates perfectly to the happy consciousness. A commodity product (just watch a few commercials), he is at one and the same time the ideal and the tool of contemporary society. Indeed, he attains the ideal only by virtue of his use as a tool; the ideal, the hope, becomes the instrument. The gratification which the masses seek—that is, to become one of the demigods—naturally can never be fulfilled.

This denial of gratification occurs in order to maintain maximum productivity and quiescence on the part of the masses. It comes to be psychologically insured through societal controls. Of course, these controls

26. Ibid., p. 70.
27. Reimut Reiche, *Sexuality and Class Struggle,* trans. Susan Bennett (New York: Praeger, 1971), p. 71.

affect the relationship between the *oeuvre* and the audience. Here, Freud's influence on Marcuse, once more, manifests itself. Yet, this influence is not psychoanalytic in the strict sense, but rather refers to the metapsychology which Marcuse took over from Freud, often using it mainly for symbolic purposes.

Paul Robinson is quite right, for example, when he sees an allegory on the rise of capitalism in Marcuse's treatment of the primal crime.[28] For Marcuse, human history does not begin with the revolt of the sons and brothers against the primal father. Rather, history begins with the original ascension of the father, who in monopolizing the mother(s), limited enjoyment to himself alone, while imposing labor on the sons. With his rise to power, exploitation and domination resulted and there occurred an unequal distribution of work and enjoyment.[29] With each revolt of the sons, they continually found it necessary, because of guilt, to resort to a repression which originated, or imitated that of, the father (i.e., the institutionalization of religion). The guilt remains, and the repression continues, even in the present when repression of this sort is no longer necessary.

Strictly speaking, for Freud "the essence of repression lies simply in the function of rejecting and keeping something out of consciousness."[30] Consequently, the act instigated by that which is repressed is unconscious and non-directed; a specific object is not to be transformed or created. So, while nothing can be created, it is quite easy, through the non-direction of the libidinal energy, for something to be destroyed. Sublimation, on the other hand, involves desexualized libido, which is directed towards some specific object. An act of sublimation is necessarily creative, "for it would still retain the main purpose of Eros—that of uniting and binding—insofar as it helps towards establishing the unity or tendency to unity which is particularly characteristic of the ego."[31]

Now, when these concepts are applied to a work of art in advanced industrial society, a cyclical process may be seen as going into effect. In advanced industrial society repression is brought to bear upon the individual through institutionalized controls. As the individual gives vent to his libidinal energy through sublimated activity in the creation of a work of art, the society which the work is supposed to act against or negate transforms the

28. Paul A. Robinson, *The Freudian Left* (New York: Harper & Row, 1969), p. 208.

29. Marcuse, "Progress and Freud's Theory of Instincts," in *Five Lectures,* p. 37.

30. Sigmund Freud, "Repression," in *General Psychological Theory,* ed. Philip Rieff (New York: Collier Books, 1963), p. 105.

31. Freud, *The Ego and the Id,* trans. Joan Rivière (New York: Norton, 1960), p. 35.

work and "absorbs" the erotic libido which gives the work its "truth." Thus, a work such as Don Quixote becomes *Man of La Mancha*. In the novel, the critical faculty, the pathos, and the despair are retained. However, once it becomes a hit on Broadway, it also becomes a commodity product and people see it as a "hit play." As the play becomes more and more popular, both it and the original work lose their negative value. There is no integration or unity; what occurs is rather an enjoyable escape from the society and the self. Thus, Shierry Weber can say, when speaking of the "spectacle," that it is

> the perversion of the aesthetic: whereas the aesthetic is a totality
> formed by sublimation of the instincts, the spectacle releases
> instinctual energies but does not bind them into forms. On the other
> hand, the spectacle as aesthetic and as consumption prevents the
> individual from experiencing action and process; he is an actor only
> as an object and a subject only as a spectator; he consumes rather
> than makes.[32]

Another example may be seen in much of rock music, wherein the repetition of the basic rhythm and the noise "act to break down the ego to permit the diffuse release of sexual and aggressive energy, thus substituting annihilation and explosion—escape from the self—for discovery and integration."[33]

In each case, the existing reality principle is greatly strengthened by the libido it has absorbed and/or diffused. It is this which Marcuse calls "repressive desublimation"; that is to say, the sublimated activity is channeled and the critical quality and the erotic potential are transvalued into a repressively desublimated form.

Now, it is probable that the catharsis produced by the work of art, of which Aristotle spoke, in fact never affected the mass of the Athenians. The people were paid to go to the theater and a comedy was played after the tragedy to prevent them from "walking out shaken." Under present circumstances, however, the invalidity of catharsis, for Marcuse, is assured. Even were the catharsis to be effective, it would simply foster the illusion that liberation is a private affair of the heart. Consequently, since the catharsis is invalid, and the negativity of the traditional forms are absorbed, in order to preserve itself as the negation, art must transvalue and alienate itself from the society of alienated individuals. As the work and the elements within the work are removed from society, the artistic effect must be one of estrangement. It is only through this estrangement that the "inner truth" of

32. Shierry M. Weber, "Individuation as Praxis," in Paul Breines, ed., *Critical Interruptions* (New York: Herder & Herder Inc., 1970), p. 37.
33. Ibid., p. 55.

what can be, *"la promesse de bonheur,"* can be recaptured and preserved from societal absorption. Consequently, to the degree that art relates itself to society, then to that degree, also, is it invalidated through the controls of the society.[34]

Yet, at least in his latest work, Marcuse becomes extremely critical of anti-art (i.e., painting without color, music without score, destruction of language and form as such). Through its total denial of what is, art *qua* negation becomes a negative absolute, reified and itself one-dimensionalized, which tends to undermine both the dynamic of culture and the dialectical process itself. Though it may well be that art responds to administrative society by alienating itself from it, Marcuse asks whether the point has not been reached "where the oeuvre drops out of the dimension of alienation, of *formed* negation and contradiction, and turns into a sound game, language game—harmless without commitment [employing] shock which no longer shocks. . . ."[35]

Hegel conceived of art as that which "supplies out of the real world what is lacking to the notion."[36] However, within the anti-art genre, what occurs is that the positive value of that which is to be supplied, is itself denied. It is for this reason that, at best, anti-art comes to be simply the opposite of what is, rather than *that which is not*. It is this which vitiates the force of the imagination, the erotic content, and the function of art.

Consequently, Marcuse sees "the passing of anti-art, the reemergence of form. And with it, we find a new expression of the inherently subversive qualities of the aesthetic dimension, especially beauty as the sensuous appearance of the idea of freedom."[37] The form which must come into existence is an *aesthetic form*, which, embodied in the "style," subjects "reality to another order, subjects it to the 'laws of beauty.' "[38] Now, these laws are not, in themselves, either "intellectual" or subjective. Harmony, balance, etc., are elements of

> the aesthetic form in art [which] has the aesthetic form in nature
> (das Naturschöne) as its correlate, or rather desideratum. If the idea
> of beauty pertains to nature as well as to art, this is not merely an
> analogy, or a human idea imposed on nature—it is the insight that
> the aesthetic form, as a token of freedom, is a mode [or moment?]
> of existence of the human as well as the natural universe, an
> objective quality.[39]

34. Marcuse, *Counterrevolution and Revolt,* p. 101.
35. Marcuse, "Art and Revolution," in *Partisan Review* (Spring 1972), p. 178.
36. Hegel, op. cit., p. 27.
37. Marcuse, "Art and Revolution," p. 179.
38. Marcuse, *Counterrevolution and Revolt,* p. 98.
39. Marcuse, *Counterrevolution and Revolt,* p. 67.

In this context, Schiller's influence on Marcuse's thought becomes readily apparent. It is Schiller's concept of phantasy which is to become the vehicle for estrangement and recovery of the "inner truth."[40] Phantasy is seen as carrying within itself the "play impulse" which, through mediating between the "sensuous impulse" (which is receptive and ethereally passive) and the "form impulse" (which is marked by its desire for mastery), actually inculcates both within itself.[41] This play impulse may be thought of as having for its ideal object "*a living shape,* a concept which serves to denote all aesthetic qualities of phenomena and—in a word—what we call *Beauty* in the widest sense of the term."[42] Quoting Schiller, Marcuse feels that this play impulse, with its "objective as beauty and its goal as freedom,"[43] would become, if introjected into the individual and/or realized by him, the sensibility whereby the utopian liberation of humanity would manifest itself.

Within Schiller's conception of "play,"[44] an essential quality is that of lightness (*Leichtheit*). Traditionally, it was this quality which allowed art to remove itself from earthly want and transcend societal reality. But for Marcuse, this transcendence is, at present, denied through the controls of advanced industrial society. Traditional form, now simply creates the "element of Semblance (*Schein*) [which] necessarily subjects the represented reality to aesthetic standards and thus deprives it of its terror."[45] Since, in keeping its traditional form, art decreases the distance between itself and the concrete reality, more likely is the possibility of its being integrated and repressively desublimated. Therefore, art can survive "only where it cancels itself, where it saves its substance by denying its traditional form, thereby denying reconciliation."[46]

Unbounded by this traditional form, and compelled by this quality of "*leicht,*" phantasy transcends societal reality. That "harmonious truth" of the imagination, which becomes utopian when compared to the present state of reality and its performance principle, enables phantasy to retain the faculty of negativity. What we find, is that

> the truth value of imagination relates not only to the past, but also
>
> to the future: the forms of freedom and happiness which it invokes

40. Indeed, Freud saw phantasy as the only thought activity which was preserved from reality testing and which still remained subordinate to the pleasure principle. See Freud, "Two Principles in Mental Functioning," in *General Psychological Theory.*

41. Friedrich Schiller, *On the Aesthetic Education of Man* (New York: Frederick Ungar, 1965), p. 76.

42. Ibid.

43. Marcuse, *Eros and Civilization,* p. 170.

44. Schiller, op. cit., p. 78.

45. Marcuse, *Eros and Civilization,* p. 131.

46. Ibid., p. 132.

claim to deliver the historical reality. In its refusal to accept as final
the limitations imposed upon freedom and happiness by the reality
principle, in its refusal to forget what can be, lies the critical
function of phantasy.[47]

It is at this point that the relation between art and utopia becomes clear.
Art serves as a "container," the medium of that "truth" which is to become
the consciousness of the utopian man: indeed, the erotic truth it contains
becomes, for Marcuse, the very justification of that utopian condition. The
revolutionary and utopian potential of phantasy lies in the fact that it
inherently seeks "to satisfy those wishes that reality does not satisfy."[48]

Since, in Marcuse's legacy from Schiller, one must pass through the
aesthetic in order to solve the political, the surrealist protest against isolating
the material from the cultural revolution follows logically in Marcuse's
thought. Breton, also, believes that the Great Refusal must negate the totality
of existence in capitalist society. Simultaneously, however, it must hold forth
the possibility of sociocultural liberation through new modes of expression
and by expanding what is "real" to include the subconscious and what is
revealed to it in hallucinations, dreams, etc. In fact, the surrealist influence on
Marcuse is quite pronounced. Art in revolt and the artist as nonconformist,
the utopian desire to reconcile all contradiction, especially the imaginary and
the real, and the concern with the "new man," are all major tenets of
surrealist thought and art.[49] Also, since for Breton, the refusal had to be
total, it also had to be political. Thus, he linked surrealism to the Communist
party, so that it could take a political stand and gain a political outlet for its
content. So, too, for Marcuse, "The fight for Eros is a political fight." And
what this means, is that the potential truth of art can not be fulfilled until the
works "explode" the given society—that is to say, become realized
(*verwirklichen*) in the manifestation of the erotic content and the "play
impulse" in concrete reality.[50]

This is not to say, however, that art would "disappear." Thus, "At the
optimum, we can envisage a universe common to art and reality, but in this
common universe, art would retain its transcendence."[51] Art can disappear

---

47. Ibid., p. 135.

48. Freud, "The Theme of the Three Caskets," in *Character and Culture,* ed. Philip
Rieff (New York: Collier Books, 1963), p. 76.

49. André Breton, *What is Surrealism?* trans. David Gascoyne (London: Faber &
Faber, 1936) pp. 50-73.

50. A very real basis and justification for Marcuse's argument lies in the emphasis
Freud put on the "libidinal character" of Eros. See Freud, *Beyond the Pleasure
Principle,* trans. James Strachey (New York: Bantam Books, 1959), p. 92.

51. Marcuse, "Art and Revolution," p. 182.

for Marcuse, only if a stage of civilization would come about in which men could no longer distinguish between beauty and ugliness, good and evil. This would involve a "barbarism at the height of civilization."[52]

For Marcuse, the relationship between art and praxis is not the simple "dismissal" of art into praxis—that is, drawing the consequences and then going on to realize the idea. Rather, the potential truth cannot be fulfilled without revolutionary praxis. At the same time, however,

> [A]rt cannot submit to the actual requirements of the revolution without denying itself. But art can and will draw its inspirations, and its very form, from the then prevailing revolutionary movement—for revolution is in the substance of art.[53]

Thus, by their interaction, the erotic content of art would be set free through the revolutionary action, while praxis would dedicate itself to the destruction of the institutions of surplus repression, since this free Eros and an art which draws its strength and inspiration from the praxis would enable the individuals to realize the irrationality of these institutions. In lowering the level of repression, a "new man" would emerge.

Yet, Marcuse sees that the problem lies in the fact that in order to effect the revolution, it would already require the existence of that type of individual who is unable to tolerate this unnecessary societal repression, and who is to some degree freed from its indoctrinating influence. If it is necessary that there occur a "junction of art and revolution in the aesthetic dimension,"[54] then it is only logical that the interrelation and conjunction of the aesthetic and the revolution must become incarnate within the revolutionaries themselves.

Marcuse's whole utopian conception is, of course, based on the achievement of a high level of abundance, equally distributed throughout the population. Once the material conditions are assured, however, within the universe common to art and reality, art might change its character completely, in that it might no longer necessitate objectification (*Vergegenständlichung*). For in this new situation,

> techniques would then tend to become art, and art would tend to form reality: the opposition between imagination and reason, higher and lower faculties, poetic and scientific thought, would be invalidated. Emergence of a new Reality Principle: under which a new sensibility and a desublimated scientific intelligence would combine in the creation of an aesthetic ethos.[55]

52. Ibid.
53. Ibid., p. 178.
54. Ibid., p. 180.
55. Marcuse, *An Essay on Liberation*, p. 24.

Technology would no longer produce products for its own sake, and man would become the true master of the machine. The operationalist rationality under which the society functions, and the divisions between technology and art would come to be replaced by a new rationality. Within this rationality, "art's ability to 'project' existence, to define yet unrealized possibilities would then be envisaged as validated by and functioning in the scientific transformation of the world."[56] As man would come to recognize nature as a subject in its own right, he would interrelate with it—an interrelation which would foster the "pacification of existence." As the "natural" and erotic content of beauty and the "eternal myths" come to be recaptured,[57] they would enter the very infrastructure of man. He would become "playful" and "beautiful" in terms of Schiller's "living shape."

This "play" would manifest itself as part of the "new sensibility"—a sensuousness in which man need no longer be ashamed of himself and the atrocities which he committed in the past. The guilt of the primal crime would be expiated by the newly found liberating potential of memory. Time would no longer be thought of in unilinear terms, but rather as a circular process, as an "eternal recurrence" (Nietzsche)—a process which would allow man to fully recapture his past.

A new man and a new society would be created with a new guiding paradigm, in which art, while retaining its transcendence, would enter into harmony with societal reality, as man would enter into harmony with nature. This utopia would reflect an order in which men would be "biologically" incapable of committing violence[58]—an order in which evil would be banished and Thanatos overcome. Sexuality would turn into sensuality as the erogenous zones would begin to spread themselves over the whole body, abolishing any type of genital organization. As Marcuse's quote of Baudelaire, a world would come into being in which "La, tout n'est qu-ordre et beauté; Luxe, calme et volupté."

*   *   *   *

In formulating his conception, Marcuse relies on a tradition and a mode of thought which is alien to most Americans. The use of this tradition, however, is quite understandable given his purposes, since, as Lukács points out, "For anyone wishing to return to the revolutionary traditions of Marxism, the revival of the Hegelian traditions is obligatory."[59]

56. Marcuse, *One-Dimensional Man*, p. 239.
57. Marcuse, "Art and Revolution," p. 175.
58. Marcuse, *An Essay on Liberation*, pp. 21-28.
59. Georg Lukács, *History and Class Consciousness*, trans. Rodney Livingstone (Cambridge, Mass.: Massachusetts Institute of Technology Press, 1968), p. xxi. It is worthwhile to add that not only did Marx and Engels recognize their indebtedness to the idealist tradition in their works, but also, that Engels founded a Schiller *Verein* in Manchester.

In keeping with this tradition, the essence of art, for Marcuse, lies in its critical faculty and in the truth of the erotic content which is retained (*aufgehoben*) in the work. For Hegel, however, art is a categorical entity within the absolute spirit (*Geist*), by which it can *intuitively* become conscious of itself. Therefore, it acts as a *mediation*, rather than as a "container" of truth.

Indeed, in Marcuse's conception, the real dialectical relationship is suppressed in favor of this supposed "erotic" truth. The thing of beauty does not represent any "truth"—erotic or otherwise. Rather, it is something new, unique, built from the materials of the world, *at the urging of* the repressed instinct. The repressed Eros prompts the creative process; it is the motive, but not necessarily the object, that is being expressed. This, of course, does not contradict the fact that it also can be the object in a specific case, as for example, *Tristan and Isolde.*

Truth, if such it can be called, comes out of the interaction between the audience, the artist and the work. Once the creation is completed, the artist loses control of it. It is an objectification (*Vergegenstaendlichung*) and "creates its own audience of art lovers" (Marx). But as an objectification, it is not reified (*Verdinglichung*), in that through the work the audience and the artist are able to interrelate in their humanity through the force of imagination. Thus, if the work contains a truth, it is an essentially human truth a particular and concrete truth, with its own *specific "promesse de bonheur."*

One of the central problems in the distinction between affirmative and negative culture is that both terms become abstractions. Whether or not a specific work of art becomes part of an affirmative or of a negative culture depends neither exclusively upon the culture as such, nor upon the work treated autonomously as an end unto itself. Each work is directed towards a certain public,[60] within the community at large, and it is the interaction it achieves with this public which gives it negativity, or its opposite. There is no inherent "negativity" within art without a correlative effect upon a given public.

In this context, certain of Marcuse's ideas on censorship become relevant. Though he would censor certain ideas where "the pacification of existence, where freedom and happiness are at stake,"[61] he goes on to say that

censorship of art and literature is regressive under all circumstances.

There are cases where an authentic oeuvre carries a regressive

60. Jean-Paul Sartre, *What is Literature?* trans. Bernard Frechtman (New York: Harper & Row, 1965), p. 117. Sartre, also, speaks of affirmative art, and in, I think, a more persuasive manner, but in a different context.

61. Marcuse, "Repressive Tolerance," in Robert Paul Wolff, Barrington Moore, Jr., and Herbert Marcuse, *A Critique of Pure Tolerance* (Boston: Beacon Press, 1969), p. 88.

> political message—Dostoievski is a case in point. But then the
> message is canceled by the oeuvre itself: the regressive political
> content is absorbed (*aufgehoben*) in the artistic form: in the work as
> literature.[62]

Once more, the idealist influence breaks through. For at the base of this
conception lies, once more, the inherent value of "truth," with a consequent
neglect of the real and concrete effects of the work on the consciousness of
the audience. Of course, it is possible to make the argument that the
regressive political message is canceled in Dostoevski's work, or perhaps in
Lawrence's, but what about in the case of Céline's vicious anti-Semitism,
which most certainly had an effect upon his reading public? Also, this
conception ignores the whole area of art known as non-fiction fiction, or
journalistic fiction, as exemplified in some of Norman Mailer's works. Should
works such as these, many of which carry an explicit political appeal, be
regarded as politico-cultural tracts, or as artistic *oeuvres*?

What is forgotten is that the *oeuvre* can have a sharply, and even strictly,
political effect, with the potential of influencing the consciousness and/or
mores of a given society. On the one hand, to make the claim that censorship
is necessary when there is a political threat to the "pacification of existence"
and then to ignore the same threat when it is leveled from the artistic sphere,
is not only inconsistent, but involves a theoretical attempt to separate the
work from the effects it has on the audience. A separation between
intellectual and aesthetic appreciation, which it is impossible even to
consider.

Since, for Marcuse, art must continually strive to alienate itself from
reality, the atypical character,[63] in the form of the hero, assumes
importance. Interestingly enough, it is Kierkegaard, whom Marcuse vigorously
attacks in *Reason and Revolution,* who first realizes the negation of all
society, including the transcendence of the traditional hero, in the "knight of
faith."

To be sure, the tragic hero has his truth, in the sacrifice he makes for
society. It is a universal truth, for each man can relate to it. It is
communicable and the truth shames the petty bourgeois desires and passions
of the society. It is the truth of human nobility and grandeur, stemming
from the depth of the hero's heart. However, the knight of faith goes beyond
this, for in his faith there is

> this paradox, that the particular is higher than the universal—yet in
> such a way, be it observed, that the movement repeats itself, and

62. Ibid., p. 89.

63. For an interesting discussion of typicality and atypicality, see Lukács, "The
Ideology of Modernism," in *Realism in Our Time,* trans. John Mander and Necke Mander
(New York: Harper Torchbooks, 1964).

> that consequently the individual after having been in the universal,
> now as the particular isolates himself as higher than the universal.[64]

This "truth" is something which only the individual involved can relate to, the sacrifice something which only he can fully comprehend. It is both the resignation and the paradox, which encompassed in faith propel this truth above the aesthetic-universal.[65]

The tragic hero creates or exemplifies his truth by the nobility of his character in a given situation. It is there, within him, and the suffering he takes upon himself, be it physical, moral, or both, is taken on in such a way that it is universally comprehensible. The choices are made in the ethical realm, according to an ethical standard whereby both he and his actions can be judged by society and himself.

The knight of faith, the religious hero, does not relate to a "universal" ethical standard, but to God alone. Indeed, it is precisely in his existing with men, while relating only to God, that the suffering occurs.

> The ethical expression for what Abraham did is, that he would
> murder Isaac; the religious expression is, that he would sacrifice
> Isaac;·but precisely in this contradiction consists the *dread* which
> can well make a man sleepless, and yet, Abraham is not what he is
> without this *dread.*[66]

The concern here, is not with the "freedom" of the religious hero—a freedom which is purely private in character—but, rather, with a number of points which become extremely important. First, the dread implies a "suspension of the telos," that is, it moves itself outside the continuum of the dialectic. Second, there is the subjectivism, the pure particularity of the subject, in that he has no one to relate to besides God, while, finally, there is the removal of the subject from the temporal and the concrete.

In spite of the resignation and the paradox, the subject has an internal power through the very faith which compels him to perform the act. However, once this faith is lost, once the individual is secularized and encounters the dread from this vantage point, his faith becomes a vacuum and his power turns to impotence. In this situation, the collectivity is still negated, while through the loss of God, the individual becomes an atomized entity, an absolute particularity. This condition is pushed to its extreme in advanced industrial society,[67] where art "guides us in the direction of

64. Søren Kierkegaard, *Fear and Trembling and The Sickness Unto Death,* trans. Walter Lowrie (Princeton: Princeton University Press, 1969), p. 65.
65. Ibid., p. 58.
66. Ibid., p. 41.
67. Here, a direct relation to the substructure is evident, for as Lukács points out, "The more the general influence of capitalism extends into reality, the more difficult this [artistic] struggle becomes. For as social relations grow increasingly abstract, the less

madness; and, indeed, for modern man there is no other way. Only the madness is inaccessible to the machine."[68] Whether there is, indeed, "no other way" remains open to question; however, the first part of the observation is certainly correct.

Man as a particularity—dwarfed, isolated, and alone—trembles when thrown into the complexity and size of the technological state. That one major response should be an extreme subjectivism, which negates the collectivity entirely, is only natural. Still, a subjectivism of this type appears wanting, as Hegel quite correctly perceived,

> in that the subject desires to penetrate into truth and has a craving
> for objectivity, but yet is unable to abandon its isolation and
> retirement into itself, and to strip itself free of this unsatisfied
> abstract inwardness [of mind], and so has a seizure of sickly
> yearning.[69]

A specific case in point is William Burroughs's *Naked Lunch,* which describes a junkie's vision of the world. In this work, there is an energy of bitterness and a cynicism, which manifests itself in the "algebra of need"—an addiction which takes different forms in each individual, either as an addiction to power, money, drugs, etc.—a cynicism, extreme and all-inclusive, which precisely due to this, becomes cheap. There is no erotic content within the work, but rather an overriding negativism.[70] A negativism, which because of its egocentric, at times self-pitying, and all-pervasive character, is indeterminate (*unbestimmt*).

To be sure, at moments, Burroughs is both provocative and incisive. Yet, his bitterness, and the ugliness which is consistently exhibited throughout the work, stands in sharp contradistinction to the deep sense of humanity which rested beneath the satire of a Molière, a Swift, or a Musil.

Similarly, from *Waiting for Godot,* through *Endgame* and *Krapp's Last Tape,* Beckett draws us inward, in a technically excellent and often absorbing manner to the final silence. It is this silence, perhaps, he is thinking of, when Marcuse calls the work of Beckett, "the most uncompromising, most extreme

---

possible it becomes to disentangle the beauty of the human essence; to see and express artistically the unity of man despite the fragmentation caused by the capitalist division of labor." Lukács, *Goethe and His Age,* trans. Robert Anchor (New York: Grosset & Dunlap, 1969), p. 242.

68. Ellul, op. cit., p. 404.

69. Hegel, op. cit., p. 99.

70. Freud would consider this type of negation "the derivative of expulsion, [which] belongs to the instinct of destruction. The passion for universal negation, the 'negativism' displayed . . . is probably due to be regarded as a sign of the defusion of the instincts due to the withdrawal of the libidinal components." See Freud, "Negation," p. 216.

indictment . . . which precisely because of its radicalism repels the political sphere. . . . [As] there is no hope which can be translated into political terms, the aesthetic form excludes all accommodation and leaves literature as literature. And as literature, the work carries one single message: to make an end with things as they are."[71] Still, what does this silence hold for us? There is no anger, no questioning, no unity, and no integration: there is only silence. Finally, in denying discourse itself, the estrangement-effect is impaired, the negation is rendered ineffective, and the interaction of the audience, the artist, and the work, destroyed.

For Brecht, the estrangement-effect (*Verfremdungseffekt*), attempts to overcome alienation (*Entfremdung*) through distance. One is brought to realize that he is watching a play, which is not life, but a representation of life; at no time is the play to serve as an illusion. Distance becomes the bond between the members of the audience, in that, through a form which is intrinsically social and which negates aesthetic illusion, they are made to realize intellectually that alienation which they have in common.

But here, the *Verfremdungseffekt* is transvalued. As art continually alienates itself from society and its reality principle, it also alienates itself from the mode of discourse, which can not be separated from the members of the society themselves. It is not enough to say that because anti-art has fallen out of "the dimension of alienation" it becomes an unformed negation. Nor is it simply a question of societal absorption of the work's negative value. Rather, it is within the very nature of being incommunicable that the "revolt" of the artist loses any potential effect it might otherwise have had. It is precisely because of this that the negativity of the work becomes ineffective, in that it does not make *manifest* the freedom of the imagination and the potential it contains.

Indeed, Marcuse holds that within the aesthetic form, "the surrealist program must still be valid." We find that "the dream must become a force of changing rather than dreaming the human condition: it must become a political force."[72] But precisely because it is a dream, its images need not take on an objectively cognitive quality. What can be manifested within a dream is a form which is inherently subjective—a subjectivity which becomes extreme in its alienation within anti-art, which is itself an offshoot of surrealism and expressionism.

The aesthetic *form* is itself alienated and opposed to societal reality, so that there is no mediator between the dream and the populace. Indeed, if the effect cannot be rationally grasped and internalized, then it can have no impact upon the consciousness of the audience, other than in an irrational manner.

71. Marcuse, "Art and Revolution," p. 179.
72. Marcuse, *Counterrevolution and Revolt*, p. 102.

Marcuse has always been extremely critical of the anti-intellectualism which appears in many New Left trends. However, he does not take into account the unmediated nature of anti-art, which is non-dialectical and which opens the door to a dangerous irrationalism. In anti-art, comprehension is immediate, subjective, and purely emotional. One cannot intellectually comprehend or evaluate a white canvas, or a composition without score.

Although the aesthetic form, when desublimated, does attempt to reach the intellect, it must be "immediate" art, in that it would attempt to activate a "natural" sense experience, freed from the constraints and requirements of present-day society as well.[73] However, within the Hegelian construct, immediate knowledge and reason are irreconcilable. It is this very immediacy, which makes for irrationality.

Consequently, form is not something abstract, alienated from societal reality. Form is precisely the societal reality which is introjected into the aesthetic realm. Form is, indeed, "the embodiment of man's mastery over matter; [wherein] transmitted experience is preserved and all achievement is kept safe. . . . Form is social experience solidified."[74]

It is this common sense of "social experience" that allows form to act as, what I should like to call, an *interactive mediation.* The creative experience of the artist is itself taken from the world and given his own stamp. (Even for the realist, no matter how closely he wishes to mirror reality, his choice of subject is necessarily arbitrary, while for the surrealist, dreams can bear a real relation to external reality.) The artist's characters take on a life of their own (*Lebensanschauung*), gaining their uniqueness or typicality, by reacting against the world which the author creates in his work (*Weltanschauung*) from the materials of the society. It is this dialectical tension between the author's world, his characters, and the external world, which allows the dynamic of the content (i.e., hopes, emotions, questions, probings, and power) to arise.

There is no arbitrary or reified distinction between form and content; however, without a form which is inherently socially communicable, this dynamism evaporates. The manner in which it is brought to the audience is through form; through mastery, technique, symbolism, or realism, the objective world of the audience is able to meet and interact with the subjective world of the author. Therefore, while acting upon the public, since it is form which makes content understandable, it also affects the content of the work itself. Form refines content and gives it that lightness (*leicht*) which Marcuse sees as being inherent within content alone.

Form, in this sense, could well be that which could allow

73. Marcuse, *Counterrevolution and Revolt,* p. 81-82.
74. Ernst Fischer, *The Necessity of Art: A Marxist Approach,* trans. Anna Bostock (London: Penguin Books, 1959), p. 15.

>art [to] lead us back to the origins of rebellion, to the extent that it
>tries to give its form to an elusive value which the future perpetually
>promises, but of which the artist has a presentiment and wishes to
>snatch from the grasp of history.[75]

From this position, it does not follow that art must become the propagandistic servant of the society and its politics, as with, say, socialist realism. In fact, it may be argued that socialist realism is simply extreme subjectivism and/or negativism turned on its head, with the same antidialectical implications.

Marcuse, himself, sees socialist realism as at best a perversion of art, at worst as not being art at all.[76] In this case, "objectivity" incorporates the subject, subjugating the *oeuvre* itself to the given societal "purpose."[77] In its later stages, form was overemphasized, and its critical quality was consciously repressed in favor of a politically "objective" truth.

It should be observed here that the pure formalists, among them the nonrepresentational painters and the writers of the "new novel," such as Robbe-Grillet, also ignore both the interrelationship of form and content and of subject and object. These works often move towards either simple decoration, or adopt an attitude which totally denies the critical quality of the content.[78] Often conceiving of form as that which is purely subjective representation, the objective conditions of interpersonal experiences are negated in favor of an exercise in pure technique.

However, what is interesting, even with regard to socialist realism, is that a truly great work unconsciously retains a certain critical insight. Every major work, in some way, interacts with the foundations of society, and criticizes even when such is not the intent; here, it becomes a case of the work breaking through the "style." In Sholokov's *And Quiet Flows the Don,* in spite of its socialist realist style, we see the basis for the impending mechanization, standardization, and drudgery of that "second revolution" which was to follow. As it can break through the style, so, too, can the work transcend the author's own perspective and intent. As Engels rightly noted, this occurs with Balzac, who above all was

>politically a Legitimist; his work is a constant elegy on the
>irretrievable decay of good society; his sympathies are all with the
>class doomed to extinction. But for all that, his satire is never
>keener, his irony never bitterer, than when he sets in motion the

75. Albert Camus, *The Rebel,* trans. Anthony Bower (New York: Vintage Books, 1956), p. 258.

76. Marcuse, *Soviet Marxism* (New York: Vintage Books, 1961), p. 113.

77. For a fuller explication of the "purpose" of socialist realism, see Abram Tertz, *The Trial Begins and On Socialist Realism* (New York: Vintage Books, 1960).

78. Herbert Read, *Art and Society* (New York: Schocken Books, 1966), p. 124.

> very men and women with whom he sympathizes the most
> deeply—the nobles.[79]

It is certainly true that art must involve itself with that which is not. But, it is no less true that art must define and mirror the subtlest societal mores and make tangible that nonquantifiable level of sensitivity (or lack of it) and the innermost strivings of the society. The question is not one of divorcing reality from art (or dominating the latter by the former), but rather of relating the two through their interaction. Thus, for example, in literature, form, as it has previously been defined, must interact with content. Through its mediation, the subject and object, while distinct, are still interrelated, and what occurs is that the individual and/or human condition (if that is what the individual is to reflect) becomes an integral part of the specific collective conditions. It is only from here that the work can formulate its vision and transcend what is. It is only in this manner that the critical quality can manifest itself and retain the artistic authenticity of the work.

Attempting to separate art from societal reality can also lead to an indulgence in idealism. In fact, in describing "art for art's sake," Walter Benjamin saw it as "a negative theology in the form of the idea of 'pure' art."[80] This "theology" seeks to separate art not only from its social function and its "contextual integration" with tradition, but also from its quintessential humanism. On the other hand, pure formalism and/or socialist realism generically lose their transcendental potential. Lukács is quite correct, in that

> "the more developed capitalist society is, the more developed are
> both its poles; the increasingly abstract and empty stylization as
> well as the increasingly servile and photographic naturalism which
> clings to immediate surfaces."[81]

In the same vein, the nullification of the negation, and the one-dimensionalization of society, through its introjection of the "happy consciousness" into the populace, has a pronounced effect upon the artist. Sartre, looking back upon his early childhood when he first started to write, recognizes the power of indoctrination and the importance of contradiction for artistic creation.

> "I had armed myself to defend mankind against terrible dangers,
> and everyone assured me that it was quietly on its way to
> perfection. Grandfather had brought me up to respect bourgeois

79. Marx and Engels, *Selected Correspondence* (Moscow: Progress Publishers, 1965), p. 403.

80. Walter Benjamin, *Illuminations,* ed. Hannah Arendt (New York: Schocken Books, 1969), p. 224.

81. Georg Lukács, *Goethe and His Age,* p. 105

democracy; I would have gladly unsheathed my pen for it. But with de Fallieres as President, the peasant voted: what more could I ask? And what does a republican do if he has the luck to live in a republic? He twiddles his thumbs, or else he teaches Greek and describes the monuments of Aurillac in his spare time. I was back where I had started from, and I thought I would stifle in that world without conflicts which left the writer unemployed."[82]

The present power exerted by society over art, however, does not suggest that it is necessary for a return to the concerns and forms of a previous age. Still, even today, art can enter 'the absurd' in an attempt to define the individual's relation to it, as well as his concrete existence, in intrinsically personal terms as is demonstrated so brilliantly in Camus' *The Fall*. Lyricism, also, retains its importance, even in a revolutionary context, for "if art will not help this new man to educate himself, to strengthen and refine himself, then what is it for? And how can it organize the inner life, if it does not penetrate it and reproduce it?"[83]

Still, the encounter with destiny takes place as much within the world as within the mind or the heart. But the attempt at defining the individual's position in reality may well bear its fruit in futility, since:

"none of us has time to live the true dramas of the life that we are destined for. This is what ages us—this and nothing else. The wrinkles and creases on our faces are the registration of the great passions, vices, insights that called on us; but we, the masters were not home."[84]

Yet, strangely enough, it could well be within this futility and pathos, which is so real to every individual, that humanity identifies itself. The scope of the individual is broadened in the unravelling of the metaphysical and concrete alternatives. In enabling the individual to project himself into certain situations and know the despair of choice, or in making him feel beauty and the most sublime sorrow, his consciousness expands. It is herein that the liberating and critical function of art manifests itself, and not in the vacuum of pure negation.

But it is still not so simple, for a paradox ensues. Indeed, it is certainly true that:

"modern music is shattering forms, breaking away from conventions, carving its own road. But exactly to whom does it speak of liberation, freedom, will, of the creation of man by

82. Jean-Paul Sartre, *The Words* trans. Bernard Frechtman (Conn.: Fawcett Crest Books, 1964), p. 110.

83. Leon Trotsky, *Literature and Revolution* trans. Rose Strunsky (Ann Arbor: University of Michigan Press, 1971), p. 138.

84. Op. cit. Benjamin, p. 211.

> man–to a stale and genteel listener whose ears are blocked up by an
> idealist aesthetic. Music says 'permanent revolution' and the
> bourgeoisie hear 'Evolution, progress.' And even if, among the young
> intellectuals, a few understand it, won't their present impotence
> make them see this liberation as a beautiful myth, instead of their
> own reality."[85]

As subjectivism becomes more and more intense, the emphasis on the ego as an *absolute particularity* decreases the power to love, and forces back on itself its own frustration and bitterness, while society transforms and extends this into repression. Yet, again, subjectivity need not be destroyed, especially since it is from the community itself "that the determining principle for the content of art, as well as for the medium which represents it in outward form, comes to be particularization, individualization, and the subjectivity which they require."[86]

Within this dialectical tension between the subject and his world–between the particular and the universal–at least two qualities are brought into being, which besides madness are inaccessible to the machine. One has already been mentioned, which is pathos, and the other is striving.

It is noteworthy that Freud, in his own terms, perceived this, in that "the proneness to decay of all that is beautiful and perfect can, as we know, give rise to two different impulses in the mind. The one leads to the aching despondency ... while the other leads to rebellion against the fact asserted."[87]

This despondency, if it does not turn into self-indulgence or self-pity, is in the *oeuvre* turned into a poignant pathos. The individual's ultimate lack of control over all of the consequences of his actions, the cruelty of the "cunning of history," man's struggle against his own mortality–all make for pathos. And to be grasped as real, this pathos must be presented in humanly comprehensible terms, as much through the technical skill of the artist as through the breadth of his vision.

The marvelous grandeur of the struggle and the nobility of pathos is beautifully expressed by Dylan Thomas.

> Though wise men at their end know dark is right,
> Because their words had forked no lightening they
> Do not go gentle into that good night.[88]

Phantasy, for Marcuse, is the vehicle of liberation. However, there is within the very nature of phantasy, as it is so construed, the element of escape.

85. Jean-Paul Sartre, "The Artist and His Conscience" in *Situations* trans. Benita Eisler (Conn.: Fawcett Crest Books, 1965), pg. 145.

86. Hegel, op. cit., p. 122.

87. Freud, "On Transcience," in *Character and Culture,* p. 148.

88. Dylan Thomas, *Collected Poems* (New York: New Directions, 1957), p. 128.

Creation, on the other hand, even in the most mundane sense, involves mastery: a mastery not simply of that which is abstract and ethereal, but of that which is concrete. Of course, this is not to say that phantasy is irrelevant to creation. Indeed, "The artist being aware of his internal world which he must express, and of the external materials with which he works, can in all consciousness use the material to express the phantasy."[89]

By the same token, phantasy may also become an allegorical weapon, in that it can exhibit a critical quality of art, when joined to social experience and description, as in the case of Abram Tertz's *The Makepeace Experiment.* Even this type of work becomes a viable form of realism. As Brecht said,

> Whether a work is realist or not cannot be seen merely from having a look whether it is similar or not to existing works that are called realist and were realist in their own epoch. In each case the description of life must be compared not with other descriptions of life but with life itself. A work is comprehensible not merely because it is written exactly like the other works before it. Something had to be done to make them comprehensible. So we, too, must do something to make new works comprehensible. It is not a question merely of what is popular, but of what can be made popular.[90]

The writer writes to be read, and the ego longs for recognition. As it is within society that the artist creates, it may well be that the artist's desire to bring his vision across to as wide a public as possible, interacting with and paralleled by his striving for excellence, gives rise to the *oeuvre*. The mutual recognition of the self and the other in creation—the quest for a popular excellence. So, Sartre can write in *Nausea:*

> A book. A novel. And there would be people who would read this book and say: "Antoine Roquentin wrote it, a red-headed man who hung around cafés," and they would think of my life as I think about the negress's: as something precious and almost legendary. A book. Naturally, at first it would only be a troublesome tiring work, it wouldn't stop me from existing or feeling that I exist. But a time would come when the book would be written, when it would be behind me, and I think that a little of its clarity might fall over my past. Then perhaps, because of it, I could remember my life without repugnance.[91]

89. Hannah Siegel, "A Psycho-Analytical Approach to Aesthetics," in eds., Melanie Klein, Paula Heimann, P.E. Money-Kyrle, *New Directions in Psychoanalysis* (London: Tavistock, 1955), pp. 397-398.

90. Martin Esslin, "Solzhenitsyn and Lukács," in *Encounter* (March 1971), p. 48.

91. Sartre, *Nausea,* trans. Lloyd Alexander (New York: New Directions, 1964), p. 178.

Turning from the individual artist to society, one can see that although Marx never devoted a major work to aesthetic theory, he saw art as part of the superstructure which emanates from the socioeconomic conditions of a given period. Both Marx and Engels always stressed the realistic over the purely idealistic,[92] and neither conceived of art as being the container of liberation. For Marx, it was not necessary to pass through the aesthetic in order to enter and then change the political world. Rather, this liberation was to be brought about through the proletarian revolution and a class consciousness which is to stem from the realization by the proletariat of their own economic interests and their subsequent existential needs. These needs are what Marcuse expands into the overriding need for a "pacification of existence." But Marx did not go this far, and, therefore, Marcuse considers the new popularity of Fourier extremely important, since he "was the only one to have made clear this qualitative difference between free and unfree society."[93] Now, it may be that Marx refrained from speaking of such a society because he lived in a time of scarcity and might have considered utopian speculation frivolous; however, there may well be deeper reasons.

This new society, which Marcuse conceives of, would in the Hegelian manner reconcile all contradictions and "end the segregation of the aesthetic from the real,"[94] as well. Art would lose its need to remain outside of reality; instead, it would be actualized within it (*Verwirklichung*). The aesthetic would become the "mode in which reason and the sensuous are harmonized."[95] This very reality would then be constituted within a framework in which there would no longer be "the painful transcendence toward the future but the peaceful recapture of the past. Remembrance, which has preserved everything that was is 'the inner and the actually higher form of the substance.' "[96] Art, as "attained and sustained fulfillment" would become manifest as the "pacification of existence."

So too, time would be conquered in that spirit which "overcomes its temporal form, negat[ing] time." In Marcuse's thought, the conquest of time assumes tremendous importance, for, "unless the power of time over life is broken, there can be no freedom." This power, which stands in the way of man's fulfillment and which must be broken is "the tyranny of becoming over being."[97] Though, of course, men will die, it lies within the very nature

---

92. Marx, in fact, says that his view of the drama "consists in not forgetting the realistic for the idealistic, Shakespeare for Schiller," in *Selected Correspondence*, p. 119.
93. Marcuse, "The End of Utopia," p. 68.
94. Marcuse, *An Essay on Liberation*, p. 32.
95. Weber, "Individuation as Praxis," p. 24.
96. Marcuse, *Eros and Civilization*, p. 106.
97. Marcuse, *Eros and Civilization*, pp. 106-110.

of this fulfillment and the new sensibility of sensuality and eroticism, that the fear and dread of death will be negated.

With the change in the sensibility of man and the world which he relates to, with the conquest of time, art must change radically both its locus and function within the new society. A change so radical that what we now know as art would be unrecognizably altered. While the art object, at least as we now know it, assumes an objectified form, in the utopian condition, man will realize himself through his own self-externalization (*Entäusserung*)[98] rather than through art as objectified *oeuvres*. The aesthetic form will realize itself, will emerge from the social process of production, and it is this which would make for the pacification of existence.

Still, through the reconciliation of contradictions, a condition could come about which would negate the very idea of individual fulfillment. This would involve the integration of the subject into the object, or in Freudian terms, Roheim's dual-unity situation.[99] As the society takes on the role of the mother, who equally distributes her bounties to all (the brothers), any private existence, any personal life at all would by its very nature emerge both as a threat to the brothers and to the societal mother. Under these conditions, the very desire to create an individual personality would re-impose the guilt from crimes beginning with the overthrow of the father, which was expiated only through humanity as a whole.

Although Marcuse implicitly denies it,[100] a true pacification of existence would involve not only making tension "non-aggressive" and "non-destructive," but also lowering ego boundaries, which both Freud and Roheim see as "a characteristic feature of schizophrenia."[101] Furthermore, Freud points out, that instincts aside, a state of society may occur which he terms a *psychologisches Elend,* in which identification between the members of a society is so close that those who possess a special ability receive no recognition at all.[102]

With regard to the recapture of *"les temps perdus,"* Hegel found that the truth of a given period is retained as it is superseded (*aufgehoben*) by the notion in its next phase of development. It does not need to be "recaptured," precisely because the truth of the past is absorbed into the present—in the higher level of consciousness which has been achieved. On the other hand, for

98. Géza Roheim, *Magic and Schizophrenia* (Bloomington, Ind.: University of Indiana Press, 1970), p. 4.

99. Marcuse, *Eros and Civilization,* p. 106.

100. Marcuse, *Negations,* p. 237.

101. Roheim, op. cit., p. 111.

102. Freud, *Civilization and Its Discontents,* trans. and ed. James Strachey (New York: Norton, 1961), pp. 62-63.

Marx, though he throws off the idealist trappings of Hegel's dialectic, the concept of progress is fundamental. Although, he occasionally looks back to feudalism with a type of nostalgia, Marx clearly realizes the necessity for progress, in the higher development of the means of production in the capitalist stage.[103]

Marx, himself, was acquainted with Schiller's work, and yet he refrained from taking on the "play impulse." Possibly, this may have been simply due to a fear of abandoning the materialist method, or perhaps he foresaw the possibility of what Lukács calls a "mythologization" of "intuitive comprehension (*Verstehen*)" were the aesthetic realm to take over the sociopolitical world. But perhaps it was that, rather than desiring a pacification of existence, Marx dreamed of a society in which existence would be intensified and dynamic.

While, for Marcuse, play can become creative, for Marx, creativity is always somewhat closer to productivity, even were this productivity only to result in a heightened consciousness, self-awareness and/or fulfillment; for Marx, man is *homo faber*. It is for this reason that in the Manifesto, Marx and Engels write that "in bourgeois society, living labour is but a means to increase accumulated labour. In communist society, accumulated labour is but a means to widen, to enrich, to promote the existence of the labourer."[104]

Although Marcuse sees the necessity of labor and a "limited" mastery, this labor is desexualized and becomes a form of "play." Indeed, "In this utopian hypothesis labor would be so different from labor as we know it or normally conceive of it that the idea of the convergence of labor and play does not diverge too far from the possibilities."[105]

But mastery is not quantitative; it is inherent within creation, and this creativity also implies a certain technical proficiency, a proficiency which inculcates within it an *ésprit sérieux*.

Art can, indeed, "be an integral factor in shaping the quality and 'the appearance' of things, in shaping the reality, the way of life...."[106] However, it cannot do this through its "convergence" with technology. Art must, and can only, project utopia. This it can do only by projecting new categories of *perceiving* truth (not by projecting the 'truth' itself)—by projecting new forms of feeling, seeing, thinking. And art becomes imperative, because of this, in a revolutionary sense not only by negating the cruelty and

103. See *The Communist Manifesto* and *The German Ideology*.
104. Marx and Engels, *Selected Works*, 1:36.
105. Marcuse, "The End of Utopia," p. 78.
106. Marcuse, *An Essay on Liberation*, p. 32.

stagnation of the status quo for what can be, but by helping change the consciousness and the sensibility of men through education and refinement.

Marcuse's vision is both idyllic and pastoral; it is a movement "toward an ever more peaceful, joyful struggle with the inexorable resistance of society and nature." But, in order to allow man full freedom and the free play of all human faculties—in order to allow him to create—one must allow man to feel pain; he must be given the freedom to fail. If fulfillment implies experience—the highest and the lowest, the mad and the sane, the very separation of the emotions and the feeling and knowing of each one—then pacification might well negate fulfillment, by the very literal meaning of the word.

Perhaps, rather, a state must be reached in which man is able to delve into the intensity of his life—a state which capitalism can never reach. Possibly the goal, utopia, itself is a process which embodies the feeling which inspired the creation of that goal in the first place. Perhaps it is in the striving itself, not suffering in a Dostoevskian sense, that man furthers his nobility and enhances himself in the consciousness of his humanity and the growth of his love. For it could well be that the striving, at a given point, breaks as would a line of light into its components when coming into contact with a prism, without any of the parts losing that quality which originally gave them birth.

Perhaps the despair of Faust is the despair of every man—that life cages him in, while he knows that even were he to burst free of the prison, still there would not be enough life to satiate him. Possibly each of us could be able to stake our hope and our dignity on our inability to say *"Verweile doch! Du bist so schön."* And as art lets us know our striving and our common anguish, it may well reinforce upon each one of us the belief, in a secular context, that:

> no, not one shall be forgotten who was great in the world. But each was great in his own way and each in proportion to the greatness of that which he loved. . . . Everyone shall be remembered, but each became great in proportion to his expectation. One became great by expecting the possible, another by expecting the eternal, but he who expected the impossible became greater than all. Everyone shall be remembered, but each was great in proportion to the greatness of that with which he strove.[107]

---

107. Kierkegaard, op. cit., p. 31.